Current Trends in Slavery Studies in Brazil

Dependency and Slavery Studies

Edited by
Jeannine Bischoff and Stephan Conermann

Volume 7

Current Trends in Slavery Studies in Brazil

Edited by
Stephan Conermann, Mariana Dias Paes,
Roberto Hofmeister Pich and Paulo Cruz Terra

DE GRUYTER

Gefördert durch die Deutsche Forschungsgemeinschaft (DFG) im Rahmen der Exzellenzstrategie des Bundes und der Länder – Exzellenzcluster Bonn Center for Dependency and Slavery Studies (BCDSS) EXC 2036/1-2020, Projektnummer: 390683433

Funded by the Deutsche Forschungsgemeinschaft (DFG, German Research Foundation) under Germany's Excellence Strategy – Cluster of Excellence Bonn Center for Dependency and Slavery Studies (BCDSS) EXC 2036/1-2020, Project No.: 390683433

ISBN 978-3-11-102610-7
e-ISBN (PDF) 978-3-11-102652-7
e-ISBN (EPUB) 978-3-11-102698-5
ISSN 2701-1127
DOI https://doi.org/10.1515/9783111026527

Library of Congress Control Number: 2022951744

Bibliographic information published by the Deutsche Nationalbibliothek
The Deutsche Nationalbibliothek lists this publication in the Deutsche Nationalbibliografie; detailed bibliographic data are available on the internet at http://dnb.dnb.de.

Cover image: Illustration from Jean-Baptiste Debret. *Voyage pittoresque et historique au Brésil*, 3 vols. (Paris: Firmin-Didot, 1834,1835,1839), Wikimedia Commons, Public Domain. Image mirrored.
Typesetting: Integra Software Services Pvt. Ltd.
Printing and binding: CPI books GmbH, Leck

www.degruyter.com

Contents

Paulo Cruz Terra

Introduction

Through the texts gathered here, the present book aims to offer some of the current trends in Brazilian slavery studies to the international public.[1] Furthermore, in this introduction, we intend to discuss the broader picture of the relevance of slavery studies in the Brazilian academic context. Slavery lasted in Brazil for more than three centuries. Equally, this country received the largest number of enslaved African people in the Americas and was the last state in the Western world to abolish slavery. These elements indicate the importance of slavery in Brazil's history; the question is to try to identify its significance in academic studies in the recent past, more specifically in historical studies. In terms of presenting the relevance of slavery in academic history, several graduate courses in history already had research areas dedicated exclusively to slavery from the very beginning, in the 1970s. This is the case, for example, of Fluminense Federal University, which had a research area called "Slavery and Abolition." The Pontifical Catholic University of Rio Grande do Sul, with the subject "Slavery in Brazil," and the Federal University of Pernambuco, with its course on "Slavery in the Northeast in the Transition to Free Labor," provide similar examples.[2] Another element that points to the theme's relevance in Brazilian academic studies is the vast number of theses and dissertations dedicated to it. From 1996 to 2019, there were around 2,500 theses and dissertations on this subject. The vast majority were in history (49%), followed by law (5%). In history alone, around 1,200 theses and dissertations involved the subject of slavery in this period, 8.81% of total production in the field.[3]

The number of historical studies on slavery has grown over the years: while there were only 13 in 1996, in 2018 they reached a peak of 89. The four universities with the most significant number of studies are the University of São Paulo, the Federal University of Bahia, Fluminense Federal University, and the State University of Campinas. Three of them are represented in this book. It is also crucial to remark that this work on slavery is currently spreading to many other parts of the country, from north to south. We can infer some reasons for this increase. A first possibility is the expansion of history graduate courses in Brazil. From 1971 to 2018, there was an increase of more than 500% in the number of master's courses in history and 1,900% in similar doctoral courses. This growth was mainly concentrated between 2000 and

1 Initial versions of the chapters were discussed at an event organized by the Bonn Center of Dependency and Slavery Studies on current trends in Brazilian slavery studies, which reunited Brazilian researchers on December 10 and 11, 2020.

2 Carlos Fico and Ronald Polito, *A História no Brasil (1980–1989): elementos para uma avaliação historiográfica* (Ouro Preto: Editora Universidade Federal de Ouro Preto, 1992).

3 Capes' catalogue on dissertations and theses: http://catalogodeteses.capes.gov.br/catalogo-teses/#!/ [accessed 02.08.2022].

https://doi.org/10.1515/9783111026527-001

2018.[4] This increase in graduate courses was directly related to the growth of public investment in research. The two central public research funding agencies at the federal level, CNPq and CAPES, grew significantly between 2000 and 2015. CNPq, for example, had an increase in its budget of around 200% over this period.[5]

Another aspect to consider when understanding the growth of work on slavery is the approval of law 10.639, which makes the teaching of Afro-Brazilian and African history and culture mandatory in elementary and high schools. The law, approved in 2003, is the result of the struggle of black movements to re-evaluate the role of black people in Brazilian history and the appreciation of black culture. In this sense, we can relate the establishment of the law to the emergence of graduate programs dedicated to the theme, such as the professional master's in the history of Africa, diaspora, and indigenous people at the Universidade Federal do Recôncavo da Bahia. A large amount of research on slavery is being internally disseminated. Articles are published in prominent journals, such as Revista Brasileira de História, which, as perhaps the country's most important journal, had two special issues entirely dedicated to the subject between 1997 and 2020.[6] In terms of publications, it is also necessary to mention the journal Afro-Ásia, which first appeared in 1965: published periodically since 1995, it is a national journal entirely dedicated to Afro-Brazilian and African subjects.[7] The same is true of events. The biennial congresses of the National History Association, a meeting that brings together many historians in Brazil, usually have at least one thematic symposium dedicated to slavery.[8] Besides, since 2003 there has also been the conference "Slavery and Freedom in Southern Brazil" (Encontro Escravidão e Liberdade no Brasil Meridional), which has already convened ten times, most recently in 2019. Here, there were 27 sessions with the presentation of around 80 papers.[9]

However, it is important to emphasize that while works on the history of slavery have increased in Brazil, the field currently faces some challenges. The first is a drastic decrease in funding, especially after 2016. The budget for CNPq and CAPES in 2021 is 73.4% lower than it was in 2015.[10] Meanwhile, the government of President Jair Bolsonaro began in 2018: it has cut the research budget and significantly reduced space

4 Carlos Fico, Claudia Wasserman and Marcelo de S. Magalhães, "Expansão e avaliação da área de História – 2010/2016," *História da Historiografia: International Journal of Theory and History of Historiography* 28 (2018): 267–302.

5 Gabriel Zanlorenssi and Caroline Souza, "Orçamentos da Capes e do CNPq caíram 73,4% desde 2015," *Nexo Jornal*, 20/10/2021, https://www.nexojornal.com.br/grafico/2021/10/20/Orçamentos-da-Capes-e-do-CNPq-ca%C3%ADram-734-desde-2015 [accessed 02.08.2022].

6 The *Brazilian History Journal* website: https://www.scielo.br/j/rbh/ [accessed 02.08.2022].

7 The *Afro-Ásia* website: https://periodicos.ufba.br/index.php/afroasia [accessed 02.08.2022].

8 One source of information is the National History Association (ANPUH) website: https://anpuh.org.br/index.php/quem-somos/simposio-nacional-de-historia [accessed 02.08.2022].

9 See website of the conference: "Slavery and Freedom in Southern Brazil": http://www.escravidaoeliberdade.com.br/site/index.php?option=com_content&view=article&id=53&Itemid=63 [accessed 02.08.2022].

10 Zanlorenssi and Souza, "Orçamentos da Capes."

for the humanities, which are understood as superfluous. In addition, Bolsonaro's government has brought other symbolic challenges. If studies on slavery were already of political importance in Brazil, they gained even greater weight in the face of statements by government officials that slavery was positive for Africans or the remark by the deputy president on November 20, 2021 (Black Awareness Day), that there is no racism in Brazil.[11] The picture presented so far points to a broad, consolidated, and growing amount of work about slavery in Brazil. In 2010, Herbert S. Klein and Francisco Vidal Luna pointed out that "Brazilian historians and economists are doing more studies on their institution of slavery than" in the United States, "despite the imbalance in the size of the historical profession in the two countries."[12] Brazilian works have outlets within the country and are written in Portuguese. But how well they are known in the international context? In 2013, Jean Hébrard published a review of studies on slavery in Brazil. According to him, among "the countries where colonial slavery existed, present-day Brazil has undoubtedly produced the richest and most abundant research into this terrible part of its history." However, he indicated that "due to linguistic barriers, this decisive contribution to the understanding, and therefore the memory, of the institution of slavery is little known outside Brazil's borders."[13]

The language barrier can indeed be a problem. Portuguese does not wield influence outside Portuguese-speaking countries, and publishing in English can present some obstacles. Studies on academic literacy show that the evaluation of Anglophone journals is not only affected by the mastery of English literacy and rhetorical practices, but also imbalanced power relations between center and periphery with regards to knowledge production.[14] This means that knowledge of the language is not enough: it is also necessary to know Anglo academic literacy practices. When analyzing the journal Slavery & Abolition, perhaps one of the leading international journals on the subject, it is possible to verify that between 2000 and 2020, 17 articles were published

---

11 Guilherme Mazui, "'No Brasil, não existe racismo', diz Mourão sobre assassinato de homem negro em supermercado," in *G1*, 20/11/2021, https://g1.globo.com/politica/noticia/2020/11/20/mourao-lamenta-assassinato-de-homem-negro-em-mercado-mas-diz-que-no-brasil-nao-existe-racismo.ghtml [accessed 02.08.2022]; "Presidente da Fundação Palmares diz que escravidão foi 'benéfica'," in *R7*, 27/11/2019, https://noticias.r7.com/brasil/presidente-da-fundacao-palmares-diz-que-escravidao-foi-benefica-27112019 [accessed 02.08.2022]; Gabriela Ramos, "'Aqui no Brasil não existe isso de racismo', diz Bolsonaro em Fortaleza," in *O Estado de S. Paulo*, 28/06/2018, https://politica.estadao.com.br/noticias/eleicoes,aqui-no-brasil-nao-existe-isso-de-racismo-diz-bolsonaro-em-fortaleza,70002375442 [accessed 02.08.2022].

12 Herbert S. Klein and Francisco V. Luna, *Slavery in Brazil* (Cambridge: Cambridge University Press, 2010): IX.

13 Jean Hébrard, "L'esclavage au Brésil: le débat historiographique et ses racines," in *Brésil: quatre siècles d'esclavage. Nouvelles questions, nouvelles recherches*, ed. Jean Hébrard (Paris: Karthala, 2012): 7–61.

14 Theresa Lillis and Mary Jane Curry, "Professional Academic Writing by Multilingual Scholars. Interactions with Literacy Brokers in the Production of English-Medium Texts," *Written Communication* 23 (2006): 3–35.

that explored slavery in Brazil in detail.[15] Of these, only six were written by Brazilians, about 35%. Of course, it is important to remark on the interest in the subject shown by researchers from other countries. Equally, it is also necessary to reflect on the possible difficulties encountered by researchers from peripheral countries, such as Brazil, when publishing in English-language journals.

So, while only a tiny part of Brazilian works on slavery are published in other languages, one cannot fully agree with Hébrard that they are so unknown. In any case, it is essential to emphasize the importance of an initiative like this book (financed by the Bonn Center for Dependency and Slavery Studies) in enabling Brazilian researchers to present current trends in slavery studies to a broader audience. As mentioned previously, Brazil has produced a vast number of theses and dissertations on slavery, around 1,200 in history alone between 1996 and 2019. These theses, dissertations, conference papers, and journal articles offer multiple perspectives and discuss varied subjects, making it hard to represent this diversity in one book. That being said, even though this publication does not show all the current trends of slavery studies in Brazil, it does portray the significant ones. And, since the institution of slavery lasted for more than 300 years in Brazil, we try to offer a wide chronological selection, providing papers that range from the seventeenth century to the post-abolition era at the beginning of the twentieth century. However, most of the chapters discuss the imperial Brazilian period, which covers much of the nineteenth century.

The "negro folk songs" in places affected by the African diaspora, especially Brazil, in the late nineteenth and early twentieth centuries are analyzed by MARTHA ABREU. She mentions that "the music of the slave quarters was really open territory for disputes over meanings and the creation of new hierarchies about the place of African descendants in the post-abolition period." On the one hand, it is possible to verify the reconstruction and existence of racism in the musical and artistic milieu, as the songs "served to belittle the black population and spread stigmas about their bodies and behavior." On the other hand, "these songs were also important in the anti-racist fight carried out by black musicians and artists who invented paths for promotion and empowerment in this same cultural world."

The connections between Brazil and Africa are explored by CRISLAYNE ALFAGALI, who examines iron and gold mining and smelting in the eighteenth century in Minas Gerais, Brazil, and the region of Ilamba in the "Kingdom of Angola and its conquests." As well as showing that "the knowledge of metallurgy was an essential element of the overseas expansion and the exploration of valuable metals such as iron," Alfagali presents how metallurgy was part of African traditions that were reinvented in the colonial context as a form of resistance.

MARIA HELENA PEREIRA TOLEDO MACHADO points out that if the more traditional historiography recognizes only the generic figure of the slave, exempt from gender and

15 See the Slavery & Abolition website: https://www.tandfonline.com/journals/fsla20 [accessed 02.08.2022].

sex, even more recent studies, which have gradually particularized the experience of captivity, have also neglected the specificities of gender in slavery: this includes maternity. The author explores this subject as she addresses the case of the murder of two slave children in São Luís, the capital of the northern province of Maranhão, in 1876. Analyzing it, she examines not only the issue of slave maternity, but also manumission and the separation of mothers and children.

The rights of liberated Africans in Brazil are analyzed by BEATRIZ G. MAMIGONIAN, who discusses "the circumstances, regulations, and juridical proceedings surrounding the implementation of the peculiar statute, the exploitation of mandatory labor, and their definitive emancipation." While the history of liberated Africans in this country is connected to the complex dynamics of nation formation, "marked by the continuation of the illegal trade in enslaved Africans as well as by intense British pressure for its abolition," a comparison with groups of liberated Africans in other parts of the globe allows the author to see the Brazilian case as an illustration of the shifting worlds of labor in the nineteenth century.

MARIANA DIAS PAES mentions the importance of documents produced by judicial institutions to the historiography of Brazilian slavery, at least over the last thirty years. While other studies have already found that the courts were an "arena of struggle," Paes suggests in her text that we can go further and "consider them to be spaces of normative production as well, with enslaved persons and other actors involved in legal proceedings as agents of that production." In this sense, the law was not only disputed in courts but was also created, as people produced specific meanings for norms: the author shows that this process was permeated by various normative frameworks.

TÂMIS PARRON analyses a historical process that began between 1790 and 1830 and reached its high point from 1830 to 1860, the three decades preceding the American Civil War: this involved Brazil, Cuba, and the United States. He points out a cluster of relations between these spaces, "a trans-regional framework within which events and processes in one place began to have impact, influence, and significance on events and processes in the others." Although this was originally anchored in commodity exchanges, it "evolved into a fundamental source of political and geopolitical power for each slaveholding country in their relationship with the capitalist world economy as a whole."

ROBERTO HOFMEISTER PICH analyzes the context and contents of *In supremo apostolates*, published in 1839 by Pope Gregory XVI, the first papal document to explicitly condemn and prohibit the enslavement and traffic of *both* indigenous and black people and to unambiguously ban the transatlantic slave trade, the suppression of which was being especially pressed by Great Britain. The chapter's second goal is to offer a view of how the document impacted the Catholic Church in nineteenth-century Brazil, connecting Catholic Christians and institutions to emancipatory discourses and abolitionist movement(s). He investigates the thought of Antônio Vicente Ferreira Viçoso, who was consecrated bishop of Mariana in 1844. The analysis of a text by Viçoso characterizes the many ways the Catholic Church in Brazil, despite many ambiguities and hesitations, was – through several of its authorities – engaged with abolitionist ideas and influenced people's opinions and attitudes towards abolitionism.

The lynchings that occurred in the nineteenth century have only recently been analyzed by historians, as mentioned by RICARDO F. PIROLA. His contribution examines lynchings during "the period prior to abolition, especially in the 1880s, when the movement to abolish slavery exacerbated tensions between slaves and masters and intensified the political struggle to expansion of civil rights in Brazil." Among the different questions he answers in the text are: why were enslaved people lynched, who took part in the lynchings, and, in the case of the lynching of free individuals, what led members of the public to take the law into their own hands?

Female street vendors or peddlers (*quitandeiras*) in Brazilian urban centers in in the second half of the nineteenth century are the subject of FABIANE POPINIGIS' text. She shows that whether "enslaved or free, these women were fundamental for the operation of the production and consumption economy, paying taxes and using credit; they were likewise essential for basic services involving the preparation of food, cleaning, and the provision of care." These laboring women of African descent established relations, economic and emotional, with their peers and people of different social and political statuses. At the same time, they formulated expectations and attributed specific meanings to their freedom, influencing the political debates of the time.

LILIA SCHWARCZ investigates the presence of slavery in the iconography produced about Brazil by Europeans. The "reiteration of themes and a given visual logic" in "this iconography conforms to a 'politics of visual representation' and the creation of 'otherness'." They "also conform to perceptions capable of producing and rooting racial stereotypes." Comparing paintings and photographs, she shows that, later, artists had less control over the attitudes of their "models." The expressions and body language of black models could reveal another type of slave agency: "their refusal to embody the passive, exotic stereotypes slave-owning society cast for them."

PAULO CRUZ TERRA shows that while there is a great deal of academic work on abolition in Brazil, the investigation into social labor history is still incipient. His objective is to analyze how vagrancy and labor intertwined in the legislation – and the debates – of the Brazilian abolition process, which culminated with the abolition law in 1888. As the process of constructing vagrancy criminalization in Brazilian abolition cannot be understood only within national borders, he proposes approaching this subject from the perspective of global labor history, seeking connections and comparisons with the Portuguese Empire.

Regarding the vital issue of indigenous slavery, CARLOS ZERON points out the notions the Jesuit priest António Vieira shared with other colonization agents in the seventeenth century and those that set him apart. Concerning the acceptance of indigenous enslavement, Zeron argues that the similarity between settlers, royal administrators, and Jesuits in Portuguese America resulted from a long period of cultural sedimentation, which was conceived, justified, and made possible by Roman law, interpreted in the light of Christian theological precepts.

Indigenous slavery; gender; racism; the representation and presence of black people in artistic expression; rights; justice; relations with labor history; slavery and its economic connections and impacts; connections between the Catholic Church and abolitionism; perspectives that try to overcome methodological nationalism: these are some of the trends present in texts gathered in this book. Several of these trends relate to academic work about slavery in places like the USA, France, and Germany.[16] However, Brazilian slavery studies are not only on the receiving end of new trends established in the historiographies of these countries: indeed, the collaboration of Brazilians with international scholars is essential for asking new questions.

Given the broad, consolidated, and growing work on slavery in Brazil, it is evident that not all current trends are represented here. We believe that the book is only a taste of this vibrant historiography, whetting the appetite of the international public for more.

Bibliography

Websites

Capes' catalogue on dissertations and theses, http://catalogodeteses.capes.gov.br/catalogo-teses/#!/ [accessed 02.08.2022].

The *Brazilian History Journal* website, https://www.scielo.br/j/rbh/ [accessed 02.08.2022].

The *Afro-Ásia* website, https://periodicos.ufba.br/index.php/afroasia [accessed 02.08.2022].

The National History Association (ANPUH) website, https://anpuh.org.br/index.php/quem-somos/simposio-nacional-de-historia [accessed 02.08.2022].

The Website of the conference "Slavery and Freedom in Southern Brazil," http://www.escravidaoeliberdade.com.br/site/index.php?option=com_content&view=article&id=53&Itemid=63 [accessed 02.08.2022].

The *Slavery & Abolition* website, https://www.tandfonline.com/journals/fsla20 [accessed 02.08.2022].

Secondary Literature

Fico, Carlos, and Ronald Polito. *A História no Brasil (1980–1989): elementos para uma avaliação historiográfica* (Ouro Preto: Editora Universidade Federal de Ouro Preto, 1992).

Fico, Carlos, Claudia Wasserman and Marcelo de S. Magalhães. "Expansão e avaliação da área de História – 2010/2016," *História da Historiografia: International Journal of Theory and History of Historiography* 28 (2018): 267–302.

---

16 See, for example, Michael Zeuske's discussion on the historiography of slavery. Michael Zeuske, "Historiography and Research Problems of Slavery and the Slave Trade in a Global-Historical Perspective," *International Review of Social History* 57 (2012): 87–111.

Hébrard, Jean. “L’esclavage au Brésil: le débat historiographique et ses racines,” in *Brésil: quatre siècles d’esclavage. Nouvelles questions, nouvelles recherches*, ed. Jean Hébrard (Paris: Karthala, 2012): 7–61.

Klein, Herbert S., and Francisco V. Luna. *Slavery in Brazil* (Cambridge: Cambridge University Press, 2010).

Lillis, Theresa, and Mary Jane Curry. “Professional Academic Writing by Multilingual Scholars. Interactions with Literacy Brokers in the Production of English-Medium Texts,” *Written Communication* 23 (2006): 3–35.

Mazui, Guilherme. “‘No Brasil, não existe racismo’, diz Mourão sobre assassinato de homem negro em supermercado,” *G1*, 20.11.2021, https://g1.globo.com/politica/noticia/2020/11/20/mourao-lamenta-assassinato-de-homem-negro-em-mercado-mas-diz-que-no-brasil-nao-existe-racismo.ghtml [accessed 02.08.2022].

Mazui, Guilherme. “Presidente da Fundação Palmares diz que escravidão foi ‘benéfica’,” *R7*, 27.11.2019, https://noticias.r7.com/brasil/presidente-da-fundacao-palmares-diz-que-escravidao-foi-benefica-27112019 [accessed 02.08.2022].

Ramos, Bagroela. “‘Aqui no Brasil não existe isso de racismo’, diz Bolsonaro em Fortaleza,” *O Estado de S. Paulo*, 28.06.2018, https://politica.estadao.com.br/noticias/eleicoes,aqui-no-brasil-nao-existe-isso-de-racismo-diz-bolsonaro-em-fortaleza,70002375442 [accessed 02.08.2022].

Zanlorenssi, Gabriel, and Caroline Souza. “Orçamentos da Capes e do CNPq caíram 73,4% desde 2015,” *Nexo Jornal*, 20.10.2021, https://www.nexojornal.com.br/grafico/2021/10/20/Orçamentos-da-Capes-e-do-CNPq-ca%C3%ADram-734-desde-2015 [accessed 02.08.2022].

Zeuske, Michael. “Historiography and Research Problems of Slavery and the Slave Trade in a Global-Historical Perspective,” *International Review of Social History* 57 (2012): 87–111.

Martha Abreu

Slave Songs and Racism in the Musical World: Rio de Janeiro and the Black Atlantic, 1880–1910

> [. . .] And so by fateful chance the Negro folk song – the rhythmic cry of the slave – stands today not simply as the sole American music, but as the most beautiful expression of human experience born this side the seas. It has been neglected, it has been, and is, half despised, and above all it has been persistently mistaken and misunderstood; but notwithstanding, it still remains as the singular spiritual heritage of the nation and the greatest gift of the Negro people. William E.B. Du Bois, "The Sorrow Songs," 1903.[1]

Back in 2002 or 2003, Hebe Mattos invited me to attend a *jongo*[2] at the São José da Serra *quilombo* in Valença, the state of Rio de Janeiro, and begin to take part in the study on "memories of captivity" she was then working on with Ana Lugão Rios and Robson Martins. I can say with all certainty that from that point on, my life was never the same. Besides discovering that the *jongo* had not died out, as many folklorists claimed, I also became an historian of the present. The places of the past in the present, the memories of captivity in post-abolition struggles, the role of slave songs and intangible heritage – like the *jongo* – in the contemporary development of black *quilombola* identity began to take over my every thought, plan, writing, orientation, undergraduate and graduate course, and teacher training workshop.

One of the outcomes of this investment was the 2017 publication of the book *Da Senzala ao Palco, canções escravas e racismo nas Américas, 1870–1930* (From the Slave Quarters to the Stage, Slave Songs and Racism in the Americas).[3] In that book, I try to show the history and importance of slave songs, not only for the development of modern world music, but also for the propagation of racism in the world of musical and cultural entertainment. Ironically, these songs were also important in the antiracist fight carried out by the black musicians and artists who invented paths for promotion and empowerment in this same cultural world. In order to do this, it was vital that the legacy of the slave songs be understood from the demands of black and

1 William E.B. Du Bois, *The Souls of Black Folk* (Boston/New York: Bedford Books, 1997): 186.

2 We can define *jongo* as a round dance, with movements in pairs, the beating of drums, chants, and challenges in verses. Today the *jongo* is considered Brazilian cultural heritage. Hebe Mattos and Martha Abreu, "Jongo, Recalling History," in *Cangoma Calling: Spirits and Rhythms of Freedom in Brazilian Jongo Slavery Songs*, ed. Pedro Meira Monteiro and Michael Stone (Dartmouth, MA: University of Massachusetts Dartmouth, 2013): 77–88.

3 Martha Abreu, *Da Senzala ao Palco, canções escravas e racismo nas Américas, 1870–1930* (Campinas: Editora da Unicamp, 2017). See also the vídeo "Slave Songs and Racism in the Americas," https://www.youtube.com/watch?v=agZPb-uEVto [accessed 10.01.2022].

https://doi.org/10.1515/9783111026527-002

quilombola social and cultural movements, which, throughout Brazil, had transformed their memories of captivity and freedom into a fight against racism and for land, rights, equality, and justice. To a great extent, the book is also the fruit of my learning about racism in the cultural field, no easy thing, I must say, for someone raised within the parameters of whiteness and lulled by the legends of Brazil's alleged racial democracy.[4]

1 From the Slave Quarters to the Stage

In 1903, Du Bois, historian and great leader of the American and Black Atlantic movement, was able to define like few others the disputes that had raged around what he called "the Negro folk song – the rhythmic cry of the slave." In his words, the songs came to be despised, misunderstood, and forgotten, but they were the "sole American music," "the most beautiful expression of the human experience born this side the seas," "the singular spiritual heritage of the nation and the greatest gift of the Negro people." On the one hand, he was aware of the songs' devaluation, neglect, and misrepresentation; on the other hand, he championed their positive identity (national and ethnic), political, and cultural meanings.[5] The history of black music in the Americas has always been characterized by disputes over its significance and meanings. And, since it is my intent to highlight the field of music throughout the nineteenth and twentieth centuries, it became an important arena of conflict among musicians, black musicians, scholarly white artists, and entrepreneurs of the theater, piano scores, and the recording industry. No doubt it was also a powerful forum for the propagation of racism and the anti-racist fight. From very early on and throughout the nineteenth century, "Negro folk songs" attracted a wide variety of white attention and opinions: from repressive gentlemen, religious authorities, and politicians concerned about the practices; from curious musicians and dancers interested in artistic novelties; and from cultural entrepreneurs thirsty for new audiences and new businesses in the field of entertainment. And we could also highlight the interest of erudite scholars, like folklorists, especially in Brazil, who worried about the dangers of the "survival" of African cultural and musical expressions. They ended up betting on the disappearance of the African musical memory and invested in the valorization of Brazilian popular and mestizo music, fruit of the contributions of Africans and Portuguese for a

---

4 I cannot go without noting the contributions my students have made to studies about slave songs in various parts of Brazil. These included studies of *batuques*, *lundus*, *maxixes*, *jongos*, *congados*, and sambas in the southeast, and *maracatus*, sambas, and *bois* in the northeast. See Martha Abreu, Giovana Xavier, Livia Monteiro and Eric Brasil, *Cultura Negra, Novos Desafios para os Historiadores*, vol. 1 and 2 (Niterói: Editora da Universidade Federal Fluminense, 2017).

5 Debates about the musical contribution of Africans and their descendants to national development, in both the United States and Brazil, became an important agenda item for musicians, intellectuals, folklorists, and black movements throughout the twentieth century.

supposed national harmony.[6] With some delay, if we compare it with historians' studies of slave music, dance, and poetry in the United States,[7] there has been renewed interest in the "rhythmic cry of the slave" in Brazil. Without a doubt, this renewal involved the greater presence of historians in the subject and the resulting understanding of the cultural phenomena (musical, festive, and religious) from the action of the social subjects, of black social subjects. As historiography in Brazil has shown, the "Negro folk songs," in their most varied forms as songs, festivals, dances, poetry, and religious songs, even if wrapped in European musical traditions, were part of the negotiation strategies and claims of the slaves and their descendants.[8] During captivity, they were a part of the desire for autonomy and freedom, alongside other important demands such as family life, the possibility of freedom from slavery, and access to land. Once free or after abolition, they were a part of the right to celebrate and the political affirmation of their legacy, values, and feelings.

In this paper, amid the many possibilities for discussion regarding the "Negro folk songs" in places affected by the African diaspora, I will try to call attention to one important aspect: their presence on stage and in the prosperous commercial market for sheet music. Without a doubt, the songs became coveted attractions and products in the world of musical entertainment in the late nineteenth and early twentieth centuries wherever there had been slavery. What did their presence mean when they arrived in places far from the slave quarters? And what was the purpose of their promotion on the international Atlantic musical circuits of New York, Paris, Rio de Janeiro, Havana, and Buenos Aires?[9] As they circulated through circuses, modern stages, and piano scores, these songs constantly made reference to memories and scenes of captivity, whether in the

6 Studies on black music and festivals in Brazil throughout the twentieth century were in close dialogue with North American anthropological studies about possible "African cultural survivals" in the Americas. See Arthur Ramos, *As culturas negras no novo mundo* (São Paulo: Companhia Editora Nacional, 1979); Melville Herskovits, "El estúdio de la música negra en el hemisfério occidental," *Boletin Latino Americano de Musica* 5 (1941): 133–42.

7 For a few references, see, Roger D. Abrahams, *Afro-American Folktales: Stories from Black Traditions in the New World* (Nova York: Pantheon Books, 1985); Laurence W. Levine, *Black Culture and Black Consciousness* (Nova York: Oxford University Press, 1977); Eugene Genovese, *Roll, Jordan, Roll, The World the Slaves Made* (New York: Vintage Books, 1976).

8 See João José Reis, "Tambores e Temores, a Festa Negra na Bahia na primeira metade do século XIX," in *Carnavais e Outras Frestas*, ed. Maria Clementina P. Cunha (Campinas: Ed. Unicamp, 2002): 108–56; Robert Slenes, "Eu venho de muito longe, eu venho cavando: jongueiros cumba na senzala centro-africana," in *Memória do jongo. As gravações históricas de Stanley Stein, Vassouras, 1949*, ed. Silvia Lara and Gustavo Pacheco (Rio de Janeiro: Folha Seca; Campinas: Cecult, 2007): 109–58; Wlamyra Albuquerque, *O jogo da dissimulação: Abolição e cidadania negra no Brasil* (São Paulo: Cia das Letras, 2009); Maria Clementina P. Cunha, *'Não tá sopa': Sambas e sambistas no Rio de Janeiro, de 1890 a 1930* (Campinas: Editora da Unicamp, 2016).

9 Given the constraints of this paper, I will not go into the closely related discussion of sound recordings of ragtime, blues, jazz, tangos, and *maxixes* in the nascent transnational recording industry.

titles, illustrations, verses, or genres. That is why starting here, I will refer to them as *slave songs*. I use italics to differentiate them from the songs sung by slaves during captivity. Constantly revived in the diversity of the cakewalk, rags, blues, and jazz in the United States, the rumba and the *son* in Cuba, the calypso in the English-speaking Caribbean, and the *lundus, tangos, maxixes,* and *sambas* in Brasil, there was a great variety of *slave songs* identified with the heritage of slavery in the vast territory of the Americas.[10] They invaded the modern cultural circuits of the American Atlantic and European Atlantic, where the new colonial expansion attracted views about very different peoples and cultures. And they were successful in the sheet music market, in salons, in concerts, on stages and in the young recording industry, starting in the late nineteenth and early twentieth centuries. The world of entertainment and Atlantic musical entrepreneurs produced appealing shows and modern dance entertainment for white audiences from genres, rhythms, and themes identified with the Negro population in the Americas – at around the same time and certainly not by chance.[11] My main argument, in dialogue with the North American bibliography, is that when *slave songs* arrived in show business, brought mainly, but not only, by white artists or entrepreneurs, they promoted appraisals of the past and the legacy of slavery with racialized and racist representations of Afro-American peoples – before or after abolition. These were appraisals that formed the basis of the words of Du Bois with regard to the "misunderstanding" of and "disdain" for "Negro folk songs." This view of the *slave songs* has been studied more extensively in the North Atlantic reality.[12] My research sought to find exact parallels in Brazil, establishing a series of comparisons with the United States in the field of music from 1870 to 1930. For this, I started from common problems (racism and anti-racism in the musical field) and equivalent sources (theater announcements, scores, and phonographic recordings), contributing to a broadened horizon of transnational studies on post-abolition and racism in the Atlantic world. Without a doubt, the differences between the United States and Brazil are already quite well-known, but the strategy of my research, more than reinforcing the known specificities between the two countries, was to seek possible similarities in the field of music. The results were positive, and it was impressive to see how here and there the musical field constitutes a fundamental place for not only the projection of African-American genres and musicians but also for the propagation (and subversion) of racist ideas from the late nineteenth through the early

---

10 It is important to note that this discussion can no longer be thought of in purely national terms.

11 For a few references, see Robin Moore, "O teatro bufo: teatro *blackface* cubano," in *Música e História no longo século XIX*, ed. Antônio H. Lopes, Martha Abreu, Martha T. de Ulhoa and Mônica P. Velloso (Rio de Janeiro: Fundação Casa de Rui Barbosa, 2011): 357–82; John Charles Chastten, *National Rhythms, African Roots. The Deep History of Latin American Popular Dance* (Albuquerque: University of New Mexico Press, 2004); Bryan Wagner, *Disturbing the Peace. Black Culture and the Police Power After Slavery* (Cambridge: Harvard University Press, 2009): chapters 3 and 4; Tim Brooks, *The Lost Sound: Blacks and the Birth of the Recording Industry, 1890–1919* (Champaign: University of Illinois Press, 2005).

12 Paul Gilroy, *The Black Atlantic: Modernity and Double Consciousness* (London: Verso Books, 1993).

twentieth centuries.[13] By using some examples from the United States and Brazil, I plan to show how interest in the music and dance of slaves and their descendants in the Atlantic entertainment world of the late nineteenth century naturalized, hierarchized, and ridiculed musical and racial differences and identities. The racist maxims of the pseudo-scientific treatises that circulated throughout the Atlantic were projected upon the world of music. The meanings attributed to black characters and their musical genres in theaters, song lyrics, and on the covers of sheet music editions created powerful possibilities for the propagation of allegories about the inferiority and supposed degeneration of African descendants precisely in the final hours of modern slavery, when

Figure 1: Bert Williams, https://en.wikipedia.org/wiki/Bert_Williams#/media/Ficheiro: BertWilliamsPhotoPortraitWithCigarette.jpg, Samuel Lumiere studio, New York City [accessed 15.09.2021].

13 Micol Seigel, *Uneven Encounters. Making Race and Nation in Brazil and United States* (Durham, NC: Duke University Press, 2009); Kim Butler, "New Negroes: Negritude e movimentos Pós-Abolição no Brasil e na diáspora africana," in *Histórias do Pós-Abolição, Histórias do pós-Abolição no mundo atlântico*, vol. 1–3, ed. Martha Abreu, Carolina V. Dantas, Hebe Mattos, Beatriz Loner and Karl Monsma (Niterói: Eduff, 2014): 137–48. Kim Butler and Petrônio Domingues, *Diásporas Imaginadas: Atlântico Negro e História Afro-Brasileiras* (São Paulo: Perspectivas, 2020).

there were also discussions about the citizenship rights of former slaves.[14] Due to the constraints of this article, I will not be able to delve more deeply into the strategies black musicians used to deal with and transform racism. But no doubt the commercial rise of rhythms, themes, and genres identified with the memories of slavery and the Negro population may have broadened the work opportunities for black musicians – and this certainly made some difference in the possibilities offered by the artistic field to subvert the racial hierarchies being propagated after the abolition of slavery. Even if they had to negotiate the traditional stereotypes of the spectacles offered by *slave songs*, new meanings and new dimensions reached the cakewalks and the *lundus*, for example, when performed by black artists like Bert Williams (1874–1922) in the United States and Eduardo das Neves (1874–1919) in Brazil (See Fig. 1 and 2).[15]

Figure 2: Eduardo das Neves, O Malho, Ano 1917, Edição 747, p. 44, available at http://memoria.bn.br/ [accessed 06.12.2022].

14 See Ana Lugão Rios and Hebe Mattos, *Memórias do Cativeiro: Família, Trabalho e Cidadania no Pós-Abolição* (Rio de Janeiro: Civilização Brasileira, 2005).

15 See Martha Abreu, "Slave Songs and Racism in the Post-Abolition Period: Eduardo das Neves and Bert Williams, Brazil and the United States," in *The Boundaries of Freedom: Slavery, Abolition, and the Making of Modern Brazil*, ed. Brodwyn Fischer and Keila Grinberg (Cambridge: Cambridge University Press, 2022): 388–419.

2 The Case of the Cakewalk

As Abrahams points out, the cakewalk of the plantations featured a caricatured mimicry of the masters' quadrille through exaggerated walking and dance movements. It was a stylized and improvised practice that could also reveal the deep critical and ironic attitude of the slaves, although, according to Lawrence Levine, the masters did not always seem to notice subversion.[16] On the contrary, they understood that the dance imitating the performance of the rich white masters confirmed some impressions they had of slaves: that they were naturally naïve, happy, laughing, and musical. The cakewalk was already born wrapped in various interpretations, disputes, and meanings. According to Petrine Archer-Straw, as artistic expression outside the plantation, the dance recognized as the cakewalk would initially have been an urban phenomenon performed by blacks who migrated from the south to the north in search of better living conditions after slavery ended. In general, it involved the performance of gaudy, bowed, and arrogant gestures to the sound of ragtime, with the hips almost always prominent and in motion.[17] In 1890, the cakewalk could already be seen in Manhattan at the end of a well-known music theaters: the Creole Show. From then on, it was regarded as a "fever,"[18] a real epidemic that affected whites and blacks alike, and successfully reached revue theaters and musical shows in the United States, Europe, and South America (Fig. 3).[19] No doubt because of all the imagery it brought from life in the slave quarters, the new dance became one of the most important expressions of *slave songs* on the stage and one of the most effective ways to propagate, revive, and discuss racist stereotypes regarding the black population.

The cakewalk type of performance, characterized by parody, irreverence, and humor, was easily incorporated into the famous blackface minstrel shows, with their Ethiopian melodies, and Coon shows (a genre with stereotypical representations of the black and slave population), which were successful from the mid-nineteenth century in the United States, based on comical white minstrels painted black. With black greasepaint and exaggerated lips and eyes, made up into grotesque and racist caricatures, the blackfaces ridiculed the presumed childishness and musical joy of slaves on the old plantations of the south on the stage through costumes, comic skits, mocking performances, speech, and dances. They also conveyed pejorative and laughable images of

16 Roger Abrahams, *Singing the Master, the Emergence of African-American Culture in the Plantation South* (New York: Penguin Group, 1992): 101, 185; Levine, *Black Culture*: 17.

17 Petrine Archer-Straw, *Negrophilia, Avant-Garde Paris and Black Culture in the 1920s* (New York: Thames & Hudson, 2000): 44.

18 The characterization of the cakewalk as a virus, epidemic, fever, and contagion, later also attributed to jazz, allows us to understand it, according to Astrid Kusser, as a dance that broke borders and divisions of class and race. Astrid Kusser, "The Riddle of the Booty . . .," http://www.radicalriddims.de/txt-riddleofbooty-e.html [accessed 27.07.2016].

19 With regard to the success of the cakewalk in Paris, see also Gérard Noiriel, *Chocolat clown nègre. L'histoire oubiée Du premier artiste noir de la scène française* (Montrouge: Bayard Editions, 2012): 166–69.

Figure 3: 1907 postcard from the digitized collection "Colonialism and the African diaspora on postcards." University and the Cologne State Library, http://www.radicalriddims.de/txt-riddleofbooty.html [accessed 02.11.2020]. *The Brooklyn Cake Walk, German Orchestra*, 1908, https://www.youtube.com/watch?v=8nqkXIHQgCU [accessed 20.07.2016].

black characters, such as Sambos (laughing, naïve, mischievous, grotesque, animalized, and inconsequential figures), Mamies, and Old Uncles (like Uncle Remus and Uncle Tom), along with well-dressed Dandies and their pretension in appearing cultured and refined in the cities after abolition. To Robin Moore, all of these representations reinforced the justifications of segregationist policies.[20] There is a vast specialized bibliography about blackface shows in the United States. Generally, the most recent works hold the view that minstrel shows had considerable significance in disseminating ideas about race, class, and gender at the same time as they made "blackness" an American cultural commodity.[21] In fact, the stereotypical illustrations of slaves and their descendants, and

20 Robin Moore, "O Teatro Bufo: o teatro *blackface* Cubano" in *Música e História no longo século XIX*, ed. Antônio H. Lopes, Martha Abreu, Martha T. de Ulhoa and Mônica P. Velloso (Rio de Janeiro: Fundação Casa de Rui Barbosa, 2011): 358.

21 Annemarie Bean, James V. Hatch and Brooks McNamara, eds., *Inside the Minstrel Mask. Readings in Nineteenth-Century Blackface Minstrelsy* (Middletown: Wesleyan University Press, 1996): XII. See also William Fitzhugh Brundage, ed., *Beyond Blackface: African Americans and the Creation of American Popular Culture, 1890–1930* (Chapel Hill: University of North Carolina Press, 2011); Samuel A. Floyd, Jr., *The Power of Black Music: Interpreting Its History from Africa to the United States* (Oxford: Oxford University Press, 1999); Eric Lott, "Blackface and Blackness," in *Inside the Minstrel Mask. Readings in Nineteenth-Century Blackface Minstrelsy*, ed. Annemarie Bean, James V. Hatch and Brooks McNamara (Middletown: Wesleyan University Press, 1996): 3–34; Daphne Brooks, *Bodies in Dissent: Spectacular Performance of Race and Freedom (1850–1910)* (Durham, NC: Duke University Press, 2006). Tracking all the meaning of their spectacles, however, continued to pose a challenge because, by bringing forth the notion of race and rekindling racist imagery, they carnivalized these convictions and opened the door to critical responses that were far more plural than is possible to predict. As Abrahams pointed out, minstrel shows, with their slave and black characters like the famous Uncle

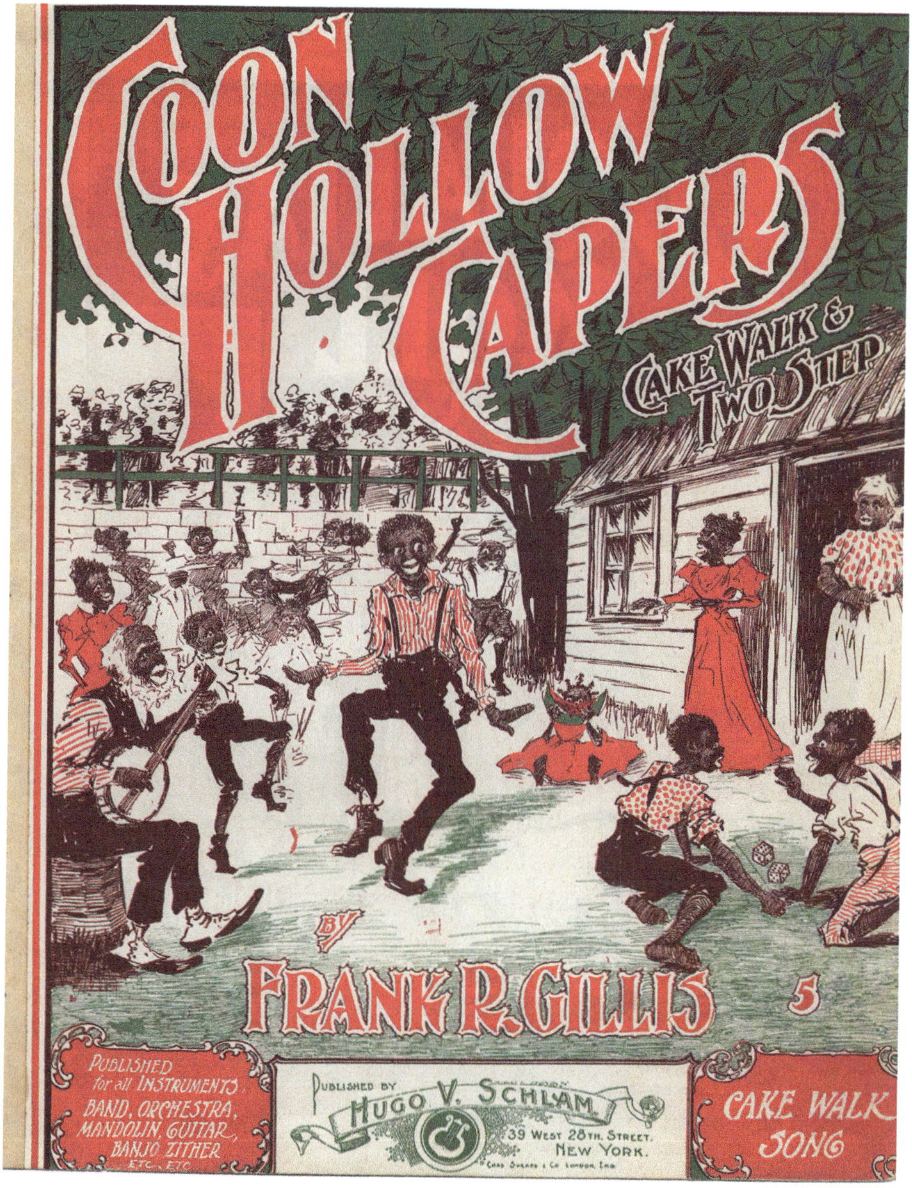

Figure 4: Coon hollow capers: cake walk & two step, 1899. Sheet Music Collection. African-Americana. Brown University.

Tom, could also reveal critiques of slavery, the slaveholding South, and the dehumanization of slaves, especially when they began to incorporate black artists into their casts and among their musicians.

Figure 5: Sam Bennett, *Loquatias Moll* (*cakewalk*), Armstrong Music, New York, 1900. *Historic American Sheet Music*, Duke University.

of the modern cakewalk found in theatrical performances and on printed covers, effectively helped spread a devastating racist ideology about black identity in American homes that owned pianos.[22] They also disseminated to the general public the maxims of the period's scientific thought about the idea of races through repetition of certain patterns of drawings that projected the alleged inferiority of the black population and their proclaimed natural vocation for music and dance (See Fig. 4 and 5).

Micol Seigel and I have documented to a considerable extent the presence of the cakewalk in Brazil.[23] Always together with the *maxixe*, which was also found in the United States, these genres revealed modern, transnational, and Atlantic tastes and challenged traditional European dances, valuing exotic and lascivious choreographies (characterized by the attractive swaying of the hips) historically identified with the legacy of slavery[24] and with the black and poor population. Performances of the cakewalk and *maxixe* in Brazil were along the same lines, and generated similar effects and meanings in different locations of the diaspora.

3 *Slave Songs* on the Stages of Brazil

As in the United States, *slave songs* in Brazil reached other public spaces, with different meanings and representations. Throughout the nineteenth century, these representations were documented in the literary texts of Manoel Antônio de Almeida and could be seen and heard in the musical performances of the tent theaters of popular festivals in downtown Rio de Janeiro, like the festival of the Divino Espírito Santo do Campo de Santana and the festival of the Largo de Santa Rita I studied some time ago.[25] In these tents, comedies such as those by Martins Pena were staged, featuring *lundus*, *fados*, *cateretês*, *récitas*, *mágicas*, duets, and many dances, from the waltz to the *batuque rasgado* and including *miudinhos*, belly rolls, *saracoteios*, *requebros*, polkas, *chulas*, *jongos*, and, most probably, *maxixes*. At least since the 1870s, "Negro dances" became attractions in theaters, and their adaptations for piano were traded in the growing and lucrative market for sheet music in Brazil. I need to acknowledge that historiographical research has made significant discoveries about the presence of music and dances inherited from African cultures and slavery in the music theaters of Rio de Janeiro. Without these discoveries, it would be impossible to suggest any kind of dialogue between minstrel shows and Brazilian performances. As I plan to show, based on this new research and my survey of scores, the relationships between *slave songs* in Brazil and the United

22 Stephanie Dunson, "Black Misrepresentation in Nineteenth-Century Sheet Music Illustration," in *Beyond Blackface: African Americans and the Creation of American Popular Culture, 1890–1930*, ed. William Fitzhugh Brundage (Chapel Hill: University of North Carolina Press, 2011): 45–65, here 54.

23 I found similar references in the *Correio da Manhã*. Between 1903 and 1908, I found 33 news stories involving the cakewalk. Seigel, *Uneven Encounters*: 73.

24 See Denis-Constant Martin, "A herança musical da escravidão," *Revista Tempo* 15, no. 29 (2011): 15–42.

25 Martha Abreu, *O Império do Divino, Festas religiosas e Cultura Popular no Rio de Janeiro, 1830–1900* (Rio de Janeiro: Nova Fronteira, 2009): chapter 1.

States, between cakewalk, ragtime, *jongo, lundu, maxixe,* and tango in representations about blacks and the world of slavery, are closer than previously thought and shown. The growth of musical theaters and their success in Brazil was also accompanied by the eventual incorporation of dances and music inherited from slavery and Afro-Brazilian sources and expressions that interacted with European music.[26] To Fernando Mencarelli, the presence of *jongos* and *lundus* on stage, especially at the end of operettas and revues, was not just a fad, but something that became almost obligatory in translated texts, parodies, or texts by white Brazilian authors and artists.[27] As Silvia Martins de Souza and Cristina Magaldi have pointed out, although one can recognize (and positively value) the addition of Afro-Brazilian musical expression to the stage, composed mostly by white classical musicians and performed by white artists, musical presentations in general infantilized the figure of the slave and the black population, sometimes emphasizing traits of joy and resignation, disorder and malice in grotesque and comic caricatures, many of them set on coffee farms or in low income housing in the cities, with obvious parallels to minstrel shows in the United States.[28] Characters from the Afro-Brazilian world, such as the *bahianas* and mulattos, played by white actresses, also became the center of attention, and were often associated with delicious and appealing "typical" food dishes. The recurrence of hip shaking, in turn, called attention to movement of the hips, a major interest of cakewalk and *maxixe* dancers in the salons. At the same time, it provided the association between what was defined as the "Negro race" and exotic and erotic bodies prone to licentiousness.[29] With doses of laughter, humor, and racism, they brought African descendants and their cultural expressions to the stage. The chances were good that audiences would leave these shows reasonably convinced that African descendants were primitive, inferior, and unprepared for citizenship.

There were many examples of the transformation of *slave songs* into theatrical and musical performances. In 1871, Henrique Alves de Mesquita, a black musician who had studied in France, with support from the imperial government, organized a "Negro chorus," a *fado* and a "big *jongo*, accompanied by *batuque*," to open the operetta *Trunfo às Avessas* (Upside-Down Joker), by França Jr, at the Fênix Dramática Theater. *Trunfo às Avessas*, with comedy and political satire, was set on a farm in Madureira at the time of

26 Cristina Magaldi, "Música, sátira e política no Rio de Janeiro Imperial," in *Música e História no longo século XIX*, ed. Antônio H. Lopes, Martha Abreu, Martha T. de Ulhoa and Mônica P. Velloso (Rio de Janeiro: Fundação Casa de Rui Barbosa, 2011): 409; Cristina Magaldi, *Music in Imperial Rio de Janeiro. European culture in tropical milieu* (Lanham, MD: The Scarecrow Press, 2004).

27 Fernando Antonio Mencarelli, "A Voz e a Partitura. Teatro musical, indústria e diversidade cultural no Rio de Janeiro (1868–1908)" (PhD diss., Universidade Federal de Campina Grande, 2003): 223–37; Magaldi, "Música, sátira e política": 401.

28 Silvia Cristina Martins de Souza, "A alquimia cultural do teatro musicado de Francisco Correa Vasques: Rio de Janeiro, segunda metade do século XIX," in *Música e História no longo século XIX*, ed. Antônio H. Lopes, Martha Abreu, Martha T. de Ulhoa and Mônica P. Velloso (Rio de Janeiro: Fundação Casa de Rui Barbosa, 2011): 354.

29 Magaldi, "Música, sátira e política": 418–19.

debates over the approval of the Free Womb Law of September 1871.[30] In 1880, in Artur Azevedo's comic opera, *Os Noivos* (The Newlyweds), Francisco de Sá Noronha, Portuguese by birth, composed a *jongo* and a *cateretê*. The setting was a farm in interior Rio de Janeiro state, and the *jongo* opened the second act as a kind of show for visitors. Just before that, in 1877, Arthur Azevedo had already included two *jongos* in his 1877 revue *Nova Viagem a Lua* (New Trip to the Moon).[31] In the 1880s, a good example of *slave songs* on the stage is the presence of the *Jongo dos sexagenários* (*Jongo* of the Sexagenarians) by Henrique de Magalhães, which, in 1885, was a success in the theatrical play *A mulher homem* (The Woman Man). The song made direct reference to the debate over Law 3270, passed by parliament in September of that year, which authorized the freeing of slaves over the age of 60. The lyrics accompanying the score were entitled *Ai! ai! Sinhô*. According to Silvia Martins de Souza, who extensively discusses its verses and newspaper reports, the *Jongo dos sexagenários*, with African words, expressed the passivity of the old Negro, the pain and suffering of slavery, and conveyed the image of submissive, resigned, dependent, and unprepared slaves.[32] The cover of the sheet music sold by a prosperous and elegant firm features a list of 81 songs from the *Collection of Tangos and Havaneras for Piano.* Included among the tangos and *havaneras* were two *lundus* and several themes associated with "Negro songs": *los negros, el negrito, la negrita, araúna* (*quisomba*), *quebra quebra minha gente*, and *lundu das mulatinhas*.

In 1887, another *jongo* was presented at the *O Mercúrio* Revue, a mix of the comedic and the fantastic, by Artur Azevedo and Moreira Sampaio, starring white actor Xisto Baía, who played, in addition to a journalist, a *capadócio*, a figure connected to the world of capoeira and bravery. The *jongo*, composed by scholarly musician Abdon Milanez (1858–1927), director of the Conservatory of Music of Rio de Janeiro, appeared as a "group of negros" (probably in blackface) who accompanied the Olympian god Mercury in a discussion about "widening the street of the *zungus*" (Negro meeting houses) (Fig. 6a and 6b).

Finally, in the year of abolition itself, the *Revista do ano de 1888* (1888 Revue) heralded Francisco G. de Carvalho's *Tango do Bendegó* and a new *jongo* by Henrique Alves de Mesquita for the second act. The lyrics were by white writer Dr. Oscar Pederneiras. The *jongo* and tango in the year of abolition brought to the stage the historical celebrations taking place throughout the southeast. On the cover of the score published

30 Ibid.: 402–3; Antonio J. Augusto, *Henrique Alves Mesquita . . . Da pérola mais luminosa à poeira do esquecimento* (Rio de Janeiro: Folha Seca, 2014): 151.

31 Silvia Cristina Martins de Souza, "Que venham negros à cena com maracas e tambores: jongo, política e teatro musicado no Rio de Janeiro nas últimas décadas do século XIX," *Afro-Asia* 40 (2010): 159; Magaldi, "Música, sátira e política": 408.

32 De Souza, "Que venham negros": 162–63. For the author, even if one considers the participation of many authors, actors, and musicians of musical theater in the struggles for abolition, like Chiquinha Gonzaga, Arthur Azevedo, Francisco Correa Vasques, Cavalier Darbilly, and Henrique Mesquita, they were not far removed from the prejudice or paternalistic vision that sought to protect the action of slaves and freedmen.

(a)

(b)

Figure 6a–b: Sheet music. Abdon Milanez, "jongo," Narciso & Arthur Napoleão. Acervo digital, Biblioteca Nacional, RJ, http://objdigital.bn.br/acervo_digital/div_musica/mas233029/mas233029.pdf [accessed 23.09.2022].

by the company Buchman & Guimarães, the drawings featured stereotypical images of dancers, as well as of a supposedly well-dressed black couple, in the very year that everyone would be equal, officially or ironically. These were the hurdles, limits, and challenges that black musicians themselves had to deal with when projecting themselves into the musical world with their artistic talents (Fig. 7).

Figure 7: Sheet music. Francisco G. de Carvalho, Henrique A. de Mesquita, Oscar Pederneiras. *Revista de 1988.* Biblioteca Nacional, RJ, http://objdigital.bn.br/acervo_digital/div_musica/mas198175/mas198175.pdf [accessed 23.09.2022].

4 *Slave Songs* in the Sheet Music Market

According to Marcelo Cazarré, since the mid-nineteenth century, the affluent society of Rio de Janeiro was growing wealthier, buying pianos and sheet music for their favorite past-times: family parties, dances, and soirees, mainly to the sound of waltzes, French and Italian arias, and polkas.[33] The decrease in the price of pianos also signaled the transformations of a city that, due to the prospects created by the coffee economy, was getting closer and closer to Atlantic musical novelties. If the taste for European opera arias and waltzes was widespread among the more refined sectors – and predominated in the published music catalogs – songs from the land, such as *modinhas, lundus,* tangos, *jongos,* and "negro dances," an expression used in compositions, also had their place in the successful sheet music market. Through the work of Monica Leme on popular music and music publishing (1820–1920), a world of business around sheet music, led by powerful publishers like Casa Bevilácqua, Narciso & Arthur Napoleão, Buschmann & Guimarães, and Casa Levy, begins to emerge.[34] With accessible and even reduced prices (some at $1000 and $500), sheet music scores could have editions and covers with special and individualized designs, matching the theme of the compositions, as is the case of some *batuques* and sambas. The score for *Danse Nègre, caprici caráctéristique* by J. Ascher for piano, found in the *Álbum de Família* (Family Album) no. 6, of the Villa Lobos Institute, is a good example of how piano players in "family homes" knew the repertoire associated with *slave songs.* The publication is French and the composer was Dutch (1829–1869), with a career between London and Paris, but sales received the seal of the Casa Isidoro Bevilácqua of Rio de Janeiro. In the background of the illustration of Ascher's composition, there are small images of black men and women in scenes that refer to African or African-American slave imagery. In defining the style, *caprici caráctéristique,* there is the promised touch of fantasy and exoticism. The cover features the profile of a woman's face and she is wearing a scarf on her head, a common feature in representations of black dancers in the United States as well (Fig. 8).

No doubt renditions and representations of *slave songs* did not occupy a preferred place in the scores of the catalogs published and consulted, but they were clearly visible there in the song titles, the genres and, less frequently, on some covers.[35] When analyzing the 1913 catalog of Casa Bevilácqua, one of the most important houses from the late nineteenth and early twentieth centuries, Monica Leme has indicated the

33 Marcelo Macedo Cazarré, *A trajetória das danças de negros na literatura pianística brasileira* (Pelotas: Editoria da Universidade Federal de Pelotas, 2001): 50.

34 Monica Neves Leme, "E 'Saíram à Luz': As novas coleções de polcas, modinhas, lundus, etc. – Música popular e impressão musical no Rio de Janeiro (1820–1920)," 2 vols. (PhD diss., Universidade Federal Fluminense, 2006).

35 The score covers were consulted at the Moreira Salles Institute, the Music Division of the National Library, and the Villa Lobos Institute, Rio de Janeiro.

Figure 8: Sheet music. J. Ascher, *Danse Nègre*. Instituto Villa Lobos. "Álbum de Família" 61.

predominance of waltzes and polkas. But *habaneras, lundus*, and tangos were also advertised. I was pleasantly surprised to see that nine cakewalks were printed.[36] Another musical work, subtitled *Dança de negros* (Dance of the Negroes) but explicitly named *Batuque*, was published in a score by Alberto Nepomuceno (1864–1920) in the Brazilian series for orchestra in 1891. The cover of the score I located, *Primeira suite braziliene* (First Brazilian Suite), published by Arthur Napoleão, features a carefully designed final proof. *Batuque* was presented for the first time in 1888 at the Iracema Club in Fortaleza, shortly before abolition, when we know the drums had been beating for many days and weeks all over farms in the coffee-growing southeast. The depiction comes close to the descriptions and images of nineteenth-century travelers and of what was then known as *jongo*, but generically referred to as *batuque* (See Fig. 9a and b). Palm trees, especially banana trees, quite present in *jongo* verses, the bonfire, the long drums, the

36 Leme, "E 'Saíram à Luz'": 312.

(a)

(b)

Fig. 9a–b: Sheet music. Alberto Nepomuceno. Suite Brezilienne. Catálogo de Partituras. DIMAS, Biblioteca Nacional, M786.1 N-IV-59.

couple in the center with "distinctive" gestures and performance, set the scene and the location. All the characters in the image appear to be slaves; they are barefoot and drawn with crude and deformed features, especially the faces. A woman on the left, smoking a pipe, probably represented the old African ancestors always present in the *jongo* circles. The illustrator, identified as "Lucas" in a signature beside the campfire, demonstrated that he knew something of what he was representing.

For Avelino Romero, who conducted a reference study on the composer's career, *Batuque* is a work associated with his concerns for land themes and the development of Brazilian concert music.[37] No doubt he was also associated with the abolitionist intellectual milieu of which he was a member, together with Coelho Netto, Artur Azevedo, Rodolfo Bernadelli, and Angelo Agostini. Unlike other musicians associated with the conservatory, like Henrique Mesquita and Cavalier Darbilly, Nepomuceno did not devote himself to the musical world of the revue theater, but did engage in dialogue with the sheet music business and completed some compositions using a pseudonym. Among them, to my great surprise, he published a cakewalk in 1911 for the operetta *La Cigale.*[38] According to Avelino, the musical piece has a "strong descriptive character," allowing one to visualize or feel what would be a *dança de negros*, as it was disseminated and stereotyped by travelers' or literary accounts: grotesque and obscene movements in leaps, flips, belly rolls, twisted arms, and hips; verses repeated in chorus, with monotonous, discordant, unpleasant singing, "of a very soft sadness" that "echoed through the woods in the silence of night, with a melancholy and strange grandeur." At the climax of the dance, the belly roll, Nepomuceno "sought to portray" the scene through "furious fortissimo."

From a certain perspective, it is possible to consider that the composer broke with the vision of those who denied that the sound of the slave quarters had any value when he successfully transposed *Batuque* to concert music. Avelino goes so far as to consider that Nepomuceno accomplished "harmonic racial integration" in classical musical language. On the other hand, however, Avelino himself calls attention: Nepomuceno "dressed the *batuque* in a dress coat," or as one critic said, it was a Brazilian theme seen and felt "through the great German symphonists."[39] The music of the slave quarters was really open territory for disputes over meanings and the creation of new hierarchies about the place of African descendants in the post-abolition period. If *slave songs* left the slave quarters, distorted representations of the black population were sure to be generated. The *batuque* could come into concerts, but it would come without its protagonists and with new violence and prejudice. As we have seen, all this interest and valorization of *slave songs* was in parallel with reconstruction and the existence of racism in the musical and artistic milieu of the post-abolition period. Although they

---

37 Avelino Romero Pereira, *Música, Sociedade e Política. Alberto Nepomuceno e a República musical* (Rio de Janeiro: Editoria da Universidade Federal do Rio de Janeiro, 2007): 228.
38 Ibid.: 225.
39 Ibid.: 55.

were able to pave the way for black musicians and their talent, they also served to belittle the black population and spread stigmas about their bodies and behavior. It is also worth remembering that the presence of *jongos* and *lundus* in performances and scores did not keep them from being beleaguered and banned from the streets of Rio de Janeiro in the second half of the nineteenth century. Black musicians who achieved some success in the United States, like Bert Williams, Scott Joplin, Marion Cook, and Ernest Hogan, and in Brazil, like Henrique Alves Mesquita, Joaquim Antonio da Silva Callado, Patápio Silva, Benjamim de Oliveira, Geraldo Magalhães, Eduardo das Neves, and João Cândido (Le Chocolat), had to deal with and face all the prejudices and racist stereotypes attributed to African descendants and their songs. But the music of the slave quarters and its legacy had really come to stay, establishing its presence in all the places of the African diaspora in the Americas. They would still have a long career throughout the twentieth century in the recording, motion-picture, and radio industry, revolutionizing modern musical canons and modernity itself, as Du Bois noted, and subverting racial theories. This, though, is another story.

Bibliography

Abrahams, Roger D. *Afro-American Folktales: Stories from Black Traditions in the New World* (New York: Pantheon Books, 1985).

Abrahams, Roger. *Singing the Master, the Emergence of African-American Culture in the Plantation South* (New York: Penguin, 1992).

Abreu, Martha. *Da Senzala ao Palco, canções escravas e racismo nas Américas, 1870–1930* (Campinas: Ed. Unicamp, 2017).

Abreu, Martha, Giovana Xavier, Livia Monteiro and Eric Brasil. *Cultura Negra, Novos Desafios para os Historiadores*, vol. 1–2 (Niterói: Editora da Universidade Federal Fluminense, 2017).

Abreu, Martha. "Slave Songs and Racism in the Post-Abolition Period: Eduardo das Neves and Bert Williams, Brazil and the United States," in *The Boundaries of Freedom: Slavery, Abolition, and the Making of Modern Brazil*, ed. Brodwyn Fischer and Keila Grinberg (Cambridge: Cambridge University Press, 2022): 388–419.

Augusto, Antonio. *Henrique Alves Mesquita: Da pérola mais luminosa à poeira do esquecimento* (Rio de Janeiro: Folha Seca, 2014).

Archer-Straw, Petrine. *Negrophilia, avant-garde Paris and Black culture in the 1920s* (New York: Thames & Hudson, 2000).

Bean, Annemarie, James V. Hatch and Brooks McNamara, eds. *Inside the Minstrel Mask. Readings in Nineteenth-Century Blackface Minstrelsy* (Middletown: Wesleyan University Press, 1996).

Brooks, Daphne. *Bodies in Dissent: Spectacular Performance of Race and Freedom (1850–1910)* (Durham, NC: Duke University Press, 2006).

Brooks, Tim. *The Lost Sound: Blacks and the Birth of the Recording Industry, 1890–1919* (Champaign: University of Illinois Press, 2005).

Brundage, W. Fitzhugh, ed. *Beyond Blackface: African Americans and the Creation of American Popular Culture, 1890–1930* (Chapel Hill: University of North Carolina Press, 2011).

Butler, Kim. "New Negroes: Negritude e movimentos Pós-Abolição no Brasil e na diáspora africana," in *Histórias do Pós-Abolição, Histórias do pós-Abolição no mundo atlântico*, vol. 1–3, ed. Martha Abreu, Carolina V. Dantas, Hebe Mattos, Beatriz Loner and Karl Monsma (Niterói: Eduff, 2014): 137–48.

Butler, Kim, and Petronio Domingues. *Diásporas Imaginadas: Atlântico Negro e História Afro-Brasileiras* (São Paulo: Perspectivas, 2020).

Cazarré, Marcelo M. *A trajetória das danças de negros na literatura pianística brasileira* (Pelotas: Editoria da Universidade Federal de Pelotas, 2001).

Chastten, John Charles. *National Rhythms, African Roots: The Deep History of Latin American Popular Dance* (Albuquerque: University of New Mexico Press, 2004).

Cunha, Maria Clementina P. *'Não tá sopa': Sambas e sambistas no Rio de Janeiro, de 1890 a 1930* (Campinas: Editora da Unicamp, 2016).

Dunson, Stephanie. "Black Misrepresentation in Nineteenth-Century Sheet Music Illustration," in *Beyond Blackface: African Americans and the Creation of American Popular Culture, 1890–1930*, ed. William Fitzhugh Brundage (Chapel Hill: University of North Carolina Press, 2011): 45–65.

Du Bois, William E.B. *The Souls of Black Folk* (Boston/New York: Bedford Books, 1997).

Floyd, Samuel Jr. *The Power of Black Music: Interpreting its History from Africa to the United States* (Oxford: Oxford University Press, 1999).

Genovese, Eugene. *Roll, Jordan, Roll: The World the Slaves Made* (New York: Vintage Books, 1976).

Gilroy, Paul. *The Black Atlantic: Modernity and Double Consciousness* (London: Verso Books, 1993).

Herskovits, Melville J. "El Estúdio de La Música Negra En El Hemisfério Occidental," *Boletin Latino Americano de Musica* 5 (1941): 133–42.

Kusser, Astrid. "The Riddle of the Booty . . .," http://www.radicalriddims.de/txt-riddleofbooty-e.html [accessed 27.07.2016].

Leme, Monica Neves. "E 'Saíram à Luz': As novas coleções de polcas, modinhas, lundus, etc. – Música popular e impressão musical no Rio de Janeiro (1820–1920)," 2 vols. (PhD diss., Universidade Federal Fluminense, 2006).

Levine, Laurence W. *Black Culture and Black Consciousness* (New York: Oxford University Press, 1977).

Lott, Eric. "Blackface and Blackness," in *Inside the Minstrel Mask. Readings in Nineteenth-Century Blackface Minstrelsy*, ed. Annemarie Bean, James V. Hatch and Brooks McNamara (Middletown: Wesleyan University Press, 1996): 3–34.

Magaldi, Cristina. "Música, sátira e política no Rio de Janeiro Imperial," in *Música e História no longo século XIX*, ed. Antônio H. Lopes, Martha Abreu, Martha T. de Ulhoa and Mônica P. Velloso (Rio de Janeiro: Fundação Casa de Rui Barbosa, 2011): 263–86.

Magaldi, Cristina. *Music in Imperial Rio de Janeiro: European Culture in Tropical Milieu* (Lanham, MD: The Scarecrow Press, 2004).

Martin, Denis-Constant. "A Herança Musical Da Escravidão," *Revista Tempo* 15, no. 29 (2011): 15–42.

Mattos, Hebe, and Abreu, Martha. "Jongo, Recalling History," in *Cangoma Calling: Spirits and Rhythms of Freedom in Brazilian Jongo Slavery Songs*, ed. Pedro Meira Monteiro and Michael Stone (Dartmouth: University of Massachusetts Dartmouth, 2013): 77–88.

Mattos, Hebe and Ana L Rios. *Memórias do Cativeiro. Família, Trabalho e Cidadania no Pós-Abolição* (Rio de Janeiro: Civilização Brasileira, 2005).

Mencarelli, Fernando A. "A Voz e a Partitura: Teatro musical, indústria e diversidade cultural no Rio de Janeiro (1868–1908)" (PhD diss., Universidade Federal de Campina Grande, 2003).

Moore, Robin. "O teatro bufo: teatro *blackface* cubano," in *Música e História no longo século XIX*, ed. Antônio H. Lopes, Martha Abreu, Martha T. de Ulhoa and Mônica P. Velloso (Rio de Janeiro, Fundação Casa de Rui Barbosa, 2011): 357–82.

Noiriel, Gérard. *Chocolat clown nègre: L'histoire oubiée Du premier artiste noir de la scène française* (Montrouge: Bayard Editions, 2012).

Pereira, Avelino Romero. *Música, Sociedade e Política: Alberto Nepomuceno e a República musical* (Rio de Janeiro: Editoria da Universidade Federal do Rio de Janeiro, 2007).

Ramos, Arthur. *As culturas negras no novo mundo* (São Paulo: Companhia Editora Nacional, 1979).

Reis, João José. "Tambores e Temores, a Festa Negra na Bahia na primeira metade do século XIX," in *Carnavais e Outras Frestas*, ed. Maria Clementina P. Cunha (Campinas: Ed. Unicamp, 2002): 108–56.

Seigel, Micol. *Uneven Encounters: Making Race and Nation in Brazil and United States* (Durban: Duke University Press, 2009).

Slenes, Robert. "Eu venho de muito longe, eu venho cavando: jongueiros cumba na senzala centro-africana," in *Memória do jongo: As gravações históricas de Stanley Stein, Vassouras, 1949*, ed. Silvia Lara and Gustavo Pacheco (Rio de Janeiro: Folha Seca; Campinas: Cecult, 2007): 109–58.

de Souza, Silvia Cristina Martins. "A alquimia cultural do teatro musicado de Francisco Correa Vasques: Rio de Janeiro, segunda metade do século XIX," in *Música e História no longo século XIX*, ed. Antônio H. Lopes, Martha Abreu, Martha T. de Ulhoa and Mônica P. Velloso (Rio de Janeiro: Fundação Casa de Rui Barbosa, 2011): 327–56.

de Souza, Silvia Cristina Martins. "Que Venham Negros À Cena Com Maracas E Tambores: Jongo, Política E Teatro Musicado No Rio de Janeiro Nas Últimas Décadas Do Século Xix," *Afro-Asia* 40 (2010): 145–71.

Wagner, Bryan. *Disturbing the Peace: Black Culture and The Police Power After Slavery* (Cambridge: Harvard University Press, 2009).

Wlamyra Albuquerque. *O jogo da dissimulação: Abolição e cidadania negra no Brasil* (São Paulo: Cia das Letras, 2009).

Crislayne Alfagali

Iron, Gold, and Labor in Eighteenth-Century Ilamba and Minas Gerais

This article sums up my research in recent years on iron and gold mining and smelting in the eighteenth century in Minas Gerais, Brazil, and in the region of Ilamba, then called the "Kingdom of Angola and its conquests." Its starting point is the experience of blacksmiths, smelters and miners from diverse origins and social levels, as well as the knowledge, techniques and strategies involved in their activities. This topic is approached from a local perspective that considers the political and social processes of each location and in connection with each other, while establishing the links that forged South Atlantic history. In my MSc studies, I surveyed a group of artisans linked to iron smelting and forgery in the Brazilian cities of Vila Rica and Mariana in the eighteenth century. By comparing lists with the names of local artisans in the records of local councils with the indexes of names at notary offices in these gold-producing villages, I documented 50 artisans for whom it was possible to find an inventory and/or testament, along with other types of documents: the final set covered a total of 44 inventories, 8 testaments, 31 civil suits, and 2 criminal suits. These 85 documents contain information on a group of 50 artisans: 16 from Portugal, 8 from Minas Gerais (one "*pardo*/brown" and one "freed man"), one from the "Coast of the Mine" ("black" and "freed"), one "*pardo*/brown freed man," one "*crioulo* freed man," and one "brown man."[1] As we analyze the slave assistants of these artisan masters, we also find other identities. In inventories dating from 1728 to 1768 in Vila Rica and Mariana, the percentage of Africans among the slaves who became the possessions of iron lords reached 70.97%. Among them, 36.37% represented the Mina nation; 54.55% were captives from Angola, Benguela, Congo, and Caburu; and 9.08% corresponded to the Calabar and Courano nations. These figures correspond to the standards found for this region in the first half of the eighteenth century. The Mina group was the largest, and there is a higher incidence of slaves from West Central Africa.[2] The composition of the slave assistants of blacksmiths, farriers, and coppersmiths in Vila Rica underwent a drastic transformation in the second half of the century, following the changes identified in the structure of slave ownership in the region. The big shift was that slightly over half of all captives (50.42%) started encompassing *crioulos, cabras, pardos*/brown, and *mulatos*/mulattoes. The groups representing West Central Africa became a majority among Africans, amounting to 34,45% of all slaves. The Mina nation, in turn, decreased to represent only 7.08% of blacksmiths' slaves. Only 22 of the 269 captives in the consulted inventories are identified as iron

1 No information regarding the origin, color, or legal status of the others was found. Crislayne Alfagali, *Em casa de ferreiro: Os artesãos do ferro nas Minas Gerais do século XVIII* (São Paulo: Alameda, 2018).
2 Ibid.: 147–49.

https://doi.org/10.1515/9783111026527-003

artisans, nine of them from Africa. They include four official blacksmiths (Antonio Benguela, Serafim Angola, Francisco Angola, and José Courano), one blacksmith and locksmith (Manoel Benguela), one farrier (Antonio Mina), one official coppersmith (José Angola), one tinsmith (José Benguela), and one official gunsmith (Francisco Angola). Two of them, therefore, were from West Africa (Courano and Mina), while seven were from West Central Africa (Angola and Benguela). Even though the data is not substantially representative from a quantitative standpoint, this could evince that African captives from these groups were better acquainted with iron smelting. The 60-year-old José Courano and Manoel Benguela had a distinction vis-à-vis their masters' other slaves, since they had "a blacksmith initiation" – Manoel Benguela, in particular, was a "good blacksmith and locksmith initiate."[3] It is also known from the studies of Flávio Gomes that the *quilombos* – communities of fugitive slaves, which abounded in Minas Gerais – included a "blacksmith house and forge," as shown in the map below (6), which depicts the locality of Quilombo de Samambaia. Note that the iron foundry stood at the side of what seemed to be the center of political decisions, the House of Hearings (1). In West Central Africa, blacksmiths were associated with leadership, as we will see later. In Quilombo de São Gonçalo, there was also a "blacksmith's house," while in Quilombo da Cabaça, there were "dozens of fragments of molten iron, metal plates, and tin strips."[4]

The presence of slaves from African regions where smelting techniques were identified and the metallurgical records of Brazilian Quilombos provide evidence that African iron smelting techniques were used in Minas Gerais. In accounts from the nineteenth and early twentieth centuries, some groups of African origin are recurrently associated with mastery over the mining and metallurgy techniques found in Minas Gerais in the eighteenth century. The relevance of African iron production knowledge in Brazil is found in the works of travelers and naturalist authors such as José Vieira Couto, Intendente Câmara, and Baron von Eschwege, as well as in the writings of researchers from the School of Mines of Ouro Preto who pioneered narratives regarding the history of the steel industry, such as Paul Ferrand, Henri Gorceix, and Bovet. For these authors, the local techniques largely stemmed from African knowledge. The German traveler von Eschwege even argued that iron was produced for the first time in the district of Antônio Pereira by a slave of Major Captain Antônio Alves, "and in Inficionado by a slave of Captain Durães."[5] It is emphasized that the practice

3 Ibid.

4 Flávio dos Santos Gomes, *A hidra e os pântanos. Mocambos, quilombos e comundades de fugitivos no Brasil (séculos XVII–XIX)* (São Paulo: Editoria da Universidade Estadual Paulista, Ed. Polis, 2005): 371–78.

5 Wilhelm Ludwig von Eschwege, *Pluto Brasiliensis* (Belo Horizonte: Itatiaia, 1833; São Paulo: Editora da Universidade de São Paulo, 1979): 203; Cf. Henri Gorceix, "Estudo químico e mineralógico das rochas dos arredores de Ouro Preto," in *Anais da Escola de Minas de Ouro Preto: coleções de memórias e de notícias sobre a mineralogia, a geologia e as explorações das minas no Brasil* (Ouro Preto, MG: Escola de Minas de Ouro Preto, 1883): 5–23; Henri Gorceix, "A indústria Mineral na Província de Minas Gerais," in *Annaes da Escola de Minas de Ouro Preto: coleções de memórias e de notícias sobre a*

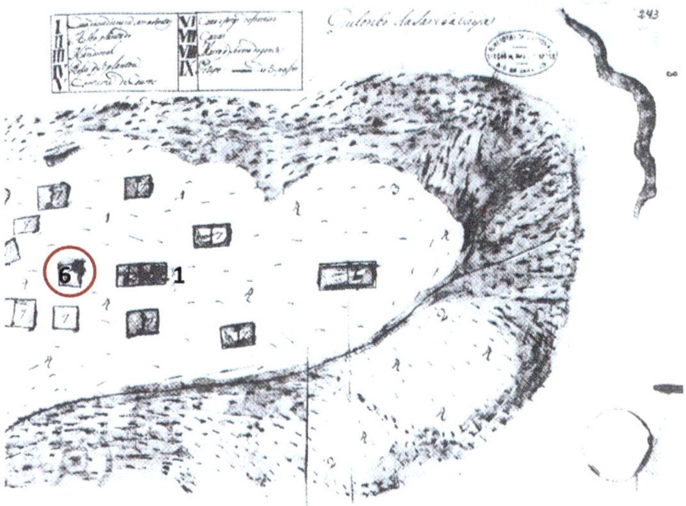

Fig. 1: Blacksmith house and forge in Quilombo de Samambaia. Legend: 1 – House of Hearings with seats; 2 – planted corn; 3 – manioc field; 4 – cultivated field; 5 – tannery; 6 – house and forge of blacksmiths; 7 – houses; 8 – hill that served as guardhouse; 9 – map scale equivalent to 5 steps. In Flávio dos Santos Gomes, *A hidra e os pântanos*: 374.

of a manual craft could be a way of saving to purchase one's freedom. And the practice of *coartação*[6] was indeed found among the masters of slave artisans. *Coartação* was an agreement enabling slaves to gradually pay for their manumission, with biannual or annual instalments over three, four, or five years. In their testaments, iron masters expressed the desire that their blacksmith slaves should continue working in their workshops after manumission, "so they may earn inside it the aforementioned gold of their freedom." This excerpt is taken from the testament of Luis Pacheco Ferreira, who expressed his will in 1789 in the following terms:

> I declare that I own a slave by the name of Felix, a blacksmith whose *coartação* I agreed to grant at the price of 100 octaves of gold; and I own another slave by the name of Agostinho, a Mina black man, whose *coartação* I am granting at the price of 80 octaves of gold, so they may pay

---

mineralogia, a geologia e as explorações das minas no Brasil (Ouro Preto, MG: Escola de Minas de Ouro Preto, 1883): 24–40; Paul Ferrand, *L'or a Minas Gerais* (Belo Horizonte: Imprensa Oficial do Estado de Minas Gerais, 1913).

6 *Coartação* was a conditional manumission procedure found in many slave areas in America. It was more frequently found in the region of Minas Gerais as a result of the wide range of economic activities at the reach of slaves. As one historian puts it, "in the case of Minas, the advantages of the urban setting were compounded by certain particularities of the mining work." These features enabled some slaves to engage in "freelance, unsupervised activities from which they would strategically obtain pecuniary benefits more easily." Laura de Mello e Souza, *Norma e conflito: aspectos da história de Minas no século XVIII* (Belo Horizonte: Universidade Federal de Minas Gerais, 1999): 168.

> them over a period of four years, provided that both the aforementioned Felix and the aforementioned Agostinho continue working at my workshop, which I am leaving to them so they may earn inside it the aforementioned gold of their freedom.[7]

Master Luís Pacheco also left "a pan to Felix the blacksmith, so he may have better conditions to earn what he must pay me." The blacksmith's trade was a decisive skill for earning and maintaining the freedom of Felix and Agostinho. Conditional manumission, in the case of *coartação*, was also the fate of the captives under the blacksmiths Manoel Rodrigues Rosa, Eusébio da Costa Ataíde, Francisco Martins Campos, and Rodrigues Pereira da Cunha, who were *coartados* in their masters' testaments.[8] Finally, iron craftsmanship was seen as a dangerous activity when practiced by African and indigenous people, as it could involve the production of weapons. Out of fear that blacks, Carijós (i.e., descendants of Indians), Mulattos, bastards, or "any other person absent of nobility" could produce their own weapons, the crown prohibited "tinsmiths, blacksmiths, coppersmiths and tinkers arrived from Portugal from teaching their work with metals to those populaces." The key issue was not about producing weapons *per se* but, instead, an attempt to ensure that the secrets of the manipulation of metals would not end up in the wrong hands. Under this norm, the crown failed to consider that the knowledge held by "those populaces" could be even more refined than that of Portuguese masters.[9] In a general way, even though organizations such as *Casa dos Vinte e Quatro de Lisboa* and *Casa dos Doze* (located in the city of Salvador) were not found in Minas Gerais, iron craftsmen still experienced the practical aspects of institutional structuring, for they shared experiences, customs, beliefs, uses, knowledge forms, and common techniques expressed in the control of their work journey, in the opening of new workshops and points of sale, and other regulations. Their participation in the *Corpus Christi* celebrations in Vila Rica, in the cortege of St George (the patron saint of the monarchy and of the iron and firearms trade in the Kingdom), demonstrates the continuity of some monarchical traditions. Structural slavery underpinned the internal hierarchies among apprentices, masters, and slaves, as well as the official knowledge, recognized by the councils, was more valued than knowledge deriving from African metallurgy.

---

7 Record of the will of Luis Pacheco Ferreira, Mariana (Minas Gerais), 1789. Arquivo Histórico da Casa Setecentista de Mariana (AHCSM), Livro de Registro de Testamento 46, fl. 80v, 1789.

8 Crislayne Alfagali, *Em casa de ferreiro*: 177–84.

9 Ângela Botelho, "Arma de fogo," in *Dicionário Histórico das Minas Gerais*, ed. Adriana Romeiro and Ângela Botelho (Belo Horizonte: Autêntica, 2003): 27.

1 From Minas Gerais to Ilamba (Kingdom of Angola, Eighteenth Century)

The study of blacksmiths in Minas Gerais and the references to African techniques prompted me to look for further information about what was taking place on the other side of the Atlantic in the eighteenth century. This is how I began to study the Royal Iron Foundry located in Nova Oeiras in the region of Ilamba, to the north of the Kwanza River in the Kingdom of Angola, which was built and became operational in the second half of the eighteenth century. This foundry was a sumptuous site planned to operate along the same lines as northern Spain's hydraulic iron production. Four Biscayan master blacksmiths (*mestres biscainhos*) were dispatched to Angola to ensure the proper execution of the plans laid down by the governor of Angola. But the foundry that effectively operated was erased both from the ground and from memory. Between the lines of the official documents, we find the "smelting house of the blacks" where local blacksmiths worked and where all blacksmithing in Nova Oeiras took place. This is the place where the Atlantic links involving ironwork techniques intersect and become even more plausible.[10] The Royal Foundry of Nova Oeiras is not a new topic in the historiography on eighteenth-century Angola. On the contrary, different generations of historians, with equally diverse perspectives, have revisited the project of the famous philosopher-administrator and governor, who became the highest expression of the reform effort in the Portuguese Enlightenment.[11] That is why I begin this story differently, by searching for local logics and determinants in the company of Pedro Manoel, a smelter from the Angolan countryside. His occupation was complex and exhausting, and for this reason he counted on the help of assistants and apprentices. He was always with two bellows operators, known as *foleiros* or *tocadores de foles*. His assistants cut iron hills open in search of iron ore, which was then broken into small pieces so it could be better smelted. This was only the beginning of their work: it was necessary to split wood, prepare the coal, build the furnace, collect papyri leaves, and meticulously control the bellows, among other tasks. Using methods that mixed practical knowledge with secret ones from the invisible world, obtained by his ancestors and enhanced over many generations, Pedro could

---

10 I reproduce here the information and arguments published in my book *Ferreiros e fundidores da Ilamba: Uma História Social da Fábrica de Nova Oeiras (Angola, segunda metade do século XVIII)* (Luanda: Fundação Dr. António Agostinho Neto, 2018).

11 Among others: António da Silva Rego, "A Academia Portuguesa da História e o II Centenário da Fábrica do Ferro de Nova Oeiras, Angola," in *Colectânea de Estudos em Honra do Prof Doutor Damião Peres* (Lisbon: Academia Portuguesa da História, 1974): 387–98; Catarina Madeira Santos, "Um governo 'polido' para Angola: Reconfigurar dispositivos de domínio (1750– c.1800)" (PhD diss., Universidade Nova de Lisboa, 2005).

produce iron and steel of excellent quality.[12] Pedro and the names of other local blacksmiths and smelters were not previously cited. For my purposes, it is extremely important to ask: what did Pedro Manoel, the smelter, think about all this? An answer can be hardly found in the available sources, inasmuch as his name and his occupation are practically all we know about him today. However, as a group of artificers (blacksmiths and smelters), Pedro and his colleagues have left some impressions on the iron foundry between the lines of the official documents. It was these tracks that I sought to follow.

The *sobas* – local leaders of the old Kingdom of Ndongo, which became the Kingdom of Angola in the eighteenth century – and local blacksmiths had been mining iron for centuries in the region, including from underground mines. The news reached the Portuguese that the jurisdictions of Golungo (Ilamba and Lumbu), Ambaca, Cambembe, and Caconda (a region and prison in the Kingdom of Benguela) were rich in iron, in addition to far-off sites where the lack of rivers did not facilitate ore transport. In 1759, we find accounts reporting on the existence of two mines, Kituxe and Kalombo, characterised by "ferruginous land," located in the lands of a leader named Kabanga kya Mbangu in Ilamba. These mines were exploited by excavating the "deep caverns," at a "high risk and mortality rates among the blacks" due to frequent landslides resulting from the humidity.[13] The construction of Nova Oeiras itself led to a great inventory of local forests, rivers, and ore mines, as well as to the expropriation of lands previously held by *sobas*, settlers, and other figures in the Kingdom of Angola's countryside. At the small foundry located to the side of the large foundry, furnaces were dug into the ground, bellows were covered with kidskin, and rocks served as the tools of the local smiths and smelters, who exported nearly 60 tons of iron and steel from 1765 to 1800, in addition to a monthly supply of 30–40 *quintais* (equivalent to 1.8 to 2.4 tons), to the Kingdom of Angola.[14]

The "children" under tutelage of the *sobas* were known as the "black inhabitants," "black ploughmen," "working blacks," "*soba* blacks," "peoples," "weaving blacks," "confined peoples" (i.e., confined to the prisons), "black croppers," "helpers," "servants," "naturals," "bush dwellers," "peoples subjected to the *sobas*," "black poor," and "workable children." Their identity was readily associated with their work: they ploughed,

12 Certificate from José Francisco Pacheco, inspector of works at the foundry, on the state of the iron foundry, São Paulo de Assunção de Luanda, March 13, 1773. Arquivo Histórico Ultramarino, Conselho Ultramarino, AHU_CU_001, Cx. 52, D. 28.

13 Letter from Antonio de Vasconcelos, governor of Angola, to Francisco Xavier de Mendonça Furtado, secretary of state for the navy and overseas. São Paulo de Assunção de Luanda, May 9, 1762. Biblioteca Nacional de Portugal (BNP), Códice 8553, microfilme (F) 6362, fl. 2 e 3.

14 These figures were obtained from shipments recorded by the Portuguese administration in several sources. AHU_CU_001, Cx. 45, D. 68; Cx. 51, D. 1; Cx. 51, D. 44; Cx. 52, D. 15; AHU_CU_001, Cx. 52, D. 73; AHU_CU_001, Cx. 119, D. 15; Cx. 119, D. 16; Arquivo Histórico Nacional de Angola (AHNA), C–14–3; C–14 –4; A–2–2, fl. 166; D–2–5; A–20–2; Instituto Histórico e Geográfico Brasileiro (IHGB) – Projeto Acervo Digital Angola-Brasil (PADAB), DVD9,19 DSC00153; DVD9,19 DSC00198; DVD10,20 DSC00415; BNP, C 8742, F6364; F3315; Instituto de Estudos Brasileiro/USP, Coleção Alberto Lamego, AL–082–024.

weaved, and raised crops; they were "work-able" and produced wealth. In the Portuguese legal system, the status of "dependents" (or, as they are called in the documents, subjects or "children" of the *sobas*) was one of free men not subject to slavery. Therefore, they should not have been subjected to the same living and working conditions of slaves. However, it can be ascertained that since the conquest, these populations were recruited for countless services under precarious living conditions, where they frequently did not receive the bare minimum for nourishment. The military officer Cadornega, for instance, stated that since the arrival of the first conquerors, they were served by the *soba*'s dependents "at the workshops of their homes and in their crops," and in the construction of fortifications and trenches.[15] The *sobas* who owed vassalage to the Portuguese (either subdued in war or as political and commercial allies) agreed with the governor that in exchange for the dispatch of workers to Nova Oeiras, they should be exempted from paying the tithe, a tax that caused them troubles in the form of collectors who either extorted them or abused their hospitality. They received the exemption and provided the necessary workers. The inventories compiled by the workers of iron foundries described the local leaders who assigned workers to the foundries; the number of "work-able children," i.e., how many people the *sobas*, in addition to the *Ilambas* and *Imbaris* (other local authorities related to war), declared they had; how many of these individuals would be sent each month; the sum of the tithe either in the form of products or salt stones for which they would be exempted; and the tithe sum in *réis*. The list with the largest number of vassal authorities and workers cites over 3,000 "able" workers, of which 500 were sent for foundry services every month. This inventory corresponded to only one third of all individuals "capable of working" under the *sobas*, since foundry workers should not overwhelm the *sobados*. Foundry work should not take workers away from agriculture and other important activities for the *sobados*.[16]

For the governor, it was necessary to change the "character of the blacks" and turn them into "active workers." But he wanted to do this without "frightening them." For this reason, Sousa Coutinho determined that labor conditions should be strictly observed. Iron bars should not be carried on the backs of the Ambundos but, instead, on the donkeys he had brought from Brazil; punishment for the lack of work would be a reduction in their daily fee, and "by no means with blows." He also established "a half hour for lunch and two hours for dinner," with the option of choosing the most appropriate moment "to avoid the sun." Furthermore, the *sobas* should send a third of the workers they had, so that each worker would serve for four months per year in the foundries. In this

---

15 Antonio de Oliveira Cadornega, *História Geral das Guerras Angolanas*, 3 vols., ed. José Matias Delgado (Lisbon: Divisão de Publ. e Biblioteca, Agência Geral das Colónias, 1680/Agência-Geral do Ultramar, 1972): vol. 1, 45; vol. 2, 67.

16 Inventory of *sobas*, *ilamba* and *imbares* from the district of Golungo who worked in the iron foudries of Nova Belém and Nova Oeiras. IHGB, DL81, 02.19.

regard, there was also a concern that enough workers should remain in *soba* areas for the development of local agriculture.[17]

A type of "attendance book" was also established to record the absences of workers. From this book, "by the end of each month, the registrar" obtained the lists that informed the payment of workers' daily fees. In addition to this procedure, workers were inspected three times a day: "all workers would be searched in the morning, by dinner time and at night."[18] Their remuneration was paid with subsistence provisions such as salt, flour, beans, fish, and textiles. In the expenses recorded by Antonio de Lencastre from 1766 to 1773 (except for the expenses for the foundrymen hired from Biscay by the governor, amounting to a daily fee of 2$ and 400 rs), the largest were those of the ordinary fees, i.e., those related to non-specialized workers. Gathering workers in a controlled work setting placed at risk the technical supervision of the work process, productivity, and the trading of products. But the available sources indicate that what took place in the foundry buildings contrasts in many aspects with the colonial plans. The first aspect to be considered in this regard was the strong instability of those workers who depended on local leaders, which was caused – or, better, was made more visible – by the work at the foundries. On the one hand, with the advent of iron foundries, the *sobas* whose subjects had been already recruited as taskmasters, missionaries, and traders had to handle additional burdens. On the other, these figures from the countryside of the Kingdom of Angola had no interest in losing the familiar "aid" of the *soba* domains, and fiercely contested control over the labor force. In their attempt to escape the violence of tithe collectors, those bosses ended up experiencing the abuses of the government of Luanda and its employees at the iron foundries. The narratives about the reasons for the escapes of *soba* workers – *soba* subjects – from the village of Nova Oeiras are numerous. A representation of *soba* leader Don Manoel Mendes Kisala to the governor of Angola explains the reasons for which his dependents were deserting work at the foundries. He complains that his children experienced "much punishment, insolence, prison, and theft" in Nova Oeiras. Furthermore, contrary to the rules laid down by the ordinances of 1768 and 1770, Kisala's subjects were not being paid for cleaning the village – since, for the governor, such a task was a "common good" and did not need to be remunerated.[19] In 1770, foundry labor inspector José Francisco Pacheco was admonished by the same governor, who was by then explicitly aware of the reasons behind desertion: "the 'working blacks' complain about the blows they are receiving, and this is the reason for their

17 Instruction that Antonio Anselmo Duarte de Siqueira must guard, serving as the general intendant of the iron foundry, from the governor, Francisco Inocência de Sousa Coutinho. São Paulo de Assunção de Luanda, January 17, 1767. AHU_CU_001, Cx. 52, D. 73.

18 Ordinance establishing the remuneration of workers at the Nova Oeiras iron foudry. São Paulo de Assunção, October 20, 1768. IEB/USP, AL–083–138.

19 Letter from Francisco Inocêncio de Sousa Coutinho, governor of Angola, to Joaquim de Bessa Teixeira, general intendant of the Nova Oeiras iron foundry. São Paulo de Assunção, March 19, 1772. *Arquivos de Angola*, v. III, n. 30–33, 1937: 401–45.

desertions; you shall avoid such tyranny."[20] As one may see, a cycle of abuses was taking place: the workers suffered maltreatment at the foundries and pressured their taskmasters, who would refrain from sending them to work. They would then suffer, in their villages, the abuses of the soldiers sent to punish them and force them to meet their obligations. The *sobas* and their subordinates fought against such abuses, i.e., against conduct not prescribed by the treaties signed with the crown. Thus, the foundry setting was a mechanism designed to control, discipline, and establish hierarchies in the iron production process. The temporal changes of work that occurred in Nova Oeiras did not correspond to the expectations regarding productive labor and the meanings of work among the local people. The notion of labor among local blacksmiths followed other rhythms and was structured according to other logics. These conceptions clashed in Nova Oeiras, not only in terms of opposite worldviews, but also among the individuals who represented the two systems of thought. Such was the context that allows us to understand the reasons for the constant escapes, for the blows, and for the fact that the workers were seen as lazy and lackadaisical by the governors. The foundry undermined the autonomy of itinerant work, the prestige of the *Jingangula*, and the sacred dimension by which human work could not be dissociated from other realms of life. Sousa Coutinho not only underestimated the local people's ability to subvert the meaning of Nova Oeiras: he also failed to take into consideration the techniques and rustic instruments that produced the high-quality iron and steel he praised so vividly, since this work process yielded, in his eyes, a small amount of iron overall. To grasp the governor's misconception, it is necessary to know some details of the metallurgy techniques of Central Africans, as well as their potential. It may not be evident at first sight, but rites and ceremonies, in addition to the use of plants during the smelting process and the rhythm of operating the bellows, have a lot to do with the knowledge of chemistry – in fact, they transcend this technical function. At the foundry, the workers with such knowledge were the best paid. In this regard, the governor also ordered:

> In the sledgehammer work with such violent fire exercise exceeding the common allotment, a higher sum shall be paid to them beyond the aforementioned daily fees: between 10 réis and one vintém a day. The same shall apply to those destined for apprenticeship, after they sufficiently show their distinguishing light. A much higher fee shall be ensured to them as soon as they become proficient in this occupation, in such a way that they may come to replace their masters.[21]

---

20 Letter from Francisco Inocêncio de Sousa Coutinho to José Francisco Pacheco, foundry labor inspector. São Paulo de Assunção de Luanda, May 14, 1770. BNP, C–8743, F–6377, fl. 189v.

21 Letter from Antonio de Vasconcelos, governor of Angola, to Francisco Xavier de Mendonça Furtado, secretary of state for the navy and overseas. São Paulo de Assunção, November 18, 1768. AHU_CU_001, Caixa 52, D. 44.

2 Metallurgy Knowledge, Power, and Myth

The available references reiterate the prestige of blacksmiths as described in missionary narratives since the seventeenth century. In several foundational myths of Central African societies, the association between the blacksmith and political power was frequent. According to Antonio de Oliveira Cadornega, the first king of Ndongo was a blacksmith, denominated *gongolhas* (*sic*) in Kimbundu and Kikongo, *ngangula*, and, in plural form, *jingangula*. For this reason, the blacksmith occupation was highly appreciated and surrounded by social and economic prestige. Additional words for "blacksmith" were *musuri, kateli, unsugula, muxiri,* and *unguoxilaekete*.[22] Experts on the history of language have found two variations of the word "blacksmith" in the Lower Congo: *ngangula* and *npangula*. Both derive from the Bantu verb *pàngʊd*, which means "to cut, separated."[23] Thus, the word was not directly linked to the propagation of metallurgy in the region. In the course of time, it is possible that the political title *ngangula* became a metaphor for the blacksmith figure, who, similar to a leader, was also tasked with settling disputes ("setting things apart"). Metallurgy and royalty shared a common understanding of the nature, sources, and control of power. In Kongo, local leaders and blacksmiths were individuals initiated in similar circumstances via collective "cults of affliction." They could even be in the same lineage, observing common alimentary taboos and wearing the same jewels and bracelets. Blacksmiths were also priests and interceded before the *bisimbi*, the creative metallurgy spirits. In the twentieth century, the narratives of the anthropologist Mertens (1942) describe the participation of blacksmiths in the rites of investiture and burial of local leaders.[24] Even when blacksmiths were not exclusively kings or noblemen, they still participated in these societies as respected leaders. In other narratives of the seventeenth century, such as those by Cavazzi or Antonio Gaeta, the lineage of the king of Ndongo was also linked to the mastery of blacksmith techniques.

22 De Oliveira de Cadornega, *História geral das guerras angolanas*, v. 1, 56. Antonio da Silva Maia, *Dicionário complementar: português-kimbundu-kikongo* (n.p, 1964); Antónia de Assis Júnior, *Dicionário Kimbundu-Português* (Luanda: Argente, Santos e Comp. Lda., n.d.); Karl Edvard Laman, *Dictionnaire kikongo-français avec une carte phonétique décrivant les dialectes les plus importants de la langue dite Kikongo* (Bruxelles: Falk, 1936).

23 Koen Bostoen, Odjas Ndonda Tshiyayi and Gille-Maurice de Schryver, "On the Origin of the Royal Kongo Title Ngangula," *Africana Linguistica* 19 (2013): 56.

24 Joseph Mertens, *Les chefs couronnés chez les Ba Kongo orientaux: étude de régime successoral* (Brussels: G. van Campenhout, 1942); Eugenia W. Herbert, *Iron, Gender and Power: Rituals of Transformation in African Societies* (Bloomington: Indiana University Press, 1993): 136–44; Wyatt Macgaffey, *Religion and Society in Central Africa: the Bakongo of Lower Zaire* (Chicago: University of Chicago Press, 1986); Robert Slenes, "L'Arbre Nsanda replanté: cultes d'affliction Kongo et identité des esclaves de plantation dans le Brésil du Sud -Et (1810–1888)," *Cahiers du Brésil Contemporain* 67–68, no. 2 (2007): 217–313; Jan Vansina, "Linguistic Evidence for the Introduction of Ironworking in Bantu-Speaking Africa," *History in Africa* 33 (2006): 321–61; John Thornton, "The Regalia of the Kingdom of Kongo, 1491–1895," in *Kings of Africa: Art and Authority in Central Africa*, ed. Erna Beumers and Hans-Joachim Koloss (Maastricht: Foundation Kings of Africa, 1992): 56–63.

The principal *soba* of Ilamba Alta or Lumbu, called Mubanga, was this lineage's heir. It was in this region that an iron foundry was built in the eighteenth century. For Cavazzi, the blacksmith was "the most notable of all artificers." In the words of Cadornega, the *ngangula* "was a very appreciated activity among these people, and by exercising it they would obtain slaves and yield, since it was the most needed for their crops. This shows how necessary the effective presence of blacksmiths was for the development of agriculture, hunting, and war."[25] In December 1768, the Kilamba Ngongue, a Kamukala by the name of Antonio Pedro, informed the intendant of the iron foundry Novo Belém that he had 42 sons to offer to its works, including 12 smelters (called *pulungu* in the "language of the land"), two blacksmiths, and 28 bellows operators. In the same region, at a place called Cathari (in the jurisdiction of Golungo Alto), army major and assistant-of-orders Antonio Salinas de Benevides described the smelters and blacksmiths in 1800 as *pulungus* and *gangulas*, respectively.[26] In the dictionaries of the Bantu language, a meaning cannot be identified for the word *pulungu* that might somehow be related to the work of smelters. The only hypothesis that seems plausible is based on the studies of Colleen Kriger. Words for "furnace" sharing this root (*-lungu*) are found in a diversity of regions of Central Africa – Lwena, Luba – Shaba, Hemba, Tabwa, Bemba, and Fipa. For Kriger, such a recurrence is representative of the exchanges of technical knowledge among smelters and blacksmiths of various origins. *Pulungu*, therefore, has links with the smelting furnace and the work of smelters.[27]

We find iron artisans playing leadership roles according to their position in society. Such roles were backed both by dependence on their practical knowledge and by their guardian spirits. Objecting to the iron foundries, "blacks and tradesmen" in Ambaca complained about the lack of metal. In such a situation, "blacks, blacksmiths, and smelters" could no longer meet the demands of the jurisdiction and Nova Oeiras at the same time. Overwhelmed by intrigues and resistancs, the governor ordered the regent of Ambaca: "you shall leave the black smiths and smelters at their own convenience so they may proceed as best suits them, for there is no other way of steering such peoples."[28] At the end of the day, "such peoples" seemed not to have been so easily co-opted, or "steered," as the governor had expected: neither by "persuasion" nor by "moderate salaries." As a result of these pressures, in 1769, Sousa Coutinho ordered that his subjects under the heads of Ambaca should no longer be sent to the foundry. Therefore, artificers working

---

25 Antonio Cavazzi de Montecúccolo, *Descrição histórica dos três Reinos do Congo, Matamba e Angola*, vol. 1 (Lisbon: Junta de investigações do Ultramar, 1965): 253; Antonio da Gaeta, *La meravigliosa conversione a lla Santa Fede di Cristo d ellaregina Singa e del suo regnodi Matamba* (Nápoles: Francisco de Maria Gioia, 1669).

26 Letter from Antonio Salinas de Benavides. São Paulo de Assunção de Luanda, November 15, 1800. *Arquivos de Angola*, v. IV, nº 52, 1939: 323.

27 Colleen E. Kriger, *Pride of Men: Ironworking in 19th Century, West Central Africa* (Portsmouth: Heinemann, 1999): 84.

28 Letter from Francisco Inocêncio de Sousa Coutinho, governor of Angola, to José Antunes de Campos, ruler of Ambaca. São Paulo de Assunção de Luanda, January 25, 1768. IEB/USP, AL–083–002.

with iron and the "violent exercise of fire" staked the material, cultural, and cognitive resources at their disposal to assert their will and negotiate both the terms of their work in Oeiras and the extent of their collaboration with the governor's projects. Their relevance and ability to coordinate politically were so strong that the governor of Angola ordered the foundry authorities to leave them "at their own convenience."[29] A particular reference crosscuts the blacksmith's occupation, access to spiritual powers, and political predominance; in contrast to the usual historiographical narratives, this is the reference to a smelter. In March 1800, mineralogist José Álvares Maciel described the expenses he had incurred due to some iron smelting experiences. Among them, we find: "to the *soba* from Ilamba who laid down his first furnace in observance of his rites," together with the notes on a payment of 2$ and 400 rs – a considerable amount, if compared with the record of payments to Biscayan taskmasters in previous years.[30] On this occasion, the principal authority of the village – the *soba* leader himself – was the smelter. This suggests that many political leaders could be also smelters and blacksmiths, controlling both iron mines and the large number of subjects with that occupation. The blacksmiths and smelters refused to obey the work rhythm and demands that the Royal Iron Foundry sought to impose on them. They were accustomed to another rhythm that had nothing in common with the foundry's discipline: they smelted and forged "in observance of their own rites." What can we affirm about these rites? Many ritual records were produced by ethnologists in the twentieth century. Evidently, one cannot state that the rites bearing a relation to smelting in the late eighteenth century correspond to those observed over 200 years later. Yet, as historian Hampatê Bá rightly points out, "the traditional occupations are the key vectors of oral tradition." He considers the practice of an occupation as the greatest example in oral tradition, since it encompasses more than actions and gestures; by conveying his knowledge to an apprentice, a master is also sharing "effectual moral, social and legal codes intrinsic to each group, which have been faithfully passed down and observed by oral tradition."[31] An example of this continuity is the use of *pemba*, a white type of clay mentioned by Joseph Miller as a sacred powder employed by some local lineages to ensure the fertility of women. In approximately 1950, José Redinha recorded the rituals of an iron foundry that also used *pemba* in the village of Tchiungo-Ungo.[32] The furnaces of the foundries recorded by Redinha were modelled on feminine contours – with breasts, navel, and female genitalia, the place from which the smelted

29 Letter from Francisco Inocêncio de Sousa Coutinho, governor of Angola, to Antonio Anselmo Duarte. São Paulo de Assunção, November 7, 1769. BNP, C 8743, F 6367.

30 Letter from José Álvares Maciel to Miguel Antonio de Melo, governor of Angola. Trombeta, March 2, 1800. BNP, C 8553, F6362.

31 Amadou Hampatê Bá, "A tradição viva," in *História Geral da África I. Metodologia e pré-história da África*, ed. Joseph Ki-Zerbo (São Paulo: Ed. Ática/UNESCO, 1980): 202.

32 José Redinha, *Campanha etnográfica ao Tchiboco (Alto-Tchicapa)* (Lisbo,: Companhia de Diamantes de Angola/Museu do Dundo, 1953–1955); José Bacellar Bebiano, *Museu do Dundo: notas sobre a siderurgia dos indígenas de Angola e de outras regiões africanas* (Lisbon: Publicações culturais da Companhia de Diamantes de Angola, 1960): 36–43.

iron would flow. Redinha noticed that the foundry's operation was simulated childbirth. Within this context, the use of *pemba* seems quite allusive to the effort to ensure good childbirth results, as its use by the women of local lineages was accredited with increasing their fertility. At this foundry in the 1950s, the complete process took approximately 11 hours, since, during the smelting process, the master smelter – the son of the *soba* leader – officiated several rites in addition to the one described above: he wore special attire ("a doe skin") and uttered prayers "aimed at the air's entry point," while evoking "the grandparents, uncles, and aunts who had successively been masters of the craft, and asking for their good graces so the foundry would work perfectly."[33] In the consulted eighteenth-century records – which primarily comprise administrative sources – the work rhythm of local blacksmiths is described as an obstacle to "industriousness" and a sign of "laziness." The use of their local tools and techniques is seen as "coarse" and "barbarous." An example of such a view is the depiction produced by Governor Antonio de Vasconcelos in 1759:

> [. . .] since they [the blacksmiths and smelters] are naturally lazy and poorly industrious, they only do the necessary to meet the requests at an infinite waste of time due to the lack of instruments, and remain content with a piece of kid skin per blowpipe and a stone to lay the iron on, while they do not count on something that they can use as a sledgehammer.[34]

As we learned with *soba* smelter Cokwe, the work rhythm of any traditional occupation in Africa had two necessary rituals aimed at earning the approval of the ancestors and – in this case – attain good smelting results. The local techniques were underestimated by the colonial authorities. While using the *prima facie* coarse instruments described above, the blacksmiths of Central Africa had developed sophisticated iron production techniques by which they could control and delicately balance the amount of air blown into the furnace by the bellows. Thus, they could determine the quality of the iron they produced, as well as its ductility, fusibility, and malleability. The "smelting house of the blacks" operated following local iron smelting methods. When the foundry's intendant received from the governor a request of 150 *quintais* (equivalent to nine tons) of iron, he recruited 138 specialized workers, including smelters, blacksmiths, and bellows operators. They worked in groups of three "daily" for "over five months" to meet the goal stipulated by the governor. The smelting furnaces produced an overall average of two to two and a half arrobas of iron (30 to 45 kg) per day with 10 smithing forges, which turned the smelted iron into small bars (*barretas*).[35] During this process, a foundry employee annotated that each day, a total of 50 ore loads were used at the foundry. Since

33 Ibid.: 37.

34 Letter from Antonio de Vasconcelos, governor of Angola, to Francisco Xavier de Mendonça Furtado, secretary of state for the navy and overseas. São Paulo de Assunção de Luanda, January 18, 1759. BNP 8553, F 6362.

35 Letter from José Francisco Pacheco. Iron foundry of Nova Oeiras, March 5, 1773. AHU_CU_001, Cx. 57, D. 28.

the ore was obtained three leagues (nearly 15 km) from the foundry's location and carried by 50 workers, transport would take place only once a day. A total of 188 individuals participated in these works every day only to produce iron.[36] Moreover, each of the 46 smithing forges required a daily total of three coal bags, adding to an overall total of 138 bags. Therefore, there were still those individuals who worked cutting firewood, producing charcoal, and transporting it to the foundry. The number of workers involved in the subsidiary activities of the foundry must have been even larger. The names of six "blacks" who worked at the foundry have reached us: Pedro, Manoel, Damião Antonio, Sebastião Antonio, Cristóvão João, Ismão Sebastião, and João André. Their names show that they were baptized vassals of the Portuguese Crown. They were recruited to verify how much iron its method was yielding. Pedro Manoel, the smelter with whom we began this article, together with his two bellows "servants," used 60 pounds of "raw ore," that is, an average of 28 kg of mined ore from the hills in the foundry's vicinity. Pedro built his furnace and, with the help of his bellows operators, began to smelt the ore. After the first day of smelting, 40 pounds were left; and after the second day, 20 pounds – approximately nine kilos – remained. Therefore, two smelting sessions were carried out for obtaining the iron. These nine kilos of iron ore were then sent to the smithing forge to be "refined" by removing the slag; and with the help of two other assistants, he reduced the iron produce to a small bar of four and a half pounds (2 kilos). All other smelters followed the same procedure and obtained similar results, varying between four and four and a half pounds of iron. Together, the smelters, bellows operators and blacksmith who produced the little bars received $80 rs(réis) per day, adding to 3$ 200 rs. A total of 12 kg of iron was produced from 168 kg of raw ore in 48 hours.[37] For the governor, this amount of iron was still too little. He desired higher yields, such as those obtained by the Biscayan workers at their hydraulic iron foundries. The point was that work in Biscay was carried out day and night, six days per week; workers even slept in the foundries. One could then ask: which *ngangula* and *pulungu* would want that?

In Ilamba, blacksmithing seems to have been an exclusively male occupation. In 1800, Antonio Salinas Benevides noted that blacksmiths in Golungo Alto left their women cultivating the fields so they could devote themselves to iron smelting. Women's isolation and exclusion were frequent characteristics of this occupation in Central and Western Africa. Eugene Herbert considers that taboos around the feminine presence at the time of smelting must be understood in terms of social control of sexuality

36 Letter from José Francisco Pacheco. Iron foundry of Nova Oeiras, March 5, 1773. AHU_CU_001, Cx. 57, D. 28. Letter from Antonio de Vasconcelos, governor of Angola, to Francisco Xavier de Mendonça Furtado, secretary of state for the navy and overseas. São Paulo de Assunção de Luanda, May 6, 1769. IEB/USP, Al –082–156.

37 Certificate from José Francisco Pacheco, inspector of works at the foundry, on the state of the iron foundry, São Paulo de Assunção de Luanda, March 13, 1773. AHU_CU_001, Cx. 52, D. 28.

and reproduction.[38] We must also consider, as Colleen Kriger remarks, that rituals, secrecy, and the exclusion of some groups from fire and iron occupations are related to the strategies of artificers to maintain control over an activity, which, as we have seen, gave them some social, economic, and political privileges. Thus, the increased rhythm, the discipline, and the idea of the smelting house meant to them an intrusion into a closed and sacred practice.[39] In Central Africa, smelting took place during the dry season (*cacimbo*, as it is called, from March to August), since the trees and stone or ground ore became drenched during the rainy season, affecting the quality of the charcoal and the iron to be smelted. This appears twice in the consulted sources. Governor Sousa Coutinho ordered the construction of the "smelting house of the blacks" as a covered place, so that they could work during all seasons of the year and prevent "the excuses that rains give people, which preclude the work of the blacksmiths."[40] In one of his letters, Sousa Coutinho comments that in Ilamba it was not possible to recruit all blacksmiths and smelters, as some would remain at the location to smelt iron "in the *cacimbo* months."[41] Thus, blacksmiths worked in their villages during specific seasons, while, in the case of the smelting house, they operated the furnaces during the entire year. If the smelting house had already troubled the internal processes of the craft, hydraulic blacksmithing would completely alter the relations of Ambundo smiths and smelters with their occupation. Many of them became expendable, since in a hydraulic foundry, an average of only six workers, including master smelters and blacksmiths, were needed to operate the foundry and produce 40–50 tons of iron annually. The "smelting house of the blacks" produced an estimated 18 tons per year with the work of 138 smiths and smelters. If Nova Oeiras began operating with water wheels, it would threaten the survival of an occupation and its prestige and social meaning both inside and outside the foundry. Pedro Manoel and his colleagues, the Soma smelter, and rebel "black smiths and smelters" from Ambaca realized the governor's intentions, even without first-hand knowledge of Biscayan reality, and probably did not appreciate the idea. In Biscay, the trade associations of smiths and smelters refused to adhere to smelting in blast furnaces as they threatened the survival of their occupations. Why would it be different with the Ambundos, who noticed all these changes and attempts at interference? As Colleen Kriger correctly notes, the blast furnaces developed in Europe were not more sophisticated or technically developed than the bloomery furnaces of Africa. It was believed for a long time that bloomery furnaces could not reach high temperatures, and that the melt temperatures of some metals could only be reached with blast furnaces. But in reality, bloomery furnaces

38 Letter from Antonio Salinas de Benavides. São Paulo de Assunção de Luanda, November 15, 1800. *Arquivos de Angola*, v. IV, nº 52, 1939, 323. Herbert, *Iron, Gender and Power*: 96.

39 Kriger, *Pride of Men*: 57.

40 Letter from the governor of Angla to Antonio Anselmo Duarte, general intendant of the iron foundry. São Paulo de Assunção de Luanda, December 10, 1766. BNP, C 8742, F6364.

41 Carta de FISC para Francisco Matoso de Andrade, ruler (*capitão-mor*) of Ambaca. São Paulo de Assunção de Luanda, May 25, 1767. BNP, C 8742, F 6364.

can not only reach high temperatures, but also maintain them. Experimental bloomery furnaces have been capable of reaching temperatures around 1,600 °C. The objective of African smelters was not only to reach high temperatures. The challenge previously was to maintain the temperature at 1,200°C–1,300°C; as a result, the furnace's "atmosphere of reduction" would be enough for producing molten iron "with great resistance to traction and relatively low carbon content." This material "could be conveniently transformed by a blacksmith into various types of products."[42] Furthermore, the slag of bloomery iron has higher fusibility, which allows iron bits to be welded without a smelting agent. This, in turn, enables the instruments produced with such iron to be easily repaired, reshaped, and sharpened. Considering this, it is interesting to re-read some comments written by Sousa Coutinho about the iron produced by the Ambundos. The governor considered this metal superior "to all existing ones for cutting instruments," and the tools produced with it were neither undermined by long "duration" nor by different uses – in his words, "adoptions."[43] José Álvares Maciel wrote the most comprehensive account of the details involved in the iron smelting process at Nova Oeiras, including all the technical elements described above. The mineralogist successively visited the region of Ilamba (then called *Trombeta*) between 1795 and 1800, and produced drawings and annotations based on the observations of local smelters and smiths. Maciel was a prominent naturalist educated at the School of Natural Philosophy of the University of Coimbra and had vast experience with mineralogical studies. In his *Narrative about the Iron Foundry of Nova Oeiras in the Kingdom of Angola,* Maciel identified the tools and the iron production process. Two figures follow describing two smelting processes.[44]

This process could last one hour with three workers in the first figure representing the smelting of iron bars (a re-smelting process); and it would last four hours in the second figure, in which only two workers appear, in a process involving the smelting of iron ore. Maciel also depicts the bodily movements of the smelter and bellows operators. The smelter is in a squatting position (or sits on the floor) and controls the process and the rhythm of the bellows. The other two workers are standing and operate the bellows in a repetitive and cadenced movement. Blowing the bellows was indispensable for controlling the quality of the produced iron. One may imagine that specific smelting songs were sung then to determine the cadence as the bellows were blown.[45] Maciel did not consider additional stages of the smelting process: the necessary time for building the furnace, the mining tasks at the hills from which the ferruginous rocks were extracted,

42 Kriger, *Pride of Men*: 33, 34, 88.

43 Letter from the governor of Angola to Francisco Ferreira Guimarães. São Paulo de Assunção de Luanda, February 13, 1768. AHNA, Códice 79, fl. 78v–80.

44 José Álvares Maciel, *Notícia da Fábrica de Ferro da Nova Oeiras do Reino de Angola*. São Paulo de Assunção de Luanda, December 15, 1797. Arquivo Histórico do Tribunal de Contas (AHTC), Erário Régio, 4196.

45 For a similar process in Burkina Faso, see Christopher D. Roy, Jean-Baptiste Kientega, Jacob Bamogo and Abdoulaye Bamogo, *From Iron Ore to Iron Hoe: Smelting Iron in Africa* (DVD, CustomFlix, 2005).

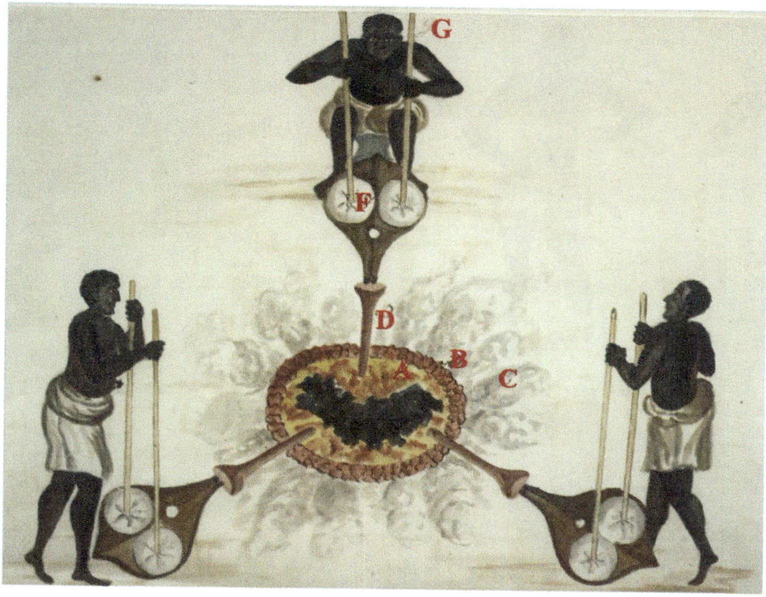

Fig. 2: Iron smelting in Nova Oeiras, 1797. José Álvares Maciel, "Narrative about the Iron Foundry of Nova Oeiras in the Kingdom of Angola," AHTC, Erário Régio, 4196. Legend: A – the foundry's furnace, where the iron ore and bars are introduced. After being molten, they remain under the charcoal; B – this is the furnace's wall, with a tile shard grid; C – the smoke exiting the wall openings; D – this is the clay tube through which the bellows blow; F – their leather; G – sticks for operating the bellows. This smelting procedure is carried out for a brief period; it will take slightly over an hour.

and the time for crushing those stones, cutting trees, and preparing charcoal. Nor did he consider the work after the smelting process, when the blacksmith hammers the slag out of his forge and prepares the metal for producing a wide variety of instruments. In any case, the point is that bloomery smelting does not require high investments in terms of energy, ore, and fuel, and all the necessary resources could be abundantly found across the entire region of Ilamba. The bellows were operated manually and access to ore was easy and recurrent. The "practical blacks," as local blacksmiths and smelters were called, as well as the *sobas* and Makotas who ruled them, interpreted royal initiatives as the intrusions of explorers and naturalists into an activity that enclosed sacred elements and as a constant exploitation of their skills in Nova Oeiras, imposing on them a strenuous rhythm and labor conditions that affronted their ways of living and working. Worker escapes and *soba* resistance to continue recruiting their "sons" demonstrate that Central Africans did not intend to collaborate with a foundry that only did them harm. Governor Sousa Coutinho's diligent attempts to show how his projects could bring prosperity to the region proved to be ineffective. At any rate, despite using prejudiced expressions such as "imperfect" or "faulty" in his depiction of the labor of Africans, and despite judging the rustic tools they used as illustrative of their "ignorance" and

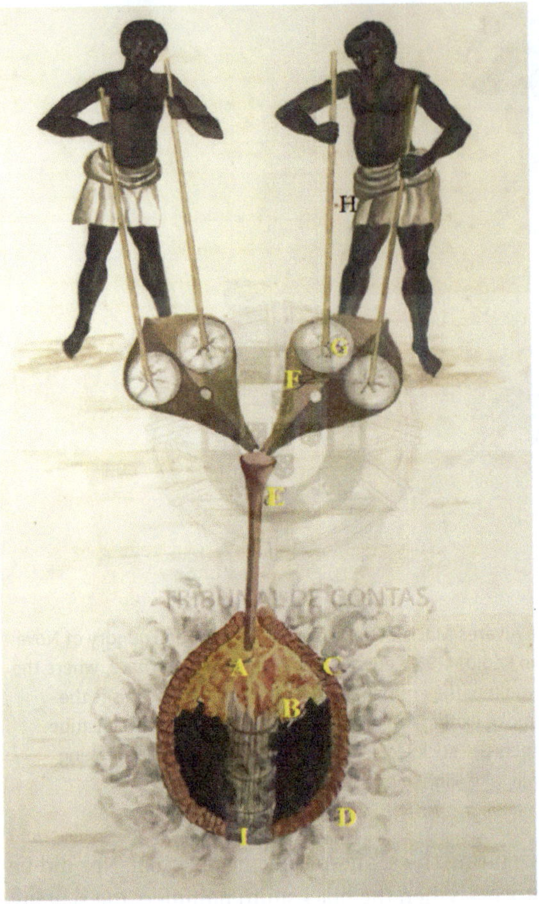

Fig. 3: Iron smelting in Nova Oeiras, 1797. José Álvares Maciel, "Narrative about the Iron Foundry of Nova Oeiras in the Kingdom of Angola," AHTC, Erário Régio, 4196. Legend: "A – this is a mabú[46] or straw drench, which is placed at the furnace's center; B – this is the iron covered with charcoal, which is placed on the sides of the same straw, which, in turn, is covered with the same charcoal. The clay tube is used to keep the fire lit and control the temperature; C – this is the furnace's wall with a tile shard grid. D – this is the smoke exiting the openings of the same wall; E – equally at the reach of the bellows; F – the tube reaches the ore; G – this is the leather of the bellows; H – this is the stick; I – the iron smelted from ore, at the reach of the bellows. This is the smelting of the ore itself, and I placed two arrobas and six pounds of iron ore. In four hours, I saw the smelting of [the number is missing on the manuscript] pounds of iron".

"poverty," the cultured governor did recognize their merit. In 1768, in a letter to the majorant of Mateus (governor of São Paulo, Brazil), he wrote: "many better and countless blacks I have, who not only provided for the existence of this iron-less kingdom of

46 A group of papyrus stems.

Europe for four years, but also produced many hundreds of quintais which I have shipped to His Majesty."[47] Reflection on African scientific contributions like metallurgy allows us to "decolonize" the history of the sciences, intellectual history, and the history of concepts and discourses. The blacksmiths and smelters of Ilamba continued mining iron after the foundry's closure and sold their small iron bars in exchange for tithe exemptions – a conquest negotiated by the *sobas* in previous years with the governor of Angola. They thereby protected their occupation and ancestral techniques. In 1830, Governor José Almeida e Vasconcelos recalled the large sums spent on the foundry, which was then in complete ruins: "the building and the machinery, everything there is reduced to perfect nullity; the weir and canal through which the foundry's water derived are now demolished." At that point, he reported a "covered space" in Trombeta (Golungo), a simple construction where "black people [. . .] are forced by contract to pay the tithe in [iron] bars, which have been sent to the Royal Navy's arsenal in this city for the price of twenty-five réis each *arrátel* (or pound)."[48]

3 Gold Mining in Angola, and Back to Minas Gerais

When the governor regulated the recruitment of workers for the iron foundry, he warned that it was necessary to avoid the "means by which service was assisted in Lombige" because the local populations resisted working for the colonial agents.[49] In the mid-eighteenth century, gold mining on the Lombige River (near Luanda, in Angola, north of the Kwanza River, see figure 4) was characterized by silence. Beyond its chroniclers,[50] no studies have been produced to examine the theme more closely, nor does the archaeological information available come close to the abundance of data about other Southern African locations. For this reason, I found no additional elements that prove the local exploitation of gold before the Lombige River prospections. But miners were sent to assess its mines, and hundreds of thousands of workers were recruited following family norms. Local leaders became important intermediaries (and, sometimes, obstacles) between the Iberian crown and access to the mines.

47 Letter from the governor of Angola, Francisco de Sousa Coutinho, to Luis Antonio de Sousa, governor of São Paulo (Brazil). São Paulo de Assunção de Luanda, November 30, 1768. Arquivo Nacional da Torre do Tombo (ANTT), Projeto reencontro Morgado Mateus mf. 12.

48 Letter from José Maria de Sousa Macedo Almeida e Vasconcelos, governor of Angola, to Nuno Caetano Álvares Pereira de Melo. Luanda, December 6, de 1830. IHGB – PADAB (Projeto Acervo Digital Angola-Brasil), DL76,02.35.

49 Letter from Francisco de Sousa Coutinho, governor of Angola. São Paulo de Assunção de Luanda, March 8, 1766. BNP, C–8742, F–6364.

50 Francisco Salles Ferreira, *Minas em Angola: Ouro, prata e carvão no Golungo Alto e Cambambe* (Lisbon: Typographia de A. da Costa Braga, 1896).

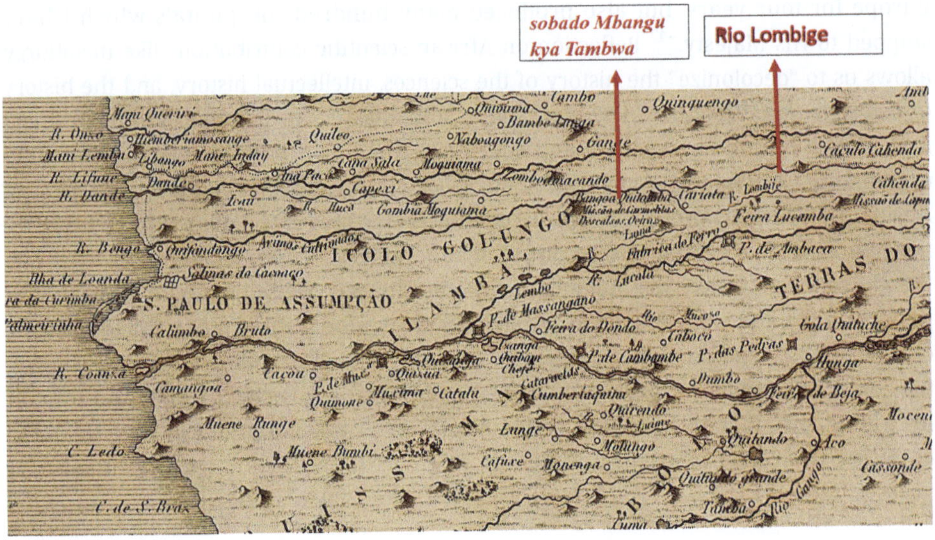

Fig. 4: The Lombige River, gold, and iron in Angola (1790). Luis Candido Pinheiro Furtado, Carta Geográfica de la Costa Ocidental de África (. . .) 1790/1825. Gabinete de Estudos Arqueológicos de Engenharia Militar- Lisboa (GEAEM), 4172-1A-9-13.

In 1754, the first rumors circulated that Friar Lourenço de Jesus Maria and the miner Caetano Álvares de Araújo had found gold in the Lombige and Lifua rivers and were carrying out mining activities in the region. The governor of the Kingdom of Angola obtained a sample of the ore and sent it to the Portuguese king, who ordered that he should continue to investigate the discovery and calculate the daily costs of labor per local worker. The workers sent – most of them, living as dependents of Portuguese vassals – were paid according to the system described above for iron smelting.[51] Álvares de Araújo was born in Angola and lived for 18 years in Minas Gerais before he escaped Brazil and returned to his homeland to evade his debts. His findings (together with his partner, who had since long abandoned his friar's habit) propelled gold prospecting for three years along the Lombige River and its tributaries. As a result of the exploratory journeys sponsored by the Portuguese, successive gold shipments were sent to Lisbon between 1754 and 1757. According to this documentation, the Portuguese concluded that the local populations were not exploiting alluvial gold ("they have not reached the point of being able to wash it"). But the governor feared that if the mines were found, they would never be safe and mining would be rapidly seized locally, since the Africans were skillful and could learn to embezzle the gold. For this reason, he worried that any

51 Letter from de Antonio Alvares da Cunha, governor of Angola. São Paulo de Assunção de Luanda, undated. Arquivo da Universidade de Coimbra (hereafter AUC), Coleções Condes da Cunha, Livro VI-III, 1754–1757.

attempt to guard the mines militarily and submit them to a taxation system would be useless. There is no evidence that gold had a special meaning either as a symbolic or costly object for the inhabitants of the region. Copper, by contrast, was considered valuable. For this reason, "they were very careful to hide it."[52] This does not mean that mining techniques did not exist, since they had tools and expertise for smelting and forging other metals and metal alloys, as we saw. Future archaeological studies may shed new light on this topic. The local leaders generally refrained from revealing the location of ores and from giving any information about the mines, which were protected under great severity. In the incursions searching for gold along the Lombige River, the governor of Angola ordered the arrest of *soba* leader Mbangu Kya Tambwa, a longstanding ally of the Portuguese who refused to show the location of gold mines. The *soba* was imprisoned for three years.[53] Álvares da Cunha' successor ordered his release after confirming that there was no gold in his lands, but only gravel with some gold specks. But in 1798, new expeditions were sent throughout the lands of Mbangu Kya Tambwa in search of gold mines. The silence of *soba* leaders and colonial persistence in promoting new incursions serve as additional evidence of the existence of gold, and of how much *soba* leaders and their subjects resisted sharing information on the natural resources of their lands.[54] In the Lombige River expeditions, the Africans who guided the group of miners, soldiers, and royal officials also sought to confound the colonial explorers by taking longer routes than necessary with circuitous paths to reach their destination. On one occasion, a five-day trip from Luanda to the Lombige River took 24 days with the local guides.[55] The prospecting expeditions followed the Lombige River upstream in search of alluvial gold mines. The expeditions included miners, soldiers for inspecting the mines, work directors and supervisors and, evidently, many workers to dig mines, wash/pan the gold, carry supplies, hunt, and provide for the crossing of rivers. João Paes do Amaral, a miner from Vila Rica in Minas Gerais, was sent to Angola to help with gold prospecting. The mining techniques and knowledge were applied to circuits more complex than he expected. Caetano learned his knowledge in the Brazilian Minas to go work in Angolan mines. João Paes do Amaral, a miner imported from Minas, narrates about the search for timber along the Bengo River to produce *bateias* (an instrument described by travelers as an African technique, probably originating with West African miners). Amaral appreciated the local timber:

52 Letter from Antonio de Vasconcelos, governor of Angola. São Paulo de Assunção de Luanda, June 28, 1762. AHU_CU_001, Cx. 45, D. 58.

53 Letter from Álvares da Cunha, governor of Angola. São Paulo de Assunção de Luanda, February 18, 1756. AHU_CU_001, Cx. 43, D. 4027.

54 Letter from Miguel Antonio de Melo, governor of Angola. São Paulo de Assunção de Luanda, January 22, 1798. AHNA, Códice 322.

55 AUC, Coleções Condes da Cunha, Livro VI–III, 1754–1757.

> [. . .] it takes a longer way to fetch wood in Vila Rica do Ouro Preto, and its quality is neither better nor grander. Men spend 8 to 10 days, and, sometimes, longer, to go get this wood and bring it to the Vila. And in Rio de Janeiro, wood does not come from near, and there is a certain circumstance; the heavier wood chunks sink into water; but by tucking a nail into one of their heads, or by gathering them, they can be pulled above water, and so people take them where they want.[56]

The governor sent for two other miners in Portuguese America – more specifically in Minas Gerais. He was assisted by "a Greek by nation" named George Tadeo, "a very practical man in this art of mining" and counted on many soldiers and royal aides. These specialized workers were well paid and did not involve themselves in harder and more perilous tasks, such as opening new mines, which were undertaken by the *soba* dependents. Working instruments such as gold pans, hoes, leverages, and mining shovels were sent from Lisbon. Despite their efforts, fever and death became the fate of most individuals sent on these expeditions. Local diseases and the unstable natural environment, in addition to the long drought and rain periods, made the countryside of Angola a justifiably feared destination. At least three *arraiais* (mission camps) were established during the expeditions: Arraial de Nossa Senhora de Nazaré, Arraial de Nossa Senhora do Cabo, and Arraial de Nossa Senhora do Bom Sucesso. Each *arraial* of the mining expedition had "no less than 500 or 400" workers. A total of 170,400 individuals were recruited. For two and half years, they worked as carriers and with "other things as needed." The figure may be exaggerated, but it was calculated by the six miners who were on the spot. The workers were sent by local vassals of the Portuguese crown in a rotary system, so they could also dedicate time to agricultural activities.[57] I have not found in the consulted documents a specific reference to distinctions in the work of by men and women, in contrast to what occurred in other Southern African regions. I know that in Angola, "servants carrying materials"[58] in public works were women, so it is possible that women also worked in the mines, carrying materials and raw ore. This may be related to Herbert's thesis that women's work in connection with mining in Sub-Saharan Africa, "collecting, pulverising, and winnowing ores," was associated with their work in agriculture. Consequently, the mining tasks would be an "agriculture analogy."[59] *Empacaceiros* (hunters of African forest buffalo), *mexiluandas* (inhabitants of the island of Luanda, probably male and female), and skillful fishermen and paddlers were also essential for the subsistence of the mining communities. Some records indicate that they

56 Letter from João Paes do Amaral, director of Lombige gold mines. Minas do Lombige, February 29, 1756. AUC, Coleções Condes da Cunha, Livro VI–III, 1754–1757.

57 Letter from Antonio de Vasconcelos, governor of Angola. São Paulo de Assunção de Luanda, January 6, 1759. *Arquivo das colônias*, v. V, n. 30, 1930, p. 148.

58 Letter from Antonio de Vasconcelos. São Paulo de Assunção de Luanda, May 14, 1760. AHU_CU_001, Cx. 46, D. 4261.

59 Eugenia Herbert, "Mining as Microcosm in Precolonial Sub-Saharan Africa: An Overview," in *Social Approaches to an Industrial Past. The Archaeology and Anthropology of Mining*, ed. Arthur Bernard Knapp, Vincent C. Pigott and Eugenia W. Herbert (London: Routledge, 1998): 138–54.

were paid with "fabric," since textiles were a valuable currency in trade.[60] Two regiments were instituted by the governor to define the rules to be followed by the directors of the *arraiais*. The aim of these norms was: to establish the workers' remuneration in accordance with the "custom of the land" and the "customary ration, which is, for eight days and ten (persons), a provision of flour and half a provision of beans."[61] The living conditions of *soba* dependents contrasted starkly with these rules. They not only were *not* remunerated, but underwent physical punishment inflicted by the directors and soldiers of the expedition and did not receive the stipulated food rations. On empty stomachs, the workers underwent long journeys of over six days between their *soba* regions and the mining site. Such a situation resulted in frequent deaths and escapes, which were punished by the soldiers, who pursued the fugitives, "mistreating and scaring off everything."[62] It was nothing new that although *soba* dependents were free, they still were "treated as slaves"[63] by the royal administrators – as the Portuguese king acknowledged. The social and legal condition of a dependent of the local leaders did not seem enough, therefore, to ensure labor conditions free from coercion. On the one hand, labor relations were mediated by local leaders, who, as subjects of the Portuguese crown, were obliged to provide workers. On the other, the workers were forced to treatment identified with a context of slavery, such as physical punishments and the lack of remuneration.

Both freedom and slavery were interpreted by the Portuguese according to the Western standards being defined in the modern era. That set of meanings cannot be associated with the liberal notion of individual rights, nor should they be uncritically applied in an attempt to grasp the notions that the Kimbundos from Angola had about labor, freedom, and slavery. The aim, in this text, is to demarcate concrete labor conditions and forms of treatment that were identified by contemporary subjects themselves as those of a slave and, in this case, by the workers from the Kingdom of Angola as unacceptable. Based on the consulted documents and on records from other southern African regions, it is understandable that escapes were the main strategy adopted by the workers to deal with the conditions imposed on them. Consequently, they did not return to their original dwelling places: "they would leave their lands unattended and stray deep into the country."[64] The migration of peasants could produce deficits in agricultural production and cause the social and political disaggregation of communities near the mines. In 1761, the king of Portugal decreed "perpetual silence" regarding

60 AUC, Coleções Condes da Cunha, Livro VI–III, 1754–1757.

61 Statutes from June 24, 1755 and January 13, 1756. AUC, Coleções Condes da Cunha, Livro VI–III, 1754–1757.

62 Letter from Antonio de Vasconcelos. São Paulo de Assunção de Luanda, January 6, 1759.

63 AUC, Coleções Condes da Cunha, Livro VI–III, 1754–1757.

64 Letter from Antonio de Vasconcelos. São Paulo de Assunção de Luanda, January 6, 1759.

the mines along the Lombige River and threatened to arrest any person who defied it.[65] His resolution was so serious that even the vestiges of the *arraiais* where the gold activities took place were destroyed. This decision directly points to the fragility of the Portuguese rule in Angola. The African kingdoms and potentates meant an internal threat to the frail limits of Portuguese occupation, in addition to the French, British, and Dutch, who could rapidly co-opt trade networks capable of taking them to the gold. Worse, gold could lead to even sharper disputes for the region and put at risk the profits from exploitation in Brazil, since the enslaved subjects who supplied the economies of Portuguese America were mostly from this region of Africa. The attempt to avoid speaking about the disastrous experience of administering the laborers also seems to have been one of the aims of the king's ruling. At the end of the day, secrecy within the colonial administration did not differ much from secrecy among local authorities, since both wanted to control the natural resources, the land, and the work force to exploit them. Even though silence reverberated in memory and through the historiography, other official and private enterprises were undertaken along the Lombige River in the nineteenth century, resulting in records of the reports and in the obtaining of gold samples by travelers such as Douville and Francina, by Angola's governor Nicolau de Abreu Castellobranco, and by the tradesmen Francisco Antonio Flores (1866) and Salom Bensaúde (1884). In his memoirs published in Lisbon in 1896, Francisco Salles Ferreira narrates how his brother, the civil engineer José Damásio de Salles Ferreira, collaborated with Francisco Antonio Flores by discovering a vast area rich in gold in the form of sparks and nuggets in the riverbed and along the banks of rivers and streams, disseminated in the ferruginous sands as a powder invisible to the naked eye. There is no doubt that gold was present in the Lombige region, in its tributaries and neighboring hills. When José Salles Ferreira prospected the region in the second half of the nineteenth century, he found local miners busy with panning systems that used concave pans or wooden bowls, "hairy bullock leather," and locally produced wooden tools such as gutters for panning the sand. At this point, there is no way of knowing whether such techniques had been used in mining along the Lombige before, that is, in the eighteenth century, or whether they were learned, for instance, from miners from Minas Gerais (Brazil) who worked in Angola. What is apparent is that gold mining entered the nineteenth century with the knowledge and adaptations of local miners. The military officer finishes his memoirs on the mines of Angola (1896) vindicating the resumption of mining along the Lombige.[66]

65 Letter from Francisco Xavier de Mendonça Furtado, November 13, 1761. AHU, Códice 472.

66 Salles Ferreira, *Minas em Angola*: 47–48.

4 Closing Remarks

Knowledge of metallurgy was an essential element in overseas expansion and for the exploitation of valuable metals such as iron. In Minas Gerais, the non-existence of iron tools to help in gold mining activities was a recurrent issue for the authorities, travelers, men of letters, and miners. Governor Rodrigo José de Menezes (1784–1788) said: "what a loss it would be for the Royal Treasury if work at the mines should be stopped for a lack of iron." In the same text, Menezes narrates that he once requested a local blacksmith to tell him "the secret of his production" and received from him, in reply, a bar of "good iron." Not yet satisfied, the governor requested that the bar be turned into a lock, which was obeyed by the mysterious blacksmith. The royal official feared that such knowledge could escape the purview of the Portuguese crown and requested this entire experience to be kept confidential.[67] In addition to gold, war objects and the exploration of iron and saltpeter were under the same purview, as both were used in explosives for new gold exploitation techniques and in the production of military devices.[68] Therefore, keeping the "secret" of metallurgical knowledge meant being inserted into power relations. This remark may seem rather too generic, but it takes on specific meanings as we examine the history of metallurgy in the South Atlantic – or, better yet, as we refer to historical actors within a society under the asserted domination of whites and mostly composed of Africans and their descendants (and for this reason, the whites sought to enslave not only the labor force, but, above all, beliefs, knowledge forms, and expectations). In Minas Gerais, domination processes were linked to a consolidated tax apparatus, to the trafficking of the enslaved, and to the consolidation of slave structures that permeated all social relations, including both public and private life. In Ilamba, Portuguese domination was permeated by unstable social relations with the local powers – the *soba* vassals – and the potentates that controlled the trafficking routes, such as Imbangala Kasange. Local slavery was marked by the rhythm of trafficking activities and increasing Atlantic demands, as well as by the values and visions of the local people themselves regarding slavery and freedom. The contexts were different but, on both ends, forms of resistance to such attempts at domination, as well as the efforts to negotiate better working and living conditions, did exist and expressed themselves in different ways. Knowing the "secret" of ore mining and smithing ensured some scope for action and, in some cases,

---

67 Exposition of Rodrigo José de Menezes, governor of Minas, August 4, 1780, in: Livro Primeiro de registro dos ofícios dirigidos à Corte Pelo Ilmo. e Exmo. Senhor D. Rodrigo José de Menezes, Governador e Capitão General desta Capitania de Minas Gerais, Arquivo Público Mineiro (APM – Seção Colonial), Códice 224, f. 139 e ss.

68 The mineral richness of the "Iron Quadrangle" (*Quadrilátero Ferrífero*) in the central region of Minas Gerais was the object of the testimonies of naturalists and travelers. In his "Brief Corographical Depiction of the Capitaincy of Minas Gerais" of 1782, João José Teixeira Coelho informs us that the region had "mines of potash alum, saltpetre, and iron," which were not explored solely "out of lack of industry."

enabled the attainment and maintenance of freedom. The *coartação*, which resulted from the possibility of buying one's own manumission and was facilitated by access to gold, was an intermediary condition between freedom and slavery. On the other side of the Atlantic, being involved in kinship relations, or being the "son" of a local authority figure, further complicated the definitions of what it meant to be free. This article described distinct modalities of slavery, labor, and dependency. A relevant point not dealt with on this occasion is the fact that alongside the *jingangula* and *pulungus*, there were Portuguese individuals, Biscayans, Frenchmen, convicts, soldiers, slaves, and the so-called "slaves of profit."[69] There were also "voluntary bondmen," that is, smiths from the foundry of Figueiró dos Vinhos in Portugal, who were forced onboard and went to Angola to teach their craftsmanship.[70]

The African leaders' persistent defense of their ore-rich territories by means of secrecy, concealment, and confounding the Europeans is an important and still little-known facet of the environmental and political history of metallurgy in the eighteenth century. And the negotiations of *sobas* and their dependents to avoid the colonial tithe needs to be recognized as a political strategy that changed the organization of labor at the iron foundry in terms of remuneration, recruitment, and daily routine of labor. The local people's lack of interest in gold is also indicative in the sense that ascribing gold exploration techniques in the Americas to Africans in a general way is a mistake that obscures the diversity of histories of the African continent. Still, knowing the details of iron smelting and forging in Ilamba considerably helps us analyze and understand the activities of African smiths and their descendants in the New World, bearing in mind that the ports of Luanda and Benguela were the departing points of most enslaved individuals who lived in Minas Gerais. In his efforts to establish a foundry in Vila de Sorocaba (São Paulo, Brazil), then-governor Luis Antonio de Sousa maintained continuous dialogues with Angola via his brother-in-law, who held the position of local governor at the time, and the official who established the iron foundry in Ilamba. He even proposed to his brother-in-law that they should send for "other Biscayan masters, for a second time" for the two foundries. In Brazilian lands, seen as "healthier" lands with a better climate than those of the Kingdom of Angola, it would not be difficult to instruct and train many smelters, who would then be sufficient for establishing the two foundries.[71] In one of his letters, Luis Antonio de Sousa narrates that at the foundry of Sorocaba, iron was produced in small amounts because of the

69 In this case, "slaves of profit" (*escravos ao ganho*) were captives allowed to earn a daily fee paid by inhabitants of neighbouring villages and even from Luanda. They also worked in Nova Oeiras. The consulted bibliography mentions at least 12 carpenter and bricklayer slaves who earned such daily fees between 1768 and 1772, including four professionals and one apprentice. AHTC, Erário Régio 4191.

70 Alfagali, *Ferreiros e fundidores da Ilamba*: 243.

71 Letter from Luis Antonio de Sousa, governor of São Paulo (Brazil) to Francisco de Sousa Coutinho, governor of Angola. São Paulo (Brazil), October 30, 1769. In *Publicação Oficial de documentos interessantes para a história e costumes de São Paulo*. v. XIX, 1896: 406–8.

"crude intelligence of a black man who, after initiating work with a master, obtain[ed] the best smelting when he conducted them." The origin of this skillful slave who replaced his Portuguese master is not known – it is not even known whether he was an African or not. But this is more evidence that may help bring together the two shores of the Atlantic regarding the exploration of African knowledge of metallurgy.[72] The Africans brought to the captaincy of São Paulo, "despite the radical parting from their societies of origin, strove [. . .] to structure" their lives based on Bantu sociocultural elements.[73] As an ancient form of knowledge and wisdom from West and West Central Africa, metallurgy – as well as other intellectual contributions, such as medical and culinary practices – was part of a set of African traditions that were reinvented in the colonial situation as a form of resistance and struggle for survival. My own comings and goings across the Atlantic are nothing but a reflection of the many travels of the characters I have investigated. I sail in incomparably better conditions, which result from my economic, racial, and social privileges (during the days of Covid-19, they were only imaginary trajectories). However, the crossing continues to reveal historical aspects of the exclusionary society in which I live, which, in turn, continues its attempt to dominate, enslave, and hide the histories I recount, as well as the descendants of Ilamba's proud and rebel *jingangulas* and *pulungus*.

Bibliography

Primary Sources

Published Primary Sources

Arquivos de Angola (AA): v. III, n. 30–33, 1937; v. IV, nº 52, 1939.

Arquivo das colônias: v. V, n. 30, 1930.

Publicação Oficial de documentos interessantes para a história e costumes de São Paulo (São Paulo: Arquivo do Estado de São Paulo, Typographia da Companhia Industrial de São Paulo, 1896).

Manuscript Sources

Arquivo Histórico da Casa Setecentista de Mariana (AHCSM): Livro de Registro de Testamento 46, fl. 80v, 1789.

Arquivo Histórico Ultramarino (AHU): Códice 472.

72 Letter from Luis Antonio de Sousa, governor of São Paulo (Brazil) to Francisco de Sousa Coutinho, governor of Angola. São Paulo (Brazil), October 30, 1769.

73 Robert W. Slenes, *Na Senzala, uma Flor: Esperanças e recordações na formação da família escravista*, 2nd ed. (Campinas: Editora da Unicamp, 2014): 155.

Conselho Ultramarino(CU)_Angola (001): Cx. 43, D. 4027; Cx. 45, D. 58; Cx. 46, D. 4261; Cx. 52, D. 28; Caixa 52, D. 44; Cx. 45, D. 68; Cx. 51, D. 1; Cx. 52, D. 15; Cx. 52, D. 73; Cx. 57, D. 28; Cx. 119, D. 15; Cx. 119, D. 16.
Arquivo Público Mineiro (APM – Seção Colonial): Códice 224, f. 139.
Arquivo Nacional da Torre do Tombo (ANTT): Projeto reencontro Morgado Mateus mf. 12.
Arquivo Histórico do Tribunal de Contas (AHTC): Erário Régio, 4196.
Arquivo da Universidade de Coimbra (AUC): Coleções Condes da Cunha, Livro VI–III, 1754–1757.
Arquivo Histórico Nacional de Angona (AHNA): Códice 322; Códice 79, fl. 78v–80; C–14–3; C–14–4; A–2–2; D–2–5; A–20–2.
Biblioteca Nacional de Portugal (BNP): C–8742, F–6364; C- 8743, F-6367; C- 8553, F-6362.
Instituto de Estudos Brasileiro (IEB/USP), Coleção Alberto Lamego: Al–082–156; AL–082–024; AL–083–002; AL–083–138.
Instituto Histórico e Geográfico Brasileiro (IHGB), Projeto Acervo Digital Angola-Brasil (PADAB): DL76,02.35; DL81, 02.19; DVD9,19 DSC00153; DVD9,19 DSC00198; DVD10,20 DSC00415.

Secondary Literature

Alfagali, Crislayne. *Em casa de ferreiro: Os artesãos do ferro nas Minas Gerais do século XVIII* (São Paulo: Alameda, 2018).
Alfagali, Crislayne. *Ferreiros e fundidores da Ilamba: Uma História Social da Fábrica de Nova Oeiras (Angola, segunda metade do século XVIII)* (Luanda: Fundação Dr. António Agostinho Neto, 2018).
de Assis Júnior, António. *Dicionário Kimbundu – Português* (Luanda: Argente, Santos e Comp. Lda., n.d.).
Bacellar Bebiano, José. *Museu do Dundo: notas sobre a siderurgia dos indígenas de Angola e de outras regiões africanas* (Lisbon: Publicações culturais da Companhia de Diamantes de Angola, 1960).
Bostoen, Koen, Odjas Ndonda Tshiyayi and Gille-Maurice de Schryver. “On the Origin of the Royal Kongo Title Ngangula,” *Africana Linguistica* 19 (2013): 53–83.
Botelho, Ângela. “Arma de fogo,” in *Dicionário Histórico das Minas Gerais*, ed. Adriana Romeiro and Ângela Botelho (Belo Horizonte: Autêntica, 2003): 27–28.
Cavazzi de Montecúccolo, Antonio. *Descrição histórica dos três Reinos do Congo, Matamba e Angola*, vol. 1 (Lisbon: Junta de investigações do Ultramar, 1965).
von Eschwege, Wilhelm Ludwig. *Pluto Brasiliensis* (Belo Horizonte: Itatiaia, 1833; São Paulo: Editora da Universidade de São Paulo, 1979).
Ferrand, Paul. *L’or a Minas Gerais* (Belo Horizonte: Imprensa Oficial do Estado de Minas Gerais, 1913).
da Gaeta, Antonio. *La meravigliosa conversione a lla Santa Fede di Cristo d ellaregina Singa e del suo regnodi Matamba* (Nápoles: Francisco de Maria Gioia, 1669).
Gorceix, Henri. “A indústria Mineral na Província de Minas Gerais,” in *Annaes da Escola de Minas de Ouro Preto: coleções de memórias e de notícias sobre a mineralogia, a geologia e as explorações das minas no Brasil* (Ouro Preto, MG: Escola de Minas de Ouro Preto, 1883): 24–40.
Gorceix, Henri. “Estudo químico e mineralógico das rochas dos arredores de Ouro Preto,” in *Anais da Escola de Minas de Ouro Preto: coleções de memórias e de notícias sobre a mineralogia, a geologia e as explorações das minas no Brasil* (Ouro Preto, MG: Escola de Minas de Ouro Preto, 1883): 5–23.
Hampatê Bá, Amadou. “A tradição viva,” in *História Geral da África I. Metodologia e pré-história da África*, ed. Joseph Ki-Zerbo (São Paulo: Ed. Ática/UNESCO, 1980): 167–212.
Herbert, Eugenia W. *Iron, Gender and Power: Rituals of Transformation in African Societies* (Bloomington: Indiana University Press, 1993).
Herbert, Eugenia. “Mining as Microcosm in Precolonial Sub-Saharan Africa: An Overview,” in *Social Approaches to an Industrial Past. The Archaeology and Anthropology of Mining*, ed. Eugenia W. Herbert, Arthur Bernard Knapp and Vincent C. Pigott (London: Routledge, 1998): 138–54.

Kriger, Colleen E. *Pride of Men: Ironworking in 19th Century, West Central Africa* (Porthsmouth: Heinemann, 1999).
Laman, Karl Edvard. *Dictionnaire kikongo-français avec une carte phonétique décrivant les dialectes les plus importants de la langue dite Kikongo* (Bruxelles: Falk, 1936).
Macgaffey, Wyatt. *Religion and Society in Central Africa: The Bakongo of Lower Zaire* (Chicago: University of Chicago Press, 1986).
Madeira Santos, Catarina. "Um governo 'polido' para Angola: Reconfigurar dispositivos de domínio (1750–c.1800)" (PhD diss., Universidade Nova de Lisboa, 2005).
de Mello e Souza, Laura. *Norma e conflito: aspectos da história de Minas no século XVIII* (Belo Horizonte: Universidade Federal de Minas Gerais, 1999).
Mertens, Joseph. *Les chefs couronnés chez les Ba Kongo orientaux: étude de régime successoral* (Brussels: G. van Campenhout, 1942).
Oliveira Cadornega, Antonio de. *História Geral das Guerras Angolanas*, 3 vols., ed. José Matias Delgado (Lisbon: Divisão de Publ. e Biblioteca, Agência Geral das Colónias, 1680/Agência-Geral do Ultramar, 1972).
Redinha, José. *Campanha etnográfica ao Tchiboco (Alto-Tchicapa)* (Lisbon: Compania de Diamantes de Angola/Museu do Dundo, 1953–1955).
Salles Ferreira, Francisco. *Minas em Angola: Ouro, prata e carvão no Golungo Alto e Cambambe* (Lisbon: Typographia de A. da Costa Braga, 1896).
dos Santos Gomes, Flávio. *A hidra e os pântanos: Mocambos, quilombos e comundades de fugitivos no Brasil (séculos XVII–XIX)* (São Paulo: Editoria da Universidade Estadual Paulista, Ed. Polis, 2005).
da Silva Maia, Antonio. *Dicionário complementar: português-kimbundu-kikongo* (Luanda: Ed. do Autor, 1964).
da Silva Rego, António. "A Academia Portuguesa da História e o II Centenário da Fábrica do Ferro de Nova Oeiras, Angola," in *Colectânea de Estudos em Honra do Prof Doutor Damião Peres* (Lisbon: Academia Portuguesa da História, 1974): 387–98.
Slenes, Robert W. *Na Senzala, uma Flor: Esperanças e recordações na formação da família escravista*, 2nd ed. (Campinas: Editora da Unicamp, 2014).
Slenes, Robert. "L'Arbre Nsanda replanté: cultes d'affliction Kongo et identité des esclaves de plantation dans le Brésil du Sud-Et (1810–1888)," *Cahiers du Brésil Contemporain* 67/68, no. 2 (2007): 217–313
Thornton, John. "The Regalia of the Kingdom of Kongo, 1491–1895," in *Kings of Africa: Art and Authority in Central Africa*, ed. Erna Beumers and Hans-Joachim Koloss (Maastricht: Foundation Kings of Africa, 1992): 56–63.
Vansina, Jan. "Linguistic Evidence for the Introduction of Ironworking in Bantu – Speaking Africa," *History in Africa* 33 (2006): 321–61.

Maria Helena Pereira Toledo Machado

Slavery, Motherhood, and the Free Womb Law

While it is not hard to understand the importance of maternity in the perpetuation of slavery, it took scholars a very long time to recognize the fact. In studies on the subject, one still often sees authors referring to slaves in general terms, as if they were somehow exempt from gender and sex and can be lumped together into one broad category. The slave's way of life has been frequently discussed in terms of living and working conditions, insalubrity, and specific social and community relationships, but without mention of the differences that might pertain to men and women – African or Creole – in the slave-labor system or inside the slave community. If the more traditional historiography recognizes only the generic figure of the slave, the recent studies that have gradually particularized the experience of captivity have also, at times, neglected the specificities of gender in slavery. A good example of this are studies devoted to slave families. The new historiography, which quite rightly restored the role of the slave family to history and disposed of visions that, taking only a macro view of slavery, saw the social life of the slaves as characterized by anomie, still needs to tweak its lens in order to recognize the various implications of marriage and maternity in the life of enslaved men and women. For slave women, being a wife and a mother implied a host of considerable challenges; in addition to the risks inherent to pregnancy, maternity, lactation, and child-rearing under the yoke of slavery, marriage and reproduction also entailed pulling a double shift and being submitted to a dual subjugation – to master and husband. In order to focus on the role maternity played in slavery, we therefore have to consider the fact that enslaved men and women experienced it from different places and were subjected to different levels of oppression and suffering. In her pioneering book on the role of gender and maternity in the creation and maintenance of the slave system in British America, Jennifer Morgan underscored the slave woman's centrality as both a laborer and a breeder in the constitution of the Atlantic slavery system. According to Morgan, it was after observing the role women played in different West African societies since the seventeenth century that European travelers and slave traders began to define and/or legitimize the structures of slavery. Farmers, merchants, and mothers, the women in these societies, especially the wives, served functions central to economic and social reproduction – roles the Europeans were keen to replicate and exploit in the Americas.[1] The most important principle legitimizing slavery throughout Atlantic slave societies was *partus sequitur ventrem*, which meant that offspring inherited

1 Jennifer Morgan, *Labouring Woman. Reproduction and Gender in New World Slavery* (Philadelphia: University of Pennsylvania Press, 2004): 12–49.

https://doi.org/10.1515/9783111026527-004

the legal status of the mother that bore them. This ancient Roman law, adopted wholesale in the Iberian Peninsula from the early days of slavery, was also presented as an unassailable immemorial principle, an argument for which there were no historical grounds whatsoever. By putting the slave woman in the dual role of producer of human and non-human capital, the principles mentioned above ended up highlighting the centrality of the enslaved woman's body as the very locus of slavery. Whether by stimulating reproduction or by neglecting it, slave-owners had always factored reproduction into their strategies for generating wealth.[2] The advent of laws prohibiting the separation of mothers and children came late. In Brazil, mothers and children under the age of 15 could be sold separately up until 1869.[3] However, the Free Womb Law of 1871, which freed the slave-born child whilst leaving the infant under the guardianship of the slave-owner (or the state) from the ages of 8 to 21, once again served to separate mothers and their offspring, as the owner retained all tutorial authority over the ward.[4] Mothers who had managed to obtain manumission by law were therefore obliged to leave their enslaved or free-born children behind, in the clutches of their former owners. In what follows I present an excerpt from a study I am currently working on with Antonio Alexandre Cardoso (Federal University of Maranhão – Codó Campus). The passage in question concerns the macabre case of the murder of two slave children. The wider study will give rise to an article and a book, expected to be completed in 2022.[5] The theme of the episode under examination straddles the issues of slave maternity, manumission, and the separation of mothers and children. The case is well known as the "crime of the baroness of Grajaú," and occurred in São Luís, the capital of the northern province of Maranhão, in 1876. While it has been the subject of other studies and even featured in Josué Montello's famous novel *Os Tambores de São Luiz* (*The Drums of São Luís*), published in 1975, so far no-one has endeavored to scour through the case files for an analysis of the power relations that led to this heinous crime. Our goal is to reconstruct these power relations from the point of view of the mother and grandmother of the murdered children. Tellingly, in the coverage of the baroness's crime, the victims were frequently referred to as *escravinhos* ("little slaves"), representing them simultaneously as poor children and as persons

2 Ibid.: 107–43; Kathleen M. Brown, *Good Wives, Nasty Wenches and Anxious Patriarchs. Gender, Race, and Power in Colonial Virginia* (Chapel Hill: University of North Carolina Press, 1996): 107–36; Jean Hebrard and Rebecca Scott, *Freedom Papers: An Atlantic Odyssey in the Age of Emancipation* (Cambridge: Harvard University Press, 2012).

3 Câmara dos Deputados [The Chamber of Deputies], Decree no. 1695, 15/09/1869, https://www2.camara.leg.br/legin/fed/decret/1824-1899/decreto-1695-15-setembro-1869-552474-publicacaooriginal-69771-pl.html#:~:text=Prohibe%20as%20vendas%20de%20escravos%20debaixo%20de%20preg%C3%A3o%20e%20em%20exposi%C3%A7%C3%A3o%20publica.&text=Os%20leil%C3%B5es%20commerciaes%20de%20escravos,escravo%20que%20vender%20em%20leil%C3%A3o [accessed 18.10.2020].

4 Presidência da República (Presidency of the Republic), Decree no. 2040, 28/09/1871, Free Womb Law, http://www.planalto.gov.br/ccivil_03/leis/lim/lim2040.htm [accessed 18.10.2020].

5 Maria Helena P.T. Machado and A. Alexandre I. Cardoso, *Geminiana e seus filhos. Escravidão e morte; maternidade e infância* (São Paulo: Bazar do Tempo, june 2023), in press.

without social value. It should be noted that the case files suggest that the murder of the two children took place practically in public, and not a single person of influence made any effective attempt to prevent the murderer, Ana Rosa Viana Ribeiro, from fulfilling her objective.

1 Geminiana and Her Sons: Slavery and Death; Maternity and Childhood in São Luís (Maranhão) in the 1870s

In the early hours of November 14, 1876, Geminiana, a young black freedwoman who had only recently bought her manumission and now scraped a living as a hired hand, left her home on Mocambo Street and walked to the corner of Grande, where she met with four men carrying a casket. Though the coffin was closed with lock and chain,[6] she could immediately see that it was child-sized[7] and bore no identifier whatsoever of who lay within. It would later emerge that the coffin was cobbled together in a rush, before dawn, and that its only adornment was some blue fabric lining on the inside.[8] There was no cortege, just four slaves carrying the casket on their shoulders, and they seemed to be trying to get to the hospital-owned São João chapel, which stood right beside the graveyard, as quickly and as silently as possible. For the slaves Primo (or Firmo, in some depositions), Geraldo, Anísio, and João, the four pallbearers, the task was immeasurably heavier than the box and its contents, given the exceptional and altogether nebulous circumstances surrounding the little slave's death. Naturally alarmed by the sight, Geminiana stopped and asked the coffin-carriers where they were coming from, and it was then that her very worst fears were all but confirmed: they had come from the residence of *Dona* Ana Rosa. Geminiana dashed back home, and from there made for the cemetery, now accompanied by her mother Símplicia, a freedwoman who had once belonged to the Texieira Belfort household but now was a hired worker in town. All the indications were pointing to the deceased child being Geminiana's young son Inocêncio, aged 8, who had been purchased by Ana Rosa Lamagnèr Viana Ribeiro a little over three months earlier. These suspicions were soon confirmed. When she reached the chapel, the distraught mother searched high and low for the child-sized coffin and finally found it in a backroom, awaiting the chaplain, who had not yet arrived. This was immaterial, as without the proper paperwork from the police, the chaplain could not proceed with

6 Geminiana's testimony. Autos Crime da Baronesa do Grajaú, 1876–77 (São Luiz: Ministério Público do Estado do Maranhão – Public Prosecutors' Office, 2009): 111–12 (hereafter ACB/MPEMA).
7 On child burials, see Luiz Vailati, *Morte menina. Infância e morte infantil no Brasil dos oitocentos (Rio de Janeiro e São Paulo)* (São Paulo: Alameda, 2010).
8 João Marcelino Romeu's testimony. ACB/MPEMA: 103.

the burial. Geminiana asked the pallbearers to open the coffin, but they resisted: *Dona* Ana Rosa had given them express orders only to unlock the casket in the presence of the chaplain, so he could commend the deceased unto the Lord. That done, they said, they were to lock the chain again and bring back the key. Geminiana protested, saying that she had been "denied sight of her son in life, and would not be so denied again in his death." The coffin was then opened, though there is some discrepancy in the case files as to who actually did this. The four slaves denied doing it, but some witnesses claimed it was they who removed the coffin lid, while others said it was the chaplain who ordered it done. Most likely, there is truth in both claims: the slave Primo, who had the key in his pocket, may well have disobeyed the orders and allowed the mother a peek at her dead son, only to re-open the coffin later, and for a longer period, in the presence of the chaplain.[9] The sight of the dead child sent Geminiana and Simplícia, his grandmother, into convulsions of despair. According to the mother, the boy was wearing striped shirt and trousers, and had his arms stretched by his side – not resting on the chest, with the hands entwined, as would have been customary. When she took his hands in order to place them in the correct burial position, she noticed rope burns on the wrists, indicating that the boy had been tied up. The two women undressed Inocêncio's corpse to conduct a thorough examination and found that the body was covered in scars – some older, others very recent – from various whippings and beatings, with a great deal of damage to the arms, back, and elbows.[10] A later coroner's examination identified a considerable number of marks, abrasions, and burns caused to the boy's body by ropes, whips, and other instruments. He had also suffered a brain hemorrhage, and his feet and hands were swollen. In addition to being visibly undernourished, the boy displayed rectal prolapse and injuries to the anus.[11] However hurriedly Ana Ribeiro Viana had tried to bury the "inconvenience," as she considered the death of the child in her household, the circumstances were not in her favor. As soon as it had become apparent that the young slave was at death's door, she had started planning the best way to make the whole bother disappear.[12] Hailing as she did from one of the main slave-owning clans of Codó, in the Maranhão hinterlands, and married to Carlos Ribeiro Viana, leader of the Liberal Party in the province, she had no reason to think the death of this ragamuffin would amount to more than another nuisance to be covered up – as had occurred many times before, including only weeks earlier, when Jacinto, Inocêncio's younger brother, aged 5 or 6, also died under her charge. Like his sibling, Jacinto had been buried in a rush but without attracting much attention.[13]

9 Testimony from Primo, Anísio, Geraldo, and João. ACB/MPEMA: 17–110.

10 Geminiana's testimony. ACB/MPEMA: 111–12.

11 First coroner's report. ACB/MPEMA: 156–59.

12 Deposition of Ana Rosa Ribeiro Viana. ACB/MPEMA: 179–81.

13 Numerous witnesses affirmed that Ana Rosa Viana tortured slaves on a routine basis. One of the slaves mentioned, a girl named Militina, had all her teeth pulled out for having smiled at Ana Rosa's husband, while another, Carolina, suffered punishments that were considered severe even by the

Things went a little differently with Inocêncio. On the night of November 13, when she heard the boy's death rattle, Ana Rosa summoned her private physician, Dr. Santos Jacinto, who arrived either immediately after the boy's death or during his final throes. The good doctor apparently had no problem writing a death certificate attesting that Inocêncio had died of natural causes brought on by intertropical hypoemia, a diarrhea-causing infection commonly known at the time as "the yellowness," and most likely contracted through the lad's habit of eating earth.[14] The doctor stuck to his story at the second coroner's examination, conducted under his responsibility on the boy's exhumed corpse five days after his death.[15] In the hours prior to Inocêncio's passing, Ana Rosa asked the doctor to put at her disposal his longest-serving and evidently most trusted slave, Sebastião dos Santos Jacinto, to assist in the preparations for ridding herself of the problem as swiftly as possible. Her first step was to try to get the child off her property. To this end, she chose the house of the mulatto Olímpia, who once in a while worked for her as a hired house servant. However, Olímpia refused, saying that she was sick herself, and that "a person in a ill health can't be tending to another."[16] The mistress then summoned Gregória Rosa Salustiana, a black hired servant who had done some work at the mansion a few weeks earlier. Gregória arrived a couple of hours before Inocêncio's death, so she and Sebastião were the only witnesses to his passing and the preparation of his body for burial. However, their testimony was vague and inconsistent, though they did let slip some telling details as to what took place at the house during those hours. For example, it emerged that Inocêncio had died in his usual bed, which was really just a piece of cloth extended on the floor of the first room along the house's balcony, contiguous with Ana Rosa's own bedroom, and that he was wearing only a short blue shirt at the time. It appears he had at least been bathed that day, though that did not seem to be at all habitual, even for a child suffering from diarrhea, with continual evacuations of feces

---

standards of the day. Ana Rosa was replaced in court by her brothers, who had decided to assume the charge in order to preserve a woman of the family from the shame of being sued, as discussed by Lenine Nequete in *O Escravo na Jurisprudência Brasileira* (Porto Alegre: Diretoria da Revista de Jurisprudência e Outros Impressos do Tribunal de Justiça, 1988): 61–77.

14 In 1835, Dr. Cruz Jobim characterized intertropical hypoemia as a disease typical of regions with a humid climate and most common among the lower classes, especially slaves. Key symptoms were diarrhea, anemia, and aerophagia. Later, other doctors established a connection between the sickness and the presence of the hookworm *Ancylostoma duodenal* in the sufferer's intestines. The habit or "mania" of eating earth, quite common among slaves, was frequently listed as a cause and sometimes an effect of the infection, which slave-owners considered particularly damaging to their interests. Dr. Xavier Sigaud associated the condition with *maculo*, also widespread among slaves, known to cause diarrhea and lacerations to the anus. See Flávio Edler, "Opilação, Hipoemia ou Ancilostomíase? A sociologia de uma descoberta científica," *Varia História* 32 (2004): 48–74 and José F.X. Sigaud, *Du Climat e des Maladies du Bresil ou Statistique Médicale de cette Empire* (Paris: Chez Fortin, 1844): 130–32.

15 Exhumation and autopsy report. ACB/MPEMA: 323–28.

16 Testimony of Olímpia Francisca Ribeiro and the slave Sebastião dos Santos Jacinto. ACB/MPEMA: 115–19, 156–59.

and blood. We know about the bath because, according to the hired slave Zuraida Guterres, rented out to Ana Rosa by Maria Clara Guterres, the lad, sullied with excrement, had been found that very afternoon passed out in the yard under the searing sun. Zuraida delicately washed the child, including the area around the anus, which was clearly torn. She dressed him in a clean and slightly longer shirt, fed him some cornmeal, and took him back to his room.[17] The boy was apparently alone in his final moments, as Gregória says she was sent to buy coffee, while Sebastião claimed he was already making his way back from Olímpia's house. Dona Ana Rosa tried to get rid of the boy every which way, not only by dispatching Sebastião to Olímpia's to convince her to take the dying child in, but also by sending the same messenger back again immediately after his death, asking if she would be responsible to arrange the funeral rites. Once more, Olímpia declined. So, Ana Rosa decided a hasty dawn burial, at six am, was her best bet and in a locked casket to avoid prying eyes. By allowing only the most perfunctory of ceremonies, followed by a rushed interment far from public view, Ana Rosa hoped to escape an outcry, as the people had long been asking questions about what was happening to the slaves at the mansion on São João Street. The mysterious death of little Jacinto, Inocêncio's younger brother, on October 27, less than a month earlier, had already aroused a great deal of suspicion. Not that Dona Ana Rosa seemed particularly worried. If she was at all apprehensive about any potential blowback from the death of a second slave child at her house in so short a time, she certainly did not show it. For people like her, from the wealthy, powerful families that had flooded into the backlands of the province over the previous decades, clearing vast plantations and rapidly building up huge slave stocks, everything seemed permitted. The future baroness of Grajaú was born in Codó, one of the most dynamic regions of the Maranhão interior, where sprawling cotton plantations had gone hand-in-glove with swelling slave stables, bought on credit or on consignment against future harvest yields.[18] Pressure from the owners for ever-higher productivity translated into extreme rates of punishment and the brutal exploitation of labor. Ana Rosa was married to Dr. Carlos Viana Ribeiro, leader of the Liberal Party and the owner of vast slaveholdings in Alcântara.[19]

17 Testimony of Zuraida Guterres. ACB/MPEMA: 259–61.

18 Mathias Röhrig Assunção, *De Caboclos a Bem-Te-Vis. Formação do Campesinato numa Sociedade Escravista: Maranhão, 1800–1850* (São Paulo: Annablume, 2015): 361.

19 Yuri Michael Almeida Costa, "Celso de Magalhãe e a Justiça Infame: crime, escravidão e poder no Brasil do Império" (PhD diss., Universidade do Vale do Rio dos Sinos, 2017): 169–80.

2 Jacinto and Inocêncio: Slaves, not Ingênuos (Freeborn Boys)

The events that led to the sale of two small children out from under their mother's feet started in the early months of 1876 and illustrate very clearly the dramas that faced the manumitted slave. Despite the emancipationist and liberating aspects of the Free Womb Law, especially when it came to the articles that provided for the purchase of manumission, in reality, the law ended up facilitating the separation of mothers and their children. This was the case with Geminiana. Though born in São Luiz, the state capital, Geminiana and her children – Isaura, age 12, and the two boys, Inocêncio and Jacinto – lived most of her life under the charge of Commander José Joaquim Teixeira Vieira Belford in his Recurso Sugar Mill, located near by the capital. At some point, when Maria Thereza Teixeira Vieira Belfort, the daughter's commander, married, Geminiana was offered to the newlywed couple as part of the dowry. In a few years, both of the couple was dead, and the father-in law became the administrator of couple's estate. The inventory fell under the jurisdiction of the court in São Luís, as the family owned a property there. The commander decided to sell off some slaves to cover the costs of the inventory, and, in March 1876, took a batch to São Luiz to be valued and listed in the town market. The slaves put on sale included Geminiana and her children. In the meantime, Geminiana deposited her price at court and was manumitted.[20] As there are no records that explain how she managed to raise the sum, we can only offer hypotheses. One of the most compelling is that her mother, Simplícia Maria da Conceição Teixeira Belford, former slave of the comander and resident in São Luís, where she hired herself out as daily worker, may have purchased her daughter's manumission from her hard-earned savings. Another is that Geminiana had savings of her own, accumulated from her work as a healer (*pajé*). Thanks to a later criminal case involving the faith healer Amélia Rosa, the queen of Pajelança in São Luís, we know that Geminiana was part of her inner circle.[21] What we do not know, however, is anything about her prior dabblings. Once she had acquired her manumission papers, Geminiana had to leave her three children behind, with Isaura, described in the case files as a little black girl of around 12, being sold on soon afterwards. This left the two boys, and they remained on the listings for months before finally attracting a buyer. In mid-June, the pair were acquired by the firm Silva & Teixeira, whose owners ran a bakery. Though the two Portuguese bakers said they bought the children because they "found them cute," they soon discovered that neither Jacinto nor Inocêncio had much utility, as they were too small to work and just

20 Testimony of Dr. José Joaquim Tavares Belfort. ACB/MPEMA: 120–25.

21 Mundicarmo Ferretti, ed., *Pajelança no Maranhão no Século XIX: o processo de Amélia Rosa* (São Luís: CMF/Fapema, 2004). Thanks to Flávio Gomes for kindly alerting us to the existence of this publication and, moreover, tracking this incredible lawsuit down in the Maranhão archives.

hung around the counter all day waiting for customers to buy them treats. So, looked at in a practical light, the bakers must have made the acquisition as a long-term investment. Which makes it all the stranger that, on August 9 that year, apparently on a whim, the boys were sold, against all common sense, to Ana Rosa Viana Ribeiro, already notorious around town for torturing slaves. They would both be dead within three months of this purchase, and everyone, especially the lower tiers of society, started speculating loudly about the crimes taking place at the mansion on São João. Rumors were rife, with tongues wagging to such a degree that the deputy chief of the second precinct had to order an autopsy on Inocêncio's body, which was still waiting to be put to rest in his cheap little coffin. Such was the general revolt caused by the murder of this young boy that the autopsy, conducted by a physician and a pharmacist, caused quite a tumult. A crowd packed into the small room at the cemetery to watch the proceedings, with the women, "wicker baskets in hand," railing against the high-society perpetrator of so heinous a crime.[22] Geminiana was there too, most probably surrounded by her faith-healer friends. The lowliest slaves, the ones with the hardest, most menial remits, made such a scene they had to be removed from the room. But their protest continued outside and across town, making it impossible to cover up the terrible atrocity, accusing the region's social elite of violating the best Christian principles.

Bibliography

Primary Sources

Câmara dos Deputados [The Chamber of Deputies], Decree no. 1695, 15/09/1869, https://www2.camara.leg.br/legin/fed/decret/1824-1899/decreto-1695-15-setembro-1869-552474-publicacaooriginal-69771-pl.html#:~:text=Prohibe%20as%20vendas%20de%20escravos%20debaixo%20de%20preg%C3%A3o%20e%20em%20exposi%C3%A7%C3%A3o%20publica.&text=Os%20leil%C3%B5es%20commerciaes%20de%20escravos,escravo%20que%20vender%20em%20leil%C3%A3o [accessed 18.10.2020].

Autos Crime da Baronesa do Grajaú, 1876–77 (São Luiz: Ministério Público do Estado do Maranhão – Public Prosecutors' Office, 2009)

Presidência da República (Presidency of the Republic), Decree no. 2040, 28/09/1871, Free Womb Law, http://www.planalto.gov.br/ccivil_03/leis/lim/lim2040.htm [accessed 18.10.2020].

Sigaud José F.X. *Du Climat e des Maladies du Bresil ou Statistique Médicale de cette Empire* (Paris: Chez Fortin, 1844).

22 Testimony of José Maria da Rocha Andrade. ACB/MPEMA: 238–41.

Secondary Literature

Almeida Costa, Yuri Michael. "Celso de Magalhãe e a Justiça Infame: crime, escravidão e poder no Brasil do Império" (PhD diss., Universidade do Vale do Rio dos Sinos, 2017).

Brown, Kathleen M. *Good Wives, Nasty Wenches and Anxious Patriarchs. Gender, Race, and Power in Colonial Virginia* (Chapel Hill: University of North Carolina Press, 1996).

Edler, Flávio. "Opilação, Hipoemia ou Ancilostomíase? A sociologia de uma descoberta científica," *Varia História* 32 (2004): 48–74.

Hebrard, Jean, and Rebecca Scott. *Freedom Papers: An Atlantic Odyssey in the Age of Emancipation* (Cambridge: Harvard University Press, 2012).

Machado, Maria Helena P.T., and A. Alexandre I. Cardoso. *Geminiana e seus filhos. Escravidão e morte; maternidade e infância* (São Paulo: Bazar do Tempo, june 2023).

Morgan, Jennifer. *Labouring Woman. Reproduction and Gender in New World Slavery* (Philadelphia: University of Pennsylvania Press, 2004).

Mundicarmo Ferretti, ed. *Pajelança no Maranhão no Século XIX: o processo de Amélia Rosa* (São Luís: CMF/ Fapema, 2004).

Nequete, Lenine. *O Escravo na Jurisprudência Brasileira* (Porto Alegre: Diretoria da Revista de Jurisprudência e Outros Impressos do Tribunal de Justiça, 1988).

Röhrig Assunção, Mathias. *De Caboclos a Bem-Te-Vis. Formação do Campesinato numa Sociedade Escravista: Maranhão, 1800–1850* (São Paulo: Annablume, 2015).

Vailati, Luiz. *Morte menina. Infância e morte infantil no Brasil dos oitocentos (Rio de Janeiro e São Paulo)* (São Paulo: Alameda, 2010).

Beatriz G. Mamigonian

The Rights of Liberated Africans in Nineteenth-Century Brazil

> I do not understand the rental of liberated Africans' services as constituting slavery, because, if they are free, they must enjoy the rights of men, free and only subject to the condition in which they find themselves, of foreigners with no means of living, with no education, with no knowledge of the language, and for this reason it was not possible for them to be dispersed around the country and left to their own devices; prudence, therefore, demanded a time limit from the government, and the law fixed it at fourteen years [. . .].[1]

On September 4, 1850, the Brazilian parliament passed the slave trade prohibition law that became known as the Eusébio de Queirós Law. The new legislation emerged from momentous parliamentary debates following the seizure of slavers by the British in Brazilian waters. One year later, in September 1851, Senator Montezuma cautiously introduced in parliament a motion regarding a group of Africans rescued from the slave trade and settled within the Brazilian Empire. The senator sought information on the *africanos livres*: where they worked, how much they earned, what their mortality rate was, and how many had been dismissed from compulsory service.[2] The motion was hardly ordinary. Despite the fact that thousands of liberated Africans worked alongside slaves in the capital city of Rio de Janeiro, the former rarely featured in parliamentary debates. In the months leading up to Montezuma's motion, however, the imperial capital's population had learned of a series of slavers seized and new groups of Africans sent to the city's House of Correction after decades of illegal slave trading. Liberated Africans were caught in the middle of the political turmoil, involuntarily embodying a crime in which private individuals and the state were invested. Thus, the senator's caution made sense in a context where political authorities suppressed any association between the slave trade's prohibition and the condemnation of slavery. Montezuma raised questions many wished to suppress.

1 Anais do Senado (Proceedings of the Senate), 1851, 12/9/1851: 312. In the original: "[. . .] não entendo que o arrendamento dos serviços dos africanos livres constitua escravidão, porque se são livres devem ter os direitos de homens, livres sujeitos unicamente à condição em que se acham, de estrangeiros sem nenhum meio de vida, sem nenhuma educação, sem conhecerem a língua, e assim não era possível que ficassem dispersos no país, e entregues a si próprios; a prudência, portanto, exigia do governo que determinasse um prazo, e a lei fixou quatorze anos [. . .]."

2 Ibid.: 310–18. An in-depth discussion of the occasion can be found in Beatriz G. Mamigonian, *Africanos livres: a abolição do tráfico de escravos no Brasil* (São Paulo: Companhia das Letras, 2017): 317–23.

Note: Translated from Portuguese by Gabriel Azevedo Duarte Franco and revised by the author. The author wishes to thank Mariana Dias Paes, Monica Dantas, Henrique Espada Lima, Patricia Melo, Antonia Márcia Pedroza, and Adriane Sanctis de Brito for their insights and comments on an earlier version, and Gabriel Franco for a graceful and skillful translation.

https://doi.org/10.1515/9783111026527-005

Liberated Africans' experiences in Brazil are part and parcel of the broader history of the African slave trade's abolition. As such, these experiences find parallels in other parts of the Atlantic and Indian oceans. This history goes back to the English-led abolitionist campaign comprising the trade's prohibition within the British Empire, bilateral treaties with representatives of several different nations, and a diplomatic and naval repression campaign that lasted for virtually the entire nineteenth century. Nevertheless, in each place recaptive Africans faced a particular situation, both on account of the local juridical order and of the abolition or continuation of the slave trade and slavery itself. Although grounded on shared humanitarian principles – to provide food, shelter, and education for those considered destitute and temporarily unable of maintaining themselves – the statutes of liberated Africans differed in places such as Sierra Leone, Jamaica, the Bahamas, Cuba, Brazil, Martinique, and Angola, as did corresponding practices, which varied widely between the opposite extremes of autonomy and coercion.[3] Around 11,000 people were estimated to have been emancipated by the Brazilian authorities or Anglo-Portuguese and Anglo-Brazilian mixed commissions between 1819 and 1864. These individuals lived in Brazil under the status of *africanos livres*. Although most stayed in Rio de Janeiro, many lived and worked in other coastal or inland Brazilian localities, in places where they had landed or been sent to.[4]

---

3 Studies on liberated Africans have proliferated in the last decade, focusing more on their experiences than on their statutes. See, on Sierra Leone, Suzanne Schwarz, "The Impact of Liberated African 'Disposal' Policies in Early Nineteenth-Century Sierra Leone," in *Liberated Africans and the Abolition of the Slave Trade, 1807–1896*, ed. Richard Anderson and Henry B. Lovejoy (Rochester, NY: University of Rochester Press, 2020): 45–65; on Cuba, Inés Roldán de Montaud, "En los borrosos confines de la libertad: el caso de los negros emancipados in Cuba, 1817–1870," *Revista de Indias* 71, no. 251 (2011): 159–92; on the British Caribbean, Rosanne Marion Adderley, *'New Negroes from Africa': Slave Trade Abolition and Free African Settlement in the Nineteenth-Century Caribbean* (Bloomington: Indiana University Press, 2006); Monica Schuler, "Liberated Central Africans in Nineteenth-Century Guyana," in *Central Africans and Cultural Transformations in the American Diaspora*, ed. Linda M. Heywood (Cambridge: Cambridge University Press, 2002): 319–52; and Michael Craton and Gail Saunders, "Transition, Not Transformation: Apprentices, Liberated Africans, and the Reconstructed Oligarchy, 1834–1860," in *Islanders in the Stream: A History of the Bahamian People*, vol. 2, (Athens: University of Georgia Press, 1998): 3–31; on Martinique, Françoise Thésée, *Les Ibos de l'Amélie: destinée d'une cargaison de traite clandestine à la Martinique, 1822–1838* (Paris: Editions Caribéenes, 1986). On those rescued on the way to the United States, see Sharla M. Fett, *Recaptured Africans: Surviving Slave Ships, Detention, and Dislocation in the Final Years of the Slave Trade* (Chapel Hill: University of North Carolina Press, 2017). See also, on Angola, Samuël Coghe, "The Problem of Freedom in a Mid Nineteenth-Century Atlantic Slave Society: The Liberated Africans of the Anglo-Portuguese Mixed Commission in Luanda (1844–1870)," *Slavery & Abolition* 33, no. 3 (2012): 479–500 as well as Anderson and Lovejoy, *Liberated Africans*.

4 It is reasonable to suppose that the treatment of liberated Africans varied according to the activities they assumed and their places of residence, as well as the presence of enslaved individuals and the reach of the illegal trade in those regions. Only additional case studies will be able to verify these variations. See Jaime Rodrigues, "Ferro, trabalho e conflito: os africanos livres na Fábrica de Ipanema," *História Social* 4–5 (1998): 29–42; Beatriz G. Mamigonian, "Do que o 'preto mina' é capaz: etnia

British jurisdiction did not apply to liberated Africans in Brazil, notwithstanding Britain's attempts to take responsibility for them and the imposition of this responsibility in specific cases.[5] This paper addresses the rights of liberated Africans in Brazil, discussing the circumstances, regulations, and juridical proceedings surrounding the implementation of the peculiar statute, the exploitation of mandatory labor, and their definitive emancipation. The history of liberated Africans in Brazil draws its logic from the complex dynamic of Brazilian nation formation – one marked by the continuation of the illegal trade in enslaved Africans and intense British pressure for its abolition.

1 From Naval Prize to Emancipated Person

As a legal category, liberated Africans in Portuguese possessions originated from bilateral agreements struck with Britain for the slave trade's abolition. The additional convention to the 1815 Anglo-Portuguese Treaty signed on July 28, 1817 regulated maritime

e resistência entre africanos livres," *Afro-Ásia* 24 (2000): 71–95; Beatriz G. Mamigonian, "Revisitando a 'transição para o trabalho livre': a experiência dos africanos livres," in *Tráfico, cativeiro e liberdade: Rio de Janeiro, séculos XVII–XIX*, ed. Manolo Florentino (Rio de Janeiro: Civilização Brasileira, 2005): 388–417; Alinnie Silvestre Moreira, "Liberdade tutelada: os africanos livres e as relações de trabalho na Fábrica de Pólvora da Estrela. Serra da Estrela/RJ (c. 1831–c. 1870)" (master's thesis, Universidade Estadual de Campinas, 2005); Maciel H.C. Silva, "Uma africana 'livre' e a 'corrupção dos costumes': Pernambuco (1830–1844)," *Estudos Afro-Asiáticos* 29 (2007): 123–60; Isabel Cristina dos Reis, "A família negra no tempo da escravidão" (PhD diss., Universidade Estadual de Campinas, 2007): 127–81; Adriana Santana, "Africanos livres na Bahia, 1831–1864" (master's thesis, Universidade Federal da Bahia, 2007); Cyra L.R. de Oliveira Fernandes, "Os africanos livres de Pernambuco (1831–1864)" (master's thesis, Universidade Federal de Pernambuco, 2010); Danúsia M. Von Zuben, *Os africanos livres nos aldeamentos indígenas no Paraná provincial, 1853–1862* (Curitiba: Universidade Federal do Paraná, 2010); Enidelce Bertin, *Os meia-cara: africanos livres em São Paulo no século XIX* (Salto: Schoba, 2013); Zilda Moura, "Dos sertões da África para os do Brasil: os africanos livres da Sociedade de Mineração de Mato Grosso (Alto Paraguai-Diamantino, 1851–1865)" (PhD diss., Universidade Federal de Santa Catarina, 2014); Jofre Teófilo Vieira, "Os 'Samangolês': africanos livres no Ceará (1835–1865)" (PhD diss., Universidade Federal do Ceará, 2017); Moisés Sebastião Silva, "Africanos livres em Alagoas: tráfico ilegal, escravidão, tutela e Liberdade (1849–1864)" (master's thesis, Universidade Federal da Bahia, 2017); Mariana Alice Pereira Schatzer Ribeiro, *Entre a fábrica e a senzala: um estudo sobre o cotidiano dos africanos livres na Real Fábrica de Ferro São João do Ipanema – Sorocaba – São Paulo (1840–1870)* (São Paulo: Alameda, 2017); and Mariana Alice Pereira Schatzer Ribeiro, "Trabalho e cotidiano dos africanos livres na Estrada da Maioridade: São Paulo-Santos (1840–1864)" (PhD diss., Universidade Estadual Paulista, 2019).

5 Jake Christopher Richards' argument that liberated Africans in Brazil shared "unguaranteed entitlements" with those of the British Empire is based on the idea that Britain exercised jurisdiction over the group in Brazil, and that Portugal and Brazil did not possess their own legislation. This assessment has no factual basis and it underscores important gaps and misconceptions in the Anglo-Saxon historiography. See Jake Christopher Richards, "Anti-Slave-Trade Law, 'Liberated Africans' and the State in the South Atlantic World, c.1839–1852," *Past & Present* 241, no. 1 (2018): 179–219.

repression, granting both parties the mutual right to search vessels.[6] Spain and the Netherlands also signed similar conventions with Britain between 1817 and 1818. These treaties established mixed commissions courts based on British possessions along the African coast (Freetown in Sierra Leone) and on territories held by the Spanish (Havana in Cuba), the Dutch (Paramaribo in Suriname), and the Portuguese (Rio de Janeiro in Brazil) in the Americas. The additional treaties and conventions served to regulate the commissions' operations, introducing standard procedures regarding Africans found on board seized vessels. Between their apprehension at sea and the conclusion of the adjudication by the commission in charge of their case, "recaptured" Africans remained under the watch and responsibility of the captor ship's crew, with no guarantee of emancipation.[7] According to maritime law procedures, two commissaries from each country – one judge and one arbitrator – evaluated the legality of the seizure. If, for a variety of reasons, the vessel was acquitted as an "unlawful prize," it was returned to its owners, who received compensation for the undue apprehension. In such cases, African survivors continued to suffer with the resumed Atlantic crossing and were eventually sold as slaves. Conversely, if the vessel's participation in the slave trade was proven before the mixed commission, the ship and its non-human cargo were auctioned and the revenue was split between the two countries represented in the commission. This procedure diverged from standard maritime law, which awarded the prize – that is, both the ship and its cargo – to its captors. Human cargo was emancipated and put under the responsibility of the nation where the court sat.[8] Article 7 of the regulations for the mixed commissions established:

---

6 For a discussion of Anglo-Brazilian mixed commissions, see Leslie Bethell, "The Mixed Commissions for the Suppression of the Transatlantic Slave Trade in the Nineteenth Century," *Journal of African History* 7, no. 1 (1966): 79–93; Leslie Bethell, *The Abolition of the Brazilian Slave Trade: Britain, Brazil and the Slave Trade Question, 1807–1869* (Cambridge: Cambridge University Press, 2002): 21–47. For more recent work on the topic, see also Jenny S. Martinez, *The Slave Trade and the Origins of International Human Rights Law* (New York: Oxford University Press, 2012): 67–98; and Jennifer Louise Nelson, "Liberated Africans in the Atlantic World: The Courts of Mixed Commission in Havana and Rio de Janeiro 1819–1871" (PhD diss., University of Leeds, 2015). For the implications of British pressure for slave trade abolition in Brazil, see Alan K. Manchester, *British preeminence in Brazil, its Rise and Decline: A Study in European Expansion* (Chapel Hill: University of North Carolina Press, 1933).

7 Sharla Fett has explored in detail the period between ships' capture and judgment in the United States, while Emily Haslam has done so for Sierra Leone from a legal perspective, arguing that mixed commissions' treatment of recaptives challenges the narrative put forth by the history of international criminal law. See Fett, *Recaptured Africans*; Emily Haslam, "International Criminal Law and Legal Memories of Abolition: Intervention, Mixed Commission Courts and 'Emancipation'," *Journal of the History of International Law* 18, no. 4 (2016): 420–47; Emily Haslam, *The Slave Trade, Abolition and the Long History of International Criminal Law: The Recaptive and the Victim* (Abingdon, Oxon: Routledge, 2020): 65–105.

8 Besides the works cited in note 6, see David R. Murray, *Odious Commerce : Britain, Spain, and the Abolition of the Cuban Slave Trade* (Cambridge: Cambridge University Press, 1980); Jean Allain, "The Nineteenth Century Law of the Sea and the British Abolition of the Slave Trade," *British Yearbook of*

> In case of the condemnation of a vessel of an unlawful voyage, she shall be declared lawful prize, as well as her cargo, of whatever description it may be, with the exception of the slaves who may be on board as objects of commerce; and the said Vessel, as well as her cargo, shall be sold by public sale, for the profit of the two Governments; as to the Slaves, they shall receive from the Mixed Commission a certificate of emancipation, and shall be delivered over to the Government on whose territory the Commission, which shall have so judge them, shall be established, to be employed as servants or free labourers. Each of the two Governments binds itself to guarantee the liberty of such portion of these individuals as shall be respectively consigned to it.[9]

In generic terms, both signatory countries committed to guaranteeing the freedom of Africans emancipated by commissions hosted in their territories. The terms used to describe liberated Africans outlined their status and labor arrangements. According to the mixed commission regulations, liberated Africans were to be employed as "servants or free laborers," a vocabulary that positioned them among juridically free individuals whose labor engagement would stand on a spectrum between subordination and autonomy. However, a royal decree dated January 26, 1818 further regulated the application of the 1815 treaty and 1817 convention:

> The slaves consigned to my royal treasury, in the mode of the aforementioned Article 7 of the regulations for mixed commissions, and all others liberated by the means decreed above, considering it is unfair that they be abandoned, shall be turned over to the district justices (*juízo da Ouvidoria da Comarca*) and, where they do not exist, that person is in charge of the conservatory of Indians [. . .], for them to be destined to serve as freedpersons for a period of fourteen years or in public service in the navy, at the forts, in agriculture, or in the mechanical trades, as best fit, and for this they will be enlisted in their respective stations, or auctioned off to private subjects with known establishment and probity [. . .] this period, however, may be shortened by two or more years for freedpersons who, by their good service and conduct, make themselves worthy of enjoying the right to full freedom before [the end of the aforementioned period].[10]

International Law 78, no. 1 (2007): 342–88; Adriane Sanctis de Brito, "Seeking Capture, Resisting Seizure: Legal Battles under the Anglo-Brazilian Treaty for the Suppression of Slave Trade (1826–1845)" (PhD diss., Universidade de São Paulo, 2018); and Haslam, *The Slave Trade*. Haslam insists that the procedures set up for the suppression of the slave trade neglected the victims. Her analysis of the cases adjudicated by the mixed commission courts in Sierra Leone shows that their procedures centered on the verification of apprehensions' legality – i.e. apprehended ships' nationalities, localities where trade was carried out, the presence of slaves or only equipment on board – rather than on the assurance that rescued persons would be emancipated.

9 "Regulations for the Mixed Commissions annexed to the Additional Convention Signed by Great Britain and Portugal for the Abolition of the Slave Trade on 28 July 1817," reprinted in Great Britain, Parliament, "Instructions for the Guidance of Her Majesty's Naval Officers employed in the Suppression of the Slave Trade," *Parliamentary Papers*: 1844.

10 Kingdom of Portugal and Brazil, "Alvará com força de lei de 26 de Janeiro de 1818," in *Coleção das Leis do Brasil* (Rio de Janeiro: Imprensa Nacional, 1818): 7–10. In the original: "Os escravos consignados à minha Real Fazenda, pelo modo prescrito no sobredito art. 7 do regulamento para as Comissões Mistas, e todos os mais libertos pela maneira acima decretada, por não ser justo que fiquem abandonados, serão entregues no Juízo da Ouvidoria da comarca e, onde o não houver, naquele que estiver

As goods rescued from smuggling by the fiscal authorities, these individuals were to be put under the responsibility of local judicial authorities or, in their absence, the authorities in charge of indigenous peoples. These authorities would manage their distribution for fourteen years of compulsory labor, at a public institution or under private employers. Thus, the 1818 royal decree declared that Africans would be referred to as *libertos*, though they were only to enjoy "the right to full freedom" after twelve years – with a record of good conduct – or fourteen years of service. In practice, this decree dislocated the category of liberated Africans within the Portuguese juridical order, as will be discussed later.

2 The Parallel with Indigenous Peoples: Incapacitated Subjects

As the anthropologist Manuela Carneiro da Cunha demonstrated, there was a significant convergence between the status attributed to Africans rescued from the slave trade and that of indigenous peoples in the nineteenth century. This convergence stemmed from an understanding of both groups as comprising free but incapacitated persons, thus subject to state guardianship.[11] Historian Patrícia Melo Sampaio has remarked that guardianship over indigenous groups in Portuguese America was imposed in Grão-Pará and Maranhão by the *Diretório dos Índios*, an ordinance passed in the context of the "Freedom Law" of June 6, 1755, which reiterated the prohibition on indigenous enslavement. The rationale of the Diretório was that the mobility of indigenous individuals considered idle or vagrant was to be restricted, while those considered incorrigible were subjected to forced labor at houses of correction. Governor Francisco Xavier de Mendonça Furtado assigned indigenous peoples to the jurisdiction of the judges of orphans (*juízes de órfãos*), establishing that "these people, who have no knowledge of the benefits that derive from work, shall be considered demented, and, for this reason, I have put them under the administration of the judge of orphans and ordered that a regiment to be observed for them."[12] Furtado understood

encarregado da Conservatoria dos Índios que hei por bem ampliar unindo-lhe esta jurisdição, para aí serem destinados a servir como libertos por tempo de catorze anos ou em algum serviço público de mar, fortalezas, agricultura e de ofícios, como melhor convier, sendo para isso alistados nas respectivas Estações, ou alugados em praça a particulares de estabelecimento e probidade conhecida [. . .] este tempo porém poderá ser diminuído por dois ou mais anos, àqueles libertos que por seu préstimo e bons costumes se fizerem dignos de gozar antes dele do pleno direito da sua liberdade."

11 Manuela Carneiro da Cunha, *Negros, estrangeiros: os escravos libertos e sua volta à Africa* (São Paulo: Companhia das Letras, 2012): 96.

12 Patricia Melo Sampaio, "Fronteiras da liberdade: tutela indígena no Diretório Pombalino e na Carta Régia de 1798," in *Tutela: formação de Estado e tradições de gestão no Brasil*, ed. Antonio Carlos de Souza Lima (Rio de Janeiro: E-papers, 2014): 35.

guardianship as a means of transition to freedom. He worried about landowners' abuse of authority over workers and the dreaded "disorder" that would ensue:

> Because I believe it unfailing that these Indians as they are, not only barbaric and rustic, but, besides lazy, unloving of any convenience which they have to reach through labor, as soon as they understand that they enjoy full freedom and that they cannot be mandated to reside in the properties where they find themselves, at that very instant I convince myself that they will absolutely abandon the landowners and take flight towards the *mocambos*, leaving everything in a state of confusion and disorder, because they do not now accept a compromise, and it is necessary to compel them so they remain orderly.[13]

Renewed considerations on the availability of indigenous labor prompted the state of Grão-Pará and Maranhão to issue the royal decree of May 12, 1798. It abolished the *Diretório dos Índios* and re-established vassalage rights to settled Indians who engaged in skilled trades, paid the tithe, and offered to protect colonial territory. Moreover, the new legislation instituted militia units under the administration of local legislative chambers. Participation in these units was mandatory for all landless Indians. Those contacted from the date of the decree's publication onwards would enjoy "orphans' privileges" (*privilégio de órfãos*) and be subject to guardianship – henceforth turned private and individual – managed by judges of orphans following the "Terms of Education and Instruction" (*Termos de educação e instrução*).[14] For the state of Brazil, in turn, around the time when the statute of liberated Africans came into force, both the *Diretório dos Índios* (for settled Indians) and the 1808 and 1809 royal decrees were active. Through these royal decrees, prince-regent of Portugal João VI authorized just war against Botocudo indigenous groups in the Rio Doce and Campos de Guarapuava regions, in southeastern Brazil. The prince also established that captured Indians were to be subject to mandatory labor for ten or fifteen years, while those who surrendered peacefully to live in settlements or assignation to landowners for forced labor were placed under guardianship. Whereas the *Diretório* ceased to apply in 1822, the just war and captivity authorizations were irrevocably cancelled by the law of October 27, 1831, which freed from servitude all Indians captured thus far. Following this law, they were to be considered "orphans" and remain under the jurisdiction of the judges of orphans. Years later, the Additional Act of 1834 provided provincial assemblies with autonomy to legislate on indigenous peoples. Local solutions

---

13 Ibid.: 38. In the original: "Porque tenho por infalível que estes índios como são, não só bárbaros e rústicos, mas, além de preguiçosos, não amam conveniência alguma a que hajam de chegar por trabalho, logo que se capacitarem que estão em plena liberdade e que os não podem obrigar a residir nas fazendas em que se acham, no mesmo instante me persuado a que desamparem absolutamente aos lavradores e se metam pelos mocambos, deixando tudo em confusão e desordem porque eles não admitem por ora meio termo, e é necessário que os obriguem para se conservarem em ordem."
14 Ibid.: 43–45.

and norms regarding that group proliferated after the act.[15] Admittedly, the parallels between indigenous subjects and liberated Africans are complex, especially since the norms related to both groups were applied unevenly. In any case, it must be noted that the same Old-Regime logics of destitution and incapacity that defined at least part of the indigenous peoples came to define liberated Africans as well.[16] In the nineteenth century, the system centered around the judges of orphans organized state management of forced labor supply very efficiently, for private and public demands alike. This arrangement safeguarded the economic and social-control interests of private and public actors. Although in principle the surveillance over guardianship arrangements aimed to avoid the re-enslavement of Indians and liberated Africans, in practice these groups had their right to freedom severely restricted and remained confined to the lowest rungs of the Brazilian social hierarchy, despite being juridically considered free. However, while indigenous subjects gradually assimilated into the poor and mixed populations, distancing themselves from owning land and keeping their culture but freeing themselves from guardianship, liberated Africans struggled with statute-associated restrictions for decades on end. In studies of Old-Regime colonial societies, a recurring mode of hierarchical incorporation of "others" stands out: after a given period of adaptation to colonial society's codes, non-white subjects were ready to take part in that society's rites as long as they respected the boundaries of the social place reserved for their "kind." Once manumitted, African-born individuals would participate in the administration of brotherhoods, militia units, trades corporations, and their local civic bodies – always bearing in mind the limitations imposed by blood purity requirements for assuming public posts, ecclesiastic responsibilities, and honorific orders.[17] Following this social rationale, once Africans rescued from the slave trade finished their guardianship and terms of mandatory service they would be allowed to integrate into the societies in which they now lived, enjoying "full rights" just as other freed Africans (*libertos*), since liberated Africans were legally free. Notwithstanding, the newest studies on the transformations of slavery and the

15 Patricia Melo Sampaio, "Política indigenista no Brasil Imperial," in *O Brasil Imperial*, vol. 1, *1808–1831*, ed. Keila Grinberg and Ricardo Salles (Rio de Janeiro: Civilização Brasileira, 2009): 183–84; Fernanda Sposito, "Liberdade para os índios no Império do Brasil: a revogação das guerras justas em 1831," *Almanack* 1 (2011): 52–65.

16 António Manuel Hespanha, *Imbecillitas: as bem-aventuranças da inferioridade nas sociedades de Antigo Regime* (São Paulo: Annablume, 2010).

17 On Afro-descendants' incorporation into colonial society, see Hebe M. Mattos, "A escravidão moderna nos quadros do Império Português: o Antigo Regime em perspectiva atlântica," in *O Antigo Regime nos trópicos: a dinâmica imperial portuguesa: (séculos XVI–XVIII)*, ed. João Luís Ribeiro Fragoso, Maria Fernanda Bicalho, and Maria de Fátima Gouvêa (Rio de Janeiro: Civilização Brasileira, 2001): 141–62; Anthony J.R. Russell-Wood, "Através de um prisma africano: uma nova abordagem ao estudo da diáspora africana no Brasil Colonial," *Tempo* 12 (2001): 11–50; and Mariza de Carvalho Soares, *People of Faith: Slavery and African Catholics in Eighteenth-Century Rio de Janeiro* (Durham, NC: Duke University Press, 2012). A similar logic possibly applied to unsettled indigenous subjects.

world of labor in the nineteenth century point to a restriction of manumissions, as well as of the horizons of autonomy of African-born and African-descended persons in the Atlantic world. It is in this context that we can understand liberated Africans' experiences after 1830.[18]

3 The Effects of Brazilian Legislation on the Abolition of the Slave Trade

The turbulent process of state building and definition of the boundaries of citizenship in post-independence Brazil were intrinsically related to the continuation of the illegal slave trade and expansion of slavery, affecting the landscape of the exercise of rights for liberated Africans. Whether formally or informally, these rights would be questioned, undermined, and revoked in practice, to the point that liberated Africans' experiences and expectations diverged very little from those of enslaved persons. The Anglo-Brazilian mixed commission court in Rio de Janeiro operated between 1830 and 1845. Acting in accordance with the treaty for the abolition of the slave trade, the commission emancipated and registered Africans found on board the ships engaged in illegal slave trading. That done, the commission turned the individuals over to the Brazilian authorities in charge of them, the latter proceeding according to the 1818 royal decree. The law passed on November 7, 1831 marked a break with previous understandings of recaptive Africans' rights. Its first article notably proclaimed free "all slaves, who enter the territory or ports of Brazil, coming from the outside," extending the reach of suppression activities to cover not only the sea, but also the coastal areas and the interior, and stipulating no time limit after disembarkation for apprehensions to happen. A decree dated April 12, 1832, which regulated the application of the 1831 law, stipulated that vessels were to be searched by assigned authorities and any slaves found on board were to be deposited until due trial. It also established that Africans originating in the illegal trade could turn to public authorities and claim their freedom at any point in time.[19] The 1831 legislation separated the vessel's and traffickers'

18 Among many others, see particularly Robert W. Slenes, "A 'Great Arch' Descending: Manumission Rates, Subaltern Social Mobility, and the Identities of Enslaved, Freeborn, and Freed Blacks in Southeastern Brazil, 1791–1888," in *New Approaches to Resistance in Brazil and Mexico*, ed. John Gledhill and Patience A. Schell (Durham, NC: Duke University Press, 2012): 100–118; David Northrup, *Indentured Labor in the Age of Imperialism, 1834–1922* (Cambridge: Cambridge University Press, 1995); Rebecca J. Scott and Jean M. Hébrard, *Freedom Papers: An Atlantic Odyssey in the Age of Emancipation* (Cambridge, Mass: Harvard University Press, 2012); and Ada Ferrer, *Freedom's Mirror: Cuba and Haiti in the Age of Revolution* (Cambridge: Cambridge University Press, 2014).

19 "Lei de 7 de Novembro de 1831," in *Coleção de Leis do Império do Brasil de 1831*, vol. 1 (Rio de Janeiro: Typographia Nacional, 1875): 182–84; "Decreto de 12 de Abril de 1832 – Dá Regulamento Para a Execução Da Lei de 7 de Novembro de 1831 Sobre o Tráfico de Escravos," in *Coleção das Leis do*

trials – conducted in the criminal sphere – from the adjudication of Africans' freedom – conducted in the civil sphere. In doing so, Brazilian legislators removed slave trade repression from the sphere of maritime law practiced by the mixed commissions, thus distancing their procedures from the British model. Regarding the rights of trafficked Africans, the Brazilian 1831 law applied to all those who entered national territory from that date, whether apprehended or not. In order for someone to be declared a liberated African, it would suffice to go through a summary proceeding in which his or her resemblance to a *boçal* African – unable to speak Portuguese – and the circumstances of his or her arrival in Brazil constituted enough evidence of the right to freedom. Besides Africans apprehended at sea or upon disembarking, in the 1830s and 1840s hundreds were emancipated as individuals or in small groups and recognized as new Africans (*africanos novos*) by the police and judicial authorities. The history of the 1831 law's application shows us, however, the politicization of the procedures that recognized trafficked Africans' freedom and the undermining of these procedures after the conservative turn that put in power those who defended slavery and the illegal trade in Brazil. Hundreds of thousands of individuals who arrived after 1831 and were not seized had their right to freedom neglected and lived as slaves, passing that status onto their children. For most of the period, the imperial government only recognized as liberated Africans those whose freedom had been declared by the mixed commission, by judges, or by the navy auditors. Only in the late 1860s were the procedures to apply the 1831 law and recognize African individuals' right to freedom reactivated in an abolitionist context that saw young lawyers, prosecutors, and judges strive to break state complicity with illegal enslavement.[20] As for the administrative procedures regarding those deemed liberated Africans, the 1831 law also represented a rupture with the previous model. Its second article declared slave traders criminally guilty for the enslavement of free persons, assigning to them the burden of the payment of fines and expenses related to the transportation of recaptured Africans back to the continent, where the government expected African authorities to offer them asylum.[21] The decision to send back to Africa all those recaptured from the slave trade after 1831 impacted governmental decisions regarding that group and the fates of many individual Africans, despite the fact that re-exportation negotiations never concluded and the plan was never put into practice. Besides this, Africans' freedom was associated with the British, seen as the tireless patrons of slave trade abolition to the detriment of Brazilian sovereignty. This fact also complicated the protection of liberated Africans' rights in Brazil. The following sections focus

Império, Atos do Poder Executivo, 1832 (Rio de Janeiro: Typographia Nacional, 1874): 100–102. See also Mamigonian, *Africanos livres*: 90–127.

20 Mamigonian, *Africanos livres*: 400–455.

21 Slave traders and buyers of newly-arrived Africans were subject to Art. 179 of the Criminal Code (Reducing a free person to slavery); see "Art. 179, Lei de 16 de Dezembro de 1830," in *Coleção de Leis do Império do Brasil de 1830* (Rio de Janeiro: Typographia Nacional, 1876): 142; "Lei de 7 de Novembro de 1831."

on liberated Africans' rights vis à vis their labor power and legal status. We will analyze those rights from the perspective of norms, their administration by the government, and the political and diplomatic debates surrounding that group.

4 Liberated Africans as Laborers

Labor arrangements involving recaptive Africans were initially handled by the judicial authorities of each district (*Ouvidoria da comarca*). In the 1830s, the judges of orphans took over that duty, as well as the responsibility over other individuals considered incapable of ruling themselves: minors, orphans, and native Indians. As a tutored group, these Africans were represented by a specific authority in each locality: the curator of liberated Africans. In addition to representing tutored Africans, the curator observed the fulfillment of norms regulating their legal status.[22] The labor system outlined in the 1818 royal decree functioned, *mutatis mutandis*, until the 1860s, distributing and "renting" liberated Africans' services among public and private institutions.[23] Initially, the standard distribution procedure was the auction of Africans' services to individuals able to pay in advance the amount equivalent to one year's salary. The winning bidder signed a document with the terms of responsibility over the African worker. This was the fate of Africans rescued from the schooner *Emília* and emancipated in 1821, as well as of other groups apprehended along the Brazilian coastline in the early 1830s. Faced with the practical abandonment of re-exportation measures, in October 1834 the Brazilian Ministry of Justice sought to reinstate the auctioning system. Only two months later, however, that model was replaced when Minister of Justice Aureliano Coutinho implemented a concessions protocol for liberated Africans' services. These concessions would be granted only by judges of orphans to public institutions or trusted individuals. Hirers signed the terms of responsibility in the presence of public authorities, solemnly vowing

22 The curator of liberated Africans was always summoned in bureaucratic issues involving his subject group. He did not necessarily act in favor of autonomy – in fact, curators tended to defend that liberated Africans should stay under their hirers' control for the sake of public order. See Mamigonian, *Africanos livres*: 121–22.

23 The royal decree of January 26, 1818 remained in force in Brazil, as did the Portuguese legislation more broadly, in accordance with the law of October 20, 1823. The 1818 decree served as legal base for liberated Africans' auctions until at least 1839. See "Lei de 20 de Outubro de 1823," in *Coleção de Leis do Império do Brasil de 1823*, vol. 1 (Rio de Janeiro: Imprensa Nacional, 1887): 7–10. In *Africanos livres*, I explore the Ministry of Justice's orientation for liberated Africans apprehended in Bahia in 1834 to have their services auctioned off in accordance with the 1818 decree. See Mamigonian, *Africanos livres*: 83. The emancipation letter of Geraldina Sunde, from Brigue Leal, no. 236, issued by Rio de Janeiro's Anglo-Brazilian Mixed Commission also referred to the 1818 decree. See Mamigonian, *Africanos livres*: 49.

> to sustain them, give them clothing, medical aid, and education, whether moral or religious, [. . .] to inform the same judges by means of legal proof the death or flight of [liberated Africans] and to assign to them service that corresponds to their strength and age.[24]

A priori, a maximum of eight Africans could be entrusted to a single hirer, who was mandated to keep them in the provincial capitals, turn them over for re-exportation (in case it did happen), and bring to the collectors of customs a yearly amount corresponding to Africans' "salary," fixed upon their concession.[25] All labor contracts involving liberated Africans were imposed by public authorities relying on predetermined conditions – including wages, paid directly to a fund. This system underscored the juridical incapacity experienced by liberated Africans, whatever their age. Regarding the use of their workforce, their juridical treatment did not effectively differ from that of other groups of free persons considered incapable, such as Indians and children. Nonetheless, these principles were applied in distorted ways that referred back to the political choices of the 1830s and 1840s – choices that restricted liberated Africans' rights. Records from 955 emancipated Africans across seven apprehension cases in Rio between 1834 and 1838 reveal significant differences in liberated Africans' distribution for labor purposes. Among those, 82% were distributed among private parties and 18% redirected to public service. Women were more often sent to private hirers (95% of women against 75% of men), whereas the proportion of men sent to public institutions was higher (25% of men against 5% of women).[26] This context gave rise to very distinct labor experiences among liberated Africans. Liberated Africans hired by private parties worked as domestic servants, either at their bidders' or hirers' houses or under lease to third parties. They held a number of functions in nineteenth-century homes, from laundry washing to gardening to breastfeeding. They were also at times employed under the hiring-out system (*trabalho de ganho*). In the latter case, they were to pay a previously stipulated weekly amount to their original hirers, saving any occasional outstanding revenue for themselves.[27] These labor arrangements were effectively analogous to those of urban slavery, since they withheld remuneration for performed labor and

---

24 Lauriana ou Edeltrudes, Petição de Emancipação, Arquivo Nacional (National Archives of Brazil), 6/2/1860: IJ6 523.

25 "Aviso de 29 de Outubro de 1834, Com Instruções Relativas à Arrematação Dos Africanos Ilicitamente Introduzidos No Império," in *Coleção das Decisões do Governo do Império do Brasil, 1834* (Rio de Janeiro: Typographia Nacional, 1866): 278–81; Aviso do Ministério da Justiça, Arquivo Nacional (National Archives of Brazil), 1/12/1834: IJ1 168; "Alterações Feitas Às Instruções Que Acompanham o Aviso Expedido Pela Secretaria de Estado Dos Negócios Da Justiça, Com Data de 29 out. 1834, e de Que Faz Menção o Decreto Desta Data, 19 Nov. 1835," in *Coleção das Leis do Império de 1835*, vol. 2 (Rio de Janeiro: Typographia Nacional, 1864): 125–30.

26 "Matrícula dos africanos apreendidos entre 1834 e 1838," ca. 1865, Arquivo Nacional (National Archives of Brazil), IJ6 471. See an analysis of this source in Mamigonian, "Revisitando a 'Transição Para o Trabalho Livre'"; and Mamigonian, *Africanos livres*: 90–128.

27 An African woman named Cândida, for example, ran her own business in Recife, Pernambuco. See Silva, "Uma africana 'livre'."

severely curtailed workers' autonomy regarding unpunished absences – and also because they at times included physical punishment. Liberated Africans reported excessive work, punishments, and mistreatment. Despite that, assigned authorities imposed limits on Africans' demands, legitimating hirers' behaviors. Rosa's and Agapito's cases, both from November 1836, elucidate this issue. Rosa was eleven or twelve years old and the only maid in Manoel José Simões' house in Rio. Upon being verbally and physically assaulted by Simões' wife for delayed service, Rosa fled and took refuge at the House of Correction. She was adamant not to return to her hirer's house, as became evident in her attempt to commit suicide by jumping down a well at the House of Correction. After evaluating the case, the curator of liberated Africans suggested to the police chief:

> I hold that she absolutely must be returned to the custody of her renter, so that her behavior does not become a precedent for serious abuses on the part of others. Nevertheless, in order to keep her in some degree of subjugation her renter should employ some docility, and he should have his wife assign the girl a less heavy burden of labor. If she does not submit, I recommend that she be turned over to the authorities so that strong and exemplary punishment might be applied.[28]

As the curator's statement demonstrates, accepting Rosa's complaints opened a precedent for other liberated Africans to pursue the imperial government's protection in case problems arose involving their hirers. The government expected hirers to maintain control over liberated Africans and only reach out to the public authorities in cases of extreme necessity. The referred curator followed this principle when he rejected Agapito's complaint that his hirer, Agostinho Feliciano, had been forcing him to work on Sundays and holidays, delaying his lunchtime to up to four in the afternoon, feeding him brown bread, and punishing him on top of everything. Agapito also reported doing all of his work unpaid. After investigating the case and finding no signs of mistreatment, the curator concluded that he should send the liberated African back to his bidder, advising in favor of the former's punishment "to cure the bad habit of escaping and to correct his errors, for eating brown bread late in the day is not the same as not eating at all and being mistreated."[29] Chief of police Eusébio de Queirós accepted the curator's suggestion regarding Agapito's case, while suggesting to the minister of justice the destitution of Simões' concessionary privilege over Rosa's services, seeing as she had been mistreated.[30] Liberated Africans designated to serve in public institutions provided the labor force that allowed the expansion of urban public services, the strengthening of military institutions, and the paving of public highways, besides the very construction of the capital's House of Correction. In contrast with the

28 The quotes are borrowed from Thomas Holloway's discussion of Rosa's and Agapito's cases. See Thomas H. Holloway, *Policing Rio de Janeiro: Repression and Resistance in a 19th-Century City* (Stanford, CA: Stanford University Press, 1993): 117–20.
29 Ibid.: 119.
30 Ibid.: 119–20.

work arrangements of liberated Africans entrusted to private parties, those working in public institutions had their mobility curtailed and suffered under their managers' harsh treatment. This large contingent of liberated African workforce seems to have worked under – always unpaid – labor requisites and a disposition to allocate workers according to their individual aptitudes. This strategic allocation relied on a constant reorganization of laborers among public institutions. Because they were organized into large groups, liberated Africans in many of these institutions, such as the war arsenal, the gunpowder factory, and the ironworks of Ipanema (*Arsenal de Guerra, Fábrica de Pólvora,* and *Fábrica de Ferro de Ipanema,* respectively), were able to form families that stuck together for decades. This might be the one right they were effectively able to enjoy, and it was generally an acknowledged right. Conversely, children usually started working at seven years old, frequently integrating with the many involuntary laborers in those institutions.[31] Upon the prohibition of newly-emancipated Africans' concession to private parties in 1850, the landscape of labor relations changed for that population. "New Africans" would fulfill their mandatory service period exclusively under public interest institutions, works, or entities. They were thus sent to many provinces' public works divisions, hospitals, and some private companies that claimed to be of public interest, such as Viscount Mauá's Company for Steam Navigation of the Amazon (*Companhia de Navegação a Vapor do Amazonas*) and the Mining Company of Mato Grosso (*Companhia de Mineração de Mato Grosso*), owned by investors from the province of Rio de Janeiro. Notwithstanding liberated Africans' engagement in works and activities associated with modernization, the forms taken by the state's exploitation of their labor force did not change – the management of the group demonstrated the imperial government's commitment to the reproduction of compulsory labor, instead of the promotion of free labor arrangements.[32] Contrary to impressions left by the bilateral agreements on liberated Africans, the apprenticeship system was never active in

31 On Africans' labor in public institutions, and specifically the *Fábrica de Pólvora da Estrela,* see Moreira, "Liberdade tutelada"; and Alinnie Silvestre Moreira, "Os africanos livres, sua prole e as discussões emancipacionistas: as famílias e a administração dos descendentes de africanos livres na Fábrica de Pólvora da Estrela (Rio de Janeiro, 1830–1860)," *Estudos Afro-Asiáticos* 29, no. 1–3 (2007): 161–200. On Rio de Janeiro's House of Correction and public works, see Carlos Eduardo Moreira de Araújo, "Cárceres imperiais: a Casa de Correção do Rio de Janeiro: seus detentos e o sistema prisional no Império, 1830–1861" (PhD diss., Universidade Estadual de Campinas, 2009); and Carlos Eduardo Moreira de Araújo, "A engenharia da liberdade: os africanos livres e as obras públicas no Rio de Janeiro Imperial," in *Pesquisa em ação,* vol. 2, ed. Shirley G.S. Carreira and Marcelo M. Mazzi (Belford Roxo: Uniabeu, 2014): 33–51. Also on the House of Correction, see Gustavo Pinto de Sousa, *Africanos livres: escravos, prisioneiros ou trabalhadores da Casa de Correção da Corte?* (Rio de Janeiro: Editora Multifoco, 2013). On the Ironworks of Ipanema and the construction of the Santos–São Paulo road, see Mariana Alice Pereira Schatzer Ribeiro, *Entre a fábrica e a senzala: um estudo sobre o cotidiano dos africanos livres na Real Fábrica de Ferro São João do Ipanema – Sorocaba – São Paulo (1840–1870)* (São Paulo: Alameda, 2017); Mariana Alice Pereira Schatzer Ribeiro, "Trabalho e cotidiano dos africanos livres na Estrada da Maioridade: São Paulo-Santos (1840–1864)" (PhD diss., Universidade Estadual Paulista, 2019).

32 Mamigonian, *Africanos livres*: 284–323; Moura, "Dos sertões da África para os do Brasil."

Brazil. Up to 1824, the Portuguese Empire's system of mechanical trades structured workers' training, labor opportunities, and quality control for services across different specializations. The municipal chambers regulated these systems by means of appointed "trade justices" (*Juízes de ofício*). Historian Mônica Martins brought up the debate on the extinction of trade corporations during the 1823 Constituent Assembly. For the viscount of Cairu, apprenticeship in trades or crafts guaranteed education towards labor, particularly for the destitute, whereas the liberal political project would condemn them to idleness. In any case, Cairu was defeated in the assembly and the 1824 constitution extinguished trade corporations, dismantling the system without fully eradicating it from the legislation.[33] There are no records of governmental investment in or preference for liberated Africans' training in the mechanical trades. Although several liberated African women sought to have their children learn trades under tailors and seamstresses, for instance, most of them did not enjoy enough autonomy to pursue these arrangements.[34] Neither the rights and obligations included in the 1830 law – regulating service contracts for Brazilians and foreigners – nor those in the 1837 law – regulating service rental – applied to liberated Africans.[35] As laborers, at least those entrusted to private parties ought, in theory, to have been governed by domestic service legislation as it featured in the Philippine Ordinances.[36] At any rate, as Brazilian "worlds of labor" come under increasing scrutiny, it becomes clearer that liberated Africans were ascribed a different status than "servants or free laborers" set forth in mixed commissions' regulations. This shift possibly happened in the application of the 1834 and 1835 regulations. Since the management of liberated African workforce was the duty of judges of orphans, laborers could not select their employers, negotiate their wages, or possibly seek protection under the Philippine Ordinances in legal disputes.

---

33 Mônica de Souza N. Martins, *Entre a cruz e o capital: as corporações de ofícios no Rio de Janeiro após a chegada da família real (1808–1824)* (Rio de Janeiro: Garamond Universitária, 2008); Marcelo MacCord, "A Irmandade de São José do Ribamar e o fim das corporações de ofício: Recife, primeiras décadas do Oitocentos," *Portuguese Studies Review* 18, no. 1 (2010): 135–53.

34 Petição de emancipação de Maria Rebola, Arquivo Nacional (National Archives of Brazil), 17/06/1857: GIFI 6D–136; Amália Guilhermina de Oliveira Coutinho, Pedido de emancipação para a Africana livre Carolina Congo, Arquivo Nacional (National Archives of Brazil), 02/12/1857: GIFI 6D–136. Maria's son was a tailor's apprentice. One of Amália's daughters learned sewing; another had worked under four different women masters, but had left them all for being too fidgety.

35 "Lei de 13/09/1830 – Regula o Contracto Por Escripto Sobre Prestação de Serviços Feitos Por Brasileiro Ou Estrangeiro Dentro Ou Fora Do Império," in *Coleção de Leis do Império do Brasil de 1830*, vol. 1 (Rio de Janeiro: Typographia Nacional, 1876): 33; "Lei n. 108, de 11/10/1837 – Dando Várias Providências Sobre Os Contratos de Locação de Serviços Dos Colonos," in *Coleção de Leis do Império do Brasil de 1837*, vol. 1 (Rio de Janeiro: Typographia Nacional, 1861): 76.

36 Monica Duarte Dantas and Vivian Chieregati Costa, "O 'pomposo nome de liberdade do cidadão': tentativas de arregimentação e coerção da mão-de-obra livre no Império do Brasil," *Estudos Avançados* 30, no. 87 (2016): 29–48; Henrique Espada Lima and Fabiane Popinigis, "Maids, Clerks, and the Shifting Landscape of Labor Relations in Rio de Janeiro, 1830s–1880s," *International Review of Social History* 62 (2017): 45–73.

Liberated Africans did not enjoy direct recourse to legal courts, and public authorities responsible for the protection of their rights did the bare minimum, as illustrated by Rosa's and Agapito's cases. It should be noted that the "wages" determined by judges of orphans to be paid to collectors of customs (or, in Rio, to the municipal treasury) were often not collected.[37] The imperial government thus set up for liberated Africans a condition in which they did not have access to specialized trade training, avenues of negotiation regarding their own labor power, or even any remuneration for their services. British commission and diplomatic employees in Brazil understood these signs of coercive labor as a violation of the bilateral agreement that posited liberated Africans' freedom. Their response was constrained, however, by the mixed commissions' regulations, which laid the responsibility over that group into their host nation's hands. To bypass Brazil's refusal to share guardianship or concede information about liberated Africans, in the 1840s the British Foreign Office and its representatives in Brazil devised a two-pronged policy. On one hand, they undermined the mixed commission in favor of transporting vessels for adjudication by British Admiralty courts (favoring liberated Africans' engagement in their own colonies); on the other, they started to offer individual protection to those moving into their jurisdiction. This altered the fates of many liberated Africans, among them the sailors José Majojo and Francisco Moçambique. It was also the fate of those rescued from the *Flor de Luanda*, who were distributed in 1838 among institutions and individuals trusted by British diplomats and awarded emancipation letters, with a sum equal to their salaries exactly eight years later (in 1846), in addition to the promise that they would be transferred to the British colony of Trinidad. This was a deliberate act by the British to signal to liberated Africans how they understood freedom. In following years, the British would invest heavily in the protection of liberated Africans' right to emancipation on the completion of their guardianship period. As historian Maeve Ryan points out, they traditionally did so through diplomatic avenues.[38]

5 The Right to Emancipation from Guardianship

The experiences of liberated Africans recaptured before November 1831 suggest that they displayed autonomy and broke free from the managers or hirers of their services, having sought to formalize the end of their guardianship. In a public notice from April 1845, Rio de Janeiro's curator of liberated Africans reiterated this group's right

37 Liberated Africans never received the earnings from this fund, which was eventually incorporated into the National Treasury. See Mamigonian, *Africanos livres*: 103–5.

38 Maeve Ryan, "British Antislavery Diplomacy and Liberated African Rights as an International Issue," in *Liberated Africans and the Abolition of the Slave Trade, 1807–1896*, ed. Richard Anderson and Henry B. Lovejoy (Rochester, NY: University of Rochester Press, 2020): 215–37.

to emancipation respecting the time limit outlined in the 1818 royal decree. The fulfillment of this right varied widely in practice.[39]

In September 1851, when Senator Montezuma introduced his motion regarding liberated Africans within the empire, he sought an assessment of how the issue had been addressed so far, so as to evaluate and possibly reformulate corresponding policies. The senator wondered whether that group had learned trades, and most importantly "whether liberated Africans given to labor engagements, since this system has been in practice, have achieved full governance over their own freedom upon the end of the lease."[40] Montezuma had previously served as minister of justice; as an observer of life in the city and someone who engaged in dialogue with government officials, legislators, and British representatives, he surely knew that the answer to his question was negative. He described liberated Africans' condition as analogous to servitude and insisted on calling the government's attention to liberated Africans' fates, "for the use and enjoyment of the rights they possess as free men." At times treating labor arrangements as engagements and at others as service rental, Montezuma steered clear of the imperial bureaucracy's standard terms (the "auctioning" and "concession" of services), perhaps because they were inextricably associated with involuntary arrangements and denied laborers much autonomy. His treatment of liberated Africans as free subjects aimed to ascribe to them the juridical capacity withheld from them by the bureaucracy. The reality was that liberated Africans' emancipation was a pressing topic at the start of the 1850s. Perhaps Montezuma knew that the Ministry of Justice occasionally received a few requests for emancipation from guardianship, such as one by Maria da Conceição.[41] This liberated African woman had been in service for over fifteen consecutive years and requested to be dismissed from serving a certain D. Emília Candida da Cruz, seeing as she, Maria, was sick with tuberculosis. Curator Carlos Honório Figueiredo knew that two liberated Africans had been emancipated shortly beforehand under condition of leaving the country. He forwarded Maria's request for an emancipation letter, also with the requirement of leaving the empire once her health improved. The response he received from Eusébio de Queirós claimed that Africans "can only remain in the empire by performing service while they cannot be re-exported."[42] As Rio de Janeiro's chief of police, Eusébio de Queirós sought to exercise his institutional power to restrict the numbers of free and freed blacks in the city. In doing so, he echoed legislators from other spaces where slavery thrived in the United States and the Caribbean, who imposed control over manumissions to limit the growth of a free colored population. Queirós used his authority to deport Africans considered undesirable, such as Felício Mina, who was sent to Angola.

39 Mamigonian, *Africanos livres*: 63–75, 120–27.

40 Anais do Senado (Proceedings of the Senate), 12/9/1851: 315.

41 Carlos Honório de Figueiredo, Pedido de emancipação para Maria da Conceição, Arquivo Nacional (National Archives of Brazil), 12/4/1849: IJ6 523.

42 Ibid.

Years later, Queirós recalled that the imperial government had deported liberated Africans on various occasions, "at times in large numbers" – a procedure that would be unfeasible were they recognized as Brazilian citizens.[43] Numerous liberated Africans hinted at their intention to break free from hirers' orders, ending up returned to the House of Correction. In May 1856, Anginha Rebola petitioned for emancipation for her and her fourteen-year-old daughter Sara. According to her hirer Maria Francisca dos Santos Torres, she "displayed good behavior until the beginning of last year, though thenceforth she tended to alcoholism, [and] became exceedingly proud and insolent, using as a pretext her condition as free to disobey me and disrespect me, notwithstanding the good treatment she always received from me."[44] Anginha's services had been hired by the House of Correction in 1837 until its director, Thomé Joaquim Torres, transferred her to perform domestic work at his own house when she gave birth to her daughter. Anginha was still employed at the Torres household when she presented her petition. While waiting for a decision, Anginha was returned to the House of Correction. Her emancipation letter was only issued months later, since the Torres' son had pleaded with the government to delay it so as to make up for a "very long history of misbehavior."[45]

British diplomacy in Rio increased pressure on the issue of liberated Africans' rights after the bilateral convention of 1817 expired, resulting in the shutdown of the mixed commission in 1845. The British consul in Rio, Robert Hesketh, invited to the consulate a number of liberated Africans residing in the city, listened to their complaints, and collected information on their workplaces and remuneration. Between 1849 and 1851, he compiled a list with 854 names. It is not unreasonable to speculate that he might have intended to remove them to one of the British colonies in the Caribbean, where other Africans found on apprehended ships had been sent. Actions like this were part of a broader politics of pressure on the Brazilian government, using the illegality of the slave trade as a weapon. A few weeks before Montezuma's parliamentary request for information on liberated Africans, the British Royal Navy

43 Queirós' declaration was made in the context of an assessment of the State Council's foreign affairs section regarding a decision by the Brazilian consulate in Montevidéu to protect a an African freedman. See Brazil. Fundação Alexandre de Gusmão. *O Conselho de Estado e a política externa do Império: consultas da seção dos negócios estrangeiros, 1858–1862* (Rio de Janeiro: FUNAG, 2005): 187–92. Queirós' opinion can be found on page 191. On the politics of liberation regarding freed Africans, see Cunha, *Negros, estrangeiros*; João José Reis, *Rebelião escrava no Brasil: a história do levante dos malês em 1835* (São Paulo, Brazil: Companhia das Letras, 2003): 479–85; Mary C. Karasch, *Slave Life in Rio de Janeiro, 1808–1850* (Princeton, NJ: Princeton University Press, 1987): 337. On the rights of freed Africans, see Beatriz G. Mamigonian, "Os direitos dos libertos africanos no Brasil oitocentista: entre razões de direito e considerações políticas," *História* 34, no. 2 (2015): 181–205.

44 Petição de emancipação de Anginha Rebola, Arquivo Nacional (National Archives of Brazil), 5/5/1856: Div. SDH cx.782 pc.3.

45 Ibid.

apprehended the *Piratinim* on the route from Salvador to Santos. A total of 102 enslaved people, creoles and Africans, were found on board. For Lord Palmerston, all those who were apprehended at the time would be considered "liberated Africans" – a broader interpretation of the statute that challenged the Brazilian Empire's own understanding.[46] There is no indication that the government responded to Senator Montezuma's motion in the following year's parliamentary session. The requested records existed, but they were incomplete and highly dispersed. More importantly, however, the gathering of this information depended on a political decision. No single person had a comprehensive perspective on the issue, but it was easy to see that it was a most delicate one. Up to 1850, over five thousand Africans had been emancipated and, among those who had not died, most had already fulfilled their fourteen years of mandatory service. Since the prohibition of the slave trade north of the equator in 1815 (affecting commerce with Bahia and the northern Brazilian provinces) and full prohibition in 1830, an estimated 920,000 Africans were illegally brought into Brazil.[47] Considering the popular conflation of "liberated Africans" with "Africans imported since the trade's prohibition," Montezuma's caution in addressing the subject of liberated Africans was hardly pointless. As the senator commented, before the Eusébio de Queirós Law this topic was off limits. Despite the silence on the subject of Montezuma's motion, the Brazilian Ministry moved to address liberated Africans' emancipation. In December 1853, a decree was in place granting the right to request emancipation to all those having completed fourteen years of service. It mandated "emancipated Africans" to reside in government-designated places and assume remunerated occupations.[48] When analyzed from multiple perspectives, the emancipation of liberated Africans reveals its political character. The petitions were bureaucratic and laborious administrative files that required proxies (*solicitadores de causas*), attorneys, or their own hirers to act on behalf of the Africans. The scribe in charge of liberated African records issued a certificate from their registry (*Livro de Matrícula dos Africanos Livres*), which identified the lot from which each African had been emancipated, as well as when his or her services had been entrusted and to whom. This

46 This unilateral interpretation of British law was radical in relation to the Aberdeen Act of 1845, which categorized the Brazilian slave trade as piracy while failing to determine that property could be confiscated without judgment. See Beatriz G. Mamigonian, "In the Name of Freedom: Slave Trade Abolition, the Law and the Brazilian Branch of the African Emigration Scheme (Brazil–British West Indies, 1830s–1850s)," *Slavery & Abolition* 30, no. 1 (2009): 41–66. Using a condescending euphemism, Martinez presents the British Foreign Office's extralegal measures in the campaign for slave trade repression as "creative interpretations" of the bilateral treaties. See Martinez, *The Slave Trade*: 140–44.
47 I address the issue of the extension of liberated Africans' statute to comprise illegally enslaved Africans, as well as the political implications of the illegal trade on slavery, in Beatriz G. Mamigonian, "O direito de ser africano livre: os escravos e as interpretações da lei de 1831," in *Direitos e justiças no Brasil: ensaios de história social*, ed. Silvia Hunold Lara and Joseli Maria Nunes Mendonça, Coleção Várias Histórias 22 (Campinas, SP, Brasil: Editora UNICAMP, 2006): 129–60; and Mamigonian, *Africanos livres*.
48 "Decreto N° 1.303, de 28 de Dezembro de 1853," in *Coleção de Leis do Império do Brasil, 1853*, vol. 1, 1853: 420.

certificate was then attached to a petition addressed to the emperor. The documents passed through the hands of multiple authorities within the Ministry of Justice. The judge of orphans and the curator of liberated Africans matched the paperwork to the plaintiff and verified the fulfillment of the service period, almost always confirming it. The chief of police requested information from the director of the House of Correction about the referred African's behavior and even arranged an interrogation with the plaintiff – and often also the hirer – to cross-examine his or her behavior and relationships in the city. Flights, drunkenness, and insubordination were never overlooked. At the end, a Ministry of Justice official summarized this information and forwarded it to the minister, who proffered his decision. As already mentioned, every African was required to fulfill the fourteen years of service in order to be emancipated, but this was not enough to confirm their right. The authorities in charge of petition proceedings considered a number of requirements absent from the decree, such as obedience and good conduct. Even so, Africans who fulfilled these requirements and demonstrated the financial means for self-support might have their petitions denied. The restriction of liberated Africans' right to definitive emancipation was tied to a perception that, once emancipated, they might pose a threat to the Brazilian social order, for they rejected submission. The director of the House of Correction in Rio de Janeiro resented their autonomy: "The African, once freed, hardly submits himself to regular daily work, since the resources of the country are enough to feed him, and in general they do not care about the future. In this establishment, among the large number of emancipated Africans it is notable that only a few subject themselves to salaried work."[49] An analysis of over 250 petitions sent to the Ministry of Justice revealed that the imperial government had prepared a trap: liberated Africans entrusted to private parties petitioned for emancipation, were deposited at the House of Correction to await the proceedings, and systematically had their services transferred to public institutions. Only after that move did they receive the – negative – reply to their petitions, since those who labored in public service did not enjoy the right to emancipation under the 1853 decree. Few liberated Africans managed to achieve emancipation in the 1850s. Some resorted to British diplomats for help.[50]

---

49 Report from the Director of the House of Correction of Rio de Janeiro, attached to Brazil, Relatório do Ministério da Justiça apresentado à Assembleia Geral Legislativa na 4a sessão da 12a legislatura pelo respectivo ministro e secretário de Estado José Thomaz Nabuco de Araújo (Rio de Janeiro: Typographia Universal de Laemmert, 1866): 5.

50 On the process of emancipation of liberated Africans, see Mamigonian, "Do que o 'preto mina' é capaz"; and Beatriz G. Mamigonian, "Conflicts over the Meanings of Freedom: The Liberated Africans' Struggle for Emancipation in Brazil (1840s–1860s)," in *Paths to Freedom: Manumission in the Atlantic World*, ed. Rosemary Brana-Shute and Randy J. Sparks (Columbia, SC: University of South Carolina Press, 2009): 235–64. On the support provided by British diplomacy to liberated Africans, see Daryle Williams, "'A necessária distinção entre liberdade e emancipação': noções africana, inglesa e brasileira do que é ser emancipado," in *Instituições nefandas: o fim da escravidão e da servidão no Brasil,*

In 1859, the justice section of the State Council acknowledged the injustice of the 1853 decree towards liberated Africans employed in public institutions, while acknowledging the reason might have been that they were essential for the maintenance of a public workforce. The promise of re-exportation also justified the imperial government's control over liberated Africans. State councilors reckoned that "with justice, being free, they cannot be perpetually subjected to a guardianship similar in means to slavery, waiting for a re-exportation that starts to turn into effective derision."[51] In any case, liberated Africans' autonomy was not on the horizon. Councilors themselves – among them Eusébio de Queirós – advised that the government adopt "a few measures that would subject them to some authority's inspection and that would disperse them, for example, across several settlements, since the rapid introduction of so many free blacks in the same place where they have lived, if not entirely as slaves, then at least subjected to a certain regime, cannot but generate inconvenience."[52] And the administration followed suit: instead of denying emancipation or withholding letters from their recipients, authorities issued the documents under the condition that emancipated subjects moved away from Rio de Janeiro. The records show countless such cases. In the early 1860s, many liberated Africans – officially deemed "emancipated Africans" – were transferred from the capital to the provinces, along with instructions for provincial authorities to watch them and keep them under control. The arrival of British minister William Christie in Brazil in the early 1860s raised the stakes of British pressure for liberated Africans' definitive emancipation. Christie was adamant to enforce the bilateral agreements and the Brazilian legislation regarding slave trade prohibition. For him, that meant systematically obtaining information from the Brazilian government regarding liberated Africans and their service periods in order to make sure they would be emancipated once their obligations were fulfilled. As Christie later recalled in his *Notes on Brazilian Questions*, he relied on British diplomatic archives in Rio to learn about the earlier stages of the two countries' diplomatic correspondence. Expectedly, he also made use of personal testimonies from other diplomatic officials.[53] Christie sent a series of representations to ministers of foreign affairs insisting on the right to "full freedom" owed to Africans emancipated by the Anglo-Brazilian mixed commission. He paid particular attention to the saga of the liberated Africans employed at the ironworks of Ipanema, who were transferred to the military colony of Itapura, on the border between São Paulo and Mato Grosso provinces. There, they would continue to serve the military without any remuneration or prospect

---

nos Estados Unidos e na Rússia, ed. Ivana S. Lima, Keila Grinberg and Daniel Aarão Reis (Rio de Janeiro: Fundação Casa de Rui Barbosa, 2018): 151–70.

51 "Seção Justiça Do Conselho de Estado, Resolução de 20/12/1859," in *Imperiais resoluções tomadas sobre consultas da seção de justiça do Conselho de Estado*, 2 vols, ed. José Próspero da Silva Caroatá (Rio de Janeiro: Garnier, 1884): 842–43.

52 Ibid.

53 William Dougal Christie, *Notes on Brazilian Questions* (Cambridge: Macmillan, 1865).

of emancipation. Faced with the Ministry of War's plan to change the status of those who served for six more years – with good conduct – to that of "settlers," Christie vehemently urged the imperial government to grant them emancipation letters and dismiss them from a new period of compulsory labor. Christie also discovered that many liberated Africans attained emancipation in exchange for residing and working away from Rio de Janeiro, and he insisted that no condition or restriction be imposed on them. He interfered in the management of liberated Africans sent to Amazonas province under the provincial president's care or through service for the Company for Steam Navigation of the Amazon. Christie's correspondence suggests that British diplomacy continued to serve as a resource for liberated Africans' defense of their rights and an agent of pressure on the Brazilian government. Christie strategically cultivated relationships with liberal politicians of abolitionist leaning, such as Francisco Otaviano and Tavares Bastos, who used the press to condemn the empire's unwillingness to emancipate liberated Africans. When two minor diplomatic incidents sparked a crisis that would end in the severance of diplomatic ties between Britain and Brazil – and Christie's departure from Rio de Janeiro in early 1863 – the issue of liberated Africans in Brazil surfaced in British parliamentary debates. Part of the diplomatic correspondence was published in the British *Parliamentary Papers*.[54]

In February 1863, the marquis of Abrantes, then Brazilian minister of foreign affairs, assured Christie that the empire administered the issue of liberated Africans with "the greatest earnestness and solicitude" and collected information to "proceed with all such discretion and prudence as the case requires," since "serious inconvenience and dangers might result from letting loose at once among the population, without certain precautions, a large number of uneducated individuals, and without experience to guide them."[55] In other words, although it was unsustainable for the government to maintain liberated Africans officially under guardianship, it was imperative that they remain under some form of control. This policy, which had already been announced in the 1859 resolution by the State Council's justice section, had set the dragging pace of emancipation until 1863. The same policy was inscribed in a new decree from September 1864, according to which all liberated Africans in the Brazilian Empire were to be summarily emancipated – under the obligation of informing police authorities about their places of residence and employment.[56] The following months

54 Great Britain. Correspondence respecting liberated slaves in Brazil. House of Commons Accounts and Papers, 1863, v. LXXIII (365); Beatriz G. Mamigonian, "Building the Nation, Selecting Memories: Vitor Meireles, the Christie Affair and Brazilian Slavery in the 1860s," in *Distant Ripples of the British Abolitionist Wave: Africa, Asia and the Americas*, ed. Myriam Cottias and Marie-Jeanne Rossignol (Trenton, NJ: Africa World Press, 2017): 235–64.

55 The Marquis of Abrantes to Mr. Christie, 28/2/1863, in Great Britain, Correspondence respecting liberated slaves in Brazil. House of Commons Accounts and Papers, 1863, v. LXXIII (365): 2–3.

56 "Decreto 3310 – Emancipação Dos Africanos Livres, 24 Set. 1864," in *Coleção das Leis do Império do Brasil, 1864* (Rio de Janeiro: Typographia Nacional, 1864): 160–61.

and years were marked by the processes of issuing and delivering remaining emancipation letters and the registration of all those who had lived under the status of liberated Africans. Data on Africans recaptured and distributed for service in the 1830s show that 28.5% ended up emancipated from guardianship; 46.8% died before receiving their definitive emancipation letter; 3% fled and were never retrieved; and 21.6% had an unknown fate. Africans who labored for public institutions were forced to serve for longer than those who labored for private parties. Among men, most of the emancipated worked for over twenty-five years; among women, most worked for over twenty years instead of fourteen.[57] The emancipation of remaining liberated Africans underscored the risk that accompanied their freedom, since enslaved Africans and their supporters tried to broaden the scope of the concept of "liberated Africans" to one which included all Africans imported illegally, as opposed to only those apprehended (as the government framed the category). This dispute went on to become central to abolitionism in the 1880s.[58] Now emancipated, liberated Africans and their descendants would be less intensively kept under imperial watch. It is still unclear whether they were finally able to break free from compulsory labor.

6 Liberated Africans among Free Poor Brazilians

Liberated Africans' experiences in Brazil largely depended on a juridical framework that mixed inherited Portuguese law and newer Brazilian regulations. This framework unfolded under British pressure, which combined surveillance and subversion of Brazilian jurisdiction. The exercise of freedom, understood as autonomy and juridical capacity, was nevertheless restricted for liberated Africans between the 1820s and the 1860s. As laborers, liberated Africans were not included in a system of trade apprenticeship, nor were they juridically treated as domestic servants. The guardianship that applied to them removed their autonomy vis à vis labor contracts, terms-of-service negotiations, and labor earnings' accumulation. Only those hired out had a different

57 "Matrícula dos africanos apreendidos entre 1834 e 1838." See a discussion on the issue in Mamigonian, *Africanos livres*: 387–94.

58 The argument that all Africans brought into Brazil after the 1831 law, as well as their descendants, had the right to be legally identified as liberated Africans was adopted by militant lawyers and judges. This disseminated abolitionist strategy deserves further investigation. See "Seção Justiça do Conselho de Estado, Resolução de 28/10/1874," in *Imperiais resoluções tomadas sobre consultas da seção de justiça do Conselho de Estado*, vol. 2, ed. José Próspero da Silva Caroatá (Rio de Janeiro: Garnier, 1884): 1721–1725; Elciene Azevedo, *Orfeu de carapinha: a trajetória de Luiz Gama na imperial cidade de São Paulo* (Campinas: Cecult, 1999); Ricardo Tadeu C. Silva, "O resgate da Lei de 7 de novembro de 1831 no contexto abolicionista baiano," *Estudos Afro-Asiáticos* 29 (2007): 301–40; Ricardo Tadeu C. Silva, "Memórias do tráfico ilegal de escravos nas ações de liberdade (Bahia, 1885–1888)," *Afro-Ásia* 35 (2007): 37–82; Mamigonian, "O direito de ser africano livre"; and Mamigonian, *Africanos livres*: 400–455.

experience, and even then they were forced to benefit their hirers with their earnings. Liberated Africans experienced the most extreme restriction of rights during their periods of compulsory labor, providing private hirers and public institutions with an extremely inexpensive labor force at a time of significant economic growth and the supposed "modernization" of the Brazilian economy. The curtailment of individual freedom and exploitation of compulsory labor by the Brazilian state applied to a number of groups that, as Peter Beattie argues, comprised the "intractable poor."[59] Among them we find military conscripts, indigenous persons, liberated Africans, convicted individuals assigned to work on galleys, and other subjects forcibly recruited to repress popular revolts. The majority of them were non-white and considered idle, ignorant, potentially or effectively dangerous, and ungovernable. Collectively, their citizenship rights were not acknowledged, and individually they heavily depended on ad-hoc negotiations with the authorities. The reiterated restriction of citizenship rights responded to an accumulated understanding of politics which excluded myriad political visions and alternative projects for the nation. In refusing to acknowledge citizenship for the free poor, the propertied elites and the state showcased the strength of conservative centralization, which endured in the First Republic (1889–1930).[60] Doubtless, liberated Africans resisted, both individually and in small groups, to the curtailment of their rights. However, they did so within a very limited space, seeing as the Ministry of Justice controlled all decisions regarding that group. The ministry's centralization of political power was so extensive as to preclude any provincial or local authority from addressing the issue of emancipation, even for individuals originally emancipated by local judicial authorities. All that was left for these dissenting authorities was to ensure liberated Africans were treated less harshly or to help expedite the transit of emancipation requests. Liberated Africans' rights must be analyzed in a context of wavering slave trade repression and extensive contraband, resulting in illegal enslavement *en masse* perpetrated by landowners with the support of the Brazilian state. This pro-slavery politics trivialized the restrictions on freedom for many individuals besides liberated Africans. In this sense, liberated Africans' history is part and parcel of labor history and the history of citizenship in Brazil's formation as an independent nation. Seen in comparative perspective with other groups of liberated Africans in the Atlantic and Indian oceans, as well as many other disenfranchised laborers around the globe, this case illustrates the shifting worlds of labor of the nineteenth century.

---

59 Peter M. Beattie, *Punishment in Paradise: Race, Slavery, Human Rights, and a Nineteenth-Century Brazilian Penal Colony* (Durham, NC: Duke University Press, 2015).

60 Monica Duarte Dantas, "Homens livres pobres e libertos e o aprendizado da política no Império," in *Revoltas, motins, revoluções: homens livres pobres e libertos no Brasil do século XIX*, ed. Monica Duarte Dantas (São Paulo: Alameda, 2011): 511–63.

Bibliography

Primary Sources

Arquivo Nacional – Rio de Janeiro (National Archives of Brazil, Rio de Janeiro):
Série Justiça – Gabinete do Ministro
IJ1 168 – Justiça – Registro de Avisos (fev. 1834–abr. 1835)
Série Justiça – Polícia, Escravos, Moeda Falsa, Africanos
IJ6 471 – Ofícios, relações e processos sobre africanos livres, 1834–1864
IJ6 523 – Ofícios e processos sobre africanos livres, 1834–1864.
Fundo Ministério da Justiça e Negócios Interiores
Diversos – Caixas SDH cx.782, Ofícios de ministros 1826–1840; pedidos de cartas de emancipação de escravos, 1854–1857, pc.3.
Documentação Identificada
GIFI 6D–136.
Brazil. Anais do Senado (Proceedings of the Senate), 1851.
Brazil. Coleção das Leis do Brasil (Collection of Brazilian Laws), Rio de Janeiro: Imprensa Nacional, 1808–1989.
Brazil. Fundação Alexandre de Gusmão. O Conselho de Estado e a política externa do Império: consultas da seção dos negócios estrangeiros, 1858–1862 (Rio de Janeiro: FUNAG, 2005).
Brazil. Relatórios do Ministério da Justiça (1834–1870).
Great Britain, House of Commons Accounts and Papers, 1863.
Great Britain, Parliamentary Papers, 1844.
Christie, William Dougal. *Notes on Brazilian Questions* (Cambridge: Macmillan and Co., 1865).
Caroatá, José Próspero da Silva, ed. *Imperiais resoluções tomadas sobre consultas da seção de justiça do Conselho de Estado*, 2 vols. (Rio de Janeiro: Garnier, 1884).

Secondary Literature

Adderley, Rosanne Marion. *'New Negroes from Africa': Slave Trade Abolition and Free African Settlement in the Nineteenth-Century Caribbean* (Indiana University Press, Bloomington, 2006).
Allain, Jean. "The Nineteenth Century Law of the Sea and the British Abolition of the Slave Trade," *British Yearbook of International Law* 78, no. 1 (2007): 342–88.
Anderson, Richard, and Henry B. Lovejoy, eds. *Liberated Africans and the Abolition of the Slave Trade, 1807–1896* (Rochester, NY: University of Rochester Press, 2020).
de Araújo, Carlos Eduardo Moreira. "A engenharia da liberdade: os africanos livres e as obras públicas no Rio de Janeiro Imperial," in *Pesquisa em ação*, vol. 2, ed. Shirley G.S. Carreira and Marcelo M. Mazzi (Belford Roxo: Uniabeu, 2014): 33–51.
de Araújo, Carlos Eduardo Moreira. "Cárceres imperiais: a Casa de Correção do Rio de Janeiro: seus detentos e o sistema prisional no Império, 1830–1861" (PhD diss., Universidade Estadual de Campinas, 2009).
Azevedo, Elciene. *O direito dos africanos: lutas jurídicas e abolicionismo na província de São Paulo* (Campinas: Editora da Unicamp, 2010).
Azevedo, Elciene. *Orfeu de carapinha: a trajetória de Luiz Gama na imperial cidade de São Paulo* (Campinas: Cecult, 1999).

Beattie, Peter M. *Punishment in Paradise: Race, Slavery, Human Rights, and a Nineteenth-Century Brazilian Penal Colony* (Durham, NC: Duke University Press, 2015).

Bertin, Enidelce. *Os meia-cara: africanos livres em São Paulo no século XIX* (Salto: Schoba, 2013).

Bethell, Leslie. *The Abolition of the Brazilian Slave Trade: Britain, Brazil and the Slave Trade Question, 1807–1869* (Cambridge: Cambridge University Press, 2002).

Bethell, Leslie. "The Mixed Commissions for the Suppression of the Transatlantic Slave Trade in the Nineteenth Century," *Journal of African History* 7, no. 1 (1966): 79–93.

Brito, Adriane Sanctis. "Seeking Capture, Resisting Seizure: Legal Battles under the Anglo-Brazilian Treaty for the Suppression of Slave Trade (1826–1845)" (PhD diss., Universidade de São Paulo, 2018).

Coghe, Samuël. "The Problem of Freedom in a Mid Nineteenth-Century Atlantic Slave Society: The Liberated Africans of the Anglo-Portuguese Mixed Commission in Luanda (1844–1870)," *Slavery & Abolition* 33, no. 3 (2012): 479–500.

Craton, Michael, and Gail Saunders. "Transition, Not Transformation: Apprentices, Liberated Africans, and the Reconstructed Oligarchy, 1834–1860," in *Islanders in the Stream: A History of the Bahamian People*, vol. 2, (Athens: University of Georgia Press, 1998): 3–31.

da Cunha, Manuela Carneiro. *Negros, estrangeiros: os escravos libertos e sua volta à África* (São Paulo: Companhia das Letras, 2012).

Dantas, Monica Duarte. "Homens livres pobres e libertos e o aprendizado da política no Império," in *Revoltas, motins, revoluções: homens livres pobres e libertos no Brasil do século XIX*, ed. Monica Duarte Dantas (São Paulo: Alameda, 2011): 511–63.

Dantas, Monica Duarte, and Vivian Chieregati Costa. "O 'pomposo nome de liberdade do cidadão': tentativas de arregimentação e coerção da mão-de-obra livre no Império do Brasil," *Estudos Avançados* 30, no. 87 (2016): 29–48.

Dias Paes, Mariana Armond. *Escravidão e direito: o estatuto jurídico dos escravos no Brasil oitocentista (1860–1888)* (São Paulo: Alameda, 2019).

Fernandes, Cyra L.R. de Oliveira. "Os africanos livres de Pernambuco (1831–1864)" (master's thesis, Universidade Federal de Pernambuco, 2010).

Ferrer, Ada. *Freedom's Mirror: Cuba and Haiti in the Age of Revolution* (Cambridge: Cambridge University Press, 2014).

Fett, Sharla M. *Recaptured Africans: Surviving Slave Ships, Detention, and Dislocation in the Final Years of the Slave Trade* (Chapel Hill: University of North Carolina Press, 2017).

Florence, Afonso Bandeira. "Entre o cativeiro e a emancipação: a liberdade dos africanos livres no Brasil (1818–1864)" (master's thesis, Universidade Federal da Bahia, 2002).

Haslam, Emily. "International Criminal Law and Legal Memories of Abolition: Intervention, Mixed Commission Courts and 'Emancipation'," *Journal of the History of International Law* 18, no. 4 (2016): 420–47.

Haslam, Emily. *The Slave Trade, Abolition and the Long History of International Criminal Law: The Recaptive and the Victim* (Abingdon, Oxon: Routledge, 2020).

Hespanha, António Manuel. *Imbecillitas: as bem-aventuranças da inferioridade nas sociedades de Antigo Regime* (São Paulo: Annablume, 2010).

Holloway, Thomas H. *Policing Rio de Janeiro: Repression and Resistance in a 19th-Century City* (Stanford, CA: Stanford University Press, 1993).

Karasch, Mary C. *Slave Life in Rio de Janeiro, 1808–1850* (Princeton, NJ: Princeton University Press, 1987).

Lima, Henrique Espada, and Fabiane Popinigis. "Maids, Clerks, and the Shifting Landscape of Labor Relations in Rio de Janeiro, 1830s–1880s," *International Review of Social History* 62 (2017): 45–73.

MacCord, Marcelo. "A Irmandade de São José do Ribamar e o fim das corporações de ofício: Recife, primeiras décadas do Oitocentos," *Portuguese Studies Review* 18, no. 1 (2010): 135–53.

Mamigonian, Beatriz G. *Africanos livres: a abolição do tráfico de escravos no Brasil* (São Paulo: Companhia das Letras, 2017).

Mamigonian, Beatriz G. "Building the Nation, Selecting Memories: Vitor Meireles, the Christie Affair and Brazilian Slavery in the 1860s," in *Distant Ripples of the British Abolitionist Wave: Africa, Asia and the Americas*, ed. Myriam Cottias and Marie-Jeanne Rossignol (Trenton, NJ: Africa World Press, 2017): 235–64.

Mamigonian, Beatriz G. "Conflicts over the Meanings of Freedom: The Liberated Africans' Struggle for Emancipation in Brazil (1840s–1860s)," in *Paths to Freedom: Manumission in the Atlantic World*, ed. Rosemary Brana-Shute and Randy J. Sparks (Columbia: University of South Carolina Press, 2009): 235–64.

Mamigonian, Beatriz G. "Do que o 'preto mina' é capaz: etnia e resistência entre africanos livres," *Afro-Ásia* 24 (2000): 71–95.

Mamigonian, Beatriz G. "In the Name of Freedom: Slave Trade Abolition, the Law and the Brazilian Branch of the African Emigration Scheme (Brazil–British West Indies, 1830s–1850s)," *Slavery & Abolition* 30, no. 1 (2009): 41–66.

Mamigonian, Beatriz G. "José Majojo e Francisco Moçambique, marinheiros das rotas atlânticas: notas sobre a reconstituição de trajetórias da era da abolição," *Topoi* 11, no. 20 (2010): 75–91.

Mamigonian, Beatriz G. "O direito de ser africano livre: os escravos e as interpretações da lei de 1831," in *Direitos e justiças no Brasil: ensaios de história social*, ed. Silvia Hunold Lara and Joseli Maria Nunes Mendonça (Campinas, SP, Brasil: Editora UNICAMP, 2006): 129–60.

Mamigonian, Beatriz G. "Os direitos dos libertos africanos no Brasil oitocentista: entre razões de direito e considerações políticas," *História* 34, no. 2 (2015): 181–205.

Mamigonian, Beatriz G. "Revisitando a 'transição para o trabalho livre': a experiência dos africanos livres," in *Tráfico, Cativeiro e Liberdade: Rio de Janeiro, Séculos XVII–XIX*, ed. Manolo Florentino (Rio de Janeiro: Civilização Brasileira, 2005): 388–417.

Manchester, Alan. *Preeminência inglesa no Brasil* (São Paulo: Brasiliense, 1973).

Martinez, Jenny S. *The Slave Trade and the Origins of International Human Rights Law* (New York: Oxford University Press, 2012).

Martins, Mônica de Souza N. *Entre a cruz e o capital: as corporações de ofícios no Rio de Janeiro após a chegada da família real (1808–1824)* (Rio de Janeiro: Garamond Universitária, 2008).

Mattos, Hebe M. "A escravidão moderna nos quadros do Império Português: o Antigo Regime em perspectiva atlântica," in *O Antigo Regime nos trópicos: a dinâmica imperial portuguesa (séculos XVI–XVIII)*, ed. João Luís Ribeiro Fragoso, Maria Fernanda Bicalho and Maria de Fátima Gouvêa (Rio de Janeiro: Civilização Brasileira, 2001): 141–62.

Moreira, Alinnie Silvestre. "Liberdade tutelada: os africanos livres e as relações de trabalho na Fábrica de Pólvora Da Estrela. Serra Da Estrela/RJ (c. 1831–c. 1870)" (master's thesis, Universidade Estadual de Campinas, 2005).

Moreira, Alinnie Silvestre. "Os africanos livres, sua prole e as discussões emancipacionistas: as famílias e a administração dos descendentes de africanos livres na Fábrica de Pólvora Da Estrela (Rio de Janeiro, 1830–1860)," *Estudos Afro-Asiáticos* 29, no. 1–3 (2007): 161–200.

Moura, Zilda. "Dos sertões da África para os do Brasil: os africanos livres da Sociedade de Mineração de Mato Grosso (Alto Paraguai-Diamantino, 1851–1865)" (PhD diss., Universidade Federal de Santa Catarina, 2014).

Murray, David R. *Odious Commerce: Britain, Spain, and the Abolition of the Cuban Slave Trade* (Cambridge: Cambridge University Press, 1980).

Nelson, Jennifer Louise. "Liberated Africans in the Atlantic World: The Courts of Mixed Commission in Havana and Rio de Janeiro 1819–1871" (PhD diss., University of Leeds, 2015).

Northrup, David. *Indentured Labor in the Age of Imperialism, 1834–1922* (Cambridge: Cambridge University Press, 1995).

Ramos, Pedro Brandão de Sousa Culmant. “Homens de confiança: moral, antiescravismo e o abolicionismo inglês na supressão do tráfico brasileiro de escravos (1836–1846)” (master’s thesis, Universidade Federal do Rio de Janeiro, 2016).

dos Reis, Isabel Cristina. “A família negra no tempo da escravidão” (PhD diss., Universidade Estadual de Campinas, 2007).

Reis, João José. *Rebelião escrava no Brasil: a história do levante dos malês em 1835* (São Paulo: Companhia das Letras, 2003).

Ribeiro, Mariana Alice Pereira Schatzer. *Entre a fábrica e a senzala: um estudo sobre o cotidiano dos africanos livres na Real Fábrica de Ferro São João Do Ipanema – Sorocaba – São Paulo (1840–1870)* (São Paulo: Alameda, 2017).

Ribeiro, Mariana Alice Pereira Schatzer. “Trabalho e cotidiano dos africanos livres na Estrada da Maioridade: São Paulo-Santos (1840–1864)” (PhD diss., Universidade Estadual Paulista, 2019).

Richards, Jake Christopher. “Anti-Slave-Trade Law, ‘Liberated Africans’ and the State in the South Atlantic World, c.1839–1852,” *Past & Present* 241, no. 1 (2018): 179–219.

Rodrigues, Jaime. “Ferro, trabalho e conflito: os africanos livres na Fábrica de Ipanema,” *História Social* 4–5 (1998): 29–42.

Roldán de Montaud, Inés. “En los borrosos confines de la libertad: el caso de los negros emancipados en Cuba, 1817–1870,” *Revista de Indias* 71, no. 251 (2011): 159–92.

Russell-Wood, Anthony J.R. “Através de um prisma africano: uma nova abordagem ao estudo da diáspora africana no Brasil Colonial,” *Tempo* 12 (2001): 11–50.

Ryan, Maeve. “British Antislavery Diplomacy and Liberated African Rights as an International Issue,” in *Liberated* Africans *and* the Abolition of the *Slave* Trade, *1807–1896*, ed. Richard Anderson and Henry B. Lovejoy (Rochester, NY: University of Rochester Press, 2020): 215–37.

Sampaio, Patricia Melo. “Fronteiras da liberdade: tutela indígena no Diretório Pombalino e na Carta Régia de 1798,” in *Tutela: formação de Estado e tradições de gestão no Brasil*, ed. Antonio Carlos de Souza Lima (Rio de Janeiro: E-papers, 2014): 31–52.

Sampaio, Patricia Melo. “Política indigenista no Brasil Imperial,” in *O Brasil Imperial*, vol. 1, *1808–1831*, ed. Keila Grinberg and Ricardo Salles (Rio de Janeiro: Civilização Brasileira, 2009): 175–206.

Santana, Adriana. “Africanos livres na Bahia, 1831–1864” (master’s thesis, Universidade Federal da Bahia, 2007).

Schuler, Monica. “Liberated Central Africans in Nineteenth-Century Guyana,” in *Central Africans and Cultural Transformations in the American Diaspora*, ed. Linda M. Heywood (Cambridge: Cambridge University Press, 2002): 319–52.

Schwarz, Suzanne. “The Impact of Liberated African ‘Disposal’ Policies in Early Nineteenth-Century Sierra Leone,” in *Liberated Africans and the Abolition of the Slave* Trade, *1807–1896*, ed. Richard Anderson and Henry B. Lovejoy (Rochester, NY: University of Rochester Press, 2020): 45–65.

Scott, Rebecca J., and Jean M. Hébrard. *Freedom Papers: An Atlantic Odyssey in the Age of Emancipation* (Cambridge, Mass: Harvard University Press, 2012).

Silva, Maciel H.C. “Uma africana ‘livre’ e a ‘corrupção dos costumes’: Pernambuco (1830–1844),” *Estudos Afro-Asiáticos* 29 (2007): 123–60.

Silva, Moisés Sebastião. “Africanos livres em Alagoas: tráfico ilegal, escravidão, tutela e liberdade (1849–1864)” (master’s thesis, Universidade Federal da Bahia, 2017).

Silva, Ricardo Tadeu C. “Memórias do tráfico ilegal de escravos nas ações de liberdade (Bahia, 1885–1888),” *Afro-Ásia* 35 (2007): 37–82.

Silva, Ricardo Tadeu C. “O resgate da Lei de 7 de novembro de 1831 no contexto abolicionista baiano,” *Estudos Afro-Asiáticos* 29 (2007): 301–40.

Slenes, Robert W., “A ‘Great Arch’ Descending: Manumission Rates, Subaltern Social Mobility, and the Identities of Enslaved, Freeborn, and Freed Blacks in Southeastern Brazil, 1791–1888,” in *New*

Approaches to Resistance in Brazil and Mexico, ed. John Gledhill and Patience A. Schell (Durham, NC: Duke University Press, 2012): 100–18.

Soares, Mariza de Carvalho. *Devotos da cor: identidade étnica, religiosidade e escravidão no Rio de Janeiro, século XVIII* (Rio de Janeiro: Civilização Brasileira, 2000).

Sousa, Gustavo Pinto de. *Africanos livres: escravos, prisioneiros ou trabalhadores da Casa de Correção da Corte?* (Rio de Janeiro: Editora Multifoco, 2013).

Sposito, Fernanda. "Liberdade para os índios no Império do Brasil: a revogação das guerras justas em 1831," *Almanack* 1 (2011): 52–65.

Thésée, Françoise. *Les Ibos de l'Amélie: destinée d'une cargaison de traite clandestine à la Martinique, 1822–1838* (Paris: Editions Caribéenees, 1986).

Vieira, Jofre Teófilo. "Os 'Samangolês': africanos livres no Ceará (1835–1865)" (PhD diss., Universidade Federal do Ceará, 2017).

Von Zuben, Danúsia M. *Os africanos livres nos aldeamentos indígenas no Paraná provincial, 1853–1862* (Curitiba: Universidade Federal do Paraná, 2010).

Williams, Daryle. "'A necessária distinção entre liberdade e emancipação': noções africana, inglesa e brasileira do que é ser emancipado," in *Instituições nefandas: o fim da escravidão e da servidão no Brasil, nos Estados Unidos e na Rússia*, ed. Ivana S. Lima, Keila Grinberg and Daniel Aarão Reis (Rio de Janeiro: Fundação Casa de Rui Barbosa, 2018): 151–70.

Mariana Dias Paes

Law and Slavery in the Brazilian Empire: A Research Agenda

1 Law and Slavery

The nineteenth-century city of Rio de Janeiro was very different from what we see today. After all, the reforms undertaken in the early twentieth century radically changed its urban landscape. Today, we find the Brazilian Society of Fine Art in the building on the corner of *Rua do Lavradio* and what is now *Rua da Relação*. However, in the nineteenth century, that same building – which stands between the hills of *Senado* and *Santo Antônio* – housed Rio de Janeiro's Court of Appeals (*Tribunal da Relação*). Housed in an elegant two-story building, the Court of Appeals had an architectural style similar to that of other public edifices in the nineteenth century. Standing on the next corner of *Rua do Lavradio*, the *Grande Oriente* Masonic lodge was much more imposing. In addition to being close to that bastion of freemasonry, the courthouse was located in a bustling part of the city. It was also near the Senate, the square formerly known as *Campo da Aclamação* (now *Praça da República*), the Public Promenade, and several churches and fountains. A building that physically embodied imperial law, the Court of Appeals was part of daily life for the city's enslaved and free populations.[1] When walking past the Court of Appeals from day to day, enslaved, freed, and free people of color were

1 It is estimated that, in 1819, there were 2,488,743 free persons and 1,107,389 enslaved persons in Brazil. The provinces with the largest number of slaves were Minas Gerais (168,543), Bahia (147,263), Rio de Janeiro (146,060), and Maranhão (133,332). Those with the lowest number were Amazonas (6,040), Rio Grande do Norte (9,109), and Santa Catarina (9,172). In 1872, according to the general census of Brazil, there were 8,419,672 free persons and 1,510,806 enslaved persons. The provinces containing the majority of the enslaved population were Minas Gerais (370,459), Rio de Janeiro (292,637), Bahia (167,824), and São Paulo (156,612). The provinces with the smallest number of enslaved persons were Amazonas (979) and Mato Grosso (6,667). For detailed population data, including for other years, see Fundação Instituto Brasileiro de Geografia e Estatística, *Estatísticas históricas do Brasil: séries, econômicas, demográficas e sociais de 1550 a 1988* (Rio de Janeiro: IBGE, 1990): 32. For discussions on population data in nineteenth-century Brazil, see Diego Nones Bissigo, "A eloquente e irrecusável linguagem dos algarismos: a estatística no Brasil imperial e a produção do recenseamento de 1872" (master's thesis, Universidade Federal de Santa Catarina, 2014); Tarcísio Botelho, "Censos e construção nacional no Brasil Imperial," *Tempo Social* 17, no. 1 (2005): 321–41.

Note: Translated by Dr H. Sabrina Gledhill. The original Portuguese version of this article was published in Mariana Dias Paes, "Direito e escravidão no Brasil Império," in *Constituição e poderes, constituição de sujeitos: caminhos da história do Direito no Brasil (1750–1930)*, ed. Monica Dantas and Samuel Barbosa (São Paulo: Instituto de Estudos Brasileiros, 2021): 182–203.

https://doi.org/10.1515/9783111026527-006

reminded that the law governed various aspects of their lives, and they could turn to judicial institutions to sue for freedom or debate other issues pertaining to labor relations, property, masters' abuse, and crime. It is also plausible to think that numerous *quitandeiras* (female street vendors who sold fruit, vegetables, and cooked food), barbers, flower sellers, and porters came and went in such a busy part of the city. These people talked, exchanged information and gossip, and occasionally saw judges, lawyers, litigants, and even other enslaved persons going in and out of the courthouse. Amid the Court of Appeals' everyday dealings, it is plausible to think that some cases caught the attention of the street vendors and other workers and might have provided fresh topics for lively conversation and gossip. However, it was not just the free and enslaved inhabitants of Rio de Janeiro who had a certain familiarity with the Court of Appeals and other judicial institutions in imperial Brazil. In 1868, when the jurist Candido Mendes de Almeida published his *Atlas do Imperio do Brazil* (Atlas of the Brazilian Empire), he observed that the nation's territory was divided into 123 counties (*comarcas*), and subdivided into *juízos* and *varas*.[2] Thus, even if they were not "learned judges," that is, those with a law degree, magistrates were also present in smaller towns and cities. Regardless of discussions about the effectiveness, probity, and professionalization of Brazilian judicial officials, the fact is that judicial institutions were part of people's daily lives, if only as the presence of a solemn space in small towns or in the form of a notary who was known to the community.

Over the last thirty years or so, the historiography of Brazilian slavery has been heavily based on documents produced by judicial institutions. Many of these works focus on the proceedings of the Court of Appeals of Rio de Janeiro, but several studies are analyses of legal proceedings involving enslaved persons in other instances and judicial districts of imperial Brazil. While many scholars have analyzed civil matters regarding the determination of legal status, it is also noteworthy that there has been considerable literature on aspects of the lives of freed and enslaved persons involved in criminal cases. Furthermore, it should be noted that, more recently, intense academic production has emerged which analyzes court cases in the north and northeast of the country.[3] These works rely on a wide range of source documents, particularly court

2 Candido Mendes de Almeida, *Atlas do Imperio do Brazil* (Rio de Janeiro: Lithographia do Instituto Philomathico, 1868). Further details on the division of counties, the occupancy of their offices, and statistics regarding court cases can be found in the Ministry of Justice's annual reports available at http://ddsnext.crl.edu/titles/107#?c=4&m=0&s=0&cv=0&r=0&xywh=-217%2C-250%2C4337%2C3060 [accessed 23.09.2022].

3 A partial list includes Marília Bueno de Araújo Ariza, *O ofício da liberdade: trabalhadores libertandos em São Paulo e Campinas, 1830–1888* (São Paulo: Alameda, 2014); Elciene Azevedo, *O direito dos escravos: lutas jurídicas e abolicionismo na província de São Paulo* (Campinas: Editora da Unicamp, 2010); Sidney Chalhoub, *Visões da liberdade: uma história das últimas décadas da escravidão na corte* (São Paulo: Companhia das Letras, 1990); Jéssyka Sâmya Ladislau Pereira Costa, "A trajetória de Catharina Maria Roza da Conceição e a escravidão ilegal no norte imperial," *Revista Semina* 17, no. 1 (2018): 81–101; Mariana Dias Paes, *Escravidão e direito: o estatuto jurídico dos escravos no Brasil*

cases. Despite reservations about the capacity of such cases to bring to light the "voice of the enslaved," they are certainly a valuable source for revealing their ways of life and conceptions of the law and justice. Through the narratives of these judicial proceedings, we can identify strategies for achieving and maintaining freedom, the complexities of labor relations and dependence, and repertoires of resistance, among others. These studies analyzed several aspects of slavery law, both in the colonial period and nineteenth-century Brazil. Generally, they depart from the perspective of slave agency[4] and the idea of the law as an "arena of struggle."[5] According to this literature, the enslaved, freedpersons, and free workers were actors with lay understandings of the law and justice who acted under the guidance of "customary practices" and resorted to courts to dispute and negotiate interpretations of specific laws. More recently, historians have also focused on the use of courts by free and freed persons to curb illegal enslavement and to protect themselves from the frequent threat to free status in a society marked by the structural precariousness of freedom.[6] After decades of research, we have established a body of knowledge about several questions regarding the relationship between

oitocentista, 1860–1888 (São Paulo: Alameda, 2019); Keila Grinberg, *O fiador dos brasileiros: cidadania, escravidão e direito civil no tempo de Antonio Pereira Rebouças* (Rio de Janeiro: Civilização Brasileira, 2002); Keila Grinberg and Beatriz Mamigonian, "Le crime de réduction à l'esclavage d'une personne libre (Brésil, XIXe siècle)," *Brésil(s): sciences humaines et sociales* 11 (2017); Silvia Hunold Lara, *Campos da violência: escravos e senhores da Capitania do Rio de Janeiro, 1750–1808* (São Paulo: Paz e Terra, 1998); Maria Helena Machado, *Crime e escravidão: trabalho, luta e resistência nas lavouras paulistas, 1830–1888* (São Paulo: Editora da Universidade de São Paulo, 2018); Hebe Maria Mattos, *Das cores do silêncio: os significados da liberdade no Sudeste escravista* (Rio de Janeiro: Nova Fronteira, 1998); Antonia Marcia Nogueira, *Desventuras de Hypolita: luta contra a escravidão ilegal no sertão, Crato e Exu, século XIX* (Natal: Editora da Universidade Federal do Rio Grande do Norte, 2015); Fernanda Pinheiro, *Em defesa da liberdade: libertos, coartados e livres de cor nos tribunais do Antigo Regime português, Mariana e Lisboa, 1720–1819* (Belo Horizonte: Fino Traço, 2018); Ricardo Figueiredo Pirola, *Escravos e rebeldes nos tribunais do Império: uma história social da lei de 10 de junho de 1835* (Rio de Janeiro: Arquivo Nacional, 2015); Victor Hugo Siqueira, *Entre togas e grilhões: o acesso à justiça dos escravizados no Maranhão oitocentista, 1860–1888* (São Paulo: Alameda, 2021).

4 Silvia Hunold Lara and Joseli Maria Nunes Mendonça, "Apresentação," in *Direitos e justiças no Brasil: ensaios de história social*, ed. Silvia Hunold Lara and Joseli Maria Nunes Mendonça (Campinas: Editora da Unicamp, 2006): 9–22; Maria Helena Machado, "Em torno da autonomia escrava: uma nova direção para a história social da escravidão," *Revista Brasileira de História* 8, no. 16 (1988): 143–60.

5 Sidney Chalhoub and Fernando Teixeira da Silva, "Sujeitos no imaginário acadêmico: escravos e trabalhadores na historiografia brasileira desde os anos 1980," *Cadernos AEL* 14, no. 26 (2009): 7–47; Edward Thompson, *Whigs and Hunters: the Origins of the Black Act* (London: Breviary Stuff Publications, 2013): 171–210.

6 Sidney Chalhoub, *A força da escravidão: ilegalidade e costume no Brasil oitocentista* (São Paulo: Companhia das Letras, 2012); Mariana Dias Paes, *Esclavos y tierras entre posesión y títulos: la construcción social del derecho de propiedad en Brasil, siglo XIX* (Frankfurt am Main: Max Planck Institute for Legal History and Legal Theory, 2021); Ariana Moreira Espíndola, "Papéis da escravidão: a matrícula especial de escravos (1871)" (master's thesis, Universidade Federal de Santa Catarina, 2016); Henrique Espada Lima, "Sob o domínio da precariedade: escravidão e os significados da liberdade de trabalho no século XIX," *Topoi* 6, no. 11 (2005): 289–326.

law and slavery in imperial Brazil. Faced with such a robust set of analyses and a plethora of lawsuits spread across archives found throughout the country, I believe we can go a step further and consider the courts to be not only "arenas of struggle" – that is, places where meanings of laws were disputed and negotiated – but also places where the concrete meaning of norms – that is, the law itself – was produced. I will develop this idea in the following sections, and use it as a basis for presenting a research agenda on slavery law in nineteenth-century Brazil. To that end, I will follow the paths indicated by a lawsuit filed against Joana, Ana, Flávio, and Ricardo by José Delfino da Silva in 1861.

2 The Case of Joana, Ana, Flávio and Ricardo

On July 19, 1867, as on so many other days in their careers, the black-gowned judges of the Court of Appeals of Rio de Janeiro alit from their carriages outside the courthouse entrance for another day of sessions. That year, the court would receive 85 appeals from the provinces of the empire.[7] Among them was the case the judges were going to consider that day. It was a somewhat curious case – so curious, in fact, that perhaps jocular comments about it had spread among the court staff and even among the *quitandeiras* and other street vendors who were in the area that day. The imbroglio that led to a lawsuit had begun six years earlier, in the small mining town of Itabira do Mato Dentro, in Minas Gerais province. In 1833, Itabira do Mato Dentro had a population of 2,539 inhabitants, of whom 380 were white, 1,023 were *pardo* (mixed race or brown), and 1,136 were black. Of the total population, 903 were enslaved. By 1872, the town's population had grown to 7,810 inhabitants, of whom 1,821 were enslaved. In the 1860s, 53 percent of the slaveowners in Itabira owned up to five enslaved persons. The decline in the proportion of enslaved people and the aging of this population suggest that Itabira was also affected by the interprovincial slave trade, which drained enslaved workers to the coffee-growing regions, especially after the end of the Transatlantic slave trade in the 1850s.[8] In 1861, the town received a visit from the Capuchin missionary Friar Francisco de Coriolano. The visit of a missionary, in itself, would have been enough to cause a stir among the inhabitants of a town nestled in the mountainous central region of the province. However, the friar's stay would generate even more excitement than the usual missionary visits. During his sojourn in the town, he received a report charging that José Delfino da Silva was holding his sisters-in-law Joana and Ana and his nephews Flávio and Ricardo as slaves. Then, in the presence of Father

7 Martim Francisco Ribeiro de Andrada, *Relatorio do Ministerio da Justiça apresentado à Assembléa Geral Legislativa na segunda sessão de decima-terceira legislatura* (Rio de Janeiro: Typographia Perseverança, 1868): 7.

8 Maura Silveira Gonçalves de Britto, "Com luz de ferreiro: práticas do ofício nas Minas do ferro escravistas, século XIX" (master's thesis, Universidade Federal de Ouro Preto, 2011): 47–68.

Evêncio and the vicar of Lagoa, the missionary sent for José Delfino and ordered him to set his relatives free. José Delfino refused to manumit them on the grounds that he did not own the enslaved persons, who belonged to his wife. Furthermore, he was heavily indebted, having sold Joana to Captain Felício José da Silva to pay off some of his debts.[9] Enraged, the missionary locked the door, raised a crucifix, and threatened José Delfino with excommunication and eternal damnation if the slave owner did not sign a letter of manumission for his relatives on the spot. Terrified, José Delfino signed the letter, but after he left, went about town loudly denouncing what had just occurred. Taking some people's advice, José Delfino then decided to sue to annul the freedom he had granted to Joana, Ana, Flávio, and Ricardo.[10]

Despite the peculiarities of this case and the gossip it might have caused among free and enslaved inhabitants of Itabira, it sheds light on several aspects of the relationship between enslaved and free persons and the law, which can also be glimpsed in other court cases in imperial Brazil. In the following sections, I will point out some of these aspects that merit more attention in future research on law and slavery.

3 Memories and Hopes

When they learned that the missionary had forced José Delfino to free them, Joana, Ana, Flávio, and Ricardo went to the home of Captain Felício da Silva and asked him to take them in. The four already knew the captain. A witness even stated that "Joana was always on the run and hiding in Felício da Silva's house, for which reason the defendant [José Delfino] had negotiated her [sale] with him."[11] And why did Joana, Ana, Flávio, and Ricardo adopt the strategy of seeking a safe haven with a captain? It is possible that, throughout their life in slavery, they had heard reports of other enslaved or freed persons adopting similar strategies. There was a deeply held belief among the enslaved that their owners could not be violent or arbitrary. When they were, some people understood that the enslaved could resort to the aid of the authorities, whether they were linked to the judiciary or not. Therefore, resorting to Captain Felício da Silva for protection could have been one of these cases. Another possibility often envisaged by enslaved persons was a change of owner, which, perhaps, was a goal Joana pursued, as she had frequented Captain da Silva's house before the imbroglio with the

9 For an analysis of the widespread use of enslaved persons as collateral and payment for debts, with a special focus on legal proceedings, see Clemente Gentil Penna, "Economias urbanas: capital, créditos e escravidão na cidade do Rio de Janeiro, c. 1820–1860" (PhD diss., Universidade Federal do Rio de Janeiro, 2019).

10 Arquivo Nacional do Rio de Janeiro, processo 11.232, fundo 84 Relação do Rio de Janeiro, série apelação cível, código de referência 84.0.ACI.00093, apelante Ana, apelado José Delfino da Silva, ano inicial 1861, ano final 1867, caixa 3.684, local Itabira, microfilme NA_063_2006.

11 Arquivo Nacional do Rio de Janeiro, processo 11.232, f. 38.

missionary. It is important to point out that not even the captain considered the manumission José Delfino granted to be valid, as he argued that José Delfino could not free a slave owned by another person. The fact that the captain did not consider Joana free makes the actions taken by Joana, Ana, Flávio, and Ricardo even more complex.[12] In recent years, Brazilian historiography has identified cases in which captives sought to "change masters" or find patronage to renegotiate their living conditions in captivity. These acts were guided by shared knowledge among the enslaved population regarding the limits of captivity and the power to punish, as well as expectations regarding masters' behavior in the master-slave relationship.[13] Sometimes, this shared understanding is portrayed as the result of the circulation among captives of legal interpretations and debates which were taking place in imperial Brazil.[14] It is true that enslaved and freed persons shared information about norms, and that, in the course of these interactions, they formed their own understandings and interpretations of slavery law.[15] My proposal is to add a new layer to this knowledge, which is already firmly established in Brazilian historiography.

In his classic work on the enslaved family, Slenes works with the term "memories and hopes" to refer to the "formation of memories, plans, worldviews and identities" among enslaved Africans in Brazil.[16] He argues that the vast majority of enslaved people in the southeast – where most of the enslaved workforce was concentrated in the nineteenth century – either came from regions of West Africa that shared several aspects of a common cultural background or were direct descendants of those Africans. Thus, despite all the violence of the process of enslavement and the Transatlantic slave trade, these captives did not lose their cultural "memories," which were fundamental to their life strategies, the formation of identities, and their "hopes" for freedom, autonomy, and rights in Brazil.[17] The law is one of the main cultural expressions of any society. Thus, conceptions of norms, institutions, and legal principles of their societies of origin were part of the cultural framework – the "memories" – of enslaved Africans in Brazil, as well as one of the structuring elements of their relationship with the courts and other judicial institutions of imperial Brazil.[18] Furthermore, after their capture, enslaved

12 Arquivo Nacional do Rio de Janeiro, processo 11.232, f. 48–49.

13 Lara, *Campos da violência*: 57–72, 238; Ricardo Figueiredo Pirola, "Escravos e rebeldes na justiça imperial: dois casos de assassinatos senhoriais em Campos dos Goytacazes (RJ), 1873," *Afro-Ásia* 51 (2015): 52–54.

14 Pirola, "Escravos e rebeldes na justiça imperial": 51–66.

15 Luiz Geraldo Silva, "Esperança de liberdade: interpretações populares da abolição ilustrada (1773–1774)," *Revista de História* 144 (2001): 107–49.

16 Robert Slenes, *Na senzala, uma flor: esperanças e recordações na formação da família escrava, Brasil Sudeste, século XIX* (Campinas: Editora da Unicamp, 2011): 17–27.

17 Robert Slenes, "Malungo, ngoma vem! África coberta e descoberta do Brasil," *Revista USP* 12 (1992): 48–67.

18 Mariana Dias Paes, "Ser dependente no Império do Brasil: terra e trabalho em processos judiciais," *Población & Sociedad* 27, no. 2 (2020): 8–29.

Africans could be held for months in Africa's colonial port cities before being embarked for the Americas.[19] While they were being held in those ports, they came into contact with the specific norms and institutions of colonial hubs, which also shaped their conceptions of the law. This created new "memories" that would play a central role in shaping their experiences of slavery and freedom in Brazil, as well as the strategies they would adopt in the judicial struggle for better living conditions and autonomy.

In Benguela (in present-day Angola), there were cases of slaves who adopted strategies such as committing petty crimes with the aim of being sold to different owners.[20] However, some documents indicate that the possibility of getting a different master and seeking out authority figures to negotiate the conditions of slavery also existed in African societies not directly subject to Portuguese colonial rule. For example, between 1849 and 1857, Ladislaus Magyar travelled through the interior of Angola, in the Bié region, and reported situations in which slaves were unhappy with the treatment they received from their owners and fled. However, when they escaped, they went to the house of another master who was powerful, influential, and already known to the enslaved person. There, the captive would kill an animal and offer himself as a slave to the new owner to compensate for the damage. This practice was recognized by local law, and former masters rarely recovered slaves who had changed owners in this way.[21] Therefore, the actions of Joana, Ana, Flávio, and Ricardo can be interpreted in the light of the already established historiographical perspective – that is, information about the law circulated among slaves and influenced their strategies. But, it can also be interpreted by taking into account the possibility that enslaved persons retained "memories" about the law in their African communities of origin, and these "memories" played an important role in their interactions with the law in imperial Brazil. What were these memories, how were they mobilized in Brazil, and how did they shape the making of imperial law? These are questions that can be developed in the future, mainly in dialogue with the extensive literature on African history produced in Brazil in recent years.[22]

19 Luiz Felipe de Alencastro, *O trato dos viventes: formação do Brasil no Atlântico Sul* (São Paulo: Companhia das Letras, 2000): 146–47; Mariana Candido, *An African Slaving Port and the Atlantic World: Benguela and Its Hinterland* (Cambridge: Cambridge University Press, 2013); Daniel Domingues Silva, *The Atlantic Slave Trade from West Central Africa, 1780–1867* (Cambridge: Cambridge University Press, 2017).

20 Mariana Candido, *Fronteiras da escravidão: escravatura, comércio e identidade em Benguela, 1780–1850* (Benguela: Edições Universidade Katyavala Bwila/Ondjiri Editores, 2018): 234. Esteban Alfaro Salas is studying more details on these cases of changing owners in Benguela as part of his doctoral research at Notre Dame University.

21 Ladislaus Magyar, *Reisen in Süd-Afrika in den Jahren 1849 bis 1857* (Leipzig: Verlag von Lauffer & Stolp, 1859): 287–90.

22 Escaping to other slave owners' homes is not the only "memory" found in court proceedings. In Dias Paes, "Ser dependente no Império do Brasil," for example, I analyze how "memories" may have influenced the enslaved persons' strategies regarding the acquisition and recognition of land rights.

4 A Kaleidoscope of Norms

Joana, Ana, Flávio, and Ricardo waged a hard-fought battle in the courts over the legal status of free, conditionally freed, or enslaved persons. At the first instance, lawyer Claudino Pereira da Fonseca defended the interests of José Delfino, while the curator (*curador*), Pedro Anacleto da Silva Lopes, defended those of Joana, Ana, Flávio, and Ricardo. Fonseca was a newly qualified lawyer, having obtained a bachelor's degree in law from the São Paulo Law School in 1858, three years before the proceedings began.[23] However, the curator, Lopes, did not have a law degree.[24] He was what was called a "provisioned" advocate (*advogado provisionado*) – someone who had not attended law school, but wanted to act as a lawyer and had obtained authorization to do so from the judicial authorities.[25] Both parties spared no effort to defend their clients. In this battle, they resorted to a kaleidoscope of norms: the decrees and laws of the imperial government, the imperial constitution, law books published between the sixteenth and nineteenth centuries, Roman law, the Philippine Ordinances, and charters from the colonial period. Resorting to norms and legal texts from the nineteenth century and earlier periods was common practice in legal proceedings involving enslaved persons.[26] This phenomenon was not due to supposed gaps in slavery law, but to the structure of the Brazilian Empire's legal framework, which was largely based on so-called *ius commune*.[27] *Ius commune* was the legal framework which operated within the centuries-old Iberian courts of the modern age, and was profoundly different from "liberal" legal systems.[28] Written laws were not hierarchically superior to

23 Information available at https://arcadas.org.br/antigos-alunos/ [accessed 23.09.2022].

24 Antonio de Assis Martins, *Almanak administrativo, civil e industrial da Provincia de Minas-Geraes do anno de 1869 para servir no de 1870* (Rio de Janeiro: Typographia do Diario do Rio de Janeiro, 1870): 137.

25 "Provisioned" lawyers and "solicitors" were common throughout the Portuguese Empire. For details on their appointment in imperial Brazil and their relationship with slavery law, see Siqueira, *Entre togas e grilhões*. For a discussion of their role in Goa, see Luís Cabral de Oliveira, "Quem sabe o que é um advogado? A resposta de Luís Manuel Júlio Frederico Gonçalves às tentativas de reforma dos provisionários goeses em 1869," *Jahrbuch für Geschichte Lateinamerikas* 52, no. 1 (2015): 207–29. In Imperial Brazil, outstanding provisioned lawyers include Antonio Pereira Rebouças and Luiz Gama. Elciene Azevedo, *Orfeu de carapinha: a trajetória de Luiz Gama na imperial cidade de São Paulo* (Campinas: Editora da Unicamp, 2005); Ligia Fonseca Ferreira, *Lições de resistência: artigos de Luiz Gama na imprensa de São Paulo e do Rio de Janeiro* (São Paulo: Edições Sesc São Paulo, 2020); Grinberg, *O fiador dos brasileiros*.

26 Dias Paes, *Escravidão e direito*: 22; Grinberg, *O fiador dos brasileiros*: 221, 244, 250–51, 258–59; Pinheiro, *Em defesa da liberdade*.

27 Dias Paes, *Esclavos y tierras entre posesión y títulos*.

28 Several proposals for liberal legal systems came from the so-called "legal enlightenment," an eighteenth-century movement that, among other issues, proposed that legislation – in the sense of written rules issued by state authorities – was the source of law *par excellence* and superior to the others sources which, many times, were not even considered valid sources at all. Paradigmatic of these

other norms as a source of law. Written legislation was not intended to regulate every aspect of life. Neither was it the embodiment of the "law," as late eighteenth- and nineteenth-century movements pro codification defended. In this sense, as they did not play a major role within *ius commune*, written legislation could be challenged, contradicted, and reformulated by judicial decisions and doctrinal texts. Deciding "against" a "law" was part of the "rules of the game."[29]

Thus, the absence of a given piece of legislation – in the "liberal" sense of the term – did not mean the absence of legal norms. In nineteenth-century Brazil, there was no overlap between "written legislation" and "the law." As historians, we must have a clearer idea of the legal framework of the time and, therefore, work with an idea of "norms" that is much broader than that which is generally found in works on slavery and law. By doing so, we will avoid falling into traps, such as believing that something that was not expressly regulated by written laws was "customary practice," and that what was against the letter of pieces of legislation was automatically "illegal." Furthermore, we should not assume that two recurrent narratives among nineteenth-century jurists were valid: first, the idea that the absence of a specific code or written law on slavery generated chaos, confusion, and uncertainty in imperial courts, leaving room for all kinds of arbitrary behavior and, secondly, the argument that the norms governing slavery were rooted in a Roman law that was lost in the mists of time. In *ius commune*, when making decisions on specific cases, no norms – whether written or otherwise – had absolute force. Judges' decisions were supposed to be guided by "equity" and "social peace." When deciding a specific case, judges were supposed to assess its unique circumstances and, so far as possible, seek to maintain "order" and the "status quo," even if that meant making a decision that went against the strict letter of one or another legislative device. In this sense, *ius commune* did not have universalizing and hegemonic pretensions, as is the case of liberal legal systems, which aim to be the only legitimate normative system applied by states in the jurisdictions they control.

---

proposals was that of Cesare Beccaria, according to whom judges should be the only "voice of the law," not its producer. For an introduction to this subject, see Raffaele Ajello, *Arcana juris: diritto e politica nel Settecento italiano* (Napoli: Jovene, 1976); Italo Birocchi, *Alla ricerca dell'ordine* (Torino: Giappichelli, 2002); Pietro Costa, *Il progeto giuridico: richerche sulla giurisprudenza del liberalismo classico* (Milano: Giuffré, 1974); Jean-Louis Halperin, *L'impossible code civil* (Paris: Presses Universitaires de France, 1992); António Manuel Hespanha, *Guiando a mão invisível: direitos, Estado e lei no liberalismo monárquico português* (Coimbra: Almedina, 2004); Michel Villey, *A formação do pensamento jurídico moderno* (São Paulo: Martins Fonts, 2006). For criticisms of legal liberalism's proposals, see Lynn Hunt, *A invenção dos direitos humanos: uma história* (São Paulo: Companhia das Letras, 2007); Barbara Welke, *Law and the Borders of Belonging in the Long Nineteenth Century United States* (Cambridge: Cambridge University Press, 2010).

29 Gustavo César Machado Cabral, *Ius commune: uma introdução à história do direito comum do Medievo à Idade Moderna* (Rio de Janeiro: Lumen Juris, 2019); Dias Paes, *Esclavos y tierras entre posesión y títulos*; Tamar Herzog, *A Short History of European Law: The Last Two and a Half Millennia* (Cambridge: Harvard University Press, 2019).

In *ius commune*, as long as the ultimate goals of sustaining order and social stability were maintained, there was no problem with resorting to other normative systems. An example of this is the concomitant existence of *ius commune* and ecclesiastical law in all Portuguese colonial jurisdictions and imperial Brazil. Ecclesiastical law and its courts are a subject yet to be explored by the historiography that deals with slavery and law in nineteenth-century Brazil.[30] Just as the law was part of people's daily lives throughout imperial Brazil, so were the Church and its institutions, which had the power to "administer justice." It should be noted that in the case of Joana, Ana, Flávio, and Ricardo, there were three ecclesiastical authorities involved in the imbroglio: a missionary, a priest, and a vicar. In general, vicars could have jurisdiction. In the aforementioned case, just before ordering the letter of manumission to be drafted, the missionary asked the priest and the vicar if they would acquit the defendant and, in view of their negative response, understood "that the sentence had been passed."[31] In the context of imperial Brazil, saying "the sentence had been passed" was not just a figure of speech, but an explicit allusion to the jurisdictional functions of the Church and its officers.

The organization of ecclesiastical courts was similar to that of their secular counterparts. The first instance (the equivalent of the lower court) was episcopal justice, exercised by the vicars-general and, when there were none in the locality, by vicars-forane. The second instance was the Metropolitan Court of Appeals (*Relação Metropolitana*), a superior ecclesiastical court located in the city of Salvador.[32] Imperial Brazil was not a secular state. The presence of church agents involved in issues related to slavery and freedom was not limited to the colonial period, nor was it unique to the case of Joana, Ana, Flávio, and Ricardo. The presence of these agents in cases tried in the empire's secular courts indicates a layer of nineteenth-century slavery law that, as yet, has not been the subject of detailed study.

Just as the centuries-old judicial archives hold a wealth of documents that tell the story of slavery law,[33] the ecclesiastical archives also contain valuable documents for understanding other aspects of that history. However, these documents have rarely been used in the analysis of slavery law in imperial Brazil. Like the well-established branch of historical research that works with these sources to analyze slavery law in other parts of Latin America,[34] the article published by Farias shows the vast potential

30 There are works on the colonial period which analyze cases involving enslaved persons within the scope of the Inquisition, such as Charlotte de Castelnau-L'Estoile, *Páscoa et ses deux maris: une esclave entre Angola, Brésil et Portugal au XVIIe siècle* (Paris: Presses Universitaires de France, 2019).

31 Arquivo Nacional do Rio de Janeiro, processo 11.232, f. 52.

32 For more details on the organization of the ecclesiastical courts, see Manoel do Monte Rodrigues de Araujo, *Elementos de direito ecclesiastico publico e particular em relação à disciplina geral da Igreja e com aplicação aos usos da Igreja do Brasil* (Rio de Janeiro: Antonio Gonçalves Guimarães & Ca, 1857).

33 Monica Dantas and Filipe Nicoletti Ribeiro, "A importância dos acervos judiciais para a pesquisa em história: um percurso," *Lex Cult* 4, no. 2 (2020): 47–87.

34 Michelle McKinley, *Fractional Freedoms: Slavery, Intimacy, and Legal Mobilization in Colonial Lima, 1600–1700* (Cambridge: Cambridge University Press, 2016); Brian Owensby, "How Juan and Leonor Won

of ecclesiastical legal proceedings to enrich the history of slavery law in imperial Brazil. In it, Farias analyzes divorce proceedings filed by *Mina* African women in which notions of honor and honesty and discourses about gender and race played a central role. The judicial cases Farias analyzed show how judges, lawyers, priests, and enslaved and freed persons took part in processes of normative production within ecclesiastical courts.[35]

In nineteenth-century Brazil, many of the *Minas* were Muslims.[36] Historians have been analyzing the presence of enslaved Muslims in Brazil in the 1800s, their life strategies, and cultural practices for some time.[37] However, Islam is not just a religion. It is also a legal system. The Quran, which was even sold in imperial Rio de Janeiro,[38] is not only a sacred book, but one of the main sources of norms in Islamic law. In that light, to what extent would "memories" of Islamic law have shaped enslaved persons' relations with the Brazilian courts?

Furthermore, Islamic law was also closely related to *ius commune* on the Iberian Peninsula. When referring to the Philippine Ordinances, just mentioning that the rules of the law of slavery present there refer primarily to Muslim slaves is not enough to understand the real influence that Islamic law may have had in shaping the laws on slavery in the Portuguese Empire and, later, imperial Brazil. Studies on Islamic slavery law in general,[39] and research on slavery on the Iberian Peninsula in particular,[40] indicate that the prolonged presence of Muslims in the region and the intense economic and cultural exchange between Christian and Islamic societies in the Mediterranean might have had a huge impact on the making of law in both cultures, which may also have influenced the norms governing slavery in the Americas.

Their Freedom: Litigation and Liberty in Seventeenth-Century Mexico," *Hispanic American Historical Review* 85 (2005): 39–79.

35 "Mina" was the generic term used in Brazil to designate enslaved Africans embarked in ports located on the Costa da Mina (Gold Coast and Slave Coast) in West Africa. Juliana Barreto Farias, "Diz a preta mina: cores e categorias sociais nos processos de divórcio abertos por africanas ocidentais, Rio de Janeiro, século XIX," *Estudos Ibero-Americanos* 44, no. 3 (2018): 470–83.

36 Juliana Barreto Farias, "Mercados Minas: africanos ocidentais na Praça do Mercado do Rio de Janeiro, 1830–1890" (PhD diss., Universidade de São Paulo, 2012): 20.

37 Marcus Carvalho, *Flávio dos Santos Gomes and João José Reis, O alufá Rufino: tráfico, escravidão e liberdade no Atlântico Negro, c. 1822–c. 1853* (São Paulo: Companhia das Letras, 2010); João José Reis, *Rebelião escrava no Brasil: a história do Levante dos Malês de 1835* (São Paulo: Companhia das Letras, 2003).

38 Alberto da Costa e Silva, "Buying and Selling Korans in Nineteenth-Century Rio de Janeiro," in *Rethinking the African Diaspora: The Making of a Black World in the Bight of Benin and Brazil*, ed. Kristin Mann and Edna Bay (London: Frank Class, 2001): 83–90.

39 Chouki El Hamel, *Black Morocco: A History of Slavery, Race, and Islam* (Cambridge: Cambridge University Press, 2013); Joshua White, "Slavery, Manumission, and Freedom Suits in the Early Modern Ottoman Empire," in *Slaves and Agency in the Ottoman Empire*, ed. Stephan Conermann and Gül Şen (Göttingen: Vandenhoeck & Ruprecht, 2020): 283–320.

40 Debra Blumenthal, *Enemies and Familiars: Slavery and Mastery in Fifteenth-Century Valencia* (Ithaca: Cornell University Press, 2009).

In short, with regard to the kaleidoscope of norms that operated in imperial Brazil, we must be careful not to fall into the traps of fetishizing written legislation and believing in the myth of Roman law. It was not just written laws and supposedly Roman law that determined the legal terms of master-slave relations. The normative repertoires available in that society were much more complex and varied. Counter-readings of sources can provide a more detailed analysis of how they operated and how they were used by different historical subjects in the process of creating slavery law. How was the law of imperial Brazil formed through an intertwining of *ius commune* rules, ecclesiastical law, various African legal systems, and Islamic law? How was this normative framework given new meaning by the liberal projects that became hegemonic in the second half of the nineteenth century? Questions like these are important for the development of the field of law and slavery in the coming years.

5 Who Produces Slavery Law?

Let us return to the case of Joana, Ana, Flávio, and Ricardo. The first party who went to court to discuss the issue was José Delfino. His lawyer filed a petition requesting that the case be assessed, as his client considered Joana, Ana, Flávio, and Ricardo to be enslaved but could not sell them because potential buyers claimed to have heard they were free. In the petition, there is no indication of the type of lawsuit being filed, just a request to resolve the issue of the alleged slaves' legal status.[41] This was normal practice from the standpoint of *ius commune*. Unlike liberal procedural law, in which procedures are mostly specified and differentiated, *ius commune* guaranteed the right to petition in broad terms, especially to those considered to be "miserable persons." The procedure by which the remedy was sought was not so important. For example, it was common practice for requests about the same conflict to be made to different authorities, such as judges and governors.[42]

Following a recurrent trend in court cases, after José Delfino filed his petition, the first legal debate was precisely about the type of procedure to be followed. Debates such as this were relatively common in Brazilian courts.[43] Shortly after being appointed curator of Joana, Ana, Flávio, and Ricardo, Pedro Anacleto argued before the judge that

41 Arquivo Nacional do Rio de Janeiro, processo 11.232, f. 3.

42 Mariana Candido, "African Freedom Suits and Portuguese Vassal Status: Legal Mechanisms for Fighting Enslavement in Benguela, Angola (1800–1830)," *Slavery & Abolition* 32, no. 3 (2011): 447–59; Pinheiro, *Em defesa da liberdade*. On the subject of petitions and their central role in the production of law in colonial Latin America, see Adrian Masters, "A Thousand Invisible Architects: Vassals, the Petition and Response System, and the Creation of Spanish Imperial Caste Legislation," *Hispanic American Historical Review* 98, no. 3 (2018): 377–406.

43 Mariana Dias Paes, "O procedimento de manutenção de liberdade no Brasil oitocentista," *Estudos Históricos* 29, no. 58 (2016): 339–60; Dias Paes, *Escravidão e direito*: 55–111; Pinheiro, *Em defesa da liberdade*.

José Delfino should file a "slavery suit" against his clients, since, in view of their condition as "miserable persons," the status of defendants would be more beneficial to them than that of plaintiffs in a "freedom suit." However, the judge disagreed. In his view, the appropriate legal action was a "freedom suit," since this was the procedure used in cases of people treated as slaves who wanted to have their "natural freedom" restored. To support this decision, the judge cited the well-known book *Doutrina das Ações* (Legal Actions Doctrine) by Portuguese jurist José Homem Corrêa Telles.[44] Corrêa Telles's book presented three types of judicial procedures that discussed people's legal status as free or enslaved: "freedom suits," "slavery suits," and "suits to exhibit a free person." This tripartite classification, however, was not exactly verified in several of the courts under Portuguese jurisdiction. For example, most of the lawsuits studied by Pinheiro (2018), which were filed in Lisbon and Mariana in the eighteenth and early nineteenth centuries, received the designation of *libelos*. There were also "requests," "notifications," "justifications," and "embargoes," among others. There are some "freedom *libelos*" and "reduction to captivity *libelos*," but these are few. In Benguela, the types of procedures used from 1850 onwards were "deposit," "[the crime of] enslaving a free person," "justification," and "claim of freedom (*reivindicação de liberdade*)."[45] In Cape Verde, the following types were identified: "evaluation (*louvação para avaliação*)," "civil suits of manumission (*autos cíveis de alforriado*)," and "civil suits of petition (*autos cíveis de petição*)."[46]

In nineteenth-century Brazil, the many different types of lawsuits used to determine a person's legal status were extensive. Like those in Lisbon, Benguela, and Cape Verde, they did not correspond to Côrrea Telles's tripartite classification, which the judge evoked in the case under analysis. The outlines of court cases in imperial Brazil, the requirements considered essential for processing them, and the types of procedures to be adopted also varied extensively, depending on the period and location.[47] It was the daily agency of historical subjects that ended up determining procedural rites. Judicial procedures were consolidated through each strategic choice that each enslaved person or curator made when filing a lawsuit, seeking to mold it within a specific procedure, through each challenge from masters and their lawyers to these procedures, through each judicial decision that enforced a rite, and through each reproduction of forms and formalities performed by court clerks, other judicial agents, and common folk. These everyday practices did not take place in a vacuum. They interacted with the most solemn sources of law – such as legislation and legal doctrine,

44 Arquivo Nacional do Rio de Janeiro, processo 11.232, f. 9–12.

45 Mariana Candido, Mariana Dias Paes, and Juelma de Matos Ngãla, *Introdução à história do direito em Angola* (forthcoming).

46 Preliminary survey of five randomly selected boxes from Cape Verde National Archives (Tribunal da Praia do Arquivo Nacional de Cabo Verde).

47 Dias Paes, "O procedimento de manutenção de liberdade": 347; Fernanda Pinheiro, "Transformações de uma prática contenciosa: as ações de liberdade produzidas em Mariana (1750/69 e 1850/69)," *Locus: revista de história* 17, no. 1 (2011): 253–71.

like Côrrea Telles's book – and with the various kinds of non-solemn normative knowledge that guided people's actions and strategies.

It is also worth remembering that, strictly speaking, there was no written legislation in nineteenth-century Brazil that explicitly granted the right for the enslaved to go to court or defined the process for doing so. However, by no means would we deny that this right existed. After all, thousands of lawsuits filed by enslaved persons abound in the Brazilian archives, and numerous judicial decisions and legal texts assumed that this was a possibility. This is a good example of what I have been calling the everyday production of law. Since colonial times, each lawsuit filed by an enslaved individual in all parts of the country was fundamental for the consolidation and conformation of captives' "right of action." "Memories" might have played an important role in the creation of this right. For example, the possibility of contesting illegal enslavement existed in West-Central African judicial institutions, such as the so-called Courts of Mucanos (*Tribunais de Mucanos*), and in Portuguese colonial hubs in West Africa.[48] Lawsuits for the definition of legal status were also a well-established practice on the Iberian Peninsula – involving both Christians and Muslims – and in other jurisdictions in the Americas.[49] Therefore, it is plausible to raise the hypothesis that, based on these various normative frameworks, a wide range of actors – jurists and non-jurists – mobilized norms and gave them new meanings. In these daily practices, in which understandings and knowledge were shared and habits and formalities were reproduced, the slavery law acquired concrete meanings. In this sense, these practices themselves were producers of slavery law in imperial Brazil.

---

48 Candido, "African Freedom Suits"; José Curto, "Struggling Against Enslavement: the Case of José Manuel in Benguela, 1816–20," *Canadian Journal of African Studies* 39, no. 1 (2005): 96–122; Mariana Dias Paes, "Shared Atlantic Legal Culture: the Case of a Freedom Suit in Benguela," *Atlantic Studies, Global Currents* 17 (2020): 419–40; Roquinaldo Ferreira, *Cross-Cultural Exchange in the Atlantic World: Angola and Brazil During the Era of the Slave Trade* (Cambridge: Cambridge University Press, 2012); Toby Green, "Baculamento or Encomienda? Legal Pluralisms and the Contestation of Power in the Pan-Atlantic World of the Sixteenth and Seventeenth centuries," *Journal of Global Slavery* 2 (2017): 310–36; Catarina Madeira-Santos, "Esclavage africain et traite atlantique confrontés: transactions langagières et juridiques (à propos du tribunal de mucanos dans l'Angola des XVIIe et XVIIIe siècles)," *Brésil(s): sciences humaines et sociales* 1 (2012): 127–48.

49 Blumenthal, *Enemies and Familiars*; Magdalena Candioti, "Free Womb Law, Legal Asynchronies, and Migrations: Suing for an Enslaved Woman's Child in Nineteenth-Century Río de la Plata," *The Americas* 77, no. 1 (2020): 73–99; Carmen Luz Cosme Puntiel and Aurora Vergara Figueroa, eds., *Demandando mi Libertad: mujeres negras y sus estrategias de Resistencia en la Nueva Granada, Venezuela y Cuba, 1700–1800* (Cali: Universidad Icesi, 2018); Alejandro De La Fuente, "Slaves and the Creation of Legal Rights in Cuba: coartación and papel," *Hispanic American Historical Review* 87, no. 4 (2007): 659–92; McKinley, *Fractional Freedoms*; Owensby, "How Juan and Leonor Won Their Freedom"; María de los Ángeles Meriño Fuentes and Aisnara Perera Díaz, *Estrategias de Libertad: un acercamiento a las acciones legales de los esclavos en Cuba, 1762–1872* (La Habana: Editorial de Ciencias Sociales, 2015); Keila Grinberg and Cristina Nogueira da Silva, "Soil Free from Slaves: Slave Law in Late 18th–Early 19th Century Portugal," *Slavery & Abolition* 32, no. 3 (2011): 431–46.

Legal history in general, and the history of slavery law in particular, are marked by a widespread dichotomy between "the law" vs. "reality" that unfolds into "the law" vs. "social practice," "law-in-action" vs. "law-in-the-books," "the law" vs. "customs," etc. These distinctions end up being unproductive, as they obscure the complex interactions that guide the everyday and non-solemn production of law. Legal categories and institutes do not have any meaning *per se* (although they are presented as if they did). Their concrete meanings are the result of shared understandings, habitual practices, and daily reiteration of forms.[50] In this sense, "practice" plays a decisive role in the construction of the concrete meanings of norms. In other words, "practice" is a key part of the process of normative production. Therefore, it is not just "practice" – it is also the law.[51] Let us take the example of possession. In general, this category is defined as the ability to hold something as one's own. But what is to hold something as one's own? What does it mean to possess someone as a slave? The validity or otherwise for a situation to be considered "possession" is determined by the shared understandings and practices of a given community. For example, in nineteenth-century Brazil, evidence of "possessing someone as a slave" included how a person was addressed, the fact that neighbors had always recognized them as being a slave, themselves or their children having been baptized as slaves, having been sold, tax having been paid on them, and so on. In other words, the concrete meaning of "possession" was given and reiterated by these small and recurrent everyday acts. These acts, in turn, were entangled with conceptions formed in more solemn spheres of normative production, such as legal doctrine, legislation, and so on.[52]

As a result of processes of assigning specific meanings to the legal category of "possession" that took place in Brazilian society, the legal idea of "possession of freedom," that is to "live as a free person," gained such strength in courts that a specific type of lawsuit was developed to address this matter: the so-called "maintenance of freedom suits."[53] Maintenance suits were used in Portuguese jurisdictions to deal with possession of assets in general. In addition, the idea of "possession of freedom" was also markedly present in Spanish and Portuguese jurisdictions.[54] However, the intertwining between debates on possession of freedom and the creation of a specific

50 Mariana Dias Paes, "Legal Files and Empires: Form and Materiality of the Benguela District Court Documents," *Administory: Zeitschrift für Verwaltungsgeschichte* 4 (2019): 53–70.

51 For a discussion on "normative production" and "normative knowledge," see Thomas Duve, "Rechtsgeschichte als Geschichte von Normativitätswissen?" in *Rechtsgeschichte – Legal History* 29 (2021): 41–68.

52 Dias Paes, "Legal Files and Empires"; Dias Paes, *Esclavos y tierras entre posesión y títulos.*

53 Dias Paes, "O procedimento de manutenção de liberdade."

54 Blumenthal, *Enemies and Familiars*; Dias Paes, "Shared Atlantic Legal Culture"; Dias Paes, *Esclavos y tierras entre posesión y títulos*; Vernon Valentine Palmer, *Through the Codes Darkly: Slave Law and Civil Law in Louisiana* (Clark: Lawbook Exchange, 2012): 135–49; Rebecca Scott, "Social Facts, Legal Fictions, and Re-Enslavement in the Diaspora of the Haitian Revolution," *Law and History Review* 35, no. 1 (2017): 9–30.

lawsuit to address this issue seems to have been unique to Brazilian society. Throughout the nineteenth century, maintenance of freedom lawsuits were recurrent in imperial courts and various debates on its procedures took place among jurists. At the current stage of research, we can assess that despite the fact that possession of freedom was a legal ideal present in other slavery jurisdictions, it did not necessarily generate a specific and regular kind of legal procedure, as it did in Brazil. Therefore, this specific process of normative production was not the act of one authority, of solemn legal rites, but the result of the daily reiteration of practices and repeated reproduction of formulas, formalities, and procedures.

It is also important to emphasize that the reiteration and habitual daily reproduction of practices and procedures could become entwined with the circumstances of a broader political context. A good example of this process is the Free Womb Law of 1871 and the debates over summary procedures in court cases discussing freedom. In the 1860s, the argument that suits regarding legal status should follow summary procedure began to appear in court proceedings. Although there was no consensus in the courts that summary procedure should be used in suits to determine legal status, jurist Agostinho Marques Perdigão Malheiro also stated that this was the appropriate procedure for such cases. The development of this legal argument took place in the context of debates about gradual emancipation, and the subject of procedures was taken up in debates within the Council of State. In the end, when the Free Womb Law was enacted, article 7 determined the use of summary procedure in freedom suits. After the enactment of the law, several legal texts were published to publicize the new rules on slavery law. The new regulations were also to be read and made public at Sunday masses. Within the courts, some lawyers put forward an extensive interpretation of article 7, arguing that, since freedom suits should follow summary procedure, it meant government recognition that the courts should favor freedom. Consequently, according to these same jurists, slavery suits should follow ordinary procedure, as it was a kind of procedure that acted against freedom.[55]

In other words, discussions about summary procedure in the context of the debates on the Free Womb Law shed light on how the daily process of normative production can be permeated by the political situation. In a context of debates about gradual emancipation, reiterated judicial practices, and arguments, engaged in dialogue with other legal texts, reached the highest levels of the empire and ended up being covered by the Free Womb Law. However, that law was not the final step in this process. Soon after its enactment, new legal interpretations were built up in courts, and shared understandings about its provisions were formed through the reading of books, daily

55 For detailed analysis of this entire debate involving the summary procedure in the context of the Free Womb Law, see Mariana Dias Paes, "Para além do ventre livre: a Lei de 1871 e as mudanças na arena dos tribunais," in *Ventres livres? Gênero, maternidade e legislação*, ed. Luciana da Cruz Brito, Flávio dos Santos Gomes, Maria Helena Machado and Iamara da Silva Viana (São Paulo: Editora Unesp, 2021).

conversations, priests' sermons at mass, newspaper articles, and so forth.[56] Generally speaking, when enslaved and free persons resorted to the courts of imperial Brazil, they were not acting *tabula rasa*. On the contrary, throughout their lives, in their daily interactions, these people had built up shared legal knowledge.

Let us return to the case of Joana, Ana, Flávio, and Ricardo to make this argument clearer. After he signed the manumission letter and the missionary unlocked the door so he could leave, José Delfino went out into the streets "like a madman," according to reports from people who met him on the road.[57] Let us make an effort to visualize this scene. At the time, Itabira do Mato Dentro had roughly seven thousand inhabitants. It was a small town nestled in the mountains of Minas Gerais. He photo below (Figure 1) was taken in 1955, that is, almost a century after the case of Joana, Ana, Flávio, and Ricardo. Therefore, at the time of the lawsuit, it was even smaller than the town we see in the photograph.

Fig. 1: Itabira do Mato Dentro in the mountains of Minas Gerais, 1955. Source: Arquivo Nacional do Rio de Janeiro, BR_RJANRIO_PH_0_FOT_04198_0073, https://commons.wikimedia.org/wiki/File:Itabira_(MG).tif.

The spectacle of someone going about "like a madman" and telling passersby that the missionary had just forced him to free his slaves certainly did not go unnoticed. We can assume that José Delfino became the "talk of the town." When commenting on the case, it is very likely that people – both free and enslaved – discussed the legitimacy of

56 Dias Paes, "Para além do ventre livre."

57 Arquivo Nacional do Rio de Janeiro, processo 11.232, f. 48.

manumissions issued "under duress." After all, the fact that the door was locked at the time of manumission was reiterated by several witnesses in the case, as they perceived it as an important element for demonstrating the invalidity of the legal act. Here again, it is clear that the attribution of concrete meaning to norms also occurs in non-solemn spaces. What did coercion and duress concretely mean in the context of drafting a legal document? According to the witnesses in Itabira, it meant locking the door and threatening the plaintiff with eternal damnation and excommunication. Thus, in the small town of Itabira, shared legal knowledge was being formed regarding the meaning of coercion, duress, control, and so forth.

Those closest to José Delfino, in turn, advised him on what he should do to retrieve his alleged slaves: he should go to the notary who had registered the letter and file a complaint that the document had been issued under duress. Although it is not as clear in the narrative of the court case, it seems that the simple fact of having gone to the notary, as advised, had no effect, so José Delfino ended up making a formal request to the judge for his complaint to be included in the letter of manumission. When taking these measures, José Delfino was assisted by Professor Honorato Caetano de Souza, who, as far as I could ascertain, was neither a bachelor-in-law nor a provisioned lawyer.[58] Getting legal advice from members of one's own community – as José Delfino had done – was also common practice in other legal cases. This indicates that people talked about the law and shared legal knowledge, even if it was lay legal knowledge. Also, Captain Felício da Silva's behavior indicates that knowledge of the law was shared among members of certain communities. As soon as he learned of what had occurred, he immediately had José Delfino cited in a lawsuit to safeguard the captain's rights over Joana.[59]

Thus, after manumission was granted in the missionary's presence, the different actors in this imbroglio took the steps they deemed most appropriate to safeguard what they considered to be their rights. Joana, Ana, Flávio, and Ricardo went to Captain Felício da Silva's house. José Delfino went to the notary and then to court, with the aim of inscribing in the letter of manumission the fact that it had been issued under duress. And Captain Felício da Silva sent a summons to José Delfino to safeguard his rights of ownership over Joana. The actions of each of these people were guided by notions of law and justice immersed in their experiences, memories, and daily learning about norms and legal procedures. Furthermore, each of these actions reflected specific meanings of norms, which produced and configured slavery law on a daily basis in imperial Brazil. Our knowledge of how these understandings and meanings were shared among the most diverse historical actors in imperial Brazil is still very incipient. Baltazar and Cardim show how laws were read out during Sunday services in colonial times.[60] As I

58 Arquivo Nacional do Rio de Janeiro, processo 11.232, f. 45.

59 Arquivo Nacional do Rio de Janeiro, processo 11.232, f. 48.

60 Miguel Baltazar and Pedro Cardim, "A difusão da legislação régia (1621–1808)," in *Um reino e suas repúblicas no Atlântico: comunicações políticas entre Portugal, Brasil e Angola nos séculos XVII e XVIII*, ed. João Fragoso and Nuno Gonçalo Monteiro (Rio de Janeiro: Civilização Brasileira, 2017): 161–207.

mentioned, this practice was reiterated in the context of the Free Womb Law. Silva recounts how the Portuguese Charter of 1773 was published and debated by slaves and freedmen in Paraíba.[61] Cowling, in turn, emphasizes the role of everyday conversations and gossip in the circulation of information among enslaved women.[62] This is a subject that remains to be explored and can help us better understand the process of producing slavery law.

6 Conclusion

Let us return to that day on July 19, 1867, when the judges of the Rio de Janeiro Court of Appeals met to consider the case of Joana, Ana, Flávio, and Ricardo. They decided that the appeal against the lower court's decision had been filed after the legal deadline. This decision, in turn, reaffirmed the idea that, to be valid, legal acts should be carried out with "free expression of will," that is, without coercion. The testimony of witnesses, their descriptions of the closed door, and the terrifying threats uttered by the missionary – already known among the local residents as someone who "mistreated everyone for the smallest thing, telling them to shut up, and cursing"[63] – were decisive for the judge to determine that a "free expression of will" was lacking when José Delfino signed the manumission letter for Joana, Ana, Flávio, and Ricardo. Thus, this case allows us to glimpse different paths and perspectives that can guide our future research on slavery law. We have already found that norms, information, and interpretations circulated among enslaved and freed persons. We can go a step further and, in addition to identifying other aspects of this movement, consider that there was also the presence of "memories" of other legal systems that were shared within these communities.

We have already found that courts were an "arena of struggle." We can go a step further and consider them to be spaces of normative production as well, with enslaved persons and other actors involved in legal proceedings as agents of that production. In the courts, law was not only disputed, it was created. After all, through memories, shared legal knowledge, daily practice, and reiterated formalities, people created specific meanings for norms. This process of normative production did not take place in a vacuum. In addition to entangle with more general political and economic contexts, it was permeated by various normative frameworks: African legal systems, *ius commune*, ecclesiastical law, Islamic law, and, perhaps, others still to be discovered. Finally, it is important to emphasize that this was also an asymmetric

61 Silva, "Esperança de liberdade."

62 Camillia Cowling, *Conceiving Freedom: Women of Color, Gender, and Abolition of Slavery in Havana and Rio de Janeiro* (Chapel Hill: University of North Carolina Press, 2013): 145–48.

63 Arquivo Nacional do Rio de Janeiro, processo 11.232, f. 46.

process that was marked by violence. If it is true that, in imperial Brazil, enslaved persons managed to forge certain configurations of slavery law, it is also true that they were unable to stop the institutionalization of illegal enslavement.

Bibliography

Primary Sources

Arquivo Nacional do Rio de Janeiro, processo 11.232, fundo 84 Relação do Rio de Janeiro, série apelação cível, código de referência 84.0.ACI.00093, apelante Ana, apelado José Delfino da Silva, ano inicial 1861, ano final 1867, caixa 3.684, local Itabira, microfilme NA_063_2006.

Almeida, Candido Mendes de. *Atlas do Imperio do Brazil* (Rio de Janeiro: Lithographia do Instituto Philomathico, 1868).

Andrada, Martim Francisco Ribeiro de. *Relatorio do Ministerio da Justiça apresentado à Assembléa Geral Legislativa na segunda sessão de decima-terceira legislatura* (Rio de Janeiro: Typographia Perseverança, 1868).

Magyar, Ladislaus Magyar. *Reisen in Süd-Afrika in den Jahren 1849 bis 1857* (Leipzig: Verlag von Lauffer & Stolp, 1859).

Martins, Antonio de Assis. *Almanak administrativo, civil e industrial da Provincia de Minas-Geraes do anno de 1869 para servir no de 1870* (Rio de Janeiro: Typographia do Diario do Rio de Janeiro, 1870).

Secondary Literature

Ajello, Raffaele. *Arcana juris: diritto e politica nel Settecento italiano* (Napoli: Jovene, 1976).

Alencastro, Luiz Felipe de. *O trato dos viventes: formação do Brasil no Atlântico Sul* (São Paulo: Companhia das Letras, 2000).

Araujo, Manoel do Monte Rodrigues de. *Elementos de direito ecclesiastico publico e particular em relação à disciplina geral da Igreja e com aplicação aos usos da Igreja do Brasil* (Rio de Janeiro: Antonio Gonçalves Guimarães & Ca, 1857).

Ariza, Marília Bueno de Araújo. *O ofício da liberdade: trabalhadores libertandos em São Paulo e Campinas, 1830–1888* (São Paulo: Alameda, 2014).

Azevedo, Elciene. *Orfeu de carapinha: a trajetória de Luiz Gama na imperial cidade de São Paulo* (Campinas: Editora da Unicamp, 2005).

Azevedo, Elciene. *O direito dos escravos: lutas jurídicas e abolicionismo na província de São Paulo* (Campinas: Editora da Unicamp, 2010).

Baltazar, Miguel, and Pedro Cardim. "A difusão da legislação régia (1621–1808)," in *Um reino e suas repúblicas no Atlântico: comunicações políticas entre Portugal, Brasil e Angola nos séculos XVII e XVIII*, ed. João Fragoso and Nuno Gonçalo Monteiro (Rio de Janeiro: Civilização Brasileira, 2017): 161–207.

Birocchi, Italo. *Alla ricerca dell'ordine* (Torino: Giappichelli, 2002).

Bissigo, Diego Nones. "A eloquente e irrecusável linguagem dos algarismos: a estatística no Brasil imperial e a produção do recenseamento de 1872" (master's thesis, Universidade Federal de Santa Catarina, 2014).

Blumenthal, Debra. *Enemies and Familiars: Slavery and Mastery in Fifteenth-Century Valencia* (Ithaca: Cornell University Press, 2009).

Botelho, Tarcísio. "Censos e construção nacional no Brasil Imperial," *Tempo Social* 17, no. 1 (2005): 321–41.

Britto, Maura Silveira Gonçalves de. "Com luz de ferreiro: práticas do ofício nas Minas do ferro escravistas, século XIX" (master's thesis, Universidade Federal de Ouro Preto, 2011).

Cabral, Gustavo César Machado. *Ius commune: uma introdução à história do direito comum do Medievo à Idade Moderna* (Rio de Janeiro: Lumen Juris, 2019).

Candido, Mariana. "African Freedom Suits and Portuguese Vassal Status: Legal Mechanisms for Fighting Enslavement in Benguela, Angola (1800–1830)," *Slavery & Abolition* 32, no. 3 (2011): 447–59.

Candido, Mariana. *An African Slaving Port and the Atlantic World: Benguela and Its Hinterland* (Cambridge: Cambridge University Press, 2013).

Candido, Mariana. *Fronteiras da escravidão: escravatura, comércio e identidade em Benguela, 1780–1850* (Benguela: Edições Universidade Katyavala Bwila/Ondjiri Editores, 2018).

Candido, Mariana, Mariana Dias Paes and Juelma de Matos Ngãla. *Introdução à história do direito em Angola* (forthcoming).

Candioti, Magdalena. "Free Womb Law, Legal Asynchronies, and Migrations: Suing for an Enslaved Woman's Child in Nineteenth-Century Río de la Plata," *The Americas* 77, no. 1 (2020): 73–99.

Carvalho, Marcus, Flávio dos Santos Gomes, and João José Reis. *O alufá Rufino: tráfico, escravidão e liberdade no Atlântico Negro, c. 1822–c. 1853* (São Paulo: Companhia das Letras, 2010).

Castelnau-L'Estoile, Charlotte de. *Páscoa et ses deux maris: une esclave entre Angola, Brésil et Portugal au XVIIe siècle* (Paris: Presses Universitaires de France, 2019).

Chalhoub, Sidney. *Visões da liberdade: uma história das últimas décadas da escravidão na corte* (São Paulo: Companhia das Letras, 1990).

Chalhoub, Sidney. *A força da escravidão: ilegalidade e costume no Brasil oitocentista* (São Paulo: Companhia das Letras, 2012).

Chalhoub, Sidney, and Fernando Teixeira da Silva. "Sujeitos no imaginário acadêmico: escravos e trabalhadores na historiografia brasileira desde os anos 1980," *Cadernos AEL* 14, no. 26 (2009): 7–47.

Cosme Puntiel, Carmen Luz, and Aurora Vergara Figueroa, eds. *Demandando mi Libertad: mujeres negras y sus estrategias de Resistencia en la Nueva Granada, Venezuela y Cuba, 1700–1800* (Cali: Universidad Icesi, 2018).

Costa, Jéssyka Sâmya Ladislau Pereira. "A trajetória de Catharina Maria Roza da Conceição e a escravidão ilegal no norte imperial," *Revista Semina* 17, no. 1 (2018): 81–101.

Costa, Pietro. *Il progeto giuridico: richerche sulla giurisprudenza del liberalismo classico* (Milano: Giuffré, 1974).

Cowling, Camillia. *Conceiving Freedom: Women of Color, Gender, and Abolition of Slavery in Havana and Rio de Janeiro* (Chapel Hill: University of North Carolina Press, 2013).

Curto, José. "Struggling Against Enslavement: The Case of José Manuel in Benguela, 1816–20," *Canadian Journal of African Studies* 39, no. 1 (2005): 96–122.

Dantas, Monica, and Filipe Nicoletti Ribeiro. "A importância dos acervos judiciais para a pesquisa em história: um percurso," *Lex Cult* 4, no. 2 (2020): 47–87.

De La Fuente, Alejandro. "Slaves and the Creation of Legal Rights in Cuba: coartación and papel," *Hispanic American Historical Review* 87, no. 4 (2007): 659–92.

Dias Paes, Mariana. "O procedimento de manutenção de liberdade no Brasil oitocentista," *Estudos Históricos* 29, no. 58 (2016): 339–60.

Dias Paes, Mariana. *Escravidão e direito: o estatuto jurídico dos escravos no Brasil oitocentista, 1860–1888* (São Paulo: Alameda, 2019).

Dias Paes, Mariana. "Legal Files and Empires: Form and Materiality of the Benguela District Court Documents," *Administory: Zeitschrift für Verwaltungsgeschichte* 4 (2019): 53–70.

Dias Paes, Mariana. "Shared Atlantic Legal Culture: The Case of a Freedom Suit in Benguela," *Atlantic Studies, Global Currents* 17 (2020): 419–40.

Dias Paes, Mariana. "Ser dependente no Império do Brasil: terra e trabalho em processos judiciais," *Población & Sociedad* 27, no. 2 (2020): 8–29.

Dias Paes, Mariana. *Esclavos y tierras entre posesión y títulos: la construcción social del derecho de propiedad en Brasil, siglo XIX* (Frankfurt am Main: Max Planck Institute for Legal History and Legal Theory, 2021).

Dias Paes, Mariana. “Direito e escravidão no Brasil Império,” in *Constituição e poderes, constituição de sujeitos: caminhos da história do Direito no Brasil (1750–1930)*, ed. Monica Dantas and Samuel Barbosa (São Paulo: Instituto de Estudos Brasileiros, 2021): 182–203.

Dias Paes, Mariana. “Para além do ventre livre: a Lei de 1871 e as mudanças na arena dos tribunais,” *Ventres livres? Gênero, maternidade e legislação*, ed. Luciana da Cruz Brito, Flávio dos Santos Gomes, Maria Helena Machado and Iamara da Silva Viana (São Paulo: Editora Unesp, 2021): 429–48.

Duve, Thomas. “Rechtsgeschichte als Geschichte von Normativitätswissen?” *Rechtsgeschichte – Legal History* 29 (2021): 41–68.

El Hamel, Chouki. *Black Morocco: A History of Slavery, Race, and Islam* (Cambridge: Cambridge University Press, 2013).

Espíndola, Ariana Moreira. “Papéis da escravidão: a matrícula especial de escravos (1871)” (master’s thesis, Universidade Federal de Santa Catarina, 2016).

Farias, Juliana Barreto. “Mercados Minas: africanos ocidentais na Praça do Mercado do Rio de Janeiro, 1830–1890” (PhD diss., Universidade de São Paulo, 2012).

Farias, Juliana Barreto. “Diz a preta mina: cores e categorias sociais nos processos de divórcio abertos por africanas ocidentais, Rio de Janeiro, século XIX,” *Estudos Ibero-Americanos* 44, no. 3 (2018): 470–83.

Ferreira, Ligia Fonseca. *Lições de resistência: artigos de Luiz Gama na imprensa de São Paulo e do Rio de Janeiro* (São Paulo: Edições Sesc São Paulo, 2020).

Ferreira, Roquinaldo. *Cross-Cultural Exchange in the Atlantic World: Angola and Brazil during the Era of the Slave Trade* (Cambridge: Cambridge University Press, 2012).

Fundação Instituto Brasileiro de Geografia e Estatística. *Estatísticas históricas do Brasil: séries, econômicas, demográficas e sociais de 1550 a 1988* (Rio de Janeiro: IBGE, 1990).

Green, Toby. “Baculamento or Encomienda? Legal Pluralisms and the Contestation of Power in the Pan-Atlantic World of the Sixteenth and Seventeenth Centuries,” *Journal of Global Slavery* 2 (2017): 310–36.

Grinberg, Keila. *O fiador dos brasileiros: cidadania, escravidão e direito civil no tempo de Antonio Pereira Rebouças* (Rio de Janeiro: Civilização Brasileira, 2002).

Grinberg, Keila, and Beatriz Mamigonian. “Le crime de réduction à l’esclavage d’une personne libre (Brésil, XIXe siècle),” *Brésil(s): sciences humaines et sociales* 11 (2017).

Grinberg, Keila, and Cristina Nogueira da Silva. “Soil Free from Slaves: Slave Law in Late 18th-Early 19th Century Portugal,” *Slavery & Abolition* 32, no. 3 (2011): 431–46.

Halperin, Jean-Louis. *L’impossible code civil* (Paris: Presses Universitaires de France, 1992).

Herzog, Tamar. *A Short History of European Law: The Last Two and a Half Millennia* (Cambridge: Harvard University Press, 2019).

Hespanha, António Manuel. *Guiando a mão invisível: direitos, Estado e lei no liberalismo monárquico português* (Coimbra: Almedina, 2004).

Hunt, Lynn. *A invenção dos direitos humanos: uma história* (São Paulo: Companhia das Letras, 2007).

Lara, Silvia Hunold. *Campos da violência: escravos e senhores da Capitania do Rio de Janeiro, 1750–1808* (São Paulo: Paz e Terra, 1998).

Lara, Silvia Hunold, and Joseli Maria Nunes Mendonça. “Apresentação,” in *Direitos e justiças no Brasil: ensaios de história social*, ed. Silvia Hunold Lara and Joseli Maria Nunes Mendonça (Campinas: Editora da Unicamp, 2006): 9–22.

Lima, Henrique Espada. “Sob o domínio da precariedade: escravidão e os significados da liberdade de trabalho no século XIX,” *Topoi* 6, no. 11 (2005): 289–326.

Machado, Maria Helena. “Em torno da autonomia escrava: uma nova direção para a história social da escravidão,” *Revista Brasileira de História* 8, no. 16 (1988): 143–60.

Machado, Maria Helena. *Crime e escravidão: trabalho, luta e resistência nas lavouras paulistas, 1830–1888* (São Paulo: Editora da Universidade de São Paulo, 2018).

Madeira-Santos, Catarina. "Esclavage africain et traite atlantique confrontés: transactions langagières et juridiques (à propos du tribunal de mucanos dans l'Angola des XVIIe et XVIIIe siècles)," *Brésil(s): sciences humaines et sociales* 1 (2012): 127–48.
Masters, Adrian. "A Thousand Invisible Architects: Vassals, the Petition and Response System, and the Creation of Spanish Imperial Caste Legislation," *Hispanic American Historical Review* 98, no. 3 (2018): 377–406.
Mattos, Hebe Maria. *Das cores do silêncio: os significados da liberdade no Sudeste escravista* (Rio de Janeiro: Nova Fronteira, 1998).
McKinley, Michelle. *Fractional Freedoms: Slavery, Intimacy, and Legal Mobilization in Colonial Lima, 1600–1700* (Cambridge: Cambridge University Press, 2016).
Meriño Fuentes, María de los Ángeles and Aisnara Perera Díaz. *Estrategias de Libertad: un acercamiento a las acciones legales de los esclavos en Cuba, 1762–1872* (La Habana: Editorial de Ciencias Sociales, 2015).
Nogueira, Antonia Marcia. *Desventuras de Hypolita: luta contra a escravidão ilegal no sertão, Crato e Exu, século XIX* (Natal: Editora da Universidade Federal do Rio Grande do Norte, 2015).
Oliveira, Luís Cabral de. "Quem sabe o que é um advogado? A resposta de Luís Manuel Júlio Frederico Gonçalves às tentativas de reforma dos provisionários goeses em 1869," *Jahrbuch für Geschichte Lateinamerikas* 52, no. 1 (2015): 207–29.
Owensby, Brian. "How Juan and Leonor Won Their Freedom: Litigation and Liberty in Seventeenth-Century Mexico," *Hispanic American Historical Review* 85 (2005): 39–79.
Palmer, Vernon Valentine. *Through the Codes Darkly: Slave Law and Civil Law in Louisiana* (Clark: Lawbook Exchange, 2012).
Penna, Clemente Gentil. "Economias urbanas: capital, créditos e escravidão na cidade do Rio de Janeiro, c. 1820–1860" (PhD diss., Universidade Federal do Rio de Janeiro, 2019).
Pinheiro, Fernanda. "Transformações de uma prática contenciosa: as ações de liberdade produzidas em Mariana (1750/69 e 1850/69)," *Locus: revista de história* 17, no. 1 (2011): 253–71.
Pinheiro, Fernanda. *Em defesa da liberdade: libertos, coartados e livres de cor nos tribunais do Antigo Regime português, Mariana e Lisboa, 1720–1819* (Belo Horizonte: Fino Traço, 2018).
Pirola, Ricardo Figueiredo. *Escravos e rebeldes nos tribunais do Império: uma história social da lei de 10 de junho de 1835* (Rio de Janeiro: Arquivo Nacional, 2015).
Pirola, Ricardo Figueiredo. "Escravos e rebeldes na justiça imperial: dois casos de assassinatos senhoriais em Campos dos Goytacazes (RJ), 1873," *Afro-Ásia* 51 (2015): 41–80.
Reis, João José. *Rebelião escrava no Brasil: a história do Levante dos Malês de 1835* (São Paulo: Companhia das Letras, 2003).
Scott, Rebecca. "Social Facts, Legal Fictions, and Re-Enslavement in the Diaspora of the Haitian Revolution," *Law and History Review* 35, no. 1 (2017): 9–30.
Silva, Alberto da Costa. "Buying and Selling Korans in Nineteenth-Century Rio de Janeiro," in *Rethinking the African Diaspora: the Making of a Black World in the Bight of Benin and Brazil*, ed. Kristin Mann and Edna Bay (London: Frank Class, 2001): 83–90.
Silva, Daniel Domingues. *The Atlantic Slave Trade from West Central Africa, 1780–1867* (Cambridge: Cambridge University Press, 2017).
Silva, Luiz Geraldo. "Esperança de liberdade: interpretações populares da abolição ilustrada (1773–1774)," *Revista de História* 144 (2001): 107–49.
Siqueira, Victor Hugo. *Entre togas e grilhões: o acesso à justiça dos escravizados no Maranhão oitocentista, 1860–1888* (São Paulo: Alameda, 2021).
Slenes, Robert. "Malungo, ngoma vem! África coberta e descoberta do Brasil," *Revista USP* 12 (1992): 48–67.
Slenes, Robert. Na senzala, uma flor: esperanças e recordações na formação da família escrava, Brasil Sudeste, século XIX (Campinas: Editora da Unicamp, 2011).
Thompson, Edward Thompson. *Whigs and Hunters: The Origins of the Black Act* (London: Breviary Stuff Publications, 2013).

Villey, Michel. *A formação do pensamento jurídico moderno* (São Paulo: Martins Fonts, 2006).

Welke, Barbara. *Law and the Borders of Belonging in the Long Nineteenth Century United States* (Cambridge: Cambridge University Press, 2010).

White, Joshua. "Slavery, Manumission, and Freedom Suits in the Early Modern Ottoman Empire," in *Slaves and Agency in the Ottoman Empire*, ed. Stephan Conermann and Gül Şen (Göttingen: Vandenhoeck & Ruprecht, 2020): 283–320.

Tâmis Parron

Slavery and the Power of Trade: Markets and Geopolitics in the Nineteenth-Century Americas

> The intercourse which we now have with the single Island of Cuba is of more value to the United States, in one year, than that with Mexico would be in ten! James Yard, trader from Philadelphia, 1818.[1]

> Our own commerce is immense. It is said nearly 7 millions of dollars of our own capital has been invested this year in coffee alone. William Hunter, US diplomat in Rio de Janeiro, 1835.[2]

Written nearly two decades apart, these epigraphs represent two snapshots of the economic relations between the United States and the next most powerful slaveholding spaces in the Americas during the nineteenth century, Cuba and the Empire of Brazil. The author of the first is James Yard, a trader from Philadelphia involved with Caribbean commerce who also had some personal experience in Portugal and Spain. Yard worried about the world order after the Congress of Vienna (1815). Since the return of peace to Europe, the United States had been facing competition from Europeans in the Caribbean trade circuits they had monopolized during the revolutionary wars, when American vessels plied the Atlantic as neutral carriers between Europe and the West Indies. As a result, American trade in the Caribbean declined after the fall of Napoleon. The only exception to offset that shortfall was Cuba, because Spain had allowed the island, then under a coffee and sugar revolution, to deal directly with the United States. But now, Yard reasoned, the new trade balance was at risk. Whole regions of Hispanic America had declared their independence, and the American press was pushing the Union to acknowledge their cause based on ideological affinity. Yard opposed it. He thought that if Congress followed their advice, Madrid would retaliate by blocking American access to the treasures of Cuba. Yard decided to act. In 1818, he wrote a pamphlet, revised by James Biddle, future president of the Second Bank of the United States, arguing that trade with colonial Cuba was worth the independence of an entire continent. "The humble article of molasses imported into the United States [. . .] from Cuba is of more commercial and we may add as a corollary, of more

1 James Yard, *Spanish America and the United States or the Views of the Actual Commerce of the United States with the Spanish Colonies* (Philadelphia: Carey, 1818): 23.
2 Official letter from William Hunter to John Forsyth, December 10, 1835, US National Archives, Record Group 59, microfilm 121, roll 12.

Acknowledgment: This study was funded by Capes-Print 41/2017 (grant number 88881.310263/2018-00) and FAPERJ Jovem Cientista do Nosso Estado (grant number E-26/201.462/2022).

https://doi.org/10.1515/9783111026527-007

national importance than all the ordinary articles imported into this country from all the ports and places of Spanish America."[3] "The single port of the Havanna consumes from 80 to 100.000 barrels of our flour annually."[4] Figures, not republican ideals, should guide Washington's diplomatic efforts in the New World.[5]

In the year Yard and Biddle prepared their pamphlet, Brazil's position in the United States' trade balance was insignificant. It purchased little – less than China, Italy, Portugal, Spain, the Danish Antilles, and almost all the British dominions, including Gibraltar. And it sold almost nothing: it was seventh in supplying sugar, alongside the Swedish West Indies, and sixth in coffee, on the same level as Martinique and Guadeloupe. By 1835, that scenario had changed thoroughly. William Hunter, the US representative in Rio de Janeiro, a shrewd man who had married his daughter into the family of the biggest American trader in Rio, noticed that the Brazilian Empire was turning into a valuable commercial partner for the United States. Ten years earlier, Brazil had become the largest customer for American wheat flour, and by 1834, its largest supplier of coffee. He wrote to the State Department: "We have perhaps committed a mistake in placing Brazil on the same platform with other American powers." He thought that because of the

> immense extent of her territories [. . .], her feelings of rising superiority over Portugal, and by consequence a diminishing dependence on England [. . .] we ought to become towards this country [. . .] a *tutelary* friend, a promoter of its stand as a respectable American power.[6]

By the end of the 1830s, like Cuba twenty years earlier, trade in slave-made goods meant Brazil was on the rise in American geopolitics, placing it above the continent's free republics as well.

Establishing a solid trading network with Cuba and Brazil was one of the systemic sources of economic and geopolitical power for US slaveholders in the nineteenth century. Both materially and ideologically, it strengthened the institutional stability of slavery in the three countries just as anti-slavery forces were emerging as a decisive factor for social change in the world arena. This network enriched local slaveholders, gave Cubans and Brazilians easier access to North American ships, technology, and capital, increased the relative importance of Cuba and Brazil for the United States, and recast the republic as a buffer state against world anti-slavery. Nevertheless, its development was not as solid as it may seem, and it fell far short of manifest destiny. The American-Cuban-Brazilian commodity circuit had made progress at the dawn of the century, but stalled in terms of goods and capital traded between 1815 and 1830. Only

3 Yard, *Spanish America and the United States*: 14.

4 Ibid.: 13.

5 Ibid.: 56–58.

6 Official letters from William Hunter to John Forsyth, Official letter from William Hunter to John Forsyth, December 10, 1835, US National Archives, Record Group 59, microfilm 121, roll 12; and February 10, 1837, USNA, RG 59, m. 121, roll 13.

after the Nullification Crisis (1828–1833), which overhauled US tariff policy, did material integration and political alignment between the three regions take off. This chapter provides an overview of that story. First, it describes the trade relations between the United States, Cuba, and Brazil before 1830. Next, it focuses on the Nullification Crisis and measures its impact on the economic integration of these three economies. Finally, it sketches out an attempt to frame this process of material convergence as a key component in the evolution of slavery in the United States, Brazil, and Cuba – the *oikoumene* of slavery in the Americas.

1 Revolutionary Wars, 1795–1815: Tentative Beginnings

From the slave emancipation in the French Caribbean in 1795 to Napoleon's invasion of the Iberian Peninsula in 1807, the United States exploited its status as a neutral country in the Revolutionary Wars to become the main redistribution center of West Indian products bound for Europe. Following old patterns of trade, the republic bought sugar, coffee, molasses, indigo, and tobacco in exchange for timber, small manufactured goods, and, above all, wheat flour, used as an international currency since colonial times.[7] In the 1780s, its main trading partner in the region had been the colony of Saint-Domingue, the world's leading producer of sugar and coffee, which could directly trade with the republic after the French loosened monopoly regulations in 1786. After 1791, the slave revolution in Saint-Domingue limited the colony's productive capacity. From 1789 to 1800, sugar and coffee production dropped by 86% and 44%, respectively, opening a window of opportunity for global competitors such as Cuba and Brazil.[8]

Contrary to expectations, however, Hispano-Cuban slaveholders did not immediately come to dominate the American market. According to data from the *American State Papers*, the French West Indies, an entity consisting primarily of Saint-Domingue and Haiti, sold more brown sugar to the United States than Cuba between 1795 and 1808: 196,000 *vs.* 129,000 metric tons (mt), surpassing it in every single year except for 1798–1801. In the coffee trade, Saint-Domingue's dominance was even stronger. The French colony shipped 168,000 mt to the republic, compared to Cuba's paltry 19,000 mt, capturing 55% of the American market. Despite its unimpressive beginnings, conditions for economic expansion in Cuba were more promising than in the neighboring island.

7 John J. McCuster and Russell R. Menard, *The Economy of British America, 1607–1789* (Chapel Hill: University of North Carolina Press, 1991).

8 Pierre Pluchon, *Toussaint Louverture de l'esclavage au pouvoir* (Paris: l'Ecole/Port au Prince, Editions Caraïbes, 1979): 275; William C. van Norman Jr., *Shade-Grown Slavery: The Lives of Slaves on Coffee Plantations in Cuba* (Nashville: Vanderbilt University Press, 2013): 38.

Endowed with extensive unexplored tracts in the fertile plains of Artemisa, Cuban elites received a constant influx of capital, enjoyed an unrestricted Transatlantic slave trade, received refugees from Saint-Domingue with expertise in agronomy, and benefited from an enlightened policy geared toward economic growth, carefully designed by local elites and Bourbon policymakers.[9] In an acute moment of the revolutionary conflict, rife with reciprocal embargoes, Cuba finally beat Haiti to become the United States' primary supplier of sugar and coffee.

Renewed war between France and Great Britain (1804), as well as the defeat of the French-Spanish naval coalition in the Battle of Trafalgar (October 21, 1805), allowed the American entrepôt trade to reach unprecedented levels, with values 20% higher than for domestic exports (1804–1808). The republic even supplanted Great Britain in the sugar trade, trading 20% to 30% more than its former colonial masters.[10] America's luck would turn in the following years, however. After Napoleon issued the Berlin Decree prohibiting continental trade with Britain in 1806, London retaliated with Orders-in-Council forbidding citizens of Britain and neutral countries (i.e., the United States) from engaging in continental trade. Against this backdrop, Virginian presidents Thomas Jefferson and James Madison convinced Congress to embargo London several times, creating the hostile environment that led to the Anglo-American War of 1812.[11] At the same time, popular resistance to Napoleon in the Iberian Peninsula in 1808 placed Spain on the British side in the European wars; Cuban slaveholder and intellectual Francisco de Arango y Parreño seized on this opportunity to read out the longest defense of free trade ever made by the colonists before the island's royal consulate in November of that year.[12] Allowed to trade freely during the wars, Havana became North America's main source of sugar, a position that it would not lose until the twentieth century, and coffee, a place it occupied for twenty-five years.

Before 1808, Brazil remained out of the US's commodity circuits, focusing its trade on Africa and other Portuguese possessions, while Lisbon re-exported Brazilian goods to the Mediterranean and North Atlantic markets. Benefiting from enlightened reforms

9 Levi Marrero, *Cuba: Economía y Sociedad: Azucar, Ilustración y Conciencia (1763–1868)*, vol. 3 (Madrid: Editora Mayor, 1981); Torres-Cuevas, Eduardo. "De la Ilustración reformista al reformismo liberal," in *Historia de Cuba. La Colonia, evolución socioeconómico y formación nacional de los origines hasta 1867*, ed. María del Carmen Barcia, Gloria García and Eduardo Torres-Cuevas (Havana: Editora Política, 1994): 314–59; David A. Brading, "La España de los Borbones y su império americano," in História de América Latina, vol. 2, *America Latina Colonial In los siglos XVI, XVII, XVIII*, ed. Leslie Bethell (Barcelona: Editorial Crítica, 1990): 85–126; Ada Ferrer, "Cuban Slavery and Atlantic Antislavery," in *Slavery and Antislavery in Spain's Atlantic Empire*, ed. Josep M. Fradera and Christopher Schmidt-Nowara (New York: Bergham Books, 2013): 134–57.

10 Manuel Moreno Fraginals, *O engenho: complexo sócio-econômico açucareiro cubano*, 3 vols (São Paulo: Hucitec, 1989): vol. 2, 234–37.

11 Donald R. Hickey, "American Trade Restrictions during the War of 1812," *Journal of American History* 68, no. 3 (1981): 517–38.

12 Francisco Arango y Parreño, *Obras* (Havana: Imagen Contemporanea, 2005): 467–521.

by the Braganza crown, Brazil also responded well to the new market opportunities at the turn of the nineteenth century. Its "agricultural renaissance" included cocoa farming in Pará, rice and cotton in Maranhão, wheat in the southern captaincies, and the expansion of the traditional sugar regions of Bahia and Pernambuco. At the same time, new sugar centers emerged north of Rio de Janeiro and in western São Paulo, and coffee was introduced around Rio de Janeiro.[13]

Until 1807, therefore, Brazil and Cuba belonged to different commodity circuits. While Cuba fed American re-exports, Brazil boosted the foreign trade of its colonial master, Portugal.[14] After the reciprocal embargoes and the invasion of Iberia by Napoleon (November 1807), Brazilian trade was channeled off from Portugal to Great Britain. One month after Jefferson signed his first embargo law, the Portuguese regent, Dom João, opened Brazilian ports to neutral countries. In the following years, Brazil became the main foreign buyer of British goods in the Americas, second only to the United States.[15] The Rio de Janeiro-London economic axis mirrored what existed between Havana and Washington. Brazil stored its sugar and coffee in London's waterfront warehouses, while Cuba did the same in Philadelphia, New York, and Baltimore. Neither Brazil nor Cuba had their colonial masters as their leading economic partners anymore, and both the United States and Britain mostly re-exported rather than consumed – Brazilian and Cuban goods.

---

13 Andrée Mansuy-Diniz Silva, "Portugal y Brasil: la reorganización imperial, 1750–1808," in *História de América Latina,* vol. 2, *America Latina Colonial en los siglos XVI, XVII, XVIII,* ed. Leslie Bethell (Barcelona: Editorial Crítica, 1990): 150–84; Dauril Aldin, "El Brasil colonial tardío, 1750–1808," in *História de América Latina,* vol. 3, *America Latina Colonial: economía,* ed. Leslie Bethell (Barcelona: Editorial Crítica, 1990): 306–58; Kenneth Maxwell, *Chocolate, piratas e outros malandros: Ensaios tropicais* (Rio de Janeiro: Paz e Terra, 1999): 89–124, 157–208; Rafael Marquese and Dale Tomich. "O Vale do Paraíba escravista e a formação do mercado mundial do café no século XIX," in *O Brasil imperial,* vol. 2, *1831–1870,* ed. Keila Grindberg and Ricardo Salles (Rio de Janeiro: Civilização Brasileira, 2009): 339–83.

14 Valentim Alexandre, *Os sentidos do império: questão nacional e questão colonial na Crise do Antigo Regime português* (Porto: Edições Afrontamento, 1993): 25–77; Jorge M. Pedreira, "From Growth to Collapse: Portugal, Brazil, and the Breakdown of the Old Colonial System (1750–1830)," *Hispanic American Historical Review* 80, no. 4 (2000): 839–64; Jorge M. Pedreira, "Economia e política na explicação da independência do Brasil," in *A Independência Brasileira: novas dimensões,* ed. Jurandir Malerba (Rio de Janeiro: FVG Editora, 2006): 55–97.

15 José Jobson de Andrade Arruda, *Uma colônia entre dois impérios: a Abertura dos Portos brasileiros, 1800–1808* (São Paulo: Edusc, Bauru 2008): 52–58.

2 The New World Order, 1815–1830: Converging Paths

Before 1815, re-exports played a key role in American international trade. Data available for 1802–1804 suggests that sugar and coffee made up 20% of the country's aggregate exports and 45% of its re-exports. In contrast, cotton was 10% of its exports.[16] Coffee and sugar stimulated the development of the country's merchant fleet, helping the United States become a significant player the world economy in the early nineteenth century. While sugar and coffee balanced the republic's foreign trade, however, the American market for coffee and sugar could expand, as it actually did, but only at small rates. From 1815 onward, new macroeconomic conditions boosted the consumption of Cuban and Brazilian goods in the US market.

With the peace of 1815, markets for cotton boomed. The British demand for raw cotton, held back by the war for many years, was unchained by new markets in the Atlantic and beyond, which fostered the cultivation of short-staple cotton in the Piedmont soils of Georgia and South Carolina, the black limestone soils of the Black Prairie (Alabama and Mississippi), and the alluvial lands along the lower Mississippi Valley.[17] Supported by the political agreements known as the Missouri Compromise, which shielded the interstate slave trade from federal restrictions, American cotton achieved unprecedented growth rates in 1816–1820 (77%), 1821–1825 (50%), and 1826–1830 (47%), increasing its global market share from 30% to 50% over a single decade (1820–1830).[18] The average annual value of cotton exports alone (US$ 25 million) exceeded all capital inflows from the entrepôt trade (US$ 21.5 million).

In theory, the surplus from the cotton trade could allow the US to allocate more capital to the international trade in coffee and sugar, either shipping them to Europe or keeping them for domestic consumption. This commodity circuit, however, faced two obstacles. After 1815, European powers resumed direct trade with the Americas, breaking the monopoly that the United States had enjoyed as neutral carriers during the Revolutionary Wars. Just as importantly, American protectionism, set up in the wake of the wars under the name of American System, overtaxed coffee and sugar, inhibiting the

16 For all figures until 1821, data were taken from the *American State Papers. Documents, Legislative and Executive, of the Congress of the United States. Commerce and Navigation*, vol. 1–2 (Washington: Gales and Seaton, 1832). For the following years, they come from the *Report of the Secretary of the Commerce and Navigation of the United States* (Washington: Gales and Seaton, 1824–1839). See also *American State Papers*, "Commerce with Great Britain and Her Dependencies, and All Ports of the World": vol. 5, 640–66; and Michelle C. McDonald, "From Cultivation to Cup: Caribbean Coffee and the North American Economy, 1765–1805" (PhD diss., University of Michigan, 2005).

17 Gavin Wright, *The Political Economy of the Cotton South: Households, Markets, and Wealth in the Nineteenth Century* (New York: Norton, 1978): 10–29.

18 Stuart Bruchey, ed., *Cotton and the Growth of the American Economy: 1790–1860. Sources and Readings* (New York: Harcourt, Branc & World, 1967): 18–25.

growth of the US domestic market for these commodities. This second point, given its relationship with Cuba's and Brazil's foreign trade, merits further consideration.

The American System was born out of conviction, necessity, and convenience, and to a certain extent its purpose was to maintain national control over the rise of the cotton commodity chains. Generally speaking, the cotton economy involved a plurality of interests. Northern business communities mediated credit to Southern planters, who in turn promised to ship future crops of cotton to Northern ports, especially New York. Once inspected, the bulk of cotton (up to 85%) would go on to Liverpool, while the rest supplied the burgeoning mills of New Jersey, New York, and Pennsylvania – their development during the Revolutionary Wars was the first successful case of import substitution industrialization in the New World. At the beginning, this national capital-cotton-navigation-manufacturing complex developed under the protection of wars and blockades. After the fall of Napoleon, Britain seemed to threaten it.[19]

On July 3, 1815, London and Washington signed a treaty providing for reciprocal tariffs on shipping tonnage in the commerce between the two countries. Nevertheless, the British government was careful enough to keep Americans out of its colonial and domestic markets. While excluding the West Indies from the 1815 agreement, keeping them under metropolitan monopoly, Westminster also barred foreign flour from Britain through new Corn Laws. Washington politicians protested, claiming that this framework would allow Britain to take over American foreign trade. In their view, British vessels would carry manufactures to the United States, sail away with timber or food products for the West Indies, then return to Europe with sugar. Alternatively, they would take "cotton, rice, and tobacco" from nearby ports, such as "Charleston, Savannah and New Orleans," and make their way back home. Apparently, they were not wrong. Between 1815 and 1817, the share of US vessels in the cotton export trade from Southern ports dropped by 15%.[20]

A series of initiatives were adopted to react against British policies. Efforts were made to diversify the portfolio of wheat buyers in the Americas as alternatives to the British market.[21] From 1816 to 1822, Cuba emerged as the main costumer for American flour; hence the words by James Yard ("[t]he single port of the Havanna consumes from 80 to 100.000 barrels of our flour annually"). From 1823 onward, another slaveholding power, Brazil, became the largest buyer of American flour, which in due time would create a commodity circuit linking American wheat to Brazilian coffee, a precondition for

19 John R. Killick, "The Cotton Operations of Alexander Brown and Sons in the Deep South, 1820–1860," *Journal of Southern History* 43, no. 2 (1977): 169–94; Walter Johnson, *River of Dark Dreams: Slavery and Empire in the Cotton Kingdom* (Cambridge, MA: Belknapp Press, 2003).

20 "Commercial Intercourse with Foreign Nations," opinion by the Commerce Committee of the House of Representatives, read on March 15, 1822, in *American State Papers: Commerce and Navigation*: vol. 2, 646 (opinion on p. 632–57); Wray Vampley, "The Protection of English Cereal Producers: The Corn Laws Reassessed," *The Economic History Review* 33, no. 3 (1980): 382–95.

21 Brian Schoen, *The Fragile Fabric of Union: Cotton, Federal Politics, and the Global Origins of the Civil War* (Baltimore: The John Hopkins University Press, 2009).

importing Brazilian coffee into the US.[22] Just as importantly, in 1817 Congress passed an Act of Navigation nationalizing intercoastal trade, expelling the British from the cotton routes between the South and New York. On April 18, 1818, Congress also forbade British ships from direct trade between the United States and the West Indies, affecting the import of Jamaican goods (primarily coffee). At the same time, higher tariffs were required to pay off war debts or to stop the British from dumping their manufactures on American markets. In this context, coffee came to cost 5¢ per pound (compared to 3¢ in wartime) and sugar 3¢ per pound (versus 2.5¢).[23] From 1824 to 1828, the protectionist lobby managed to raise import duties further, from an average of 25% to almost 50% of the value of imported goods. The tariff law of 1828 would be known to history as the "Tariff of Abominations."

These measures and countermeasures from both sides of the Atlantic had mixed results. For one, cotton exports relieved sugar and coffee from their role of redressing the American balance of trade as entrepôt articles. Cotton money could now take over that role. Indeed, the share of coffee re-exported to Europe fell from 85% (pre-1808 level) to 40% in the 1820s, while sugar dropped from 65% to 25%. This means that both goods were transitioning from means of exchange to domestic consumption goods. On the other hand, protectionism inhibited trade. The sheer volume of the American coffee trade had been larger in 1795–1807 than it was in 1816–1828: 287,000 mt v. 199,000 mt, for an average of 22,000 mt v. 15,300 mt per year. Sugar volumes decreased even more sharply: from 670,000 mt (1795–1807) to 447,000 mt (1816–1828), for an average of 51,000

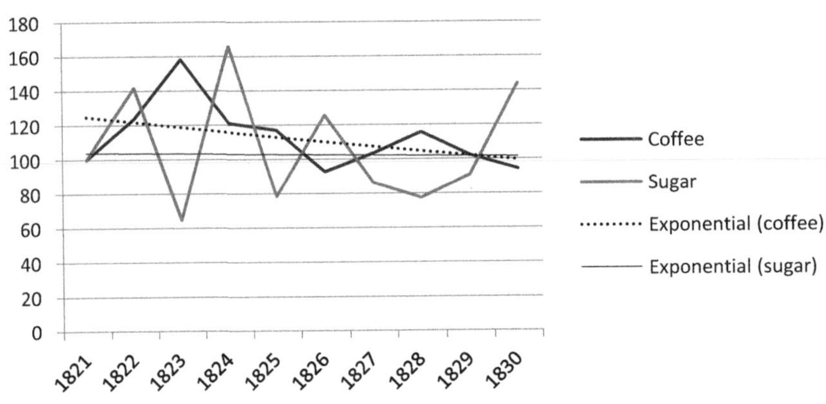

Fig. 1: American capital invested in the coffee and sugar trade (1821 = 100).[24]

22 Gregory Brown, "The Impact of American Flour Imports on Brazilian Wheat Production: 1808–1822," *The Americas* 47 (1991): 315–36.
23 Richard Follet, *The Sugar Masters: Planters and Slaves in Louisiana's Cane World, 1820–1860* (Baton Rouge: Louisiana State University Press, 2005): 25–26.
24 Data for all figures extracted from the sources mentioned in note 16.

mt vs. 34,0000 mt per year. US capital invested in the cotton and sugar trade over the 1820s stagnated or trended slightly downward, as seen in Fig. 1.

In short, the financial capacity of US foreign trade, backed by the Southern cotton boom after 1815, did not automatically lead to deep market integration between the three slaveholding powers of the nineteenth century. An additional event would still be required to interweave the destinies of cotton, sugar, and coffee – a passionate sectional conflict that targeted and weakened America's post-war protectionism.

3 The Nullification Crisis, 1828–1833: Slavery and Free Trade

Tariffs were raised and debated in Congress in 1816, 1820, 1824, and 1828. These four tariff laws came into being thanks to a coalition of interests in which planters, manufacturers, and traders could see themselves as beneficiaries of protectionism. As the years went by, however, many Southern representatives deserted the alliance. They feared that Britain could retaliate by raising duties on American raw cotton or rice and turn instead to "Brazil and the East Indies, [which] can even now furnish her with these articles."[25] Prices also pulled them out of the American System. Seeing the value of short-staple cotton fall abruptly from 27.3¢ (1815) to 15.2¢ (1820) to 9.8¢ (1828), Southern politicians became unwilling to pay out more capital for foreign goods to sponsor a minoritarian sector of the national economy, i.e., Northern manufacturing. In the House of Representatives, Southerners reached an unprecedented degree of political cohesion and coherence. At least eight out of every ten southern representatives tried to lower tariffs in 1820, 1824, and 1828. Apart from Kentucky, a wheat producing state harmed by the Corn Laws and interested in new domestic industrial consumer regions, the rate of opposition to protectionism reached 95% among Southern representatives.[26] It was a formidable resistance, but had meager practical results, as the South consistently lost every congressional vote on tariffs during those years. Southerners felt for the first time what a social minority (the manufacturing sector) could do to convince other groups (e.g., traders) to defeat their solid political phalanx on a topic considered strategic for the South. Put in perspective, it seemed to be extraordinarily dangerous. Abolitionism was on the rise in England, with obvious consequences for the

---

25 Remonstrance against an Increase of Duties on Imports (1820), in *American State Papers*, Finance: vol. 3, 563–67; Schoen, *The Fragile Fabric of Union*: 113.

26 For the parliamentary votes, *Annals of Congress, House of Representatives* (hereafter, *AC, HR*), 14th Congress, April 8, 181: 1351–1352; *AC, HR*, 16th Congress, April 28, 1820: 2139–2140; *AC, HR*, 18th Congress, April 16, 1824: 2429–2430; *Register of Debates* (hereafter, *RD*), *HR*, 20th, April 22, 1828: 2471–79. The quotation is from "Remonstrance against an Increase of Duties on Imports," from Charleston, cited in Schoen, *The Fragile Fabric*: 113.

US. At the same time, demographic growth was giving the North more seats in the House of Representatives, indicating that Southern political power would diminish accordingly. The tariff defeats of the 1820s sounded like a tragic sign of slaveholders' weakness in a dynamically changing world.[27]

Against this backdrop, Southern politicians started to develop a new kind of constitutional theory, known as the Nullification doctrine. Its key tenets were already circulating in periodicals, pamphlets, and speeches throughout South Carolina, Georgia, and Virginia when South Carolina's John Calhoun, the sitting vice-president, developed it coherently in his *Exposition and Protest* (1828). Known for his sharp mind and erudition, Calhoun marshaled ideas from political economy and constitutional law to convince Americans that the South could legally reject protectionism even without congressional consent. High tariffs, he explained, made life equally expensive both in the North and the South, but had unequal effects across regions due to the nature of their respective markets. For industrializing regions, a higher cost of living represented no problem, since tariffs stabilized a domestic market where losses could be transferred to consumers. For slaveholders, this reasoning was a fairy tale. Mark-ups in consumer goods were deadly, since most planters operated in free markets across the Atlantic. "Our market is the world," Calhoun wrote. "We have no monopoly in the supply of our products; one-half of the globe may produce them. Should we reduce our production, others stand ready, by increasing theirs, to take our place." "We are thus compelled to produce, on the penalty of losing our hold on the general market."[28] "We have no monopoly" is poetic license. The South was about to command 50% of the market for raw cotton in the Atlantic, a monopoly acquired through aggressive competitiveness.

Calhoun developed the second part of his argument in the field of constitutional law and political theory. In a classical syllogism of two premises and one conclusion, he taught that

> If it be conceded [. . .] that the sovereign powers delegated are divided between the General and State Governments, and that the latter hold their portion by the same tenure as the former, it would seem impossible to deny to the States the right of deciding on the infractions of their powers, and the proper remedy to be applied for their correction.[29]

The individual state, raised here as the source of the political compact of the Union, could call a special convention to decide whether federal laws hurting its interests

27 William W. Freehling, *The Road to Disunion*, vol. 1, *Secessionists at Bay, 1776–1854* (Oxford: Oxford University Press, 1990): 253–88; Manisha Sinha, *The Counterrevolution of Slavery: Politics and Ideology in Antebellum South Carolina* (Chapel Hill: University of North Carolina Press, 2000): 33–62.

28 John C. Calhoun, "Exposition and Protest reported by the Special Committee of the House of the Representative of South Carolina, on the Tariff," in *The Statutes at Large of South Carolina*, ed. Thomas Cooper (Columbia: A.S. Johnston, 1836): 247–73 (quote on 257).

29 Ibid.: 265–66.

were unconstitutional to a "palpable and dangerous"[30] extent so as to justify a state veto. Such a doctrine transferred constitutional decision-making from the Supreme Court to state conventions, where slaveholders had full control of political processes. For Calhoun, the tariff laws were a clear instance of unconstitutionality. He claimed that, according to the Constitution, the Union could collect "import duty," but only "for the sole purpose of revenue."[31] When the Union used import duties as "an instrument of rearing up the industry of one section of the country on the ruins of another," it abused powers originally delegated by the individual states.[32] Consequently, the interested state could nullify the law and even secede from the republic if the Union insisted on its error. Calhoun, in his endeavor to redefine the locus of sovereignty in the United States, formalized a constitutional doctrine of separatist federalism.

From 1829 to 1831, Southern politicians eschewed the ultimate consequences of radical Nullification ideas and tried to revise the American System within the bargaining channels of Congress. A key figure in this process was George McDuffie, an ally of Calhoun's, also hailing from South Carolina. McDuffie held a key position in Congress as chairman of the Ways and Means Committee, in charge of tariff issues in the House of Representatives alongside the Manufactures Committee. In 1830, McDuffie started a full-fledged assault on the Tariff of Abominations. First, he simply proposed ending high tariffs on iron, cotton, and wool, as well as molasses and salt. This wholesale approach failed miserably. He then tried a softer method: lowering tariffs article by article. His committee drafted a bill cutting the duty on a bushel of salt to 15¢ in 1830 and to 10¢ the next year. It passed. And then another to cut duties on molasses from 10¢ to 4¢ per gallon. It also passed.[33]

McDuffie did more. As chairman of the Ways and Means Committee, he asked that Congress slash the duty on coffee from 5¢ to 2.5¢ per pound. A representative from Maryland took the opportunity to suggest cutting the tax down to 1¢ – Maryland had mostly voted against the tariffs of 1828, and it was home to the big merchant houses involved in the wheat-coffee commodity circuit linking Brazil to the United States. It was further alleged that coffee "did not come into competition with any domestic product"; that "the article was no longer one of luxury but had become one of general and necessary use"; and that it was illogical to put it in the basket of protected articles. In 1827, Congress had tried to lower coffee duties. Three years later, it actually did so. After some hesitation, the House designed a plan to gradually lower duties on coffee, from 5¢ to 2¢ in 1831 and 1¢ in 1832.

Free trade for slaveholders opened the American market to molasses and coffee. Sugar was the next domino to fall. The untiring McDuffie presented a new plan for replacing the "Tariff of Abominations" in 1832. His bill aimed at lowering duties on cotton

---

30 Ibid.: 266.

31 Ibid.: 248.

32 Ibid.

33 For salt, *RD, HR*, 21th Congress, May 19, 1830, 1049 (presentation of the bill) and May 28, 1830: 1138–1139 (enactment). For molasses, *RD, HR*, 20th Congress, March 4, 1828, p. 1727 (10-cent tariff); 21st Congress, May 21, 1830: 1121 (presentation of McDuffie's bill) and May 28, 1830: 1139 (its enactment).

textiles, iron goods, and sugar. By then, Nullification had already morphed into an unofficial party in South Carolina and gained ranks of sympathizers, supporters, and allies in neighboring states. This environment gave McDuffie confidence to speak out for his bill along the lines of[34] Nullification on the floor of the House of Representatives. In a four-hour speech, he demanded lower tariffs, hinting here and there at the possibility of secession. The resulting law, sanctioned by the Executive and the Manufactures Committee, cut the average tariff by half in 1828. Some of the changes were of great interest to producers in Cuba and Brazil. The duty on brown sugar fell from 3¢ to 2.5¢, that on white sugar from 4¢ to 3.3¢, and that on coffee to zero. In 1833, the new tariff law came into effect.[35]

One might think that Southerners were able to bend both Congress and the executive to their will through ideological radicalism. But this is only part of the story. An even more important factor behind the reforms was the general decline of prices in the Atlantic. Low prices for articles such as coffee, sugar, and molasses were rendering the "American System" too burdensome for the Northern traders that had been supportive of protectionism since 1816. The following figures (Fig. 2, Fig. 3, and Fig. 4) illustrate the price movements of commodities between 1821 and the year when Congress lowered the duties on each one.

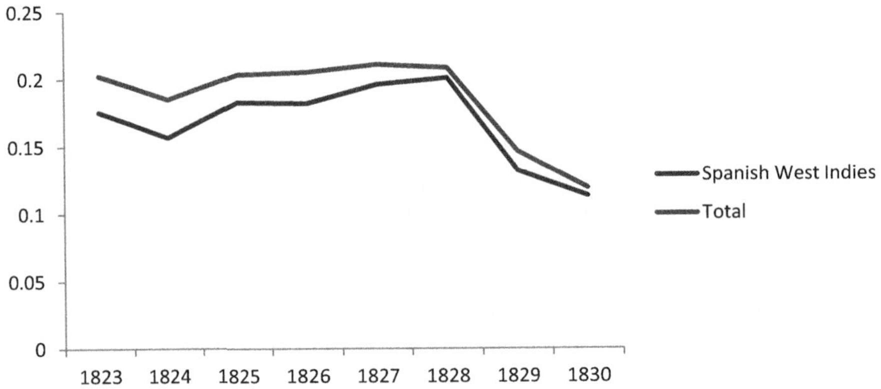

Fig. 2: Average price of molasses per year (per gallon, in US$ cents).

34 About coffee, *RD, HR*, 21st Congress, April 15, 1830: 803 and April 20, 1830: 807–8.

35 For McDuffie, *RD, HR*, 22nd Congress, February 8, 1832: 1763 passim. His speech in defense of the bill was published in a pamphlet. *Speech of Mr. McDuffie of South Carolina on the Bill Proposing a Reduction of the Duties on Imports*. Washington, D.C.: Duff Green, 1832. The tariff reductions are in the *Journal of the House of Representatives of the United States of America*. Washington, D.C.: Duff Green, June 22, 1832: 915–18; and *Journal of the Senate of the United States of America*. Washington, D.C.: Duff Green, July 5, 1832: 407.

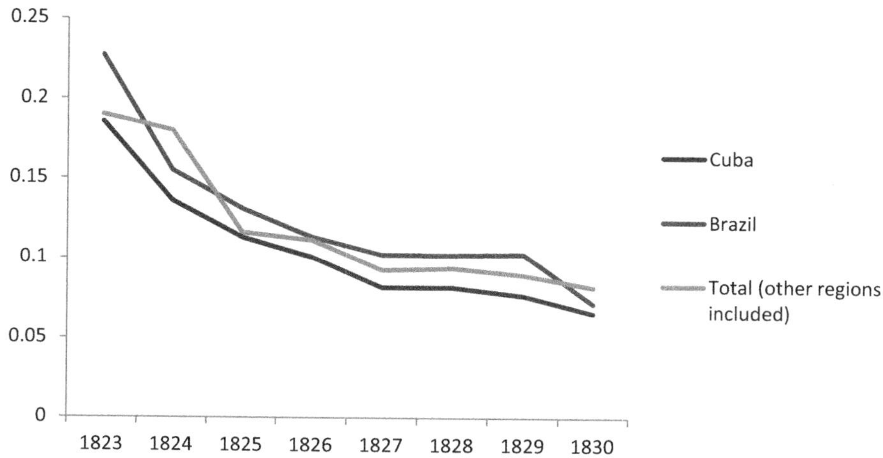

Fig. 3: Average price of coffee per year (per pound, in US$ cents).

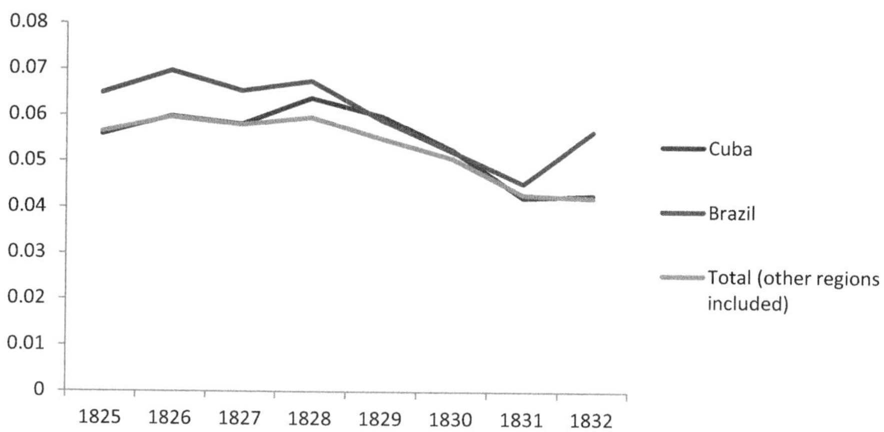

Fig. 4: Average price of brown sugar per year (per pound, in US$ cents).

Molasses prices seem to have been directly affected by the Tariff of Abominations, which raised duties on molasses from 4¢ to 10¢. As a consequence, molasses fell from 20¢ to 11¢ in the same year, and the tariff came to amount to 91% of their market value. When McDuffie asked that it be revised from 10¢ to 4¢, the traders thanked him and Congress accepted. The same happened to coffee. The average price fell from over 20¢ to 6.5¢ (Cuba) or 7.1¢ (Brazil), so that the 5¢ tariff jumped from 25% to over 70% *ad valorem*. When Congress tried to bring the duty down in 1827, it still met resistance, as prices were around 8¢ to 10¢. During the downturn in 1830, Congress finally lowered the duty on coffee from 5¢ to 2¢. Once again, McDuffie offered a bill, the traders thanked him, and Congress took it. Sugar's turn came only in 1832, when the price of brown sugar reached its lowest value between 1823 and 1840, falling from almost 6¢ to 4.2¢ per pound. The tariff decreased from 3¢ to 2,5¢, returning levels from before the War of 1812, in a move identical to the previous ones: McDuffie offered a bill, the traders thanked him, and Congress took it. As the Atlantic markets were reconfigured during the fifteen years following the Congress of Vienna, prices were an intrinsic component of both the North American intersectional alliances and the Nullification Crisis. The vociferous ideologues from South Carolina would never accept this wording, but the fact is that a few cents spoke louder and worked more wonders in the late 1820s than the hundreds of swaggering pages they published.

The North's concessions to the South on tariffs were selective. As acknowledged by a Rhode Island representative in 1833, the duties lowered by that point only applied to food for free workers, like coffee and sugar, and not to the products either consumed by slaves or made of iron, wool, and cotton. Even worse, the specific concessions by the North turned out to be part of a parliamentary strategy to shield protectionism with the clout of constitutionality. The budget deficit resulting from lower duties on coffee, molasses, sugar, salt, and other staples meant that higher duties on cotton, wool, and iron manufactures would become fiscal necessities, and so perfectly constitutional. When South Carolinians realized the maneuver, they put into practice their new constitutional theory of separatist federalism. During a quasi-war between the Union and the state, with military mobilizations on both sides in late 1832 and early 1833, Congress hammered out a compromise scaling down duties on manufactures and other commodities over the decade until they reached 20% *ad valorem* in 1842.[36] Sugar was among them.[37]

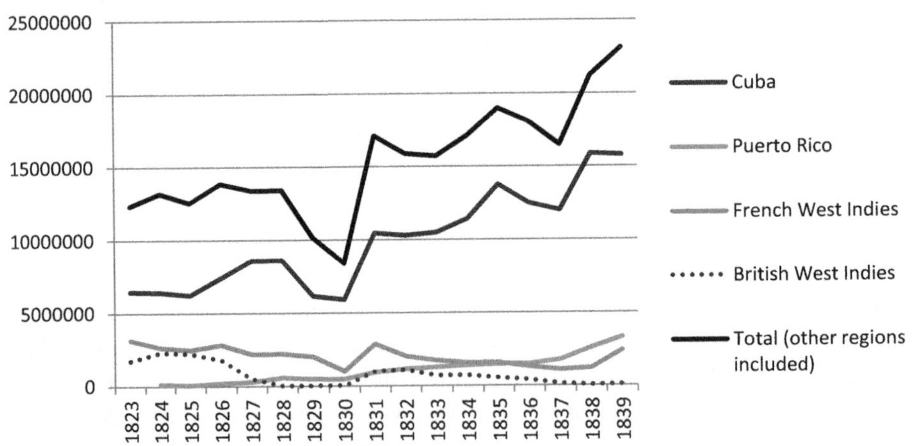

Fig. 5: American import of molasses by region (in gallons).

36 Freehling, *The Road to Disunion*: 273–85.

37 Follet, *The Sugar Masters*: 27.

It is hard to overstate the impact of the new fiscal framework on the import of tropical goods into the United States. Figure 5 shows that molasses imports, used in American distilleries to manufacture rum, had stagnated during the 1820s at around 13 million gallons per year, dropping to an average of 9 million in the 1829– 1830 two-year period because of the Tariff of Abominations. After McDuffie's bill, purchases of molasses rose to 17 million, 30% above the average of the previous decade. Since Cuba snapped up 65% of the American market and, conversely, the United States purchased 97% of Cuban molasses,[38] lower duties meant the island was newly flush with American capital. In the early 1830s, molasses sales amounted to two thirds of the white and brown sugar bought by the U.S. Not bad for a good considered a byproduct of the sugar economy.

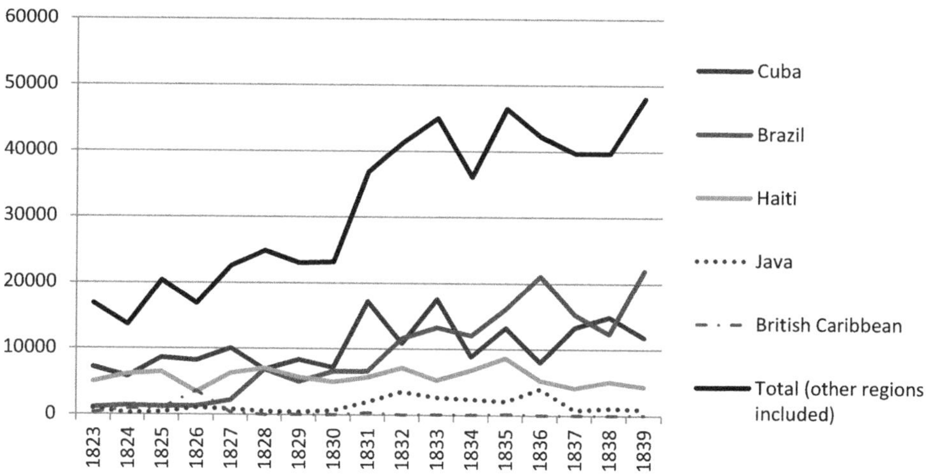

Fig. 6: American coffee imports by region (in mt).

Figure 6 presents American coffee imports over the same period. Coffee imports had been expanding in the 1820s, but boomed after Congress slashed tariffs in the early 1830s. Whereas importers bought approximately 49 million pounds, or 22,000 mt, in the five-year period of 1826 to 1830, the trade doubled during the next five years, to 91 million pounds or 41,000 mt. This unprecedented increase established a new benchmark for the coffee trade in the United States, which stabilized around 40,000 mt in the years 1836–1840. Among global suppliers, Brazil was the only one capable of increasing its exports at the same rate as Americans increased their imports, thanks largely to a combination of ecology, the built environment inherited from sugar and gold production, unexploited lands in the Paraíba Valley, and a diplomatic corps capable of keeping the Transatlantic slave

38 Moreno Fraginals, *O engenho*: vol. 3, n.p., table 2.

trade legal as late as 1830.[39] Jamaica, listed as the British Caribbean in the figure, which at one point had been the republic's third largest supplier of coffee after the 1815 peace, faced tariff retaliations by the US in 1818 and structural limits to coffee production due to the scarcity of land and labor. Although Java, a Dutch colony, went through a coffee revolution during this period,[40] the Dutch sent about 90% of its output to European markets: it was of a higher quality and was more valuable than what was consumed in the United States. Haiti had dominated the American market before the system of reciprocal blockades, and from 1809 to 1828 it was second only to Cuba, but Brazil later surpassed it by a wide margin. Haiti's production stalled at around 20 million mt, as seen in Fig. 7.[41]

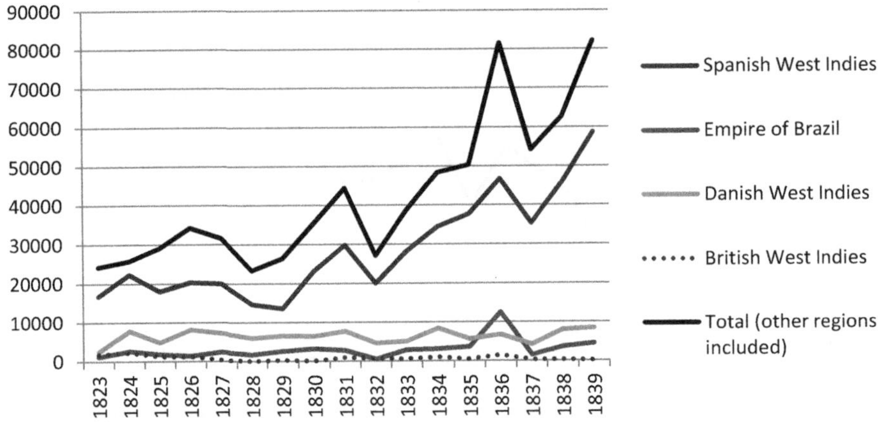

Fig. 7: American brown sugar imports by region (in mt).

The US bought increasing quantities of brown sugar in the 1820s, but the growth rate of this trade was so small that its exponential line predicted an annual import of 40,000 mt by 1840. Thanks to tariff reductions, imports rose to 80,000 mt in 1839, twice as much as projected. The physical volume of sugar purchased by the US was comparable to those years preceding the French invasion of Spain and Portugal. Cuba, in command of the American market since 1809, was naturally the main beneficiary of this windfall.

In the decades following the Nullification Crisis, the United States, Cuba, and Brazil went through a period of growing market integration, a large-scale material transformation with considerable implications for the political stability of New World slavery in the nineteenth century. Scholars usually discuss the politics of slavery from nation-centered

39 Marquese and Tomich, "O Vale do Paraíba."; Tâmis Parron, *A política da escravidão no Império do Brasil, 1826–1865* (Rio de Janeiro: Civilização Brasileira, 2011): 72–84.

40 Mario Samper and Radin Fernando, "Historical Statistics of Coffee Production and Trade from 1700 to 1960," in *The Global Coffee Economy in Africa, Asia, and Latin America, 1500–1989*, ed. W.G. Clarence-Smith and Steven Topik (Cambridge: Cambridge University Press, 2003): 411–62, here 436.

41 Ibid.: 428.

perspectives, and it is natural that they do so. National politics is where the struggle for the state is explicitly staged. This view, however, can be misleading. The enclaves producing cotton in the South, sugar in Cuba, and coffee in Brazil belonged both to sovereign states and to the global economy. American, Cuban, and Brazilian planters were no less involved in the political struggles over state control than they were subject to the competitive pressures of world markets. No wonder that some of their decisions, even when targeting local issues like the Nullification Crisis, went well beyond the national arena and achieved systemic relevance. This mechanism explains in large part the material integration of the United States, Cuba, and Brazil during the nineteenth century.

4 Unified Paths, c. 1830–1860: The *Oikoumene* of the Second Slavery

Led by a small section of the master class of the United States, the Nullification Crisis did not establish commercial and financial ties between the three most dynamic slaveholding spaces of the New World out of nothing. What it did do was bring those relations to a new level, helping to broaden the US domestic market for coffee and sugar and to make popular demand for those coveted articles more sensitive to small rises in consumer income (elasticity of demand). This rising commodity circuit played an important role in the histories of the United States, Brazil, and Cuba. Let us take a closer look at the issue.

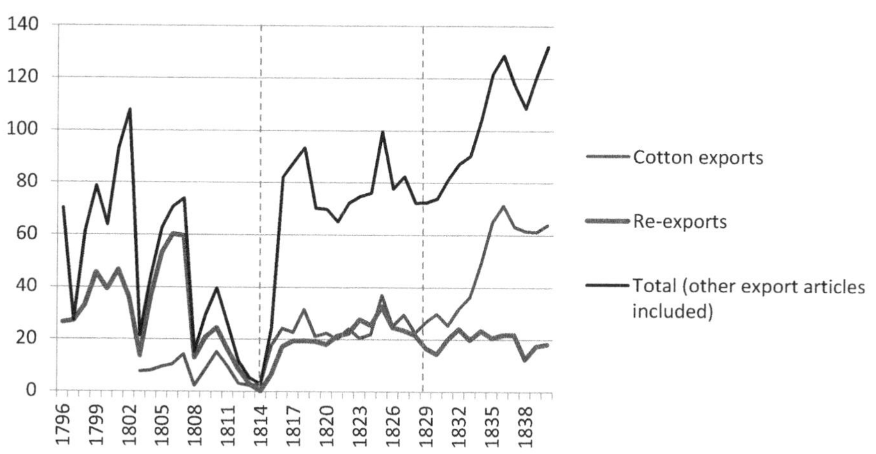

Fig. 8: US cotton exports and re-exports (in US$ millions).

Figure 8 shows three phases or moments: from 1796 to 1814, from 1815 to 1828, and from 1829 onward. Their distinction lies in the role that cotton and the re-export trade played in the American trade balance over the years. In *Moment I*, when the Revolutionary

Wars shaped commercial relations between the US and the greater Caribbean, re-exports turned out to be the leading sector of the young republic's foreign commerce. While large-scale commercialization of short-staple cotton had begun in the 1790s, the amounts it generated, available for the years after 1802, were well below those attained by resales of foreign merchandise. Coffee reshipment alone moved more money than the total sale of cotton in the first years of the century. It may be that the role played by tropical goods in foreign trade limited their domestic consumption in the United States.

In *Moment II*, the return of peace in 1815 allowed European powers to resume direct trade with the New World, reducing the value of American re-exports by 40%. This shift was offset by the rise of cotton exports, which now generated as much money as re-exports, and by exports of wheat to new partners like Brazil. Thanks to these changes, the total revenue from foreign trade (exports plus re-exports) in *Moment II* was like that of *Moment I*, thereby providing the means to retain a larger share of coffee and sugar for domestic consumption without straining the balance of trade. Two factors seem to have prevented a more aggressive expansion of coffee and sugar consumption in the American market. Re-exports were still relevant in those years and, above all, high tariffs made prices of tropical articles burdensome for middle- and low-income consumers throughout the 1820s.

Those two obstacles disappeared in *Moment III*. From 1829 on, the value of cotton exports rose well beyond that of the American re-export trade, coming to perform a critical role in the republic's trade balance. In theory, the surplus capital generated by cotton could be used to buy larger amounts of coffee and sugar and keep them for domestic consumption. Before that could happen, however, tariffs still had to be reduced, and this is precisely what happened during the Nullification Crisis. From this perspective, the Nullification Crisis readjusted the American tariff system to the new scenario supported by the cotton boom. Figures 9 and 10 show how *Moments I, II*, and *III* fit perfectly into the overall evolution of sugar and coffee imports to the republic.

In *Moment I*, 85% of coffee and 65% of sugar were re-exported; in *Moment II*, 40% and 25%; and in *Moment III*, after a short period of adjustment, 10% and 13%. The third period stands out even more in absolute terms. From *Moment I* to *Moment II*, average annual coffee and sugar imports dropped significantly, from 22,000 mt to 15,300 mt for coffee and from 51,000 mt to 34,000 mt for sugar. In other words, the rates of retention expanded over a smaller physical volume. Not so in *Moment III*. Retention rates for coffee and sugar dropped to 10% and 13%, while annual coffee imports tripled to 43,000 mt and sugar imports doubled to 70,000 mt. By then, the United States was starting to play a leading role in expanding key markets for tropical goods and, by extension, in fostering slavery in other countries. In 1827, for example, the two main European markets for coffee were Hamburg and Antwerp. Each bought 28,000 mt, almost a quarter more than the US (22,000 mt). By 1834, Hamburg had become relatively less important (23,000 mt), followed by Amsterdam (20,000 mt), while the United States outpaced both by far (46,000 mt). In 1843, while Hamburg remained at 20,000 mt, now second to France

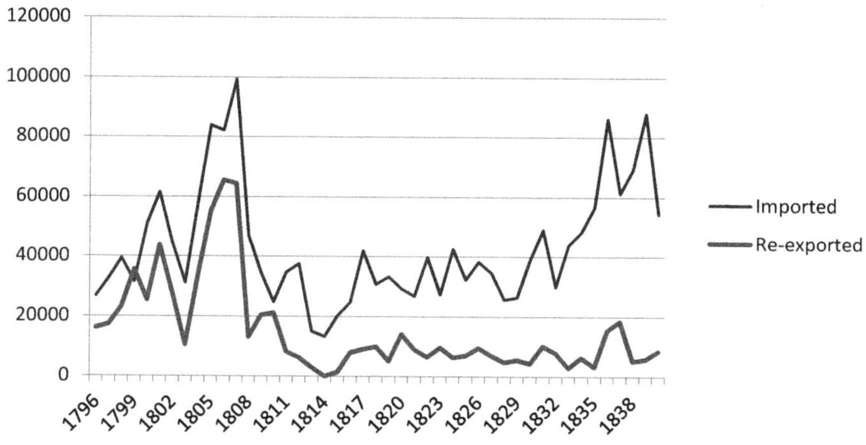

Fig. 9: Destination of white and brown sugar imports (in mt).

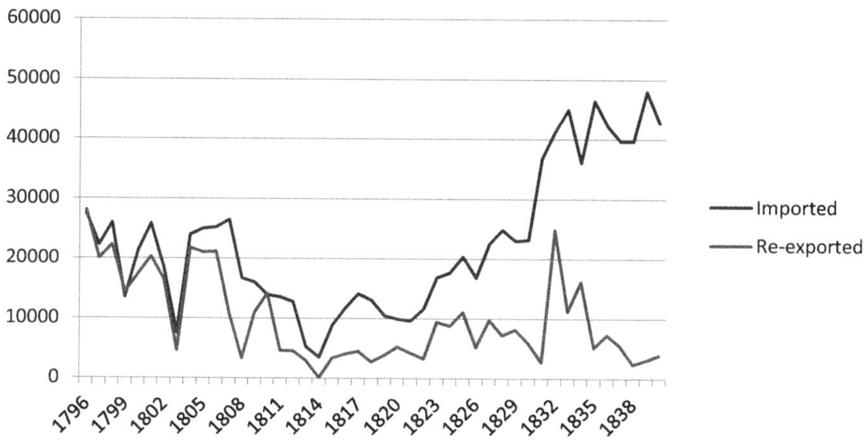

Fig. 10: Destination of coffee imports (in mt).

(29,000 mt), the United States was moving ahead towards 70,000 mt. In those years, the American republic re-organized the geography of coffee world markets.[42]

Capital volumes employed in sugar and coffee trading also reached a new level of magnitude in *Moment III*. Data available for the years 1802–1804, 1821–1830, and

42 European Data in Friedrich Benedict Weber, *Historisch-statistisches Jahrbuch in Bezug auf Nationalindustrie und Staatswirtschaft mit besonderer Berücksichtigung Deutschlands und namentlich Preussischen Staats. Erster Doppel-Jahrgang: Die Jahre 1830–1831* (Breslau: Mar und Comp., 1834): 438; August Schiebe, ed., *Universal-Lexikon der Handelswissenschaft*, vol. 2 (Leipzig: Friedrich Fleischer; Zwickau: Gebrüder Schumann, 1838): 137–46; Karl August, Müller, ed., *Statistisches Jahrbuch für 1845* (Leipzig: Hinrichsen Buchhandlung, 1845): 19.

1831–1840 suggests that the amount of dollars invested fluctuated, trending negatively in the 1820s. The annual average value of the coffee trade was US$ 7.3 million in the early 1800s, US$ 5 million in the 1820s, and almost US$ 9 million in the 1830s. The corresponding values for sugar were US$ 5.7 million, US$ 4.2 million, and US$ 7.8 million. Tariffs explain these abrupt changes, though deeper underlying factors support the broader upward trend. In general terms, coffee consumption stimulated that of sugar, since the former is a bitter stimulant usually taken with the latter, and both rose in tandem with

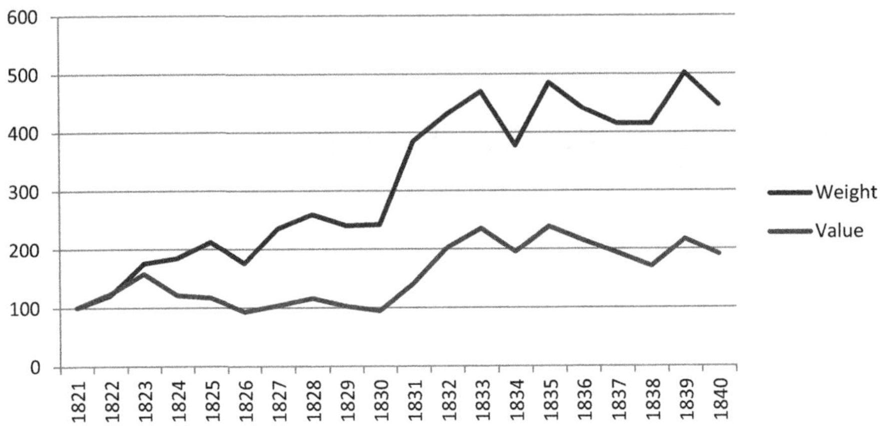

Fig. 11: Ratio of volume traded to capital invested (coffee, 1821 = 100).

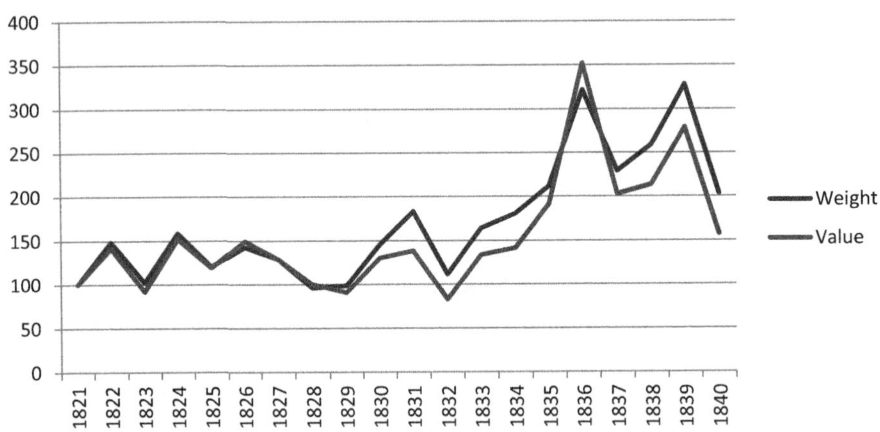

Fig. 12: Ratio of volume traded to capital invested (sugar, 1821 = 100).

demographic growth, urbanization, and the increasing connection between farming output and market-based relations. These trends are visible in Figures 11 and 12.[43]

Over the years, the leading commodity frontiers of slavery in Brazil and Cuba became dependent on the economic strength and political power of the American master class, who boosted capital surplus through cotton exports and challenged the American System under the banner of free trade. One may wonder if the emerging gradual market integration between these slaveholding regions did not become a source of geopolitical power at the time. To explore this idea, we can take as our starting point the phrase "Caribbean *oikoumene*," coined in a well-known essay by Sidney Mintz.[44] Mintz used the concept to define the Caribbean region as a geohistorical unit forged within a process of "cultural stripping and rebuilding" designed to discipline an enslaved immigrant workforce in order to meet the demands of distant markets. The expression does not describe cultural contents (language, beliefs, ideology), but rather a common process of cultural remodeling imposed on Caribbean people by capitalist modernity. Behind their differences in language and values, the West Indies, taken as a whole, experienced demographic imbalance, productive specialization, reduced availability of land, intercontinental supply chains, and colonialism.[45]

The United States, Cuba, and Brazil also went through a shared process of historical convergence during the nineteenth century. As Dale Tomich suggests, the reconfiguration of world markets and accumulation under the hegemony of British capital changed both the temporality and the spatiality of slavery in the Americas. Thanks to the environment, material life, economic conditions, and political compacts, new commodity frontiers – coffee in Brazil, sugar in Cuba, and cotton the United States – could rise as a historical unit against older plantation enclaves in their competition for rising labor, credit, technology, and consumption markets.[46] Following Mintz, one could argue that nineteenth-century capitalism also established a shared system of exploitation, environment exhaustion, and social violence throughout culturally diverse regions such as the Paraíba Valley, the Lower Mississippi Valley, and the Matanzas flatlands of Cuba. However, that is not the argument of this essay.

Rather, what I would like to point out is that there was a cluster of relations *among the slaveholding spaces* over the nineteenth century, a trans-regional framework within which events and processes in one place began to have impact, influence, and significance on events and processes in the others. Originally anchored in commodity exchanges, this

---

43 For the values at the beginning of the nineteenth century, see *American State Papers*, "Commerce with Great Britain and Her Dependencies, and All Ports of the World": vol. 5, 640–66.

44 Sidney Mintz, "Enduring Substances, Trying Theories: The Caribbean Region as Oikoumenê," *Journal of the Royal Anthropological Institute*, v. 2, n. 2 (1996): 289–311.

45 Peter Emmer, "The Dutch and the Second Atlantic System," in *Slavery and the Rising of the Atlantic System*, ed. Barbara Solow (Cambridge: Cambridge University Press, 1991): 75–96.

46 Dale Tomich, *Through the Prism of Slavery. Labor, Capital, and World Economy* (Lanham, MD: Rowman & Littlefield, 2004).

shared framework evolved into a fundamental source of political and geopolitical power for each slaveholding country in their relationship with the capitalist world economy as a whole. This remarkable historical unit – or *oikoumene* – was set up between 1790 and 1830, reaching its high point from 1830 to 1860, the three decades preceding the American Civil War.

The *oikoumene* of slavery in the nineteenth century had many implications for geopolitics, the economy, and national politics, but for now I would like to emphasize only two. The articulation between Cuba and Brazil, on one side, and the United States, on the other, turned the latter into a key mediating instance between the other slaveholding spaces and the British political and economic powerhouse. Increasingly, American technology, credit, and human resources helped organize the Transatlantic slave trade of Brazil and Cuba, as well as their transportation system, warehousing facilities, and plantation machinery. From a political perspective, economic integration meant growing alignment around slavery-related issues, which reinforced the position of Brazilian and Cuban slaveholders in their double confrontation with local and British antislavery movements. At decisive moments, US diplomacy helped Brazil and Spain resist British pressure against human bondage. In addition, Cubans and Brazilians referred to the US to justify their defense of slavery.[47] Immanuel Wallerstein once wrote about sixteenth-century Spain that a country may be on the periphery of capitalism even if it is not peripheral.[48] The opposite applies to the United States three centuries later. It became central to black slavery in the Americas even though it was not the center of the world economy at the time.

Instead of understanding the reconfiguration of nineteenth-century slavery as the result of three independent answers to world capitalism, the point of this essay is that the rise of Cuba and Brazil was increasingly mediated by that of the American economy, which in turn was dependent on the globalization of the British empire, a subject beyond the scope of this essay. This *oikoumene* formed a solid cluster of relations in which the purchase, transportation, and consumption of coffee and sugar, as well as the ideological and political defense of slavery, increasingly revolved around the United States.[49] This was a break with the past. Whereas, historically, most slave-made goods from the New World had been consumed in Europe, from 1830 onward coffee and sugar from Cuba and Brazil found their key consumer market in the main

47 Tâmis Parron, "A política da escravidão na era da liberdade: Estados Unidos, Brasil e Cuba, 1787–1847" (PhD diss., Universidade de São Paulo, 2015).

48 Immanuel Wallerstein, *O sistema mundial moderno*, vol. 1, *A agricultura capitalista e as origens da economia-mundo europeia no século XVI* (Edições Afrontamento: Porto, 1990): 191.

49 See Oscar Zanetti and Alejandro García, *Sugar and Railroads: A Cuban History* (Chapel Hill: University of North Carolina Press, 1998); Jonathan Curry-Machado, *Cuban Sugar Industry: Transnational Networks and Engineering Migrants in Mid-Nineteenth Century Cuba* (New York: Palgrave MacMillan, 2011); Daniel Rood, *The Invention of Atlantic Slavery: Technology, Labor, Race, and Capitalism in the Greater Caribbean* (Oxford: Oxford University Press, 2020).

slaveholding nation of the time, an aspect that helped carve out a space of autonomy for slavery within an increasingly anti-slavery world. However, this *oikoumene* had a limit at its very core. Due to the international division of labor, the United States never internalized its cotton commodity chain: while it consumed other countries' slave-made goods, it did not consume the lion's share of its own slave-made cotton. If it had, a new sort of material integration could have led to incalculable impacts on the domestic anti-slavery movement, North-South inter-regional alliances, and political compromises regarding slavery. Ultimately, American slaveholders never stopped depending on Great Britain, and when London did not acknowledge the independence of the Confederate States of America, they belatedly realized the risk of entrusting their fate to the hands of a non-slaveholding foreign power.

Like every historical structure, this new *oikoumene* of slavery had a beginning and an end. It had its formative years (1790–1830), its heyday (1830–1860), and its crisis (1861–1865). The outbreak of the American Civil War brought it to an end by remaking the material and symbolic ties between the United States, Cuba, and Brazil. While commodity flows continued to increase afterward, they did so on an entirely new basis. Cotton's share in the republic's trade balance decreased, with its export values gradually surpassed by those of wheat, the outcome of a revolution in world markets for wheat and in wheat production in the Mid-West.[50] Coffee from Brazil and sugar from Cuba found in wheat an economic substitute for cotton, but the political lobby of the wheat industry could not give Brazilians and Cubans the ideological and geopolitical cover they had once enjoyed among Southerners. A new world was in the making, and the Second Slavery, without its *oikoumene*, eventually collapsed.

Bibliography

Primary Sources

American State Papers. Documents, Legislative and Executive, of the Congress of the United States. Commerce and Navigation, vol. 1–2 (Washington: Gales and Seaton, 1832).

Journal of the House of Representatives of the United States of America (Washington, D.C.: Duff Green, June 22, 1832).

Journal of the Senate of the United States of America (Washington, D.C.: Duff Green, July 5, 1832).

Letter from the Secretary of the Treasury of the United States for the year ending the 30th September, 1822 (Washington: Gales and Seaton, 1823).

---

50 William Cronon, *Nature's Metropolis: Chicago and the Great West* (New York, Norton: 1992); William Appleman Williams, *The Roots of the Modern American Empire: A Study of the Growth and Shaping of Social Consciousness in a Marketplace Society* (New York: Random House, 1969): 132–236; Giovanni Arrighi, *O longo século XX: dinheiro, poder e as origens de nosso tempo* (Rio de Janeiro/São Paulo: Contraponto/Unesp, 1996): 277–309.

Müller, Karl August, ed. *Statistisches Jahrbuch für 1845* (Leipzig: Hinrichsen Buchhandlung, 1845).

Official letters from William Hunter to John Forsyth, Official letter from William Hunter to John Forsyth, December 10, 1835, US National Archives, Record Group 59, microfilm 121, roll 12; and February 10, 1837, USNA, RG 59, m. 121, roll 13.

Remonstrance against an Increase of Duties on Imports (1820), American State Papers, Finance, vol. 3, 563–67.

Report of the Secretary of the Commerce and Navigation of the United States for the year ending on the 30th September, 1823 (Washington: Gales and Seaton, 1824).

Speech of Mr. McDuffie of South Carolina on the Bill Proposing a Reduction of the Duties on Imports (Washington, D.C.: Duff Green, 1832).

Schiebe, August, ed. *Universal-Lexikon der Handelswissenschaft*, vol. 2 (Leipzig: Friedrich Fleischer/Zwickau: Gebrüder Schumann, 1838).

Weber, Friedrich Benedict. *Historisch-statistisches Jahrbuch in Bezug auf Nationalindustrie und Staatswirtschaft mit besonderer Berücksichtigung Deutschlands und namentlich Preussischen Staats. Erster Doppel-Jahrgang: Die Jahre 1830–1831* (Breslau: Mar und Comp., 1834).

Secondary Literature

Aldin, Dauril. "El Brasil colonial tardío, 1750–1808," in *História de América Latina*, vol. 3, *America Latina Colonial: economía*, ed. Leslie Bethell (Barcelona: Editorial Crítica, 1990): 306–58.

Alexandre, Valintim. *Os sentidos do império: questão nacional e questão colonial na Crise do Antigo Regime português* (Porto: Edições Afrontamento, 1993).

Arango y Parreño, Francisco. *Obras* (Havana: Imagen Contemporanea, 2005).

Arruda, José Jobson de Andrade. *Uma colônia entre dois impérios: a Abertura dos Portos brasileiros, 1800–1808* (São Paulo: Edusc, Bauru 2008).

Arrighi, Giovanni. *O longo século XX: dinheiro, poder e as origIns de nosso tempo* (Rio de Janeiro/São Paulo: Contraponto/Unesp, 1996).

Bergad, Lair, *The Comparative Histories of Slavery in Brazil, Cuba, and the United States* (Cambridge: Cambridge University Press, 2007).

Brading, David A. "La España de los Borbones y su império americano," in *História de América Latina*, vol. 2, *America Latina Colonial In los siglos XVI, XVII, XVIII*, ed. Leslie Bethell (Barcelona: Editorial Crítica, 1990): 85–126.

Brown, Gregory. "The Impact of American Flour Imports on Brazilian Wheat Production: 1808–1822," *The Americas* 47 (1991): 315–36.

Bruchey, Stuart, ed. *Cotton and the Growth of the American Economy: 1790–1860. Sources and Readings* (New York: Harcourt, Branc & World, 1967).

[Calhoun, John C.] "Exposition and Protest reported by the Special Committee of the House of the Representative of South Carolina, on the Tariff," in *The Statutes at Large of South Carolina*, ed. Thomas Cooper (Columbia: A.S. Johnston, 1836): 247–73.

Cronon, William. *Nature's Metropolis: Chicago and the Great West* (New York: Norton, 1992).

Curry-Machado, Jonathan. *Cuban Sugar Industry: Transnational Networks and Engineering Migrants in Mid-Nineteenth Century Cuba* (New York: Palgrave MacMillan, 2011).

Drescher, Seymour. *Abolition: A History of Slavery and Antislavery* (Cambridge: Cambridge University Press, 2009).

Emmer, Peter. "The Dutch and the Second Atlantic System," in *Slavery and the Rising of the Atlantic System*, ed. Barbara Solow (Cambridge: Cambridge University Press, 1991): 75–96.

Fernández de Pinedo Echevarra, Nadia. *Las Balanzas del Comercio exterior de La Habana, 1803–1807* (Bilbao: Universidad Editorial del PaísVasco, 2000).
Ferrer, Ada "Cuban Slavery and Atlantic Antislavery," in *Slavery and Antislavery in Spain's Atlantic Empire*, ed. Josep M. Fradera and Christopher Schmidt-Nowara (New York: Bergham Books, 2013): 134–57.
Follet, Richard. *The Sugar Masters: Planters and Slaves in Louisiana's Cane World, 1820–1860* (Baton Rouge: Louisiana State University Press, 2005).
Foner, Eric. *Historia de Cuba sus relaciones con los Estados Unidos*, vol. 1, *1492–1845, de la conquista de Cuba hasta 'la escalera'* (Havana: Editora Universitaria, 1966).
Freehling, William W. *The Road to Disunion*, vol. 1, *Secessionists at Bay, 1776–1854* (Oxford: Oxford University Press, 1990).
Hickey, Donald R. "American Trade Restrictions during the War of 1812," *Journal of American History* 68, no. 3 (1981): 517–38.
Horne, Gerald. *The Deepest South: The United States, Brazil, and the African Slave Trade* (New York: New York University Press, 2007).
Jarnagin, Laura. *A Confluence of Transatlantic Networks* (Tuscaloosa: University of Alabama Press, 2008).
Johnson, Walter. *River of Dark Dreams: Slavery and Empire in the Cotton Kingdom* (Cambridge, MA: Belknapp Press, 2003).
Killick, John R. "The Cotton Operations of Alexander Brown and Sons in the Deep South, 1820–1860," *Journal of Southern History* 43, no. 2 (1977): 169–94.
Marquese, Rafael, and Dale Tomich. "O Vale do Paraíba escravista e a formação do mercado mundial do café no século XIX," in *O Brasil imperial*, vol. 2, *1831–1870*, ed. Keila Grindberg and Ricardo Salles (Rio de Janeiro: Civilização Brasileira, 2009): 339–83.
Marrero, Levi. *Cuba: Economía y Sociedad: Azucar, Ilustración y Conciencia (1763–1868)*, vol. 3 (Madrid: Editora Mayor, 1981).
Maxwell, Kenneth. *Chocolate, piratas e outros malandros: Ensaios tropicais* (Rio de Janeiro: Paz e Terra, 1999).
McCuster, John J., and Russell R. Menard. *The Economy of British America, 1607–1789* (Chapel Hill: University of North Carolina Press, 1991).
McDonald, Michelle C. "From Cultivation to Cup: Caribbean Coffee and the North American Economy, 1765–1805" (PhD diss., University of Michigan, 2005).
Moreno Fraginals, Manuel. *O engenho: complexo sócio-econômico açucareiro cubano*, 3 vols. (São Paulo: Hucitec, 1989).
Parron, Tâmis. *A política da escravidão no Império do Brasil, 1826–1865* (Rio de Janeiro: Civilização Brasileira, 2011).
Parron, Tâmis. "A política da escravidão na era da liberdade: Estados Unidos, Brasil e Cuba, 1787–1847" (PhD diss., Universidade de São Paulo. 2015).
Pedreira, Jorge M. "From Growth to Collapse: Portugal, Brazil, and the Breakdown of the Old Colonial System (1750–1830)," *Hispanic American Historical Review* 80, no. 4 (2000): 839–64.
Pedreira, Jorge M. "Economia e política na explicação da independência do Brasil," in *A Independência Brasileira: novas dimensões*, ed. Jurandir Malerba (Rio de Janeiro: FVG Editora, 2006): 55–97.
Pluchon, Pierre. *Toussaint Louverture de l'esclavage au pouvoir* (Paris: l'Ecole/Port au Prince, Editions Caraïbes, 1979).
Rood, Daniel. *The Invention of Atlantic Slavery: Technology, Labor, Race, and Capitalism in the Greater Caribbean* (Oxford: Oxford University Press, 2020).
Samper, Mario, and Radin Fernando. "Historical Statistics of Coffee Production and Trade from 1700 to 1960," in *The Global Coffee Economy in Africa, Asia, and Latin America, 1500–1989*, ed. William Gervase Clarence-Smith and Steven Topik (Cambridge: Cambridge University Press, 2003): 411–62.

Schoen, Brian. *The Fragile Fabric of Union: Cotton, Federal Politics, and the Global Origins of the Civil War* (Baltimore: The John Hopkins University Press, 2009).
Silva, Andrée Mansuy-Diniz. "Portugal y Brasil: la reorganización imperial, 1750–1808," in *História de América Latina*, vol. 2, *America Latina Colonial en los siglos XVI, XVII, XVIII*, ed. Leslie Bethell (Barcelona: Editorial Crítica, 1990): 150–84.
Sinha, Manisha. *The Counterrevolution of Slavery: Politics and Ideology in Antebellum South Carolina* (Chapel Hill: University of North Carolina Press, 2000).
Torres-Cuevas, Eduardo. "De la Ilustración reformista al reformismo liberal," in *Historia de Cuba. La Colonia, evolución socioeconómico y formación nacional de los origines hasta 1867*, ed. María del Carmen Barcia, Gloria García and Eduardo Torres-Cuevas (Havana: Editora Política, 1994): 314–59.
Vampley, Wray. "The Protection of English Cereal Producers: The Corn Laws Reassessed," *The Economic History Review* 33, no. 3 (1980): 382–95.
van Norman Jr., William C. *Shade-grown Slavery: The Lives of Slaves on Coffee Plantations in Cuba* (Nashville: Vanderbilt University Press, 2013).
Wallerstein, Immanuel. *O sistema mundial moderno*, vol. 1, *A agricultura capitalista e as origens da economia-mundo europeia no século XVI* (Porto: Edições Afrontamento, 1990).
Williams, William Appleman. *The Roots of the Modern American Empire: A Study of the Growth and Shaping of Social Consciousness in a Marketplace Society* (New York: Random House, 1969).
Wright, Gavin. *The Political Economy of the Cotton South: Households, Markets, and Wealth in the Nineteenth Century* (New York: Norton, 1978).
Yard, James. *Spanish America and the United States or the Views of the Actual Commerce of the United States with the Spanish Colonies* (Philadelphia: Carey, 1818).
Zanetti, Oscar, and Alejandro García. *Sugar and Railroads: A Cuban History* (Chapel Hill: University of North Carolina Press, 1998).

Roberto Hofmeister Pich

The Catholic Church and Abolitionism in Nineteenth-Century Imperial Brazil: Pope Gregory XVI's Bull *In supremo apostolatus* (1839) and Antônio Vicente Ferreira Viçoso's Anti-Slavery Thought

On December 3, 1839, Pope Gregory XVI published the apostolic letter *In supremo apostolatus fastigio*, through which he categorically prohibited the enslavement of and trade in indigenous and African slaves. In the document, the Highest Pontiff includes himself in a long tradition of predecessors who vehemently reprimanded practices of enslavement. In fact, several other pontiffs before Gregory XVI made moves against slavery to both indigenous people and blacks from West and Sub-Saharan Africa. Concretely, and concerning black slavery in particular, such statements had a very modest effect. After all, even granting a real connection between the apostolic letter by Gregory XVI and the abolitionist movement(s) in the nineteenth century, the truth is that slavery officially endured in Brazil until May 13, 1888.[1]

From the fifteenth century onwards, the relationship between the Catholic Church as a whole – including its ecclesiastical authorities, theologians, and ministers – and slavery was characterized by ambiguities and even contradictions.[2] Concerning ecclesiastical

---

1 Rebecca J. Scott, ed., *The Abolition of Slavery and the Aftermath of Emancipation in Brazil* (Durham, NC/London: Duke University Press, 1988); Mário Maestri, *A servidão negra* (Porto Alegre: Editora Mercado Aberto, 1988); Mário Maestri, *O escravismo no Brasil*, 10th ed. (São Paulo: Atual, 2002); Lilia Moritz Schwarcz and Flávio Gomes, eds., *Dicionário da escravidão e liberdade* (São Paulo: Companhia das Letras, 2018).

2 For the perception of this with regard to black slavery and the Transatlantic traffic in slaves, one should revisit works by such authors as Tomás de Mercado OP (1525–1575), Luis de Molina SJ (1535–1600), Alonso de Sandoval SJ (1576–1652), Diego de Avendaño SJ (1594–1688), Francisco José de Jaca OFM Cap (*c.* 1645–1689), and Epifanio de Moirans OFM Cap (1644–1689). See Alfredo Santiago Culleton, "Tomás de Mercado on Slavery: Just According to Law, Unjust in Practice," *Patristica et Mediaevalia* 36 (2015): 29–38; Márcio Paulo Cenci, "African Slavery and Salvation in the *De instauranda Aethiopum salute* of Alonso de Sandoval S.J. (1577–1652)," *Patristica et Mediaevalia* 36 (2015): 75–89; Roberto Hofmeister Pich, "Alonso de Sandoval S.J. (1576/1577–1652) and the Ideology of Black Slavery: Some Theological and Philosophical Arguments," *Patristica et Mediaevalia* 36 (2015): 51–74; Roberto Hofmeister Pich, "Second Scholasticism and Black Slavery," *Veritas* 64, no. 3 (2019): 1–24; Roberto Hofmeister Pich, "Second Scholasticism and Black Slavery (Continuation and End)," *Veritas* 65, no. 1 (2020): 1–13; Roberto Hofmeister Pich, "Francisco José de Jaca's (*c.* 1645–1689) and Epifanio de Moirans's (1644–1689) Plea for the Liberation of Enslaved Black People in Latin America," in *Civilization – Nature – Subjugation. Variations of (De-)Colonization*, ed. Christoph Haar, Matthias Kaufmann and Christian Müller (Berlin: Peter Lang, 2021): 69–110. Ambiguity certainly also characterizes the attitude of Jesuit missionaries in colonial Brazil towards slavery. Their conservative ideological role in shaping a colonial society that included in its structure both the

https://doi.org/10.1515/9783111026527-008

authorities, there were, on the one hand, pontiffs who, through pontifical bulls and apostolic briefs, condemned slavery; on the other hand, there were pontiffs who expressed, to a greater or less extent, acquiescence. This was initially due, above all, to the fight against the expansion of Islam in the Mediterranean and, shortly after, to the urgent need to react to the expansion of Islam in West and Sub-Saharan Africa, the Atlantic coast of which began to be more and more explored by the Portuguese. As Muslims did to Christians, too, it was considered legitimate, in principle, to enslave the followers of Islam for the alleged purpose of setting them free from a false and unfaithful religion. More specifically, in the wake of both the ambiguities in official documents by the Roman See and the movement to combat the expansion of Muslim domains, we should emphasize that several popes endorsed the project of ultramarine expansion by the Kingdom of Portugal through a series of bulls that gave religious backing to the conquest of new territories along the western African coast, even if this could lead, as a consequence, to the enslavement of pagan or unfaithful inhabitants. It has been correctly noted that the bull *Sicut Dudum* (January 13, 1435) by Pope Eugene IV (1431 to 1447) cannot be taken as an anti-slavery document, since it only contains a condemnation of the enslavement of baptized Christians or people about to receive Christian baptism[3] who happened to be found in areas of Catholic mission.

In the first of several bulls that gave explicit support to Portuguese overseas expansionism and showed toleration towards enslavement (*Dum diversas*, June 18, 1452), "Pope Nicholas V [1447 to 1455] authorized the king of Portugal [Afonso V] to attack, conquer, and subjugate Saracen Moors, pagans, and other enemies of Christ."[4] As is known today, the enslavement of black people from western Africa for commercial purposes by the Portuguese is documented from 1441 onwards;[5] with *Dum diversas*, this received ecclesiastical sanction. The same Pope Nicholas V, in the bull *Romanus Pontifex* (January 8, 1455), authorized the infant Dom Henrique to conquer and enslave not only Muslims, but all pagans found between Morocco and the Indies. These and other pontifical statements, ratified by Calixtus III (1455 to 1458), openly authorized the Portuguese to conquer, assert political sovereignty, establish commercial monopolies, and, last but not least, create the "power of spiritual jurisdiction" in Africa.[6]

slavery of black people and a Christian project of catechesis together with an ethics for the relationship between masters and slaves has been explained in several studies; see, for example, Ronaldo Vainfas, *Ideologia e escravidão. Os letrados e a sociedade escravista no Brasil colonial* (Petrópolis: Vozes, 1986); Ronaldo Vainfas, "Escravidão, ideologias e sociedade," in *Escravidão e abolição no Brasil. Novas perspectivas*, ed. Ciro Flamarion Cardoso (Rio de Janeiro: Jorge Zahar Editor, 1988): 48–56.

3 Nicole Priesching, "Die Verurteilung der Sklaverei durch Gregor XVI. im Jahr 1839. Ein Traditionsbruch?" in *Saeculum: Jahrbuch für Universalgeschichte* 59, no. 1 (2008): 145–46.

4 Laurentino Gomes, *Escravidão – Volume I: Do primeiro leilão de cativos em Portugal até a morte de Zumbi dos Palmares* (Rio de Janeiro: Globo Livros, 2019): 343.

5 Michael Zeuske, *Sklaven und Sklaverei in den Welten des Atlantiks 1400–1940. Umrisse, Anfänge, Akteure, Vergleichsfelder und Bibliographien* (Berlin: LIT, 2006).

6 Priesching, "Die Verurteilung der Sklaverei": 146–47.

At any rate, the subsequent renaissance and pre-modern popes, who, just like Nicholas V, were notably sympathetic to the idea of "plenitude of [papal] power," showed diverse attitudes. The immediate successor of Calixtus III, Pius II (a person of humanist tendencies and the author of a large work on history and cosmography, whose pontificate extended from 1458 to 1464), affirmed again, in 1462, in a letter directed to the bishop of Rubicón (on the Canary Islands), that the enslavement and trade of African slaves in conditions similar to those taken into consideration by Eugene IV[7] decades before, were a grave sin and would bring, as a consequence, the issuing of severe canonical penalties for their perpetrators. Pope Paul III (1534 to 1549) famously published the brief *Veritas ipsa* (May 2, 1537) and *Sublimis Deus* (June 2, 1537),[8] a true "Magna Charta of the law of peoples," according to Hans-Jürgen Prien.[9] Here, he prohibited all enslavement on the basis of alleged natural inferiority, thereby presenting decisive grounds for rejecting any attempt to legitimate the conquest of aboriginal peoples and American lands through the idea that Amerindians lacked a soul or were defective in reason, making them naturally incapable of wielding freedom and the right to property.[10] In turn, Pope Urban VIII (1623 to 1644) declared, or rather, following documents by Paul III, "re-declared" the prohibition of enslavement of and trade of enslaved indigenous people or original inhabitants of the western and southern Indies with *Commissum Nobis* (April 22, 1639).[11] We should keep in mind that none of the documents with critical notes about slavery mentioned so far (to which the apostolic letter *In supremo apostolatus* by Gregory XVI makes explicit reference, see Section 2,[12] with the exception of the bulls by Eugene IV and Calixtus III) constitutes an unconditional and strict condemnation of slavery: rather, they refer to specific forms of slavery and specific groups of people that were unjustly enslaved. Moreover, it is important to realize that none of these papal documents contemplate black slavery as a system of enslavement connected to the Transatlantic trade that supported the colonization and economic exploitation of the Americas.

On the slavery of black Africans within the context of the Transatlantic trade (essentially, from the western coast of Africa to the Americas from the first years of the sixteenth century),[13] there were, almost from the beginning, some critical voices inside the Church. If

---

7 Priesching, "Die Verurteilung der Sklaverei": 147.

8 In the literature, there is divergency about the dates on which these two documents were issued, which, as such, are similar in content.

9 Hans-Jürgen Prien, *Die Geschichte des Christentums in Lateinamerika* (Göttingen: Vandenhoeck & Ruprecht, 1978): 173.

10 Silvio Arturo Zavala, *Repaso histórico de la bula* Sublimis Deus *de Paulo III, en defensa de los indios* (México: Universidad Iberoamericana, 1991).

11 Priesching, "Die Verurteilung der Sklaverei": 150.

12 Further references to popes who issued documents touching the topic of slavery will be made in Section 2 of this study.

13 Herbert S. Klein, *Escravidão africana – América Latina e Caribe*, trans. José Eduardo de Mendonça (São Paulo: Editora Brasiliense, 1987): 11–57; Zeuske, *Sklaven und Sklaverei*: 97–264; Michael Zeuske,

Catholic thinkers critical of black slavery between the sixteenth to eighteenth centuries were not "abolitionists" in a strict sense, according to the view that it is always and everywhere wrong that human beings are property of other human beings and treated as such, there was, despite ambiguities on these same points, hard criticism of the legitimacy of slave trade and possession of slaves, as well as of aspects of the treatment (incompatible with a Christian ethics of serf – master relations) given to enslaved Africans sent to a regime of forced labor in the New World.[14] Moreover, in a few cases, there was also opposition to slave traffic and property *as a whole,* pleading for an end to it *with no room for ambivalence.*[15] Non-ambiguous stances and stances radically contrary to black slavery from ministers, missionaries, and intellectuals were, as a rule, not exalted or propagated. One way or another (due to internal pressure by the Church, external pressure from the civil authorities, or pressure from economic agents whose undertakings depended on forced labor), such stances were discouraged and silenced.[16]

Embarrassing as it may be, anti-slavery positions in the bosom of the Catholic Church gained strength only in the nineteenth century. They gained substance together with the emergence of a decided pressure campaign on the international scene for the end of the Atlantic slave trade in the 1830s, led by the British government above all.[17] Such pressure had repercussions for the Vatican. In order to understand anti-slavery "movements" inside the Catholic Church in the nineteenth century, especially in Latin America, we have to consider the rise of the ultramontanist model in the hierarchical structure of the Church. This was characterized by an unequivocal alignment to the Roman See and had an impact on the relationships between ecclesiastical authority and

Sklavenhändler, Negreros und Atlantikkreolen. Eine Weltgeschichte des Sklavenhandels im atlantischen Raum (Berlin/Boston: De Gruyter Oldenbourg, 2015): 296–348; Michael Zeuske, *Sklaverei. Eine Menschheitsgeschichte von der Steinzeit bis heute* (Stuttgart: Philipp Reclam, 2018): 79–119.

14 Ludovicus Molina, *De iustitia et iure* (Coloniae Allobrogum: Ed. Marci Michaelis Bousquet, 1738 [Venetiis, 1611]): I, tr. 2, disp. 32–40, 86–117; Didacus de Avendaño, *Thesaurus indicus seu Generalis Instructor pro regimine conscientiae,* vol. 1 (Antuerpia: Apud Iacobum Meursium, 1668): tit. IX, cap. XII, § 8, nn. 180–205, 324–30; Alonso de Sandoval, *Un tratado sobre la esclavitud – De instauranda Aethiopum salute,* trans. Enriqueta Vila Vilar (Madrid: Alianza Editorial, 1987): II, iv–v, 243–51; Roberto Hofmeister Pich, Alfredo Santiago Culleton and Alfredo Carlos Storck, "Second Scholasticism and Black Slavery – Some Philosophical Assessments," *Patristica et Mediaevalia* 36 (2015): 3–15.

15 Francisco José de Jaca, *Resolución sobre la libertad de los negros, en estado de paganos y después ya cristianos: La primera condena de la esclavitud en el pensamiento hispano,* ed. Miguel Anxo Pena González (Madrid: Consejo Superior de Investigaciones Científicas, 2002); Epifanio de Moirans, *Siervos libres: una propuesta antiesclavista a finales del siglo XVII,* ed. Miguel Anxo Pena González (Madrid: Consejo Superior de Investigaciones Científicas, 2007).

16 On the commited actions by Francisco José de Jaca and Epifanio de Moirans against the commerce and property of black slaves in the Caribbean, see, for example, Miguel Anxo Pena González, "Un autor desconocido y singular en el pensamiento hispano," in *Francisco José de Jaca, Resolución sobre la libertad de los negros, en estado de paganos y después ya cristianos,* ed. Miguel Anxo Pena González (Madrid: Consejo Superior de Investigaciones Científicas, 2002): XXVIII–XXXVI.

17 See references in footnotes 35 and 134.

secular states. Across the world, and in particular in Brazil,[18] ultramontanist bishops strove for an end to any intervention by civil authorities in ecclesiastical jurisdiction and for the integral application of ecclesiastical norms directly issued by the popes in bishops' ministerial domains.[19] Ultramontanism is the ideological background of *In supremo apostolatus*,[20] issued by Pope Gregory XVI (1831 to 1846), which was the *first* official document by the Catholic Church that condemned the enslavement and trade of black people and indigenous people altogether – in fact, enslavement and trade of human beings, generally speaking (*ISA*, 1839, n. 1). Until then, enslavement and the slave trade had been legitimized *lato sensu* by normative reasons (*tituli*) taken from both Roman and medieval versions of the law(s) of peoples and positive law.

The impact of this letter in Catholic countries, its role in strengthening abolitionist movement(s) in the nineteenth century, and its promotion of the more or less direct participation of lay people and clerics in these movements is an open field of research.[21] The central purpose of this study is to show the repercussions of Gregory XVI's bull on the thought of Antônio Vicente Ferreira Viçoso,[22] bishop of Mariana from 1844 to 1875.

---

18 Fabiano Glaeser dos Santos, *O Papa infalível em Porto Alegre: repercussões em terras sulinas do Concílio Vaticano I* (Porto Alegre: EST, 2020): 44.

19 Hubert Wolf, "História da Igreja Católica durante o "longo século" XIX de 1789 a 1918," in *História ecumênica da Igreja*, vol. 3, *Da Revolução Francesa até 1989*, ed. Thomas Kaufmann, trans. Irineu Rabuske and Alfred Keller (São Paulo/São Leopoldo: Edições Loyola/Paulus/Editora Sinodal, 2017): 111.

20 For the references to the apostolic letter, I shall use the abbreviation "*ISA*." The division into five numbered paragraphs follows the translation into Portuguese found in: Papa Gregório XVI, *Carta Apostólica* In supremo [1839], Montfort Associação Cultural, http://www.montfort.org.br/bra/documentos/decretos/in_supremo/ [accessed 01.10.2022]. See also Gregório XVI, "In supremo," in *Documentos de Gregório XVI e de Pio IX (1831–1878)*, ed. Lourenço Costa, trans. Darci L. Marin (São Paulo: Paulus, 1999): 49–53. The original text, in Latin, was compared with the translation into Portuguese and with the following translation into English: Pope Gregory XVI, *In supremo apostolatus*, Papal Encyclicals Online, https://www.papalencyclicals.net/Greg16/g16sup.htm [accessed 01.10.2022].

21 This is something that was only recently noticed by researchers on the philosophical and theological history of black slavery in Latin America and Brazil; see, for example, João Paulo Rodrigues Pereira, "Educação ofendida ou defendida: as consequências do ideal antiescravista de Dom Viçoso no Seminário de Mariana (1844–1875)," *Revista saberes interdisciplinares* 23, no. 2 (2019): 97–108; Lúcio Álvaro Marques and João Paulo Rodrigues Pereira, "A barbárie como operador político," in *Escritos sobre escravidão*, ed. Lúcio Álvaro Marques and João Paulo Rodrigues Pereira (Porto Alegre: Editora FI, 2020a): 70–74.

22 Although the study of "Slavery Offended and Defended 1840" is quite recent, there are some studies on Viçoso's ministerial work, theological thought, and discourses and practices related to slavery. In the last case, these studies focused on Viçoso's remaining correspondence, personal notebooks, sermons, and contributions to the review *Selecta Catholica*. See Arnaldo José de Melo, "Dom Ferreira Viçoso (1787–1875) e sua obra reformadora da Igreja de Minas Gerais: uma releitura teológica moral" (PhD thesis, Pontificia Universitas Lateranensis, 2005); Marcella de Sá Brandão, "'Em defesa dos catholicos': imprensa católica no episcopado de D. Antônio Ferreira Viçoso" (master's diss., Universidade Federal de Minas Gerais, 2015): 63–137, 141–45 (giving comprehensive information on Viçoso's own remaining writings); Ítalo Domingos Santirocchi and Manoel de J. Martins, "'Quanto ao serviço dos escravos, eu os dispenso': D. Antònio Ferreira Viçoso, bispo ultamontano e antiescravista (século XIX),"

The first step is to briefly characterize ultramontanism in the nineteenth-century Catholic Church in Brazil. Secondly, we describe *In supremo apostolatus*. Third, we make remarks on the integration of this bull into the discourse of the Catholic Church in nineteenth-century Brazil. At this point, we analyze the thought of Viçoso on the basis of a recently discovered and edited manuscript. Here, Viçoso applies the main ideas of Gregory XVI's bull, explains his own views about slavery, and defends the validity of the Brazilian laws that were promulgated in alignment with the British international campaign for the end of the Atlantic slave trade.[23] Viçoso's efforts are precious testimony to the connections between Gregory XVI's bull, anti-slavery debates among Catholic clerics, and legal measures all over the world, particularly in Brazil, to further abolitionism.

1 Ultramontanism *and* Abolitionism? A Note of Transition

Before we propose an examination of Gregory XVI's *In supremo apostolatus* and an account of the reception of abolitionist ideas, coming from the Roman See, by Brazilian Catholic intellectuals and ecclesiastical authorities, such as Antônio Vicente Ferreira Viçoso, it seems important to highlight that both Gregory XVI and Antônio Vicente Ferreira Viçoso adhered to a self-understanding of the institution of the Roman Catholic Church about ecclesiastical jurisdiction and about the limits of civil power that can be characterized as "ultramontanism." This is a significant note about what we might expect with regard to the repercussion of *In supremo apostolatus* in Brazilian Catholicism. Although its roots are much older, especially from the end of the eighteenth century onwards, after the events of the French Revolution, the ultramontanist movement began to gain strength in the Roman Catholic universe. The model of the Church intended by the ultramontanists found its consolidation in the second half of the nineteenth century. The ultramontanist group undoubtedly was the winner in the I Vatican Council (1869–70).[24] Especially in the nineteenth century, ultramontanism meant much more than regaining papal and episcopal authority and securing the Church's jurisdictional autonomy – it brought about a significant reformation of the clergy's moral behavior, theological education, and sense of religious vocation, as well as the re-education of Catholics in doctrine and religious

in *Doze capítulos sobre escravizar gente e governar escravos: Brasil e Angola – séculos XVII–XIX*, ed. Denise Vieira Demétrio, Ítalo Domingos Santirocchi and Roberto Guedes (Rio de Janeiro: Mauad X, 2017): 197–226.

23 With the expression "Brazilian laws" or "Brazilian laws in the 1830s" against the slave trade, I refer to the Law of November 7, 1831, and its ampliative decrees.

24 John W. O'Malley, *Vatican I: The Council and the Making of the Ultramontane Church* (Cambridge, MA: Belknap Press, 2018).

observance. In any case, ultramontanism was mainly characterized by the strictest ideological and political alignment of the clergy with the Roman curia and, as a consequence, both opposition to ceding important aspects of the Church's prerogatives and fostering its full freedom with regard to the exertion of its ministry and jurisdiction. Ultramontane bishops and priests were involved in fights against the state's power over the Church and were opposed to every form of state interference in ecclesiastical questions.[25] The acceptance of the prerogatives of the state over the Church is summarized in the word "gallicanism."[26] Irrespective of the spiritual crisis in European Catholicism and the loss of political power by the Roman Catholic Church that explains its institutional search once again – as in the Latin Medieval West – for authority and prerogative of religious truth only *ultra montes*, the fact is that as an ecclesiastical movement that consolidated during nineteenth-century scientificist modernity, ultramontanism represented, in principle at least, a quite reactionary creed.[27]

In Portugal, in particular, the so-called system of royal patronage had prevailed since the fifteenth century, in which the Church, in practice, was a kind of department of the state and members of the clergy were like officials of the crown.[28] Royal patronage endured in Brazil[29] until the proclamation of the Brazilian Republic in 1889, although it was already in decay from the second half of the nineteenth century onward. A decisive reason for such a decline was the increasing number of priests and bishops who adhered to the ultramontane movement and put into question the legitimacy of this juridical order between church and state. From 1840 onwards, an increasing number of ultramontane bishops and priests acted in Brazil. For the most part, they received their education either in the influential seminary of Saint-Sulpice in Paris (established in 1651 by Jean-Jacques Olier) or in the Collegium Romanum.[30] Ultramontane clerics were opposed to the basic order supported by royal patronage, which established that the bishops of a given state should be nominated by the highest political authority – in the case of nineteenth-century Brazil, after independence from Portugal on September 7, 1822, they had to be nominated by the emperor himself. Contrary to what we might expect, Dom Pedro II himself, prematurely crowned on July 18, 1841, chose for the Brazilian episcopate priests who, later on, would contribute much to the

25 Vitor Conzemius, "Ultramontanismus," in *Theologische Realenzyklopädie* 34 (2002): 254.

26 See Giacomo Martina, *História da Igreja: de Lutero a nossos dias II – A era do liberalismo*, trans. Orlando Soares Moreira (São Paulo: Edições Loyola, 1996): 241–59.

27 Walther von Loewenich, *Die Geschichte der Kirche II: Von der Reformation zur Neuzeit*, 2nd ed. (München/Hamburg: Siebenstern, 1966): 144; Walther von Loewenich, *Der moderne Katholizismus*, 4th ed. (Witten: Luther-Verlag, 1959): 38–68.

28 See Henrique Cristiano José Matos, *Nossa história. 500 anos de presença da Igreja Católica no Brasil*, vol. 1, *Período colonial*, 2nd ed. (São Paulo: Paulinas, 2005): 97–114.

29 See Riolando Azzi, "A instituição eclesiástica durante a primeira época colonial," in *História da Igreja no Brasil. Ensaio de interpretação a partir do povo – Primeira Época*, ed. Eduardo Hoornaert et al., 2nd ed. (Petrópolis: Vozes, 1979): 160–69.

30 Santos, *O Papa infalível em Porto Alegre*, 69.

end of the system of royal patronage. In principle, Dom Pedro II's background motivation was simply to prevent clergymen with "revolutionary" tendencies – or "republican" tendencies, for that matter – getting access to the episcopate and using their influence and jurisdiction on the political domain.[31]

Gregory XVI's *In supremo apostolatus* was made public little more than seven months before the coup of the age of majority perpetrated by the General Assembly on July 23, 1840, making Pedro II, who was only 14 years old, a person who has come of age and, hence, emperor. It is currently unknown whether *In supremo apostolatus* received permission – the "placet" – for publication in Brazil: apparently, the document was never published in Cuba, for example, another slave-based power in Latin America.[32] In theory at least, under the regalist regime, it was granted that every ecclesiastical document could only be translated and published in Brazil with the approval of the highest political authority. At any rate, it is possible to affirm that Brazilian clerics or clerics active in Brazil, notably Antônio Vicente Ferreira Viçoso, who, on December 29, 1840,[33] was still a priest,[34] were acquainted with *In supremo apostolatus* shortly after its publication. How they became aware of it, the practical effects demanded by the papal document on Catholic Christians, and how these effects were ideologically and practically related to abolitionism in Brazil are not very well known yet. It is arguable that the letter gave a decisive expression, in doctrinal terms, to the belief that the slavery of black people severely offended the message of the Christian Gospel, a conviction that would have a positive impact on faithful Catholics in terms of accepting the validity of the increasing number of anti-slavery laws in nineteenth-century Brazil, such as the Law of November 7, 1831 (also called the "Feijó Law" or "Lei para inglês ver [Law to Be Seen by the British]") and the Law of September 4, 1850 (also known as the "Eusébio de Queirós Law").[35] The

---

31 Dilermando Ramos Vieira, *História do Catolicismo no Brasil*, vol. 1, *1500–1889* (Aparecida: Editora Santuário, 2016): 225.

32 Priesching, "Die Verurteilung der Sklaverei": 157.

33 This is the date that we find in the end of the original manuscript, kept at the "Arquivo Eclesiástico Dom Oscar de Oliveira" or the Ecclesiastical Archive of the Archdiocese of Mariana/MG, which was identified and edited by João Paulo Rodrigues Pereira. See the details of the publication in the bibliographical references. In this edition, the reproduction of Gregory XVI's bull is found in Padre Antônio Ferreira Viçoso, "Escravatura ofendida e defendida 1840," in *Escritos sobre escravidão*, ed. Lúcio Álvaro Marques and João Paulo Rodrigues Pereira (Porto Alegre: Editora FI, 2020): 184–87.

34 He also held the position, then, of "Superior Visitor of the Brazilian Province of the Congregation of Mission." See Lúcio Álvaro Marques and João Paulo Rodrigues Pereira, "Introdução histórica," in *Escritos sobre escravidão*, ed. Lúcio Álvaro Marques and João Paulo Rodrigues Pereira (Porto Alegre: Editora FI, 2020): 27.

35 See Senado Federal, *A abolição no Parlamento: 65 anos de luta (1823–1888)*, 2nd ed. (Brasília: Secretaria Especial de Editoração e Publicações – SEEP, 2012): 141–75. The Law of September 4, 1850, declared the trade of slaves to Brazil extinguished. Navy auditors should judge those who traded slaves into the country – farmers who broke the new anti-slavery law should be brought to court by the local justice. For a history of abolitionism in Brazil on the basis of analyses of anti-slavery laws, especially after the Law of September 4, 1850, see Robert Conrad, *The Destruction of Brazilian Slavery*

Law of November 7, 1831, which will be particularly referred to in the fourth section of this study, "was the first national law to prohibit the commerce of slaves."[36]

The story of the institutional and social impact, as well as of the integration into theological discourse and practice, of Gregory XVI's bull on Brazilian Catholicism among clergymen in Brazil particularly moved by fidelity to the Roman pontiff and explicitly bound to the ultramontane movement needs thorough investigation. To this group belonged Father Antônio Viçoso, appointed on January 12, 1844, as the seventh bishop of Mariana.[37]

2 Describing an Abolitionist Bull

Gregory XVI (1765–1846), born Bartolomeo Alberto Cappellari, as a rule is taken as a conservative pope, due in particular to his rejection of liberal Catholicism and modernist trends such as democratic regimes and freedom of conscience, as we can read in *Mirari vos* (August 15, 1832). He is also strongly identified with the ultramontanist movement. His performance as the prefect of the *Congregatio de Propaganda Fide* from 1826 to 1831 reveals his interest in the missionary task of the Church and is evidence of his acquaintance with specific areas of Catholic missionary work, such as Africa and Latin America.[38] It is perceptible that Gregory XVI's pastoral-evangelical and missionary concern with Catholic communities around the world was an impulse for the promulgation of the 1839 bull, but there is also an important political background that has to be highlighted. If it is well known that international policies for the abolition of Transatlantic slave trade in the nineteenth century came from Great Britain, it sometimes goes unnoticed that its secretary for foreign affairs, Lord Palmerston, through the mediation of the British consul in Florence Thomas Aubin, explicitly

1850–1888 (Berkeley/Los Angeles/London: University of California Press, 1972). On the political influence of England in the abolition of slave trade in Brazil, see also Leslie Bethell, *The Abolition of the Brazilian Slave Trade. Britain and the Slave Trade Question 1807–1869* (Cambridge: Cambridge University Press, 1970): especially 62–179.

36 See Senado Federal, *A abolição no Parlamento*: 65–71. Beatriz Gallotti Mamigonian and Keila Grinberg, "Lei de 1831," in *Dicionário da escravidão e liberdade*, ed. Lilia Moritz Schwarcz and Flávio Gomes (São Paulo: Companhia das Letras, 2018): 285. On the facts about the Law of November 7, 1831, and the role of that law in Brazilian imperial policies, the international relationships of the Brazilian Empire, and in the history of abolitionism in Brazil, see Beatriz G. Mamigonian, *Africanos livres. A abolição do tráfico de escravos no Brasil* (São Paulo: Companhia das Letras, 2017).

37 On Antônio Viçoso's profile as an ultramontane cleric, see Tatiana Costa Coelho, "Nas malhas do discurso: a Reforma Católica em Mariana e o discurso ultramontano de Dom Viçoso (Minas Gerais 1844–1875)," *Revista Eletrônica de História do Brasil* 9, no. 2 (2007): 97–107; Tatiana Costa Coelho, "A Reforma Católica em Mariana e o discurso ultramontano de Dom Viçoso (Minas Gerais 1844–1875)," in *Anais do XXVI Simpósio Nacional de História – ANPUH*, ed. Marieta de Moraes Ferreira (São Paulo: ANPUH, 2011): 1–9; Brandão, "'Em defesa dos catholicos'": 20–62.

38 Priesching, "Die Verurteilung der Sklaverei": 156–57.

requested, for humanitarian reasons, a declaration by the Roman pontiff in favor of the abolitionist cause.[39] Gregory XVI reacted on a high level indeed. *In supremo apostolatus* is a short document, but very dense in content, which is especially due to the fact that it presupposes several other papal documents and synthetizes important theological ideas. Right in the beginning, (i)[40] Gregory XVI affirms that the bull is part of his "pastoral solicitude" to move faithful Christians away from "the inhuman slave trade in negroes and all other men" (*ISA*, n. 1). The initial statement is particularly important, because it offers the conceptual framework for a document in its entirety, namely, that, in the face of the Christian Gospel, the trade of slaves is inhuman: indeed, *the trade of slaves* is the leading thread of the letter.

As comes out from the totality of the second paragraph of *In supremo apostolatus*, Gregory XVI, having in mind enslaved people from antiquity (or, more exactly, from the the period of the primitive and ancient Church), affirms that (ii) the Gospel has brought, once it became known, some relief to those "miserable people." (iii) A major reason for people being in the condition of slavery was wars (*ISA*, n. 2). Gregory XVI indicates that (iv) the apostles were not concerned with the end of slavery, but rather with how masters should humanely and fairly treat their slaves and how slaves should give, "according to the flesh," obedience towards masters. The basis for this relationship of command-and-obedience and mutual benefit is the theological principle that masters and serfs have "a common master," and before him all people are equal in condition (*ISA*, n. 2). It is explicit, at this point, that Gregory XVI is exploring the theology of Paul's apostolic letters in order to formulate the essentials of human relationships valid for Christians. These essentials, primarily in Christian houses and large families and, in a derivative way, in Christian communities and societies, condition what *among Christians* the institution of slavery, as a kind of lord-and-serf relationship, is or can be: passages such as Eph 6:5–9, Cl 3:22–35, and Cl 4:1 inspire the document. It is important to realize that Gregory XVI does not want to confine Christian instruction about the treatment of slaves to Christian houses and societies or, in a nutshell, relationships among Christians. In this sense, he affirms that (v) the "law of the Gospel" is "sincere charity towards all." "Our next" towards whom we shall act in charity, just like towards Christ himself, is any person who finds himself in need, as according to the text of Mt 25:35–40 (*ISA*, n. 2). Obedience to evangelical law explains (vi) the tradition of the ancient Church of guiding its faithful members to set their slaves free as a reward for their merits in service, which chiefly happened, according to the Cappadocian church father Gregory of Nyssa (*c.* 335–*c.* 395), as a custom during the "Easter Feast" or "Easter solemnities." It is also because of the guiding function of

39 Ibid.: 156.

40 In the following, the points (i), (ii), (iii), etc., are not subdivisions in the *In supremo apostolatus*, but rather are employed by the author of this study. They are auxiliary tools for reading and interpreting the apostolic letter and indicate emphases of what is understood by the author as more central in the text.

the law of the Gospel, which shapes the life of the Church, (vii) that zealous Christians accepted becoming slaves in order to, in replacement for them, set other enslaved people free, a testimony Gregory XVI takes from the ancient *Epistle of Clement to the Corinthians* or *First Epistle of Clement*,[41] written by Pope Clement I, whose pontificate extended from 88 to 97 (*ISA*, n. 2).

An important perception of the role of the Christian religion in shaping mind and attitudes towards slavery appears in the last part of paragraph 2 of *In supremo apostolatus*, the scope of which is the general theological view of the apostles and the ancient Church about slavery.[42] Gregory XVI clearly understands (viii) that the evangelical law of charity, which in principle at least commands and coordinates all actions of the Christian Church and its members, helped dissipate "the fog of pagan superstition" and soften "the manners of barbarous people" over time and with the enlargement of the Church's influence over the world (*ISA*, n. 2). It is implicit in this affirmation that evangelical law, inserted or determined in the world after the institution of the Christian community, is a stimulating element of historical processes that promote civilization and humanization. It is as a consequence, and even evidence, of this historical role of Christian ethics (ix) that one might say that, finally, for "several centuries" there have been "no more slaves in the greater number of Christian nations" (*ISA*, n. 2). This positive estimation by Gregory XVI is possibly an overstatement. At any rate, it seems that he has in view the Christian world, or the whole set of Christian nations, as it existed until approximately the end of the fifteenth century, before the movements of discovery and overseas expansion by Portugal and Spain. Without specifying any dates, we can suppose (x) that the "profound sorrow" that the pontiff expresses in the face of the events that then occurred *among Christians* due to "desire for sordid gain" "in lonely and distant countries" (*ISA*, n. 2) (the western coast of Africa? The American continent?) is also a lamentation for the interruption of historical progress and regression into a condition that should have been fully surpassed since the advent of Christianity. The fact under appraisal is, in general, (xi) the renewed enslavement of "Indians, negroes, and other wretched peoples" (*ISA*, n. 2). If the condemnation of the commerce in slaves is the framework of *In supremo apostolatus*, it contains not only *a lamentation* for the reintroduction of enslavement motivated by vile greed, but also *a condemnation*; after all, such enslavement (xii) presupposes continued traffic (the Transatlantic trade?), which happens to favor and induce enslavement (*ISA*, n. 2).

In the next paragraph, Gregory XVI refers to previous pontifical documents which also contained condemnations of enslavement and the trade of indigenous and Africans slaves. The choice of documents is consciously selective and seems to have in mind, in particular, the tangency between enslavement, the *colonization of America*,

41 Douglas Powell, "Clemens von Rom," in *Theologische Realenzyklopädie* 8 (1981): 113–18.

42 See, in this regard, Henneke Gülzow, *Christentum und Sklaverei in der ersten drei Jahrhunderten* (Bonn: Rudolf Habelt Verlag, 1969); Geoffrey Ernest Maurice de Sainte-Croix, "Early Christian Attitudes to Property and Slavery," in *Studies in Church History*, ed. Derek Baker (Oxford: Blackwell, 1975): 1–38.

and the *Transatlantic trade of slaves from Africa to the New World.*[43] All documents mentioned by Gregory XVI are from the fifteenth century onwards, that is, from the pontificate of Pius II (see above) to that of Pius VII (from March 1800 to August 1823). Gregory XVI (xiii) venerates and praises these previous pontifical contributions to the condemnation of the attitude or "behavior" of Christians who reintroduced enslavement and promoted the slave trade. He affirms (xiv) that such agents compromise their "spiritual welfare," put to shame "the Christian name," and stimulate amidst the "infidel peoples" hate towards the Christian religion, the "true religion" (*ISA*, n. 3). In this last point, it is evident that Gregory XVI is concerned with the harm that slavery causes to the evangelization of the world's peoples by the Catholic Church. In order to stress this last point, (xv) two bulls connected with the Amerindians are invoked: *Sublimis Deus* by Paul III and *Commissum Nobis* by Urban VIII (see the Introduction). Gregory XVI highlighted the scope of the condemnation they contain: what was condemned were the enslavement, trade, and treatment of the indigenous people as property of others in every possible respect, both by direct and indirect actors in the slavery system, as well as indigenous people continuing to live in this status after having been unjustly enslaved. In an additional unmistakable condemnation of enslavement, we find a reference to a third pope, namely, Benedict XIV (1740 to 1758), who issued on December 20, 1741,[44] *Immensa Pastorum principis* to the Brazilian episcopate, and other places as well (*ISA*, n. 3).[45] As it turns out, the background context of Benedict XIV's bull, which in the end had little or even no practical effects, was defending Jesuit missions in the lands of the Guaranis in South America.[46] In the same paragraph, (xvi) Gregory XVI highlights two popes who promulgated condemnations of the enslavement of and subsequent trade in black people from the western coast of Africa, Pius II and Pius VII. In the case of Pius VII, his vehement condemnation of the traffic of black slaves (*ISA*, n. 3) is not registered in bulls, but rather in the political gesture by the Roman See of adhering to the Congress of Vienna in 1815, which, in a joint declaration, prohibited the traffic of slaves in the northern hemisphere,[47] as well as in communications against the slave trade addressed to the crowns of France and Portugal.

It is in paragraph 4 of *In supremo apostolatus* that Gregory XVI turns the focus to his own times and specifies for faithful Catholics the condemnation and instruction of

---

43 For a general account of positionings by the popes, on a documentary basis, about slavery from the fifteenth to the nineteenth centuries, see Priesching, "Die Verurteilung der Sklaverei": 145–55; Pius Onyemechi Adiele, *The Popes, the Catholic Church and the Transatlantic Enslavement of Black Africans 1418–1839* (Hildesheim/Zürich/New York: Georg Olms Verlag, 2017).

44 The apostolic letter by Gregory XVI from December 3, 1839, interrupted a long silence from the Roman See on the theme of slavery, which had lasted from the apostolic letter of Benedict XIV on December 20, 1741.

45 See also Adiele, *The Popes, the Catholic Church and the Transatlantic Enslavement of Black Africans 1418–1839*: 377–78, 532–34.

46 Priesching, "Die Verurteilung der Sklaverei": 153–54.

47 In the prohibition, thus, the African "Costa da Mina" or "Gold Coast," from where a significant amount of enslaved Africans were taken into the Transatlantic slave trade, was included; see Carlos

his letter. (xvii) If through the documents of his predecessors the Catholic Church had attempted to interrupt the "cruelty of the invaders" and the "cupidity of Christian merchants" with regard to indigenous and black people, the still existing and frequent traffic of black people practiced by Catholic Christians (after all, it is over Catholic Christians that Pope Gregory XVI had spiritual jurisdiction) motivated a new effort to remove "such a shame from all the Christian nations." (xviii) This thus becomes a condemnation and prohibition that all Catholics – clerics and lay people – must be aware of and be obliged to observe:

> [. . .], We warn and adjure earnestly in the Lord faithful Christians of every condition that no one in the future dare to [unjustly][48] vex anyone, despoil him of his possessions, reduce to servitude, or lend aid and favour to those who give themselves up to these practices, or exercise that inhuman traffic by which the Blacks, as if they were not men but rather animals, having been brought into servitude, in no matter what way, are, without any distinction, in contempt of the rights of justice and humanity, bought, sold, and devoted sometimes to the hardest labor. Further, in the hope of gain, propositions of purchase being made to the first owners of the Blacks, dissensions and almost perpetual conflicts are aroused in these regions (*ISA*, n. 4).

In synthesis, from this document onwards (xix) any form of enslavement of any person is condemned and prohibited for Christians. Moreover, (xx) the trade of slaves is condemned, which is nourished by enslavement, nourishes enslavement, and puts the enslaved person into an inhuman condition (above all, due to inhuman labor). In the last two aspects highlighted, the corresponding unworthy actions are condemned if committed either directly or indirectly. In the paragraph under analysis of *In supremo apostolatus*, despite the general tone of condemnation, (xxi) those who are addressed as victims of such crimes are black people: the message is primarily for them (to do justice to them) and their executioners (to stop them and to condemn their actions). (xxii) We can interpret the letter in such a way that the reasons for condemning and prohibiting these practices are essentially two: the practices are completely inhuman and completely unjust or detrimental to law or right. In this condition, these practices are in strict opposition to the evangelical law of charity, which was previously stressed (*ISA*, n. 2), and to everything that derives from it. In the end (xxiii), Gregory XVI repeats the link between the evil of slavery and the evil of wars. If in paragraph 2, focused on the primitive Church, wars are the main generators of slaves, so again in paragraph 4: if the commerce in slaves is nourished by enslavement and it creates enslavement, enslavement is nourished by wars and creates wars – in this case, among the nations of the African continent.

If the expectation that the contents of the letter would be unreservedly adopted by faithful Catholics can be taken as something quite obvious, it should not go

---

Eduardo Moreira de Araújo, "Fim do tráfico," in *Dicionário da escravidão e liberdade*, ed. Lilia Moritz Schwarcz and Flávio Gomes (São Paulo: Companhia das Letras, 2018): 231.

48 The adverb "iniuste" is used in the Latin text of the bull, although it is omitted in many translations. Certainly, its use or its omission could suggest different interpretations of what the document is condemning.

unnoticed that *In supremo apostolatus* – a binding document written by an ultramontane pope – ends with explicit words about the use of papal authority for the condemnation of the enslavement of and the traffic in black people and about the strict prohibition that any Catholic might defend the licitness of the contrary opinion and teach something in opposition to the (normative) content of the apostolic letter (*ISA*, n. 4). Gregory XVI ends up with the mention of simple measures to make sure that all Christians will, without difficulty, become acquainted with his document (*ISA*, n. 5).

There is no doubt that we have in *In supremo apostolatus* an official condemnation by the Catholic Church of the enslavement and Transatlantic trade of African slaves. Henceforth this could no longer be done, it was henceforth condemned and prohibited for Christians. This interpretation was presented by Nicole Priesching as a "narrow interpretation" (*enge Auslegung*) of the proposal, in distinction to a "broad interpretation" (*weite Auslegung*),[49] according to which the contents of paragraph 4, in particular, can be interpreted as a condemnation of slavery *as such*, since "to [unjustly] vex [or: to do violence to] anyone" and "to despoil [anyone] of [. . .] possessions" can, in fact, refer to all human beings unfairly and inhumanly enslaved. The first interpretation favors the understanding that the purpose of the document is only *partially* an anti-slavery campaign, whereas the second interpretation favors the understanding of the letter as a broadly anti-slavery document. These interpretations, in corresponding degrees, can be connected to defenses of the abolition of slavery that are less or more comprehensive. Once more following the interpretation by Nicole Priesching,[50] if the "broad interpretation" is correct (according to which all existing slavery of indigenous and black peoples should be finished and any continuation is condemnable), the apostolic letter contains two novelties in comparison with all previous pontifical documents about slavery: (a) it approaches in one single document the slavery of indigenous and black people[51] and (b) it condemns every form of slavery and commerce in slaves, and not just one or another aspect. At any rate, there is room for a note of conceptual accuracy here: the use of the expression "broad interpretation," as well as the implicit allusion to the notions (used by the author of this essay) of a "broad anti-slavery view," "broad abolitionist view," etc., should not cast a shadow on the perception that Gregory XVI makes no defense of what might be called "strict abolitionism." Again, we assume that, according to this notion, it is morally condemnable always and everywhere that human beings are the property of other human beings – or, in other words, that personal beings (rational, volitional, and, of course, conscious beings) are impoverished to such a significant extent that they lose, or even give to others, the precious good of external freedom, such as possession of one's own body and its use according to one's wishes or intentions. Under this definition, "abolitionism" in a strict sense means a

---

49 Priesching, "Die Verurteilung der Sklaverei": 144.

50 Priesching, "Die Verurteilung der Sklaverei": 154.

51 Of course, this novelty is contemplated by the "narrow interpretation" as well.

pure and simple "anti-slavery view." Rather, the anti-slavery view or abolitionism that *In supremo apostolatus* clearly represents is the condemnation of every and any inhuman and unjust form of slavery, without subscribing to the view that there is no possible form of humane and just slavery.

3 Gregory XVI's Bull, Catholic Thinkers, and Abolitionism in Brazil

Irrespective of the explicit anti-slavery normative orientation that we can read in the text of *In supremo apostolatus*, it still leaves the reader in the face of an ambiguity of no small significance. It can be formulated like this: does the letter contain normative consent for the continuation of the slavery in which so many millions of individuals *were already in*? This openness to interpretation belongs to the history of the reception of *In supremo apostolatus* in Brazilian Catholicism.[52] More generally, the discourses and practices, Gregory XVI's bull generated and helped to distribute in the context of imperial Brazil, belong to the history of its interpretation and the description of the historical potential of its theses. Here, we should locate the role of the Catholic Church in Brazil as a whole in influencing people's convictions and actions to the point of leading them to adhere to anti-slavery laws and abolitionist movement(s). It is relevant to think that as unequivocal guidance to the moral attitude of Christians, as well as their opinion about action in society, at least in a broad sense, the 1839 bull *most likely* helped give form to the relationship of the Catholic Church with the abolitionist movement, which should be here understood as plural in its motivations, but sufficiently unified in its purpose, the suppression of any form of existing or future enslavement and the commerce of slaves.[53]

There is evidence that, among ultramontane members of the Brazilian clergy, the orientations given by the apostolic letter had as a result the creation of abolitionist circles promoted by ecclesiastical agents (above all, bishops), as well as the creation of anti-slavery literature and print media, like, for example, the review *Selecta Catholica*, which circulated from 1846 to 1847, edited by Dom Antônio Vicente Ferreira Viçoso

52 About the reception of the letter among Catholics and Protestants in the United States of America, see John Quinn, "'Three Cheers for the Abolitionist Pope!': American Reaction to Gregory XVI's Condemnation of the Slave Trade, 1840–1860," *The Catholic Historical Review* 90, no. 1 (2004): 67–93; Priesching, "Die Verurteilung der Sklaverei": 157–60.

53 I believe that this basic unified view of what abolitionism could mean after Gregory XVI's bull of 1839 was already incorporated into the prohibitions clearly stated in the Feijó Law of 1831, a law which was simply, and regrettably, frustrated; see Juremir Machado da Silva, *Raízes do conservadorismo brasileiro. A abolição na imprensa e no imaginário social*, 3rd ed. (Rio de Janeiro: Civilização Brasileira, 2018): 223–62.

and Father José Antônio dos Santos.[54] Father dos Santos, years later, in 1864, would be consecrated the first bishop of Diamantina, where he articulated an "emancipatory discourse" and promoted abolitionism.[55] In fact, hasty judgments or one-sided opinions, according to which the Catholic Church in Brazil, particularly in the nineteenth century, simply endorsed or quietly accepted the system of slavery and only, and at most, attempted to mitigate its inhuman effects, should be suspended.[56] With regard to the attitudes of Catholic thinkers and ministers about anti-slavery laws and abolitionist initiatives, the figure of Antônio Vicente Ferreira Viçoso (1787–1875) stands out.[57] Being born in Peniche (Portugal), Antônio Viçoso entered in Lisbon the "Congregation of Mission" or the "Lazarists" (also called the "Vicentine Fathers and Brothers," due to its founder St. Vicente de Paulo (1581–1660)). He was formally appointed by Dom Pedro II to the episcopal office and was ordained bishop of Mariana on May 5, 1844. The purpose of the next sections is to analyze Viçoso's theological and philosophical views about slavery on the basis of a manuscript that was recently discovered and edited for the first time, *Escravatura ofendida e defendida* (1840) [*Slavery Offended and Defended* (1840)].[58] In the text, Viçoso's analyses of slavery and the slave trade go beyond the contents and reception of Gregory XVI's bull. At any rate, he explicitly includes the letter in his discourse and, in particular, connects nineteenth-century Catholic theological discourse both to a critique of slavery and to the endorsement of the Brazilian laws of the 1830s that were promulgated in clear alignment with the British international campaign for the end of the Atlantic slave trade.

---

54 Marques and Pereira, "Introdução histórica," 34–35. The role of the review *Selecta Catholica* in educating people in moral customs and the Catholic faith, including a critique of slavery, has been the object of some research; see Raquel Martins de Assis, "Psicologia, educação e reforma dos costume: lições da *Selecta Catholica* (1846–1847)" (PhD thesis, Universidade Federal de Minas Gerais, 2004).

55 Lívia Gabriele Oliveira, "A presença da Igreja nas ações abolicionistas do Norte Mineiro: o caso do Bispado de Diamantina – 1864–1888" (master's diss., Instituto de Ciências Humanas e Sociais Mariana, 2011): 71–100.

56 A good revisionist – both sober and well-informed in its critique – exposition of the attitude of the Catholic Church towards black slavery in colonial and imperial Brazil is offered by Henrique Cristiano José Matos, *Nossa história. 500 anos de presença da Igreja Católica no Brasil*, vol. 2, *Período imperial e transição republicana*, 2nd ed. (São Paulo: Paulinas, 2010), in two chapters: "A Igreja e a Escravidão Negra"/"Church and Black Slavery": 105–47, and "A Igreja e a Abolição da Escravatura"/"The Church and the Abolition of Slavery": 149–94.

57 For a short biography, see Marques and Pereira, "Introdução histórica," 26–28. Still valuable is Belchior J. da Silva Neto, *Dom Viçoso, apóstolo de Minas* (Belo Horizonte: Imprensa Oficial do Estado de Minas Gerais, 1965).

58 See Padre Antônio Ferreira Viçoso, "Escravatura ofendida e defendida 1840," in *Escritos sobre escravidão*, ed. Lúcio Álvaro Marques and João Paulo Rodrigues Pereira (Porto Alegre: Editora FI, 2020): 145–202.

3.1 Antônio Viçoso on Slavery

Viçoso's views on slavery throughout his manuscript are various. The text actually begins with the reproduction, *perhaps* in an abridged form,[59] of a pro-slavery dialogue possibly authored by Father Leandro Rebello Peixoto e Castro (1771–1841), who, just like Antônio Viçoso, was born in Portugal and was a Lazarist priest (indeed, they were sent together to Brazil in 1819).[60] Peixoto e Castro's and Viçoso's views about the topics of debate mainly oppose each other. After the reproduction of the dialogue – a description of which will be offered in Section 3.3 – we find several expositions[61] by Viçoso about the topic of slavery. The dialogue and the expositions by Viçoso have a common point, to which in the end all reflections by Viçoso are directed: the debate on the legitimacy of the Law of November 7, 1831,[62] which, in alignment with British international policies, prohibited the Transatlantic slave trade and the entry of any imported slaves from Africa into Brazil. We begin with a summary of Viçoso's philosophical and theological views on slavery.

In the text under analysis, Viçoso reveals several sources of his philosophical-juridical opinions, which will be exposed in his reaction to Peixoto e Castro's dialogue. He quotes selective passages of M. Lacroix's *Traité de morale, ou devoirs de l'homme envers Dieu, envers la société et envers lui-même* (1767), after a Portuguese edition made is Lisbon, where he finds rejections of the traditional legal grounds allowing the enslavement, possession, and trade of slaves (see below). Lacroix, and certainly Viçoso too, connected slavery with barbarism and inhumanity.[63] Viçoso's mention of the *Institutiones Juris Lusitani, cum Publici tum Privati* (1789) by the Portuguese jurist Pascoal José de Mello [Freire] (1738–1798) has the sole purpose of stressing that a nation does not have to tolerate slavery just because it needs labor: in order to make use of people's services, workers are needed, not people with the status of being someone else's property.[64] Moreover, the reference to the booklet *Memória analítica acerca do comércio de escravos e acerca dos males da escravidão doméstica* (1837) [*Analytical Memorial about the Commerce of Slaves and the Evil of Domestic Slavery* (1837)] by the Brazilian scientist, and later director of the National Museum, Frederico Leopoldo

59 Marques and Pereira, "Introdução histórica," 28–29.

60 Ibid.: 27.

61 Viçoso's own exposition, after the reproduction of Peixoto e Castro's dialogue, was divided by himself into 15 chapters; see Padre Antônio Ferreira Viçoso, "Escravatura ofendida e defendida 1840": 163.

62 Padre Antônio Ferreira Viçoso, "Escravatura ofendida e defendida 1840": 164.

63 Ibid.: 165–66.

64 Ibid.: 166–67.

Cezar Burlamaqui (1803–1866), stresses the point that slavery is a religious, moral, and political evil, endorsing the view that it is a kind of barbarism and brutality.[65] This congenial reference, by the way, is rather surprising if Burlamaqui really was the person behind the pamphlet *Memória sobre o comércio dos escravos, em que se pretende mostrar que este tráfico é, para eles, antes um bem do que um mal* [*A Memorial about the Commerce of Slaves, in Which One Intends to Show that This Traffic is, for Them, a Good Rather Than an Evil*] (1838). After all, this pamphlet's author defended the continuity of the slavery of black Africans on the basis of the judgment that, for them, the condition of slavery, combined with an ethics of serfs-and-masters, was something good. It was a good both for enslaved Africans and for all nations that made use of their labor. As a whole, it decisively contributed to the Africans' spiritual and physical development, or, in other words, to their progress in civilization.[66]

The theological sources mentioned by Viçoso are perhaps more interesting. He strongly relies on Nicolas-Sylvestre Bergier (1718–1790), a French Catholic theologian engaged in Christian apologetics whose works were especially directed against atheist philosophers. A significant contribution by Bergier as a writer was the several articles that make up the *Dictionnaire de théologie*, which happened to be part of the *Encyclopédie* (1751–1772), edited and co-edited by Bergier's friend, Denis Diderot. Viçoso focused on two dictionary entries by Bergier, "Esclaves" and "Negres," and simply quotes passages, extensively, in Portuguese. We are told by Viçoso that, for Bergier, the continuation of slavery in the colonies was unjustifiable. This is a summary of Bergier's ideas: in natural law and the domestic sphere, slavery was at a certain time both inevitable and much more humane. Thus, it is not explicitly and totally rejected by Old and New Testament laws. After having been nearly suppressed, "the irruption of barbarians" retarded that "happy revolution," and through civil law slavery was continuously allowed.[67] The most important of Bergier's ideas for Viçoso is that in his times, "that abusive right" once permitted by law "is no longer extant" – it does not exist in Europe anymore and cannot exist in the Americas any longer. In general, (a) there is no natural right to the selling and buying of African slaves because there is no natural right to put them in that condition (they are not licitly enslaved due to allegedly just wars, for example). In fact, (b) the slave trade stimulates arbitrary wars and the connected mechanism of enslavement and commerce. Moreover, (c) even if it is true that Africans were tyrannically treated in their own lands, slavery and the

65 Ibid.: 167.

66 Marques and Pereira, "A barbárie como operador político," 55–57. They seem to make a mistake here. In the web address of the "Biblioteca Brasiliana Guita e José Mindlin," where the digitized document is accessible (see https://digital.bbm.usp.br/handle/bbm/3800), we are told that the pamphlet was probably written by José Carneiro da Silva, a "mill lord" and local political leader from Campos dos Goitacazes.

67 Padre Antônio Ferreira Viçoso, "Escravatura ofendida e defendida 1840": 167.

trade of humans to other countries are harms and not gestures of compassion or humanity. Finally, (d) even if it is true that the colonies could not stand without slaves, one should rather say that the colonies – which were essentially about greed and economic advantage – might be renounced, but not values such as "humanity," "justice," "universal charity," and "sweetness."[68]

The second theological inspiration referred to by Viçoso is the opinions of theologians at the Ecclesiastical Conferences of the Diocese of Angers, taken from proceedings published in France between 1804 and 1832. As it turns out, these theologians do not affirm that slavery is always morally wrong. But they express concerns about the trade of slaves in and from Africa, since this practice seems to be against "equity," "humanity," and "conscience." Here the opinions appear in the language of moral theology still current in Viçoso's times. (a) Nobody can feel assured in conscience about the probability that the sellers of slaves in Africa are agents with moral principles and "religious feelings." The widespread discourse is that slaves are mostly war prisoners. But such wars are hardly legitimate – African political leaders only know the law "of the stronger." Moreover, (b) the trade in slaves is what gives these leaders the "convenience" they need, making the trade viciously related to their own benefit.[69]

Viçoso's own philosophical-theological judgment about enslavement and the Transatlantic slave trade is preceded by reports about how people were enslaved in Africa. These reports are from travelers. Our author mentions the tomes of *Viajante universal* (or, more exactly, *O viajante universal, ou notícia do Mundo Antigo e Moderno* [*The Universal Traveler, or Notice of the Ancient and the Modern World*], where volumes 12 and 13 proceed from the beginning of the nineteenth century).[70] Travelers report how much African societies were internally broken, in moral or normative terms, because of the possibility of trading slaves with overseas nations. Because of the need, greed, vice, and, above all, tyranny of those who had power, nearly everyone can be enslaved in Africa and sold to slave dealers. This dimension of normalizing enslavement was nourished by a decisive aspect at the core of Viçoso's reflections: because there were buyers, there were all sorts of ways of enslaving and selling people in Africa. In fact, travelers' accounts testify that African monarchs exert absolute authority over their subjects, which amounts to arbitrariness in legislation and rulership.[71] Within African nations (towards a monarch's own vassals) and among African nations (towards a nation's neighbors), political and legal violence and arbitrariness – above all in the form of despotic laws and in the connection between war and enslavement[72] – are deeply

68 Ibid.: 169.

69 Ibid.: 170.

70 See Mr. De Laporte, *O viajante universal, ou notícia do Mundo Antigo e Moderno*, vol. 12–13 (Lisbon: Typografia Rollandiana, 1800–1803).

71 Padre Antônio Ferreira Viçoso, "Escravatura ofendida e defendida 1840": 171.

72 The moral, legal, economic, and political instability caused by the Transatlantic slave trade in African societies has been explored on a historical basis by, for example, John Thornton, *Africa and Africans in the Making of the Atlantic World, 1400–1800* (New York: Cambridge University Press, 1998).

seated at the beginning of the chain of enslaving and trading people.[73] In many African cultures, wealth came to be understood according to the number of slaves that someone possesses – it was frequently also connected to a man's ability to have several women, large families, and many children, most of which were eligible to be sold by the father. Stimulated by the traffic in slaves, human beings became a major good of exportation.[74]

Viçoso's *own* philosophical-theological judgment, in general terms, about the slavery of black people is based on the opinions of jurists and theologians and on the testimonies of travelers. More exactly, it is an opinion about whether existing enslavement and the slave trade could be accepted and practiced by someone with a clear conscience, for the sake of one's own salvation. He is convinced, after having read Bergier and the theologians of the diocese of Angers, that, in his times, enslavement can neither be accepted nor practiced. The central perception is that trading slaves, as a kind of contract, demands justice, and this presupposes that enslaved people are true properties of those who sell them. But they are not, or at least they cannot be known, with certainty, to be so. Sellers and buyers, thus, cannot possibly act in good faith. Viçoso highlights Antonino Diana's (1585–1663) view in his quite popular *Resolutionum moralium* (1628–1656), which was influential in the Conference of Angers's reports on slavery. Although Diana himself was far from being a "tutiorist" or rigorist moralist with regard to the conditions of certainty for acting in good conscience, on the commerce of human beings he affirmed that the buying of slaves in good faith alone could morally justify that act – this is understood, here, as an act under the certainty that these people were enslaved with justice. Buying in bad or doubtful faith about the slaves' real condition would render that act immoral and put the obligation on buyers to restitute freedom.[75] Judging the commerce in slaves and assuming that there was no possible certainty about the real status of enslaved Africans, Viçoso can only endorse the view according to which the commerce was unjust and its agents were all exposed to acting illicitly. No honest person or pious Christian, under the moral circumstances around enslavement in Africa, could in good conscience continue to buy slaves. Those who do and trade slaves behave with a barbarism comparable to that of African sellers.[76]

3.2 Viçoso on Brazilian Laws and Gregory XVI's Bull against Slavery

We can understand Viçoso's theoretical incursions into the problem of slavery so far as a preparation for his judgment on the normative justification of Brazilian laws against the slave trade that were being issued in the years prior to his writing. Ideologically,

73 Padre Antônio Ferreira Viçoso, "Escravatura ofendida e defendida 1840": 172–73.

74 Ibid.: 173–75.

75 Ibid.: 175.

76 Ibid.: 176–77.

Gregory XVI's bull is taken by Viçoso as the synthesis of the line of thought he was pursuing with his theological-philosophical reflections and decisive support for the moral import of the Brazilian laws in question. In their turn, the sections of his exposition focused on Brazilian laws and Gregory XVI's bull give the final grounding for his debate with the author of the dialogue *Slavery Offended and Defended*, which consists of a disqualification of anti-slavery legal efforts in Brazil after the Feijó Law.

Viçoso was well acquainted with recent laws and decrees about slavery and slave traffic in Brazil. His comments presuppose and endorse the Law of November 7, 1831, or the Feijó Law. Since it officially prohibited the importation of enslaved Africans into Brazil, it had as a consequence that slaves, as soon as they entered Brazil, should be set free. Ampliative decrees, such as those on April 12, 1832, about the examination of ships, and on February 12, 1833, about the re-exportation of slaves back to Africa, were a natural extension of the Feijó Law.[77] Viçoso is particularly interested in mentioning legal "notifications" (*avisos*) from the imperial authorities to the official judges and presidents of the Brazilian provinces (such as Pernambuco, Bahia, and Minas Gerais) to be committed to applying those laws, as well as warning people of their validity and the punishments of prison and monetary penalties for importers of African slaves and those complicit in such actions. We are told by Father Viçoso that some notifications announced penalties to judges and presidents themselves.[78] It seems to be undeniable that Viçoso is praising the legal initiatives of the Brazilian government or, in other words, the measures directly proposed by the Brazilian regency. Accordingly, the Law of November 7, 1831, was expanded in several "orders" about the prohibition of importing African slaves: eleven orders in 1834, ten orders in 1835, fifteen orders in 1836, eight orders in 1837, and four orders in 1838. Through the original law and its expansions, Viçoso's believed, Brazilian legislators did a good job: they followed civilized European nations, which faced the initial costs of abolition and were able to change the structure of land cultivation. But what is Viçoso's understanding of this positive civilizational step by the European nations? Why did they suppress slavery and why was that progress in civilization? (a) Viçoso clearly believes that, in his day, societies not based on slavery are better structured in moral terms. A slave-based society meant for Europe what was then happening in Brazil: "an extreme relaxation in customs." In large families of slaves, cases of concubinage, drunkenness, and thievery are quite usual and are signs of the moral and social degradation promoted by slavery.[79] In other cases, families of slaves are described as unstructured and lacking the presence of a father.[80] (b) As a further reason for seeing in the abolition of slavery civilizational improvement, Viçoso reflects on the possible advantages of a society

77 For both Decrees, see Senado Federal, *A abolição no Parlamento*: 73–77 and 79–82. See also Mamigonian and Grinberg, "Lei de 1831": 287–88.

78 Padre Antônio Ferreira Viçoso, "Escravatura ofendida e defendida 1840": 178.

79 Ibid.: 179.

80 Ibid.: 179–80.

without slaves, even if apparently the justice of a nation can only be obtained at the cost of some economic regression. But this is not quite so: for Viçoso, we find among "publicists" quite convincing views about how much slavery diminishes the "temporal happiness of nations"[81] (in Portuguese, the word *publicista* means a "political writer" or, more generally, a person who writes on public affairs for a broader audience). It is remarkable that for both theses, especially for the second on the "temporal happiness of nations," Father Viçoso reproduces arguments by the utilitarian Jeremy Bentham (1748–1832), found in part 3, chapter 2 ("Of Slavery") of *Principles of the Civil Code*.[82]

Following Bentham's analysis, human beings' happiness is a matter of their own wishes and sensations. It consists of a life that significantly satisfies human wishes and sensations in terms of actual pleasure and the absence of pain; in human community life, the ideal of happiness has to be, to a decent extent, coordinated by political authority and institutions.[83] Slavery as such is something pleasant for slaveholders, but not for enslaved people: free men and slaves will never desire to exchange roles. Enslaved people know that they are "miserable" – they cannot be convinced of the opposite by means of any calculation that attempts to conclude in their happiness.[84] Of course, there is a gap – in happiness – between freedom and slavery; if this is not always clear, it is only because slaves usually never experience the better (freedom) rather than the worse (slavery). There are obvious empirical proofs that nobody embraces slavery by choice: experience everywhere gives no basis even for a calculation of happiness according to which, comparing a slaveholder's life and a slave's life, the sum of good and evil would be equivalent. The slaveholder is the one who has all advantages. Abolition obviously represents a loss for the holder and a gain for the enslaved person.[85]

Bentham's account also disqualifies any thesis according to which slavery favors the wealth and power of nations. Abolition will represent an economic loss for the slaveholder. But a nation will not lose in terms of economic production in the case slaves are set free: free men are much more productive than slaves.[86] Happiness increases with economic abundance, and political power too. Regarding production,

---

81 Ibid.: 180.

82 See Jeremy Bentham, *The Works of Jeremy Bentham*, vol. 1, *Principles of the Civil Code* (Indianapolis: The Online Library of Liberty, 2011) [=*The Works of Jeremy Bentham*, ed. John Bowring (Edinburgh: William Tait, 1838–1843): 624–29].

83 See, for example, Jeremy Bentham, *An Introduction to the Principles of Morals and Legislation*, ed. J.H. Burns and H.L.A. Hart (Oxford: Clarendon Press, 1996): Chapter 1, 11–16. Viçoso does not cite Bentham from this work. In any event, Viçoso's purpose in quoting ideas by Bentham lies in his theses about how slavery is connected to civilization retardment.

84 Padre Antônio Ferreira Viçoso, "Escravatura ofendida e defendida 1840": 180.

85 Ibid.: 180.

86 On the slave labor force as the basis of economic production in colonial Brazil and during most of the existence of the Brazilian Empire, see Francisco Vidal Luna and Herbert S. Klein, *Escravismo no Brasil*, trans. Laura Teixeira Motta (São Paulo: Edusp, 2010); Dale W. Tomich, *Pelo prisma da escravidão: trabalho, capital e economia mundial*, trans. A. de P. Danesi (São Paulo: Edusp, 2011).

slaves (a) lack the stimulus of economic reward; besides, (b) the insecurity of their condition affects "the industry" of which they are capable. A slave has no reason to "excel himself," doing his best.[87] If a slave shows what he is capable of, he only raises his obligations: he acquires no recognition, no property of his own, no reason for appreciating the work he does. As a result, we are told by Bentham, slaves produce less and consume more – a slave has nothing of his own to keep or save. He has no reason to serve better than what he actually does; in principle, he does not think about improvement, since such thinking requires a motive.[88] Bentham seems to see in such a disadvantageous life regarding the pursuit of happiness a factual, empirical reason, to be confirmed everywhere and always, that slaves can only tend to be bad workers and persons: they can only look for deplorable habits of immediate compensation for suffering and unfruitful participation in immediate pleasure. The link between slavery and civilization is an impossible rather than just a negative one: slavery undermines human development and a nation's happiness.[89]

While Viçoso finds support for his endorsement of the Brazilian laws that prohibit the importation of African slaves in Bentham's arguments for the connection (1) between slavery and "the retardment of public morality" and (2) between slavery and "the retardment of public wealth" (in sum, for the connection between slavery and civilizational retardment), two further reasons can be added. (3) Quoting some lines of a notification by the government from March 13, 1834, Viçoso voices the historical worry that a society economically based on the labor force of unjustly enslaved people runs the risk of self-destruction, if these people, by making use of violent means attempt to set themselves free from their condition. This is no preaching, it is rather a warning to slavery's apologists that can already be found in a legal notification.[90] The background for such a note is the Haitian Revolution (1791–1804), through which, after a series of brutal conflicts, self-liberated captives finally overthrew the French colonial regime in Saint-Domingue and, to a significant extent, established an independent country, Haiti, governed by former slaves.[91] Finally, (4) Viçoso sees in the Brazilian laws a correction to a "solemn injustice" against "innocent victims." Enslaved Africans and their enslaved descendants, generation after generation, represent a chain of injustice and barbarism: for the most part, those who were captured, enslaved, and traded were not really "true slaves."[92]

In fact, Viçoso believes that his exposition so far is able to present principles through which conclusions against slavery and slave trade can be naturally drawn. If there are doubts about these conclusions (in summary, that the prohibition of the slave trade is a just legal act), Viçoso affirms in section IX of his manuscript that

87 Padre Antônio Ferreira Viçoso, "Escravatura ofendida e defendida 1840": 181.

88 Ibid.: 182.

89 Ibid.

90 Ibid.: 183.

91 See, for example, Manisha Sinha, *The Slave's Cause: A History of Abolition* (New Haven/London: Yale University Press, 2017): chapter 15.

92 Padre Antônio Ferreira Viçoso, "Escravatura ofendida e defendida 1840": 184.

Catholics should pay attention to Gregory XVI's apostolic letter. Section IX contains a complete version of *In supremo apostolatus* in Portuguese.[93] It is not clear whether this is Viçoso's own translation or a Portuguese version made by other hands. What is clear is that the bull is an essential ideological support for the anti-slavery laws Viçoso is defending. The final lines of the bull – in which Gregory XVI stressed his authority over Catholics in condemning the enslavement and traffic of black people and in prohibiting any public or private defense and teaching of any contrary opinion – are emphasized by Viçoso. The message seems to be clear: Gregory XVI's letter was a morally binding document for Catholics and support for both international and Brazilian policies – expressed in laws and decrees – against the slave trade. At this point, Viçoso has all he needs to turn his attention back to Brazilian clerics who could be characterized both as defenders of slavery and the traffic of black people generally speaking and, more specifically, as people teaching ideas that were in contradiction to the conclusions of *In supremo apostolatus*. This is Viçoso's refutation of *Slavery Offended and Defended* (1840) by Father Peixoto e Castro. The clash of ideas, in this case, is representative of how the Catholic Church in Brazil had to face the challenge of finding and giving orientation regarding the legal-political fight against the slave trade and, increasingly, of taking a stance regarding abolitionism.

3.3 Slavery Defended?

Viçoso's expositions about slavery from 1840 are constructed around a dialogue titled *Slavery Offended and Defended*, which Father Peixoto e Castro probably wrote either a little before the promulgation of Gregory XVI's bull on December 3, 1839, or after the promulgation when the author was still unacquainted with it. The bull is not mentioned in the dialogue according to Viçoso's reproduction, and Viçoso's reactions to it (see the next sections of this study) do not seem to refer to a text he had read long before. Although many reflections advanced by Viçoso could be seen as independent of the contents of the dialogue, it is perceptible that the heart of Viçoso's text lies in opposing this pro-slavery piece in two general aspects: firstly, it does not represent Catholic theological thought about slavery and the slave trade in the nineteenth century; secondly, it mistakenly criticizes anti-slave trade laws issued by the Brazilian government that, for moral, legal, political, economic, and theological reasons, deserve support. Peixoto e Castro's dialogue does not represent Viçoso's views; it is a text full of theses that Viçoso in effect rejects. In the following, a summary of the dialogue's main ideas is provided.

Although the dialogue contains two characters, "Luiz" and "Theodoro," it turns out that "Theodoro" represents the author's views. Our résumé is focused, thus, on the opinions voiced by him around a question raised by "Luiz": "Is the commerce of

93 Ibid.: 184–87.

slavery licit in our days?"[94] The Law of November 7, 1831, is the background of the question. Theodoro wants to prove that this law is in fact no law, since it does not have what a law needs in order to obligate. It is not a *valid* law. This is initially based on two premises: its object is not "the common good";[95] even if it was, the law "prescribed and lost subsistence, for it was not used since after its promulgation."[96]

What about the first premise? The good searched for by this law relates only to imported slaves, not "the community of Brazilians." The Brazilian economy still needs a slave labor force for production, and thus more slaves to replace older ones. There are not sufficient "free arms" (including "settlers" and "Indians") to be hired to replace slaves. Freedmen are not and will not right away get used to a labor system in which they are hired after payment. Moreover, farmers and their families are not prepared to become laborers. The economic system will lack coordination, the production of basic goods will collapse, the supply of basic needs will not be provided. The recklessness of this law is confirmed by the alleged fact that the extinction of slavery can hardly be gradual, since statistics show that every year Brazil loses "one third of its slaves" – the country will totally lack slaves within approximately three years. If disgraces will be the effect of such an imprudent law, it has nothing to do with the common good: it rather harms the common good. Thus it has no force, as a law and cannot be binding "in conscience."[97] How can one know that a given civil law "is not based on the common good"? The character Theodoro admits that "legislators" and "doctors [scholars]" can be helpful in that regard, but he emphasizes that there is also a valid "consuetudinary" interpretation, "which is introduced by a constant practice in the community." The fact that the Feijó Law was not being taken seriously by the government or the authorities is a "manifest argument" that it failed with regard to the aim of promoting the common good. Regarding morality, the dialogue's author defends the view that a "safe conscience" about how to act can be achieved through what is "more probable" – he affirms that it is wiser and more probable that the Feijó Law is invalid.[98]

This is a connecting point to the second premise advanced above. The Brazilian government is not considered to have been "sufficiently free" in declaring that law. What it did was compromised by agreements with England. The aims of England's anti-slavery campaign do not seem to be good for Brazil; they can hardly be just

94 Ibid.: 145.

95 The idea that a just, valid law ordinates, in a prescriptive way, a human being's action towards the common good is a well-known Thomistic notion; see Thomas de Aquino, *Summa theologiae* [Latin-Portuguese], vol. 6, ed. C.-J. Pinto de Oliveira, 2nd. ed (São Paulo: Edições Loyola, 2012): IIaIIae q. 58, a. 5, resp., 63–64. Of course, it does not mean that the dialogue's author is interpreting correctly the connection or lack of connection to the common good in the Brazilian law he is criticizing.

96 Padre Antônio Ferreira Viçoso, "Escravatura ofendida e defendida 1840": 146.

97 Ibid.: 146–48.

98 Ibid.: 148–49.

philanthropy. The British perhaps intend to make of Brazil a politically weak and economically dependent nation. The *real* intention of the Brazilian government was to allow what was actually happening: it "shuts the eyes to the trade of Africans once they are introduced" into the country. The government is aware of the continuity of the importation of slaves from Africa and does not act to prevent the traffic or charge public authorities accordingly. The Feijó Law was promulgated, but in practice it prescribed.[99] This is more than "tacit consent," it is rather "express" consent with what really happens – the continuation of the slave trade. By so neglecting the Feijó Law, the government was showing concern for the country's needs. The dialogue's author agrees with that prudent strategy. A declaration that would officially abrogate that law should be made only in a future time, without putting international treaties at risk.[100]

At this point, the debate is strongly centered on the question of who has the power to abrogate a law. In principle, only the legislator can do it. But presupposing "non-use" of the law and that legislators are aware of it and have never punished anyone for breaking that law – presupposing, moreover, that a few cases of toleration towards non-observance suffice for the presumption of a law's nonvalidity – one is already allowed to conclude that the abrogation of the law is the legislator's own will and that he gives his consent for annulation. For this principle of abrogating a law, the author of the dialogue refers to authorities both in civil and canon law – Pascoal José de Mello [Freire] and Pope Benedict XIV (1675–1758), respectively.[101] Strict application of these principles is perceptible in the tolerant attitude of the Brazilian government towards the commerce in enslaved people from Africa. The few acts of applying the Feijó Law are an ostensive dissimulation of a strictness the government does not want to take at all. It allows the conclusion that a law so unpleasant to the community is also not taken as binding by the legislators. Brazilian subjects, thus, were justified in believing that the Feijó Law was, in practice, null.[102]

But irrespective of the nonvalidity of the Law of November 7, 1831, was such a "commerce of human flesh" not something wrong or unjust in its own nature? After all, enslaved people, as the effect of a crime against natural and divine law, were deprived of a most precious gift with which God endowed every human being. In the face of this question, the dialogue's author offered theological and philosophical considerations about

99 Ibid.: 149.

100 Ibid.: 150.

101 Ibid.: 151–52.

102 Ibid.: 152–53. That the Law of November 7, 1831, fell into disuse – it was neither observed nor was the breaking of it punished – by the time Peixoto e Castro wrote his dialogue is certainly a historical fact, although the law itself was never abrogated. Apparently, the practical boycott against the law came, above all, from judges and the juridical system as whole, which clearly favored the pro-slavery parties; see Juremir Machado da Silva, *Raízes do conservadorismo brasileiro. A abolição na imprensa e no imaginário social*, 3rd ed. (Rio de Janeiro: Civilização Brasileira, 2018): 224, 231–36. We are told that between 1831 and 1849, more than 700,000 enslaved people illegally entered into the country; see Araújo, "Fim do tráfico," 236.

slavery.[103] He at first summarizes seven reasons for not considering "slavery, in general," as something unjust and for not taking its "lords" as persons acting in "intrinsic malice." The author emphasizes that the Church historically lived together with slavery and also accepted it theoretically. Slavery – even perpetual slavery – is not explicitly condemned either in the Old or New Testament. It is not as such an offence to natural law. Moreover, there were regulations for slavery in late-ancient and medieval times, both in civil and canon law (in the *Codex Iustiniani* and in the *Decretum Gratiani*, for example). Of particular interest is the author's fifth reason, according to which Brazilian prelates never found slavery to be something strange. Documentary evidence of this is the famous "Constitutions of Bahia" or the "Constituições Primeiras do Arcebispado da Bahia," the first set of pastoral norms elaborated in Brazil on the basis of a provincial synod in 1707, called by the fifth archbishop of Bahia, Dom Sebastião Monteiro da Vide (1643–1722),[104] which contained precepts for masters and slaves.[105]

In fact, the author's central moral or normative concern is the traffic of slaves from Africa to Brazil. He is interested in justifying what slave traders do by affirming that they are not people who take away other people's freedom: they simply buy enslaved people who were brought to "that condition by laws and practice in use in that land and legitimately introduced by their rulers."[106] Regarding an ideology of black slavery, we can imagine that our author is voicing and in some way supporting a common opinion among those who opposed abolition laws in terms of the strict prohibition on importing slaves. It is particularly interesting – also because of Viçoso's use of it and because of his replies (see subdivisions 3.1 and 3.4) – that, among his sources about African laws and customs, the dialogue's author calls to his side the reports given by "respectful travelers," such as the reports about Africa found in De Laporte's *Universal Traveler*.

The author intends to show that since "time immemorial," slavery was established in Africa and became quite natural on the continent, especially due to being born from enslaved women and to punishment for several kinds of crimes. In a nutshell: Africans enslave people for reasons quite similar to those accepted in Western tradition. They do have clear notions of justice and legality, and this is something sufficiently verified: (a) the first reason for enslaving is war (war satisfaction); (b) the second is crime (punishment for crimes); (c) the third is "retaliation," which is a right that a nation has for "punishing anyone [or: any other nation] who unjustly commits [a crime], steals, and destroys it, both regarding people and properties."[107] "Retaliation" is an immediate

---

103 Padre Antônio Ferreira Viçoso, "Escravatura ofendida e defendida 1840": 153.

104 Constituições Primeiras do Arcebispado da Bahia [1853]. Edições do Senado Federal, vol. 79, https://www2.senado.leg.br [accessed 01.23.2022].

105 Padre Antônio Ferreira Viçoso, "Escravatura ofendida e defendida 1840," 153. See José Oscar Beozzo, "A Igreja e a escravidão," in *História da Igreja no Brasil: Segunda Época – Século XIX*, ed. João Fagundes Hauck et al. (Petrópolis: Vozes, 1980): 266–72.

106 Padre Antônio Ferreira Viçoso, "Escravatura ofendida e defendida 1840": 154–55.

107 Ibid.: 155.

reaction, similar to war indeed, but focused on the "right to self-defense" after an aggressive and unjust invasion which happens between two nations that do not respond to any political power above them.[108] Moreover, as in the Greek-Roman and Christian Western tradition, (d) Africans enslave people because of debts. Finally, (e) slavery by birth or applied to children born of enslaved women is also valid in African nations.[109] The author's emphasis is on the idea that these legal claims for enslaving people were known by Africans and, if they are not abused, they are as such just – they are (still) recognized in European legal, philosophical, and even religious sources as well.[110] At this point, it is central for the author's intention to stress that the legal justifications known and used by African authorities in order to legitimately enslave people essentially match those found in European natural and civil law, as well as in the *ius gentium*, as we can find in the thought of Hugo Grotius (1583–1645), author of *De iure belli ac pacis* (1625). There are reasons to think, thus, that from the beginning, i.e., already in the African nations that enslave and trade people, slavery is a legal system. The impressive amount of enslaved people in Africa is arguably a multitude of licit slaves that may be traded[111] – in principle, there is no injustice in these facts and deeds.

But if enslavement – thus, the status of slavery – is acceptable, is the trade of human beings, or "human flesh," acceptable as well? That it is acceptable is one of main theses of the dialogue. This is the argument: by accepting the condition of slavery, one accepts that a person – the "master" – has the right to demand the services of the slave(s) for their entire life. Such a right to property and work can be valued in money: it has a monetary value. If there is a law that allows it, such a value can be negotiated. The commerce in slaves, thus, "is about a true right," and a price can be estimated by those who possess slaves. This is not "commerce in human flesh." After all, a slaveholder does not have property rights over a slave as a person can have property rights over cattle. The property right over the slave is about making reasonable use of his services or even selling him according to his interests. An owner is not a torturer, his right is legally restricted by the duties of good and humane treatment. Slavery is depicted by the dialogue's author as something better than perpetual imprisonment.[112]

Even admitting that there are enslaved people that were actually robbed, just as it is possible that in other legitimate forms of commerce people trade illegitimate goods, the author of the dialogue insists in saying that – as a fact attested by travelers – this is not the rule in the slave trade, but rather the exception. As a rule, civilized people sell and trade legitimate slaves, and these people were, as a rule, enslaved on the basis of

108 Ibid.: 155–56.

109 Essentially, these kinds of legal *tituli* for legitimating slavery had been discussed in western thought since the end of sixteenth century; see, in this regard, the well-known exposition by Molina, *De iustitia et iure*: I, tr. 2, disp. 33, 87–91.

110 Padre Antônio Ferreira Viçoso, "Escravatura ofendida e defendida 1840": 156.

111 Ibid.: 157.

112 Ibid.: 158.

one of the five legal reasons mentioned above. Since this is a normative scenario about slavery in Africa, the dialogue's author demands each time a "positive proof" – a particular proof – for any accusation that a trader is selling slaves that were robbed. If people usually trust sellers about dealing legitimate goods – like horse-sellers, for example! – people should usually believe that slave traders do not buy their products from thieves.[113] Doubting sellers without positive proof is not a probable doubt.

A particularly interesting discussion in the dialogue is about the justice of considering slaves children born of enslaved women, even of women that were justly enslaved. What was these children's crime? Why do they receive a perpetual punishment like their parents? The dialogue's author offers a quite detailed answer to what he considers to be "the most difficult knot of this question"; after all, anyone could realize that in nineteenth-century colonial Brazil, politically pressed by international laws that severely restricted the Transatlantic slave trade, the slave-born were supposed to be both a successful and a most necessary source for generating slaves and a slave labor force. In order to find principles that give support to such a legal claim, the author offers what he calls "external proofs," and he then examines the "nature of things" about that practice.[114] "External proofs" that the slavery title in question is not something evil or contrary to natural law as such are actually passages from the Bible (such as Ex 21:4), some customary laws of many nations, and the contents of Roman and canon law. Moreover, in the ancient Church, the fathers, councils, and prelates never expressed any opinion contrary to the practice.[115]

The "internal proofs" are more interesting.[116] We are told that "by natural law parents are lords of their children." This is supported by the principle that "by natural law each rational being is lord and has rulership over his works," i.e., the fruits or production of one's work. As the painter is the natural possessor of his painting and the farmer of his harvest, so are the parents of their production, their children. The parents' rule over their children, thus, is true and natural, and it has to be managed through reason: if parents allow children to be hired, lent out, given, or sold, all these and other acts have to be compatible with "the purpose and conservation of human kind."[117]

The dialogue's author admits, moreover, that with the improvement of laws in human societies, paternal powers over children diminish. To a great extent, they pass over to "the society's chief" – parents rule with restrictions over children and only up to a certain age, before their emancipation. Civil law, thus, restricts paternal powers; liberty in civil terms – of a human being born in a given society – depends on the

113 Ibid.: 159.

114 Ibid.: 160.

115 Ibid.: 161.

116 On the rulership and property rights that parents legitimately have over their children and on the thesis that children born of slave women are slaves too, see again Molina, *De iustitia et iure*: I, tr. 2, disp. 33, n. 21–32, 89–91.

117 Padre Antônio Ferreira Viçoso, "Escravatura ofendida e defendida 1840": 161.

proportion to which civil laws restrict "the rights that nature has given to the parents."[118] This restriction is up to the civil authorities. This is the reason why "in some nations it is allowed that parents sell the children," while in others not. Truly, paternal rights over children are diminishing, minors are becoming freer than before – and this is civil, not natural freedom. But where the legal claim of parents ruling over their children as property is valid, children are for parents quite like slaves. They can be treated, thus, as a property which has value, and as such they can be traded and put into contracts.[119]

As it turns out, the dialogue's author believes that "freedom in which civil man is born is due to the civil laws, not to nature" – in society, the freedom with which a human being comes to the world and is, to a greater or lesser degree, the property of his parents is something determined by civil laws. In coherence with the former conclusion, "if civil laws do not dispose anything [. . .] with regard to some classes of people [for exerting their status as progenitors or parents], they will always keep their natural rights over the children."[120] While it is true that in some states in the nineteenth century, "the natural power of slaves over their children" is legally endorsed, Brazil is a state in which Roman law in particular juridically prevails; since it is a principle of Roman law that "the birth follows the womb" – or, in free translation, "the condition of the child follows the condition of the mother" – and by natural law an enslaved woman rules over and possesses her children as her own products, the following conclusion can be validly drawn: as a slave woman is the property of her master, so all her children, i.e., all her natural fruits, are property of that master, too. The slaveholder is the lord and owner of the children, so he is allowed to dispose of them as his properties and can even play the role of natural father in matters such as education and discipline – all of this is taken to be licit, so long as the master respects the "rational nature of his nigger [in Portuguese: crioulo]."[121]

Viçoso does not address any reaction to the dialogue's argument for the licitness of considering the children of enslaved women slaves too. In the too-slow history of laws that led the country to the full abolition of slavery in 1888, the idea that "the birth follows the womb" as a formal principle for enslaving people was debated by jurists in imperial Brazil, especially in the years that preceded the promulgation of the Law of September 28, 1871 (also called "Rio Branco Law" or "Law of the Free Womb").[122] According to this law, the children born of enslaved women from that day onwards should be declared free. At any rate, the Rio Branco Law also came with all the ambiguities that

118 Ibid.: 161–62.

119 Ibid.: 162.

120 Ibid.: 162.

121 Ibid.: 162–63.

122 See Eduardo Spiller Pena, *Pajens da casa imperial. Jurisconsultos, escravidão e a Lei de 1871* (Campinas: Editora da Unicamp, 2001). See also Joseli Maria Nunes Mendonça, *Entre a mão e os anéis. A Lei dos Sexagenários e os caminhos da abolição no Brasil* (Coleção Várias Histórias. Campinas: Editora da Unicamp, 1999): 97–114.

so typified legal advances towards abolition in nineteenth-century Brazil: the child should stay under the power of the slaveholder for eight years, after which he or she could be released after an indemnity of 600,000 réis – as an alternative, the minor should serve the holder until his or her twenty-first birthday.[123]

3.4 Slavery Rejected: A Clash of Ideas between Two Catholics Clerics

Viçoso's "fraternal disagreement"[124] with Peixoto e Castro's apology for the continuity of slavery initially focuses on fourteen points, always making reference to pages (ranging between page 1 and page 63) of what we can suppose was Peixoto e Castro's original manuscript. In the following, the description and analysis focus on topics that we consider to be theoretically more relevant. Special attention is given to the discussions about the legitimacy of anti-slavery laws.

(i) A first aspect to be emphasized in Viçoso's replies is his disagreement with the idea that the continuity of slavery represents a common good for Brazilian society. Viçoso's reaction contains two aspects: firstly, people should be warned about the fact that a slave-based society could at any time face the risk of self-destruction (a brutal revolution, for example) – what happened in Haiti could similarly occur in Brazil as a consequence of oppressive legal slavery, and the risk of social convolutions should be taken as much higher if slavery was nourished by illegal commerce.[125] Secondly, the common good cannot simply mean the possible good for the majority of people (or of Brazilians): it must be combined with justice, with the justice required by the *ius gentium*, which should regulate all contracts with African nations.[126]

(ii) A second important aspect in Viçoso's replies is that a society economically based in kinds of labor force other than slaves was already a reality in Europe and should be a viable possibility for Brazil, too – clearly, his judgment is motivated by

---

123 See Senado Federal, *A abolição no Parlamento*: 463–560. A "fund of emancipation" was created as well, through which the state, by payment, should have been able to set free a certain number of slaves each year. In order to properly compensate slaveholders, a system of registration of slaves was introduced. See Joseli Maria Nunes Mendonça, "Legislação emancipacionista, 1871 e 1885," in *Dicionário da escravidão e liberdade*, ed. Lilia Moritz Schwarcz and Flávio Gomes (São Paulo: Companhia das Letras, 2018): 280–82; Beatriz G. Mamigonian, "O Estado Nacional e a instabilidade da propriedade escrava: a lei de 1831 e a matrícula de escravos de 1872," *Almanack* 2 (2011): 20–37. It is interesting to note that in the "Report of the Special Commission nominated for studying the Project [i.e., the Law of the Free Womb] (containing the proposal and the amendments)," see again Senado Federal, *A abolição no Parlamento*: 465–518, theological views on slavery and texts by Roman pontiffs, called "vehement admonitions against slavery," are mentioned, including the letter by "Gregory XVI, in November [sic!] 1839" (First Part, IV, 468–69).

124 Padre Antônio Ferreira Viçoso, "Escravatura ofendida e defendida 1840": 187.

125 Ibid.: 194.

126 Ibid.: 188.

ideals, as no technical analysis is offered. Freedmen and farmers (or land owners) will have to adapt their lives in order to learn how to make land cultivation viable by hiring workers after payment; slaveholders and their family members will possibly have to engage themselves in handwork, and there is no shame in this.[127] (iii) As a third aspect, Viçoso praises the Law of November 7, 1831 – his text can be read as an explicit compliment to Brazilian legislators and "the emperor, who sanctioned it." It was by no means an untimely law – on the contrary, it was discussed in many sessions prior to its final form.[128] Viçoso also confronts the author of the dialogue in the affirmation that the government itself "shuts the eyes to the commerce in Africans." On the contrary, the 49 "orders" issued before 1838 were evidence that the imperial government (the legislators), irrespective of the disagreement or even disobedience of provincial peace judges, deputies, and/or presidents, took the Law of 1831 seriously and did not modify it.[129]

Moreover, bringing the doctrine of conscience to the debate, Viçoso claims that (iv) it is morally wrong that a subject or subjects can alone judge about the higher probability that a given law is non-existent or has no binding force, being then able to act against it "with safe conscience"[130] – after all, an improbable law can indeed be neglected in good conscience. Viçoso is sure of having old and modern probabilists and tutiorists on his side,[131] and he relies on Giovanni Vincenzo Patuzzi's OP (1700–1769) *Ethica christiana sive theologia moralis* (1770) to reject the idea that subjects decide "about the justice or injustice of laws." Disobedience towards a law has to presuppose that it is evidently unjust, on a natural basis, and so is taken in this way by pious and prudent men as well. As a rule, subjects have to obey laws, even if they deem them doubtful: by so doing, they presume that "the legislator's will and disposition" is right and just.[132] Among the several authors mentioned, Viçoso highlights Alphonsus Maria de Liguori (1696–1787), founder of the Congregation of the Most Holy Redeemer in 1732 and author of the masterpiece *Theologia moralis* (1748). In line with Francisco Suárez SJ (1548–1617), Alphonsus Liguori confirms that a doubtful law keeps obligating those

---

127 Ibid.: 188–89.

128 Ibid.: 189. Strictly speaking, the law was sanctioned in the first period of the Brazilian regency (1831–1840), that is, the period of the "Triune Regency," which was initially a "provisional" and then a "permanent" one working from 1831 to 1835.

129 Padre Antônio Ferreira Viçoso, "Escravatura ofendida e defendida 1840": 191.

130 Ibid.: 190.

131 Ibid.: 189. On these moral systems or theories of a good moral conscience, see, for example, Julia A. Fleming, *Defending Probabilism. The Moral Theology of Juan Caramuel* (Washington, DC: Catholic University of America Press, 2006): 1–6; John A. Gallagher, *Time Past, Time Future: A Historical Study of Catholic Moral Theology* (New York/New Jersey: Paulist Press, 1990): 29–47; Harald E. Braun and Edward Vallance, eds., *Contexts of Conscience in Early Modern Europe 1500–1700* (Hampshire/New York: Palgrave Macmillan, 2004).

132 Padre Antônio Ferreira Viçoso, "Escravatura ofendida e defendida 1840": 189–90.

under its authority. After all, the legislator has "a right of commanding, of governing through higher councils," and his reasons are often ignored by many.[133]

If the author of the dialogue, with his patriotic tone, shows concerns about the real political intentions of the British government and suspects it of interest in Brazil's economic collapse and in shaking Brazil's sovereignty,[134] (v) it is quite remarkable how much Viçoso praises the illustration of British policy. Evidence of the moral qualities of that government are the large sums it has spent on emancipating slaves in the Antilles and building up a civilization of freedmen and returnees in Sierra Leone.[135] For Viçoso, convincing testimony of the praiseworthy intentions of the British government is found in the "memories of Gregoire, member of the Legislative Body and the National Institute of France" – here, Viçoso invokes Henri Jean-Baptiste Grégoire (1750–1831), also referred to as "the Abbé Grégoire," a French Catholic priest, liberal left politician, defender of racial and religious equality, and, more specifically, an advocate of the abolition of slavery. In that regard, Abbé Grégoire – whose *Mémoires* appeared in 1837, in two volumes – depicted the British as "friends of humanity." After all, they acted for the abolition of slave trade and the promotion of "civilization in Africa" by organizing on the African Atlantic coast "political societies of free blacks."[136] Although the British – civilizational, Christian, and abolitionist – project of Freetown in Sierra Leone at the end of the eighteenth century cannot be discussed in any detail here, it should at least be said that Abbé Grégoire was enthusiastic about it, as well as a profound admirer of the person who first envisioned it and is taken as one of its founders, the intellectual, social activist, and pioneering campaigner for the end of slavery and the slave trade, Granville Sharp (1735–1813).[137]

If the author of the dialogue had expressed concern for the fact that the Law of November 7, 1831, would make impossible the importation of slaves who had been enslaved because of just claims – that is, as a consequence of (a) "crimes," (b) "just wars," (c) "debts," (d) "retaliations," and (e) "birth" by enslaved women – (vi) Viçoso

133 Ibid.: 190. Alphonsus Maria de Liguori is usually counted among the most notorious "equiprobabilists"; see Alfonso Maria de' Liguori, *Dell'uso moderato dell'opinione probabile* (Bassano: Remondini, 1765). See also M.P. Souza, "Norma e consciência na determinação da verdade moral," *Kairós – Revista Acadêmica da Prainha*, 4, no. 2 (2007): 297–302. As a doctrine of moral conscience, "equiprobabilism" allowed that, in cases of doubt, an agent could follow an opinion which favors freedom, so long as it was as equally probable as the opposite opinion. So, for example, if in face of some moral challenge or dilemma the agent has no notion of an existing rule or law and has doubts about the promulgation of any, he could be led by his freedom. Of course, this is not what happened with the anti-slavery laws under discussion.

134 An important study on the role of the British in Brazil's development – broadly understood – in the nineteenth century is still Richard Graham, *Britain and the Onset of Modernization in Brazil 1850–1914* (Cambridge: Cambridge University Press, 1968), containing a chapter on "Changing Patterns of Labor: Slave Trade and Slavery" (160–86).

135 Padre Antônio Ferreira Viçoso, "Escravatura ofendida e defendida 1840": 191–92.

136 Ibid.: 192.

137 Ibid.: 192–94. See Carl Watner, "*In favorem libertatis*: The Life and Work of Granville Sharp," *Journal of Libertarian Studies* 4, no. 2 (1980): 215–32.

re-establishes the old criticism of the slave trade *from* Africa based on illegitimate enslavements *in* Africa – this kind of criticism was widespread in sixteenth- and seventeenth-century anti-slavery literature.[138] Viçoso dismisses reasons (a) to (d) based on the reports by travelers that prove them for the most part unreal. There is no clear system of justice in African nations that justifiably connects grave crimes to enslavement as a punishment. Wars and retaliation generate prisoners and slaves again as a punishment, but their real justice is usually arbitrariness or simply absent. Moreover, the relation between real debts and the punishment of enslavement is disproportional. It is unacceptable that a person who owes someone else a "cow" or a "ram" can become – along with his or her family and descendants – a perpetual slave as a form of debt payment. In reality, what is claimed as a valid reason for enslaving Africans is usually just a myth. Regarding (e), Viçoso has no intention of offering any solution to the classical debate on the right parents possess to sell their children in cases of most extreme need – the debate was famously featured in sixteenth-century Brazil by the Jesuits Quirício Caxa (1538–1599) and Manuel da Nóbrega (1517–1570).[139] At any rate, we are told by Viçoso, what really happens is that African parents raise "hundreds of children in order to sell them, keeping just the oldest one as the heir." And this is a bizarre custom, unacceptable as a right.[140] Considering, finally, that the number of slaves from Africa put into that condition by having been plainly and simply being robbed is – at least – equal to the number of those who were not properly enslaved according to reasons (a) to (e), it is elementary to conclude that, for the most part, African slaves are illegitimate.[141]

(vii) Viçoso is shocked by an argument of the dialogue's author according to which, given the "extensive and multiple origins of many true slaves" in Africa, someone needs "positive proof" to judge that a trader is really selling "robbed slaves" – which seems to imply, moreover, that the burden of proof regarding illegal property is on all who raise suspicions about slaves' real status. Positive proof means here something like offering evidence for the fact that traders possess things that are not what they are said to be or, in other words, not legally or fairly possessed. Accusers must provide this evidence, traders do not need to offer evidence that their goods or possessions are what they are or legal. This issue was certainly important in nineteenth-century public discussions about the slave trade and is important in order to understand how parties *pro* and *contra* that commerce tried to offer evidence for their views. After all, that the original enslavement of people in Africa was unjust should be more than merely a rumor. Viçoso appeals several times to the objective value of reports by trustworthy travelers or, more exactly, the literature produced by

138 See the literature referred to in note 2, above. See also Roberto Hofmeister Pich, "Probabilismo e escravidão negra," *Humanidades: Revista de la Universidad de Montevideo* 8 (2020): 17–67.

139 See Alfredo Carlos Storck, "The Jesuits and the Indigenous Slavery: A Debate over Voluntary Slavery in Brazilian Colonial Period," *Mediaevalia – Textos e Estudos* 31 (2012): 69–83.

140 Padre Antônio Ferreira Viçoso, "Escravatura ofendida e defendida 1840": 195.

141 Ibid.: 195–96.

De Laporte in *The Universal Traveler*. Based on massive numbers of trustworthy testimonies and the widespread news about how people were illegally enslaved and traded in Africa, it is not possible to say that traders that bring slaves to Brazil and purchasers of slaves can act in good conscience.[142] Surely, the discussions and opinions *pro* abolition of the Transatlantic slave trade were based on testimonies. Neither testimonies nor any positive proof for the injustice of enslavement could possibly be founded on what traders or any people interested in trading slaves might hear from traffickers on the African shores. The figure of the "traveler" implicitly works, here, as a kind of impartial spectator, a kind of impartial "reporter" abroad.

At this point in the text, Viçoso creates a fictional conversation between a trader who brings his ship to Africa and tries to prove his good conscience in dealing with local traffickers. (viii) He imagines the ironic situation in which the chaplain of the ship talks to the captain about Gregory XVI's bull and the prohibition of slave trade that it promulgates to all Catholics. As an answer, the captain reports that "his Father" – that is, the author of the dialogue! – explained to him that "the pope spoke of violent and illicit slavery, which is obtained through invasions and hunting," but the bull was not addressed to persons like him, who bought slaves with his own money. The bull could rather only have in view the "black trafficker" who sold slaves to the international trader. What traders make has nothing to do with entering a country to capture people. The chaplain, then, expresses his understanding that the bull by Gregory XVI has not black people in Africa in view because they are not Christians. The apostolic letter only speaks to Christians that "make immediate invasions for hunting blacks." Therefore, if someone follows the judgement of the dialogue's author, the bull "is useless and has no place," for its contents do not affect the conscience of slave traders.[143]

Of course, Viçoso does not believe that Gregory XVI's bull allows this interpretation[144] – it is rather a clear prohibition, valid for all Catholics, of the trade of African slaves. No Catholic Christian can find, by participating in the chain of the Transatlantic slave trade from Africa to other parts of the world, a zone of safety for his conscience. Those who go to the African coast to purchase slaves – not only those who hunt people with the purpose of selling them as slaves to traders – commit a crime and do not act in ignorance. Doubts about the true condition of people sold on the market as slaves were unsolvable. But the bull, whose contents Viçoso believes to have been influenced by the theologians of the Conference of Angers, was apparently not obvious for everyone regarding the links of the slavery chain that should be taken as prohibited:[145] Catholic ministers and thinkers would have to take responsibility for its interpretation.

142 Ibid.: 196.

143 Ibid.: 197.

144 Moreover, it is not possible to affirm, so far, that Father Peixoto e Castro, by the time he wrote *Slavery Offended and Defended*, made any interpretation of Gregory XVI's bull.

145 Padre Antônio Ferreira Viçoso, "Escravatura ofendida e defendida 1840": 199–200.

A central purpose of Viçoso's exposition, totally in line with and arguably as a further interpretation or reaction to *In supremo apostolatus*, (ix) is to guide the conscience and actions of Catholic Christians. Viçoso thus decisively confronts the author of the dialogue by affirming that nobody can participate in the selling and buying of African slaves and at the same time act in sound conscience – acting within the chain of the Transatlantic slave trade is acting within an area of unsolvable doubt about the licitness of contracts. Although Viçoso's text does not offer any detailed theory of moral (good) conscience, some guidance is explicitly proposed: (a) buying things about which the person has doubts whether they are licit property or not is a mortal sin – this is an idea Viçoso takes from Pierre Collet (1693–1770), a Lazarist moral theologian and the author of a quite popular work called *Institutiones theologicae* (1757). (b) If someone is a possessor of some external goods and, after consideration, comes to believe that it is more likely that the thing was stolen, he is obliged to return it. And (c) if someone is about to acquire "something notable" and has doubts whether it was stolen or not, he sins mortally if he buys it, being then obliged to restitution – this idea Viçoso takes from Fulgenzio Cuni[g] liati OP (1685–1759), the Catholic theologian and author of *Universae theologiae moralis accurata complexio*. When applied to the problem of the slave trade, all these principles should presuppose the truth that it is more probable that Africans who happen to be enslaved are by right free. Freedom is the first thing to be – immediately – returned to black people, although not the only thing. That enslaved Africans were for the most part free persons according to right was also the conviction of theologians, Gregory XVI's bull, and Brazilian laws.[146]

4 Concluding Remarks

Viçoso provides in his exposition a massive and many-sided defense of the abolition of the slave trade and substantial support for the Law of November 7, 1831, and its subsequent ampliative decrees and notifications. In particular, he seems to point to a community of Catholic ministers and thinkers in Brazil[147] who share the same view and see in Gregory XVI's bull a decisive and explicit orientation for abolishing the slave trade. If this community of thinkers shared Viçoso's profile, it was characterized by conservatism in ecclesiology and religion and liberalism in economy and rights. Viçoso's text is an articulated and "fraternal" effort at making Catholics like the priest and theologian who wrote the dialogue change their minds about the licitness of the commerce in slaves. Granted that Gregory XVI's bull had to be taken as the binding

146 Ibid.: 198–99.

147 Regarding the abolition of slave trade and, thus, the legitimacy of Brazilian legal determinations since 1831, Padre Antônio Ferreira Viçoso, "Escravatura ofendida e defendida 1840": 199, enlists himself and "the most skillful masters of theology from Minas [Gerais]" and "the bishops of Brazil" on the same page.

guide to the problem of slavery among Catholics, writings with opposite views about the subject should be sent to bishops in order to be sanctioned or reproved.[148] At any rate, it seems that the apostolic letter would demand interpretation by Catholic authorities – Viçoso himself advances some ways how pro-slavery parties could choose some readings of it in order not to feel directly touched by its commands. It is likely that Viçoso has understood Gregory XVI's bull according to what was called above the "narrow interpretation," although his own expositions on slavery suggest that he sympathized with a broad program of abolishing slavery everywhere. Viçoso, as with most Catholic theologians, was not a strict abolitionist. It is not possible to affirm yet whether Viçoso saw in Gregory XVI's bull a substantial endorsement of convictions he already had about slavery or whether he substantially reshaped and reconceived his opinions about slavery because of the bull – there is some evidence that in an earlier phase, Viçoso, when he was still a priest and before 1839–1840, saw in slavery an opportunity for the evangelization of black people.[149] Be that as it may, and this is valid for Viçoso too, it seems fair to affirm that the apostolic letter, which was in principle a binding document, should be a guide for showing Catholic clerics a direction in thinking about slavery and the slave trade.

This way of seeing the connection between Gregory XVI's bull and Antônio Viçoso should inspire – with no presumptuousness, of course, but rather with the sobriety of well-documented information – a direction in research on the Catholic Church and abolitionism in imperial Brazil. This research, in terms of methodology, could focus on the reception of *In supremo apostolatus* by Catholic authorities (bishops),[150] priests, and theologians, as this can be tracked and described on the basis of sermons, correspondence, ecclesiastical journals, notebooks, and perhaps theological texts – many of these materials survive as manuscripts in the ecclesiastical archives. After all, these were means of influencing beliefs and attitudes towards the facts of slavery that, in theological terms, had a "pastoral" dimension, which, although it differed from the work by the "publicists" in the nineteenth century, was at least partially a "public" dimension as well.

On the political-philosophical level, it is remarkable how much and how clearly Viçoso declares his alignment with thinkers who had a legal and social plan for Brazil that included the abolition of the slave trade. The last paragraphs of his exposition are proof of his admiration for the ideas of the Brazilian naturalist and politician José

148 Padre Antônio Ferreira Viçoso, "Escravatura ofendida e defendida 1840": 200.

149 This is noted by Melo, *Dom Ferreira Viçoso (1787–1875)*: 308–9, on the basis of a sermon by Viçoso entitled "Os meios para a perseverança" ("The Means for Perseverance").

150 On the role of Catholic bishops in promoting abolitionist ideas in imperial Brazil, see also Henrique Cristiano José Matos, *Nossa história. 500 anos de presença da Igreja Católica no Brasil*, vol. 2, *Período imperial e transição republicana*, 2nd ed. (São Paulo: Paulinas, 2010): 178–88.

Bonifácio de Andrada e Silva (1763–1838), supporter of Brazilian independence from Portugal and of a liberal monarchy in Brazil. Viçoso was a reader of José Bonifácio's *Analytic Memories*.[151] He quotes and finds in them some of the same key ideas reflected in his own text: (a) the country's economic development depended on the introduction of free labor; (b) universal "freedom"[152] and "justice" are key values of civilized and developed societies; (c) a society of slaves brings the risk of a revolution; (d) abolition of the slave trade is connected to "reason," "humanity" – perpetual slavery is contrary to "religion and sound politics" – and the defense of the country's own interests, safety, and peace; (e) "individual freedom" is related both to "morality and justice" and to the power of a nation; (f) anti-slavery laws and policies represent a form of patriotism.[153] It is arguable that Viçoso not only sympathizes with all these ideas of José de Bonifácio, but also finds in Catholic social thought and doctrine, as epitomized in *In supremo apostolatus*, an ideology in harmony with them.

Bibliography

Primary Sources

Alfonso Maria de' Liguori. *Dell'uso moderato dell'opinione probabile* (Bassano: Remondini, 1765).

Alonso de Sandoval. *Un tratado sobre la esclavitud – De instauranda Aethiopum salute*, trans. Enriqueta Vila Vilar (Madrid: Alianza Editorial, 1987).

Andrada e Silva, José Bonifácio de. *Memórias sobre a escravidão*, ed. Graça Salgado (Rio de Janeiro: Arquivo Nacional, 1988).

Bentham, Jeremy. *An Introduction to the Principles of Morals and Legislation*, ed. J.H. Burns and H.L.A. Hart (Oxford: Clarendon Press, 1996).

Bentham, Jeremy. *The Works of Jeremy Bentham*, vol. 1, *Principles of the Civil Code* (Indianapolis: The Online Library of Liberty, 2011) [= *The Works of Jeremy Bentham*, ed. John Bowring (Edinburgh: William Tait, 1838–1843): 538–659].

151 See José Bonifácio de Andrada e Silva, *Memórias sobre a escravidão*, ed. Graça Salgado (Rio de Janeiro: Arquivo Nacional, 1988), especially the "Representação à Assembléia Geral Constituinte e Legislativa do Império do Brasil sobre a escravatura" (1825). In the early phase of the Brazilian monarchy, José Bonifácio de Andrada e Silva conceived a plan for a gradual, though complete and irreversible, emancipation of black slaves in Brazil. See Antonio Penalves Rocha, "Idéias antiescravistas da Ilustração na sociedade escravista brasileira," *Revista Brasileira de História* 20, no. 39 (2000): 52, 55–56.

152 At the end of his text, see Padre Antônio Ferreira Viçoso, "Escravatura ofendida e defendida 1840": 201–2, Viçoso also reproduces (from the work *O Feliz Independente do Mundo e da Fortuna*, 1779, in 3 volumes) the praise of "freedom" as a universal and "absolute and irrevocable" divine gift made by the illuminist Catholic thinker from Portugal, Teodoro de Almeida (1722–1804), himself an Oratorian or member or the Order of Saint Felipe Néri. Teodoro de Almeida features promoters and agents of slavery as "monsters of reason."

153 Padre Antônio Ferreira Viçoso, "Escravatura ofendida e defendida 1840": 200–01.

Constituições Primeiras do Arcebispado da Bahia [1853]. Edições do Senado Federal, vol. 79, https://www2.senado.leg.br [accessed 01.23.2022].
Costa, Lourenço, ed. *Documentos de Gregório XVI e de Pio IX (1831–1878)*, trans. Darci L. Marin (São Paulo: Paulus, 1999).
De Laporte, Mr. *O viajante universal, ou notícia do Mundo Antigo e Moderno*, vol. 12–13 (Lisbon: Typografia Rollandiana, 1800–1803).
Didacus de Avendaño. *Thesaurus indicus seu Generalis Instructor pro regimine conscientiae* vol. 1 (Antuerpia: Apud Iacobum Meursium, 1668).
Epifanio de Moirans. *Siervos libres: una propuesta antiesclavista a finales del siglo XVII*, ed. Miguel Anxo Pena González (Madrid: Consejo Superior de Investigaciones Científicas, 2007).
Francisco José de Jaca. *Resolución sobre la libertad de los negros, en estado de paganos y después ya cristianos: La primera condena de la esclavitud en el pensamiento hispano*, ed. Miguel Anxo Pena González (Madrid: Consejo Superior de Investigaciones Científicas, 2002).
Gomes, Laurentino. *Escravidão – Volume I: Do primeiro leilão de cativos em Portugal até a morte de Zumbi dos Palmares* (Rio de Janeiro: Globo Livros, 2019).
Gregório XVI, Papa. *Carta Apostólica* In supremo [1839]. Montfort Associação Cultural, http://www.montfort.org.br/bra/documentos/decretos/in_supremo/ [accessed 01.11.2022].
Gregory XVI, Pope. *In supremo apostolatus*, Papal Encyclicals Online, https://www.papalencyclicals.net/Greg16/g16sup.htm [accessed 01.10.2022].
Ludovicus Molina. *De iustitia et iure* (Coloniae Allobrogum: Ed. Marci Michaelis Bousquet, 1738 [Venetiis, 1611]).
Thomas de Aquino. *Summa theologiae* [Latin-Portuguese], vol. 6, ed. C.-J. Pinto de Oliveira, 2nd ed. (São Paulo: Edições Loyola, 2012).
Viçoso, Padre Antônio Ferreira. "Escravatura ofendida e defendida 1840," in *Escritos sobre escravidão*, ed. Lúcio Álvaro Marques and João Paulo Rodrigues Pereira (Porto Alegre: Editora FI, 2020): 145–202.

Secondary Literature

Adiele, Pius Onyemechi. *The Popes, the Catholic Church and the Transatlantic Enslavement of Black Africans 1418–1839* (Hildesheim/Zürich/ New York: Georg Olms Verlag, 2017).
Araújo, Carlos Eduardo Moreira de. "Fim do tráfico," in *Dicionário da escravidão e liberdade*, ed. Lilia Moritz Schwarcz and Flávio Gomes (São Paulo: Companhia das Letras, 2018): 230–36.
Assis, Raquel Martins de. "Psicologia, educação e reforma dos costumes: lições da Selecta Catholica (1846–1847)" (PhD thesis, Universidade Federal de Minas Gerais, 2004).
Azzi, Riolando. "A instituição eclesiástica durante a primeira época colonial," in *História da Igreja no Brasil. Ensaio de interpretação a partir do povo – Primeira Época*, ed. Eduardo Hoornaert et al., 2nd ed. (Petrópolis: Vozes, 1979): 153–242.
Beozzo, José Oscar. "A Igreja e a escravidão," in *História da Igreja no Brasil: Segunda Época – Século XIX*, João Fagundes Hauck et al. (Petrópolis: Vozes, 1980): 255–95.
Bethell, Leslie. *The Abolition of the Brazilian Slave Trade. Britain and the Slave Trade Question 1807–1869* (Cambridge: Cambridge University Press, 1970).
Brandão, Marcella de Sá. "'Em defesa dos catholicos': imprensa católica no episcopado de D. Antônio Ferreira Viçoso" (master's diss., Universidade Federal de Minas Gerais, 2015). diss.
Braun, Harald, and Edward Vallance, eds. *Contexts of Conscience in Early Modern Europe 1500–1700* (Hampshire/New York: Palgrave Macmillan, 2004).
Cenci, Márcio Paulo. "African Slavery and Salvation in the *De instauranda Aethiopum salute* of Alonso de Sandoval S.J. (1577–1652)," *Patristica et Mediaevalia* 36 (2015): 75–89.

Coelho, Tatiana Costa. "A Reforma Católica em Mariana e o discurso ultramontano de Dom Viçoso (Minas Gerais 1844–1875)," in *Anais do XXVI Simpósio Nacional de História – ANPUH*, ed. Marieta de Moraes Ferreira (São Paulo: ANPUH, 2011): 1–9.

Coelho, Tatiana Costa. "Nas malhas do discurso: a Reforma Católica em Mariana e o discurso ultramontano de Dom Viçoso (Minas Gerais 1844–1875)," *Revista Eletrônica de História do Brasil* 9, no. 2 (2007): 97–107.

Conrad, Robert. *The Destruction of Brazilian Slavery 1850–1888* (Berkeley/Los Angeles/London: University of California Press, 1972).

Conzemius, Victor. "Ultramontanismus," *Theologische Realenzyklopädie* 34 (2002): 253–63.

Culleton, Alfredo Santiago. "Tomás de Mercado on Slavery: Just According to Law, Unjust in Practice," *Patristica et Mediaevalia* 36 (2015): 29–38.

Fleming, Julia A. *Defending Probabilism. The Moral Theology of Juan Caramuel* (Washington, DC: Catholic University of America Press, 2006).

Gallagher, John A. *Time Past, Time Future: A Historical Study of Catholic Moral Theology* (New York/New Jersey: Paulist Press, 1990).

Graham, Richard. *Britain and the Onset of Modernization in Brazil 1850–1914* (Cambridge: Cambridge University Press, 1968).

Gülzow, Henneke. *Christentum und Sklaverei in der ersten drei Jahrhunderten* (Bonn: Rudolf Habelt Verlag, 1969).

Kähler, Christoph, "Sklaverei II. Neues Testament," *Theologische Realenzyklopädie* 31 (2000): 373–77.

Klein, Herbert S. *Escravidão africana – América Latina e Caribe*, trans. José Eduardo de Mendonça (São Paulo: Editora Brasiliense, 1987).

Klein, Richard. "Sklaverei IV. Alte Kirche und Mittelalter," *Theologische Realenzyklopädie* 31 (2000): 379–83.

Luna, Francisco Vidal, and Herbert S. Klein. *Escravismo no Brasil*, trans. Laura Teixeira Motta (São Paulo: Edusp, 2010).

Maestri, Mário. *A servidão negra* (Porto Alegre: Editora Mercado Aberto, 1988).

Maestri, Mário. *O escravismo no Brasil*, 10th ed. (São Paulo: Atual, 2002).

Mamigonian, Beatriz G. *Africanos livres. A abolição do tráfico de escravos no Brasil* (São Paulo: Companhia das Letras, 2017).

Mamigonian, Beatriz G. "O Estado Nacional e a instabilidade da propriedade escrava: a lei de 1831 e a matrícula de escravos de 1872," *Almanack* (Guarulhos) 2 (2011): 20–37.

Mamigonian, Beatriz Gallotti, and Keila Grinberg. "Lei de 1831," in *Dicionário da escravidão e liberdade*, ed. Lilia Moritz Schwarcz and Flávio Gomes (São Paulo: Companhia das Letras, 2018): 285–91.

Marques, Lúcio Álvaro, and João Paulo Rodrigues Pereira. "A barbárie como operador político," in *Escritos sobre escravidão*, ed. Lúcio Álvaro Marques and João Paulo Rodrigues Pereira (Porto Alegre: Editora FI, 2020): 36–75.

Marques, Lúcio Álvaro, and João Paulo Rodrigues Pereira. "Introdução histórica," in *Escritos sobre escravidão*, ed. Lúcio Álvaro Marques and João Paulo Rodrigues Pereira (Porto Alegre: Editora FI, 2020): 17–35.

Martina, Giacomo. *História da Igreja: de Lutero a nossos dias II – A era do liberalismo*, trans. Orlando Soares Moreira (São Paulo: Edições Loyola, 1996).

Matos, Henrique Cristiano José. *Nossa história. 500 anos de presença da Igreja Católica no Brasil*, vol. 1, *Período colonial*, 2nd ed. (São Paulo: Paulinas, 2005).

Matos, Henrique Cristiano José. *Nossa história. 500 anos de presença da Igreja Católica no Brasil*, vol. 2, *Período imperial e transição republicana*, 2nd ed. (São Paulo: Paulinas, 2010).

Melo, Arnaldo José de. "Dom Ferreira Viçoso (1787–1875) e sua obra reformadora da Igreja de Minas Gerais: uma releitura teológica moral" (PhD thesis, Pontificia Universitas Lateranensis, 2005).

Mendonça, Joseli Maria Nunes. *Entre a mão e os anéis. A Lei dos Sexagenários e os caminhos da abolição no Brasil* (Campinas: Editora da Unicamp, 1999).

Mendonça, Joseli Maria Nunes. "Legislação emancipacionista, 1871 e 1885," in *Dicionário da escravidão e liberdade*, ed. Lilia Moritz Schwarcz and Flávio Gomes (São Paulo: Companhia das Letras, 2018): 277–84.

Oliveira, Lívia Gabriele. "A presença da Igreja nas ações abolicionistas do Norte Mineiro: o caso do Bispado de Diamantina – 1864–1888" (master's diss., Instituto de Ciências Humanas e Sociais Mariana, 2011).

O'Malley, John W. *Vatican I: The Council and the Making of the Ultramontane Church* (Cambridge, MA: Belknap Press, 2018).

Pena, Eduardo Spiller. *Pajens da casa imperial. Jurisconsultos, escravidão e a Lei de 1871* (Campinas: Editora da Unicamp, 2001).

Pena González, Miguel Anxo. "Un autor desconocido y singular en el pensamiento hispano," in Francisco José de Jaca. *Resolución sobre la libertad de los negros, en estado de paganos y después ya cristianos*, ed. Miguel Anxo Pena González (Madrid: Consejo Superior de Investigaciones Científicas, 2002): XXIII–XCVIII.

Pereira, João Paulo Rodrigues. "Educação ofendida ou defendida: as consequências do ideal antiescravista de Dom Viçoso no Seminário de Mariana (1844–1875)," *Revista saberes interdisciplinares* 23, no. 2 (2019): 97–108.

Pich, Roberto Hofmeister. "Alonso de Sandoval S.J. (1576/1577–1652) and the Ideology of Black Slavery: Some Theological and Philosophical Arguments," *Patristica et Mediaevalia* 36 (2015): 51–74.

Pich, Roberto Hofmeister. "Francisco José de Jaca's (*c.* 1645–1689) and Epifanio de Moirans's (1644–1689) Plea for the Liberation of Enslaved Black People in Latin America," in *Civilization – Nature – Subjugation. Variations of (De-)Colonization*, ed. Christoph Haar, Matthias Kaufmann and Christian Müller (Berlin: Peter Lang, 2021): 69–110.

Pich, Roberto Hofmeister. "Probabilismo e escravidão Negra," *Humanidades: Revista de la Universidad de Montevideo* 8 (2020): 17–67.

Pich, Roberto Hofmeister. "Second Scholasticism and Black Slavery," *Veritas* 64, no. 3 (2019): 1–24.

Pich, Roberto Hofmeister. "Second Scholasticism and Black Slavery (Continuation and End)," *Veritas* 65, no. 1 (2020): 1–13.

Pich, Roberto Hofmeister, Alfredo Santiago Culleton and Alfredo Carlos Storck. "Second Scholasticism and Black Slavery – Some Philosophical Assessments," *Patristica et Mediaevalia* 36 (2015): 3–15.

Powell, Douglas, "Clemens von Rom," *Theologische Realenzyklopädie* 8 (1981): 113–20.

Prien, Hans-Jürgen. *Die Geschichte des Christentums in Lateinamerika* (Göttingen: Vandenhoeck & Ruprecht, 1978).

Priesching, Nicole. "Die Verurteilung der Sklaverei durch Gregor XVI. im Jahr 1839. Ein Traditionsbruch?" *Saeculum: Jahrbuch für Universalgeschichte* 59, no. 1 (2008): 143–62.

Quinn, John F. "'Three Cheers for the Abolitionist Pope!': American Reaction to Gregory XVI's Condemnation of the Slave Trade, 1840–1860," *The Catholic Historical Review* 90, no.1 (2004): 67–93.

Rocha, Antonio Penalves. "Idéias antiescravistas da Ilustração na sociedade escravista brasileira," *Revista Brasileira de História* 20, no. 39 (2000): 43–79.

Sainte-Croix, Geoffrey Ernest Maurice de. "Early Christian Attitudes to Property and Slavery," in *Studies in Church History*, ed. Derek Baker (Oxford: Blackwell, 1975): 1–38.

Santirocchi, Ítalo Domingos, and Manoel de J. Martins. "'Quanto ao serviço dos escravos, eu os dispenso': D. Antònio Ferreira Viçoso, bispo ultamontano e antiescravista (século XIX)," in *Doze capítulos sobre escravizar gente e governar escravos: Brasil e Angola – séculos XVII–XIX*, ed. Denise Vieira Demétrio, Ítalo Domingos Santirocchi and Roberto Guedes (Rio de Janeiro: Mauad X, 2017): 197–226.

Santos, Fabiano Glaeser dos. *O Papa infalível em Porto Alegre: repercussões em terras sulinas do Concílio Vaticano I* (Porto Alegre: EST, 2020).

Schwarcz, Lilia Moritz, and Flávio Gomes, eds., *Dicionário da escravidão e liberdade* (São Paulo: Companhia das Letras, 2018).

Scott, Rebecca J., ed. *The Abolition of Slavery and the Aftermath of Emancipation in Brazil* (Durham, NC/ London: Duke University Press, 1988).

Senado Federal. *A abolição no Parlamento: 65 anos de luta (1823–1888)*, 2nd ed. (Brasília: Secretaria Especial de Editoração e Publicações – SEEP, 2012).

Silva, Juremir Machado da. *Raízes do conservadorismo brasileiro. A abolição na imprensa e no imaginário social*, 3rd ed. (Rio de Janeiro: Civilização Brasileira, 2018).

Silva Neto, Belchior J. da. *Dom Viçoso, apóstolo de Minas* (Belo Horizonte: Imprensa Oficial do Estado de Minas Gerais, 1965).

Sinha, Manisha. *The Slave's Cause: A History of Abolition* (New Haven/London: Yale University Press, 2017).

Souza, M.P. "Norma e consciência na determinação da verdade moral," *Kairós – Revista Acadêmica da Prainha* 4, no. 2 (2007): 282–308.

Storck, Alfredo Carlos. "The Jesuits and the Indigenous Slavery: A Debate over Voluntary Slavery in Brazilian Colonial Period," *Mediaevalia – Textos e Estudos* 31 (2012): 69–83.

Thornton, John. *Africa and Africans in the Making of the Atlantic World, 1400–1800* (New York: Cambridge University Press, 1998).

Tomich, Dale W. *Pelo prisma da escravidão: trabalho, capital e economia mundial*, trans. A. de P. Danesi (São Paulo: Edusp, 2011).

Vainfas, Ronaldo. "Escravidão, ideologias e sociedade," in *Escravidão e abolição no Brasil. Novas perspectivas*, ed. Ciro Flamarion Cardoso (Rio de Janeiro: Jorge Zahar Editor, 1988): 46–56.

Vainfas, Ronaldo. *Ideologia e escravidão. Os letrados e a sociedade escravista no Brasil colonial* (Petrópolis: Vozes, 1986).

Vieira, Dilermando Ramos. *História do Catolicismo no Brasil*, vol. 1, *1500–1889* (Aparecida: Editora Santuário, 2016).

Von Loewenich, Walther. *Der moderne Katholizismus*, 4th ed. (Witten: Luther-Verlag: 1959).

Von Loewenich, Walther. *Die Geschichte der Kirche II: Von der Reformation zur Neuzeit*, 2nd ed. (München/ Hamburg: Siebenstern, 1966).

Watner, Carl. "*In favorem libertatis*: The Life and Work of Granville Sharp," *Journal of Libertarian Studies* 4, no. 2 (1980): 215–32.

Wolf, Hubert. "História da Igreja Católica durante o "longo século" XIX de 1789 a 1918," in *História ecumênica da Igreja*, vol. 3, *Da Revolução Francesa até 1989*, ed. Thomas Kaufmann; trans. Irineu Rabuske and Alfred Keller (São Paulo/São Leopoldo: Edições Loyola/Paulus/Editora Sinodal, 2017): 87–185.

Zavala, Silvio Arturo. *Repaso histórico de la bula* Sublimis Deus *de Paulo III, en defensa de los indios* (México: Universidad Iberoamericana, 1991).

Zeron, Carlos Alberto de Moura Ribeiro. *Linha de fé. A Companhia de Jesus e a escravidão no processo de formação da sociedade colonial (Brasil, séculos XVI e XVII)* (São Paulo: Edusp, 2011).

Zeuske, Michael. *Sklaven und Sklaverei in den Welten des Atlantiks 1400–1940. Umrisse, Anfänge, Akteure, Vergleichsfelder und Bibliographien* (Berlin: LIT, 2006).

Zeuske, Michael. *Sklavenhändler, Negreros und Atlantikkreolen. Eine Weltgeschichte des Sklavenhandels im atlantischen Raum* (Berlin/Boston: De Gruyter Oldenbourg, 2015).

Zeuske, Michael. *Sklaverei. Eine Menschheitsgeschichte von der Steinzeit bis heute* (Stuttgart: Philipp Reclam, 2018).

Ricardo F. Pirola

Lynchings in Nineteenth-Century Brazil: Slavery, the Press and the Courts

In an article entitled "A Lei de Lynch" ("Lynch's Law") published in February 1879, *A Gazeta de Notícias*, then one of nineteenth-century Rio de Janeiro's leading newspapers, reported that a mob of nearly 200 people had stormed the jail in Itu, a town in São Paulo province, and lynched an enslaved man named Nazário. Days later, the same newspaper once again used the term "Lynch's Law" regarding a case in California, in which a mob had lynched a black man accused of horse theft. For readers of the Brazilian press in the late nineteenth century, the association between the expression "Lynch's Law" and forms of extrajudicial punishment was not uncommon. Since at least the 1850s, the topic of lynchings had become extremely popular in the newspapers, whether they were reporting on cases in Brazil or reprinting news of lynched "horse thieves," "murderers" and "gold robbers" in the United States.[1] Although it is not uncommon to find reports of lynchings in nineteenth-century sources, few studies in the Brazilian literature have focused on analyzing this subject. This finding can be partly explained by the fact that the authors who have studied lynching in Brazil concentrate their analysis on more recent periods, especially the second half of the twentieth and the first years of the twenty-first centuries. As a result, lynching in Brazil has been assessed as an expression of violence in the low-income outskirts of the country's large urban centers – areas characterized by the absence of the state in the regulation of social relations.[2] Historians have only recently begun to look at the lynchings that occurred in nineteenth-century Brazil. I am particularly referring to the work of Karl Monsma and Amy Chazkel.[3] Both studies have the merit of drawing historians' attention

1 A modified version of this paper was published in Portuguese in the book entitled *Do tráfico ao pós-abolição*. See Ricardo F. Pirola, "A lei de Lynch no ocaso da escravidão: linchamentos, justiça e polícia (1878–1889)," in *Do tráfico ao pós-abolição: trabalho compulsório e livre e aluta por direitos sociais no Brasil*, ed. Regina C. Xavier and Helen Osório (São Leopoldo: Oikos, 2018): 454–81.

2 Paulo Rogério Meira Menandro and Lídio de Souza, *Linchamentos no Brasil: a Justiça que não tarda, mas falha: uma análise a partir de dados obtidos através da imprensa escrita* (Vitória: Fundação Ceciliano Abel de Almeida, 1991); Maria Victória Benevides and Rosa Maria Ferreira, "Respostas populares e violência urbana: o caso dos linchamentos no Brasil (1979–1982)," in *Crime, violência e poder*, ed. Paulo Sérgio Pinheiro (São Paulo: Brasiliense, 1983): 227–43; José Arthur Rios, "Linchamentos: do arcaico ao moderno," *Revista de Informação Legislativa* 25, no. 100 (1988): 207–38; Sérgio Adorno, "Linchamentos em São Paulo," in *Continuidade autoritária e construção da democracia: relatório final*, ed. Paulo Sérgio Pinheiro (São Paulo: Núcleo de Estudos da Violência/USP, 1999): 404–80; José de Souza Martins, *Linchamentos: a justiça popular no Brasil* (São Paulo: Editora Contexto, 2015).

3 Karl Martin Monsma, "Linchamentos raciais no pós-abolição: alguns casos excepcionais do oeste paulista," in *Políticas da raça: experiências e legados da abolição e da pós-emancipação no Brasil*, ed. Flávio Gomes and Petrônio Domingues (São Paulo: Selo Negro Edições, 2014): 195–210. See also Karl Martin

https://doi.org/10.1515/9783111026527-009

to the subject of lynching as an important key to assessing the post-abolition period in Brazil. For example, Monsma uses lynching cases to highlight the racial conflicts between Italian immigrants and formerly enslaved individuals in the years following the abolition of slavery in rural São Paulo. Chazkel emphasizes the struggle of the formerly enslaved and their descendants to assert the civil rights they acquired following the end of slavery. Although these authors have both made major contributions to the study of lynchings in Brazil, it is still essential to look at this phenomenon during the period prior to abolition, especially in the 1880s, when the movement to abolish slavery exacerbated tensions between slaves and masters and intensified the political struggle to expand civil rights in Brazil. In other words, we must analyze the interactions between the institutions of the imperial government – particularly the police and the courts – and the general public. After all, why were slaves being lynched? Was domestic punishment inflicted by slave-owners who failed to keep the enslaved in line? Did the police and the courts lack effective instruments for punishing crimes committed by captives while upholding seigneurial interests? With regard to the lynching of free individuals, what led members of the public to take the law into their own hands? Who took part in the lynchings? I conducted my research on lynchings in southeastern Brazil between 1878 and 1888 with questions like these in mind. Therefore, this article aims to analyze newspapers published in the last decade of slavery in Brazil. The golden age of abolitionism, it officially began in 1871 with the creation of the Free Womb Law and ended with abolition in 1888.

I use two series of documents in this study. The first is the annual reports produced by the police chiefs of Rio de Janeiro, São Paulo and Minas Gerais, sent to provincial presidents. In these reports, lynchings were described in the "Police" section under the heading "Public Peace." Another source that serves as a basis for this study is nineteenth-century newspapers. In order to cover the contents of newspapers spanning a decade, I used the search tool provided by the Brazilian National Library's "Hemeroteca Digital" website. The search terms used were *linchamento* and *lei de Lynch* ("lynching" and "Lynch's law").[4] Before embarking on this analysis, I should emphasize that this study does not adopt a preconceived concept of lynching. The

---

Mosma, *A reprodução do racismo: fazendeiros, negros e imigrantes no oeste paulista, 1880–1914* (São Carlos: Editora da Universidade Federal de São Carlos, 2016); Amy Chazkel, "'A Lei de Lynch': Reconsidering the View from Brazil of Lynching in the United States, 1880s–1920s," in *Global Lynching and Collective Violence*, vol. 2, ed. Michael Pfeifer (Chicago: University of Illinois Press, 2017): pos. 1661 [e-book].

4 The search for the keywords *linchamento* and *Lei de Lynch* in the Hemeroteca found 79 hits in 10 newspapers for 1870–1879. For 1880–1889, 304 hits were found in 17 newspapers. It should be noted that not all hits were confirmed as news related to lynchings, as the search system also identifies terms whose spelling is similar to the search words. For example, the search engine also found *puchamento* (asthma), *alinhamento* (alignment), *lançamento* (launch) and "general Lynch." It should be stressed that the newspaper search only found one case that was not mentioned in the reports from the chiefs of police (this is the case of the lynching of a Portuguese man in June 1885, in Mar de Hespanha, Minas Gerais).

term "lynching" is used as the contemporary sources themselves defined it in the documents consulted. The main objective is to try to avoid anachronisms when dealing with collective actions taken in the name of justice. An example taken from the book by Paulo Menandro and Lídio de Souza helps exemplify the risk of transferring current definitions of the term to the nineteenth century. Both authors understand lynchings to be "any public collective action aimed at summarily executing individuals accused of committing a crime without any type of legal trial."[5] Thus, when applying this definition to the 1800s, Menandro and Souza concluded that the earliest act of this nature recorded in the literature occurred in 1853, in Campinas. This is a case cited by Maria Helena Machado in her book *Crime e escravidão* (Crime and Slavery), in which, after seeing some of their fellow captives punished by an overseer, 12 enslaved individuals collectively retaliated by killing that controlling agent of production.[6] However much it may fit into the concept of lynching presented by those authors, this type of action was not viewed as "lynching" by contemporary sources (whether from the perspective of the police, the courts, defendants, victims, witnesses or even the press). Machado herself does not identify it as a lynching.[7] In fact, the murder of overseers (or masters) by a group of slaves was a frequent occurrence in the history of slavery in Brazil, particularly in the second half of the nineteenth century. However, the descriptions of these incidents ranged from "acts of rebellion," "barbaric acts" and "murder" to the "struggle for the restoration of natural rights" (according to the abolitionists), but never "lynching." It therefore seems more appropriate here to analyze what the sources describe as lynching than to use a modern-day concept to find events that fit the chosen definition. In fact, the identification of the meanings that this phenomenon has acquired over time is key to the construction of a history of lynching in Brazil. Otherwise, we run the risk of failing to understand the definition that a certain period lends to the concept of justice (embodied by the courts), the police and individual expectations of such institutions.

1 Lynch's Law

This study of police chiefs' reports and newspapers found 14 cases of lynchings in which 22 people were killed and 5 seriously injured between 1878 and 1888.[8] All lynching victims identified by this study were men, 22 of whom were enslaved and 5 were

5 Menandro and de Souza, *Linchamentos no Brasil*: 19.

6 Ibid.: 15.

7 Maria Helena Machado, *Crime e escravidão: trabalho, luta e resistência nas lavouras paulistas (1830–1888)* (São Paulo: Brasiliense, 1987): 67.

8 For the purposes of this article, attempted lynchings were not considered. I intend to cover those phenomena in future studies.

free. Among the captives, only 3 survived the attack by the mob, while there were 2 free individuals among the survivors. These data indicate that the lynchings that occurred in the last decade of slavery in the Brazilian southeast made the enslaved population their preferred target. Mob attacks on the enslaved were also more lethal than those on free individuals.[9] The cases found are distributed over the years as follows: one case in 1878, one in 1880, one in 1881, one in 1883, three in 1884, four in 1885, one in 1887 and two in 1888. Thus, we can see that the years with the highest rates of lynchings were 1884 and 1885, when I also found the largest number of victims. It is also essential to note that one of the characteristics of the lynchings was the fact that the mob frequently victimized more than one individual in the same attack. This situation was particularly striking in the case of the province of Rio de Janeiro, where seven lynchings resulted in a total of 19 fatalities. The attacks that resulted in the lynching of more than one victim mainly targeted slaves who had killed their masters or the managers of rural estates. Another characteristic of the sample gathered for this study is linked to the fact that they all occurred in rural areas of Brazil, while no lynching cases were reported in the provincial capitals.[10] In fact, the locations where the lynchings occurred were traditional areas of slavery that gained prominence during the imperial period due to their agricultural production and high concentration of captives. In the 1880s, most of those regions were still buying enslaved individuals through the domestic slave trade, receiving captives from other parts of the country or the city of Rio. Until abolition was decreed in Brazil in 1888, the three provinces covered in this article were the main hubs of slavery (they contained the largest number of captives), and stood out for their defense of slavery in the national parliament through their political representatives.[11] Among the motives for lynching, murder was the main catalyst for mob action. The crime of murder was the initiating factor in eleven of the 14 lynching cases identified. One of the lynching cases was also motivated by the fact that some residents of the town of Itapira, São Paulo, had accused

9 Regarding the conflicts arising from abolitionism in Brazil, see Maria Helena Machado, *O plano e o pânico: os movimentos sociais na década da abolição* (Rio de Janeiro: Universidade Federal do Rio de Janeiro; São Paulo: Editora da Universidade de São Paulo, 1994); Ângela Alonso, *Flores, votos e balas: o movimento abolicionista brasileiro (1868–1888)* (São Paulo: Companhia das Letras, 2015); Celso Thomas Castilho, *Slave Emancipation and Transformations in Brazilian Political Citizenship* (Pittsburgh: University of Pittsburgh Press, 2016).

10 In an editorial published in 1885, *Gazeta de Notícias* associates lynchings from that period with rural towns, confirming the data found in the sample. See: "Serviço da matança de gado," *Gazeta de Notícias*, January 28, 1885.

11 Regarding the domestic slave trade, see Robert W. Slenes, "A 'Great Arch' Descending: Manumission Rates, Subaltern Social Mobility and Slave and Free(d) Black Identities in southeastern Brazil, 1791–1888," in *New Histories of Resistance in Brazil and Mexico*, ed. John Gledhill and Patience A. Schell (Durham, NC: Duke University Press, 2012): 100–118. Regarding political debates in parliament in the 1880s, see Robert Conrad, *Os últimos anos da escravatura: 1850–1888*, trans. Fernando de Castro Ferro (Rio de Janeiro: Civilização Brasileira, 1978).

the local chief constable of protecting slaves. Another began with the fact that a free Portuguese man was accused of buying stolen goods from the enslaved. In one case, the motive is still unknown. Compared to the lynching processes analyzed by the literature in the second half of the twentieth century, we can see that "crime against the person" (such as murder) was already one of the main catalysts for the lynchers' actions.[12] Other peculiarities should be noted in the cases in our sample. That is, certain types of murders appeared to have had more potential to trigger mob action than others. Of the eleven lynchings initiated on account of the crime of murder, eight resulted from attacks by slaves against members of a master's family (five murders of masters, one murder of a female slave owner, two cases of deaths of the master's children). Therefore, this was the main catalyst for lynching in the nineteenth century. Two other cases also resulted from the murder of production control agents who were not related to the slave-owner (one administrator and one overseer). There was only one lynching case triggered by the murder of a family of farmers by a free man. The fact that the lynching victim killed an entire family of farmers (the husband, his pregnant wife, three children and a slave) is stressed by contemporaries as the main motive for exacting vigilante justice. Another revealing characteristic of the type of lynchings that occurred in the late nineteenth century has to do with the place where the lynching process began. Of the 14 cases in the sample, seven started with the mob breaking into a jail to remove the accused to be lynched. In one case, the victim was snatched from police custody while he was on his way to jail. In three others, the lynchings took place on the farms where the accused captives lived. Two others began with an attack on the victims' home (in one case, the lynch mob broke into a police chief's home, while in the other, it invaded the home of a municipal judge). In one case, there is no information about where the lynching began. The predominance of situations in which lynchings started with the removal of the accused from the hands of the authorities was an affront to the institutions of the police and courts of the imperial state. Many slave-owners complained in the press that slaves committed crimes and then gave themselves up to the police, seeking protection. In the view of the masters, the courts had also failed to stop captives from committing crimes, justifying the application of Lynch's law to mete out what they considered to be justice.[13] One of the main challenges for studies of lynching is trying to understand how the mob was formed and of whom it was composed. I begin with the question about the formation of crowds. In the 14 cases identified by this study, the lynch mobs' actions clearly demonstrate a high degree of organization. The fact that the vast majority of lynchings began with dragging the accused from jail or from the hands of the police when he was being taken to prison signifies that a certain level of organization was required.

---

12 Menandro and de Souza, *Linchamentos no Brasil*: 93–103; de Souza Martins, *Linchamentos*: 40, 51–54.

13 Cf. Ricardo F. Pirola, *Escravos e rebeldes nos tribunais do Império: uma história social da lei de 10 de junho de 1835* (Rio de Janeiro: Arquivo Nacional, 2015): 143–208.

The act of breaking into a jail usually required deciding the best time to act, when they would face less resistance from the police and even avoid arrest. Therefore, the mob does not seem to have been formed spontaneously by strangers who got together at the time of the crime (this is usually the pattern for lynchings in urbanized city centers).[14] Reading case reports of late nineteenth-century lynchings, the theory of mobs made up of members who knew each other becomes more plausible. For example, in the case of the lynching of the enslaved man named Nazário in Itu, in 1878, a mob formed to remove him from the jail by force (the exact number of participants is not certain, as reports mention between 150 and 1,000 people) on the same day the accused was arrested. However, the lynch mob encountered strong resistance from the police and was forced to disperse. The final tally of this confrontation was one dead (a soldier assigned to the police station) and several wounded. The following day, the mob returned to the jailhouse and succeeded in breaking in and capturing the accused. Nazário was killed in a public place, and his body was dragged through the town.[15] The lynching that took place in Rio Bonito, Rio de Janeiro, in 1884 is also paradigmatic due to the considerable degree of organization required to commit this act of vigilante justice. The police chief of Rio de Janeiro reported that the mob tried to break into the jail to capture four enslaved individuals accused of killing their master, José Martins da Fonseca Portella, on the night of the crime. However, its participants were turned back. Two months later, when the defendants were on trial, a lynch mob broke into the jail in the dark of night, took the defendants out and killed them. The police chief acknowledged that the participants had organized the lynching, waiting for about two months "to distract the attention of the authorities, who were on their guard against any plans of attempted attack."[16] In at least two other cases, the mobs were even better organized. In one of them, which took place in Valença in 1883, the police chief's reports indicate that at around two pm, one day after two enslaved men were arrested and charged with killing the administrator of a local farm, a mob of about sixty individuals, "masked or simply with faces covered, armed with sticks, shotguns and swords" and showing "a certain military order in their march" through the city streets, broke into the jail looking for the accused.[17] After lynching the two slaves in a public place, they began searching for the three other captives said to be involved in the same crime and supposedly at large. The following day, at seven am, they managed to capture and kill one of the

14 Menandro and de Souza, *Linchamentos no Brasil*: 98–103; Benevides and Ferreira, "Respostas populares e violência urbana": 229; de Souza Martins, *Linchamentos*: 71–89.

15 *Relatório apresentado à assembleia provincial legislativa de São Paulo*, 1880, Biblioteca Nacional (Rio de Janeiro), Relatórios dos Presidentes – Época do Império, MF4717: 72. Cf. Jonas Marçal Queiroz, "Da Senzala à República: tensões sociais e disputas partidárias em São Paulo (1869–1889)" (master's thesis, Department of History, UNICAMP, 1995): 225–48.

16 *Relatório apresentado à assembleia provincial legislativa do Rio de Janeiro*, 1885, Biblioteca Nacional (Rio de Janeiro), Relatórios dos Presidentes – Época do Império, MF4371: S1–5.

17 *Relatório apresentado à assembleia provincial legislativa do Rio de Janeiro*, 1883, Biblioteca Nacional (Rio de Janeiro), Relatórios dos Presidentes – Época do Império, MF4371: 8.

wanted men. The other two fugitives were more fortunate. They were eventually arrested by the police and quickly transferred to the prison in Rio de Janeiro. This case is very similar to those which occurred in the US South, and particularly in the West, where the formation of groups of vigilantes is observed. Those organizations acted outside the law, in the name of justice and racial superiority.[18] Another lynching in which the mob showed a high degree of organization occurred in Penha do Rio de Peixe (now Itapira), São Paulo. According to the police chief, what he described as a "mob of mutineers" waited until dawn on February 11, 1888, to break into the chief constable's house and lynch him. He tried to escape, but was captured in his back yard and killed. The police records do not give the size of the mob, but the press mentions more than 300 lynchers. The murdered chief constable was accused of sheltering runaway slaves. There were two captives in his home when the mob broke in, but they managed to escape. The chief of police points out that the transfer of the chief constable had already been requested, but members of the public had moved too quickly. The mob preferred to use the act of lynching to express the local community's anger at officials who protected the enslaved.[19] The lynching of the chief constable from Itapira was widely reported in the press, and even portrayed by Ângelo Agostini in his *Revista Ilustrada*, in Rio de Janeiro.[20]

It is curious to note that in these two highly organized lynchings (Valença and Itapira), the types of weapons used were different from the other cases. In these two instances, there are indications of the open use of firearms and swords (in the case of the lynching in Valença, the records show that clubs, shotguns and swords were used; in Itapira, revolvers, front-loading pistols and rifles are reported). In the other cases, according to the police reports the most frequently used weapons were sticks, stones, ropes and sickles. In the case reported in Rio Bonito, Rio de Janeiro, in 1884, the use of axes was also reported, and one of the victims was said to have been hacked to pieces. In the case of Resende, Rio de Janeiro, in 1884, the mob was armed with sticks and bayonets apparently stolen from the prison guards. These descriptions help us determine the degree of organization of the lynch mobs, and reports of the open use of firearms and swords are more closely associated with cases in which they were highly organized. With regard to the lynchers' backgrounds, the available information has left fragmented clues that can nevertheless help us build an overview of the matter. Firstly, there are no reports of enslaved individuals taking part in lynch mobs, which

18 Regarding lynchings in the US, see Stewart E. Tolnay and Elwood M. Beck, eds., *A Festival of Violence: An Analysis of Southern Lynching, 1882–1930* (Urbana-Champaign: University of Illinois, 1995); Michael Pfeifer, *Rough Justice: Lynching and American Society, 1874–1947* (Urbana-Champaign: University of Illinois, 2004); Ken Gonzalez-Day, *Lynching in the West, 1850–1935* (Durham, NC: Duke University Press, 2006).

19 *Relatório apresentado à assembleia provincial legislativa de São Paulo*, 1888, Biblioteca Nacional (Rio de Janeiro), Relatórios dos Presidentes – Época do Império, MF4717; 11.

20 Regarding Ângelo Agostini, see: Marcelo Balaban, *Poeta do lápis: sátira e política na trajetória de Angelo Agostini no Brasil Imperial (1864–1888)* (Campinas: Editora da Unicamp, 2009).

Fig. 1: Linchamento de abolicionista em Penha do Rio do Peixe, província de São Paulo.
Source: *Revista Ilustrada*, February 18, 1888, no. 485, p. 8.

were mainly composed of free men and possibly freed individuals, as in one case, at least, it was reported that a "brown" (*pardo*) man had been charged with lynching in Rio Bonito in 1884.[21] In fact, when reporting the lynching of slaves, the newspapers described the lynch mobs during that period as being made up primarily of farmers, farm workers, landowners and members of farming clubs.[22] It can also be said that, particularly in cases where the deed that motivated the lynching was murder, the mob also included the murder victim's family, neighbors, friends and acquaintances. In two of the cases found, for example, the lynch mob formed during the funeral procession or shortly after the burial of the murder victim.[23] I would also like to point

21 Relatório apresentado à assembleia provincial legislativa do Rio de Janeiro, 1885: 8, S1–5.
22 Cf. Speech by Cristiano Ottoni reprinted in "Senado," *Jornal do Comércio*, June 10, 1884; Cf. "Tópicos do Dia," *O Paiz*, March 1, 1885; Cf. "Lei de Linch," *Gazeta de Notícias*, January 14, 1885. Cf. "Joaquim Nabuco," *Gazeta da Tarde*, June 10, 1884.
23 See the case of Paraíba do Sul, Rio de Janeiro: Relatório *apresentado à assembleia provincial legislativa do Rio de Janeiro*, 1881, Biblioteca Nacional (Rio de Janeiro), Relatórios dos Presidentes – Época do Império, MF4371: 8. See the case of Cantagalo, Rio de Janeiro: Relatório *apresentado à assembleia provincial legislativa do Rio de Janeiro*, 1881, Biblioteca Nacional (Rio de Janeiro), Relatórios dos Presidentes – Época do Império, MF4371: 9.

out that as the cases in this sample took place in rural areas, in small towns in imperial Brazil, it is very likely that the members of the lynch mob were also linked by community ties. That is, in those localities, an attack on one of their members was seen as an attack on the entire community. Even in cases where the lynching was not motivated by a murder, as was the case with the chief constable in Itapira, the Portuguese man in Mar de Hespanha, Minas Gerais, and the municipal judge in Serro, Minas Gerais, it can be said that most of the people in the mob knew each other and sought to justify their actions as being in the best interests of the community with which they identified. In the case of the chief constable in Itapira, the police chief's report states that the lynch mob was made up of local farmers and their henchmen.[24] Furthermore, in his depiction of the incident, the cartoonist Ângelo Agostini highlights the presence of landowners in the foreground, portrayed wearing tall boots, hats and coats (the type of clothing commonly worn by wealthy farmers during that period). In the case of the Portuguese man lynched in Mar de Hespanha for allegedly buying stolen goods that the enslaved had taken from their masters, his lynching was an offshoot of the extrajudicial killing of slaves accused of murdering an overseer.[25] After attacking the captives from the farm for which the overseer had worked, killing one of them, the lynch mob went to the police station in search of the other captive accused of the same crime. Held off by the police, the mob turned on the Portuguese man. Their victim was tied to a pole and lynched. Therefore, in this case, it is clear that the members of the mob had the same characteristics described above for the cases in which the triggering factor for the lynching was a murder. As for the case of the municipal judge in Serro, the details are scarce. Finally, it should be noted that I have been able to identify certain rituals that were performed when lynchings took place. José de Souza Martins was the first author in the Brazilian literature to draw attention to the importance of this issue in his analysis of lynchings.[26] In fact, we can initially observe that the vast majority of cases occurred in public places. In the incidents that involved storming a jail, the lynchings always took place outside the police station. Thus, breaking into the jail proved to be just the first move in a longer series of actions that took place outdoors, in public. In the only case for which we have more details about the lynchings done on farms, the lynchers' behavior proved to be similar – that is, the mob seized an enslaved person who was locked in a room in the house, awaiting the police, and lynched him in the farmyard. In the case that involved

---

24 Regarding the lynchings in Itapira, São Paulo, cf. *Relatório apresentado à assembleia provincial legislativa de São Paulo*, 1888, Biblioteca Nacional (Rio de Janeiro), Relatórios dos Presidentes – Época do Império, MF4717: A8.

25 Cf. Fala que o Exmo. Sr. Desembargador José Antônio Alves Brito dirigiu à assembleia legislativa provincial de Minas Gerais, Relatório apresentado à assembleia provincial legislativa de Minas Gerais, 1885, Biblioteca Nacional (Rio de Janeiro), Relatórios dos Presidentes – Época do Império, MF4446: AB4–6.

26 de Souza Martins, *Linchamentos*: 45–62.

the lynching of the Portuguese man in Mar de Hespanha in 1885, the incident happened in a public place, and the victim was later dragged through the streets. In all these situations, the mob clearly intended to make the act of lynching as exemplary as possible, seeking to exhibit its victims to all members of that community. The only two lynchings we found that took place in private homes were those of the chief constable in Itapira and the municipal judge in Serro.[27] In these situations, the mob's intent seems to have been to drive their victims out of the community once and for all by threatening their lives and property (in both cases, the reports show that their houses were destroyed). It is important to note that many of the individuals appointed to the posts of chief constable and municipal judge in the nineteenth century were not born in the places where they worked. Therefore, the lynch mobs sought precisely to root them out of their communities. The municipal judge who was assaulted in Serro did not die of his injuries, but the authorities pointed out that they had arranged for his transfer. The reports on lynchings also show that, in some cases, these acts followed very specific rituals that linked the murder victims and their accused killers (those who were lynched by the mob). In the case of Nazário, which took place in Itu in 1878, the mob took the enslaved man from his jail cell, lynched him in a public place and, finally, dragged his dead body to his victims' house. The mob seemed to want to make publicly clear that revenge had been taken, insisting on ritually informing the dead and their living relatives about the lynching of the accused.[28] Another case for which the reports show a clear indication that the act of lynching was followed by a certain type of ritual took place in Cantagalo, Rio de Janeiro, in 1881. The lynch mob's victim was Antônio José dos Santos, accused of killing one F. Miranda, who worked at the Bom Jardim railway station. According to the newspaper *Gazeta de Notícias*, Miranda was "highly regarded" by the local community.[29] During Miranda's funeral, some of the mourners – around sixty people – headed for the jail, from where they took the accused, forcing him to accompany his victim's funeral procession (the *Gazeta de Notícias* goes so far as to say that the accused was forced to carry the coffin). The point seems to have been ritually to inform the deceased that his killer has been caught. After the funeral, the accused was lynched and his body dumped on a road. The lack of a proper burial was yet another way to continue the torments of lynching – or, as Martins observes, "the treatment often given to the victim's corpse constitutes a disfiguring rite that prohibits the realization of death as a crossing

---

27 Regarding the lynchings in Itapira, SP, cf. *Relatório apresentado à assembleia provincial legislativa de São Paulo*, 1888, Biblioteca Nacional (Rio de Janeiro), Relatórios dos Presidentes – Época do Império, MF4717: A8. Regarding the case in Serro, MG, see: *Relatório apresentado à assembleia provincial legislativa de Minas Gerais*, 1885, Biblioteca Nacional (Rio de Janeiro), Relatórios dos Presidentes – Época do Império, MF4446: AA–10.

28 *Relatório apresentado à assembleia provincial legislativa de São Paulo*, 1880, Biblioteca Nacional (Rio de Janeiro), Relatórios dos Presidentes – Época do Império, MF4717: 72.

29 "Lei de Lynch," *Gazeta de notícias*, November 5, 1881.

over."[30] It is also important to note that the types of torture inflicted by the mob were related to the types of crimes committed and, especially, to the status of the lynched individual's alleged victim. It is curious to note that the only case where the body of the lynching victim was thrown on a bonfire was precisely the one that involved the murder of a female slave-owner whose daughter was stabbed with a knife. Therefore, the people of the town of Cambucy, Rio de Janeiro, seem to have felt obliged to defend its more vulnerable members even more strongly. According to Christian belief, which predominated in many rural communities in nineteenth-century Brazil, it was believed that burning a corpse prevented the soul from entering Heaven, condemning the victim to eternal damnation. Therefore, lynch mobs followed rituals that sought to do much more than just killing their victims. Lynching was intended to mete out exemplary punishment, avenge the lynched individual's victims and damn his soul for eternity.

2 Lynchings in the Twilight of Slavery

When analyzing the cases covered in this chapter, what initially stands out is the widespread distrust of police and the courts, particularly in their ability to punish criminals in an exemplary manner. This conclusion is clear in the attacks on the jails to remove prisoners, as well as lynchings of individuals who personified such institutions, like the chief constable and the municipal judge. The aim of this section is to understand the reasons for the state's lack of credibility (especially the police and the courts) in the eyes of the lynchers, and how this phenomenon was related to the death throes of slavery. The news reports and articles published in the press about lynchings in the years prior to the abolition of slavery in Brazil underscore the association between vigilantism and the frequent commutations of sentences granted by the emperor. Such commutations focused particularly on cases where the defendants had been sentenced to death by hanging, commuting those sentences to hard labor in the galleys or life in prison. According to the empire's criminal code (1830), the death penalty was reserved for the most serious crimes, such as murder, murder followed by robbery and slave uprisings. Therefore, for part of the population, failure to apply that penalty meant the perpetuation of impunity. An essay published by the newspaper *Gazeta de Campinas* in 1879 aptly illustrates the criticism propagated in the press regarding commutations of capital punishment. After praising the lynching in Itu, São Paulo, in 1879, "Nho Quim," the pseudonymous writer, pointed out that the only thing missing in that case was the people "putting the disfigured corpse of the [lynched] murderer in a coffin and sending it as a gift to [Emperor] Pedro II so he could see for

30 de Souza Martins, *Linchamentos*: 56.

himself the result of his unjust pardons."[31] Although the monarch rarely granted a convict a full pardon, the use of that term in the newspaper article reinforced the message that Pedro II left defendants who had been condemned to death unpunished (as if they had been pardoned). The Brazilian constitution of 1824 determined that the so-called moderating power, exercised solely by the monarch, included the ability to commute sentences or pardon defendants sentenced by the courts. As of 1854, in particular, it was also stipulated that all cases where defendants (free or enslaved) were sentenced to death in a final decision should be referred ad hoc to the monarch for consultation. Members of the Ministry of Justice and the Council of State produced written opinions to guide the emperor's decisions. The tendency throughout the nineteenth century was for the monarch to follow his advisers' decisions (his decisions only differed from theirs in exceptional cases). In the second half of the nineteenth century, particularly after 1860, the number of commutations from capital punishment to life terms in prison or the galleys (for both free and enslaved defendants) grew significantly, to the point of abolishing capital punishment in practice by the 1880s.[32] This situation was due to the application of certain (liberal) legal interpretations when evaluating commutations, no matter if the individual was free or enslaved. For example, mitigating factors included the defendant being underage, the evidence (other than a confession) and whether the crime was committed in self-defense or in response to threats against the defendant. If one of these factors was found in case-by-case evaluations, as well as non-compliance with police or legal procedures during the process, this would serve as a justification for not applying the death penalty.[33] While the application of the death penalty had become rare by the 1880s, the beginning of the abolitionist process added new factors to social disputes. Since the enactment of the so-called Free Womb Law in 1871, when the transition to the end of slavery officially began, slave-owners had become increasingly distrustful of the emperor and, more generally, the monarchy as defenders of their interests. In fact, more than just freeing the children born to enslaved women, this law also introduced further rights for captives, such as being able to build up savings and buy their own freedom without the slave-owner's permission. It is also essential to stress that even before the Free Womb Law was enacted, parliament had passed a law in 1869

31 "Carta de um caipira," *Gazeta de notícias*, March 2, 1879. Regarding pardons granted by Pedro II, see: Ricardo Figueiredo Pirola, "Cartas ao Imperador: os pedidos de perdão de réus escravos e a decisão de 17 de outubro de 1872," *Almanack* 13 (2016): 130–52.

32 The percentages of commutations for the enslaved were 91 percent between 1876–1880 and 100 percent between 1881–1887. Cf. Pirola, *Escravos e rebeldes*: 102. Brasil Gerson, *A escravidão no Império* (Rio de Janeiro: Pallas, 1975): 142–55. Ribeiro presents non-systematized data on commutations, without explaining the makeup of his sample. João Luiz Ribeiro, *No meio das galinhas as baratas não têm razão: a lei de 10 de junho de 1835, os escravos e a pena de morte no Império do Brasil (1822–1889)* (Rio de Janeiro: Renovar, 2005): 313–15.

33 Regarding commutations of capital punishment in the nineteenth century, see Pirola, *Escravos e rebeldes*: 89–208.

that banned the breaking up of enslaved families through sale or inheritance. From the seigneurial perspective, these measures represented undue interference by the imperial government in the master-slave relationship. The slave-owners felt that any decisions regarding captives had to be theirs alone, and not determined by the state. However, times had changed. In 1885, the Sexagenarian Law freeing enslaved individuals when they reached the age of sixty was also enacted, and the abolition of punishment by whipping was approved in 1886. Thus, the masters' loss of identification with the actions of the state was strongly accentuated in the last decade of slavery in Brazil.[34] It should also be said that, since the domestic trade had grown since the transatlantic slave trade was definitively banned in 1850. That process moved in at least three directions, from small and medium-sized properties to large ones, from the major cities, especially Rio, to farms in the interior, as well as from the northeast and south to the southeast.[35] As we have seen, the provinces selected for the sample used in this study were areas that received slaves through the internal trade. This finding is highly important for our analysis of lynchings, because many contemporaries associated murders, especially those of masters, overseers and farm managers, with slaves acquired through the domestic trade. In other words, they were "outsiders" who disrupted local slavery. As a reflection of this issue, the reports from the police chiefs of Rio de Janeiro began including a specific section from 1881 onwards to report the murders of masters and overseers committed by slaves. In some cases, such as that of Itu in 1879, in which before being lynched, the enslaved man named Nazário had killed several members of a seigneurial family, the subject of captives considered "criminal outsiders" even sparked debates in the provincial assembly regarding the need for measures to put a stop to the domestic slave trade (in the Itu case, Nazário had come from Minas Gerais).[36] I do not have any data on the other lynching victims in my sample, but the perception that the alleged murderers were "outsiders" is clearly an important factor to explain the processes that triggered lynchings. The ritual function of these extrajudicial killings was to remove those who did not conform to the rules of coexistence and respect social hierarchies, whether they were, in fact,

34 Regarding abolitionist laws and their impact in the legal sphere, see Conrad, *Os últimos anos*; Regina Célia Lima Xavier, *A conquista da liberdade: libertos em Campinas na segunda metade do século XIX* (Campinas: Centro de Memória Unicamp, 1996); Joseli Maria Nunes Mendonça, *Entre a mão e os anéis: a lei dos sexagenários e os caminhos da abolição no Brasil* (Campinas: Editora da Unicamp, 1999); Eduardo Spiller Pena, *Pajens da casa imperial: jurisconsultos, escravidão e a lei de 1871* (Campinas: Editora da Unicamp, 2001); Elciene Azevedo, *O direito dos escravos: lutas jurídicas e abolicionismo na província de São Paulo* (Campinas: Editora da Unicamp, 2010). Regarding the impact in the press and the literature of debates on the Sexagenarian Law, see Ana Flávia Cernic Ramos, *As máscaras de Lélio: política e humor nas crônicas de Machado de Assis (1883–1886)* (Campinas: Editora da Unicamp, 2016). Regarding the ban on whipping, see Ricardo F. Pirola, "O castigo senhorial e a abolição da pena de açoites no Brasil: justiça, imprensa e política no século xix," *Revista de História* 176 (2017).

35 Cf. Slenes, "A 'Great Arch' Descending": 100–118.

36 Cf. Queiroz, *Da Senzala à República*: 91–152.

"outsiders" or individuals who had become "outsiders" when they protested against the established order. In this situation, frequent resistance from the police to attempts to lynch individuals accused of crimes most certainly reinforced the perception among a large part of the residents of these southeastern rural communities that the state was ignoring their interests. It not only failed to punish evildoers effectively by commuting capital punishment, but also got in the way of vigilante justice. In fact, if on one hand the police tried to prevent lynchings, on the other, the courts stopped the lynchers from being convicted in the cases where they went to trial.[37] It is possible, however, that rural communities did not even see this type of outcome as a measure taken by public officials who upheld their interests. This is because the murder cases in which lynchers stood accused were decided by a jury, which was restricted to citizens who could read and write. In practice, that rule excluded the enslaved, African freedmen and a good part of the economically dispossessed population. Literacy was still restricted to a very small percentage of the Brazilian population, generally associated with the better-off ranks of society. It is quite possible, therefore, that the individuals who made up the juries identified socially with the lynch mobs. It is also essential to return to the question of slaves surrendering to the police after committing a murder, especially of masters, overseers or farm managers. One characteristic of this type of occurrence was linked to the fact that such crimes were generally perpetrated collectively by groups of three or four captives, and mainly in the 1870s and 1880s. Several comments in the press and parliamentary debates associated such actions by the enslaved with ways of escaping captivity. From this perspective, upon learning that, most likely, they would receive a commutable death sentence, slaves committed crimes to free themselves from enforced servitude. The behavior of groups of enslaved people who went straight to the police to take responsibility for a specific murder was also a recurring phenomenon, even if those individuals had not played a direct part in the crime. More than being a strategy for escaping slavery, as several slave-owners claimed, these situations reflected open questioning of seigneurial authority itself, embodied in demands such as the right to days off, decent food, permission to farm their own allotments and a suitable place of work. They also expressed the slaves' own view of the police and courts as institutions in which they could fight for their rights.[38] Clearly, this situation reinforced the perception of social disorder on the part of the

37 Regarding the case in Resende, Rio de Janeiro, in 1884, see: *Gazeta da Tarde*, September 22, 1884. Regarding Rio Bonito, RJ, see: *Relatório apresentado à assembleia legislativa provincial do Rio de Janeiro*, 1885: 9.

38 Regarding crimes committed by the enslaved in the last decades of slavery and captives fleeing to surrender themselves to the police, see: Machado, *Crime e escravidão*; Sidney Chalhoub, *Visões da liberdade: uma história das últimas décadas da escravidão na Corte* (São Paulo: Companhia das Letras, 1990); Célia Maria Marinho Azevedo, *Onda negra, medo branco: o negro no imaginário das elites, século XIX*, 3rd ed. (São Paulo: Annablume, 2004). Maria Helena Machado, "'Teremos grandes desastres, se não houver providências enérgicas e imediatas': a rebeldia dos escravos e a abolição da escravidão," in *O Brasil Imperial*, vol. 3, *1870–1889*, ed. Keila Grinberg and Ricardo Salles (Rio de Janeiro: Civilização Brasileira Press, 2009): 367–400; Pirola, *Escravos e rebeldes*.

free rural population of the southeast. The lynchings of slaves in which those most directly accused of committing crimes were executed and the other residents of a certain rural property were beaten appear to be a response to the collective actions of the captives. If the enslaved acted in groups, either at the time of the crime or when surrendering themselves to the police, the lynchers' actions also focused on collective acts. In fact, these situations took on aspects of open conflict between masters and slaves. It is no wonder that abolitionists like Joaquim Nabuco, who favored a gradual, parliament-led process of dismantling slavery, feared that the discord sparked by lynchings could result in an armed conflict similar to the Civil War in the United States.[39] In short, these considerations help us better understand the lynchings of enslaved and free individuals that occurred in the latter years of slavery in Brazil. That is, a large part of the free populations of rural communities in the southeast came to see the state and its institutions (especially the police and courts) as ineffectual in representing their interests. The introduction of rights for the enslaved and the increasing inclusion of liberal legal principles into the analysis of the commutation of capital punishment (both for enslaved and free individuals) during the ongoing march of abolitionism were viewed as the expression of a crisis in institutions that no longer punished criminals effectively. In other words, for many in the rural southeast, the process of transforming Brazilian society at the end of the nineteenth century produced social disorder, breaking the rules of coexistence and long-established hierarchies. In this sense, that segment of the population felt they had to take the law into their own hands to shore up a structure threatened with permanent collapse.[40]

3 Conclusion

Historians seem to have little doubt today that the abolition of slavery in Brazil on May 13, 1888, and the failure to compensate slave-owners sealed the fate of the monarchy, which was overthrown by a military coup the following year. It should also be noted that, in the years after the founding of the republic, the state once again robustly represented the interests of local elites. The question then arises as to what happened with the practice of lynching during the post-abolition period. The only work that has ventured to study this topic so far is that by Monsma, who analyzed São Paulo police records for the years 1890 and 1900. That author found five cases of lynchings, the last of which reportedly occurred in 1893. Monsma explains that the small number of cases (especially when compared to the United States in the same

---

39 Joaquim Nabuco, *O abolicionismo*, 10th ed. (São Paulo: PubliFolha, 2000).

40 It is not yet clear what happened to the individuals involved in the lynching cases mentioned in this paper. The information I have gathered so far indicates that they were not prosecuted by the Justice.

period) was based on factors such as the desire to maintain law and order on the part of local representatives (in order to keep the peace), the failure of the Brazilian elite and newly arrived European immigrants to form a racial identity and the continued political dominance of that same elite group through clientelism.[41] Monsma's findings still need to be compared with the results of further archival research, but if his information is confirmed, it is quite possible that lynching entered a period of decline, particularly in the rural areas of the southeast. In fact, it seems that the resumption of close relations between state institutions and the interests of local elites ensured that the police and the courts took care of any disturbances of the peace.

Bibliography

Primary Sources

Exposição (b), Rio de Janeiro, 1881: 9.
Exposição, Rio de Janeiro, 1881: 8.
Fala que o Exmo. Sr. Desembargador José Antônio Alves Brito dirigiu à assembleia legislativa provincial de Minas Gerais, 1885: 5, AB–4, AB–6.
Relatório apresentado à assembleia provincial legislativa de São Paulo, 1880: 72.
Relatório apresentado à assembleia provincial legislativa do Rio de Janeiro, 1885: S1–5.
Relatório apresentado à assembleia provincial legislativa do Rio de Janeiro, 1883: 8.
Relatório, Minas Gerais: AA–10.
Relatório, São Paulo, 1888: A8.

Secondary Literature

Alonso, Ângela. *Flores, votos e balas: o movimento abolicionista brasileiro (1868–1888)* (São Paulo: Companhia das Letras, 2015).
Azevedo, Elciene. *O direito dos escravos: lutas jurídicas e abolicionismo na província de São Paulo* (Campinas: Editora da Unicamp, 2010).
Balaban, Marcelo. *Poeta do lápis: sátira e política na trajetória de Angelo Agostini no Brasil Imperial (1864–1888)* (Campinas: Editora da Unicamp, 2009).
Benevides, Maria Victória, and Rosa Maria Ferreira. "Respostas populares e violência urbana: o caso dos linchamentos no Brasil (1979–1982)," in *Crime, violência e poder*, ed. Paulo Sérgio Pinheiro (São Paulo: Brasiliense, 1983): 227–43.
Castilho, Celso Thomas. *Slave Emancipation and Transformations in Brazilian Political Citizenship* (Pittsburgh: University of Pittsburgh Press, 2016).

41 Monsma, "Linchamentos raciais no pós-abolição": 195–210.

Cernic Ramos, Ana Flávia. *As máscaras de Lélio: política e humor nas crônicas de Machado de Assis (1883–1886)* (Campinas: Editora da Unicamp, 2016).

Chalhoub, Sidney. *Visões da liberdade: uma história das últimas décadas da escravidão na Corte* (São Paulo: Companhia das Letras, 1990).

Chazkel, Amy. "'A lei de lynch': Reconsidering the View from Brazil of Lynching in the United States, 1880s–1920s," in *Global Lynching and Collective Violence*, vol. 2, ed. Michael Pfeifer (Chicago: University of Illinois Press, 2017): pos. 1661 (e-book).

Conrad, Robert. *Os últimos anos da escravatura: 1850–1888*, trans. Fernando de Castro Ferro (Rio de Janeiro: Civilização Brasileira, 1978).

Gerson, Brasil. *A escravidão no Império* (Rio de Janeiro: Pallas, 1975).

Gonzalez-Day, Ken. *Lynching in the West, 1850–1935* (Durham, NC: Duke University Press, 2006).

Machado, Maria Helena. *Crime e escravidão: trabalho, luta e resistência nas lavouras paulistas (1830–1888)* (São Paulo: Brasiliense, 1987).

Machado, Maria Helena. *O plano e o pânico: os movimentos sociais na década da abolição* (Rio de Janeiro: Universidade Federal do Rio de Janeiro; São Paulo: Editora da Universidade de São Paulo, 1994).

Marinho Azevedo, Célia Maria. *Onda negra, medo branco: o negro no imaginário das elites, século XIX*, 3rd ed. (São Paulo: Annablume, 2004).

Martins, José de Souza. *Linchamentos: a justiça popular no Brasil* (São Paulo: Editora Contexto, 2015).

Meira Menandro, Paulo Rogério, and Lídio de Souza. *Linchamentos no Brasil: a Justiça que não tarda, mas falha: uma análise a partir de dados obtidos através da imprensa escrita* (Vitória: Fundação Ceciliano Abel de Almeida, 1991).

Mendonça, Joseli Maria Nunes. *Entre a mão e os anéis: a lei dos sexagenários e os caminhos da abolição no Brasil* (Campinas: Editora da Unicamp, 1999).

Mosdma, Karl Martin. "Linchamentos raciais no pós-abolição: alguns casos excepcionais do oeste paulista," in *Políticas da raça: experiências e legados da abolição e da pós-emancipação no Brasil*, ed. Flávio Gomes and Petrônio Domingues (São Paulo: Selo Negro Edições, 2014): 195–210.

Mosma, Karl Martin. *A reprodução do racismo: fazendeiros, negros e imigrantes no oeste paulista, 1880–1914* (São Carlos: Editora da Universidade Federal de São Carlos, 2016).

Nabuco, Joaquim. *O abolicionismo*, 10th ed. (São Paulo: PubliFolha, 2000).

Pfeifer, Michael. *Rough Justice: Lynching and American Society, 1874–1947* (Urbana-Champaign: University of Illinois, 2004).

Pirola, Ricardo F. "A lei de Lynch no ocaso da escravidão: linchamentos, justiça e polícia (1878 – 1889)," in *Do tráfico ao pós-abolição: trabalho compulsório e livre e aluta por direitos sociais no Brasil*, ed. Regina C. Xavier and Helen Osório (São Leopoldo: Oikos, 2018): 454–81.

Pirola, Ricardo F. *Escravos e rebeldes nos tribunais do Império: uma história social da lei de 10 de junho de 1835* (Rio de Janeiro: Arquivo Nacional, 2015).

Pirola, Ricardo F. "Cartas ao Imperador: os pedidos de perdão de réus escravos e a decisão de 17 de outubro de 1872," *Almanack* 13 (2016): 130–52.

Pirola, Ricardo F. "O castigo senhorial e a abolição da pena de açoites no Brasil: justiça, imprensa e política no século xix," *Revista de História* 176 (2017).

Ribeiro, João Luiz. *No meio das galinhas as baratas não têm razão: a lei de 10 de junho de 1835, os escravos e a pena de morte no Império do Brasil (1822–1889)* (Rio de Janeiro: Renovar, 2005).

Rios, José Arthur. "Linchamentos: do arcaico ao moderno," *Revista de Informação Legislativa* 25, no. 100 (1988): 207–38.

Sérgio Adorno. "Linchamentos em São Paulo," in *Continuidade autoritária e construção da democracia: relatório final*, ed. Paulo Sérgio Pinheiro (São Paulo: Núcleo de Estudos da Violência/USP, 1999): 404–80.

Slenes, Robert W. “A ‘Great Arch’ Descending: Manumission Rates, Subaltern Social Mobility and Slave and Free(d) Black Identities in southeastern Brazil, 1791–1888,” in *New Histories of Resistance in Brazil and Mexico*, ed. John Gledhill and Patience A. Schell (Durham, NC: Duke University Press, 2012): 100–18.

Spiller Pena, Eduardo. *Pajens da casa imperial: jurisconsultos, escravidão e a lei de 1871* (Campinas: Editora da Unicamp, 2001).

Tolnay, Stewart E., and Elwood M. Beck. *A Festival of Violence: An Analysis of Southern Lynching, 1882–1930* (Urbana-Champaign: University of Illinois, 1995).

Xavier, Regina Célia Lima. *A conquista da liberdade*: *libertos em Campinas na segunda metade do século XIX* (Campinas: Centro de Memória Unicamp, 1996).

Fabiane Popinigis

Laboring Women of African Descent in Nineteenth-Century Brazil

When the *quitandeira* Maria Mina went to the notary office to register her manumission letter as a result of what she had saved from her work as a vendor in a small port city in the south of Brazil in the 1860s, she was following the steps of many other women of African descent around the Atlantic.[1] From colonial times, women like her were fundamental protagonists in the organization of the small-scale food trade, and urban labor in general, in various parts of the Atlantic world. In nineteenth-century Brazil, in different contexts and moments, they were at the center of debates about the organization and hygienization of strategic spaces in cities and the creation of modern market buildings, inspired by European models.[2]

Whether enslaved or free, these women were fundamental for the operation of the production and consumption economy, paying taxes and using credit; they were likewise essential for basic services involving the preparation of food, cleaning, and the provision of care. Moreover, the legal definition that stated that them elements of the endogenous reproduction of slavery. In this strategic economic position, carrying out production and social reproduction tasks, they were also protagonists in the struggle for freedom and the maintenance of their family and community ties. For them, the implementation of manumission plans demanded strategies that often became visible in individual trajectories, but were collectively constructed.

These laboring women were capable of saving money, acquiring freedom, and even accumulating wealth in some cases. They established relations of affections and solidarity, creating economic ties not only with their peers, but also with men and women of different social and political status and influence. In their working circuits, social

1 María Elisa Velázquez Gutiérrez and Carolina González Undurraga, *Mujeres africanas y afrodescendientes: experiencias de esclavitud y libertad en América Latina y África Siglos XVI al XIX* (México: Secretaría de Cultura, Instituto Nacional de Antropología e Historia, 2016).

2 Fabiane Popinigis, "'Aos pés dos pretos e pretas quitandeiras': experiências de trabalho e estratégias de vida em torno do primeiro mercado público de desterro – 1840–1890," *Afro-Ásia* 46 (2012): 193–226; Juliana Barreto Faria, *Mercados Minas: africanos ocidentais na praça do Mercado do Rio de Janeiro (1830–1890)* (Rio de Janeiro: Arquivo Geral da Cidade, 2015); Valter Martins, *Mercados urbanos, transformações na cidade: abastecimento e cotidiano em Campinas, 1859–1908* (Campinas: Editora da Unicamp, 2010); Richard Graham, *Feeding the City: From Street Market to Liberal Reform in Salvador, Brazil, 1780–1860* (Austin: University of Texas Press, 2010).

Note: I would like to thank Mariana Dias Paes, Paulo Cruz Terra and Stephan Conermann for the invitation to join this enterprise, as well as the participants of the workshop for the discussion of a previous version of this paper. I'm also grateful for the insightful comments and suggestions of Cristiana Schettini and for Henrique Espada Lima for his effort to make this article readable in English.

https://doi.org/10.1515/9783111026527-010

relations, and the broad networks that they wove in everyday life, women of African descent formulated expectations and attributed specific meanings to their freedom. In this way, they also influenced the political debates in the context in which they lived.[3]

This article aims to give a contribution to answer the question of "how the productive and reproductive work of women – free and unfree – created wealth."[4] Following Stanley's question, it will argue that gender analysis is central to understanding the interactions between slavery and capitalism in labor history. Without any intention of being exhaustive, a dialogue with recent scholarship in slavery studies in Brazil will allow me to include my own research to understand the role of enslaved and freed women in the production of wealth, in the organization of labor, and in social and political relations during slavery.

More recently scholarship has been interested in the life trajectories of African and Afro-descendent women, enslaved, free, and freed, during the nineteenth century, including the immediate post-abolition period (1888). This bibliography explores gender relations in different constructions of femininities and conceptions of maternity at the peak of the slave period and in its decline, in a context of the growing racialization and reformulation of labor relations.[5]

In this article, we will show the connections between increasing commercial activities and the work these women carried out in Brazilian cities in the second half of the ninetieth century as a possible form of accumulation. Although in most of cases street selling provided income that was only sufficient for day-to-day survival, vendors were fundamental

3 Sidney Chalhoub, *Visões da Liberdade – uma história das últimas décadas da escravidão na corte* (São Paulo, Companhia das Letras, 1990); Keila Grinberg, "Manumission, Gender, and the Law in Nineteenth-Century Brazil," in *Paths to Freedom: Manumission in the Atlantic World*, ed. Rosemary Brana-Shute and Randy J. Sparks (Columbia: University of South Carolina Press, 2009): 1–14; Sandra Graham, *Caetana diz não: história de mulheres na sociedade escravista brasileira* (São Paulo: Companhia das Letras, 2005); Henrique Espada Lima, "Freedom, Precariousness, and the Law: Freed Persons Contracting out their Labour in Nineteenth-Century Brazil," *International Review of Social History* 54, no. 3 (2009): 391–416; Camillia Cowling, *Conceiving Freedom: Women of Color, Gender, and the Abolition of Slavery in Havana and Rio de Janeiro* (Chapel Hill: University of North Carolina Press, 2013).

4 Amy Drew Stanley, "Histories of Capitalism and Sex Difference," *Journal of the Early Republic* 36, no. 2 (2016): 343–50.

5 Maria Helena P.T. Machado, "Corpo, gênero e identidade no limiar da abolição: a história de Benedicta Maria Albina da Ilha ou Ovídia, Escrava (Sudeste, 1880)," *Afro-Ásia* 42 (2010): 157–93; Lorena Féres da Silva Telles, *Libertas entre sobrados: mulheres negras e trabalho doméstico em São Paulo (1880–1920)* (São Paulo: Alameda, 2013); Maciel Henrique Silva, *Pretas de honra: vida e trabalho de domésticas e vendedoras no Recife do século XIX (1840–1870)* (Recife: Editoria de Universidade Federal de Pernambuco; Salvador: Editoria de Universidade Federal da Bahia, 2011); Marília Bueno de Araújo Arízia, *Mães infames, filhos venturosos: trabalho, pobreza, escravidão e emancipação em São Paulo (século XIX)* (São Paulo: Alameda, 2020); Patrícia Geremias, "Como se fosse da família: arranjos formais e informais de criação e trabalho de menores pobres na cidade do Rio de Janeiro (1860–1910)" (PhD diss., Federal University of Rio de Janeiro, 2019); Maria Helena P.T. Machado, Luciana da Cruz Brito, Flávio dos Santos Gomes and Iamara da Silva Viana, *Ventres livres? Gênero, maternidade e legislação* (São Paulo: ed. UNESP, 2021).

in the organizing and functioning of the basic services of cities. Women were engaged in many other tasks besides selling goods, and some of them managed to achieve freedom for themselves and for others with their savings and influence. They were both subjects and agents of the transformations which occurred in the second half of ninetieth century through new configurations of labor relations and the organization of cities.

1 Laboring Women in Twentieth-Century Scholarship

In Brazil is not surprising that almost all the later research on working women of African descent acknowledges indebtedness to the pivotal book by Maria Odila Leite da Silva Dias, *Quotidiano e Poder em São Paulo no século XIX*. Originally published in 1984, the book has become a classic on the history of women and labor in its approach to the forms of survival of poor women in the city of São Paulo at the beginning of the nineteenth century. Dias stated her objective was to show women as "social beings," "inserted in their specific contexts" and to redeem "their actual historic roles,"[6] in order to understand their life and labor conditions and the spaces they occupied. According to her, women had been ignored by historians, who expressed their "incapacity to deal with the participation of women in the process of the formation of Brazilian society."[7]

In the early 1980s, Dias anticipated some of the questions which the renewal of social history would explore in the following years: in a careful rereading and crosschecking of documents from various sources, including those produced by the municipal council, the Catholic Church, judicial documentation, travelers' reports, and literature, she brought to light the names, actions, and strategies of those who "were left aside in the works of historians."[8]

Dias centered her interest on the agency of those women who supported their households with their own work and were heads of families, contemplating forms of resistance and survival, from small and daily acts of circumventing fiscal authorities to the organization of strikes against poverty.[9] The protagonists of her study occupied a wide diversity of spaces in the realm of work and labor relations, fulfilling fundamental roles for the functioning of the economy. Usually regarded by historians at

6 Maria Odila Leite Dias, *Quotidiano e poder em São Paulo no século XIX*, 2nd ed. (São Paulo: Brasiliense, 1995): 55; Maria Odila Leite Dias, *Power and Everyday Life: The Lives of Working Women in Nineteenth-Century Brazil* (New Brunswick, NJ: Rutgers University Press, 1995).

7 Ibid.: 40.

8 Ibid.: 29.

9 Ibid.: 53.

that time as people without history, we know now that working women's histories were actually fundamental for the understanding of the period.[10]

The 1980s and 1990s in Brazil were a period of renewal for the paradigms of social history, with a strong expansion of the so-called "history from below." A generation of historians asked about the possibility of investigating the social experience of the working classes, and "subaltern" men and women, including the poor and the enslaved, through new methodological approaches in order to focus their attention on seldom used (or indeed ignored) documentary sources. In this analytical movement, daily life gained a central importance for the investigation of material conditions, social relations, and subjectivities.[11]

A characteristic of the disassociation between the historiographies of slavery and labor in relation to the initial developments in the 1980s and 1990s is that the discussion about the history of labor began, until recently, with the period after the abolition of slavery (1888). In the last two decades these frameworks have been imploded, placing on the agenda the themes of racism and precarious work for the post-abolition period and thematizing questions about labor and workers' movements much before 1888. Another fundamental element has been the increasing consideration of the centrality of Africa in the comprehension of historic processes.[12]

Despite these advances, the question of women's labor force as an important driver of economic development in the nineteenth century, in the terms proposed by Dias at the beginning of the 1980s, was slow to be formulated in the social historiography about nineteenth-century Brazil. The particularity which interests us is that she treated the activities of women in the first half of the nineteenth century as *work* and as central for the subsistence of their families and the social organization of the city's everyday life. This perspective is fundamental for connecting the conceptual keys of women's labor in the nineteenth century to the conditions of slavery and their relationship with daily life in the city.

10 Maria Odila Leite da Silva Dias, "Mulheres sem história," *Revista USP* 114 (1983): 31–45.

11 For an updated version of these developments, see the dossier: Paulo Fontes, Alexandre Fortes and David Mayer, "Brazilian Labour History in Global Context: Some Introductory Notes," *International Review of Social History* 62, no. S25 (2017): 1–22. See also Schettini, Cristiana and Fabiane Popinigis, "O lugar do trabalho: história social e perspectiva de gênero no Brasil," in *Recortes do Feminino*, ed. Andrea Maia (Rio de Janeiro: Telha, 2021): 265–86.

12 Fabiane Popinigis and Paulo Terra, "Diálogos entre a historiografia do trabalho e da escravidão no Brasil," in *Trabajos y Trabajadores en América Latina (Siglos XVI–XXI)*, ed. Rossana Barragán Romano, Amaru Villanueva Rance and Cristina Machicado Murillo (La Paz: Vicepresidencia del Estado Plurinacional de Bolivia/Centro de Investigaciones Sociales [CIS], 2019): 33–54.

2 The Paths of Women in Nineteenth-Century Brazilian Commerce

In the context of the history of everyday life, in line and contemporaneously with Dias' book, Luciano Figueiredo and Ana Magaldi examined women's work in street trade and prostitution among the "socially declassified" in eighteenth-century Minas Gerais. Figueiredo and Magaldi, like Dias, sought to remove women from invisibility. They argued that, although they were fundamental in the organization of the supply network for the reproduction of the mining economy, women were seen as agents of "disorder" by contemporaries.[13] Figueiredo's and Magaldi's research showed that while Portuguese men dominated the retail trade, women worked in street commerce as hawkers or as *quitandeiras* (street peddlers selling ready-to-eat food and other products). At this moment, distinctions among women were little observed, following the framework of studies about the "female condition" of that time in relation to the various experiences of "poor, free, and slave black, mulatto, and white women."[14]

This focus would change in the 1990s. In an article published in 1996, Maria Cecília Soares approached the problem from the perspective of *ganhadeiras*,[15] women of African descent working as hawkers on the nineteenth-century streets of Salvador. According to her, these women were fundamental for urban supply, which also gave them political and economic importance in city life. Soares shows that African women had special success in the sales of *quitandas* and were considered "dangerous" by the authorities, also because of their contacts with the *quilombolas* (as those who escaped slavery and lived in their own communities were known).[16]

Sheila de Castro Faria's research in the late 1990s acknowledged the pioneering role of Figueiredo, Magaldi, and Dias. Faria advances in the question, showing the forms of accumulation of wealth by these "merchant madams": strategies for the transmission of goods and partnerships in commercial activities.[17] However, she

13 Luciano Figueiredo and Ana Maria Magaldi, "Quitandas e quitutes: um estudo sobre rebeldia e transgressão femininas numa sociedade colonial," *Cadernos de Pesquisa da Fundação Carlos Chagas* 54 (1985): 50–61.

14 Luciano Figueiredo, *O avesso da memória: cotidiano e trabalho da mulher em Minas Gerais no século XVIII* (Rio de Janeiro: José Olympio/Brasília, DF, EDUMB, 1993): 249.

15 *Ganhadeiras* (or *ganhadores*, in the masculine form) was the word used to describe enslaved or free men and women of African descent who made a living on the urban streets of Brazil, providing their services as peddlers, carriers, washers, etc., and usually paying a fee to their "masters" and employers. *Ganhador(a)* can be roughly translated as "earners." See João José Reis, "'The Revolution of the Ganhadores': Urban Labour, Ethnicity and the African Strike of 1857 in Bahia, Brazil," *Journal of Latin American Studies* 29, no. 2 (1997): 355–93.

16 Cecília Moreira Soares, "As ganhadeiras: mulher e resistência negra em Salvador no século XIX," *Revista Afro-Ásia* 17 (1996): 57–71.

17 Sheila de Castro Faria, "Sinhás Pretas Mercadoras: as pretas minas nas cidades do Rio de Janeiro e São João Del Rey" (postdoctoral thesis, Universidade Federal Fluminense, 2004).

disagrees with those authors by stating that those women cannot be labelled as being in "poverty." She argued that, quite to the contrary, in eighteenth-century Minas Gerais manumitted black women, second only to white men, were the group which most left testaments and wills after their deaths, indicating that many of them were capable of accumulating at least some wealth, and can hardly be classified as "poor."[18] But they did not rise socially due to the social "stigma" they carried as former slaves.[19]

In the 1990s, these and other research projects turned to manumissions, final wills, and inventories as part of a broader historiographical movement. As there was consensus in the scholarship that enslaved women had a greater facility than men to obtain their manumissions, it sought to discover more about how women paid for their freedom, who they were, what they did, and the social relations in which they were involved. The question of ethnic-racial belonging was emphasized by studies based on quantitative and qualitative research, which showed that while enslaved women born in Brazil had more chances of getting conditional manumission letters through connections and proximity with their masters or owners and the so-called *casa grande*, as well as domestic services, African women saw profitable activities, above all in urban provision, as the principal path to purchase liberty.[20]

These researchers contradict the initial suppositions that women had greater facility in achieving freedom solely, or above all, due to connections established through sexual or affective relations with their owners. They have found that the majority of manumissions were conditional or onerous and that there were various ways to achieve them.[21] Many female slaves, such as Maria Mina quoted at the beginning of this paper, managed to carry out profitable activities and accumulate savings. The possibility of buying their own manumission obviously depended on various factors. This scholarship built a diverse and multi-faceted framework, which left space for the action and functioning of wide-ranging networks of relations.

In the last decade, research about the everyday life and working conditions of female slaves and freed women working in the food trade in the nineteenth century multiplied and intersected. The proliferation of new scholarship on the lives of these women made possible the mapping of their forms of organization and circulation in a diversity of regional contexts. Although men also occupied themselves in selling foodstuff on the

18 In this point, she is accompanied by Júnia Furtado, *Chica da Silva e o contratador de diamantes* (São Paulo: Companhia das Letras, 2003) and Graham, *Feeding the City*.

19 Sheila de Castro Faria, "Mulheres forras e estigma social," *Tempo* 9 (2000): 62–92.

20 Douglas Libby and Clotilde A. Paiva, "Manumission Practices in a Late Eighteenth-Century Brazilian Slave Parish: São José d'El Rey in 1795," *Slavery & Abolition* 21, no. 1 (2000): 96–127.

21 Mary Karasch showed that out of 1,319 slaves who received manumission between 1807 and 1831, around two thirds were women, highlighting that manumission did not come from the benevolence of slave owners, but because they were bought through numerous possibilities in the economy. See Mary Karasch, *A Vida dos Escravos* (São Paulo: Companhia das Letras, 2000): 430–79; Mary C. Karasch, *Slave Life in Rio de Janeiro, 1808–1850* (Princeton: Princeton University Press, 1987).

streets (as *quitandeiros*, or *pombeiros*),[22] or had stalls in markets, it was women who stood out as the main protagonists in this business in the heterogeneous documentation available until the end of the nineteenth century. *Quitandeiras* and *pombeiros* could be found everywhere in cities and were a constant and striking presence in market places.

Obviously, for foreigners landing in important port cities such as Rio or Salvador, the image of a massive African presence was impressive. In Salvador, which housed the capital of Portuguese America until 1763, the population in 1835 was 65,000 people, of whom 42% were slaves and 58% free or freed. Africans accounted for 33.6% of this population.[23] As Richard Graham showed, African women were especially pre-eminent among vendors. However, as in other contexts, they did not just increase horizontal solidarity. Their horizontal ties intersected with vertical ones. The physical mobility to move around the city to negotiate and deal with all kinds of people was a link in this chain of commerce, and credit allowed vendors to construct a broad network.[24]

Another important port which received a large part of the slaves brought to the Americas, as well as foreign visitors, was Rio de Janeiro. The population of the capital of the Empire of Brazil in 1849 was 226,000 people, of whom 110,000 were slaves. 74,000 Africans, both slaves and freed, lived in the capital.[25] Candelária market, the largest enclosed market building in Brazil, inspired by European constructions, was built in the 1840s. In this central market in Rio de Janeiro, small fruit and vegetable traders primarily established alliances and partnerships in relation to the *Mina* identity, but they were in constant negotiation with other groups. According to Juliana Barreto Farias, their efforts to construct expanded families, also based on their expectations of freedom, and strategies in accumulating wealth explain the visibility they acquired, observed by travelers and corroborated by the historiography.[26] We believe that it is possible that *quitandeira mina* became a synonym for peddler, with credentials such as respectability and resourcefulness in selling, as well as business skill.

22 *Pombeiros* were the intermediaries who purchased foodstuffs from the producers and sold the goods in turn to other traders or consumers; the term came from the word *pumbo*, which meant markets and fairs on the borders of the Kingdom of the Congo. Alberto da Costa Silva, *A manilha e o libambo – a África e a escravidão de 1500 e 1700* (Rio de Janeiro: Nova Fronteira, 2002).

23 João José Reis, *Rebelião escrava no Brasil: a história do Levante dos Malês de 1835* (São Paulo: Companhia das Letras, 2003): 23–25; João José Reis, *Slave Rebellion in Brazil: The Muslim Uprising of 1835 in Bahia*, trans. Arthur Barkel (Baltimore: Johns Hopkins University Press, 1993) (translated from the 1986 edition).

24 Graham, *Feeding the City*: 9–53.

25 Luiz F. Alencastro, "Vida privada e ordem privada no Império," in *História da Vida privada no Brasil: império*, ed. Fernando Novais (São Paulo: Companhia das Letras, 1997): 24–25.

26 Juliana Barreto Faria, *Mercados Minas: africanos ocidentais na praça do Mercado do Rio de Janeiro (1830–1890)* (Rio de Janeiro: Arquivo Geral da Cidade, 2015).

According to Selma Pantoja, the term *quitanda* had its roots in the Mbundu term *kitanda*, and in Luanda the term served to designate the markets where everything was sold in the seventeenth century: "throughout the centuries, the term quitandeira has referred to the people who work in those markets."[27] In Brazil, African women and their descendants dominated street commerce and the "*quitanda* business" in urban centers until the middle of the nineteenth century, as many researchers have shown. This happened because "their prestige facilitated the relationship with the consumer market, formed by various social sectors, both slaves and free people. Men did not have this appeal. *Quitandeiras* were especially popular."[28] Araújo et al. also highlight the prominence of black *minas* in this trade and describe the unmistakable figure of the *quitandeiras* in nineteenth-century Rio de Janeiro: "With their large turbanes, the back-cloths over their shoulders, the essential straw basket, the full skirt, the lace shirt, they crossed the city in all directions, and were eternalized in the pens of foreign travelers such as Thomas Ender, Jean Baptiste Debret, and Johann Moritz Rugendas."[29] To explain the presence of the *quintandeiras*, the importance of commercial experience in Africa was highlighted where women dominated this type of trade.[30]

It was no accident that Maria, who was mentioned at the beginning of this paper, had the surname "Mina" – a word that indicated her origin in West Africa. The prominence of *Mina* black women and their accumulation strategies has called the attention of researchers. The term *Mina* refers to the nomenclature of the Atlantic slave trade, designating those who left the Mina Coast, in West Africa, and it was reappropriated and resignified on the other side of the Atlantic. In nineteenth-century Brazil, the African *Minas*, above all women, became known as accomplished traders. This aspect was registered in the texts and images from accounts provided by foreign travelers visiting the Brazilian coast throughout the nineteenth century.[31]

African women and their descendants not only dominated the business of selling food on the streets of cities like Salvador, Recife, Rio de Janeiro, Campinas, São João

27 Selma Pantoja, "Women's work in the Fairs and Markets of Luanda," in *Woman in the Making of the Atlantic World: The Theatre of Shadows*, ed. Clara Sarmento (Newcastle: Cambridge Scholars Publishing, 2008): 45–67.

28 Carlos de Araújo Moreira, Juliana Barreto Farias, Carlos Eugênio Líbano Soares and Flávio dos Santos Gomez, *Cidades Negras – africanos, crioulos e espaços urbanos no Brasil escravista do século XIX* (São Paulo: Alameda, 2006): 93.

29 Araújo et al., *Cidades Negras*: 93–94.

30 Cf. "Mulheres forras e estigma social": 62–92; Graham, *Feeding the City*; Libby and Pavia, "Manumission Practices."

31 Carlos Eugênio Líbano Soares and Flávio dos Santos Gomes, "Negras minas no Rio de Janeiro: gênero, nação e trabalho urbano no século XIX," in *Rotas atlânticas da diáspora africana: da Baía do Benin ao Rio de Janeiro*, ed. Mariza de Carvalho Soares (Niterói: Editoria Universidade Federal Fluminense, 2007): 191–224. Julietta Barreto Farias, Flávio dos Santos Gomes and Carlos Eugênio Líbano Soares, *No Labirinto das nações – africanos e identidades no Rio de janeiro, século XIX* (Rio de Janeiro: Presidência da República, Arquivo Nacional, 2005).

del Rei, and Desterro, but they also played a fundamental role in credit and transit networks among the powerful, mingling in this way in the political life of the city.

3 Urban History beyond Social Control

We will take the case of Desterro to explore in a little more detail how the work of *quitandeiras* was at the center of the disputes for urban space and its reformulation, and to see why their work was not recognized as such. The first half of the nineteenth century saw the predominantly uncontested organization of black men and women in trade, the *quitandeiras* and *pombeiros* involved in street commerce, whether they were slaves, free, or freed. However, in the second half of the century there was a progressive increase in attempts at social control related to the circulation and activities of people. This process was worsened in the last quarter of the nineteenth century, in line with the influence of scientific racism in Brazil and the struggles for abolition.

After independence from Portugal in 1822, the local and regional spheres of government went through a profound process of reorganization in order to fulfill the responsibilities given by the new legal and administrative framework. This organization kept local powers under the supervision of regional spheres, which in turn were submitted to the imperial government.[32] In the following decades, public authorities became increasingly involved in the construction of market places and buildings in order to demarcate the spaces of circulation and sale of food and produce, under the justification of the need for hygiene in the more important public places, and to improve the inspection of commerce and the collection of taxes and fines. Parallel to this, there was an increase in the prices of land and slaves around 1850 – the date of the passing of the Land Law and the abolition of the Atlantic slave trade. This was added to an increasing process of racialization, which reduced the space for social ascension of freed people in the second half of the twentieth century.[33]

In this context, a great diversity of bylaws and notifications published by councils in various cities attempted to control the circulation of enslaved women and the free population of color, including through the inspection of the payment of tax and registration fees. However, their exhaustive reiteration shows that these regulations were

32 "[. . .] a law of 1928 and a major constitutional amendment of 1934, weakened city councils to allow the centrally appointed provincial president even greater power over the municipality." Graham, *Feeding the City*: X.

33 Robert Wayne Andrew Slenes, "A 'Great Arch' Descending: Manumission Rates, Subaltern Social Mobility and Enslaved, Freeborn and Freed Black Identities in Southeastern Brazil, 1791–1888," in *New Approaches to Resistance in Brazil and Mexico*, ed. John Gledson and Patience A. Schell (Durham, NC: Duke University Press, 2012): 100–18; Hebe Mattos, "Raça e cidadania no crepúsculo da modernidade escravista no Brasil," in *O Brasil imperial*, vol. 3, *1870–1889*, ed. Keila Grinberg and Ricardo Salles (Rio de Janeiro: Civilização Brasileira, 2009): 15–39.

frustrated on a daily basis by the actions of street vendors, who organized themselves to maintain their spaces of work in urban centers. At the very least, the recurrent resistance of these workers of African origin to leave the center of the city in the name of hygiene and the cleaning and cleanliness of the public square is widely documented, at least until the end of the nineteenth century.[34]

In Salvador, the *quitandeiras* were accused of providing food to the *Malê* rebels and in participating in this conspiracy, while in 1858 they were involved in a food riot that resulted in the storming of the municipal council. In Rio de Janeiro, *quitandeiras,* who had always occupied their places in the market square by the sea, went on strike against the exorbitant prices charged for the new stalls constructed in that space in 1885.[35] In both events, arguments about the "public interest" were made by different social actors, stating that the "people" had to be protected by the public authorities from greedy and hoarding merchants. The latter could be modest *pombeiros* and *quitandeiras,* as well as large business owners.

In the case of Desterro, in the south of Brazil, the presence of Africans and *quitandeiras* was always noted in the discussions about the location for the construction of the market building. The urban center of Desterro had 5,611 inhabitants, of whom 25% were slaves.[36] The view of the "black men and women *quitandeiras*" dominating the main square in the city, in front of Matriz church and the government buildings, caused the president of the province to take action against what he considered to be "bad taste." The market constructed in Desterro in 1851, like the one in Rio de Janeiro, was inspired by European models and was the reason of intense political disputes. These debates were based on the opinion about the best place for the building and the people who worked there, resulting in the formation of two different political groups in the local configuration of the liberal and conservative parties of the empire.

The first public market of Desterro had the function of organizing the trade of foodstuffs, controlling the workers who walked through the streets, beautifying central space, and making it more hygienic. Previously, "even slaves" could rent the stalls, and there were constant complaints about the lack of hygiene in the place where the foodstuffs were on display. The so-called "*quitanda* places" in the market were almost all rented by women, and many of them had names which mentioned their African

34 Maciel Henrique Silva, *Pretas de Honra – vida e trabalho de domésticas e vendedoras no Recife do século XIX (1840–1870)* (Recife: Editoria de Universidade Federal de Pernambuco; Salvador: Editoria de Universidade Federal da Bahia, 2011); Valter Martins, *Mercados urbanos, transformações na cidade: abastecimento e cotidiano em Campinas, 1859–1908* (Campinas: Editora da Unicamp, 2010); Graham, *Feeding the City*; Popinigis, "Aos pés dos pretos e pretas quitandeiras"; Baretto Farias, *Mercados minas.*

35 João José Reis and Márcia Gabriela D. de Aguiar, "'Carne sem osso e farinha sem caroço': o motim de 1858 contra a carestia na Bahia," *Revista de História* 135 (1996): 135–59; Soares, "As ganhadeiras"; Juliana Farias Barreto, "A greve nas marinhas. protestos, tradições e identidades entre pequenos lavradores, quitandeiras e pombeiros (Rio de Janeiro, século XIX)," *ArtCultura* 11, no. 19 (2009): 35–55.

36 Mappa aproximado da população da Provincia de Santa Catarina. Relatório do Presidente da Provincia, Joao José Coutinho, apresentado em março de 1855: 36.

origin, such as Simôa Mina, Anna Mina, Maria Mina, Josefa Caçange, Esperança Cabinda, Luiza Cabinda, and Zeferida Calabá.[37] At the same time, outside the market building, the presence of women was also striking. All paid charges to work as *quitandeiras*.[38]

While the enslaved Maria Mina had a space in the corridors of the recently constructed market in the 1850s, the "freed black" Joanna Prates was, for many years, the only women to rent a stall within it.[39]

This is because the market's regulation defined that *the market stalls* could only be rented to free people. Despite this, the "*quitanda* spaces," as they called the corridors in the market, could be rented to slaves once they had a written license from their owners.[40] It was thus sought to prevent the stalls in the square from being occupied by "immoral persons and even slaves," as had occurred previously in the city center. With this, although it was not totally prohibited, it was sought to define specific and well limited spaces for slaves. The regulations also prohibited "black peddlers and beggars from walking around the square."[41]

The charges collected by the municipality after the construction of the public market increased 275.74%, and the market alone was responsible for 31% of the municipality's total revenues in the middle of the 1860s.[42] However, the *quitandeiras* and *pombeiros* who worked outside the market were an important part of this figure.[43]

This is the case of Anna and Justina, who in 1831 were freed when still very young by their owner and mistress, the widow Rita de Cássia Poyção, on the condition that

37 Arquivo Histórico Municipal de Florianópolis (AHMF), Livro Caixa no. 139, Receita e despesa da Câmara Municipal (1854–1855). Taxes and charges were entered in the payment books of the municipal council, in which were recorded the revenue of the administration referring to all payments of municipal taxes, charges, and fines for the infraction of codes, as well as the payment of their employees and all services rendered to the municipality. The book *Collection of Charges for the Stalls in the Public Market* recorded the payment of rents, in other words the half yearly lease of each of the stalls within the market building, done by public auction.

38 The value of the tax paid to exercise the function of *pombeiro* was 3,200 réis, while that charged for the sale of *quitandas* on the streets of the city was 1,200 réis. AHMF, Livro Caixa no. 139, Receita e despesa da Câmara Municipal 1854–1855.

39 AHMF, Termos de arrematação das casinhas do Mercado.

40 After the construction of the building, these men and women were limited to using the so-called "*quitanda* places": spaces between the columns which, divided in two, could be rented by male and female slaves and freed people. Ofícios da Câmara Municipal a Presidência da Província 1850, Art. 24º do Regulamento do Mercado Velho: fls 120–26.

41 Arquivo Público do Estado de Santa Catarina (APESC), Florianópolis, Regulamento do Mercado, Ofícios da Câmara Municipal para a presidência da Província – 1850, ff. 120–26.

42 AHMF, Balanço da receita e despesa da Câmara Municipal da Cidade do Desterro do ano findo de 1º. de julho de 1863 a junho de 1864: Fls. 118, Livro 153, 1868–1869.

43 In the same period (between July 1863 and June 1864), the council collected 160,000 réis in relation to *pombeiro* charges, which were 6,400 each, meaning that there were 25 people exercising this function *who had paid the charges*. Although the peddler charge was more expensive, the total paid by the *pombeiros* was higher than the total amount referring to the charges paid by small taverns (89#600).

they look after their former owner and her companion until their death.[44] When Rita died, more than thirty years later, in 1864, she left property for the former slaves.[45] In this way, the widow guaranteed support and subsistence for herself and her companion in old age, while the freed slaves guaranteed their freedom and later their autonomy. The two freed slaves continued to live from selling *quitandas* until at least 1884, when they must have been around 70 and 57 years respectively, like Maria Mina and many others, who for this paid a charge to sell *quitandas* on the streets.[46] Anna and Justina adopted the surname of their former owner, who they supported through the sale of *quitandas* and from whom they received property and housing as inheritance.

As stated above, the ties of prominent people in the city were fundamental for the survival and ascension of these women. After a long period of working partnerships with African men and women in the sale of food in the market in the 1850s, Maria Mina paid for her manumission through an important politician in the city in 1860. She was the slave of the peddler Luís de Sant'anna Carpes, who had received 800,000 *réis* in cash from Captain Clemente Antônio Gonçalves as payment for the manumission of Maria.[47]

Many years later, Maria got involved in a dispute with the powerful Feliciano Alves de Brito, a wealthy merchant and colonel in the National Guard. The freed African, a well-known street vendor in Desterro, had sealed a contract with Brito to purchase Manoel in installments, who she said was her nephew. In 1883, the slave was represented by a legal representative in a law case, since Mina did not want to pay the total amount. They argued over the bad health of the young freedman and the long years of slavery. Alves de Brito was furious and argued that the freedman worked for Maria, who made money at his cost.

Thus, in addition to the broad networks of horizontal solidarities through their work as street vendors, these women also constructed verticalized relations in various environments. All these shared in the food distribution network in the capital's urban center, through which they found forms of survival and ways to guarantee their freedom.

The Catholic brotherhoods were also important places for the establishment of these relations. One such was followed by Joanna Prates, a devotee of the *Irmandade de Nossa Senhora do Rosário e São Benedito dos Homens Pretos*, founded in 1750, a

AHMF, Balanço da receita e despesa da Câmara Municipal da Cidade do Desterro do ano findo de 1º. de julho de 1863 a junho de 1864: Fls. 118. Livro 153; Registro de Correspondência da Câmara Municipal a Diversas Autoridades, Relatório da Câmara Municipal, Registro da Receita e Despesa, 1858–1869.

44 Ofício do Cartório de Desterro, "Lançamento de Escrito de Liberdade da escrava Anna," Livro 4 de notas do 2º, 1831: fls. 118v and 199.

45 Daniela Sbravati, "Mulheres de (In)certa condição," *Revista Mundos do Trabalho* 1, no.2 (2009): 85–90.

46 Cf. AHMF, Livro auxiliar da receita e despesa da Câmara Municipal, 1883–1884: fls. 29 and 33.

47 Gonçalves had been president of the municipal council of Desterro at the time of the opening of the public market building; years later, he began to work as an inspector for the council.

common devotion among enslaved and freed men and women. Some Africans held important positions among their people, judging by the roles they assumed in the brotherhood, as was the case of Joana herself. There they dealt with the "good men" of Desterro, white landholders and *senhores* with whom slaves and freed people established ties and contacts, which also developed into commercial relations.[48]

In the final decades of the nineteenth century, this transit became increasingly more difficult. The growth of the influence of the racially based hygienist ideology in public policies and the tightening of attempts at inspection and tax collection in relation to the circulation and sale of foodstuffs directly affected Africans and their descendants who worked in this trade. This movement was an essential part of progressive attempts to control the enslaved, freed, and free populations in the final years of slavery.[49]

The documents reveal the concern of the public authorities with the levying of taxes and charges in relation to street vending services and with the quality of foodstuffs and their distribution. Above all, along with other regulations from the period, they reveal the fear of the circulation of people involved in this work, Africans and their descendants, both enslaved and freed. On the other hand, the codes and publications, their content and republication, with new clauses, also showed that the determinations were constantly bypassed by these workers and their allies. After all, the municipality was not only a place of regulation and control, but also a daily space for the relationship of workers with public authorities, claims, negotiations, and conflicts.[50]

In this analysis, we anchor ourselves in the historiographic debates and research about the expansion of the actual concept of the working class to include activities and relations not previously treated as labor. We consider here the dimensions of processes and activities carried out and related to the home, life, and the community, and the complex relations between productive and reproductive work and their blurred boundaries.[51]

---

48 Cláudia M. Malavota, *Os homens pretos do Desterro. Um estudo sobre a Irmandade de Nossa Senhora do Rosário (1841–1860)* (Itajaí: Núcleo de Estudos Afro-Brasileiros [NEAB]/Casa Aberta Editora, 2011).

49 Sidney Chalhoub, *Cidade Febril* (São Paulo: Companhia das Letras, 1994).

50 Paulo Terra, Marcelo de Souza Magalhães and Martha Abreu, eds., *Os poderes municipais e a cidade* (Rio de Janeiro: Mauad X, 2019).

51 Marcel van der Linden, *Workers of the World: Essays Toward a Global Labor History* (Leiden: Brill, 2008); Marcel van der Linden, *Transnational Labour History: Explorations* (London: Routledge, 2003); Dorothy Sue Cobble, "The Promise and Peril of the New Global History," *International Labor and Working-Class History* 82 (2012): 99–107; Eileen Boris, "Reproduction as Production: Thinking with ILO to Move Beyond Dichotomy," *Labor and Society* 22 (2019): 283–98.

4 Who and Where Were the Women Workers? Domestic Service, Seamstresses, Servants, and Casual Workers

Three elements combined for the creation of an androcentric narrative about labor, which excluded the contribution of women and enslaved people to the construction of wealth and social organization: In this area 1. The idea of the inadequacy of the historic process of Desterro in relation to a broader explanatory model about the role of the ago-exporting plantations of Brazil; 2. Restricting the category of domestic labor to activities in the home and as non-productive; 3. A structural and expanded vision of the processes that does not permit the understanding of individual experiences and trajectories. The reordering of urban space in Desterro is part of a broader narrative of the history of Santa Catarina. The province had its first largescale experience of colonization and settlement when, through the subvention of the Portuguese crown, 5,000 Azorean men and women were brought to the region in mid-eighteenth century. The narrative established later, which proved to be strong and long-lived, was that the failure of these Azorean immigrants in agriculture gave way to the success of German immigrant settlements established during the nineteenth century. With this, Germans came to occupy the place of the motor of local economic development, while the Portuguese, initially more used to fishing activities than to agriculture, worked in administrative services and took employment in the bureaucracy.[52]

This narrative of the development of Santa Catarina corroborated a generalized explanatory model about the formation of the labor market in Brazil, in which the concept of free labor, exercised by European immigrants, was associated with the modernization of production and industrialization relations. The general lines of this report indicate how political disputes related to the construction of the memory of Santa Catarina excluded the significant African contribution.

In a 1959 book republished in 2000, *Negros em Florianópolis*, the sociologist Fernando Henrique Cardoso advocated two arguments to explain what he defined as "economic disorganization" in Santa Catarina, given the successful German and Italian settlements on the mainland: the failure of the Azorean farming experience and the peculiar way in which Santa Catarina adjusted to "colonial status." According to him, the poor population "had not economically organized [. . .] around colonial production." 10% of Desterro's active population were in the military. With its forts and fortifications, its importance was in the defense of territory in southern Brazil.[53]

52 For a critique of this approach, see: Adriano Duarte, "Space, Culture and Labour in Santa Catarina, 1900–1960," *Journal of Social History and the History of Social Movements* 49 (2013): 53–74.

53 Fernando Henrique Cardoso, *Negros em Florianópolis – relações sociais e econômicas* (Florianópolis: Insular, 2000): 77.

Cardoso contrasted the agricultural failure of the Azorean settlers with the productivity of German immigrants, responsible for supplying products to the central market in the city.[54] Neither slaves nor freed people, According to Cardoso, the rural world of the island was poor, plebian, and Azorean.[55] He recognized that the principal economic activity of Desterro was urban trade, which expanded continuously in the nineteenth century, leading to the ascension of a merchant elite (shipowners, importers). He also included the possibility that slave work was used in the food trade, though "in heavy services in general."[56]

Although he found evidence of enslaved labor in the circulation of merchandise, Cardoso could not conceive of its protagonist role in activities related to commerce, precisely because his framework did not permit him to consider slaves as historical actors.[57] Moreover, in his theoretical perspective, slavery was an obstacle for free labor and, consequently, for economic and social development. For this reason, even highlighting the coexistence of the work of small autonomous landholders and free employed workers alongside slave labor, the latter appears as having degraded "free labor."[58]

In the first Brazilian census in 1872, in the urban center of Desterro the majority of those classified as "domestic workers" were enslaved. No slave was classified as a "farm worker." In the other parts of Santa Catarina Island, the ratio was inverted, with a majority of the enslaved classified as farm workers. Considering the island as a whole, slaves accounted for 11% of the population, with half of these concentrated in the city of Desterro. Furthermore, almost half (49%) of the slaves in Desterro were classified as being in "domestic service" and 21% as "without a profession." For Cardoso, these numbers prove the predominance of domestic service in the enslaved labor force. The use of slaves in activities considered as non-productive thus explained a great deal of the region's backwardness and its mismatch in relation to the slaveholding system. Among the free people, women outnumbered men of the same condition in all racial categories, though there was little difference in the case of whites.

According to the census, Desterro concentrated slave labor, domestic service, and women. Female slaves were distributed among only four categories: 21 were "seamstresses," 23 "servants and casual workers," 445 were in "domestic service," and 121 "without a profession." Finally, it is important to note here: 1. the concentration of slave labor in the port city of Desterro – practically the double of the province of Santa Catarina; 2. the predominance of women among freed people; 3. the overwhelming majority of women classified under "domestic service."

54 Cardoso, *Negros*: 104.
55 Ibid.: 10.
56 Ibid.: 70.
57 For this discussion, see Chalhoub, *Visões da Liberdade*.
58 Cardoso, *Negros*: 100–115.

The census does not show any enslaved person in the category of "merchants, bookkeepers, and clerks" either in Desterro or in the province of Santa Catarina. However, this absence does not mean that there were no slaves involved in the urban trade, but only that they were not recognized as belonging to a defined place in the hierarchy of occupations in the retail trade. For this reason, it is important to define here the difference between street vendors and workers in retail: one was dominated by Africans and their descendants, above all women, while the other by Portuguese men, at least until the end of the nineteenth century in many cities in Brazil, like Rio, Salvador, and Recife. In Desterro, Germans also gained prominence in commerce, both as small producers and as merchants. The term "merchant" was, in general, reserved for the owners of businesses, whether they were from high-status or low-status commerce, and was not used for employees, clerks, servants, or street vendors.

The women involved in these activities almost did not appear in the census as "merchants." Only eight among a total of 404 merchants were women. Therefore, our hypothesis is that the black women we find paying taxes for their *quitandas* – food stalls – and circulating on the streets and the central market with their products were classified in the census as "domestic service." This interpretation can be found in the very construction of census categories: men could be classified as "clerks" or "merchants," while women were assigned to the wide-ranging category of "domestic service."

In addition to the characteristics and the inherent problems of the sources themselves, it is important to highlight a conceptual question: an inattentive reading of the contemporary meanings of the expression "domestic service" reduced domestic work, in particular that done by women, to work in the house and so-called reproductive work, and not as work which creates value and wealth. The distortion provoked by this reading is that it does not consider that in the nineteenth century, "domestic service" included women's work in activities integrated into the production and circulation of goods, evidentially fundamental for the functioning of the economy.

If we consider that the configurations existing in the term "domestic labor" have their own historicity, *as part of labor history*, it can be seen that the term assumed distinct meanings. Among the more or less known meanings are their feminization and their restriction to household work.[59] The relevance of the theme, especially in the case of Brazil (although not only), where racism was fundamental in the construction of a discursive ideal of the white and waged labor market has been increasingly indicated.[60] In the case of Santa Catarina, this reading also defined the persistence of a historiographic narrative about a province defined as "white." Sustained there is the idea

59 Sandra Graham, *House and Street: The Domestic World of Servants and Masters in Nineteenth-Century Rio de Janeiro* (New York: Cambridge University Press, 1988).

60 For a summary of the most recent research, see: Flávia Fernandes de Souza, "Trabalho doméstico: considerações sobre um tema recente de estudos na História do Social do Trabalho no Brasil," *Revista Mundos do Trabalho* 7, no. 13 (2015): 275–96.

that European immigration was uniquely responsible for propelling commercial and industrial growth in the region, through productive and modernizing work.

More recent historiography has deepened the research not only on the African presence in the region and the Atlantic connections of Desterro port and the importance of these actors in the productive process, but also in the social and cultural life of the city.[61] Like other places in Brazil, African and Afro-descendant men and women were fundamental for the economic support of Desterro's public economy and social organization as tax payers, goods suppliers, and contributors to the general wealth in the city, while they sought liberty for themselves and their relatives. However, while the food market was initially a privileged place for the mobility and autonomy of enslaved and freed women, its meaning changed and increasingly began to concentrate the organizing principles of exclusion from central spaces in the cities.

5 Conclusion

As has been shown above, during the nineteenth century the presence of African women and women of African descent in the streets of every city in Brazil was pervasive, as was their striking influence in urban social dynamics. That is why it is difficult to understand how it took so long for them to find their due place within the scholarship about slavery and in labor studies, in which they were, in the very best scenario, treated as ancillary elements, passive and subaltern helpers without agency, mere supporting figures. How can it be that, as they were central to the maintenance of the system of slavery and its dissolution, in the organization of labor activities, and the construction of wealth, the work of these women has not been sufficiently considered?

Dias' pioneering study helped open research paths for a fertile field about poor women's labor, a topic which has returned in recent years, asking about the meaning of color-based stigma, as well as the social relations engendered by slavery and freedom in the expanding labor market. The social productive and reproductive labor carried out by women and the social and material wealth that they produced have increasingly become the focus of the paths followed by the social history of slavery in the nineteenth century.

61 Beatriz Mamigonian, "Africanos em Santa Catarina: escravidão e identidade étnica (1750–1850)," in *Nas rotas do império: eixos mercantis, tráfico e relações sociais no mundo português*, ed. João Fragoso, Manolo Florentino, Antônio Carlos Jucá and Adriana Campos (Vitória: Editoria da Universidade Federal do Espírito Santo, 2006): 565–96; Paulino de Jesus Francisco Cardoso, *Negros em Desterro: experiências das populações de origem africana em Florianópolis na segunda metade do século XIX* (Itajaí, SC: Casa Aberta, 2008); Malavota, *Os Homens Pretos do Desterro*; Beatriz Mamigonian and Joseane Zimmerman, ed., *História Diversa: africanos e afrodescendentes na Ilha de Santa Catarina* (Florianópolis: Editoria de Universidade Federal de Santa Catarina, 2013).

This article intends to contribute to reflecting from a gender perspective on the processes of social exclusion and racialization in the post-emancipation period in various parts of Brazil and the Americas. We seek to demonstrate why it is important to consider the activities done by women of African descent as work, such as the production and circulation of food stuffs, the organization of urban life, and the generation of wealth in cities. It is also sought to rethink the categories of domestic service to define gendered meanings of labor as central in labor market disputes between slavery and freedom and the construction of androcentric meanings for labor.[62]

The accumulation of scholarship about the experience of enslaved people, legally free workers, and women in specific contexts and their relations, has allowed for the formulation of the new research questions, emphasizing a greater approximation between the history of slavery and labor history. Adopting a perspective sensitive to gender as one of the fundamental elements of the organization of these relations (as well as race and class), it is still possible to pose new questions revisiting classical themes. Also, only on a scale of observation which allows us to see subjects, their strategies and actions can we go beyond ideal models and stereotypes.

The final decades of the nineteenth century in Brazil, at a conjuncture of great political and social transformations, such as the advent of the republic and abolition, were also a moment of the creation of categories for the struggle for rights, which cut across by hierarchies of race and gender in the fields of labor/work. Nevertheless, the various activities carried out by women of African descent, with the main ones being paid – and which could be in commerce, domestic service, or prostitution, often alternating between them – were increasingly relegated to invisibility, devaluation, or criminalization. This occurred at a moment of the broad diffusion of theories of scientific racism and discourses of modernization and civilization, which assigned men the role of providing for the family. In this context, the growth of more aggressive processes of industrialization and the emergence of new forms of organization of social movements also constructed hierarchies for better paid and socially valued work in the demands for rights based on a masculine model of worker.

62 Henrique Espada Lima and Fabiane Popinigis, "Maids, Clerks, and the Shifting Landscape of Labor Relations in Rio de Janeiro, 1830s–1880s," *International Review of Social History* 62, no. 25 (2017): 45–73.

Bibliography

Primary Sources

Arquivo Histórico Municipal de Florianópolis (AHMF), Balanço da receita e despesa da Câmara Municipal da Cidade do Desterro do ano findo de 1º. de julho de 1863 a junho de 1864, fls. 118, Livro 153, 1868–1869.

Arquivo Histórico Municipal de Florianópolis (AHMF), Livro Caixa no.139, Receita e despesa da Câmara Municipal (1854–1855).

Arquivo Histórico Municipal de Florianópolis (AHMF), Termos de arrematação das casinhas do Mercado.

Arquivo Histórico Municipal de Florianópolis (AHMF), Livro auxiliar da receita e despesa da Câmara Municipal, 1883–1884, fls. 29 and 33.

Arquivo Público do Estado de Santa Catarina (APESC), Florianópolis, Regulamento do Mercado, Ofícios da Câmara Municipal para a presidência da Província – 1850, ff. 120–26.

Ofícios da Câmara Municipal a Presidência da Província 1850, Art.24º do Regulamento do Mercado Velho, fls. 120–26.

Ofício do Cartório de Desterro, “Lançamento de Escrito de Liberdade da escrava Anna,” Livro 4 de notas do 2º, 1831, fls. 118v and 199.

Registro de Correspondência da Câmara Municipal a Diversas Autoridades, Relatório da Câmara Municipal, Registro da Receita e Despesa, 1858–1869.

Secondary Literature

Alencastro, Luiz F. “Vida privada e ordem privada no Império,” in *História da vida privada no Brasil*, vol. 2, ed. Fernando A. Novais (São Paulo: Companhia das Letras, 1997): 11–94.

de Araújo Moreira, Carlos, Juliana Barreto Farias, Carlos Eugênio Líbano Soares and Flávio dos Santos Gomez. *Cidades negras: africanos, crioulos e espaços urbanos no Brasil escravista do século XIX* (São Paulo: Alameda, 2006).

Ariza, Marília Bueno de Araújo. *Mães infames, filhos venturosos: trabalho, pobreza, escravidão e emancipação no cotidiano de São Paulo (século XIX)* (São Paulo: Alameda, 2020).

Barragán, Rossana, Amaru Villanueva Rance and Cristina Machicado Murillo, eds. *Trabajos y trabajadores en América Latina (siglos XVI–XXI)* (La Paz: Vicepresidencia del Estado, Presidencia de la Asamblea Legislativa Plurinacional, Centro de Investigaciones Sociales, Ministerio de Planificación del Desarrollo, 2019).

Barreto Farias, Juliana. *Mercados minas: africanos ocidentais na Praça do Mercado do Rio de Janeiro (1830–1890)* (Rio de Janeiro: Archivo Geral da Cidade do Rio de Janeiro, 2015).

Farias Barreto, Juliana. “A greve nas marinhas. protestos, tradições e identidades entre pequenos lavradores, quitandeiras e pombeiros (Rio de Janeiro, século XIX),” *ArtCultura* 11, no. 19 (2009): 35–55.

Barreto Farias, Juliana, Carlos Eugênio Líbano Soares and Flávio dos Santos Gomes. *No labirinto das nações: africanos e identidades no Rio de Janeiro* (Rio de Janeiro: Presidência da República, Arquivo Nacional, 2005).

Boris, Eileen. “Reproduction as Production: Thinking with the ILO to Move Beyond Dichotomy,” *Journal of Labor and Society* 22, no. 2 (2019): 283–98.

Cardoso, Fernando Henrique. *Negros em Florianópolis: relações sociais e econômicas* (Florianópolis: Editora Insular, 2000).

Cardoso, Paulino de Jesus Francisco. *Negros em Desterro: experiências das populações de origem africana em Florianópolis na segunda metade do século XIX* (Itajaí, SC: Casa Aberta, 2008).
de Castro Faria, Sheila. "Sinhás Pretas Mercadoras: as pretas minas nas cidades do Rio de Janeiro e São João Del Rey" (postdoctoral thesis, Universidade Federal Fluminense, 2004).
de Castro Faria, Sheila. "Mulheres forras e estigma social," *Tempo* 9 (2000): 62–92.
Chalbhoub, Sidney. *Cidade febril: cortiços e epidemias na corte imperial* (São Paulo: Companhia das Letras, 2017).
Chalbhoub, Sidney. *Visões da liberdade: uma história das últimas décadas da escravidão na corte* (São Paulo: Companhia Das Letras, 1990).
Cobble, Dorothy Sue. "The Promise and Peril of the New Global Labor History," *International Labor and Working-Class History* 82 (2012): 99–107.
da Costa e Silva, Alberto. *A manilha e o libambo: a Africa e a escravidão, de 1500 a 1700* (Rio de Janeiro: Editora Nova Fronteira, Ministério da Cultura, Fundação Biblioteca Nacional, Departamento Nacional do Livro, 2002).
Cowling, Camillia. *Conceiving Freedom: Women of Color, Gender, and the Abolition of Slavery in Havana and Rio de Janeiro* (Chapel Hill: University of North Carolina Press, 2013).
Dias, Maria Odila Leite da Silva. "Mulheres sem História," *Revista de História* 114 (1983): 31–45.
Dias, Maria Odila Leite da Silva. *Quotidiano e poder em São Paulo no século XIX*, 2nd ed. (São Paulo: Brasiliense, 1995).
Dias, Maria Odila Leite da Silva. *Power and Everyday Life: The Lives of Working Women in Nineteenth-Century Brazil* (New Brunswick, NJ: Rutgers University Press, 1995).
Figueiredo, Luciano and Ana Maria Magaldi. "Quitandas e quitutes: um estudo sobre rebeldia e transgressão femininas numa sociedade colonial," *Cadernos de Pesquisa da Fundação Carlos Chagas* 54 (1985): 50–61.
Figueiredo, Luciano. *O avesso da memória: cotidiano e trabalho da mulher em Minas Gerais no século XVIII* (Rio de Janeiro: José Olympio, 1993).
Fontes, Paulo, Alexandre Fortes and David Mayer. "Brazilian Labour History in Global Context: Some Introductory Notes," *International Review of Social History* 62, no. S25 (2017): 1–22.
Furtado, Júnia Ferreira. *Chica da Silva e o contratador dos diamantes: o outro lado do mito* (São Paulo: Companhia das Letras, 2003).
Geremias, Patrícia. "Como se fosse da família: arranjos formais e informais de criação e trabalho de menores pobres na cidade do Rio de Janeiro (1860–1910)" (PhD diss., Federal University of Rio de Janeiro, 2019).
Graham, Richard. *Feeding the City: From Street Market to Liberal Reform in Salvador, Brazil, 1780–1860* (Austin: University of Texas Press, 2010).
Grinberg, Keila. *Liberata, a lei da ambigüidade: as ações de liberdade da Corte de Apelação do Rio de Janeiro no século XIX* (Rio de Janeiro: Relume Dumará, 1994).
Grinberg, Keila. "Manumission, Gender, and the Law in Nineteenth-Century Brazil," in *Paths to Freedom: Manumission in the Atlantic World*, ed. Rosemary Brana-Shute and Randy J. Sparks (Columbia: University of South Carolina Press, 2009): 1–14.
Karasch, Mary C. *Slave Life in Rio de Janeiro, 1808–1850* (Princeton: Princeton University Press, 1987).
Lauderdale Graham, Sandra. *House and Street: The Domestic World of Servants and Masters in Nineteenth-Century Rio de Janeiro* (Austin: University of Texas Press, 1992).
Lauderdale Graham, Sandra. *Caetana diz não: histórias de mulheres da sociedade escravista brasileira* (São Paulo: Companhia das letras, 2005).
Líbano Soares, Carlos Eugênio, and Flávio dos Santos Gomes. "Negras minas no Rio de Janeiro: gênero, nação e trabalho urbano no século XIX," in *Rotas atlânticas da diáspora africana: da Baía do Benin ao Rio de Janeiro*, ed. Mariza de Carvalho Soares (Niterói: Editoria Universidade Federal Fluminense, 2007): 191–224.

Libby, Douglas Cole, and Clotilde Andrade Paiva. "Manumission Practices in a Late Eighteenth-Century Brazilian Slave Parish: São José d'El Rey in 1795," *Slavery & Abolition* 21, no. 1 (2000): 96–127.
Lima, Henrique Espada. "Freedom, Precariousness, and the Law: Freed Persons Contracting out Their Labour in Nineteenth-Century Brazil," *International Review of Social History* 54, no. 3 (2009): 391–416.
Lima, Henrique Espada, and Fabiane Popinigis. "Maids, Clerks, and the Shifting Landscape of Labor Relations in Rio de Janeiro, 1830s–1880s," *International Review of Social History* 62, no. S25 (2017): 45–73.
van der Linden, Marcel. *Transnational Labour History: Explorations* (London: Routledge, 2003).
van der Linden, Marcel. *Workers of the World: Essays Toward a Global Labor History* (Leiden: Brill, 2011).
Machado, Maria Helena P.T. "Corpo, gênero e identidade no limiar da abolição: a história de Benedicta Maria Albina da Ilha ou Ovídia, escrava (Sudeste, 1880)," *Afro-Ásia* 42 (2010): 157–93.
Machado, Maria Helena P.T., Luciana da Cruz Brito, Flávio dos Santos Gomes and Iamara da Silva Viana. *Ventres livres? Gênero, maternidade e legislação* (São Paulo: ed. UNESP, 2021).
Malavota, Claudia Mortari. *Os Homens Pretos do Desterro: um estudo sobre a Irmandade de Nossa Senhora do Rosário (1841–1860)* (Itajaí: Núcleo de Estudos Afro-Brasileiros (NEAB), Casa Aberta Editora, 2011).
Mamigonian, Beatriz. "Africanos em Santa Catarina: escravidão e identidade étnica (1750–1850)," in *Nas rotas do império: eixos mercantis, tráfico e relações sociais no mundo português*, ed. João Fragoso, Manolo Florentino, Antônio Carlos Jucá and Adriana Campos (Vitória: Editoria da Universidade Federal do Espírito Santo, 2006): 565–96.
Mamigonian, Beatriz, and Joseane Zimmerman, eds. *História Diversa: africanos e afrodescendentes na Ilha de Santa Catarina* (Florianópolis: Editoria de Universidade Federal de Santa Catarina, 2013).
Mattos, Hebe. "Raça e cidadania no crepúsculo da modernidade escravista no Brasil," in *O Brasil imperial*, vol. 3, ed. Keila Grinberg and Ricardo Salles (Rio de Janeiro: Civilização Brasileira, 2009): 15–39.
Martins, Valter. *Mercados urbanos, transformações na cidade: abastecimento e cotidiano em Campinas, 1859–1908* (São Paulo: Editora Unicamp, 2010).
Pantoja, Selma. "Women's work in the fairs and markets of Luanda," in *Woman in the Making of the Atlantic World: The Theatre of Shadows*, ed. Clara Sarmento (Newcastle: Cambridge Scholars Publishing, 2008): 45–67.
Popinigis, Fabiane. "Aos pés dos pretos e pretas quitandeiras: experiências de trabalho e estratégias de vida em torno do primeiro mercado público de desterro – 1840–1890," *Afro-Ásia* 46 (2012): 193–226.
Popinigis, Fabiane, and Paulo Terra. "Diálogos entre a historiografia do trabalho e da escravidão no Brasil," in *Trabajos y Trabajadores en América Latina (Siglos XVI–XXI)*, ed. Rossana Barragán Romano, Amaru Villanueva Rance and Cristina Machicado Murillo (La Paz: Vicepresidencia del Estado Plurinacional de Bolivia; Centro de Investigaciones Sociales [CIS], 2019): 33–54.
Reis, João José. *Slave Rebellion in Brazil: The Muslim Uprising of 1835 in Bahia*, trans. Arthur Barkel (Baltimore: Johns Hopkins University Press, 1993) [translated from the 1986 edition].
Reis, João José, and Márcia Gabriela D. de Aguiar. "'Carne sem osso e farinha sem caroço': o motim de 1858 contra a carestia da Bahia," *Revista de História* 135 (1996): 135–59.
Reis, João José. "'The Revolution of the Ganhadores': Urban Labour, Ethnicity and the African Strike of 1857 in Bahia, Brazil," *Journal of Latin American Studies* 29, no. 2 (1997): 355–93.
Reis, João José. *Rebelião escrava no Brasil: a história do Levante dos Malês de 1835* (São Paulo, Companhia das Letras, 2003).
Sbravati, Daniela. "Mulheres de (In)Certa Condição," *Revista Mundos do Trabalho* 1, no. 2 (2009): 13–40.
Schettini, Cristiana, and Fabiane Popinigis. "O lugar do trabalho: história social e perspectiva de gênero no Brasil," in *Recortes do Feminino*, ed. Andrea Maia (Rio de Janeiro: Telha, 2021): 265–86.
Silva, Maciel Henrique. *Pretas de honra: vida e trabalho de domésticas e vendedoras no Recife do século XIX (1840–1870)* (Recife: Editoria de Universidade Federal de Pernambuco; Salvador: Editoria de Universidade Federal da Bahia, 2011).
Slenes, Robert Wayne Andrew. "A 'Great Arch' Descending: Manumission Rates, Subaltern Social Mobility and Enslaved, Freeborn and Freed Black Identities in Southeastern Brazil, 1791–1888," in *New*

Approaches to Resistance in Brazil and Mexico, ed. John Gledson and Patience A. Schell (Durham, NC: Duke University Press, 2012): 100–18.

Soares, Cecília Moreira. "As Ganhadeiras: Mulher e Resistência Negra em Salvador no Século XIX," *Afro-Ásia* 17 (1996): 57–71.

de Souza, Flavia Fernandes. "Trabalho doméstico: considerações sobre um tema recente de estudos na História do Social do Trabalho no Brasil," *Revista Mundos do Trabalho* 7, no. 13 (2016): 275–96.

Stanley, Amy Dru. "Histories of Capitalism and Sex Difference," *Journal of the Early Republic* 36, no. 2 (2016): 343–50.

Telles, Lorena Féres da Silva. *Libertas entre sobrados: mulheres negras e trabalho doméstico em São Paulo (1880–1920)* (São Paulo: Alameda, 2013).

Terra, Paulo Cruz, Marcelo de Souza Magalhães and Martha Abreu, eds. *Os poderes municipais e a cidade: Império e República* (Rio de Janeiro: Mauad X, 2019).

Velázquez Gutiérrez, María Elisa, and Carolina González Undurraga. *Mujeres africanas y afrodescendientes: experiencias de esclavitud y libertad en América Latina y Africa Siglos XVI al XIX* (México: Secretaría de Cultura, Instituto Nacional de Antropología e História, 2016).

Lilia Moritz Schwarcz

Images of Slavery: The Other of the Other (the Sixteenth to the Nineteenth Centuries)

We are the other's other.
José Saramago in *All the Names*

As is widely known, Brazil was the last Western nation to abolish slavery, doing so only in 1888, three years after Cuba and thirteen after the US, and then only under intense internal and external pressure. It was also the nation that imported the highest number of Africans, an estimated 45% of all those forcibly removed from the African continent.[1] What's more, the slavery system spread countrywide, north to south, and spanned the entire range of manual labor. The Jesuit Antonil described the slaves as "the country's hands and feet,"[2] and that was no exaggeration. They worked in the streets, in homes, on the fields, in the manors and the mines, on cattle ranches, in slaughterhouses, on rice paddies, cotton fields and cane, sugar and coffee plantations, and in every other post or service that required constant, daily toil. The system's longevity alone would be enough to explain the "excess" of slavery-related iconography in Brazilian archives, but there were other elements involved, too. Exotic and tropical, the Portuguese colony in the Americas, which would obtain its independence only in 1822 whilst retaining a Portuguese emperor as head of state, was visited by an untold number of wayfarers, illustrators, naturalists, and adventurers, who, paradoxically, left behind a wealth of idyllic, pacific images of the country. However, it was a land that could not claim to be entirely or only agreeable. If its nature was ripe for Edenization, its labor regime, in which one human being could own another, could be considered nothing other than violent and cruel. Furthermore, as the Portuguese colonizers did not have any tradition in genre, landscape, or even historical painting, but devoted their artistic energies solely to religious themes and scenes,[3] the works produced in and about Brazil – the colony and, later, the empire – were largely by travelers (doubly foreign, insofar as they had neither a vested nor prolonged interest in Portuguese America) from France, the Netherlands,

1 See the Website of "Slave Voyages": http://www.slavevoyages.org [accessed 27.08.2022].

2 André João Antonil, *Cultura e opulência do Brasil por suas drogas e minas* (Lisbon: n.p., 1711).

3 It should be noted that Portugal lacked a tradition in painterly education. There were academies in the colony and at home, but none devoted to painting, which was considered of lesser importance, if not a dishonorable waste of time. In Lisbon, there was no art-training infrastructure to speak of, save for schools set up in monasteries and *aulas régias*, and all art was concentrated in the royal palaces and churches. Worse still, even these initiatives were in frank decline in the early nineteenth century. The "Sketching Course," founded at Mafra monastery by Johann Ludwig in the first half of the eighteenth century, had disappeared, while the *aulas regias* – drawing, civil architecture, sculpture and engraving – introduced in the latter half of the 1900s, headed in the same direction. Adolfo Morales de Los Rios, *O ensino artístico* (Rio de Janeiro: Imprensa Nacional, 1942): 109.

https://doi.org/10.1515/9783111026527-011

Britain, Italy, or Spain. As such, most of this iconography was produced by white Europeans just passing through, who had a clearly colonial perspective. They were genuine "outsiders," and their vantage point was an "other's view of the other": that of European rovers in an exotic tropical land mainly inhabited by enslaved Africans. In their baggage they brought the conceptions and models into which they had been socialized, artistically and philosophically, in their home nations. Proof of this is that certain images – highlighting the picturesque landscapes of the colonies – were stubbornly repeated in the most varied colonies across the whole Afro-Atlantic domain. In Brazil, as in Cuba, Jamaica, Haiti, and the southern United States, certain stock scenes were hammered into a visual convention. First of all, they revealed a similar logic, as they were produced to illustrate a literary genre known at the time as "Picturesque Travel," which accentuated the bucolic, pleasant aspects of these lushly natural vistas, so very different to their European homelands. They tended, therefore, to gloss over the tensions and conflicts of mutinying, runaway slaves forming *quilombos* (maroon colonies) on the back of collective or individual break-outs and insurrections.[4] Many of these travelers continued on their way into Spanish, English, or French colonies, and rolled out the same tropes wherever they went. This "package" did include slavery, though it was usually depicted in an orderly form, airbrushed of all violence. The transport scenes of masters and their ladies being carried around on sedan chairs, protected from the sun's rays and prying eyes behind dainty curtains, became famous not only in Brazil, but in Spanish America, too. Other popular images were those of slaves dressed in rags, smoking long pipes; plantation scenes in which the slaves are seen working the fields in compositionally pleasing arrangements; slave women peddling their wares in the streets; and men struggling under unwieldy burdens. In Brazil, there was a certain visual convention, with the images circulating most widely and growing in popularity, causing a natural selection of motifs, as if no singularity were allowed to exist in these "eternally tropical" lands. Hardly coincidentally, most of these engravings, oil paintings, prints, and, later, photographs, were extolling in tone. Their placid, calm, and "picturesque" scenes were, by definition, tailor-made to please a European clientele.

4 The picturesque – a group of popular theories, ideas, and conventions that sprang up around the practice of appreciating landscapes – became a fad in the late eighteenth and early nineteenth centuries. It was an aesthetic category considered opposite to the concepts of the sublime and the beautiful, featuring quick-fire, imprecise renderings. The term was an Anglicism of the French *pittoresque* and the Italian *pittoresco* and, over time, came to apply to any pleasing themes in painting in general, not only landscape painting. On this, see Stephen Copley and Peter Garside, ed., *The Politics of the Picturesque: Literature, Landscape and Aesthetic since 1770* (Cambridge: Cambridge University Press, 1994): 1–5.

Fig. 1: Black Mina, age 26. 1866. Cuba.

1 When Slavery is an Aesthetic Form: Engravings and Drawings

Artists like Frans Post, Jean-Baptiste Debret, Rugendas, Elder, Chamberlain, Maria Graham, and many others never intended to capture the "true" reality of what they were depicting. They had their own aims and reasons for being in a colony like Brazil. One of the most recurrent approaches was to present these lands as remote and isolated, yet as the cradle of "new civilizations." As the intention was to cater to a market that was avid for this kind of image, avoiding the everyday violence that pervaded slavery was considered good form. We shall stick to two of the painters whose work most widely illustrates books and reports on Brazil to this very day: Debret and Rugendas. Both had such an influence on the local imaginary that their work seems to serve as a "visual benchmark" for the slavery period, without venturing into the specificities of its context or authorship. Jean-Baptiste Debret hailed from artistic families on both sides. He was first cousin to José Bouchet (the French master in the Rococo style that was so popular at court at the time), but he was also related to the famous Jacques-Louis David, the painter of the French Revolution. Debret was so close to

Fig. 2: Um cozinheiro de tropeiros (Muleteer cook). Brazil. Biblioteca Nacional [and Brasiliana Fotográfica].

David that he even worked for a time in his studio, first as an apprentice and later as a master. However, in 1815, after the ouster of Napoleon and David's exile from France, Debret found himself unemployed and mourning a son killed in the war. And so, he decided to try his luck in the Portuguese colony, the only one in the Americas to have a monarch.[5] He also planned to land himself a place at the French Academy of the Fine Arts, the doors to which his "Picturesque and Historical Voyage to Brazil" would eventually open for him. The artist experimented with watercolors and used the technique to render a colony and later a nation that seemed to him so full of promise, where the prevailing order and hierarchy kept its agrarian elite and "their

5 At this time, the monarch, João VI, was living in Brazil, having fled the Napoleonic invasion of Portugal. In 1815, after the Congress of Vienna, the prince not only transformed the colony into the United Kingdom of Brazil and the Algarve, but declared an end to the war with France. This measure triggered an influx of French craftsmen, industrialists, and painters into Brazil. Debret arrived at precisely this time.

slaves" in clearly demarked camps. True to David's academic technique, he drew Africans with perfect bodies and lustrous skin, just right for the Edenic tropics that dwelled in the imaginations of the artist and his European clientele. However, as the critic Rodrigo Naves points out, the "form was difficult":[6] finding moral and ethical virtues in this land of forced labor was no easy task. Only two of Debret's drawings were censored by the IHGB (Brazilian Historical and Geographical Institute): in one of these, in the foreground, the artist depicted a bound slave being flogged by a driver, whilst, in the background, as if to reinforce the normalcy of such punishments, another slave is being whipped at a tree.

Fig. 3: Jean-Baptiste Debret, *Feitor castigando negro (Driver flogging a slave)*. Watercolor on paper, 1835. Engraving published in the book *Viagem pitoresca através do Brasil*. Fundação Biblioteca Nacional Collection, RJ.

These few exceptions aside, Debret's Africans generally just go about doing what the slave system expected of them. Ostensibly descriptive, the French artist's drawings seem to "calm" the environment down a notch by presenting an orderly world with a clear hierarchy. The Bavarian Johann Moritz Maurício Rugendas was also born into a family of artists. After the Napoleonic wars he, too, temporarily left his country to

6 Rodrigo Naves, *A forma difícil* (São Paulo: Ática, 1996). See also Valéria Lima, *Uma viagem com Debret* (Rio de Janeiro: Zahar, 2006) and Valéria Lima, *Debret, historiador e pintor* (Campinas: Unicamp, 2005); Lilia Schwarcz, *O sol do Brasil* (São Paulo: Companhia das Letras, 2008).

join the mission of Baron Georg Heinrich von Langsdorff as a naturalist and painter/draughtsman. He spent only three years in Brazil, but during that time he produced a book that is largely responsible for the image Brazilians have today of what the country and slavery were like in the early nineteenth century. Slave quarters, capoeira dancers, festivities, drum rings, stately manors, slave traffickers, and slave ships all make Rugendas' oeuvre a more "scientific" and purportedly exempt depiction. Exempt they certainly weren't, and of particular note are the perspectives the naturalist allowed to seep out of the background, minor details that reveal a whole world of associations. For example, it is not unusual in these pictures to see a master or one of his drivers ogling the slave women, but while the African men nearby pretend not to be looking, you can clearly read the scorn and revolt on their faces. So, besides the opulent bounty of Brazil's nature, one can also glean the violence irrupting everywhere, even in the most humdrum situations, and which was obviously not lost on the Bavarian artist.[7]

Fig. 4: J.M. Rugendas. *Negros novos*. C.1835, watercolor. Itaú Cultural collection.

7 For a more detailed analysis of Rugendas' works, see the excellent article by Robert W. Slenes, "As provações de um Abraão africano: a nascente nação brasileira na *Viagem Alegórica* de Johann Moritz Rugendas," *Revista de História da arte e arqueologia* 2 (1995/96): 271–94.

Tension is often rife in Rugendas' paintings, and particularly so in the piece *Negros novos* (New Blacks), which depicts a batch of newly arrived slaves. There is no escaping the master's lascivious eyeballing of the bare-chested woman, who has her back turned to him. Beside her stands her son or daughter, displaying concern and discomfort, as do the three slave men depicted nearby. The man furthest on the left stares down at the ground, but his eyes betray his rage. The same holds for the captive in the bottom right, who does his best to look away, though he cannot hide his disgust. Lastly, the slave sitting just behind him sucks on a stick of cane, as if unaware of what's going on. The painting is almost a graphic novel take on the violence perpetrated daily in the bedchamber, where the white master would rape the African women, especially the "new arrivals" that pleased him the most. Understanding the conventions in which these artists were inserted and the aims they had – one was in Brazil in search of a post as court painter while the other was working as a naturalist draughtsman – helps debunk the purported "objectivity" of the engravings they produced, insofar as these evinced interests and even "patterns of intention," to use Baxandall's term.[8] What we are faced with here is a politics that, through images, justifies, at a push, the very "need for domination" over peoples with customs considered so totally different. There was, therefore, an abyss between "nature," always Edenized, and the "natives," the future of whom was still impossible to foretell. At a time when there was no concept of authorship as such,[9] these images circulated widely and were reproduced by countless hands, who repeated or even copied compositions and situations, adapting them to new contexts. Similar depictions can be found in the Caribbean in general and in works portraying plantation slavery in the southern USA and Brazil. By these means, such situations became templates for demonstrating hierarchy and laid down "colored" stereotypes: the street-hawking black woman, the muscular negro, the urban slave scurrying after his master, the sensual house slave, the well-dressed errand boy, the chain gang toiling on the fields. Whether in Brazil, Puerto Rico, Antigua, Barbados, Cuba, or Jamaica, these engravings composed hierarchized, similar worlds. They were all part and parcel of a reality being painted into posterity as a sort of "colonial model" that could be adapted to anywhere with urban or rural slavery.

This was also a world that disciplined and punished:[10] in and through the images, messages of order and control circulated. Flanders masks, whips, shackles, pronged collars, the pillory as a statement of power, and the tree trunk as a symbol of domination were forms of knowledge that likewise traveled throughout this Afro-Atlantic diaspora, revealing not only how hierarchy was installed, but how it was maintained.

---

8 Michael Baxandall, *Patterns of Intention* (New Haven: Yale University Press, 1985).

9 See Robert Darnton, *The Business of Enlightenment* (Boston: Harvard University Press, 1987).

10 This is a reference to the famous book by Michel Foucault, *Vigiar e punir* (Petrópolis: Vozes, 2009), the first chapter of which deals with the ways power is etched into the bodies of the condemned.

Fig. 5: Jean-Baptiste Debret. *Empregado do governo saindo a passeio* (Government official heading out for a stroll). Color print, 1835. Museu Castro Maya.

Fig. 6: *Cutting the sugar cane.* William Clark, 1833. Color print, 23.4 x 34.4 cm. John Carter Brown Library.

Fig. 7: *Vue de l'etablissement des missions a St Johns dans l'isle d'Antigoa aux Indes occidentales* (View of the St. John's mission settlement on the Isle of Antigua in the West Indies). Johann Heinrich Stobwasser, c. 1830. Aquatint engraving, 24.9 x 33 cm. John Carter Brown Library.

Fig. 8: *Vue de Gracebay dans l'isle d'Antigoa* (View of Gracebay on the Isle of Antigua). Johann Heinrich Stobwasser, c. 1830. Aquatint engraving, 25.5 x 33.8 cm. John Carter Brown Library.

Fig. 9: *Vue de Gracehill dans l'isle d'Antigoa aux Indes occidentales* (View of Gracehill on the Isle of Antigua in the West Indies). Johann Heinrich Stobwasser, c.1830. Aquatint engraving, 25 x 35.2 cm. John Carter Brown Library.

Fig. 10: *Slaves in Barbadoes*. Ralph Stennet, 1820. Lithographic print, 10.3 x 16.8 cm. John Carter Brown Library.

Fig. 11: *Jamaican negroes cutting cane in their work dresses*. Strand T. Cadell, 1825. Color print, 11.8 x 19.7 cm. John Carter Brown Library.

In societies that adopted the techniques of showcasing order and maintaining control, visuality played a pivotal role. Didactically, these images were sold and distributed so widely they became part of a picturesque model that exalted the exuberant beauty of nature, but also disclosed the promise of punishment. In the picture by Debret above, the perfection of the black body does not exclude a demonstration of corporal punishment even during the working day. It's all there, in the same figure, with no name, origin, or context. What we see is a synthetic, almost "didactic" form of delimiting the space of power in the mistreated body itself. This is the "spectacle of slavery" and the exemplarity of the African captive's naturalization. In this case, the slave's own face is turned against him as the instrument of punishment and upholder of the (good) order.

2 Photographing the Invisible

In this veritable politics of visibility, there is a paradox worthy of note, at least in the Brazilian case. If the country took so long to abolish slavery, it was much sprightlier when introducing a technique that promised modernity and speed: photography. In 1834, Hercule Florence conducted his first photographic experiments; on December 28,

Fig. 12: *A Spanish planter of Puerto Rico*. Ralph Stennet, 1820. Print, 16.7 x 10 cm. John Carter Brown Library.

1839, an ad in the *Jornal do Commercio* announced the arrival of the daguerrotype, promising the myriad of the world duplicated in a matter of minutes:

> One would have to see it with one's own eyes to believe the rapidity and the result of the operation. In less than nine minutes [. . .] all those objects will be found reproduced in all their minutiae with the most perfect fidelity and precision, [so] that there is no doubting the thing was made by nature's own hand, and almost without the artist's intervention at all.[11]

11 See Boris Kossoy, *Hercule Florence, a Descoberta Isolada da Fotografia no Brasil*, 3rd ed. (São Paulo: Eitoria da Universidade de São Paulo, 2006); Boris Kossoy, *Origens e Expansão da Fotografia no Brasil: Século XIX* (Rio de Janeiro: Edição Funarte, 1991); Boris Kossoy, *Fotografia e História* (São Paulo: Ática, 1999).

Fig. 13: *The Old Plantation*, painted in the late eighteenth century by John Rose, courtesy of the Colonial Williamsburg Foundation.

Fig. 14: Family of negro slaves from Loango, 1792, plate 69 from Narrative of a Five-Year Expedition against the Revolted Negroes of Surinam, engraved by William Blake (1757–1827), pub. 1806.

Fig. 15: *The mode of training blood hounds in St Domingo, and of exercising them by chasseurs*. Marcus Rainsford, 1805. Engraving, 21.1 x 18.1 cm. John Carter Brown Library.

In the paper's printed photography, as if by magic, there was the royal palace, with the troop out front and the spire of the imperial chapel to the left; in the middle, there was bell tower of the Third Order of Monte Carmo; further to the right, Hotel de France. And it was in this manner – as a copy of the real – that photography was, at first, incorporated into historical research and documents. It was here to adorn,

Fig. 16: *Repression contre lés esclaves* (Slave beatings). Surinam, Guyana, 1772.

Fig. 17: Jean-Baptiste Debret. *Negros acorrentados levando para a cadeia o jantar que foram buscar no Hospital da Misericórdia* (Chained blacks carrying home the dinner fetched at the Hospital da Misericórdia), c. 1820–30. Watercolor on paper,14.5 x 22.2 cm. Museu Castro Maya, Rio de Janeiro.

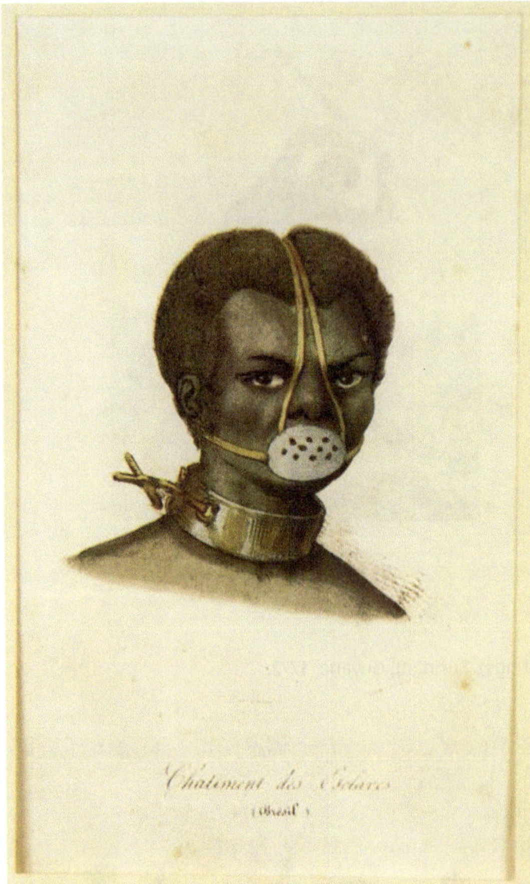

Fig. 18: Jacques Arago, *Castigo de escravos*. FBN.

sometimes to corroborate, other times to simply justify previously established theories. Over time, photographs would become a sign of status, illustrating the news, filling up photo albums. The supposition was that photography *reflected* the context; it was a product of its time, not a producer. Those who believed this were very much mistaken. Photography, as Susan Sontag wrote, "was born to lie," and the more widespread it became, the more truth it told; or rather, the more it became reality.[12] And in this exotic terrain – a tropical, slavocratic monarchy with elites avid for this kind of status symbol – professional photographers multiplied, and most of them were foreigners. Starting with Florence and followed by Gilberto Ferrez, Gainsly, August Stahl, Victor Frond, Militão, Cristiano Jr., Augusto Riedel, and others, this new technology won over

12 Susan Sontag, *Sobre a fotografia* (São Paulo: Companhia das Letras, 2000).

Fig. 19: Jean-Baptiste Debret. *Máscara que se usa nos negros que tem o hábito de comer terra* (Mask used on blacks who have the habit of eating dirt). c.1820–1830. Watercolor, 18.7 x 12.5 cm. Museu Castro Maya Collection – IBRAM/MINC.

Brazil and took a firm hold.[13] Emperor D. Pedro II, for example, liked to see himself and be seen as the world's first emperor photographer; among the palace's many expenses were fees for the private tutor hired to teach Princess Isabel how to take her first pictures.[14] As the technique became more refined and affordable, the imperial nobility began to have fun with the novelty, which promised to eternize families and individuals with a simple "poof." Photography developed so swiftly that it was soon not only fixing

13 For an excellent perspective on imperial photographers, see Ana Maria Mauad, *Poses e flagrantes – Ensaios sobre história e fotografia* (Niteroi: Eduff, 2008). For a first-rate analysis of Brazilian photographers during the empire, see Natália Brizuela, *Fotografia e Império: paisagens para um Brasil moderno* (São Paulo: Companhia das Letras, 2012).

14 Lilia Schwarcz, *The Emperor's Beard* (New York: Hill and Wang, 2003).

images, but duplicating and triplicating them, turning them into postcards and a whole variety of formats that could finally offer and deliver visual posterity. One way or another, because of the combination of these two factors – Brazil being the last country to abolish slavery and having taken so quickly to the technique of photography – the nation ended up amassing a large archive of photographs of slavery, perhaps the largest among nations with a slave-owning past. Sometimes slaves were photographed by surprise, as they walked in the streets. On other occasions, they were arranged, like part of the landscape. In some cases, they posed for the camera at photographic studios, where they were cast to type, while in others they served as mere props to aggrandize their masters or mistresses. Just like the traveling artists and naturalists, foreign photographers created certain visual conventions that were in vogue throughout the Americas and the Caribbean. The head of the family, standing proud and surrounded by his offspring, was the only one who bore a name and surname. The well-dressed ladies, their hands and faces the only skin shown, were another symbol and extension of their husbands' power, as were the groomed, well-behaved children, with their starkly delimited genders: boys in sailor tunics and Bermuda shorts, the girls sporting elaborate plaits and ribbons in their hair. The setting was also carefully chosen so as to best convey the image of the "well-structured family." The walls they posed before were often adorned with tropical or Alpine landscapes, fancy drapery, or a classical column. Some professional photographers moved to Brazil and set up studios – many with royal support. Others operated on an itinerant basis, lugging their equipment about on their backs, scouting for just the right vista or street scene. In a nation based on forced labor, it was hardly surprising that the slave cut "an insistent figure." They are a constant, if varied, presence in photographs from the period: sometimes they are a background blur, other times the main subject. Many appear embarrassed or discomfited, but some are proud and dignified. Sometimes the sitters are wearing ill-fitting clothes clearly borrowed for the occasion. In others, they are portrayed in the tribal dress of their home nations or alongside the tools of their trades: hoes, shoeshiner's boxes, and other paraphernalia that signaled their station. The hierarchy was reinforced through photography: masters in their top hats and boots; ladies in their jewelry and tailored dresses. The slaves, on the other hand, are seen barefoot, and, almost always, with the exception of house slaves, wearing fewer clothes. Their bodies, invariably, wear the stoop of "submission." The techniques of the body and body language that set the mold for visual tropes, showed where each stood in this rigidly stratified society.[15] If Brazil clearly had a superior quantity and quality of this kind of photography, it is because photographers moved within the complex world of the Afro-Atlantic slave trade. Many professional photographers made a name for themselves recreating the work environments of slaves at their ateliers.

15 On techniques of the body, see the classic essay by Marcel Mauss, "As técnicas do corpo," in *Sociologia e Antropologia* (São Paulo: Casac Naify, 2003): 399–422. On the ways bodies remember, cf. Didier Fassin, *La force de l'ordre: Une anthropologie de la police des quartiers* (Paris: Seuil, 2011).

The pictures were produced for sale domestically, but also abroad. One of the best-known purveyors of this line of photography was Cristiano Junior, who, in the artificial setting of his studio, erected neutral backdrops, stripped of every hint of violence, where he presented slaves "in action," carrying things, selling vegetables, cooking, fighting, chatting. The picture portraits were shot at his studio and printed in standard *carte-de-visite* format, then sold in sets to foreigners – as an 1865 AD in the *Jornal do Commercio* shows – under such titles as "Black types collection." These *carte-de-visite* sets depicting slaves engaged in various trades and forms of labor were sold directly from Cristiano

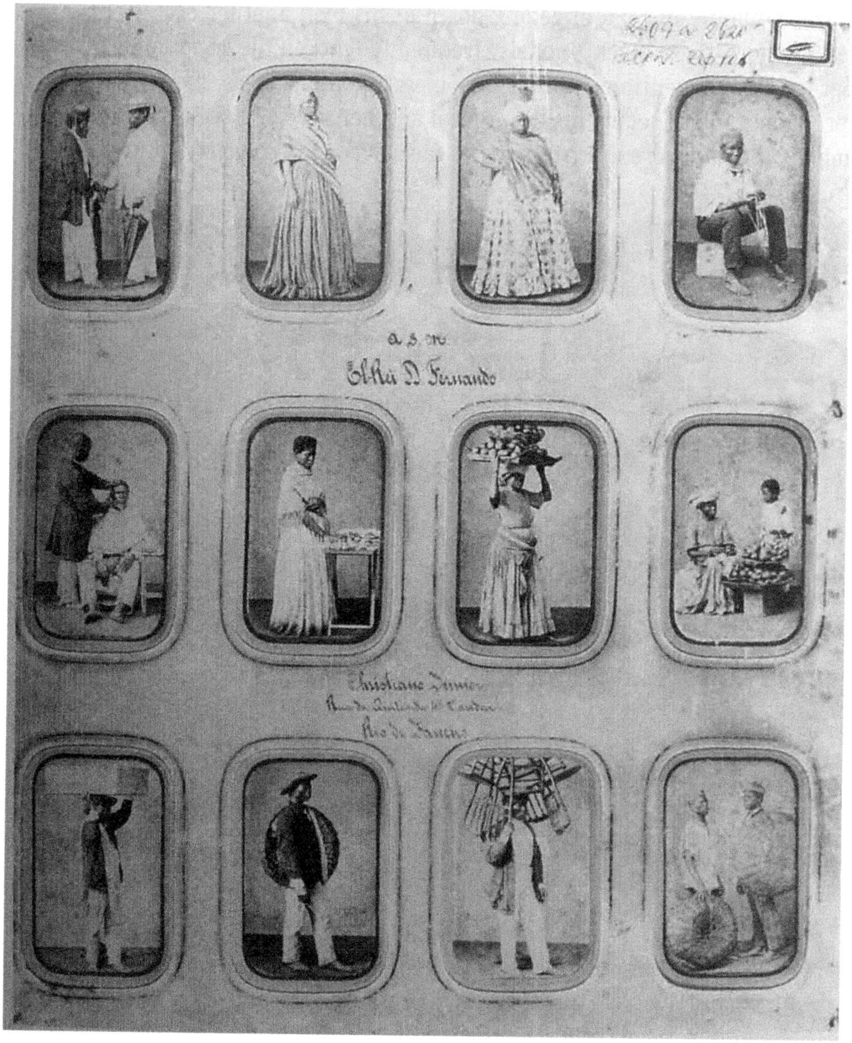

Fig. 20: Christiano Jr. *Conjunto representando negros em seus diversos ofícios* (Picture set depicting negroes at their various trades). Rio de Janeiro, 1865. Albúmen. Acervo Museu Histórico Nacional.

Jr.'s studio or through the house Leuzinger, the most famous intermediary in the field. The collections were often branded abroad as "memories of Brazil," satisfying Old World curiosity about these distant lands, fast becoming the "other" of the "other," a colonial world wholly and necessarily distinct from the European.

But there's a lot more we can see in these pictures. First off, the discomfort and self-consciousness of the slaves submitted to these situations is palpable. In fact, this perhaps one of the standout characteristics of photography compared to painting. In photographs, the artist has less control over the attitudes the "models" exude: one refuses to take off his hat and looks straight into the camera instead of ignoring it, while another stares defiantly instead of gazing down at his feet; another crosses his arms and winces. In short, these black "models" frequently ignored the script and thwarted the photographer's conventions with unexpected reactions. Here, we see body language, expressions, and deportments that reveal another type of slave agency: their refusal to embody the passive, exotic stereotypes the slave-owning society cast for them.

Fig. 21: Militão Augusto de Azevedo. *Senhor e seus escravos* (Master and his slaves). São Paulo, s.d., Albúmen, 6.3 x 8.3 cm. Photographic proof print album o n.° 6, photo 10.165. Acervo Museu Paulista.

There are other details, too, which, perhaps because they are not part of professional portfolios, reveal forms of identity that seem truer to internal languages. Pictures showing slaves with distinctive scarifications on their faces and backs are often found among the photographs taken in Brazil, the Caribbean, South America, and the southern states of the USA. These scars, which clearly fascinated photographers, were, in truth, the ethnic markings of the many Africas that made up the Afro-Atlantic diaspora.

Fig. 22: Isla de Pinos, Cuba c. 1830 (Llevat family and their slaves), http://familiallevat.com/isla-de-pinos-en-cuba-en-1900/ [accessed 23.09.2022].

Portraits of women wrapped in kangas from the West African coast often relegate traditional dress to a mere generic detail in the titles, but they still serve as records of belonging. These were no ordinary "wraps" or fabrics, but expressions of identity and sociability.

Fig. 23: Augusto Stahl. *Escrava envolta em panos* (Slave wrapped in cloth). Rio de Janeiro, c.1865. Albúmen, 15.3 x 12 cm. Acervo Instituto Moreira Salles.

But there is another way of capturing "slave attitudes," and that's by looking at the details, through the chinks these photographs left disclosed. When enlarged, many of these pictures reveal a world of otherwise imperceptible behaviors which the photographer had certainly not intended. In photos taken of slaves working the plantations, the idea was basically to exalt the order and diligence with which they went about their daily toil, but, when you blow these images up, not only does the staged artificiality of the composition come to the fore (far too symmetrically arranged to be true, and with the driver serving as director's assistant, "getting everyone in position"), but a whole world of reactions transpires, going from outright revolt to total embarrassment.

Fig. 24a: ale do Para. Slaves on a coffee-drying patio, Vale do Paraíba. c. 1882. Gilberto Ferrez collection/ Acervo Instituto Moreira Salles.[16]

Other slaves end up being caught in frame by accident, snapped standing on the streets, the sidewalks, the street corners. There they are, even though they aren't supposed to be. Another favorite in the photographic repertoire of slave-owning lands was the "black momma" series. Such portrayals were so frequent they formed a convention in their own right; a way of revealing "benign, maternal slavery." However, once again, when looked at up-close, these pictures reveal tangled tensions and contradictions: the borrowed clothes, the effort made to keep the kids from squirming

16 The cropping and enlarging of photos was done in conjunction with Sergio Burg and Maria Helena Machado for an exhibition and seminar called "Abolitions," held 2008.

Fig. 24b: Zoom of 24a.

Fig. 24c: Zoom of 24a.

(and ruining the picture), the nervous expressions of those forced to sit in the glare of the photographer's attention, but also that of the owner who commissioned the photo. These are just some of the discomforts the slaves were made to endure. There's little point in trying to gauge whether these relationships were based on affection or violence, because it is far more likely that they were based on affection *and* violence. Perhaps these black mothers, gently holding the offspring of their white masters, encapsulate a universe of contradictions that comprised the reality slavery created. Once again, anonymity discloses the politics of invisibility present in these images. These slaves are seldom, if ever, named. The fact is that in these photographs, the "black models" sometimes "let themselves be shown" and in other cases "made themselves be seen,"[17] seizing control of the situation and, as far as possible, their own image. If the photographer or master intended to exercise total control over the scene being staged, they had no way of preventing a slew of tensions from irrupting through the details of the finished product. Maurício Lissovsky wrote that photographs are like ghosts, they condense time in such a way that they are never truly present nor past; they linger somewhere between the living and the dead.[18] Exploiting the opportunities afforded by the photographic lens, the fleeting moment between the click and the captured image, slaves could (however briefly and slightly) express their revolt. Bound to the past just like ghosts, these images couldn't be more contemporary.

3 Images of Abolition as Examples of Reconciliation

It was only from the late 1850s that images began to appear connected with abolitionism. Even so, the vast majority of this work was still being produced by white Europeans and so tends to be self-referential. One of the most common tropes was the African demonstrating gratitude, as if freedom were a "gift" rather than a right and a victory. One thing stands out in these abolition-flavored images, and that's the total lack of agency attributed to Afro-descendants. Shackles being broken, kneeling slaves with arms raised, gushing with gratitude, all of this composes an iconography that keeps the ball in the white court and denies the blacks any active participation in their own emancipation. It would seem there formed a network of traveling artist abolitionists who always worked with the same stock visual elements that induced a univocal message: the victim status of the slaves and their due recognition for the gift

17 Sandra Sofia Machado Koutsoukos, "Fotografias com corpo e alma," *Afro-Ásia* 48 (2013): 439–46 and, by the same author, *Negros no estúdio do fotógrafo, segunda metade do século XIX* (Campinas: Edunica, 2010).

18 Maurício Lissovsky, "Dez proposições acerca do futuro da fotografia," *Facom. Revista da Faculdade de Comunicação e Marketing da FAAP* 23 (2011): 9.

received. A good example of this type of conception is found in the work of François-Auguste Biard.[19] Painter, draughtsman, and caricaturist, he was a Frenchman who made his debut at the Paris Salon of 1824.[20] In 1838 he traveled as official court painter for King Louis-Phillippe (1773–1850), a post he occupied until the fall of the monarchy in 1848. He was no stranger to the movements shaking Europe at that time and which, in France, would culminate in the deposition of the monarch. The artist became known for his historical paintings, travel pictures showing exotic locations,[21] and his works critical of slavery. This denunciation of bondage crept into Biard's repertoire with the painting *La traite des nègres*,[22] presented at the Paris Salon in 1835. In the scene, a slave market more closely resembles an exotic bazaar, given the orientalist treatment proffered to the figures, their garb, and behaviors.[23] In the center, a slave is seen lying on the ground, having his teeth checked by a prospective buyer. The woman to the left is having her arm cattle-branded, while, in the top left-hand corner, another slave is being flogged; a third, with a noose around his neck, looks resigned to impending death. A small child in the foreground is a lonely testament to the separation of mothers from their children. The white men in-scene are all armed, denoting the absolute coercion at play, further reinforced by the presence of four black men who seem to be negotiating the sale of some captives. From this painting on, Biard was identified as a painter engaged with the abolitionist cause.[24] However, if the theme was revolutionary, the overall impression these paintings convey is always one of conciliation, with the end of slavery presented as a "gift" from white men and women. A case in point is *Proclamation de la liberte des noirs aux colonies.*

In this painting, which became emblematic, the tone of harmonization is evident: the blacks are seen giving thanks for their liberty, holding aloft their broken shackles under the condescending gaze of the whites nearby. The image of the breaking of chains in such a respectful manner by the former slaves is telling, depicting abolition as orderly and trauma-free, with the liberated blacks still beholden to their old

---

19 The information about Biard is taken from an article I co-wrote with Lucia Stumpf, entitled "Os fugitivos que vêm do sul," forthcoming. On the author, see also Ana Lúcia Araujo, *Brazil through French Eyes* (New Mexico: University of New Mexico Press, 2015).

20 Karel David, *Dictionnaire des Artistes de Langue Française en Amérique du Nord, peintres, sculpteurs, dessinateurs* (Quebec: Presses de l'Université Laval, 1992).

21 In 1827, Biard embarked on his first voyage, a tour of the Mediterranean, with calls at Malta, Cyprus, Syria, and Egypt. In 1839, the painter joined a scientific expedition directed by Paul Gaimard to Spitzberg and Lapland, in the Arctic. In 1858, the artist set sail for Brazil, where he spent two years. On the return voyage, in 1860, Biard stopped off in the United States.

22 *La traite des nègres*, 1835. Oil on canvas, 162 x 228 cm. Wilbeforce House, Hull City Museums and Art Galleries, Kingston-upon-Hull.

23 Pedro de Andrade Alvim, "Le monde comme spetacle: l'ouvre du peintre François-Auguste Biard (1798–1882)" (PhD diss., University of Paris, 2001).

24 Cf. Ana Lúcia Araujo, *Brazil through French Eyes* (New Mexico: University of New Mexico Press, 2015); De Andrade Alvim, *Le monde comme spectacle.*

Fig. 25: Biard, 1849. Versailles Museum.

Fig. 26: *Scène d'ouverture d'une vente publique de nègres. Marchant de nègres et son maquignon.* Paul Harro Harring, 1840. India ink, watercolor, and gouache on paper. Instituto Moreira Salles.

Fig. 27: *Inspection de négresses nouvellement debarquées de l'Afrique. Homme d'affaires de Mrs Quickly. Les modernes Mr. Quickly et Dolly.* Paul Harro Harring, 1840. India ink, watercolor, and gouache on paper. Instituto Moreira Salles.

masters. This painting, or reproductions of it in whole or in part, did the rounds of the Afro-Atlantic circuit that visually united the various slave societies.[25]

Another painter who plied the African diaspora with abolitionist images was the Dane Harro Harring, who traveled widely to campaign against slavery. Didactic, as if intending to get a message across, the painter's first watercolor contrasts the Africans' despair with the blasé poise of the traders (Fig. 26). In the second picture (Fig. 27), Harring rails against the "notorious trade," as it was then called. A woman prods an African girl with her umbrella, as if to test the quality of the "merchandise," while, to the left, a prospective buyer examines another girl, who appears to shrink under his touch. The artist reveals the atrocities of the system through its own stereotypes. On the other hand, he calls attention to the Africans' passivity, and once again abolition is understood as a "white" endeavor. And that is true, insofar as the owners were, in the vast majority, white. But these paintings also underscore a process that bears a striking resemblance to the international abolitionist discourse, which generally denied the slaves any agency or reaction even in the emancipation process. Once again,

25 Paul Gilroy, *The Black Atlantic: Modernity and Double Consciousness* (London: Verso, 1987). Biard was also in Brazil in the 1850s. He traveled for a period of two years and stopped off at the United States on his way home.

we see the affirmation of a genuine visual politics that reproduced, recreated, and propagated the models of the day. Faced with the inevitable demise of the system, the model to be followed spoke of fidelity and continuity, not social convulsion.

4 Representing the "Other"

This body of images contains another subset of visual politics: the production of anonymity and invisibility. In the vast majority of cases, we do not know (because we are not told) who these "models" are. They are described (merely) as "slaves" at work. Photographs of wet nurses almost always give the names of the suckling masters on the slave women's laps or pinned to their shoulders so as not to squirm and blur the image at the last moment. But we are almost never given the identities of the women themselves. The same occurs in scientific illustrations, in which individuals were photographed exclusively in the interests of science.[26] Frontal or profile photos of naked Africans purport to represent evolutionary stages, offering nothing in terms of individuality: the subjects are scientific types, nothing more.

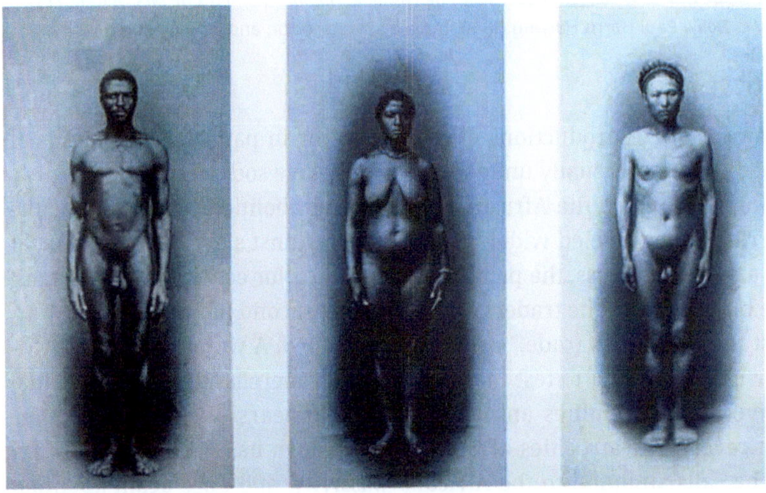

Fig. 28: Augusto Stahl. *Estudo antropológico* (Anthropological study). Rio de Janeiro, c.1865. Albúmen, 21 x 28 cm. Peabody College collection, Harvard.

26 Cf. Camillia Cowling, *Conceiving Freedom. Women of Color, Gender and Abolition of Slavery in Havana and Rio de Janeiro* (Chapel Hill: University of North Carolina Press, 2013); Maria Helena Machado, "Entre dois Beneditos: Histórias de Amas de Leite no ocaso da escravidão," in *Mulheres negras no Brasil escravista e do pós-emancipação*, ed. Giovanna Xavier, Juliana Barreto Farias and Flavio Gomes (São Paulo: Selo Negro, 2012): 199–213.

The same occurs in representations of work. In this case, the captives are there to illustrate the functions they fulfilled on a daily basis. No names or specificities are given. This ambiguity of looking at but looking through, identifying but never naming, of coining or constructing "types," was all part of the well-assembled architecture that structured the body of photographic work that circulated in the Afro-Atlantic world. They became so common and widespread that they dispensed entirely with context, locality, and, especially, authorship. In Brazil, for example, even today images that really only make sense in Rio de Janeiro, in part in Pernambuco and Bahia, and, at a push, in São Paulo, are laid out indiscriminately in history books, especially those of a didactic nature, as if they applied to the country as a whole, without distinction. On the other hand, it's interesting to note how, even in more recent institutions, such as the National Museum of Afro-American History and Culture in Washington, engravings produced in Brazil are shown with no caption, date, or author at all, as if they pertain to some "stock imagery of slavery," with no specific time, geography, or place. Not that this iconography is exactly "Brazilian," as it was largely produced by foreigners just passing through. But to use these pictures without due identification transforms them into "universal" representations of a wider Afro-Atlantic reality. It also means depoliticizing them, turning them into data and evidence-exhibits on a given period without questioning the reasons and schemas that lie behind them. Visual representations have the capacity not only to copy reality, but also to produce it. Put another way, they are not mere mirrors held up to the everyday world that simply presents what was seen; every artist fills his or her work with imagination, intention, and craft. Especially when it comes to representing "others" so "exceptionally other," the pictures end up mixing ethnography with heady doses of emotion, a strong injection of feeling, anxiety, and even fear. Taken as a body of work, and with reference to their reiteration of themes and a given visual logic, this iconography conforms to a "politics of visual representation" and the creation of "otherness."[27] They also conform to perceptions capable of producing and rooting racial stereotypes. Fleshy lips, stark colors, toned bodies, flaring nostrils, crispy hair, all of this swirled around this diasporic circuit whose largely European artists had the power to pin down external features and make them seem like mere derivations from an internal (because biological) structure. Hardly coincidentally, in the late nineteenth century, racial determinism came to the fore, arguing for the existence of rigid biological differences that spawned degeneration when mixed.[28]

---

27 Cf. Stuart Hall, "The Spectacle of the Other," in *Representation: Cultural Representations and Signifying Practices*, ed. Stuart Hall (London: Sage/The Open University, 1997): 223–90.

28 I dealt with this theme in the book Lilia Schwarcz, *The Spectacle of the Races* (New York: Hill and Wang, 1999).

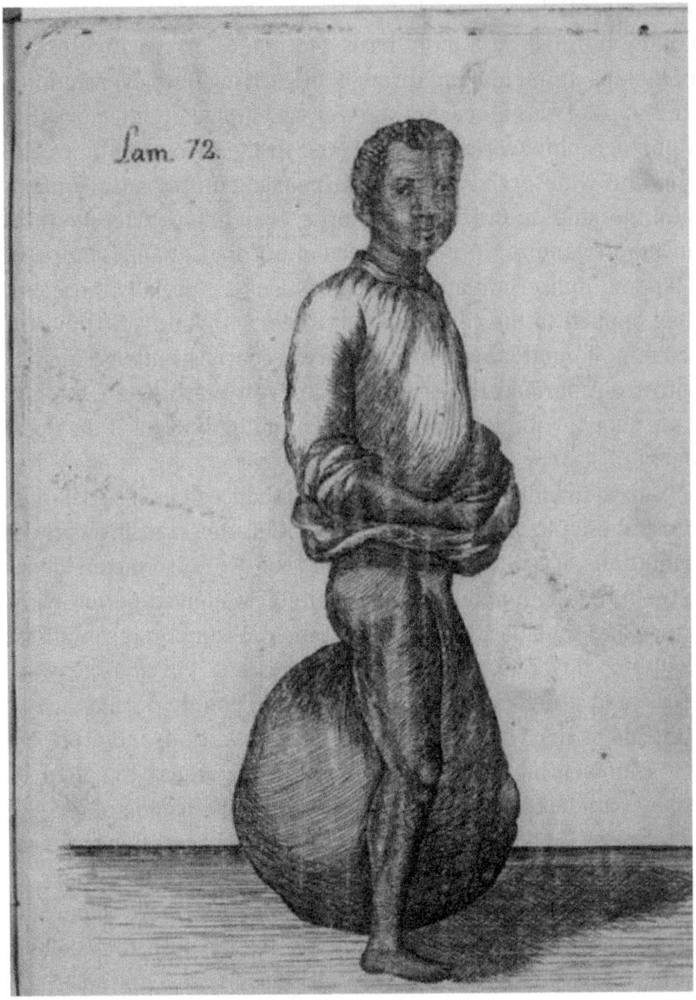

Fig. 29: Negro hernia disforme. Antonio Parra, 1798. Gravura, 17.2 x 13.2. John Carter Brown Library.

Once again, and with the blessing of science, diverse groups were reduced to blocks, this time biological blocks. So, rather than describe the various African nations that comprised this modern diaspora or introduce their different histories – as complex as they were hybrid – the approach taken was always to annul and deny all plurality. Terms like "black" in the US and "negro" in Brazil now served as umbrella terms that simply did not exist in Africa, where there were countless tribal realities. These descriptors ended up becoming concepts that only functioned in relation, never in isolation. They corresponded to articulated responses – counterpositions, basically – that argued blankly that these people are *not* white. As such, theirs were not pure "colors," but rather, first and foremost, metaphors that indicated "lack": of origin, of agency, of identity.[29] On the other hand, the immense set of visual representations of the slave system produced over the course of four centuries also strove to transform, visually, the diverse into the common. Produced by Europeans, these images rendered the slaves as if they were all the same. They were just slaves, blacks, bodies that toiled. Unfortunately, when compared with this array of images produced by Europeans, visual counter-narratives created by Africans and Afro-descendants are nowhere near as abundant. Because of the severity of the slave system, this type of activity was limited to a few metaphorical spaces: sculptures, kanga wraps, scarrings, amulets, and jewellery, for example.[30] There therefore remains little by way of a visual record – paintings, watercolors, and photos – produced by slaves. However, following the method proposed by the historian Carlo Ginzburg,[31] one can explore the clues and traces embedded in the details, little signs that resisted the Eurocentric schemas of the painters and photographers we've been talking about thus far. Below are two final and significant examples: one a drawing (Fig. 30) and the other a photograph (Fig. 31).

Fig. 30: J.M. Rugendas. *Mercado de escravos* (Slave market).1835. Fundação Biblioteca Nacional.

29 Cf. Marcus Wood, *Blind Visual Representations of Slavery in Memory* (London: Routledge, 2009).
30 For a broader analysis of contemporary black art, see Richard Powell, *Black Art: A Cultural History* (London: Thames and Hudson, 1997).
31 Carlo Ginzburg, *Clues, Myths and the Historical Method* (Baltimore: Johns Hopkins University Press, 2013).

In the watercolor above, the traveler Rugendas rendered a "slave market" as if it were a calm, "business" environment. A mother holds her infant to her chest, lashed to her by a sling of kanga, while recently arrived Africans talk and socialize around the fire. The scene little resembles the descriptions of such places left to us by other travelers, who spoke of the horrors and cruelty of these markets, where mortality was high, the stench rancid, and the mood set by wailing children and men and women fighting back or despairing of the situation in which they found themselves.[32] But the picture by Rugendas presents an orderly, workaday environment, the kind that prevailed in the depictions left to us by European travelers at the time. In other words, as we have shown, the idea was to offer a pleasant version of this "New World" to counter the language of colonization and the violence intrinsic to slavery. And yet, the eye is drawn to the activity of a small group of Africans further to the left, where a slave is seen drawing or writing something on the wall, certainly a register of his memories or history, as some fellow captives look on. It's hard to tell exactly what Rugendas intended by including something like this in a place designed to do just the opposite, namely naturalize and dehumanize. The naturalist may have just been depicting what he actually saw, as it's something commonly witnessed in analogous institutions, such as prisons and other forms of lockup. Leaving your mark is the last expression available to those deprived of everything else, especially their liberty. All it takes is a wall and a sharp object to scratch it with. Be that as it may, this detail could also be an act of reflection, an imaginative gesture that was always present in these nations riven by the Afro-Atlantic diaspora. Hidden in plain sight (in this case, at a slave market), they represented forms of exercising freedom even in the most extreme situations. Understood in these terms, a minor detail can be translated as one of various forms of "slave agency." Even where free will is stifled, humanity and creativity always find a way.

On to the second example. Portrait pictures of masters and mistresses being carried about in sedan chairs by slaves apparently capable of shouldering super-human burdens were so common that they formed a visual convention all of their own. Before the advent of photography, sedan chair scenes had already been a staple of painterly representation in Brazil and the Caribbean. It was a visual symbol of how people could be transformed into "beasts of burden."[33] When inserted into the urban context,

---

32 Brand, a European traveler who was visiting Valongo, a sprawling slave market in downtown Rio de Janeiro, when a huge consignment of slaves disembarked at port, left the following sad description: "The first meat shop we entered contained about three hundred children of both sexes; the eldest of them couldn't have been more than twelve or thirteen, while the youngest were six or seven at the most [. . .] The stench and heat inside were stifling and repugnant. I had my thermometer in my pocket, and it read 33 degrees, though it was winter [. . .]" .

33 In *Dicionário da escravidão e da liberdade* (São Paulo: Companhia das Letras, 2017), which I edited in conjunction with Flávio Gomes, we presented sets of drawings and photos of the famous sedan chairs from the 1800s.

Fig. 31: Unidentified photographer. *Mulher da familia Costa Carvalho e escravos* (Woman from the Costa Carvalho family and slaves). S.l., c.1860. Albúmen, 5.5 x 8.1 cm. Instituto Moreira Salles Collection.

these scenes acquire new meanings. First off, they enable us to discern other modes of slavery, such as the house slave, whose form of dress mirrored the master's own. Wearing jackets, top hats, carrying umbrellas, but never wearing shoes, they represented the submission necessary for this type of system, parading in the streets the social hierarchy imposed on them at the manors where they worked. On the other hand, as slave-powered sedan-chair transport was imbued with a metonymic function, this type of scene was often staged at photographic studios, lending a certain aesthetic refinement or souvenir, postcard quality to what actually went on in the streets. The photograph above is a case in point. The composition closely follows the routine "forms of seeing" slave society created: in the center, a haughty, well-dressed woman sits on the edge of a sedan chair built as a prop in a photographic studio. Unlike in the actual street scenes, where the master or mistress would be all but hidden from view behind the curtain, here the lady of the manor is content to "let herself be seen." She is wearing expensive, but decorous clothes, with a pair of earrings providing the only touch of bling. She seems, however, a little ill at ease with the artificiality of the situation, her hands folded before her rather tensely. Interestingly, her name is not given, as the caption mentions only the family surname: Costa Carvalho. There is no way to be sure, but we can suppose that this woman is some relation to José da Costa Carvalho, the marquis of Monte Alegre, a well-known politician, magistrate, and journalist in the Brazilian Empire. The surname carries such weight that it seems to make further specification unnecessary. There is, therefore, another politic of anonymity at work here, namely that women don't need to be identified; they are merely "part of the family." We can also note other silencing strategies at play. The caption we have today reads “woman from the Costa Carvalho family” and “slaves.” As you can see, it doesn't seem to matter whether there are two of them, three, or more. They are simply slaves, and so barefoot and nameless, even if, by being well-dressed, they mirror the importance of their owners. The caption notes only what the scene was intended to show. Of course, it doesn't reveal the identities of the slaves, because they are just props in a set, as equipmental as the sedan itself. In other words, they don't feature as individuals, only as background. That said, their contrasting poses do reveal – and impose – some personality upon the photographer and photograph. The man on the left seems to be more or less acting as instructed. His demeanor is submissive, hat in-hand, eyes downcast, back slightly curved – as it should be. After all, this was a world that didn't hide, but rather naturalized its everyday, pervasive violence. But, as we said earlier, the photographer could not always control his models. Daguerrotype lenses opened slowly, so a photograph could take up to twenty minutes to register, and a lot can happen in twenty minutes. In this sense, there's no mistaking the out-of-character posture of the slave on the right. He seems more relaxed, irreverent even, hat on his head, looking straight at the photographer or – who knows? – maybe at his master, who would most probably have been accompanying the process. He has an arm cocked, legs crossed, his elegant bearing speaking volumes. Result: he steals the show, which must have really irked the photographer and his client. In short, here are two isolated examples that, each in its own way, evince the obvious: how images don't just let themselves be seen. They exude what Baxandall calls “patterns of intention”; they purposefully erase the address on the package, as Carlo Ginzburg shows; and they go about their everyday social production, just as analyzed by Clark.[34] What's more, through minor acts of will they exude major gestures of autonomy and revolt. In the case of images produced during the period of slavery, if examined carefully, in detail, against the grain, as it were, and despite their reiteration, they reveal the malaise that surrounded slavery wherever it laid down its roots. Hence the works examined here share a common profile that visually translated an “other's other,” the “slave other” registered by usually foreign travelers and photographers. Images are extremely powerful documents of wide circulation and reflexibility. If we cannot help but reconstruct the details of their production, it is also certain that even in the watertight representations of slavery, there were leaks of liberty and space for the recognition of imaginative processes that are, by definition, limitless.

34 Michael Baxandall, *Patterns of Intention* (New Haven: Yale University Press, 1985); Timothy J. Clark, *Modernismos* (São Paulo: Cosac & Naify, 2007). Analysis of the painting “A morte de Marrat.” Carlo Ginzburg, *Indagações sobre Piero: O Batismo, o ciclo de Arezzo, a Flagelação* (São Paulo: Paz e Terra, 1989).

Bibliography

Antonil, André João. *Cultura e opulência do Brasil por suas drogas e minas* (Lisbon: n.p., 1711).

Araujo, Ana Lúcia. *Brazil through French Eyes* (New Mexico: University of New Mexico Press, 2015).

Brizuela, Natália. *Fotografia e Império: paisagens para um Brasil moderno* (São Paulo: Companhia das Letras, 2012).

Clark, Timothy J. *Modernismos* (São Paulo: Cosac & Naify, 2007).

Copley, Stephen, and Peter Garside, eds. *The Politics of the Picturesque: Literature, Landscape and Aesthetic since 1770* (Cambridge: Cambridge University Press, 1994).

Darnton, Robert. *The Business of Enlightenment* (Boston: Harvard University Press, 1987).

David, Karel. *Dictionnaire des Artistes de Langue Française en Amérique du Nord, peintres, sculpteurs, dessinateurs* (Quebec: Presses de l'Université Laval, 1992).

de Andrade Alvim, Pedro. "Le monde comme spetacle: l'ouvre du peintre François-Auguste Biard (1798–1882)" (PhD diss., University of Paris, 2001).

Fassin, Didier. *La force de l'ordre: Une anthropologie de la police des quartiers* (Paris: Seuil, 2011).

Foucault, Michel. *Vigiar e punir* (Petrópolis: Vozes, 2009).

Gilroy, Paul. *The Black Atlantic. Modernity and Double Consciousness* (London: Verso, 1987).

Ginzburg, Carlo. *Clues, Myths and the Historical Method* (Baltimore: Johns Hopkins University Press, 2013).

Ginzburg, Carlo. *Indagações sobre Piero: O Batismo, o ciclo de Arezzo, a Flagelação* (São Paulo: Paz e Terra, 1989).

Hall, Stuart. "The Spectacle of the Other," in *Representation: Cultural Representations and Signifying Practices*, ed. Stuart Hall (London: Sage & The Open University, 1997): 223–90

Kossoy, Boris. *Fotografia e História* (São Paulo: Ática, 1999).

Kossoy, Boris. *Hercule Florence, a Descoberta Isolada da Fotografia no Brasil*, 3rd ed. (São Paulo: Eitoria da Universidade de São Paulo, 2006).

Kossoy, Boris. *Origens e Expansão da Fotografia no Brasil: Século XIX* (Rio de Janeiro: Edição Funarte, 1991).

Lima, Valéria. *Debret, historiador e pintor* (Campinas: Unicamp, 2005).

Lima, Valéria. *Uma viagem com Debret* (Rio de Janeiro: Zahar, 2006).

Lissovsky, Maurício. "Dez proposições acerca do futuro da fotografia," *Facom. Revista da Faculdade de Comunicação e Marketing da FAAP* 23 (2011).

Machado Koutsoukos, Sandra Sofia. *Negros no estúdio do fotógrafo, segunda metade do século XIX* (Campinas: Edunicamp, 2010).

Machado Koutsoukos, Sandra Sofia. "Fotografias com corpo e alma," *Afro-Ásia* 48 (2013): 439–46.

Machado, Maria Helena. "Entre dois Beneditos: Histórias de Amas de Leite no ocaso da escravidão," in *Mulheres negras no Brasil escravista e do pós-emancipação*, ed. Giovanna Xavier, Juliana Barreto Farias and Flavio Gomes (São Paulo: Selo Negro, 2012): 199–213

Mauad, Ana Maria. *Poses e flagrantes – Ensaios sobre história e fotografia* (Niteroi: Eduff, 2008).

Mauss, Marcel. "As técnicas do corpo," in *Sociologia e Antropologia* (São Paulo: Casac Naify, 2003): 399–422

Baxandall, Michael. *Patterns of Intention* (New Haven: Yale University Press, 1985).

Morales de Los Rios, Adolfo. *O ensino artístico* (Rio de Janeiro: Imprensa Nacional, 1942).

Naves, Rodrigo. *A forma difícil* (São Paulo: Ática, 1996).

Powell, Richard. *Black Art: A Cultural History* (London: Thames and Hudson, 1997).

Schwarcz, Lilia and Flávio Gomes, eds. *Dicionário da escravidão e da liberdade* (São Paulo: Companhia das Letras, 2017).

Schwarcz, Lilia. *O sol do Brasil* (São Paulo: Companhia das Letras, 2008).

Schwarcz, Lilia. *The Emperor's Beard* (New York: Hill and Wang, 2003).
Schwarcz, Lilia. *The Spectacle of the Races* (New York: Hill and Wang, 1999).
Slenes, Robert W. "As provações de um Abraão africano: a nascente nação brasileira na *Viagem Alegórica* de Johann Moritz Rugendas," *Revista de História da arte e arqueologia* 2 (1995/96): 271–94.
Sontag, Susan. *Sobre a fotografia* (São Paulo: Companhia das Letras, 2000).
Wood, Marcus. *Blind Visual Representations of Slavery in Memory* (London: Routledge, 2009).

Paulo Cruz Terra

Vagrancy, Labor, and Legislation in Brazilian Abolition: A Perspective from Global Labor History (1871–1890)

In June 1871, the commission responsible for formulating the bill for the Free Womb Law (*Lei do Ventre Livre*) presented its opinion in the Brazilian House of Representatives. According to the document, the law aimed at freeing the children of slaves born after its enactment. These children would be under the power of their mother's masters until they were eight years old; after that period, the masters would either receive compensation from the state or use their services until they reached the age of 21.[1]

The commission pointed out that the proposal was precisely to promote gradual abolition, considering that an immediate abrogation would be a disaster for state security, for the owners, and for the enslaved themselves, "to whom freedom in mass and without transition would be a Greek gift."[2] According to the document, the enslaved had not been educated in freedom and were incapable of exercising citizenship; if they were not coerced or encouraged, they would become vagabonds. This idea of the atavistic idleness of the enslaved was embodied in an article that provided for the punishment for vagrancy in relation specifically to those released under the law, even though a punishment for vagrancy in general was already provided for in the criminal code.

Throughout 1871, both the House of Representatives and the Senate debated the prosecution of vagrancy in the Free Womb Law bill. Senator Silveira da Motta, for example, stated that arresting idlers and vagabonds would not be enough to coerce them. For him, this would only fill prisons: he affirms that the freedman "comes out of detention worse than he entered." According to him, the solution was to invest in "special rules for leasing freedmen services," as "it is not possible to equate the service of a free man with the service of a man who" was not free.[3] The law was also debated in newspapers; in Rio de Janeiro, the country's capital, some discussed the control of vagrancy and the regulation of employment contracts as concerns to be considered at the time of abolition.[4]

1 Annals of the Chamber of Deputies, Meeting of June 30, 1871.

2 Ibid.

3 Ibid.

4 The theme was constantly discussed in the press, as e.g.: *Diário do Rio de Janeiro*, April 16, 1871, 2; *Jornal do Commercio*, July, 1871: 5.

Note: The present text shows some results of a research project that received financial support from CAPES, CNPq, FAPERJ, and the Alexander von Humboldt Foundation.

https://doi.org/10.1515/9783111026527-012

The Free Womb Law was approved on September 28, 1871, and is considered an important step in the gradual abolition process of Brazilian slavery, which is still being completed 150 years later, as I write this text (in 2021). The objective of this chapter is to analyze how vagrancy and labor intertwine in the legislation – and in the debates around them – of the Brazilian abolitionist process, which culminated with the abolition law itself in 1888. The idea is to approach these themes from the perspective of global labor history, seeking connections and comparisons with the Portuguese Empire.

There is much academic work on the abolition process in Brazil,[5] but investigations in the field of the social labor history are still few and far between. Thus, the first part of the text seeks to provide a brief overview of the relationship between the historiography of labor, slavery, and abolition, pointing out recent developments and challenges. The next part, in turn, intends to add to recent efforts at dialogue between the two fields by proposing the analysis of the relationship between vagrancy, work, and legislation in the Brazilian abolition process.

1 Labor History, Slavery, and Abolition

In the late 1990s, despite all the developments in academic research on the social history of Brazil, it was possible to verify the absence of black workers, whether enslaved or free.[6] This was because in Brazil, as in other parts of the world,[7] labor history was equated with free wage labor. In Brazil, this happened because abolition

---

5 The academic literature on the abolition process in Brazil is vast, and some examples are: Robert Conrad, *Os últimos anos da escravatura no Brasil: 1850–1888* (Rio de Janeiro: Civilização Brasileira, 1975); Celia Maria Marinho de *Azevedo, Onda Negra, Medo Branco: o negro no Imaginário das elites – Século XIX* (Rio de Janeiro: Paz e Terra, *1987)*; Maria Helena P. T Machado, *O Plano e o Pânico: Os Movimentos Sociais na Década da Abolição* (Rio de Janeiro/São Paulo: Editoria da UFRJ/Editora da Universidade de São Paulo, *1994)*; Wlamyra R. de Albuquerque, *O Jogo da Dissimulação- abolição e cidadania negra no Brasil* (São Paulo: Companhia das Letras, 2009); Ângela Alonso, *Flores, votos e balas: o movimento abolicionista brasileiro (1868–1888)* (São Paulo: Companhia das Letras, 2015); Maria Helena P. T Machado and Celso Thomas Castilho, eds., *Tornando-se livre: Agentes históricos e lutas sociais no processo de abolição* (São Paulo: Editora da Universidade de São Paulo, 2015).

6 Silvia Hunold Lara, "Escravidão, cidadania e história do trabalho no Brasil" in *Projeto História* 16 (1998): 25–38. Balances on the Labor History produced in Brazil can be found at: Claudio H.M. Batalha, "A Historiografia da classe operária no Brasil: trajetória e tendências," in *Historiografia brasileira em perspectiva*, ed. Marcos C. De Freitas (São Paulo: Contexto, 2001): 145–58; Claudio H.M. Batalha, "Os desafios atuais da história do trabalho," *Anos 90* 13, no. 23–24 (2006): 87–104; Sidney Chalhoub and Fernando Teixeira da Silva, "Sujeitos no imaginário acadêmico: escravos e trabalhadores na historiografia brasileira desde os anos 1980," *Cadernos AEL* 26 (2009): 13–45.

7 For analyses on labor history in international contexts, see: Marcel van der Linden, *Workers of the World: Essays toward a Global Labor* (Leiden: Brill, 2008); Leon Fink, "The Great Escape: How a Field Survived Hard Times," *Revista Brasileira de História* 64 (2012): 15–32.

was seen as a landmark, with labor history taking place right after the end of slavery and being directly related to the history of the organized labor movement.

From the beginning of the 1950s in the field of sociology (and in the 1970s in historical studies), although academic studies about the worlds of labor in Brazil focused on free work, slavery was reintroduced as a subject due to its deleterious effects on the organization of the working class. Boris Fausto, in a pioneering work published in 1976, pointed out, for example, the differences between the organization of port workers in the post-abolition period in the Brazilian cities of Santos and Rio de Janeiro. While in Santos a majority of foreigners could help to explain the existence of a more combative labor movement, in Rio de Janeiro foreigners had to coexist with national workers, and disputes between them favored internal class divisions. Furthermore, national workers, among whom were many former enslaved men, tended towards paternalistic and conciliatory positions, which could be explained by the considerable weight of slavery.[8] Sheldon Maram, in an analysis similar to that by Fausto, pointed out that the Brazilian working class, synonymous with black workers, lacked "a class tradition on which it could be based," in addition to resentment towards the "sense of cultural and even racial superiority that the immigrant worker boasted about it."[9]

The historiography of Brazilian labor has undergone important transformations since the 1980s, and its approach has gone beyond looking at the organization and mobilization of workers, exploring other aspects of worker experience, such as daily life and culture. Another important change was questioning the paradigm of absence, which indicated that while in Europe dense customs and traditions favored worker struggles, in Brazil "slavery had bequeathed the absence of political culture, to be supplied by heads and ideologies imported from the center of the world, exclusive propellants of the Brazilian labor movement in its first phase."[10] Sidney Chalhoub and Fernando Silva pointed out that the Brazilian working class "began to be sought out in precise historical circumstances and to be considered as a political subject that articulated understandings of their reality and struggle strategies within a set of different constraints."[11]

Despite all these transformations, studies addressing black workers in the pre-abolition and post-abolition periods were very scarce until at least the 2000s.[12] On

8 Boris Fausto, *Trabalho Urbano e conflito social* (Rio de Janeiro: Difel, 1976): 127.

9 Sheldon Leslie Maram, *Anarquistas, imigrantes e o movimento operário brasileiro, 1890–1920* (Rio de Janeiro: Paz e Terra, 1979): 30.

10 Chalhoub and Teixeira da Silva, "Sujeitos no imaginário acadêmico," 16. On the paradigm of absence, see also Álvaro Pereira Nascimento, "Trabalhadores negros e 'paradigma da ausência': contribuições à história social do trabalho no brasil," *Estudos Históricos* 59 (2016): 607–26.

11 Chalhoub and Teixeira da Silva, "Sujeitos no imaginário acadêmico": 30.

12 Some exceptions are: Sidney Chalhoub, Gladys S. Ribeiro and Martha C. Esteves, "Trabalho escravo e trabalho livre na cidade do Rio: vivências de libertos, galegos e mulheres pobres," *Revista Brasileira de História* 8–9 (1985): 85–116; Sidney Chalhoub, *Trabalho, lar e botequim: o cotidiano dos trabalhadores no Rio de Janeiro na Belle Epoque* (São Paulo: Brasiliense, 1986); João José Reis, "A greve negra de 1857 na Bahia," *Revista USP* 18 (1993): 6–29.

another occasion, Fabiane Popinigis and I showed that the contingent of researchers dedicated to exploring the forms of expression and organization of captives, former captives, and their descendants, as well as the impact on the mobilization and organization of workers in the early republican period, has grown substantially since the 2000s.[13] Marcelo Mattos, for example, pointed out that rather than necessarily having been a demobilizing element, the struggle for the end of slavery was a catalyst for worker organization. The approximation of free and enslaved workers in the struggle for freedom created a shared arsenal that made possible "an accumulation path of fundamental experiences for working-class formation."[14]

Despite developments over the last few years regarding the inclusion of black workers, whether enslaved or free, in social labor history, some points still deserve greater attention. Among them is the development of research on race relations and racism in the worlds of labor, especially from the mid-twentieth century.[15] In addition, the historiography of Brazilian labor still undertakes analyses that are very restricted to national borders, becoming rather self-centered and parochial, as analyzed by Paulo Fontes, Alexandre Fortes, and David Mayer. According to them, there was even resistance on the part of Brazilian historians in relation to global history.[16] The dialogue with global labor history, initiated by Marcel van der Linden, could therefore be an opportunity to move away from methodological nationalism, which is considers the nation-state as a basic and self-evident analytical unit. Global labor history proposes comparisons between different countries and/or the analysis of international interactions, addressing processes that cross or subvert national borders.[17]

Currently, there are different views on what global history is, as well as an intense debate about its possibilities.[18] This text approaches perspectives that think of the global as "emphasizing on space and connections that extend beyond cultural boundaries," rather than as the whole world. Christian De Vito presented his proposal for a micro-

13 Paulo Cruz Terra and Fabiane Popingis, "Classe, raça e a história social do trabalho no Brasil (2001–2016)," *Revista Estudos Históricos* 66 (2019): 307–28.

14 Marcelo Badaró Mattos, "Trajetórias entre fronteiras: o fim da escravidão e o fazer-se da classe trabalhadora no Rio de Janeiro," *Revista Mundos do Trabalho* 1 (2009): 64.

15 Cruz Terra and Popingis, "Classe, raça e a história social do trabalho no Brasil (2001–2016)."

16 Paulo Fontes, Alexandre Fortes and David Mayer, "Brazilian Labour History in Global Context: Some Introductory Notes," *International Review of Social History* 62 (2017): 1–22.

17 Van der Linden, *Workers of the World*. There is a wide debate about global labor history. See, e.g., Franco Barchiese, "How Far from Africa's Shore? A Response to Marcel van der Linden's Map for Global Labor," *International Labor and Working-Class History* 82 (2012): 77–84; Dorothy Sue Cobble, "The Promise and Peril of the New Global Labor History," *International Labor and Working-Class History* 82 (2012): 77–84; Christian G. De Vito, "New Perspectives on Global Labour History: Introduction," *Workers of the World* 3 (2013): 7–31; Tom Brass, "Who These Days is not a Subaltern? The Populist Drift of Global Labor History," *Science & Society* 81 (2017): 10–34.

18 See e.g., Peter Winn, "Global Labor History: The Future of the Field?" in *International Labor and Working-Class History* 82 (2012): 85–91; John-Paul A. Ghobrial, "Introduction: Seeing the World Like a Microhistorian," *Past & Present* 242 (2019): 1–22.

spatial perspective, which intends to bring together "the epistemological perspective of microhistory and the spatially sensitive methodology of global history." Micro-spatial history differs from other analyses that "are based on the assumed associations of micro as local and macro as global," as well as moving away from perspectives that consider the micro as a sphere of agency and the macro as a sphere of structures.[19]

Another area of Brazilian historiography still marked by methodological nationalism, despite all the developments since the 1980s, is that dedicated to abolition.[20] Although some efforts have already been made,[21] the absence of deeper comparisons with the abolitionist process in Africa is noteworthy. This absence can also be observed in some research dedicated to abolition from the Portuguese Africa perspective. In fact, the possible connections between Africa and Brazil from the perspective of labor history are still little explored, even though Brazil was the main destination for captives transported from Africa.[22] This chapter is, therefore, part of the recent effort to bring labor history closer to the history of slavery and abolition by focusing on how the relations between vagrancy and work are described in the process of Brazilian abolition. Considering legislation and the debates around it, this chapter intends to make an analysis from the perspective of global labor history by comparing and connecting it with abolition in Portuguese Africa.

2 Vagrancy and Legislation in the Abolition Process

The Free Womb Law, enacted in 1871, provided a specific punishment for vagrancy, as mentioned above. However, the criminal code from 1830 was in force, which already punished vagrancy. According to the code, a vagrant was defined as any person who did not have "an honest and useful occupation, from which one can live, after being warned by the justice of peace, not having sufficient income."[23] Leisure, therefore, was considered wrong only for those who had no income to enjoy it, and poor people were criminalized for not being able to support themselves.

---

19 Christian G. De Vito, "History Without Scale: The Micro-Spatial Perspective," *Past & Present* 242 (2019): 348–72.

20 Alain El Youssef, *O Império do Brasil na segunda era da abolição, 1861–1880* (Tese Doutorado em História – Universidade de São Paulo, São Paulo, 2019): 2.

21 Ibid.; Marcelo Badaró Mattos, "Abolicionismo e formação da classe trabalhadora: uma abordagem para além do nacional," in *Políticas da raça: experiências e legados da abolição e do pós-emancipação no Brasil*, ed. Flávio Gomes and Petrônio Domingues (São Paulo: Selo Negro, 2014): 97–120.

22 Alfagali's and Mamigonian's texts in this volume are important exceptions. See also: Reis, "A greve negra de 1857 na Bahia"; Maria Cecília Velasco e Cruz, "Tradições negras na formação de um sindicato: Sociedade de Resistência dos trabalhadores em trapiche e café, Rio de Janeiro, 1905–1930," *Afro-Ásia* 24 (2000): 243–90; João José Reis, *Ganhadores: a greve negra de 1857 na Bahia* (São Paulo: Companhia das Letras, 2019).

23 Código Criminal do Império do Brasil anotado (1830) pelo Juiz de Direito Antonio Luiz Ferreira Tinoco (Rio de Janeiro: Imprensa Industrial, 1886).

The penalty provided for in the criminal code was "imprisonment with work for eight to twenty-four days." This penalty was increased in 1831 from one to six months of imprisonment with work, and doubled in the case of recidivism. In punitive terms, this was a considerable change from the Philippine Ordinances, which had been in force in the Portuguese Empire since 1603 and was present in Brazil even after independence in 1822. In the ordinances, the punishments for vagrancy were whippings or banishment "to Africa for a year."[24] Thus, the criminal code of 1830 represented "a break from the punishing penalties of Portuguese codification"[25] and joined the liberal codification movement "from the West underway at the turn of the 18th to the 19th century."[26] By proposing the combination of prison and work, the Brazilian code joined those of other countries influenced by the punitive theories of Cesare Beccaria, Karl Roeder, and Jeremy Bentham and their "ideals of penal utility and rehabilitation of criminals through labor."[27]

Despite all these transformations, the Brazilian code of 1830 allowed that if the defendant was enslaved and incurred a punishment other than death or the galleys, he could be sentenced to whipping: "after being whipped, he will be given back to his master, who will be forced to bring him with an iron for the time and the way designated by the judge."[28] Thus, the criminal code showed the coexistence of a new legal culture and a traditional one inherited from colonial times[29] with regard to the enslaved. The definition of vagrancy in the 1830 law is made in conjunction with the crime of begging, which was defined when a person was able to work but insisted on begging. In the legislation, there was a confluence between begging and vagrancy, since both were included in the criminalization of poverty. It became important both in the legislative effort and police practice[30] to distinguish those who continued to beg due to incapacity ("true" beggars) from "false" beggars, who begged out of laziness and falsity; the latter should be forced to work.

Two years after the promulgation of the 1830 code, the criminal procedure code brought a new particularity to vagrancy punishment. Vagabonds, as well as "beggars,

24 *Ordenações Filipinas. Livro V*, http://www1.ci.uc.pt/ihti/proj/filipinas/l5ind.htm [accessed 31.08.2022].

25 Gláucia Tomaz de Aquino Pessoa, "Código Criminal do Império," *Memória da Administração pública brasileira* (2016), http://mapa.an.gov.br/index.php/menu-de-categorias-2/281-codigo-criminal [accessed 31.08. 2022].

26 Vivian Chieregati Costa, "Codificação e formação do Estado-nacional brasileiro: o Código Criminal de 1830 e a positivação das leis no pós-Independência" (PhD diss., Universidade de São Paulo, 2013).

27 Ibid.: 277.

28 Código Criminal do Império do Brasil anotado (1830) pelo Juiz de Direito Antonio Luiz Ferreira Tinoco.

29 Luciano Rocha Pinto, "Sobre a arte de punir no Código Criminal Imperial," *Anais do XIV Encontro Regional da ANPUH-Rio: Memória e Patrimônio* (Rio de Janeiro: Numen, 2010).

30 Thomas H. Holloway, "Doing Favors for Street People: Official Responses to Beggars and Vagrants in Nineteenth-Century Rio de Janeiro," in *Cast Out: Vagrancy and Homelessness in Global and Historical Perspective*, ed. A. Lee Beier and Paul Ocobock (Athens, OH: Ohio University Press. 2008): 162–83.

drunks by habit, prostitutes, people who disturb the public peace, turbulent individuals, who, by words or actions, offend good values, public tranquility, and the peace of families," were required to sign a set of agreements.[31] These documents were part of criminal cases and established that the defendant promised not to repeat the offense.[32] The code also determined that the crimes mentioned above could be punished with a "fine up to thirty thousand *réis*, imprisonment for up to thirty days, and three months in a house of correction or public offices."[33]

This was the punishment for vagrancy that existed at the time of the Free Womb Law in 1871, which provided that slaves freed would be under government inspection for five years and "forced to hire [their] services under penalty of being constrained, if they live idle, to work in public establishments."[34] It created, therefore, a specific determination for freedmen different from the criminal code, as they should prove that they were being employed by someone rather than just demonstrate that they had an occupation. Furthermore, the period of punishment was not stipulated. Thus, forms of control and coercion were further reinforced, as freed black workers were forced to submit to a boss.

What was used to justify the new and specific regulation of vagrancy in the context of abolition was the image of the freedman as a potential vagrant. As mentioned earlier, the racist sense of atavistic black idleness appeared in the opinion of the committee responsible for the Free Womb Law project, which indicated that the prematurely freed slave, "lacking coercion or encouragement, becomes a vagabond."[35] An editorial in the newspaper *Diário do Rio de Janeiro*, commenting on the aforementioned law in December 4, 1871, pointed out that the

> black person, suddenly set free, has, as has happened everywhere, given himself up to absolute idleness at the beginning of his freedom, [for] such is his ideal paradise; or, if the law promised him freedom on a certain date, [he has], in anticipation of that fortunate time and in keeping his right done for his master, as little work as possible.[36]

The repression of vagrancy specific to freedmen generated debate in the Brazilian parliament. Deputy Duque-Estrada Teixeira, in the session of July 20, 1871, questioned what guarantees the owners and nation of labor would have when the unborn "know the state of freedom without the slightest moral and religious preparation, without family ties that inspire the work habit." He also questioned what would guarantee work when

31 Criminal Procedure Code, 1832, http://www.planalto.gov.br/ccivil_03/leis/lim/lim-29-11-1832.htm [accessed 31.08.2022].

32 Guilherme Miranda Dutra, "Bêbados, vadios e turbulentos: termos de bem viver e controle social no Segundo Reinado" (bachelor's thesis, Universidade Federal do Rio Grande do Sul, 2013): 38.

33 Criminal Procedure Code, 1832, http://www.planalto.gov.br/ccivil_03/leis/lim/lim-29-11-1832.htm [accessed 31.08.2022].

34 Law of September 28, 1871, http://www.planalto.gov.br/ccivil_03/leis/lim/lim2040.htm [accessed 31.08.2022].

35 Annals of the Chamber of Deputies, meeting of June 30, 1871.

36 Diário do Rio de Janeiro, April 12, 1871: X.

adults were torn from slavery by annual manumission and "thrown without any preparation into the vast and risky territory of freedom?"[37] Duque-Estrada Teixeira pointed out that the measure provided in the bill of the Free Womb Law was the repression of vagrancy. However, he argued that such a proposal was "sterile and illusory," given that legislation in this regard already existed. Furthermore, he considered that the 1871 law could represent "a hateful and unqualified privilege in favor of the freedman, who will be in more favorable conditions than the Brazilian citizen is today, busy taking up an honest occupation, not only for five years, but always and under penalty not simply of work in public establishments," but under penalty of imprisonment and penitentiary work.[38]

Deputy Pereira da Silva, in a session of August 24, 1871, in turn, indicated the inconsistency of the law: while allowing the children of enslaved women to gain all the political rights of Brazilian citizens when they reached 21 years old, it would take their civil rights away by placing them under government inspection. He asked: "what use are political rights to them, if civilians are in an inferior position in relation to freed slaves?" How "can you forbid them to invest themselves in this or that industry of choice, to occupy themselves with what they want, to change residence to improve their situation?"[39]

In parliamentary debates on the aforementioned law, abolitionist processes in other locations were also mentioned. The commission that drafted the Free Womb Law showed that the inspiration for a gradual transition lay in the experiences of England, Denmark, and Portugal.[40] Deputy Pinto de Campos, on the other hand, referred, in the session of August 19, 1871, to an article published in the *Jornal do Commercio* by the correspondent journalist in New York. According to the correspondent, in the slave states of the South before complete abolition, there was a belief that black people were "naturally stupid" and that they were made to be governed and work under the whip; after manumission, they would leave the plantations and work and would go to the most obscure places where they would "spend their days in complete and idle uselessness." The correspondent, however, stated that after five years of emancipation, the result in the southern states was quite different from what had been imagined, and that complete inactivity, a criminal environment, and barbarism had not prevailed there.[41]

Another constant reference in the debate was the Portuguese Empire. Senator Antão, in a session of October 14, 1871, stated that the Free Womb Law seemed to have been copied from a similar measure adopted in Portugal in 1856.[42] In turn, Senator Visconde do Rio Branco, in September of the same year, pointed out that womb freedom was how slavery was abolished in Portugal and New Granada.[43]

37 Annals of the Chamber of Deputies, meeting of July 20, 1871.
38 Annals of the Chamber of Deputies, meeting of July 20, 1871.
39 Annals of the Chamber of Deputies, meeting of August 24, 1871.
40 Annals of the Chamber of Deputies, meeting of June 30, 1871.
41 Annals of the Chamber of Deputies, meeting of August 24, 1871.
42 Annals of the Senate, meeting of October 14, 1871.
43 Annals of the Senate, meeting of September 15, 1871.

Sá da Bandeira, an important abolitionist and formulator of abolitionist laws in Portugal, inserted the 1856 law into a broader framework, which determined "that all children of slave women who were born since its date would be free." Added to it were "the decree of December 14, 1854, which ordered the registration of slaves and defined the rights of freed slaves," "the decree of November 3, 1856, which abolished forced labor, called the porter service; and that of April 24, 1858, which established the end of the state of slavery, after twenty years of the decree enactment."[44]

The law that freed the wombs of the Brazilian enslaved resembled that of the Portuguese Empire, as pointed out by Senator Antão. In the Portuguese case, children were forced "to serve the masters of their mothers free of charge until the age of twenty-one," an obligation that would cease if the master was financially compensated.[45]

An important difference is that, unlike its Brazilian equivalent, the Portuguese law did not contain any specific discussions about vagrancy. The inclusion of specific penalties for vagrancy in the context of Portuguese abolition occurred in 1875, with the approval of a law also presented by Sá da Bandeira, which proposed that the following year workers in the colonies who were freedmen would become free. These workers would be subject to state guardianship and obliged to contract their services for two years (that is, until 1878), preferably with their former employers.[46]

According to the opinion of the commission that considered the referred law, this guardianship sought to protect ex-captive men "from giving up the benefits of freedom before having acquired its habits."[47] In this perspective, the state had to civilize blacks through compulsory labor and thereby protect them from the traps of sudden freedom. Vacrancy, according to the aforementioned commission, was "the first and most pernicious vice to be prevented" in the period of transition.[48] Article 27 provided that individuals made free by law and under state guardianship would be put on trial as such, following the conditions of article 256 of the Portuguese penal code dating from 1852. This article stipulated as a vagrant someone who did not have "a certain abode to live in, nor means of subsistence, nor habitually exercise any profession or trade or other business in which to earn a living."[49]

While the punishment provided for vagrancy in the Portuguese penal code was up to six months of correctional imprisonment, the 1875 law determined a much stricter penalty for colony workers, since those judged as vagrants would be "subject to compulsory work for up to two years in state establishments specially created for this purpose, or in

44 Marquês de Sá da Bandeira, *A emancipação dos libertos: carta dirigida ao excelentíssimo senhor Joaquim Guedes de Carvalho e Menezes, presidente da relação de Loanda* (Lisbon: Imprensa Nacional, 1874): 17.

45 Law of July 24, 1856, https://thefreewombproject.com/portugal/ [accessed 31.08.2022].

46 Law of April 29, 1875, https://www.fd.unl.pt/Anexos/Investigacao/1425.pdf [accessed 31.08.2022].

47 Chamber of the Worthy Peers of the Kingdom (Câmara dos Dignos Pares do Reino), meeting of March 31, 1874.

48 Ibid.

49 Código Penal aprovado por Decreto de 10 de dezembro de 1852 (Lisbon: Imprensa Nacional, 1855).

fortresses and public works in the province, and they will receive a salary established by the respective governor." The possibility also opened up for convicts to contract "at any time their services with private persons, in which case the obligation of public service ceases."[50] It was still considered vagrancy to cause a disturbance, attempting to in employers' establishments, or enticing employees to leave the same establishments.

In 1875, a regulation was also implemented that further specified service provision contracts.[51] The regulation established a maximum of nine and a half hours of work, day of rest on Sundays, and the offer of a bed raised from the floor by the boss. In addition, it stipulated that absence from work for fifteen consecutive days "without reason shall be considered vagrancy, and, as such, subject to the penalties" established in the regulation.[52]

Vagrancy prevention in the context of abolition in the Portuguese Empire was highly debated in pamphlets from the 1870s onwards. Henrique Augusto Dias de Carvalho, in a text addressed to the marquês de Sá da Bandeira, addressed the perspective of the owners of São Tomé and Príncipe. According to him, the punishments inflicted on slaves and freedmen were barbaric and inhuman. However, "everyone knew" that if there were no punishments, "this class would have done nothing for the prosperity of agriculture and therefore of the province." The said class was made up of men "without fear of our laws, without respect for authority," who had the climate and vegetation in their favor, whose leafy groves "allow them to go great distances" and hide. In fact, the ease of "using the natural products they feed on" would make them "not a bunch of savages, but evildoers."[53] These men are "given to idleness and all the most harmful vices, and they are constantly likely to live off someone else."[54]

Other contemporaries also wrote about the association between Africans and idleness, which justified a resurgence in vagrancy criminalization.[55] If there was agreement on the repression of vagrancy, the reasons for indolence among workers in the colonies were different, and not all reinforced the idea that blacks would necessarily reject work. Sá da Bandeira himself commented on a letter from Joaquim Guedes de Carvalho e Menezes, president of the Luanda relationship, in which he explained "that the indolence now attributed to black people is due, in large part, to the conviction that their efforts and work do not benefit themselves, but third parties."[56] Sá da Bandeira himself

50 Law of April 29, 1875, https://www.fd.unl.pt/Anexos/Investigacao/1425.pdf [accessed 31.08.2022].

51 A more in-depth analysis of the aforementioned regulation can be found in Maysa Espíndola Souza, "A Liberdade do contrato: o trabalho africano na legislação do Império Português, 1850–1910" (master's thesis, Universidade Federal de Santa Catarina, 2017).

52 Law of April 29, 1875, https://www.fd.unl.pt/Anexos/Investigacao/1425.pdf [accessed 31.08.2022].

53 Henrique A. D Carvalho, *Liberdade para o povo, que ainda em terras portuguesas, vive debaixo do jugo da opressão* (S. Thomé: Imprensa Nacional, 1875): 8.

54 Ibid.: 9.

55 Other examples are: Alfredo de Oliveira Pires, *Algumas reflexões sobre a questão do trabalho nas possessões portuguesas d'Africa* (Lisbon: Typografia Progresso, 1874); Felix Meyer, *O trabalho livre em Angola e o estado desta província* (Lisbon: Typografia Progresso, 1874).

56 De Sá da Bandeira, *A emancipação dos libertos*: 3.

pointed out that "black people refuse to work when their salary is not paid or is insufficient, and when they are mistreated: and in this case, they behave like the European." According to him, on the Cabo Verde islands there was "a demonstration that indigenous people are willing to work when they are paid properly."[57] Therefore, if treated well and properly paid, black people would readily work.

Like Sá da Bandeira, abolitionists elsewhere also waged a symbolic battle to point out that blacks were not naturally indolent and therefore repelled by work. In the Brazilian abolitionist newspaper *Gazeta da Tarde*, a text entitled "The Genesis of Slavery" (*Gênese da escravidão*), and published in October 1880, stated that slavery was born when "a man fighting with another managed to subjugate him and tie him up like an animal; on that day, he had the foul idea of making him work like his domestic animals, while he enjoyed the cynical delights of idleness and parasitism."[58] An inversion is posed in this statement: idleness is instilled not in blacks, but in white gentlemen.

In a similar sense, the text "Aristocratic Charlatanism" (*Charlatanismo Aristocrático*), published in *Gazeta da Tarde* in December 1880, indicated that the slaver aristocracy of the Brazilian Empire has the "astute pretension of making believe that laziness, idleness, absenteeism, waste, luxury, and games are essential elements for agricultural production."[59] For Ennes de Souza, on the other hand, in an article published in the same newspaper in February 1885, the general rule after the liberation of the enslaved

> is their later occupation and not vagrancy, which is for them the exception, as it is, for the so-called *free population* (free of birth) of Brazil, more than a general rule vagrancy and laziness, due to the poor social education and the null professional training received, as well as the terrible economic conditions of our territorial and work organization.[60]

In Ennes' reading, therefore, vagrancy was something characteristic of the freeborn population that did not receive a professional education, in addition to the economic conditions of the country. According to Celia Azevedo, this was part of the abolitionist movement that sought to show "that freed slaves continued to work as resignedly and actively as they did as slaves." In addition, they presented as propagandistic objectives the struggle for abolition, at the same time calming the feelings of masters and enslaved people, "ensuring the possibility of a peaceful reformulation of labor relations and the preservation of the power of the large landowner"[61] These intentions were also on Sá da Bandeira's horizon, who insisted on reinforcing the docile and hardworking character of black people.

57 Marquês de Sá da Bandeira, *O trabalho rural africano e a administração colonial* (Lisbon: Imprensa Nacional, 1873): 76.

58 *Gazeta da Tarde*, October 20, 1880: 1.

59 *Gazeta da Tarde*, December 18, 1880: 1.

60 *Gazeta da Tarde*, February 27, 1885: 2.

61 Marinho de Azevedo, *Onda Negra*: 96.

Azevedo also pointed out the case of the positivist abolitionists[62] Miguel Lemos and Teixeira Mendes, who, in a work of 1888, indicated that "due to biological laws that governed the human body, individuals accustomed to work, and especially painful work such as those of slaves, did not indulge in vagrancy."[63] The inspiration was Auguste Comte, for whom the African is "naturally worshiper, and that is why he submits." Veneration could explain "the possibility of ex-slaves becoming peaceful free workers in the service of agricultural owners."[64] Although the abolitionists tried to intervene in the public debate in order to reinforce that it was not necessary to fear that freed slaves would fall into idleness, some of the attacks against them were precisely because they allegedly encouraged indolence. In a publication in the February 27, 1885, edition of the *Jornal do Commercio*, an unidentified author stated that "abolitionists do not think" and lived "poetizing by weaving chants to freedom, light, space, infinity and to idleness." The republic dreamed of by the abolitionists did not admit the need to work for a living; for this author, the "blacks freed from captivity leave the hoe to be condemned by a lawyer." In this formulation, the abolitionists were "dreamers of impossible worlds."[65] The manorial demand for measures to curb the supposedly pernicious vagrancy of freedmen did not end with the 1871 law. In agricultural congresses, which brought together farmers in Recife and Rio de Janeiro in 1878, several calls for a greater repression of idleness were identified. This would force vagrants "to lend themselves to the service of farming."[66] There was also a demand for the greater regulation of contracts, ensuring that workers complied with them.[67] The answer came in 1879 with the decree governing employment contracts, which, among other things, toughened the penalties for workers who were absent and those who refused to work.[68]

The biggest repression against vagrancy was the approval of what is known as the "Sexagenarian Law" (*Lei dos Sexagenários*) on September 28, 1885. One of its main points was the liberation of slaves over 60 years old. However, the condition was that they should work for another three years for their former masters as a way to compensate for their freedom. The law also foresaw that slaves whose manumission was financed by the

62 On positivist abolitionism, see Rafael Reis Pereira Bandeira de Mello, "A militância do Apostolado Positivista do Brasil em favor da abolição da escravidão por intermédio de opúsculos e correspondências (1881–1888)," in *Anais do XV Encontro Regional da ANPUH-RIO* (Rio de Janeiro: Numen, 2012).

63 Marinho de Azevedo, *Onda Negra*: 96.

64 Ibid.

65 *Jornal do Commercio*, February 27, 1885: 2.

66 *Congresso Agrícola do Rio de Janeiro, 1878. Anais* (Rio de Janeiro: Fundação Casa de Rui Barbosa, 1988): 182.

67 Ibid.: 58.

68 Decree no. 2.827 of March 15, 1879, https://www2.camara.leg.br/legin/fed/decret/1824-1899/decreto-2827-15-marco-1879-547285-publicacaooriginal-62001-pl.html [accessed 31.08.2022]. On the Service Lease Act from 1879, important analysis was conducted by Maria Lucia Lamounier, "Formas da transição da escravidão ao trabalho livre: a Lei de Locação de Serviços de 1879" (master's thesis, Universidade de Campinas, 1986).

emancipation fund would be obliged to remain in the municipality where they had been emancipated for five years. Those who left their domiciles would be considered vagabonds and arrested by the police: they would be employed in "public works or agricultural settlements." In addition, any freed slave found without an occupation would be "obliged to employ himself or hire out his services within a time that the police determined." If the freed slave did not comply within the period established, he would be brought before the judge of orphans, "who will force him to enter a service lease contract, under pain of 15 days imprisonment with labor and to be sent to an agricultural settlement in case of recidivism."[69] The punishment for vagrancy became even more complex and specific than in the 1871 law: it was designed to immobilize the freed slave in the municipality where he had always worked, keeping him within the jurisdiction of his former master. There was also a specified prison term for those found without an occupation.

Again, the discussion in parliament revolved around the need for abolition not to be immediate, with the justification that the enslaved would not be ready for freedom. Senator Lourenço de Albuquerque, in the session of July 18, 1885, pointed out that agriculture, as well as all other branches of the economy, would be immediately abandoned because "the first impulse of the one who, after many years of captivity, receives the great gift of freedom is to enjoy the adventure." In his view, they were synonymous for the slave: "labor and slavery, liberty and idleness."[70]

Deputy Valladares, on the other hand, in the session of August 1, 1885, presented four attempts to "replace slave labor by free labor in the person of freedman." In the case of Baron Simão Dias' project, "all the freedmen have withdrawn, chosing to live on robberies and are constantly drunk." What happened in these experiences was that workers with good behavior left "because they didn't want to cover the work of the vagabonds and lazy men." The deputy also stated that the freedmen said "that work is only for captives, not for them": the idea they had of freedom was the same as "absence of work."[71]

The main objective of the liberation of enslaved people over 60 years old was questioned by Senator Barão de Cotegipe in the session of September 21, 1885. According to him, the emancipation of these enslaved people would be harmful to them, because, in the absence of asylums, they would be left "idle and unable to earn a living easily; either by nature and by their later weakness, they will die of misery or disasters."[72]

Owners who were not members of parliament also sought to intervene in the debate. A representation signed by 82 farmers from the Campos region, in the north part of the state of Rio de Janeiro, was sent to the Brazilian House of Representatives in February 1885 and presented some proposals so that the transformation of slave labor into free work would take place without major disturbances. One proposal would be to set "a period of

69 Law of September 28, 1885.

70 Annals of the Senate, meeting of July 18, 1885.

71 Annals of the Chamber of Deputies, meeting of August 1, 1885.

72 Annals of the Senate, meeting of September 21, 1885.

seven years for the extinction of slavery in Brazil," or even a "law that compels the freed and free to work, repressing idleness and vagrancy, which cause so much damage to peace and to public wellness." In addition, it suggested the creation of "agricultural settlements, with penitentiary regulations for the punishment of habitual offenders."[73]

When analyzing the parliamentary debates around the Sexagenarian Law, Joseli Mendonça suggests that they presented the expectations of dominant groups, pointing out that: "the freedom dreamed of was the one that produced individuals dependent on their former masters."[74] This occurred because "personal dependency networks had meanings other than just assuring the owners of the availability of workers who would maintain their fortune." According to Mendonça, the law sought to guarantee "mechanisms that would make it possible to maintain a relationship of control beyond the limits of freedom," which would include, for example, the compulsion of the freedman regarding work and the control of his place of residence.[75]

The concern with vagrancy was revived in the enactment of the complete abolition of slavery in Brazil in 1888. A few days before the enactment of the law, Princess Isabel delivered a speech in which she addressed the need to extinguish the servile element, bringing up, at the same time, the importance of improving "our repressive legislation on idleness."[76] The abolitionist newspaper *Gazeta da Tarde* questioned whether the government intended to increase the penalties of the criminal code or to invent new crimes. It argued that the government was imbued with the "idea that the freedman becomes an enemy of work and public order," which experience proved to be the opposite. The newspaper also questioned why there were threats "of useless embarrassment and persecution"; did the government want "to free blacks and then to put them in jail?"[77]

Minister of Justice Ferreira Vianna, following the princess's position, proposed, a month after abolition in June 1888, a specific project in relation to vagrancy. In presenting the aforementioned project, he indicated the urgent need to repress idleness, "the source of all vices." Vianna drew attention to the need for a change in the way vagrancy was punished, since simple imprisonment, instead of correcting, encouraged idleness: if "the prisoner no longer had provisions for work, there he acquires the habit of loitering, becomes perverted, sometimes contaminated by others, or, if he is more hardened in vice, contaminating his companions."[78] The minister warned, however, of a necessary distinction between the idle, who should be harshly repressed, and the older disabled people who had come from captivity. Those who were

73 *Gazeta de Notícias* February 21, 1885: 1.
74 Joseli Maria Nunes Mendonça, *Entre a Mão e os Anéis: A Lei dos Sexagenários e os Caminhos da Abolição no Brasil* (Campinas: Editora da Unicamp, 1999): 102.
75 Ibid.
76 Annals of the Senate, meeting of May 3, 1888.
77 *Gazeta da Tarde* May 7, 1888: 1.
78 *Gazeta da Tarde* June 21, 1888: 2.

"condemned to the service of a lifetime, as instruments of an owner," Brazil could not "allow them to wander the roads and die in misery."[79]

The minister also pointed out that "the vagrant, the beggar, and all kinds of idlers are not exactly criminals [. . .] they are threats of crimes and transgressions, who are averse and foreign to work"; in his words, they would necessarily follow the path of crime.[80] When analyzing the parliamentary debates on the bill, Sidney Chalhoub stated that in this context, the term "dangerous classes" was introduced as a synonym for "poor classes." According to Chalhoub, this "means to say that being poor makes the individual automatically dangerous to society." The poor were understood to be "filled with vices, less moralized," people who could "easily 'roll into the abyss of crime'."[81]

The project presented by Vianna foresaw the creation of "establishments destined for the correction" of those accused of vagrancy, with the punishment also being increased to three months to a year. In addition, it was included as aggravations to the articles of the 1830 criminal code on vagrancy (art. 295) and begging (art. 296), "habitual drunkenness," "abandonment of employment or occupation," or even "the refusal of honest work that is offered or that has been bound by contract."[82] This bill, however, ended up not being voted on by parliament, and the change in relation to the punishment of vagrancy only took place after the beginning of the republic with the new penal code of 1890.

In the Portuguese Empire, 1878 marked the end of the transition period to freedom: the government issued a new regulation for employment contracts, largely re-editing the previous regulation from 1875.[83] The justification in the document was that "the state of the indigenous people does not yet enable them to promote, by themselves, the maintenance of their rights as free citizens, and, for this reason, a special protection from the authority becomes essential to them."[84] Thus, the same determinations regarding vagrancy for Africans remained.

It is possible to verify that both in Brazil and in the Portuguese Empire, the criminalization of vagrancy was an important device in the abolition period. Although vagrancy was

---

79 Ibid.

80 Ibid.

81 Chalhoub, *Trabalho, lar e botequim*: 62.

82 Annals of the Chamber of Deputies, meeting of July 10, 1888.

83 Esmeralda Martinez discusses the 1878 regulation in more detail. Esmeralda Simões Martinez, "O trabalho forçado na legislação colonial portuguesa: o caso de Moçambique (1899–1926)" (master's thesis, Universidade de Lisboa, 2008).

84 Regulamento para os contratos de serviçais e colonos nas províncias da África portuguesa, 1878, https://www.fd.unl.pt/Anexos/Investigacao/1426.pdf [accessed 31.08.2022]. Isabel Castro Henrique pointed out that the indigenous term acquired in this context "a pejorative, disqualifying use and serves to designate those who for this reason are condemned to compulsory work." Isabel Castro Henriques, *Os Pilares da Diferença. Relações Portugal-África (Séculos XV–XX)* (Lisbon: Caleidoscópio, 2004): 294. This, according to the author, took place through a re-elaboration of the representation of the African, whose objective was to highlight "the congenital character of savagery," and that "the savagery of the image itself serves to justify the imposition of a most ferocious discipline of work." Ibid.: 287–88.

already typified as a crime in these locations, which had many connections and similarities between their laws, the governments created specific applications for former captives. In this sense, punishing vagrancy was understood by the ruling classes as a resource for maintaining order, both in terms of guaranteeing labor for economic production and preserving the existing relations of dependency.

Although the Brazilian and Portuguese processes had many similarities, differences also existed. Thus, for example, while in the Portuguese colonies the strategy after the end of the transition period was to maintain existing rules aimed exclusively at black workers, in Brazil there was a shift to linking vagrancy to the broader concept of dangerous classes, a project that would materialize with the beginning of the republic.

3 Final Considerations

Throughout this text, I have analyzed how the issues of vagrancy and labor intertwine in the legislation of the Brazilian abolitionist process, focusing more specifically on the period between the Free Womb Law in 1871 to the Abolition Law of 1888. I tried to show that the writing of legislation took place through constant references to similar international experiences, which legitimized and reinforced arguments. In this sense, one of the main references was the Portuguese Empire, and I sought to demonstrate the approximations and connections between this and the Brazilian experience.

However, vagrancy legislation was not only used in the Brazilian and Portuguese abolitionist process. Alessandro Stanziani has pointed out that although the repression of vagrancy was heavily criticized in France in the mid-nineteenth century, it "was introduced in the colonies after emancipation and justified by the 'natural indolence' of former slaves and new immigrants as well as the need to maintain order in post-abolition society."[85] In both the French and British empires, the official abolition of slavery "was followed by extremely coercive rules regarding vagrants, issued in the name of public order and economic growth as an antidote to poverty." The anti-vagrancy policy in these spaces is, for this historian, an example that even after the end of slavery, the dividing line between freedom and its absence was not clear in the labor world, which "continued to be a world of unequal exploitation and sometimes extreme violence."[86]

In Cuba, according to Christian G. De Vito, there was a broad debate about vagrancy between 1881 and 1889, which "aimed at designing legal measures that would allow the immobilization of previously enslaved labor force on the plantation." These measures ranged from "compulsory enlistment in the army of all blacks between the ages of eighteen and twenty-eight" to the establishment of correctional facilities. De Vito suggests that

85 Alessandro Stanziani, *Labor on the Fringes of Empire: Voice, Exit and the Law* (London: Palgrave Macmillan, 2018): 193–94.
86 Ibid.

the repression of vagrancy is an "example of the adaptability of punishment to changing social and labor relations and to different spatial contexts." The author argued that policies changed as the "conceptualization of vagrancy evolved to reach different groups and achieve different goals."[87] According to him, anti-vagrancy policies "take center stage as a highly dynamic punitive tool to control urban and rural populations and as a way to expel and immobilize distinct social groups" before and after abolition.[88]

The process of vagrancy criminalization in Brazilian abolition cannot be understood, therefore, only within national borders, as it was precisely inserted into a global context of slavery abolition. In the global profound transformation of labor relations, the criminalization of vagrancy became an important resource for the ruling classes to maintain order and production.

Furthermore, the punishments for vagrancy in the Brazilian case, and also in the Portuguese Empire, elucidate a point recently highlighted by the international labor historiography, that the boundaries between free and non-free labor were not so clear at the time.[89] By breaking the rooted dichotomy between slavery and freedom, the analysis of Brazilian legislation regarding vagrancy in the abolition process allows for an approximation with studies that have sought to explore different forms of coercion.[90] Thus, it is possible to verify that under the guise of persecuting atavistic black idleness, the intention was, for example, to place freedmen under government inspection, to coerce them into becoming employees, preferably of their former masters, and keeping them where they already worked and were identified.

Bibliography

Primary Sources

Annals of the Chamber of Deputies (Anais da Câmara dos Deputados), https://bd.camara.leg.br/bd/handle/bdcamara/28839 [accessed 31.08.2022].

Annals of the Senate (Anais do Senado), https://www.senado.leg.br/publicacoes/anais/asp/ip_anaisimperio.asp [accessed 31.08.2022].

Carvalho, Henrique A.D. *Liberdade para o povo, que ainda em terras portuguesas, vive debaixo do jugo da opressão* (S. Thomé: Imprensa Nacional, 1875).

87 Christian G. De Vito, "Punishment and Labour Relations. Cuba between Abolition and Empire (1835–1886)," *Crime, Histoire & Sociétés/Crime, History and Societies* 22 (2018): 53–79.

88 Ibid.

89 Van der Linden, *Workers of the World*; Stanziani, *Labor on the Fringes of Empire*; De Vito, "New Perspectives on Global Labour History: Introduction."

90 Julia Winnebeck, Ove Sutter Adrian Hermann, Christoph Antweiler and Stephan Conermann. "On Asymmetrical Dependency," Concept Paper 1, Bonn Center for Dependency and Slavery Studies (2021), https://www.dependency.uni-bonn.de/images/pdf-files/concept-papers/bcdss_cp_1-_on-asymmetrical-dependency.pdf [accessed 01.08.2022].

Chamber of Deputies of the Portuguese Nation (Câmara dos Senhores Deputados da Nação Portuguesa) (1822–1910), https://debates.parlamento.pt/catalogo/mc/cd [accessed 31.08.2022].

Chamber of Peers of the Kingdom (Câmara dos Pares do Reino) (1842–1910), https://debates.parlamento.pt/catalogo/mc/cp2 [accessed 31.08.2022].

Código Criminal do Império do Brasil anotado (1830) pelo Juiz de Direito Antonio Luiz Ferreira Tinoco (Rio de Janeiro: Imprensa Industrial, 1886).

Código Penal aprovado por Decreto de 10 de dezembro de 1852 (Lisbon: Imprensa Nacional, 1855).

Congresso Agrícola do Rio de Janeiro, 1878. Anais (Rio de Janeiro: Fundação Casa de Rui Barbosa, 1988).

Criminal Procedure Code, 1832, http://www.planalto.gov.br/ccivil_03/leis/lim/lim-29-11-1832.htm [accessed 31.08.2022].

Decree no. 2.827 of March 15, 1879, https://www2.camara.leg.br/legin/fed/decret/1824-1899/decreto-2827-15-marco-1879-547285-publicacaooriginal-62001-pl.html [accessed 31.08.2022].

Diário do Rio de Janeiro, April 16, 1871, 2.

Diário do Rio de Janeiro, April 12, 1871, X.

Gazeta de Notícias February 21, 1885, 1.

Gazeta da Tarde May 7, 1888, 1.

Gazeta da Tarde June 21, 1888, 2.

Gazeta da Tarde, October 20, 1880, 1.

Gazeta da Tarde, December 18, 1880, 1.

Gazeta da Tarde, February 27, 1885, 2.

Jornal do Commercio, July, 1871, 5.

Jornal do Commercio February 27, 1885, 2.

Law of July 24, 1856, https://thefreewombproject.com/portugal/ [accessed 31.08.2022].

Law of September 28, 1871, http://www.planalto.gov.br/ccivil_03/leis/lim/lim2040.htm [accessed 31.08.2022].

Law of September 28, 1885, http://www.planalto.gov.br/ccivil_03/leis/lim/LIM3270.htm [accessed 31.08.2022].

Law of April 29, 1875, https://www.fd.unl.pt/Anexos/Investigacao/1425.pdf [accessed 31.08.2022].

Meyer, Felix. *O trabalho livre em Angola e o estado desta província* (Lisbon: Typografia Progresso, 1874).

Ordenações Filipinas. Livro V, http://www1.ci.uc.pt/ihti/proj/filipinas/l5ind.htm [accessed 31.08.2022].

Pessoa, Gláucia Tomaz de Aquino. "Código Criminal do Império," *Memória da Administração pública brasileira* (2016), http://mapa.an.gov.br/index.php/menu-de-categorias-2/281-codigo-criminal [accessed 31.08.2022].

Pires, Alfredo de Oliveira. *Algumas reflexões sobre a questão do trabalho nas possessões portuguesas d'Africa* (Lisbon: Typografia Progresso, 1874).

Proceedings of the Agricultural Congress of Rio de Janeiro, 1878 (Rio de Janeiro: Fundação Casa de Rui Barbosa, 1988).

Regulamento para execução da lei de 29 de abril de 1875, https://www2.ifch.unicamp.br/cecult/lex/web/uploads/da927b9b0aa93e489c21965e78286b6f922c070d.pdf [accessed 31.08.2022].

Regulamento para os contratos de serviçais e colonos nas províncias da África portuguesa, 1878, https://www.fd.unl.pt/Anexos/Investigacao/1426.pdf [accessed 31.08.2022].

de Sá da Bandeira, Marquês. *A emancipação dos libertos: carta dirigida ao excelentíssimo senhor Joaquim Guedes de Carvalho e Menezes, presidente da relação de Loanda* (Lisbon: Imprensa Nacional, 1874).

de Sá da Bandeira, Marquês. *O trabalho rural africano e a administração colonial* (Lisbon: Imprensa Nacional, 1873).

Secondary Literature

de Albuquerque, Wlamyra R. *O Jogo da Dissimulação- abolição e cidadania negra no Brasil* (São Paulo: Companhia das Letras, 2009).

Alonso, Ângela. *Flores, votos e balas: o movimento abolicionista brasileiro (1868–1888)* (São Paulo: Companhia das Letras, 2015).

Badaró Mattos, Marcelo. "Trajetórias entre fronteiras: o fim da escravidão e o fazer-se da classe trabalhadora no Rio de Janeiro," *Revista Mundos do Trabalho* 1 (2009): 51–64.

Badaró Mattos, Marcelo. "Abolicionismo e formação da classe trabalhadora: uma abordagem para além do nacional," in *Políticas da raça: experiências e legados da abolição e do pós-emancipação no Brasil*, ed. Flávio Gomes and Petrônio Domingues (São Paulo: Selo Negro, 2014): 97–120.

Barchiesi, Franco. "How Far from Africa's Shore? A Response to Marcel van der Linden's Map for Global Labor," *International Labor and Working-Class History* 82 (2012): 77–84.

Batalha, Claudio H.M. "A Historiografia da classe operária no Brasil: trajetória e tendências," in *Historiografia brasileira em perspectiva*, ed. Marcos C. De Freitas (São Paulo, Contexto, 2001): 145–58.

Batalha, Claudio H.M. "Os desafios atuais da história do trabalho," *Anos 90* 13, no. 23–24 (2006): 87–104.

Brass, Tom, "Who These Days is Not a Subaltern? The Populist Drift of Global Labor History," *Science & Society* 81 (2017): 10–34.

Castro Henriques, Isabel. *Os Pilares da Diferença. Relações Portugal-Africa (Séculos XV–XX)* (Lisbon: Caleidoscópio, 2004).

Chalhoub, Sidney. *Trabalho, lar e botequim: o cotidiano dos trabalhadores no Rio de Janeiro na Belle Epoque* (São Paulo: Brasiliense, 1986).

Chalhoub, Sidney, Gladys S. Ribeiro and Martha C. Esteves. "Trabalho escravo e trabalho livre na cidade do Rio: vivências de libertos, galegos e mulheres pobres," *Revista Brasileira de História* 8–9 (1985): 85–116.

Chalhoub, Sidney, and Fernando Teixeira da Silva. "Sujeitos no imaginário acadêmico: escravos e trabalhadores na historiografia brasileira desde os anos 1980," *Cadernos AEL* 26 (2009): 13–45.

Cobble, Dorothy Sue. "The Promise and Peril of the New Global Labor History," *International Labor and Working-Class History* 82 (2012): 77–84.

Conrad, Robert. *Os últimos anos da escravatura no Brasil: 1850–1888* (Rio de Janeiro: Civilização Brasileira, 1975).

Costa, Vivian Chieregati. "Codificação e formação do Estado-nacional brasileiro: o Código Criminal de 1830 e a positivação das leis no pós-Independência" (PhD diss., University of São Paulo, 2013).

Cruz, Maria Cecília Velasco e. "Tradições negras na formação de um sindicato: Sociedade de Resistência dos trabalhadores em trapiche e café, Rio de Janeiro, 1905–1930," *Afro-Ásia* 24 (2000): 243–90.

Cruz Terra, Paulo, and Fabiane Popingis. "Classe, raça e a história social do trabalho no Brasil (2001–2016)," *Revista Estudos Históricos* 66 (2019): 307–28.

Dutra, Guilherme Miranda. "Bêbados, vadios e turbulentos: termos de bem viver e controle social no Segundo Reinado" (bachelor's thesis, Universidade Federal do Rio Grande do Sul, 2013).

Espíndola Souza, Maysa. "A Liberdade do contrato: o trabalho africano na legislação do Império Português, 1850–1910" (master's thesis, Universidade Federal de Santa Catarina, 2017).

Fausto, Boris. *Trabalho Urbano e conflito social* (Rio de Janeiro: Difel, 1976).

Fink, Leon. "The Great Escape: How a Field Survived Hard Times," *Revista Brasileira de História* 64 (2012): 15–32.

Fontes, Paulo, Alexandre Fortes and David Mayer. "Brazilian Labour History in Global Context: Some Introductory Notes," *International Review of Social History* 62 (2017): 1–22

Ghobrial, John-Paul A. "Introduction: Seeing the World Like a Microhistorian," *Past & Present* 242 (2019): 1–22.

Holloway, Thomas H. "Doing Favors for Street People: Official Responses to Beggars and Vagrants in Nineteenth-Century Rio de Janeiro," in *Cast Out: Vagrancy and Homelessness in Global and Historical Perspective*, ed. A. Lee Beier and Paul Ocobock (Athens, Ohio: Ohio University Press, 2008): 162–83.

Hunold Lara, Silvia. "Escravidão, cidadania e história do trabalho no Brasil," *Projeto História* 16 (1998): 25–38.

Lamounier, Maria Lucia. "Formas da transição da escravidão ao trabalho livre: a Lei de Locação de Serviços de 1879" (master's thesis, Universidade de Campinas, 1986).

van der Linden, Marcel. "Labour History: The Old, the New and the Global," *African Studies* 66 (2007): 169–80.

van der Linden, Marcel. *Workers of the World: Essays toward a Global Labor* (Leiden: Brill, 2008).

Machado, Maria Helena P.T. *O Plano e o Pânico: Os Movimentos Sociais na Década da Abolição* (Rio de Janeiro/São Paulo: Editoria da Universidade Federal do Rio de Janeiro/Editora da Universidade de São Paulo, 1994).

Machado, Maria Helena P.T., and Celso Thomas Castilho, eds. *Tornando-se livre: Agentes históricos e lutas sociais no processo de abolição* (São Paulo: Editora da Universidade de São Paulo, 2015).

Maram, Sheldon Leslie. *Anarquistas, imigrantes e o movimento operário brasileiro, 1890–1920* (Rio de Janeiro: Paz e Terra, 1979).

Marinho de Azevedo, Celia Maria. *Onda Negra, Medo Branco: o negro no Imaginário das elites – Século XIX* (Rio de Janeiro: Paz e Terra, 1987).

Nascimento, Álvaro Pereira. "Trabalhadores negros e 'paradigma da ausência': contribuições à história social do trabalho no brasil," *Estudos Históricos* 59 (2016): 607–26.

Nunes Mendonça, Joseli Maria. *Entre a Mão e os Anéis: A Lei dos Sexagenários e os Caminhos da Abolição no Brasil* (Campinas: Editora da Unicamp, 1999).

Pinto, Luciano Rocha. "Sobre a arte de punir no Código Criminal Imperial," *Anais do XIV Encontro Regional da ANPUH-Rio: Memória e Patrimônio*, Rio de Janeiro, 2010, http://www.encontro2010.rj.anpuh.org/resources/anais/8/1276652470_ARQUIVO_SobreaartedepunirnoCodigoCriminalImperial.pdf [accessed 23.09.2022].

Reis, João José. "A greve negra de 1857 na Bahia," *Revista USP* 18 (1993): 6–29.

Reis, João José. *Ganhadores: a greve negra de 1857 na Bahia* (São Paulo: Companhia das Letras, 2019).

Reis Pereira Bandeira de Mello, Rafael. "A militância do Apostolado Positivista do Brasil em favor da abolição da escravidão por intermédio de opúsculos e correspondências (1881–1888)," in *Anais do XV Encontro Regional da ANPUH-RIO* (Rio de Janeiro: Numen, 2012).

Simões Martinez, Esmeralda. "O trabalho forçado na legislação colonial portuguesa: o caso de Moçambique (1899–1926)" (master's thesis, Universidade de Lisboa, 2008).

Stanziani, Alessandro. *Labor on the Fringes of Empire: Voice, Exit and the Law* (London: Palgrave Macmillan, 2018).

de Vito, Christian G. "New Perspectives on Global Labour History: Introduction," *Workers of the World* 3 (2013): 7–31.

de Vito, Christian G. "Punishment and Labour Relations. Cuba between Abolition and Empire (1835–1886)," *Crime, Histoire & Sociétés/Crime, History and Societies* 22 (2018): 53–79.

de Vito, Christian G. "History Without Scale: The Micro-Spatial Perspective," *Past & Present* 242 (2019): 348–72.

Winn, Peter. "Global Labor History: The Future of the Field?" *International Labor and Working-Class History* 82 (2012): 85–91.

Winnebeck, Julia, Ove Sutter Adrian Hermann, Christoph Antweiler and Stephan Conermann. "On Asymmetrical Dependency," Concept Paper 1, Bonn Center for Dependency and Slavery Studies (2021), https://www.dependency.uni-bonn.de/images/pdf-files/concept-papers/bcdss_cp_1-_on-asymmetrical-dependency.pdf [accessed 01.08.2022].

El Youssef, Alain. "O Império do Brasil na segunda era da abolição, 1861–1880" (PhD diss., Universidade de São Paulo, 2019).

Carlos A. de M. R. Zeron

The Concept of Justice Shared in Portuguese America and the Disputes over its Application to Slavery

> In the domain of law it is the doctrine of natural law, that is, of the law as it ought to be, which fits the ideological needs of imperialism. (Hans Morgenthau, *Politics among Nations*, 1946)

1 Introduction

It was only three years after the publication of Lewis Hanke's *All Mankind Is One* (1974) that Giuliano Gliozzi published *Adamo e il Nuovo Mondo* (1977), where he proposed an extensive and organized mapping of the various hypotheses about the origin of the Amerindians lined up between the sixteenth and eighteenth centuries. In addition to polygenist theories, what stood out in his study was a diversity of positions even among authors who affirmed the unity of mankind. Although there was a certain schematism in his analysis, Gliozzi gave an enormous contribution when he expanded the debate on the origin of the Amerindians beyond the strictly theological-philosophical foundations privileged by Hanke, contextualizing it in the different processes of conquest and colonization of America driven by European states and their respective legitimizing justifications. In fact, the *situation* of the authors of the modern era in relation to the colonial enterprises about which they wrote, justifying or blaming them, was the main factor explaining the wide variety of positions among them regarding the question of the unity of mankind.

In this article, I situate the distinctive position of the Jesuit priest António Vieira, pointing out which notions he shared with other colonization agents and which set him apart. For just as not all the coeval authors who wrote about the relations between Europeans and natives during the colonial period can be aligned exclusively on the basis of the acceptance or rejection of the premise of the unity of mankind, they also cannot be reduced to mere adherence to the economic foundation of the colonial enterprise. Vieira firmly adopted that premise and enthusiastically joined the Portuguese colonial project; however, his conviction and enthusiasm were guided and motivated by his eschatological belief. Understanding Vieira's distinctive position is, therefore, a good point of observation to describe, by contrast, the dominant positions shared in the Portuguese court and in Luso-Brazilian colonial society, including by his Jesuit companions.

Note: I am grateful to CNPq for the research grant that made this work possible and to the members of the "Grupo de Pesquisa sobre o Trabalho Indígena nas Américas (Laborindio)" and the "Seminários teóricos e práticos de metodologia da pesquisa histórica," with whom I discussed an earlier version of this text.

https://doi.org/10.1515/9783111026527-013

Therefore, I do not start with Lewis Hanke or Giuliano Gliozzi. For, especially in Portuguese colonization, I see a remarkable proximity between the colonizers and the Jesuits with regard to the relationship they proposed, and in fact entertained, with the Indians, which definitely does not align with either of these two positions. In fact, Jesuits and settlers were not distinguished by whether or not they accepted the unity of mankind: both treated the Indians occasionally as animals,[1] and, although they commonly accepted the premise, it did not prevent them from acknowledging the slavery of the Amerindian as much as that of the African. When the Jesuits came into conflict with the colonists, it was not, therefore, only for *economic* reasons, since both conceived and adhered to the practices of a slave colonial society and disputed this contingent of labor, but also because they had some irreconcilable *moral and legal* positions, which unfolded and were expressed in different political proposals for the formation and reproduction of colonial society. Or, to put it another way, morality and law were the fields in which economic disputes found the most totalizing form of expression (even though they constituted only an "apparent totality"), where the modality of appropriation of the work of the Indian or the African made sense.[2]

The historical memory that Jesuits built about themselves from the sixteenth and seventeenth centuries was expressed precisely in these terms, praising their missionaries as "protectors" of the freedom of the Indians and the only "zealous" agents of their conversion and opposing them to the settlers, qualified as "bad Christians" and "tyrants" due to greed, anger, and lust in dealing with the Indians, who they enslaved and exploited without scruple.[3] In the Portuguese colonization of America, for example, we find this polarization in the first historiographical texts, written by José de Anchieta[4] and Simão de

---

1 In the *Diálogo sobre a conversão do gentio* (1556–1557), for example, Father Manuel da Nóbrega wrote that the Indians "are dogs in eating and killing each other, and are pigs in addictions and in the way they treat themselves"; "more forgotten by creation than the brute animals, and more ungrateful than the children of vipers that eat their mothers" ("são cães em se comerem e matarem, e são porcos nos vícios e na maneira de se tratarem"; "mais esquecidos da criação que os brutos animais, e mais ingratos que os filhos das víboras que comem suas mães") etc. Manuel da Nóbrega, "Diálogo sobre a conversão do gentio," in *Monumenta Brasiliae*, 5 vols., ed. António Serafim Leite (Rome: Monumenta Historica Societatis Iesu, 1957): vol. 2, 320–22. See note 59, below.

2 The theoretical references to which I can refer to support this last formulation are the writings of György Lukács (*Prolegômenos para uma ontologia do ser social* [São Paulo: Boitempo Editorial, 2010]), Jean-Paul Sartre (*Critique de la raison dialectique* [Paris: Gallimard, 1960–1985]) and Maurice Godelier (*L'idéel et le matériel: pensée, économies, sociétés* [Paris: Fayard, 1984]).

3 Carlos A. de M. R. Zeron, *Linha de fé: a Companhia de Jesus e a escravidão no processo de formação da sociedade colonial (Brasil, séculos XVI e XVII)*, trans. Antonio de Padua Danesi (São Paulo: Edusp, 2011): 432–79 (or Carlos A. de M. R. Zeron, *Ligne de foi. La Compagnie de Jésus et l'esclavage dans le processus de formation de la société coloniale en Amérique portugaise (XVIe–XVIIe siècles)* [Paris: Honoré Champion, 2009]: 430–77).

4 "Fragmentos históricos," in *Obras Completas*, ed. José de Anchieta (São Paulo: Loyola, 1970–1989): 475–501. João Capistrano de Abreu titled José de Anchieta's notes as "historical fragments," when they were published. Anchieta's lost manuscript was called *Brasilica Societatis Historia et Vitae clarorum*

Vasconcelos,[5] who took the topic from the work of Manuel da Nóbrega, who, in turn, had already been writing about it with a clear political purpose since the middle of the sixteenth century. Historians have uncritically repeated this opposition ever since, despite its lack of historical grounding; for, in fact, the Jesuits working in the Portuguese Empire were not "protectors" or "defenders" of the natives' freedom, but only asked for the application of some legal titles to reduce Amerindians to slavery, as well as Africans.[6] When this representation is criticized in the historiography, it tends to reduce the Society of Jesus to a mere servile instrument of the commercial interests of the Portuguese crown and of colonial domination,[7] as I pointed out above.

Colonial domination, it must be recognized, is a powerful explanatory category; but it does not explain the *process* by which such domination was historically constructed. That is to say, it summarizes the final result of the process in a totalizing notion, but it does not allow any explanation of why such commercial interests, however fundamental they may have been for the reproduction of social relations within the Portuguese Empire, were insufficient to construct the *historical forms* of "internal organization"[8] of colonial societies. In short, it is a retrospective category because it indicates a point of convergence (colonial domination), but the process that led to that point is more complex and multifaceted, since it interwove not only material conditions and

---

Patrum qui in Brasilia vixerunt in Southwell's bibliography, reproduced in Carlos Sommervogel's *Bibliothèque de la Compagnie de Jésus*, vol. 1 (Paris: A. Picard, 1932): 312.

5 Especially in Simão de Vasconcelos, Crônica da Companhia de Jesus do Estado do Brasil (com as Notícias Curiosas e Necessárias das Cousas do Brasil (Petrópolis: Vozes, 1977).

6 Zeron, *Linha de fé*: 23–43 (*Ligne de foi*: 17–38).

7 Ibid.

8 The expression is employed by Godelier, *L'idéel*: 21. According to the French anthropologist, "we can see an internal link emerging between the productive capacities on the one hand, and the forms of appropriation of nature and social organization on the other" (I quote from the English translation, *The Mental and the Material. Thought, Economy and Society*, trans. Martin Thom [Thetford: Verso, 1986]: 109). Thus, to uncover the historical process of the formation of Luso-Brazilian colonial society and the engendering of its reproduction mechanisms, we consider, following Godelier, that "any social relation contains a mental element [*une part idéelle*], an element of thought, of representations which are not merely the form that this relation assumes in our consciousness, but are part of its content." In this sense, there is a distinction that is not clearly expressed in the Portuguese language ("*idéelle*" and "*idéale*," are translated by one sole word, "*ideal*"), nor in English: "Do not confuse 'mental' [*idéelle*] with 'ideal' [*idéale*] or imaginary. Not all representations present pre-existing realities to the mind 'after-the-event' as it were (where these realities are conceived as having been born independently of and unaided by these representations). Ideas are not an instance separate from social relations; they are not merely appearances, nor are they deformed and deforming reflections in social consciousness. Rather, they are an integral part of social relations as soon as the latter begin to take shape, and they are one of the conditions of their formation." (ibid.: 129). In other words: cosmogonic, theological, moral, legal, and even political conceptions cannot be seen as mere "effects of social relations in thought, [including relations with nature,] but as one of the internal components of these relations and as *a necessary condition of their formation (as well as of their reproduction)*" (ibid.: 151; italics by the author; the words inside brackets were suppressed in the English translation).

commercial interests, but also legal and political theological categories that structured social practices, whenever they were shared. What I propose in this article is that the similarity between Jesuits, royal administrators, and settlers in Portuguese America, with regard to the acceptance of the enslavement of the Indians, resulted from the long duration of cultural sedimentation,[9] that is, of certain organizing principles of social practices, originally derived from Roman law, but *reread from a theocentric perspective, according to parameters determined by the second scholasticism*: in addition to commercial interests, and beyond them, the imposition of a mode of production based on the compulsory work of Africans and Amerindians (whether the latter were called slaves or "administered") *was conceived, justified, and made possible based on ius gentium*, interpreted in the light of Christian theological precepts.

However, even if they started from the premise of the unity of the human race and, by extension, that *jus gentium* guided relations between all human groups, the differences reappeared in circumstances in which Indian and African resistance arose (especially in environments hostile to the Portuguese, and where their technology was inadequate). Differences also reappeared among the Portuguese themselves, when divergent interests broke out between royal administrators, religious orders, colonists, and their internal factions. Such differences were expressed through disputes – whether in tribunes or in texts – around the definition of "just," in civil and ecclesiastical courts, and in the practice of justice in economic activity and socio-political relations.

If there was a public debate among these agents of colonization, it was because some fundamental premises were shared: there is extensive evidence that religious orders in the Portuguese Empire guided their relations with the Indians and Africans based on a concept of justice that was barely distinguished from that used by colonists or by royal judges and administrators. The legal ordering established by these agents, from the royal council to the local chambers, sanctioned by the Jesuits who acted as advisers or confessors and legitimized by their theologians at the universities of Coimbra and Évora, made sense of the social practices of colonial societies, organizing them according to their common interests, expressed under the designation "common good."[10] The foundation of these new societies[11] lay in the exploitation of Indian and African

9 João Adolfo Hansen, "Ler & ver: pressupostos da representação colonial," *Veredas. Revista da Associação Internacional de Lusitanistas* 3, no. 1 (2000): 76.

10 Carlos A. de M. R. Zeron, "A construção de uma ordem colonial nas margens americanas do império português: discussões sobre o 'bem comum' na disputa de moradores e jesuítas pela administração dos índios (séculos XVI–XVIII)" (habilitation thesis, Universidade de São Paulo, 2010).

11 I refer here to the concept initially developed by Darcy Ribeiro and taken up by several authors since then. Darcy Ribeiro, *Estudos de antropologia da civilização: as Américas e a civilização, processo de formação e causas do desenvolvimento desigual dos povos americanos* (Petrópolis: Vozes, 1983). 87–99, 206–18. See also Darcy Ribeiro, *O povo brasileiro* (São Paulo: Companhia das Letras, 1995). For a critique of this position, see Florestan Fernandes, "Formação e desenvolvimento da sociedade brasileira," in *O Brasil de Florestan*, ed. Florestan Fernandes and Antônio David (Belo Horizonte: Autêntica, 2018): 99–115, especially 110–15.

labor, and there was agreement between the various colonizing groups on this; disagreements only arose afterwards, as to the *forms of control* of the indigenous contingent (villages – *aldeamentos* – under the tutelage of Jesuits or royal administrators, or under direct administration by the settlers, in their properties) and as to the *forms considered legitimate to appropriate the benefit of their work* (a myriad of variations that ranged from slavery, *repartição*, ecclesiastical, private or state-owned administration to free wage labor).[12] The legal order expressed existing conflicts with the populations that resisted the imposition of colonial domination under construction in America and Africa, but also among the agents of colonization that, despite finding common interests in colonial domination, often subdivided themselves into groups and fractions with divergent material interests, political views, and moral and religious values.

What I will try to demonstrate in this article is that *natural law was the fundamental concept in the Portuguese (and also Iberian and European) attempt to link populations with diverse characteristics within a single theological-political-economic system*, as they reacted to conquest and colonization; and that *it was around the same natural law that the said agents of colonization centered their controversies* when differences arose between them. The recognition of the universal in the apparent diversity of human nature and, specifically, the adoption of the premise of the unity of the human race, accordingly legitimized attempts by the Portuguese (and other Europeans) to make one (*uni vertere*) the empire's political body, especially through a legal order that aimed at the "common good" (over which, then, they disputed among themselves).[13] What was presented to them as diverse, irreducible, or contradictory demanded that they analyze precise and differentiated local contexts, to look beyond what appeared to them as semblance, or to understand why such a thing had effectively departed from the original unity. It is here that I intend to situate the particular position of the Jesuit priest António Vieira.

As I look for the process by which colonial domination was historically built, it is important to note that the questions I pose here were not foreign to the agents of colonization either, although they formulated it in their own way, with the concepts available or dominant at the time. The Jesuit José de Acosta, for example, was not the first nor the only one to classify so-called "barbarians" in categories based on criteria of social-political organization.[14] In his case, Acosta aimed to propose catechetical methods based on a relationship between dominance and conversion:[15] except for the first category of

12 These issues are being worked on within the *Grupo de Pesquisa sobre o Trabalho Indígena nas Américas (Laborindio).* See http://laborindio.fflch.usp.br/ [accessed 23.09.2022].

13 Zeron, "A construção de uma ordem colonial."

14 Domingo de Soto reports that Bartolomé de Las Casas proposed this division during the Valladolid controversy, in 1550 and 1551. Domingo de Soto, *Relecciones y opusculos. I: Introducción general, De dominio, Sumario, Fragmento: An liceat civitates infidelium seu gentilium expugnare ob idololatriam*, trans. Jaime Brufau Prats (Salamanca: Editorial San Esteban, 1995): 231–32.

15 José de Acosta, *De procuranda indorum salute*, vol. 1 (Madrid: Consejo Superior de Investigaciones Científicas, 1984–1987): 63–69.

"barbarians," which included the Chinese, the Japanese, and some groups in eastern India with whom it would be possible to converse and convince, the other two categories required the exercise of authority and force, respectively. These final two categories of barbarians brought together the various populations of the world known to Europeans at the end of the sixteenth century, including all the diversity of Amerindian societies, from the sophisticated Aztecs, Mayans, and Incas, whose empires they conquered without great difficulty, to the feared Chichimecas, Mapuches, Tupinambás, and Aimorés, who resisted them more vigorously, as well as the sub-Saharan African societies with whom they were often forced to negotiate. My argument is that although missionaries, colonizers, and royal administrators formulated different proposals to institutionalize relations between Europeans and Amerindians, or between Europeans and Africans, according to the classifications and qualifications that they attributed to groups with whom they had relations, the notions of "justice" that supported them refer to the same matrix. This matrix did not go back to what was argued by the sophist Thrasymachus, who maintained that "the just is nothing else than the advantage of the stronger,"[16] nor to the updating of this same matrix by Machiavelli, who, inspired by Roman ideas of strength and effectiveness, wanted to apply these as a political medicine against the fragmentation of the Italian peninsula. As realistic as the views of the Iberian colonists were, neither Thrasymachus nor Machiavelli were openly admitted as a source of authority.[17] However, nor were they needed, for the matrix of notions of "justice" that the Iberians used was just as effective. What I propose here is that the contradictions in the context in which Iberian colonial societies were born and evolved could not be reduced to dichotomies between might and right, between the just and the useful, and found in the principles of natural right and jus gentium, the justification of right as an exercise of power, as well as of the asymmetry – naturalized and Christianized – of relations between Europeans and natives. This is especially evident in their application of the principle of just war, but also in the identification of the circumstances that allowed the rescue of Indians and Africans, at the price of slavery, because of extreme necessity.[18] This rule led to different ways of incorporating Amerindians and Africans into colonial societies and appropriating the benefit of their work (conversely, the reactions of indigenous and African nations to those processes triggered by Europeans were also diverse, although they did not generate an institutional order in colonial society, except as isolated, non-systemic jurisprudence). This was expressed in conceptions of law and justice, whether in economic activity, in legal texts, and in theological-legal treaties, which all declined according to specific contexts. Observing such related practices and concepts from the singular

16 Plato, *Republic*: 338c.

17 Giuseppe Marcocci, "Machiavelli, la religione dei romani e l'impero portoghese," *Storica* 41–42 (2008): 62–68 and Giuseppe Marcocci, "Construindo um império à sombra de Maquiavel," in *Maquiavel no Brasil. Dos Descobrimentos ao século XXI*, ed. Rodrigo Bentes Monteiro and Sandra Bagno (Rio de Janeiro: Editora Fundação Getúlio Vargas, 2015): 68–72.

18 Zeron, *Linha de fé*: 206, 290.

position adopted by António Vieira allows to distinguish their contours more clearly, because, as I will try to demonstrate, he singularized himself by distinguishing a fourth category of barbarians, for whom he proposed a peculiar form of political-juridical relationship, although always within the parameters of natural law and jus gentium.

2 Basis

I start with a seminal author, Francisco de Vitoria, who affirmed the perfect *dominium* of the Indians over their lands, over their own people, and over the product of their work: *veri domini, tam publice quam privatim*. Despite this, his *Lesson on the American Indians* considers several concrete situations that would legitimately annul the principle of true *dominium*, through a just war moved against them: (1) when they prevented the natural right of communication, trade, and access to natural resources to Spaniards, or when they denied the right of soil to their children born in America; (2) when they prevented evangelization; (3) or to protect converts. On the other hand, their freedom – due to the public *dominium* they were recognized as having, and understood at the time as political independence obtained through self-government – could be legitimately restricted (4) when the converted Indians, being numerous, had a Christian prince appointed by the pope, (5) to prevent the tyranny of indigenous chiefs, especially when they promoted ritual sacrifices of innocents, and (6) by free and voluntary election of the majority of the Indians, who "recognized the wisdom and humanity of the Spaniards' administration."[19] (7) Such freedom could even be suppressed as a consequence of wars waged with "allies and friends," through which "the barbarians and their lands may or might have come into the possession and dominion [*dominium*] of the Spaniards."[20]

In relation to these titles, there were not many controversies among Spaniards, nor, more broadly, among Europeans, as they were based on shared principles, derived from natural and divine law. The disputes began with the interpretation of the *circumstances* that gave rise to them. On the other hand, although the second part of his *Relection*, on the "unjust titles the barbarians of the New World passed under the rule of the Spaniards," provoked the displeasure of the emperor and the pope and brought some unease to Vitoria, the most fragile and problematic point of his argument lies, in my view, in the eighth and last legitimate title, with which he ends his *Relection*. In this, *Vitoria mixes*[21]

19 Francisco de Vitoria, *Political Writings* (Cambridge: Cambridge University Press, 2010): 288.

20 Ibid.: 290.

21 I was only able to check Palencia's codex, but I also rely on the definitive editions printed in Lyon (1557) and in Salamanca (1565), as well as on the French edition by Maurice Barbier (Francisco de Vitoria, *Leçons sur les Indiens et sur le droit de guerre*, trans. Maurice Barbier [Genève: Droz, 1966]), who collated different manuscripts (see his note: xix–xx).

two incompatible concepts: tutelage and natural slavery. In the conclusion of the first part of the *Relection*, Vitoria already faced one of the most commonly alleged justifications for the domination of the Indians by the Spaniards: "*these barbarians are insufficiently rational to govern themselves* and so on"[22] (in the original: *quod isti videntur servi a natura, quia parum valent ratione ad regendum etiam ipsos*; emphasis added). Based on this argument, the Dominican rejected the idea that the Spaniards could acquire *dominium* over the Indians. To this end, he takes up the distinction that Aristotle made between natural slavery and civil slavery:

> Aristotle certainly did not mean to say that such men [*qui parum valent ingenio*,] thereby belong by nature to others [*alieni iuris*] and have no rights of ownership over their own bodies and possessions (*dominium [et] sui et [aliarum] rerum*). Such slavery is a civil and legal condition, to which no man can belong by nature [*qua nullus est servus a natura*]. Nor did Aristotle [*Philosophus*] mean that it is lawful to seize the goods and lands, and enslave and sell the persons, of those who are by nature less intelligent. What he meant to say was that such men have a natural deficiency, because of which they need others to govern and direct them. It is good that such men should be subordinate to others, like children to their parents until they reach adulthood, and like a wife to her husband. That this was Aristotle's [*Philosophi*] true intention is apparent [*patet*] from his parallel statement that some men are 'natural masters' [*natura domini*] by virtue of their superior intelligence [*valent intellectu*]. He certainly did not mean by this that such men had a legal right to arrogate power to themselves over others on the grounds of their superior intelligence, but merely that they are fitted by nature to be princes and guides [*imperare et regere*]. Hence, granting [*dato*] that these barbarians are as foolish and slow-witted [*inepti et hebetes*] as people say they are, it is still wrong to use this as grounds to deny their true dominion ([*verum*] *dominium*); nor can they be counted among the slaves [*servorum civilium*].[23]

That is to say, unlike civil slavery, natural slavery does not imply loss of *dominium*.[24] It is based on these Aristotelian concepts and distinctions that Vitoria concluded the first part of his *Relection*: "It may be, as I shall show, that these arguments can provide legal grounds for subjecting the Indians,"[25] referring to the eighth "just title by which the barbarians of the New World passed under the rule of the Spaniards," with which he ends his lesson. There, in the midst of supposed hesitations ("There is one further title which may be mentioned for the sake of the argument, though certainly not asserted with confidence; it may strike some as legitimate, though I myself do not

22 De Vitoria, *Political Writings*: 251.

23 Ibid. The English translation unfortunately is not always good. I am inserting the Latin expressions between brackets when required to understand the original meaning and to bring back the actual concepts that Vitoria used.

24 It must be noted, though, that for Aristotle the slave is "one division of property" (Aristotle, *Politics*, trans. Harris Rackham [London: William Heineman; Cambridge: Harvard University Press, 1959]: 1256 a), so that "the slave is not merely the slave of the master but wholly belongs to the master" (ibid.: 1254 a).

25 De Vitoria, *Political Writings*: 251.

dare either to affirm or condemn it out of hand. It is this: [. . .]"),[26] Vitoria confirms that the Amerindians effectively are natural slaves:

> these barbarians, though not totally mad, as explained before, are nevertheless so close to being mad, that *they are unsuited to setting up or administering a commonwealth both legitimate and ordered in human and civil terms.* Hence they have neither appropriate laws nor magistrates fitted to the task. Indeed, they are unsuited even to governing their own households *(res familiaris)*; hence their lack of letters, of arts and crafts (not merely liberal, but even mechanical), of systematic agriculture, of manufacture, and of many other things useful, or rather indispensable, for human use.[27]

Therefore, he concludes that "they could be governed as servants," provided that it was for their own good, according to the Aristotelian definition of natural slavery:

> It might therefore be argued that for their own benefit the princes of Spain might take over their administration, and set up urban officers and governors on their behalf, or even give them new masters, so long as this could be proved to be in their interest.[28]

Vitoria's solution is ambiguous, though, because while until now he had followed the Aristotelian distinctions properly, he then introduces a confusion:

> As I have said, this argument would be persuasive if the barbarians were in fact all mad; in that case, it is beyond doubt that such a course would be not merely lawful, but wholly appropriate, and princes would be bound to take charge of them as if they were simply children.[29]

Natural slavery and minority are absolutely distinct categories: natural slavery, as its name says, is a perennial and determined condition, while minority is a transitory condition. There is no *dominium* over minors, just as there is no domination over slaves by nature: both the tutelage and "government of the wisest" are instituted for the usefulness of those submitted; but tutelage is temporary while natural lordship, on the contrary, is permanent; the fact that both are aimed at the benefit of the governed does not authorize extrapolating the validity of this statement to make different categories equivalent. The use, by Vitoria, of the verb in the conditional and the expression "as if"[30] does not mitigate the impropriety of the confusion. For Aristotle (who serves as a reference to Vitoria), madmen and children are comparable, but they are not confused with each other:

---

26 Ibid.: 290.

27 Ibid. The italics are from the English translation; in note 88, the editor correctly observes that, in this passage, Vitoria is "returning to the question of natural slavery."

28 Ibid.

29 Ibid.

30 *Imo tenerentur ad hoc principes, sicut, si omnino essent infantes.*

> children and the sick and insane have many opinions which no sensible man would discuss, for these persons need not argument but the former time in which to grow up and alter and the latter medical or official [*politikos*] chastisement.[31]

Vitoria's ambiguity acquires even greater proportions when we take into account his references to the Epistle to the Galatians, which equates the child heir, under tutelage, and the slave (Gl 4, 1). The question in this passage concerns whether children before the age of reason can be legal masters. All the more: in the immediately preceding question, Vitoria wonders if "irrational creatures can have any dominion," where he concludes that "irrational creatures clearly cannot have any dominion";[32] "only rational creatures have mastery over their own actions"[33] and, "although this argument may seem a mere quibble over words, it is quite improper and contrary to normal usage [to concede *dominium* to irrational creatures]."[34]

The whole issue raised here about Vitoria's ambiguity seems to effectively converge on the similarity or difference between children and the irrational ("if the barbarians were in fact all mad [. . .] princes would be bound to take charge of them as if they were simply children"). He states that "children seem [*videtur*] in this respect not to be any different from irrational beings."[35] But, here, in the first part of the *Relectio* (where he defends the thesis of the perfect *dominium* of the Amerindians), immediately afterwards he restores the difference between children and irrational beings, since the minor heir is a legitimate and true owner, concluding that "the same does not hold of an irrational creature, since the child does not exist for another's use [*propter alium*], like an animal, but for himself [*propter se*]."[36] This position is consistent with what he wrote in *De Lege. Commentarium in Primam Secundae*, where he reiterated Thomas Aquinas' position that natural law is a habit,[37] which can be acquired through education (which also aligns with Aristotle's position). However, in the last part of the *Relectio*, and particularly in the passage quoted and commented on in the previous paragraph, such distinctions are overlooked by Vitoria. After all, according to Thomas Aquinas, men contract dullness in judgment *from a natural indisposition*, as in the case of idiots.[38] Furthermore, it is worth noting that Thomas Aquinas differentiates *insipientia*, which only concerns the ignorance of divine things (*solum circa divina*), *stultitia*, which deals with divine and human things, *fatuitas*, which concerns those who lack the sense of judgment (*fatus caret sensu iudicandi*),

---

31 Aristotle, *Eudemian Ethics*: I, 3: 1214b (https://anastrophe.uchicago.edu/cgi-bin/perseus/citequery3.pl?dbname=GreekAug21&query=Arist.%20Eth.%20Eud.%201214b&getid=1 [accessed 15.08.2022]).

32 De Vitoria, *Political Writings*: 247.

33 Ibid.: 248.

34 Ibid.

35 Ibid.: 249.

36 Ibid.

37 Tomás de Aquino, *Suma teológica*, 4th ed. (São Paulo: Loyola, 2014): I–II, q. 94, a. 1.

38 Ibid.: II–II, q. 46, a. 2; italics are mine; see also II–II, q. 15, a. 2.

and *amentia*, an absolute stupidity like that of the insane, who do not discern what is mischief (*iniuria*)[39] – so that, for Thomas Aquinas, as I understand it, madmen could not acquire natural law and judgment by habit or education, as this is not a transitory condition. Now, in the passage under consideration, Vitoria brings together barbarians, madmen, and children without making these distinctions, nor between divine and human things.[40] Vitoria does not undo the confusion mentioned at the end of his *Relectio*, either. On the contrary:

> there is scant difference between the barbarians and madmen; they are little or no more capable of governing themselves than madmen, or indeed than wild beasts. They feed on food no more civilized and little better than that of beasts. On these grounds, they might be handed over to wiser men to govern. And an apparent confirmation of this argument is if some mischance were to carry off all the adult barbarians, leaving alive only the children and adolescents enjoying to some degree the use of reason but still in the age of boyhood and puberty, it is clear that princes could certainly take them into their care and govern them for as long as they remained children. But if this is admitted, it seems impossible to deny that the same can be done with their barbarian parents, given the supposed stupidity which those who have lived among them report of them, and which they say is much greater than that of children and madmen among other nations.[41]

I quote this whole section to show how Vitoria transits from the qualification of the Amerindians as "slaves by nature" (*quod isti videntur servi a natura; sunt natura servi*) and "demented" – perennial conditions[42] – to "children" – a transitional condition. In

39 Ibid.: II–II, q. 46, a. 1.

40 Anthony Pagden does not comment on the difference in the condition of the child and the madman, being content to accompany Vitoria in the "resolution" through tutelage, education, and habit (referring to Aristotle and psychology): "by insisting that it was education that was responsible for the Indian's behaviour, Vitoria had effectively liberated him from a timeless void of semi-rationality and set him into an historical space where he would be subject to the same laws of intellectual change, progress and decline as other men are, be they Christian or non-Christian, European or non-European." Anthony Pagden, *The Fall of Natural Man: The American Indian and the origins of comparative ethnology* (New York: Cambridge University Press, 1986): 99.

41 Ibid.: 290–91.

42 Which, as we have seen, he denies. In denying this, he would not be alone, though: most of the theologians of the School of Salamanca follow him in this point. Luis de Molina, for example, who is influenced by Vitoria with regard to the question of the *dominium*, affirms in his treatise *De iustitia et iure*: II, 18, 3 that *amentes* and the children are both legitimate owners, since the *dominium* precedes the use of reason, and because it is based on a potentiality (Luis de Molina, *De Justitia et Jure*, 3rd ed. [Cologne: n.p., 1613–1614]). As Fernando Rodrigues Montes D'Oca comments, if the capacity for reason is a necessary constituent for the human species, then the existence of permanent demented beings cannot be accepted, since in nature there is no privation of what is necessary for the species (Fernando Rodrigues Montes D'Oca, "Francisco de Vitoria e a teoria aristotélica da escravidão natural," *Thaumazein* 7, no. 14 [2014]: 3–31). Roberto Hofmeister Pich interestingly suggests that, in reality, Vitoria's propositions are made in degrees, from potential to actual: "Vitoria knows perfectly well that in the Aristotelian tradition [the *amentes*] were understood not as virtual possessors of reason, but as 'perpetual fools', whose part in reason is so small that it is definitely not hoped that they *will make* use of reason. Their status is one of insufficient participation in rationality. Against the expectation of

the last quote, he starts from real children ("if some mischance were to carry off all the adult barbarians"), "that princes could certainly take them into their care and govern them for as long as they remained children" (note the transience of the condition of children, recognized and affirmed in "as long as they remained children") to return to their "barbarian" and "stupid" parents, to whom, however, "it seems impossible to deny that the same can be done," that is, "govern them" while they are in such a state of "stupidity." That is to say, at this point he no longer equates "barbarians" with "slaves by nature," insofar as he suggests that their condition could be remedied through education.[43]

In summary, up to this point: if the conclusion of the first part correctly followed Aristotelian concepts and distinctions, the final conclusion of the *Relection* is *doubly ambiguous*: in the proper sense of the word, i.e. in raising doubts and uncertainties when approaching contrary concepts (tutelage and natural slavery), but also because it does not explicitly explain the distinction existing in the foundation of those concepts (minority and amentia).

Why does he leave the ambiguity unresolved? Since he had already been careful, in the first part, in distinguishing natural slavery from civil slavery, why did he not distinguish it from minority? I assume he sought to reconcile the equality derived from the recognition of the unity of mankind with the theological, moral, legal, and political viability of the colonial enterprise; the *Relection* is inconclusive, but *the*

---

this tradition, Vitoria believes that the *amentes* also, if they exist, 'can be owners'; following the premise of the relationship between dominion and right, it is worth repeating that the *amentes* can suffer injury, therefore they have rights; therefore, they also have dominion. Although this still does not resolve the question of whether the 'barbarians' can have civilian dominion, Vitoria does not hesitate to say that 'dementia' or 'disability in reason' does not prevent them from 'owning' something or their assets. The deliberation *is not clear* in all its aspects. One can have the impression that Vitoria's propositions about the condition of the Indians as *amentes* are made in degrees, in which a different critical step to the thesis that they have no dominion is made each time. In the first step worked on here, one has the impression that Vitoria still places them on the same level as the 'children', which is why he hesitates to concede them civilian dominion or effective control of material goods and assignment of government functions. After all, the debated proposition speaks of the barbarians *being able* to own something, and not *already* owning something. The next proposition will suggest that they *own* something, and that in the civil sphere." Roberto Hofmeister Pich, "*Dominium* e *ius*: sobre a fundamentação dos direitos humanos segundo Francisco de Vitoria (1483–1546)," *Teocomunicação* 42, no. 2 (2012): 388–89 (my translation; italics are from the author).

43 Comparatively, it can be observed that Juan Ginés de Sepúlveda's argument does not suffer from these ambiguities, since, for him, Amerindians are "barbarians and slaves by nature" (*barbari sunt, et natura servi*); their barbarism, expressed in their uses and customs (their second nature), confirm their natural condition. Juan Ginés de Sepúlveda, *Democrates segundo, o de las justas causas de la guerra contra los indios* (Madrid: Consejo Superior de Investigaciones Científicas/Instituto Francisco de Vitoria, 1984): 86. For Nestor Capdevilla, who comments on the differences and the similarities between the imperialist perspectives of Vitoria and Sepúlveda: "La brutalité (ou la charité!) de Sepúlveda est de ne pas attendre la faute pour justifier l'assujetissement puisque le barbare est soumis du fait de sa nature." Bartolomé de Las Casas, *La controverse entre Las Casas et Sepúlveda* (Paris: Vrin, 2007): 19 (see 15–20).

ambiguity pointed out left loopholes that opened up possibilities. Indeed, the last question of the *Relection* raises again the hypothesis of the qualification of the Indians as fully empowered beings from the moral and political point of view, that is, regarding natural and civil law. He answers this question in the negative, however:

> if all these titles were inapplicable, that is to say if the barbarians gave no just cause for war and did not wish to have Spaniards as princes and so on, *the whole Indian expedition* [peregrinatio] *and trade would cease*, to the great loss of the Spaniards. And this in turn would mean a huge loss to the royal exchequer, which would be intolerable.[44]

In other words, even with perfect and true *dominium*, (1) the Spaniards still would have the right to trade with the natives (since trade is understood as a natural right, for the subsistence of men) and to exploit natural resources (given by God to all men[45]); (2) the crown would have the right to tax "a fifth part of the value or more" of the gold and silver brought by the Spaniards, "since the sea passage was discovered by our prince, and our merchants would be protected by his writ." (3) The third answer, however, denies the very premise of the question about the true and perfect *dominium* of the Amerindians:

> it is clear that once a large number of barbarians have been converted, it would be neither expedient nor lawful for our prince to abandon altogether the administration of those territories.[46]

That is to say, the conversion of "many barbarians" (*multorum barbarorum*) would imply the loss of *dominium* and political autonomy, and submission to the Christian prince – although belonging to the Church's mystical body should not imply belonging to the political body of a particular republic. In summary: (a) if the Amerindians could be qualified as slaves by nature, it would be up to the Spaniards to apply the "requirements of charity, since the barbarians are our neighbors and we are obliged to take care of their goods,"[47] in a Christian rereading of the Aristotelian "usefulness" that would benefit both the Indians and the Spaniards (private capital and the monarchy); (b) if they were qualified as minors, the Spaniards would have to tutor them for the benefit of the natives, and, by extension, control their properties; (c) if perfect and true *dominium* was recognized to the Amerindians – a hypothesis that he considered from the first part of the *Relection*[48] – it would be up to the Spaniards to maintain

44 Ibid.: 291. The italics are from the English translation; I inserted the word inside brackets.
45 Gen. 1: 26–28.
46 De Vitoria, *Political Writings*: 292.
47 Ibid.: 291.
48 "They are not in point of fact madmen, but have judgment like other men. This is self-evident, because they have some order (*ordo*) [*aliquem ordinem*] in their affairs: they have properly organized cities, proper marriages, magistrates and overlords (*domini*), laws, industries, and commerce, all of which require the use of reason. They likewise have a form (*species*) of religion, and they correctly apprehend things which are evident to other men, which indicates the use of reason." Ibid.: 250.

trade and the unrestricted exploitation of natural resources (with the consequent taxation of Spanish traders by the crown); (d) finally, in any situation, if a "large number" of the Amerindians were converted, whatever this "large number" amounts to, "it would be neither expedient nor lawful for our prince to abandon altogether the administration of those territories."[49]

This conclusion attenuates, perhaps, the impact of the second part of the *Relection*,[50] where Vitoria contested the universal jurisdiction of the pope and the emperor,[51] but does not undo the ambiguity pointed out above; on the contrary, to the natural lordship and tutelage of the Spaniards over the natives, he adds the Spanish domination over free Indians, derived from conversion. With these questions still left open and the *Relection* inconclusive, we can only go back to the premise of his presentation before the first part:

> I say that it [the discussion on the justice or injustice of the *negotium* of the Spanish among the barbarians][52] is not the province of lawyers, or not of lawyers alone, to pass sentence in this question. Since these barbarians we speak of are not subjects [of the Spanish crown] by human law (*iure humano*), as I shall show in a moment, their affairs cannot be judged by human statutes (*leges humanae*), but only by divine ones, in which jurists are not sufficiently versed to form an opinion on their own. And as far as I am aware, no theologian of note or worthy of respect in a matter of such importance has ever been called upon to study this question and provide a solution. Yet since this is a case of conscience, it is the business of the priests, that is to say of the Church, to pass sentence upon it.[53]

In other words: contrary to what the commentators of Vitoria commonly do (reduce him to a position unequivocally favorable to the true and perfect *dominium* of the Indians), we are obliged to note the ambiguity pointed out, as well as the many openings he makes for the "legitimate" loss of *dominium*, for reasons derived from natural law and divine law. Is this an inconsistency in Vitoria? A contradiction? I think that *the meaning of the* Relection *does not end in the text, but is projected in the concrete reality of the conquest and colonization of America.* Indeed, after half a century of an ultraviolent relationship that decimated the native population,[54] the justifications he grants for the loss of *dominium* and the ambiguity between minority and natural slavery that he admits in his text *open the way for a new form of political activity* by religious orders in the formation and reproduction of colonial society. Despite being based on the information of

49 Ibid.: 292.

50 "By what unjust titles the barbarians of the New World passed under the rule of the Spaniards."

51 Carlos V prohibited Vitoria from teaching colonial questions by means of a letter addressed to the prior of the San Esteban convent in Salamanca, dated November 10, 1539 . . . before making him his counsellor in this matter. See Camilo Barcia Trelles, "Francisco de Vitoria et l'école moderne du droit international," in *Recueil des cours*, vol. 17, ed. Académie de Droit international (Paris, n.p., 1928): 136–48.

52 De Vitoria, *Political Writings*: 237.

53 Ibid.: 238.

54 Obviously, he could not incorporate a scientific explanation of the spread of diseases and their consequences.

"those who have lived among them,"[55] the speculations he made in Salamanca about what the relations between Europeans and Native Americans should have been soon became the foundation of a new practice in America and of the corresponding legal system; for, the praxis contains contradictions that only theory has difficulty in sustaining.

3 Deployments

The first Jesuit provincial in Brazil, Father Manuel da Nóbrega, who was also a student at the University of Salamanca when Vitoria gave his *Relection* on the Indians,[56] accepted the premise of the unity of the human race and, consequently, of the rights of Indians to grace and salvation:

> I am imagining all the souls of men to be one and all them of the same metal, made in the image and likeness of God, and all capable of glory and created for it; and the soul of the Pope is worth the same before God as the soul of your slave Papaná.[57]

Such a statement did not prevent him from proposing something very concrete for what Vitoria had only suggested in his *Relection*: based on the same ambiguity (the Indians are our neighbors (*"próximos"*),[58] but, in other passages of that same text, he says that they are as "bestial" as "dogs," "pigs," and "vipers"[59]) and based on the same justifications derived from natural law ("they do not keep the natural law"[60]) and from divine law (they are "inconstant"[61]), Nóbrega suggested that the Indians should be reduced to villages (*aldeamentos*) under the tutelage of the Jesuits, where laws and justice should be imposed on them – "given"[62] by the priests, as he writes, and only endorsed by the

---

55 Ibid.: 291.

56 De Vasconcelos, *Crônica da Companhia de Jesus*: vol. 1, 174. See also João Adolfo Hansen, *Manuel da Nóbrega* (Recife: Fundação Joaquim Nabuco/Editora Massangana, 2010): 18; Carlos A. de M. R. Zeron, "Salamanca em contexto colonial: a teologia política de Manuel da Nóbrega (1517–1570)", in La Escuela de Salamanca: la primera versión de la modernidad, ed. David Torrijos-Castrillejo; Jorge Luis Gutiérrez (Madrid: Ediciones San Dámaso e Editorial Sindéresis, 2022): 286–287.

57 "Estou eu imaginando todas as almas dos homens serem umas e todas de um metal, feitas à imagem e semelhança de Deus, e todas capazes da glória e criadas para ela; e tanto vale diante de Deus por natureza a alma do Papa, como a alma do vosso escravo Papaná." Da Nóbrega, "Diálogo": 331–32.

58 Ibid.: 325–26.

59 Ibid.: 320–22. See note 1 above.

60 Ibid.: 345; see also 327 and 344.

61 Ibid.: 320.

62 "The law that must be given to them is to prohibit the consumption of human flesh and the initiative of the war without the permission of the governor; force them to have only one wife; oblige them to dress, as they have so much cotton, at least once they become Christians; prohibit their sorcerers; maintain harmony among them and with the Christians; force them to live in peace, in a sedentary way, if not among the Christians, on enough land distributed to them, and with the fathers of the Society to

governor-general of Brazil.[63] While in the *Relection* Vitoria only suggested that the clergy were the sole zealous agents of the conversion of the Gentile and, therefore, authorized to tutor them, Nóbrega claimed for the Jesuits *exclusive control* of the main colonization areas, alongside the sugar mills and the colonial cities: the *aldeamentos*.

Thus, since the middle of the sixteenth century, grounded on a decisive impulse by Nóbrega, which was effectively supported by the king of Portugal and by the governor-general of Brazil, the Jesuits assumed not only spiritual but also temporal control of the royal villages where Indians of different ethnic groups were gathered.[64] With that, they started to control the main reserves of labor of the Luso-American colony, along with the main forces of defense of the Portuguese conquests. This was a situation that, despite strong opposition from the settlers, lasted for more than a century, until the death of Father António Vieira, at the very end of the seventeenth century. António Vieira also started from the premise of the unity of mankind to affirm the *dominium*, or natural right to sovereignty, of the indigenous nations in terms equivalent to those used by Vitoria and Nóbrega:

> What they are not, despite all this [i.e., the "injustice" and "tyranny" with which the settlers treated them], is that they are not slaves, nor yet vassals. Slaves they are not, because they have been not taken in just wars; nor vassals either, because like a Spanish or Genoese captive in Algiers is still a vassal of his king and of his republic, so the Indian remains an Indian, even though he is a captive and forced to work, as he is a member of the body and political head of his nation, equally mattering for the sovereignty of freedom, both the crown of feathers and the one of gold, and both the bow and the scepter.[65]

teach them the doctrine." Manuel da Nóbrega, "Carta ao Pe. Miguel de Torres (Bahia, 8 de maio de 1558)," in *Monumenta Brasiliae*: vol. 2, 450. It is important to note the verb chosen by Nóbrega: the law should be "given" to the Indians, that is to say, "*posta.*" As Michel Villey recalls, the expression "positive" right "served, since the Middle Ages, to translate the Greek *nomikon*, for the very nature of the laws is to be put: *ponere leges.*" Michel Villey, *Questions de Saint Thomas sur le droit et la politique* (Paris: Presses Universitaires de France, 1987): 135. In the same sense, see António Vieira, *Clavis prohetarum. Chave dos profetas. Livro III*, ed. Arnaldo do Espírito Santo (Lisbon: Biblioteca Nacional 2000): 375.

63 Carlos A. de M. R. Zeron, "Les *aldeamentos* jésuites au Brésil et l'idée moderne d'institution de la société civile," *Archivum Historicum Societatis Iesu* 76, no. 151 (2007): 38–74.

64 Zeron, *Linha de fé*: 85, no. 77. After the model developed by Nóbrega in the captaincy of São Vicente spread along the rest of the Luso-Brazilian coast, a board composed of the governor general, the bishop, and the main Jesuits, approved, in 1584, that the Jesuits should assume the two swords in the government of the royal villages (*aldeamentos reais*). This decision was confirmed by a royal decree three years later. Archivum Romanum Societatis Iesu, *Lus. 68*: f. 343 and *Bras. 15*: f. 388r-v, § 40.

65 "O que não são, sem embargo de tudo isto [i.e. a "injustiça" e a "tirania" com que os colonos os tratavam], é que não são escravos, nem ainda vassalos. Escravos não, porque não são tomados em guerra justa; e vassalos também não, porque assim como o espanhol ou genovês cativo em Argel é contudo vassalo do seu rei e da sua república, assim o não deixa de ser o índio, posto que forçado e cativo, como membro que é do corpo e cabeça política da sua nação, importando igualmente para a soberania da liberdade, tanto a coroa de penas, como a de ouro, e tanto o arco como o ceptro." António Vieira, "Voto sobre as dúvidas dos moradores de S. Paulo acerca da administração dos índios," in *Obras escolhidas: obras várias (III) em defeza dos índios*, ed. António Vieira (Lisbon: Livraria Sá da Costa, 1951): 341–42.

However, for the Indians who had already been incorporated into colonial society,[66] Vieira still endorsed and advocated, exactly 136 years after Nóbrega, *the same system of tutelage of the Indians reduced in villages*:

> all other Indians who do not have this love for their so-called lords [the *Paulistas*], divided by the most accommodated places, must be placed in numerous villages with their priests and administrators, where in the spiritual sphere they can be indoctrinated and live under the law of Christians, and temporarily governed so that they are preserved and serve the Portuguese by their stipend.[67]

The breadth of the tutelage proposed by Vieira affects not only the Indians, but also the administrators and the colonists (*moradores*),[68] which leads him to promote ecclesiastics as tutors of the entire socioeconomic system, as Nóbrega had already proposed, in the middle of the sixteenth century (Vieira's retreat, in the specific adverse circumstances he faced in São Paulo, was to grant that such ecclesiastics were neither regular nor specifically Jesuits):

> and because there are no laws so fair and light that they do not need anyone to make them execute and keep them, for this purpose it seems convenient that, just as in Pernambuco and Rio de Janeiro there were formerly ecclesiastical administrators, so there must be in São Paulo one of known zeal and justice that visits those captaincies every year and takes care that everything said is observed, and, in the cases that are presented to him, he can and knows how to decide.[69]

For Vieira, as for Nóbrega, Jesuit tutelage guaranteed the conditions for the institutionalization of colonial society in religious, moral, and political parameters different from those proposed by the colonists, who conceived and practiced ways of reducing Indians to slavery that they described as not complying with natural law.[70] However, this tutelage also implied a severe restriction on indigenous freedom; this point of their argument is subtle and worth examining further.

---

66 Ibid.: 355–56.

67 "Todos os outros índios que não tiverem este amor a seus chamados senhores [paulistas], divididos pelos lugares mais acomodados, se ponham em numerosas aldeias com seus párocos e administradores, onde no espiritual possam ser doutrinados e viver à lei dos cristãos, e temporalmente ser governados de modo que eles se conservem e sirvam por seu estipêndio aos Portugueses." Ibid.: 356.

68 See the entirety of his proposal: 356–58.

69 "E porque não há leis tão justas e leves que não necessitem de quem as faça executar e guardar, para este fim parece conveniente que, assim como em Pernambuco e no Rio de Janeiro houve antigamente administradores eclesiásticos, assim haja em S. Paulo um de conhecido zelo e justiça, que todos os anos visite aquelas capitanias e tenha cuidado de que tudo o dito se observe, e, nos casos que se oferecerem, os possa e saiba decidir." Ibid.: 358.

70 "[. . .] não só eram pecados dos Portugueses as guerras injustas, os roubos, os incêndios, as mortes e os cativeiros com que tiranizavam os gentios do sertão; nem só eram outrossim pecados dos Portugueses as torpezas, os adultérios, os estupros, as forças, as violências, os escândalos, as impiedades, com que tratavam aos índios livres e cristãos das aldeias, tomando-lhes suas mulheres e filhas, servindo-se deles, de seus filhos e delas, sem lhes pagarem seu serviço, e testando deles e deixando-os a seus herdeiros, como se foram seus escravos [. . .]." António Vieira, "Resposta aos capítulos que deu contra os religiosos da Companhia, em 1662, o procurador do Maranhão Jorge de Sampaio," in ibid.: 276.

Nóbrega and Vieira recognized in the Indians the human characteristics essential to achieve grace. But, in them, the three potentialities of the soul – namely, intelligence, memory, and will, according to the distinction established by St Augustine[71] – were not developed. The difficulty is that they did not think that such a situation was necessarily transitory; not because they understood that the Indians were like slaves by nature, but because they believed that *the Indians were not capable of improving themselves to achieve grace*, since they were prisoners of a degenerated cultural condition, perpetuating uses and customs contrary to natural and Christian norms and obeying false prophets (the shamans, the main competitors of the missionaries in their catechetical activity). Vitoria, as I pointed out above, did not develop this point clearly, but Nóbrega, Vieira, and the other Jesuits active in Portuguese America did not hesitate to characterize the Indians as "savages," "ignorant," and "inconstant" because of their incapacity to save themselves by their own means. Ignorance and inconstancy were mainly due to the lack of writing – the core criterion used by Acosta, it is worth remembering, to distinguish the three categories of "barbarians." The Indians had the memory, the will, and the intelligence; but the memory of the first divine teachings disseminated by the Apostle Thomas would have been distorted over time by oral transmission – according to what the Jesuits identified, for example, as variations in the narratives of the Creation and the Flood, or even in the transformation of himself Thomas (Tomé) into a "civilizing god," Zumé. Since the memory had become deformed, losing the purity and accuracy of the first apostolic teachings, their will, as a result, had become weak and inconstant, as their bad customs attested; and their intelligence, finally, was no longer enough to give them civil and policed behavior. The conclusion of Nóbrega and Vieira was that, in order to transform the potentialities of the indigenous soul for salvation in actuality, "moderate subjection" needed to be imposed on them.[72]

Such moderate subjection was understood based on Thomas Aquinas, for whom there are two types of fear: "servile fear," which is the fear of punishment engendered by divine wrath, and "filial fear," that is, the fear inspired by subjection to divine parental authority. Faith is produced filial fear, while its lack is the cause of servile fear; he who ignored the faith could be led to fear God through servile fear, which the Christians simulated through war. Coherent and in line with this opinion by Thomas Aquinas, Nóbrega proposed that, if the preaching and invitation to the voluntary descent of the Indians from the interior regions known as the *sertão* to the Jesuit villages

---

71 Agostinho, *De Trinitate. Livros IX–XIII*, trans. Arnaldo do Espírito Santo, Domingos Lucas Dias, João Beato and Maria Cristina Castro-Maia de Sousa Pimentel (Covilhã: Universidade da Beira Interior, 2008): X, 11, 17–19; the same distinction can be found in Tomás de Aquino, *Suma teológica*, I, q. 79, a. 7. Cf. Manuel da Nóbrega, "Diálogo": 332, and Ignace de Loyola, *Écrits*, trans. Maurice Giuliani (Paris: Desclée de Brouwer, 1991): 80–84.

72 Carlos A. de M. R. Zeron, "Vieira in movimento: dalla distinzione tra Tapuias, Tupis e Neri alla rottura nella dottrina cristiana sulla schiavitù e sulla legge naturale," in *Schavitù del corpo e schiavitù dell'anima: Chiesa, potere politico e schiavitù tra Atlantico e Mediterraneo (sec. XVI–XVIII)*, ed. Carlos A. de M. R Zeron, Emmanuele Colombo, Marina Massimi and Alberto Rocca (Rome: Bulzoni; Milano: ITL-Biblioteca Ambrosiana, 2018): 155.

located along the coast were not successful, it was legitimate to compel them to do so through force;[73] subsequently, it was up to the missionaries to induce the passage from servile fear to filial fear in the villages, where the Indians needed to receive strict religious and civic instruction, supported by constant vigilance and punishment. All this despite Vitoria affirming that "to come to the mysteries and sacraments of Christ merely out of servile fear would be sacrilege."[74] In fact, in this respect, Nóbrega's thought follows, rather, that of Thomas Aquinas, for whom

> The primary and formal object of faith is the good which is the First Truth; but the material object of faith includes also certain evils; for instance, that it is an evil either not to submit to God or to be separated from Him, and that sinners will suffer penal evils from God: in this way faith can be the cause of fear.[75]

Subjection and conversion should take place in the villages, or reductions.[76] The ways of exercising this tutelage implied, above all, the presence of the example embodied by the virtuous missionary;[77] but also to induce them to settle down and acquire discipline through compulsory work, which would make their will constant, which, in turn, would make possible the moral and political, or civic, education of the villagers and, only then, their religious education. It can be seen that law and justice, even if imposed with moderate force, were *previous and necessary conditions* for conversion: servile fear would prepare the souls of the Indians to receive the Christian faith, not constituting a direct instrument of conversion (in this sense, he could pretend not to contradict his master in Salamanca), whereas politics, inside the villages, would play an auxiliary role, but one necessary for catechesis.

In other words, and in summary: starting from the assumption of the unity of the human race, Vitoria, Nóbrega, and Vieira (as well as so many other authors, especially religious) worked with the concept of "universal." In the context of the colonial domination being established in America, however, the operation of converting variety and diversity into a unity (*uni vertere*) implied relativizing or even denying the natural *dominium*, or sovereignty, of the Amerindians, which was justified and legitimized based on the description of their particular moral and historical situation – a description that was no longer undertaken and analyzed by theologians in European universities like Vitoria, based on letters sent from the mission lands, but directly by theologians active in mission lands, like Nóbrega and Vieira, who then jumped autonomously to grounded theological conclusions.

73 The Jesuits were then accompanied by armed allied Indians. See, among other references, Guillermo Wilde, *Religión y poder en las misiones de guaraníes* (Buenos Aires: SB, 2009): 77, 93–99.

74 De Vitoria, *Political Writings*: 272. For, "the barbarians cannot be moved by war to believe, but only to pretend that they believe and accept the Christian faith; and this is monstrous and sacrilegious." Ibid.

75 Tomás de Aquino. *Suma teológica*: II–II, q. 7, a. 1.

76 From the Latin, *reducere*, i.e., lead or guide back, reconcile; for, as pointed out, initial preaching had already been done by St Thomas.

77 Manuel da Nóbrega, "Diálogo": 323–25, 329–31, 339–40.

It should be noted that "particular," and all variations of this word, derive from the Latin *pars, partem*, but "apart" comes from *a parte rei*, an expression often used by scholastic philosophy to signify that something is according to its own nature, and not from an operation of understanding (*secundum intellectum*).[78] In the case of the Indians, if their "particular" moral and historical condition could be considered transitory, their moderate subjection and tutelage, as proposed by the Jesuits, were required, thus helping them to overcome a condition in which they found themselves circumstantially prisoners and from which they could not free themselves; on the other hand, if the Indians had historically distanced themselves from the divine and moral precepts that underpinned natural law and the law of nations, they should be reduced to civil slavery and, by this means, brought back to the prop of Christian theological and political precepts. However, if their moral condition was considered "apart" from other men, that is, constitutive and essential, their submission by natural slavery was required, as the colonizers and royal administrators normally proposed.

The operation of recognizing the *universal*, of "making one" that which appeared as *particular* or *apart* implied and even demanded to describe and analyze precise local contexts, thus disambiguating Vitoria's statements. However, even when this operation was carried out by the literate men active in America, some parts were still left out of what was intended or should be unified. This is especially noticeable in António Vieira as he dealt with different contexts, from Bahia to Maranhão, from Ceará to São Paulo. In the next section, I will try to demonstrate that *natural law was the fundamental concept that allowed him to balance domination and accommodation* in the articulation of different spaces and populations with different political and cultural characteristics, who manifested different reactions to Portuguese conquest and colonization.

4 Peculiarities

While Plato, whom I evoked at the end of the introduction of this article,[79] was not so much read, despite his ideas being widely disseminated, Quintilian, on the contrary, was read and practiced daily in the rhetorical lessons of the Jesuit schools, where missionaries and children of the wealthy classes were educated, in Portuguese America; this means that the partition of the universal, as far as nations were concerned, may have had his *Institutio oratoria* as a model. In fact, for the Roman orator and professor of rhetoric, different nations have different customs, which implies that a barbarian, a

78 Michel Villey, *Questions de Saint Thomas sur le droit et la politique* (Paris: Presses Universitaires de France, 1987). See also "Universal and Particular," in *The Great Ideas. A Syntopicon of Great Books of the Western World*, ed. Mortimer J. Adler and William Gorman (Chicago: Encyclopaedia Britannica, 1952): 957–73.

79 See note 16, above.

Roman, and a Greek have a different perception of the nature of things and, so, "there is a like diversity in the laws, institutions, and opinions of different states."[80]

Starting from the evidence of the regular reading of the *Institutio oratoria* in seventeenth-century Brazil, João Adolfo Hansen and Marcello Moreira showed how the Bahian satirical poet Gregório de Matos Guerra – a contemporary of Vieira who also studied at the Jesuit College in Bahia – unfolds and amplifies the analogies that topic allowed: "the Spaniards are arrogant; French, meretricians; Italians, sodomites; Germans, muckers; Jews, Muslims and new Christians, heretics; Indians, Blacks, *mamelucos* and mulattos, animals." As for the Portuguese, suffice it to say that the capital of their American colony "is personified as 'stepmother of the natives' and qualified as a 'giddy and smug city' composed of two Fs, 'one for filch (*furtar*), another for fuck (*foder*)'."[81]

The writings of the Jesuits, however, whose primary mission was to "make one" all peoples and nations within the mystical body of the Church, do not endorse Gregório de Matos' mordacity and hopelessness. Nevertheless, the priests recognized that the Portuguese colonists constituted the main obstacle to their project, insofar as they treated the enslaved Indians with feelings of greed (filching their freedom), lust (fucking them), and fury (treating them with cruelty). That is why they were qualified by Nóbrega as "bad Christians" (*maus cristãos*), an expression that repeatedly appeared from his first letters; but, not so often as "particulars" (*particulares*), an expression preferred by Vieira and whose use denotes precisely, at each step, the opposition to the common good of the Portuguese Empire, which, in his view, would be the instrument of the universal conversion of all peoples into the mystical body of the Church.

In a controversy with aldermen shortly before the expulsion of the Jesuits from the state of Maranhão and Grão-Pará, he refused to attribute the causes of the misery of the state solely to the lack of Indian slaves (slavery which, it should be noted, he said he did not oppose: "I approve of it very much, and requested it with the King, His Majesty insisting that everyone should be free").[82] For Vieira, experience revealed that the Indians were never enough to sustain economic activity due to the fragility of their health and their incapacity for the kind of work required by the sugar, cotton, or tobacco cultures, but also due to their resistance by war, flight, or even "longing" (*saudade*). In light of all these obstacles, only slaves from Angola were suitable.

---

80 Marcos Fábio Quintiliano, *Instituição oratória*, trans. Bruno Fregni Bassetto (Campinas: Editora da Unicamp, 2015): V, X, 25. https://www.perseus.tufts.edu/hopper/text?doc=Perseus%3Atext%3A2007.01.0063%3Abook%3D5%3Achapter%3D10%3Asection%3D25

81 João Adolfo Hansen and Marcello Moreira, *Para que todos entendais: poesia atribuída a Gregório de Matos e Guerra: letrados, manuscritura, retórica, autoria, obra e público na Bahia dos séculos XVII e XVIII* (Belo Horizonte: Autêntica, 2013): 417–18. It should be noted that the two "Fs" in overplus in Bahia contrast with the one "F" that, in a complementary topic, the Indians lack: "F" for faith.

82 António Vieira, "Resposta que deu o Padre António Vieira ao Senado da Câmara do Pará sobre o resgate dos índios do sertão," in *Obra completa do Padre António Vieira*, t. IV, vol. 3, ed. Pedro Calafate and José Eduardo Franco (São Paulo: Loyola, 2014): 155.

His explanation for the state's misery referred to five other causes: the tangled hydrography of the region, which hindered trade; the scarcity of supplies, as a result of intensive hunting and fishing; the absence of public spaces, which meant that each house had to provide all its needs autonomously; the war against Spain, which inflated the prices of imported products while bringing down the prices of sugar and tobacco on the international market; "the fifth, and very notable, vanity, which has grown in recent times, with spending not being measured, as in the past, with possessions, but with appetite."[83]

Vanity is defined in the first Portuguese dictionary, by Raphael Bluteau, as "an immoderate desire for glory, for praise, for honors."[84] In the aforementioned excerpt by Vieira, the term takes on a very precise meaning, however, as it is also precisely contextualized by linking it to social stratification in the colony. In fact, colonial society had some distinct and peculiar characteristics[85] compared to metropolitan society: in addition to being a slavish society, mestizos, free Indians and freed Africans defined the layers underneath the poorest Portuguese. For Vieira, the settlers cynically and hypocritically used their poverty to claim more than, in his understanding, they could aspire to, through the capital – material and symbolic – of Indians subordinate to them, regardless of whether they were free or slave. That fifth cause, which Vieira described as "very notable," was at the heart of the discussions about the "just," insofar as it was defined based on social relations in the colony. As the governor of Rio de Janeiro puts it, "even those whose very poverty does not allow them to have anyone to serve them, rather subject themselves to walking many years through the backlands in search of someone to serve them than to serve others for a single day."[86]

---

83 Ibid.: 154. I collated this with the manuscript kept at the Biblioteca da Ajuda: 54-XI-27, no. 12 a-p, because the fifth cause, "vanity" (*vaidade*), however "notable" it may be for Vieira, appears erroneously spelled in several editions: "validade" (in Bernardo Pereira de Berredo, *Anais históricos do Estado do Maranhão, em que se dá notícia do seu descobrimento, e tudo o mais que nele tem sucedido desde o ano em que foi descoberto até o de 1718* (Rio de Janeiro: Tipo editor Ltda., 1988): 253; but the transcription is correct in the original 1749 edition; "variedade" (in José Carlos Sebe Meihy, *Escritos instrumentais sobre os índios do padre Antônio Vieira* [São Paulo: EDUC/Loyola/Giordano, 1992]: 48); in the edition by António Sérgio and Hernâni Cidade, many lines were deleted, jumping from the second cause to the conclusions of the text (António Vieira, *Obras escolhidas: obras várias (III) em defeza dos índios*: 135–39); João Lúcio de Azevedo partially quotes the document, interrupting it halfway through, but correctly reporting the word "vanity" (João Lúcio de Azevedo, *História de António Vieira* [Lisbon: Clássica editora, 1992]: 275). In addition to the two editions cited, I only found the correct text printed in António Vieira, *Obras várias do Padre António Vieira*, vol. 1 (Lisbon: J.M.C. Seabra & T.Q. Antunes, 1856): 138.

84 Raphael Bluteau, *Vocabulário portuguez e latino* (Coimbra: no Colégio da Companhia de Jesus, 1712–1728).

85 See note 11 above.

86 "Até aquelles, cuja muita pobreza, lhe não permitte ter quem o sirva, se sogeita antes a andar muitos annos pello certam em busca de quem o sirva, do que a servir a outrem hum só dia." Antonio Paes Sande, "Relatório do Governador Antonio Paes de Sande, em que indica as causas do malogro das

The theme of vanity had already been dealt with extensively by Vieira in the *Sermão da Primeira Dominga da Quaresma*, preached in the Royal Chapel in Lisbon in 1655: commenting on a passage from Ecclesiastes 1:2, "*vanitas vanitatum et omnia vanitas*" ("vanity of vanities, all things are vanity"), he addressed the topic of the temptation of the devil, who proposed to exchange man's soul for the riches of the world. The question raised by Vieira was: how is it possible that, for the devil, my soul is worth more than everything else in the world? His answer: the devil uses cunning, preventing, through the illusion of vanity, that man thinks, weighs, and judges; in short, preventing reason from overcoming affections. For Vieira, of course, the soul is the true "everything" (*omnia*), and not the world, even the entire world, which is nothing more than a false universality that the devil promises in exchange. According to José Gonçalves Gama:

> The oratory resource is manifested in the connection it makes between the analysis of the devil's temptation and the urgency to awaken a consciousness of responsibility and of intervention in the conversion of so many souls entrusted to the kings and to the kingdom of Portugal. The devil, in the temptation he makes to Christ, offers the whole world for someone else's soul. It is this openness of interest for the souls of others that must be part of the remedy to overcome temptation, as it distances us from the vain glory of riches and honors for our own benefit, and allows Vieira to go beyond the compromises of the tempting words. [. . .] Vieira inverts the demon's strategy, making possession and conquest of the kingdoms the highest and grandest objective, since diverted from the satisfaction of human vanity to the zeal for the conversion of souls, in total and disinterested mission of service. Prudence is superimposed on vanity, and the disorderly affection of the heart opens up to a new order of love for the salvation of souls, which can accumulate kingdoms and glories, as these will be put at the service of the same cause, but free from attachments to appearances and false illusions.[87]

In this sense, Vieira can develop the analogy of interest in the salvation of his own soul with interest in the salvation of everyone's soul. Before that, however, it was necessary to watch over the salvation of the republic, whose government and administration, if conducted with a view to the common good, would favor the salvation of all.

In short: the first two reasons named by Vieira to explain the misery of the state of Maranhão could even be remedied with the regulated work of rowing Indians and with the organization of the colonial economy; but the other reasons depended fundamentally on decisive political intervention by the prince, organizing public spaces and imposing fair social relations within the sovereign Portuguese monarchy. In the distant state of Maranhão and Grão-Pará, however, the intervention of the Jesuits in the matter of the Indians, regulating their dealings with the settlers and governing their villages, was justified with a view to the salvation of the Portuguese Empire,

pesquizas das minas do Sul e propõe o alvitre para se obter de uma maneira segura o seu descobrimento," *Anais da Biblioteca Nacional do Rio de Janeiro* 39 (1917): 199. Undated document, but Antônio Paes de Sande was governor of Rio de Janeiro between March 25, 1693, and October 7, 1694.

87 José Gonçalves Gama, "Vieira e a vaidade: da tentação fazer remédio," in *Padre António Vieira: Colóquio*, ed. José Cândido Martins (Braga: Universidade Católica Portuguesa, 2009): 213–14.

destined to carry out the project of universal conversion. In Maranhão, as in Brazil, this would be done through the exercise of indirect power, the *potestas indirecta* whose formulation, outlined at the end of Vitoria's Relection, appeared already clearly specified and contextualized in Nóbrega's texts and, then, untill Vieira through the protagonism claimed and assumed by the Society of Jesus.

Justice within a republic was defined, at the time, in Aristotelian terms: giving each individual what is theirs by right or duty, according to his place or social condition.[88] Justice was aimed at the common good through distributive and commutative justice, always according to the Aristotelian partition.[89] Now, Vieira noted that, in a slave colonial society far from the kingdom, where there is a "lack of political government" (*falta de governo político*) and where "vanity" has grown "not with possessions, but with appetite," certain adjustments should be made. In this sense, he demanded the interventionist action of the state (from the king and his local representative, the governor, to the city councils) to distribute justice within a socioeconomic order that was still in the process of institutionalization, as much as he claimed the exercise of the indirect power of the Church, especially of the Jesuits, to guarantee the salvation of men, whether they were Portuguese, Brazilian, or Indians, whether they were poor or rich. In other words, Vieira claimed for the Jesuits the right to interfere directly and indirectly in the realization of justice: in the justice which aimed to repair damage caused, whether voluntarily or not, by transactions between individuals, especially when involving the Indians (commutative justice), and in the justice manifested through the distribution of goods, of positions and of charges according to the merits and to the degree that each one occupied in society (distributive justice). In the first case, people were not distinguished, but attention was paid to the disharmony resulting from damage in terms of trade or contracts, or crimes; in the second case, the merit of each individual was considered, so that the unequal were treated in an unequal way and the equal in an equal way. It was up to the judge to make equity, or justice, reign. He was responsible for adapting the law to the particular circumstances of each case. To this end, he drew on legal texts, but also evaluated and weighed concrete situations, anchored in specific social and economic contexts, which demanded a specific analysis and a specific appraisal. In the exercise of prudence, a judge should combine these elements, restoring the harmony that allowed the reproduction of the social order. In Vieira's assessment (consistent with what has been affirmed since Nóbrega), in a slavish colonial society, disordered because it was still in the process of formation and far from the kingdom, the Jesuits, more than the judges, should exercise this prudence, or at least tutor it, due to the risk of condemning the souls of both the Indians and the settlers.[90] Such was the line of continuity between

88 "Distributing [. . .] to each what is proportionately equal." Aristotle, *Nicomachean Ethics*, http://data.perseus.org/citations/urn:cts:greekLit:tlg0086.tlg010.perseus-eng1:1134a.1 [accessed 23.09.2022].
89 Ibid.: 1131a–1132b.
90 In that very sense, Father Antônio de Matos also pronounced himself, among other Jesuits, in 1619: "agree disagreements and enmities with each other, prevent injuries [and] deaths, thefts and other

these two missionaries[91] in the claim they always made regarding the exercise of the *potestas indirecta* only sketched by Vitoria.

This reading and interpretation are confirmed in the *Voto sobre as dúvidas dos moradores de São Paulo acerca da administração dos índios*, a text written just over three decades after the controversy with the aldermen in Pará and referring to another area still heavily dependent on indigenous labor, at the opposite end of Portuguese America. Unlike the *Resposta ao Senado do Pará*, Vieira does not resort here to a description of the land, nor to the historical situation. It is a text with few pages aimed at restrict circulation, in which he basically refers to concepts: there are almost forty.[92] But the fundamental problem was the same: the colonists (*particulares*) opposed to the Christian universalizing project; in this case, the *Paulistas*, who had acquired a sinister reputation for having decimated Paraguay's missions, tyrannically reducing their population to slavery. The solution he proposes in São Paulo thus finds that which had already been proposed in Maranhão and Grão-Pará: the tutelage of colonial society and, especially, of the Indians gathered in the villages (*aldeamentos*).[93] The concession he makes here – in a separate and written *Voto*, which is explained by the seclusion and silence that his confreres had imposed on him[94] – is that the tutelage was exercised not specifically by Jesuits, *in loco*, but by ecclesiastical administrators, in annual visits.

---

sins [among others] occupations in the service of God and of the Republic in which the Society's Religious in these parts are concerned." Antônio de Matos, "Informação do Colégio do Rio de Janeiro pelo Padre António de Matos," in *História da Companhia de Jesus no Brasil*, vol. 6, ed. António Serafim Leite (Lisbon: Portugália, 1938–1945): 564.

91 In which they were continually relayed by other missionaries, between them. See Zeron, *Linha de fé*: 159–88, 367–68.

92 Domination, freedom, natural freedom, restitution, consent, free will, administration, slavery, *encomienda*, proportion, laziness, captivity, [capacity for] self-government, human and political life, grace, tutelage, villages (*aldeias*), political body, violence, tyranny, land, homeland, "new and unprecedented" administration, miscegenation [i.e., families that are created "mixed and domestically"], love, regret, will, tax vassals, pact, oath, justice, free men moderately obliged to work, bond (social and loving), conscience, conservation, service, medicine, indirect power.

93 "[. . .] ecclesiastical administrators [. . .] of known zeal and justice that visit those captaincies every year and take care that everything said is observed, and, in the cases that are presented to him, he can and knows how to decide." António Vieira, "Voto sobre as dúvidas dos moradores de S. Paulo acerca da administração dos índios," in *Obras escolhidas: obras várias (III) em defeza dos índios*, ed. António Vieira (Lisbon: Livraria Sá da Costa, 1951): 358. See the full quotation in note 69, above.

94 Carlos A. de M. R. Zeron, "From Farce to Tragedy. António Vieira's Hubris in a War of Factions," *Journal of Jesuit Studies* 2, no. 3 (2015): 387–420.

5 Controversies

In the *Voto*, despite the thirty-eight notions and concepts employed, it stands out that he cites only two references of authority in addition to the Bible (which, it should be noted, is only brought up on two occasions):[95] theologians and jurists frequently cited in texts on Amerindians give way to those who had practical experiences in America, the Jesuit José de Acosta and the *oidor* of the Real Audiencia de Lima Juan de Solórzano Pereira.[96]

The same authors are also cited in a text contemporary to the *Voto*, where Vieira analyzes again the situation in Maranhão: the *Clavis prophetarum*. Here, however, there was another obstacle to the universalizing Christian project, in addition to the Portuguese colonists: the general conversion of all nations was also opposed by the "barbaric Tapuias."[97] These were contrasted with the Indians of the *aldeamentos*, who, although under coercion, had already been incorporated into the mystical body of the Church and to the political body of the Portuguese Empire.[98]

Vieira was particularly concerned with some Tapuia groups inhabiting the surroundings of the Ibiapaba mountain range, a strategic region for the connection between the state of Maranhão and Grão-Pará and the State of Brazil.[99] According to Vieira, these Tapuias were allies of the Dutch against the Portuguese, when the Batavians occupied the northeast captaincies of Portuguese America.[100] After the expulsion of the Dutch, several Tapuia groups migrated towards those mountains, so that

95 Rm 3:8; Ex 21:5–6. António Vieira, "Voto sobre as dúvidas": 352, 355.

96 Ibid.: 347–48, 351–52.

97 According to Father José de Anchieta, *Arte de Grammatica da Lingoa mais usada na Costa do Brasil* (Coimbra: por Antonio de Mariz, 1595) "Tapuia" means any indigenous person from a non-Tupi tribal group, or an Indian who does not speak the Tupi language prevalent on the South American Atlantic coast. By extension, it may mean the enemies of the Tupis, who were the main allies of the Portuguese; that is, Tapuias could refer to all the Indians from the hinterland of the American continent who had not submitted or who still resisted the Portuguese on the coast; by extension, finally, Tapuia can also mean slave, or captive, according to the *Vocabulário na língua brasílica*, a Portuguese-Tupi manuscript from the beginning of the seventeenth century.

98 As Acosta said about the third category of barbarians, "*per potentiam et honestam vim quandam, ne Evangelium impediant, coercendi sunt, et in officio continendi, quos de sylvis transferri ad urbes et humanam vitam, et quodam modo invitos ad regnum compellere expediet*". De Acosta, *De procuranda indorum salute*: 68. I analyzed the uses of the topic "*compelle intrare*" (Lc 14:23) in overseas missions in Carlos A. de M. R. Zeron, "Different Perceptions on the Topic of Forced Conversion, after the South Atlantic Experience," in *Compel People to Come In. Violence and Catholic Conversions in the Non-European World*, ed. Vincenzo Lavenia et al. (Rome: Viella, 2018): 49–68.

99 Due to the difficulties of communication by land and sea, the Maranhão mission was sometimes subordinated to the province of Brazil, sometimes to the province of Portugal. See António Serafim Leite, *História da Companhia de Jesus no Brasil*: vol. 4, 213–22.

100 "[. . .] the Dutch occupied Pernambuco and shortly afterwards became lords of the fortress of Ceará and reduced all the Indians of that neighborhood to themselves." António Vieira, "Relação da missão da Serra de Ibiapaba," in *Obras escolhidas: obras várias (III) em defeza dos índios*: 77.

"Ibiapaba was truly the Geneva of all the backlands of Brazil, because many of the Pernambucan Indians were born and raised among the Dutch," becoming "Calvinists and Lutherans, as if they were born in England or Germany."[101]

In order to deal with this situation, Vieira adopted a singular position, diverging both from coreligionists like Nóbrega, whom he had always followed in these issues, and from prominent theologians, including from the Society of Jesus, such as Francisco Suárez. Nóbrega had been emphatically in favor of a strategy of confronting the Tapuias, at least since the death of Bishop Pedro Fernandes Sardinha, eaten in an anthropophagic ritual by the Caeté Indians, together with part of the ship's crew taking him back to Portugal, in 1556:

> Those who killed the people of the bishop's ship can be immediately punished and subjected, as well as all those that are touted as enemies of the Christians, and those who want to break the peace, and those who have slaves of the Christians and do not want to give them back, and all the more that do not want to suffer the fair yoke they will be given and because of that will rise against the Christians.[102]

In this letter addressed to the provincial of Portugal and confessor to the queen regent, Nóbrega gives a favorable opinion not only to the war against the Caetés, but also against any other Amerindian nation hostile to the Portuguese, extrapolating the doctrinal parameters of just war adopted by Vitoria, insofar as he authorizes *preventive attacks* against "those who want to break the peace" and against those who resisted Portuguese colonial occupation, that is "all the more that do not want to suffer the fair yoke they will be given and because of that will rise against the Christians." Nóbrega added, after the passage quoted above:

> Subjecting the gentile, many unjust ways to obtain slaves and many scruples will cease, because the men will have legitimate slaves, taken in just wars, and they will have the service and vassalage of the Indians, and the land will be populated and our Lord will win many souls, and H.M. will have a lot of income in this land, because there will be many livestock and sugar mills, since there is not much gold or silver.[103]

---

101 Ibid.: 81 and 114, respectively.

102 "Os que mataram a gente da nau do Bispo se podem logo castigar e sujeitar, e todos os que estão apregoados por inimigos dos cristãos, e os que querem quebrantar as pazes, e os que têm escravos dos cristãos e não os querem dar, e todos os mais que não quiserem sofrer o jugo justo que lhes derem e por isso se alevantarem contra os cristãos." Manuel Nóbrega, "Carta ao Pe. Miguel de Torres": 449. Fr. Luís da Fonseca pronounced the same judgement shortly afterwards: "Informação dos Primeiros Aldeamentos da Bahia," in *Cartas, Informações, Fragmentos Históricos e Sermões*, ed. José de Anchieta (Belo Horizonte: Itatiaia, 1988): 363.

103 "Sujeitando-se o gentio, cessarão muitas maneiras de haver escravos mal havidos e muitos escrúpulos, porque terão os homens escravos legítimos, tomados em guerra justa, e terão serviço e vassalagem dos Índios e a terra se povoará e Nosso Senhor ganhará muitas almas e S. A. terá muita renda nesta terra, porque haverá muitas criações e muitos engenhos já que não haja muito ouro e prata." Ibid.

Violating the doctrine of just war, he tried to reconcile the interests of the Portuguese colonists (legitimizing the war against the Tapuias as a source of obtaining slaves for the emerging sugar industry), the crown (populating the colony with vassal Indians and increasing royal incomes with the growth of economic activity), and the Jesuit mission itself ("our Lord will win many souls"). It was at that same time that Father José de Anchieta, backed by Nóbrega, declared that "[. . .] for such people, there is no better preaching than the sword and the iron rod [Ps. 2, 9], preaching where, more than in any other, it is necessary for the *compelle eos intrare* to be fulfilled [Lk 14, 23]."[104] Nóbrega and Anchieta contradict Vitoria, therefore, who understood that the Indians should not be separated by force from sins against natural law.[105] For Nóbrega,

> the Gentile must be submitted and forced to live as rational creatures, obliging them to keep the natural law. [. . .] The proof of this is that those from Bahia, being well treated and indoctrinated, became even worse, as they saw that the bad and the guilty of past deaths were not punished; but with severity and punishment they become humble and submissive.[106]

Anchieta, on the other hand, was always more impatient and intolerant than Nóbrega:

> [the Indians] are of such a restful nature that, if they are not constantly pricked, little will be enough for them not to go to mass, nor seek other remedies for their salvation. All these impediments and customs are very easy to take out if there is fear and submission, as we have seen from experience, so far, since the time of Governor Mem de Sá.[107]

104 "[. . .] para este gênero de gente, não há melhor predicação que espada e vara de ferro, na qual, mais que em nenhuma outra, é necessário que se cumpra o *compelle eos intrare.*" "José de Anchieta a Diego Laynes (São Vicente, 16 de abril de 1563)," in *Monumenta Brasiliae*: vol. 3, 554. The biblical reference is made to Luk 14:23, *Et ait dominus servo: Exi in vias et sepes et compelle intrare, ut impleatur domus mea* ("The master then ordered the servant: 'Go out to the highways and hedgerows and make people come in that my home may be filled'.").

105 De Vitoria, *Political Writings*: 272, quoted above, note 74.

106 "O gentio se deve sujeitar e fazê-lo viver como criaturas que são racionais, fazendo-lhe guardar a lei natural. [. . .] A prova disto é que estes da Baía sendo bem tratados e doutrinados com isso se fizeram piores, vendo que se não castigavam os maus e culpados nas mortes passadas; e com severidade e castigo se humilham e sujeitam." da Nóbrega, "Carta ao Pe. Miguel de Torres": 447. He returns to this point on pages 448–49: "This Gentile is of such quality that he cannot be treated by good means, but by fear and submission, as has been experienced; and so if H.M. wants to see them all converted, he must order them to be subjected and extend the Christians inland and apportion the service of the Indians to those who will help to conquer and submit, as is done in other parts of the new land; and I do not understand how the Portuguese generation, which is the most feared and obeyed beyond all nations, is suffering and almost being subjected, along all this coast, to the vilest and saddest Gentile in all the world."

107 "[Os índios] são de uma natureza tão descansada que, se não forem sempre aguilhoados, pouco bastará para não irem à missa nem buscarem outros remédios para sua salvação. Todos estes impedimentos e costumes são mui fáceis de se tirar se houver temor e sujeição, como se viu por experiência desde o tempo do governador Mem de Sá até agora." José de Anchieta, "Informação do Brasil e de suas capitanias," in *Cartas, Informações, Fragmentos Históricos e Sermões*: 341.

The nefarious consequences of the warmongering proposals of the two Jesuit provincials for the indigenous population soon became evident, however, impacting the colonial economy.[108] Devastating military campaigns were unleashed by Mem de Sá, governor general of Brazil from 1558 to 1572, after which a process of re-evaluation of the forms of contact, submission, and coexistence with the Amerindians began among the Jesuits and in conjunction with the colonial administration. This was a long process that went through some stages: the participation of the Jesuits in the *juntas* gathered in the state of Brazil, in 1566 and 1574, to regulate the legitimate titles of the war; then, already supported by the *ouvidores gerais*, demands were formulated to the king and his counsellors in Portugal for greater restrictions on the titles of just war and for the enactment of special indigenous laws.

Despite this apprenticeship, Vieira eventually also yielded to the interests and strength of the settlers, as when he created the odd juridical figure of the "slaves of condition" (*escravos de condição*)[109] in Maranhão and Grão-Pará, or when he acquiesced that despite the unjustly servile condition of the natives, "the families of the Portuguese and Indians in S. Paulo are so connected with each other" that "to break up this so natural or so naturalized union would be a kind of cruelty among those who grew up and have lived this way for many years."[110] These positions are not remembered by the historiography, which, as I pointed out in the introduction, usually follows the parameters defined by Jesuit historical memory, especially in the case of António Vieira, "the Great."[111]

On the other hand, when Vieira gave in to the force of "barbaric Tapuias," his position was expressed not by calling on sources of authority with American experience (which would be unserviceable), but, on the contrary, by confronting Francisco Suárez. Suárez faced the discussion about the limits of legitimate forms of conversion, especially in *De mediis quibus infideles possint licite ab hominibus ad fidem adduci.*[112] There, he asks (q.4) "whether the Church has the right to preach the Gospel" [*utrum Ecclesia habeat ius ad praedicandum Evangelium*, to which he answers that the Church has the right to preach the Gospel everywhere, to defend its preachers, and to delegate its right of defense (*delegare suum ius*) to any Christian prince.[113] Suárez contemplates situations, in his text,

108 I have analyzed this situation in detail in Zeron, *Linha de fé*: 109–58.

109 António Vieira, "Direções a respeito da forma que se deve ter no julgamento e liberdade no cativeiro dos índios do Maranhão," in *Obras escolhidas: obras várias (III) em defeza dos índios*: 28–32. I analyzed this issue in Carlos A. de M. R. Zeron, "Antônio Vieira e os 'escravos de condição': os aldeamentos jesuíticos no contexto das sociedades coloniais," in *A Companhia de Jesus e os índios*, ed. Eunícia Barros Barcelos Fernandes (Curitiba: Prismas, 2016): 235–62.

110 Vieira, "Voto sobre as dúvidas": 355.

111 António Serafim Leite, *História da Companhia de Jesus no Brasil* (Lisbon: Portugália, 1938–1945): vol. 9, 192.

112 Francisco Suárez, "De mediis quibus infideles possint licite ab hominibus ad fidem adduci," in Juan de la Peña, *De bello contra insulanos. Intervención de España en America*, vol. 2 (Madrid: Consejo Superior de Investigaciones Científicas, 1982): 384–407. On the likely date of writing this text (1580–1585?), see the considerations of Carlos Baciero ibid.: 335.

113 Ibid.: 384–86.

that show an update of the discussion, integrating the Iberian overseas experience but still remaining faithful to the principles and situations previously delimited by Vitoria. Thus, he affirms that the right of war should prevail when tyranny and injury are mixed: if the province wants to receive preachers and its ruler does not, the Christian prince can protect and kill, as it is a way to prevent tyranny in matters of utmost importance, concerning salvation, and also because the Church cannot be deprived of its right. Conversely, if the king wants the preachers and the province does not, the same reasons apply. If only a few people want them, the same argument and reason is still valid. If everyone refuses them, however, they can also be compelled, because it is against natural law to prevent the free transit of people without just cause and without fear of probable damage, just as it is against divine right to impede the activity of preachers, thus justifying, as in the previous cases, a just war with all its consequences.[114]

We do not know whether Vieira had access to any copy of this Suárez manuscript; in the *Clavis prophetarum*, he only explicitly mentions *De gratia* and *De legibus*, and I am not aware of any reference to that booklet in any of his texts. Whatever the case may be, he faces the *Doctor Eximius et Pius* at a point *prior* to resistance to the preaching of divine law and even to obedience to the precepts of natural law, inasmuch as he attributes to the Tapuias an *invincible ignorance*. According to Vieira, those nations would not even have heard the preaching of the Apostle Thomas, "rejected and expelled by the Indians because he would have prohibited polygamy,"[115] nor did they know God by the "natural insight of wit and intelligence,"[116] that is to say by the natural light of reason. With Paul (Rm 10, 18), he asks: "Did they not hear?" For Vieira, Suárez "exposes and defines the difficulty excellently, although without expressing exactly the Apostle's thought":[117]

> [. . .] it must be firmly stated that not only is it possible to have an invincible ignorance of God, but also that it does exist. However, since after this statement the same issue is already a matter of fact, we need only witnesses, not philosophers or doctors. And, to prove it, I will present such witnesses that among the witnesses they are not only eyewitnesses, but the most learned among the learned.[118]

---

114 Ibid.: 386–89.

115 "Rejeitado e expulso pelos Índios porque teria proibido a poligamia" António Vieira, *Clavis prohetarum. Chave dos profetas. Livro III*, ed. Arnaldo do Espírito Santo (Lisbon: Biblioteca Nacional, 2000): 457 (I am quoting from the excellent Portuguese translation by Arnaldo do Espírito Santo; the original Latin original text can be found in the facing page).

116 "Perspicácia natural do engenho e da inteligência." Ibid.: 459.

117 "Expõe e delimita excelentemente a dificuldade, embora sem exprimir exatamente o pensamento do Apóstolo." Ibid.: 175.

118 "[. . .] deve ser firmemente afirmado que não só é possível existir uma invencível ignorância de Deus, mas também que de fato existe. Entretanto, como depois dessa asserção a mesma questão seja já uma questão de fato, necessitamos apenas de testemunhas, não de filósofos nem de doutores. E, para prová-la, apresentarei testemunhas tais que entre as testemunhas são não apenas testemunhas oculares, mas as mais doutas entre os doutos." Ibid.: 337. The learned eyewitnesses referred to by Vieira are Acosta and Solórzano Pereira, to whom he adds the bishop of Quito, Alonso de la Peña

On the other hand, Vieira also disputes Suárez regarding the impossibility of ignoring all natural law.[119] According to the summary of the *Clavis prophetarum* made by Father Carlo Antonio Casnedi, Vieira conceded to the Tapuias, "among whom he lived for a long time, not only an invincible ignorance of God, throughout the entire course of their lives, but also ignorance of all of natural law."[120]

> For this reason, the author states: if the theologians of Europe (who deny that totally invincible ignorance of God and of natural law is possible) practiced with these barbarians, they would give in their opinion.[121]

Vieira then asks if the Tapuias "should be subject to eternal punishment for their sins."[122] He answers: "the barbarians raised in the jungles, who have not heard the Gospel or by any other source have not been cleansed of the innate ignorance of God, just as they are immune from all mortal guilt, so they are also exempt from all immortal punishment."[123] Why, after all, does Vieira make so many concessions to the Tapuias in matters so widely and rigorously demanded by theologians, to the point of practically delimiting a fourth category of barbarians, blameless whether by divine or natural laws? Ultimately, in order to assist[124] the emergence of the Fifth Empire, which he predicted would be Portuguese. To this end, he launched himself at times in oppositions and confrontations, at times in compositions and negotiations, according

Montenegro. With a lesser priority, he refers to Peter Martyr d'Anghiera and Thomas Bozio, described as "*litteris, religione, et publica auctoritate insignes*". Ibid.: 366.

119 Ibid.: 338.

120 "Entre os quais por muito tempo viveu, não só uma ignorância invencível de Deus, por todo o decurso das suas vidas, mas também ignorância de todo o Direito Natural" António Vieira, "Clavis prophetarum: Resumo que dela escreveu o P. Carlos António Casnedi," in *Obras escolhidas. História do futuro*, vol. 9 (Lisbon: Livraria Sá da Costa, 1953): 181.

121 "Por esta razão diz o Autor: se os teólogos da Europa (que negam ser possível a ignorância de Deus e do Direito Natural totalmente invencível) praticassem com estes bárbaros, cederiam da sua opinião." Ibid.: 201.

122 "Devem ser sujeitos às penas eternas pelos seus pecados" Vieira, *Clavis prophetarum*: 321.

123 "[. . .] os bárbaros criados nas selvas, os quais não ouviram o Evangelho ou por outra fonte não foram purificados da ignorância inata de Deus, assim como estão imunes de toda a culpa mortal, assim também estão isentos de toda a pena imortal [. . .]." Ibid.: 327.

124 Second scholasticism understood that eternal law is a free decree derived from the will of God that establishes the order that must be observed and fulfilled by rational beings in their free actions; that is, divine law has the character of impulse and source of inclination, but also of obligation to free actions, under determined circumstances. Francisco Suárez, *De Legibus*, vol. 2 (Madrid: Consejo Superior de Investigaciones Científicas, 1974): 3, 6 and 3, 10. In this respect, Vieira seems to be closer to Suárez than to Vitoria or Domingo de Soto, for whom the law is essentially *ordinatio rationis*. The difference between Vieira and Suárez appears only afterwards, in the qualification of the capacity of action of particular groups of men.

to the conjuncture.[125] In this sense, he deepened the distinction between Tapuias and Tupis previously grammatized by Anchieta.[126] It was necessary to educate both, because both had forgotten the most basic precepts of natural law and because their will was corrupted. But this would be done in different environments: the Tupis, in the villages (*aldeamentos*), where they should be led and reduced by means of moderate subjection, whereas the Tapuias should only receive missions, after diplomatic negotiations that allowed the preachers to visit their lands.[127] We can assume, in both cases, the evaluation of the disastrous consequences of the war against the Caetés and so many others that followed it. On the other hand, if might could create the "right of the villages" among the Indians of the coast, neither the Jesuits nor the Portuguese settlers had the means to impose it on the barbaric Tapuias of the *sertão* – just as Thomas had not in America or Paul in Jerusalem (Acts, 22, 18), as Vieira points out. In other words, the Tapuias of the hinterland were the ones that finally imposed the modalities of coexistence between their nations and the Europeans. Vieira's position in the *Clavis prophetarum* (as well as in the *Relação da Serra de Ibiapaba*) is not only theological,[128] therefore, but also and above all the result of the analysis of the *historical circumstances* in which men should freely obey divine commands, especially in the zones of expansion of the Portuguese Empire. The underlying problem posed by Vieira, and characteristic of these border regions of the Iberian empires, is whether there could be salvation outside the Church, contrary to what the bull *Unam Sanctam* (1302) and the *Decree for the Jacobites* (1442) stated; more specifically, if invincible ignorance was an excuse for sin against the implicit faith in Christ.[129]

Suárez quotes Jo 15:22 and Rm 10:4 to, in principle, excuse the "infidels" who had never heard the Gospel or had not heard it to a sufficient extent.[130] However, the former should at least follow the principles of natural law; that is, they were not to be blamed for rejecting faith, nor for breaking moral precepts of natural law, and they were to manifest implicit desires to seek the truth and belong to the Church. Now, this

---

125 Since eternal law is binding over time, every law is contingent, including eternal law. Ibid.: II, 4, 2.

126 Vieira, *Clavis prophetarum*: 381–83; see note 97, above. This distinction is overlooked by Ana T. Valdez in her scholarly article "Tracking António Vieira's *Clavis Prophetarum*: The St. Bonaventure, Franciscan Institute, Manuscript 28," *The Catholic Historical Review* 103, no. 4 (2017): 663–97.

127 However, we should observe that this concession is not made to the neighbors of the Tapuias in Ibiapaba, the *quilombolas* of Palmares, as shown in Carlos A. de M. R. Zeron, "Vieira in movimento: Dalla distinzione tra Tapuias, Tupis e negri alla rottura nella dottrina cristiana sulla schiavitù e sulla legge naturale," in *Schavitù del corpo e schiavitù dell'anima*, ed. Carlos A. de M. R. Zeron, Emmanuele Colombo, Marina Massimi and Alberto Rocca (Rome: Bulzoni; Milano: ITL-Biblioteca Ambrosiana, 2018): 158–63.

128 "[. . .] a highly technical theological discourse." Valdez, "Tracking António Vieira's *Clavis Prophetarum*": 688.

129 Affirmed by Tomás de Aquino in *Suma teológica*: II–II, q. 1, a. 7, based on Hb 11:6.

130 Francisco Suárez, *De fide theologica*: I, disp. XVII, 1, 7–9, where he appeals to the authorities of Francisco de Vitoria and Thomas Cajetan.

was not the case with the Tapuias. For Suárez, these infidels would fit in what he writes in the *De legibus* (in passages that will be criticized by Vieira):

> Can this ignorance of natural precepts be insurmountable? [. . .] My opinion, in short, is that ignorance of the first principles is absolutely impossible, and even less insurmountable. While the precepts of a particular character can be ignored, which are self-evident or easily deduced from those who are, but cannot be ignored without guilt, at least for a prolonged period, since it is possible to get to know them with a minimum of diligence. Nature itself and conscience bark with such force in the acts that refer to these precepts that it is not possible to ignore them without guilt. Such are the precepts of the Decalogue and the like.[131]

Nor does Suárez consider the mitigation of circumstances – as decisive for Vieira as invincible ignorance:

> Finally, we must affirm that there is only one natural law at all times and in any human circumstances. [. . .] The reason is the same: natural law is not a consequence of a certain state of human nature, but of nature itself. There are those who think that this is true with respect to the universal principles of natural law, but that it is not with respect to the conclusions. It is necessary to distinguish, according to them, a double state of nature – of integrity or corruption – and to designate a distinct natural right. In the state of natural integrity, natural law demanded, for example, the freedom of all men, the community of goods and other things alike. While in a state of corruption it claims slavery, private property, etc., as it appears in *Manumissiones*, ff. De iustitia et iure, and § *Ius autem* Institutionum, *De iure naaturali*.[132]

131 "an haec ignorantia naturalium praeceptorum possit esse invincibilis? [. . .] mea sententia breviter est prima principia ignorari non posse ullo modo, ne dum invincibiliter. Praecepta vero particularia quae vel per se nota sunt vel facillime ex per se notis collingutur ignorari quidem posse, non tamen sine culpa saltem per longum tempus, quia et facillima diligentia cognosci possunt et natura ipsa et conscientia ita pulsat in actibus eorum ut non permittat inculpabiliter ignorari, et huiusmodi sunt praecepta Decalogi, ac similia." Suárez, *De legibus*: II, 8, 7. According to Suárez, it is not necessary to have a relationship with God to think about the *ens*, because he is thinkable before God himself; that is, such a relationship is necessary in theology, but not in metaphysics. The paradox raised by Suárez is that to think about the concept of creature, it is necessary to consider, first, the concept of *ens*; but, to think about the concept of *ens*, it is not necessary to assume the concept of creature. When one thinks of the creature as an entity, therefore, a relationship with God is not required; the relationship arises when one thinks of the being as a creature, and not the creature as a being or an entity. For the creature is a determined being, that is, the concept of creature plus its finite determination. That is, when we think of the creature as *ens*, we must abstract the relationship to God; only when we think of the being as a creature should we add the relationship with God. See Francisco Suárez, *Disputationes metaphysicae*: XXVIII, 3, 15–16. See also Costantino Esposito's considerations in the "Introduction" to the edition of this Suárez work (Francisco Suárez, *Disputazioni metafisiche I–III*, ed. Costantino Esposito [Milano: Bompiani, 2007]) and Constantino Esposito, "Suárez and the Baroque Matrix of Modern Thought," in *A Companion to Francisco Suárez*, ed. Victor M. Salas and Robert Fastiggi (Leiden: Brill, 2015): 124–47. In other words, it is possible for Vieira to philosophically conceive the situation of ignorance of the Tapuias based on Suárez's own metaphysics.

132 "Ultimo dicendum est hanc legem naturalem etiam esse unam in omni tempore et statu humanae naturae. [. . .] Ratio vero est eadem, quia haec lex non sequitur ex aliquo statu huius naturae; sed ex ipsa natura secundum se. Sunt autem qui dicant, licet hoc sit verum quoad universalia principia

Vieira's disagreement with Suárez lies in these points: for the Jesuit missionary, the Tapuias had an invincible ignorance of God. Equally, some sin they committed against natural law was "purely philosophical and not theological sin," whereas "the sin of Christians and idolaters against natural reason is not purely philosophical, but it is also theological."[133] Therefore, those who violated natural and positive laws were the Portuguese, "captivating [the Indians] not only against the royal laws, but against all natural and nations' rights and using them in excessive work, with which they killed and consumed them, even more than with wars."[134] For Vieira, unlike Suárez, it is, therefore, a deferred grace, and not a denied one: God saves the Tapuias through ignorance, because otherwise they would sin.

> The testimony, the example and the infallible proof of Divine Providence are clearly inferred and demonstrated, whom, as we sustain, provides by not providing. Indeed, Christ, by denying them and expressly forbidding the preaching of the Gospel, and, what is more, even that they hear of his name, makes it clear and evident that he did not provide them with the absolutely necessary means for the knowledge of the true God and that he finally preferred that they remain in ignorance, natural and invincible, of the same God. But this same improvidence was a kind of providence for them, because, by way of this ignorance, the merciful Lord deigned to save them the eternal penalty of the senses, those who, by his foreknowledge, he knew that from the misuse of knowledge and faith would be condemned to a total and complete punishment.[135]

huius legis, tamen quoad conclusiones non ita esse. Sed distinguendum esse duplicem statum huius naturae, scilicet vel integrae vel corruptae, et illis tribuendum esse diversum naturale ius. Nam in natura integra ius naturale petebat v. g. libertatem omnium hominum et dominia communia et similia. In natura vero corrupta petit servitutes, rerum divisionem, etc., ut sumitur ex lege *Manumissiones*, ff. De iustitia et iure, et § *Ius autem* Institutionum, *De iure naaturali.*" Suárez, *De legibus*: II, 8, 8.

133 Vieira, "Clavis prophetarum": 201, 204. The thesis condemned by Pope Alexander VIII in 1690 does not entirely coincide with that sustained by Vieira, since it referred only to the ignorance of God. See the entry "Philosophical Sin" in Arthur Charles O'Neill, s.v. "Sin," in *The Catholic Encyclopedia*, ed. Charles G. Herbermann et al. (New York: Robert Appleton Co., 1912).

134 "Cativando [os índios] não só contra as leis reais, mas contra todo o direito natural e das gentes, e servindo-se deles em trabalhos excessivos, com que os matavam e consumiam, mais ainda que com as guerras." António Vieira, "Informação sobre o modo com que foram tomados e sentenciados por cativos os índios do ano de 1655," in *Obras escolhidas: obras várias (III) em defeza dos índios*: 35.

135 "Donde claramente se infere e fica demonstrado o testemunho, o exemplo e a infalível prova daquela Providência Divina que, como afirmamos, providencia não providenciando. Com efeito, Cristo, negando-lhes e proibindo sob preceito expresso a pregação do Evangelho, e, o que é mais, até o ouvirem falar do seu nome, torna certo e evidente que não lhes providenciou um meio absolutamente necessário para o conhecimento de Deus verdadeiro e que preferiu que, por fim, permanecessem na ignorância, natural e invencível, do mesmo Deus. Mas esta mesma improvidência foi para eles uma espécie de providência, pois que, por essa ignorância, o Senhor misericordioso se dignou salvar da eterna pena dos sentidos aqueles que, pela sua presciência, sabia que do mau uso do conhecimento e da fé iriam ser condenados a um castigo total e completo." António Vieira, *Clavis prophetarum*: 473–75. I am quoting here from the Portuguese translation by Arnaldo do Espírito Santo. The Latin original text can be found in the same edition, intercalated: 472–74.

There are two ways of salvation, therefore: by conversion and by "inculpability" (by innocence). The analogy is still with Paul in Jerusalem, from where God wanted him to leave, just as Thomas left America.[136] All things considered, it is interesting to observe that Vieira chose Suárez as an opponent, a theologian who had been noted for his reasonably radical positions regarding the idea of popular sovereignty.[137] In fact, Suárez distinguishes himself from other theologians in stating that *jus gentium* differs from natural law, in which it is based on customs more than in nature, that is, classifying it as a positive human right (although it is not confused with civil law, since it is common and shared by "almost all nations").[138] For Suárez, *jus gentium* is common, but it is not natural: they are just conclusions, or deductions, taken from the principles of natural law. In its institution and in its precepts, the will prevails over reason, with a view to equity and justice and in consideration of historical circumstances. It is, thus, a custom useful to almost all men, instituted by custom, tradition, and imitation, so that it can even allow evil due to the fragility of the human condition.[139] The law of nations is, therefore, a product of freedom, of will, and not the result of logical deductions from human nature; it is not an intrinsic obligation and can thus socially and historically delimit political evil, as it depends on opinion (on deliberation) and on the free political will of men in light of their uses and customs. For this very reason, perhaps, Vieira chose Suárez as an opponent in the *Clavis prohetarum*: despite his voluntarism, the emphasis that the Grenadian theologian placed on the political dimension of the law of nations does not contribute to the voluntarism that Vieira attributes to God and to the missionary Jesuits seeking the salvation of Gentile nations like the Tapuias and, consequently, for the advent of the Fifth Empire.

---

136 At this point, Vieira is not even accompanied by Solórzano Pereira, who quotes St Ambrose to affirm that "ignorance is a worse condition than slavery, so that slavery is beneficial for her" de Solórzano Pereira, *De Indiarum iure*: II, 7, 61. See also II, 10, 78–79 ("Can invincible ignorance be admitted in matters of faith?"), II, 13, 67–75 ("It does not seem that ignorance can justify the Indians who sinned against natural law") and II, 15, 33 ("The natural precepts of the first class do not admit the excuse of ignorance"). For Solórzano Pereira, sins against natural law (combined under the notion of "barbarism") justify just war and the loss of *dominium*; in addition, he adds the principles previously put forward by Vitoria, concerning the natural right of trade, transit, hospitality, defense of the innocents, and even tyrannicide. Only Alonso de la Peña Montenegro goes as far as Vieira, and even surpasses him in certain aspects, because, for him, not only does the *custom* explain the condition of the Indians, but also the *physical distance* of the converts in relation to colonial society from the moment that they returned to their villages or were abandoned by the colonizers: if the bishop of Quito does not excuse the ignorance of the primary precepts, he does so, however, with regard to the secondary precepts, depending on these circumstances.

137 Carlos A. de M. R. Zeron, "Political Theories and Jesuit Politics," in *The Oxford Handbook of the Jesuits*, ed. Ines G. Zupanov (New York: Oxford University Press, 2019): especially 194–97.

138 Suárez, *De legibus*: II, 19, 2–4 and 6.

139 Ibid.: II, 20.

6 Conclusion

None of the authors commented on here deny the unity of humankind, while everyone stands in favor of the legitimacy of colonial enterprises, arguing only about the *ways of controlling* the incorporated indigenous population and of *appropriating the benefit* of their work. In other words, the theological, moral, and legal parameters of colonization unfold and are expressed, in their texts, in political proposals that differ only in the filigree of the definition of "just." In fact, positive law, deduced from the principles of natural law and natural right, was, alongside war and made compatible with it, one of the foundations of the formation and reproduction of a new, slave-based, and colonial society, where distributive justice should contemplate an original social structure, different from the European one, since, below the poorest peasant farmers, there were other layers, of mestizos, of free but tutored Indians, of freed Africans, and of Indian and black slaves. The link between these two foundations – law and war – was given by the *law of nations which, in each circumstance, justified right as an exercise of might*. The historical process by which the formation of Luso-American colonial society took place and its systemic articulation with the European world economy and with African societies, on both slave and Christian bases, therefore extrapolated the organizing power of mere economic interest, influenced as it were by a theological-political discourse and a related praxis.

Such discourse and praxis were not without ambiguity, however. On the contrary, the explanations and justifications that these authors allowed for the loss of *dominium* of the Amerindians the confusion that hovers in the qualification of their minority at the same time that they were liable to be reduced to slavery, and the frequent intrusion of the Aristotelian concept of natural slavery opened space for vigorous disputes between the main colonizing groups. On several occasions, such disputes culminated either in the expulsion of the Jesuits by the settlers (effective in 1640, 1661, 1684, and 1759; imminent in 1610–1611, 1655, 1666, 1682, and 1687), or in the punishment of prominent representatives of the settlers and the colonial administration (for example, in 1684). As for the crown, at least until the Pombaline reforms, it tended to delegate the resolution of conflicts over the forms of reproduction of colonial society to the direct agents of colonization, endorsing the provisional commitments they reached through laws that had an equally provisional validity (a reason of state that the historiography has interpreted – mistakenly, in my view – as an "oscillating" position).[140]

In the interstices of these disputes, the Jesuits stubbornly endeavored to engage in openly political activity throughout the colonial period and despite the equally persistent hostility of opposing groups, whether at court, among settlers, or other religious orders; they did so in councils and in *juntas*, in confessionals and pulpits, but also and above all, by controlling the royal villages (*aldeamentos reais*) that, together

140 Zeron, *Linha de fé*: 372–73 and especially 380–81.

with the Jesuit villages, brought together almost the entire reserve of labor and the defense army of the Portuguese conquests, governing, through them, the conditions of reproduction of colonial society. In fact, the heart of the disputes concerned the *control of this network of aldeamentos* spread along the coast.

In the villages, the Jesuits intended to exercise a tutelage regime over the Indians through a circumstantial adaptation of the Thomistic concept of "moderate subjection," which unfolded in several successive stages: constraining the Indians to "descend" from the *sertão* to the villages, sedentarizing them in an urbanized space, disciplining them by means of compulsory and continuous work in order to make their wills constant, with a view to allowing their civic, moral, and, only then, religious education. This arrangement, inverted in its order in relation to what was found in stoic and scholastic literature, was justified on the basis of the empirical description of a reality undertaken by missionaries active in the mission lands: as in other fields of knowledge, the argument founded in "experience" was often opposed to "authority."[141] The justifications for the inversion (starting from the positive law to teach divine law) and for the method (moderate subjection followed by tutelage) lay in the alleged inability of the Indians to free themselves both from the wicked action of the devil and from their bad usages and customs. This (dis)qualification of the Indians was the breach where the Aristotelian concept of "natural slavery" ceaselessly returned, while the refusal of moderate subjection and tutelage by the Indians justified the wars that generated civil slavery.

Similarly, but vituperating the Portuguese settlers as well as the royal administrators and judges, Vieira preached the *Sermão da sexagésima* in the Royal Chapel in 1655, when he demanded that, in order to make a fair indigenous policy feasible, in accordance with natural and divine laws, he was to obtain "some instruments"[142] from the king. Such instruments were civil laws intended to regulate the behavior of the Indians and of the settlers – since, although for different reasons, both were unable to properly carry out the "synderesis with which the good imprints the design of its light in the consciences, advising the judgment in the free acts":[143] in the case of the Portuguese settlers, it was by "willing the forbidden and yearning the denied" that

141 Within a few years, Nóbrega abandoned the European model of mobile missions and started to defend the village model he developed on the plateau of São Paulo, despite the opposition of his superiors in Portugal and Rome. Zeron, *Linha de fé*: 42–43, 82–83, 123–24. On the opposition of the Society's generals, see ibid.: 85, no. 77.

142 António Vieira, "Sermão da Sexagésima," in *Sermões*, vol. 1 (Lisbon: Lello e Irmão, 1945): 5.

143 "sindérese com que o Bem imprime na consciência o desígnio da sua Luz aconselhando o juízo nos atos livres." João Adolfo Hansen, "Vieira e os estilos cultos: *ut theologia rhetorica*," *Letras* 21, no. 43 (2011): 38. It is important to note that the "Sermão da Sexagésima" is closely linked to the "Sermão do Bom Ladrão," preached in the same Lent of 1655, when he attacked the royal preachers who badly advised the king about the predatory acts underway in colonial administration.

specific laws should be imposed on them; in the case of the Amerindians, due to their "ignorance of all natural right."[144]

Although Vieira distinguished the reduced and Christianized Tupis from the Tapuias, he understood – like Vitoria and Nóbrega before him – that, once a step of deviation from the norm was taken, it was difficult, or even impossible, for a community to reform itself in order to recover the good precepts to be extracted from natural law. Customs were understood as a "second nature" that, in the case of the Indians, provided disorderly or even unfinished societies (without kings, without laws), according to the topic taken up by so many chroniclers. In these circumstances, the intervention of an outside element or agent was required. For Vieira, this agent was above all the zealous missionary.

Christian truth, which should be the basis of all moral law, and of which traditionalist Christian knowledge, through the voice of theologians, wanted to be the sole depository and guardian, fulfilled its vocation through the missionary task delegated to the preachers sent to America to fight against the *humana impedimenta*:[145] subjecting and tutoring the Indians on the one hand, and, on the other, coercing the settlers. In both cases, however, this always *through civil laws*. There is a difference of position of the Jesuits in relation to the settlers, aldermen, and royal administrators, therefore, even though everyone understood that might creates right. This principle was not disputed, rather the discussion was about the *content* of that right.

These were, in general, the theory and the praxis related to it, as proposed by the Jesuits, in the long era that began with the first provincial, Manuel da Nóbrega, in the middle of the sixteenth century until the death of António Vieira at the end of the seventeenth century, a period during which they had the support of the crown of Portugal and Spain.[146] The persistence of the method developed in São Paulo and from there spread to the rest of America[147] denoted the Jesuits' ability to balance colonial domination and accommodation in the progressive articulation of different spaces and populations with diverse political and cultural characteristics, which manifested different reactions to the conquest and Portuguese colonization. This did not prevent, however, the opposition of expressive factions of the settlers – soon qualified as "bad Christians." In each conflict, the Jesuits demanded political intervention from the monarch to defend and support their political activity. Such intervention was guided and tutored by the clergy themselves, however, based on the theory of indirect power (that is, the power and obligation of political intervention of the Church whenever the salvation of souls was at risk, whether these souls were those of the Indians or of the settlers and colonial administrators themselves).

144 "apetecer o proibido e anelar ao negado"; "ignorância de todo o Direito Natural". Vieira, *Obras escolhidas. História do futuro*: vol. 8, 2 and vol. 9, 181, respectively.

145 Zeron, *Linha de fé*: 391.

146 On this chronology, see Zeron, "From Farce to Tragedy."

147 Carlos A. de M. R. Zeron, "Mission et espace missionnaire: les bases matérielles de la conversion," *Archives des Sciences Sociales des Religions*, 169 (2015): 307.

This method not only had lasted a long time, but also had a wide geographical application in Portuguese America, from the north of the state of Maranhão and Grão-Pará to the south of the state of Brazil. It was not efficient, though, where there was tenacious resistance, especially from Indians (but also, in more limited regions or situations, from *quilombolas* and settlers). Such was the case, particularly, of the Tapuias of the Ibiapaba Mountains, a strategic region in the land connection between those two states. The resistance of the Tapuias led Vieira, who had contact with them, to identify them in a separate category of barbarians, different from those predicted by Acosta.

Distancing himself from Vitoria and even from Nóbrega, Vieira refused to apply the rigors of the just war doctrine to these Tapuias, striving to find theological justifications to excuse them; justifications that denote, in the last instance, a geopolitical analysis that he harmonizes with the prophecy of the advent of the Fifth Empire. The "invincible ignorance" of the Tapuias, persistent despite the natural light of reason, was the providential means of incorporating them into the Fifth Empire. As the Tapuias had greater strength, they had to be convinced by a religious discourse, and not dominated by military maneuvers or by the imposition of a right – measures that would both be, in fact, ineffective. Having strength in their favor, the Tapuias maintained their habits and customs and imposed them in their relations with the Portuguese. Vieira found that such customs were inconsistent with the principles of natural law and that, consequently, relationships with those nations were not guided by the law of nations; nevertheless, he explained them by their invincible ignorance and justified them by divine providence, which "provided by not providing." Their salvation was consummated, then, with the redemptive help of the missionaries, intermediaries between the Portuguese state, the Tapuias, and the Christian God himself, who had left them covered for 1,400 years, waiting precisely for this mediation.

The incapacity recognized by Vieira to, by force, create the "right of the villages" and "give"[148] it to the barbaric Tapuias from the backlands is thus explained only on the providential level, which the Jesuit discerns in his prophetic texts. In other words, *Vieira dismisses and refuses to apply the principles of natural law to these Tapuias*. When the Portuguese did not have the power to create law and define the just according to the principles of natural law and to their interests, the power of the Tapuias was interpreted as inscrutable divine power and design, discernible through prophecies combined with the analysis of the historical circumstances in which the Portuguese should obey divine commands. The agency of the Jesuits, here, is manifested in Vieira's singular ability to recognize and prophetically interpret such conjunctures. In the case of the barbaric Tapuias, the political dimension of the law of nations did not contribute to Suarezian voluntarism, which Vieira confers, after all, not to men, but to God and, then, to the Jesuit missionaries, with a view to the salvation of these Gentile

148 See note 62, above.

nations, the beginning of the general conversion of all nations, and the advent of the Fifth Empire.

I did not set out to analyze here the prophetic statements of Vieira, however, but to highlight the uniqueness of his position in relation to the Tapuias of the Ibiapaba Mountains, in contrast with the positions he himself adopted in São Paulo in 1694, when he gave in to the demands of the settlers,[149] and especially with the different positions he adopted, successively, during his stay in Maranhão and Grão-Pará between 1653 and 1661, when he moved from defending the freedom of the Indians to defending the *escravidão de condição* and attempting to exercise indirect power by the Jesuits.[150] Such singularity evinces the practical consensus around the principle that the might (of the Tapuias of Ibiapaba, of the settlers of São Paulo and Maranhão, of the Jesuits here and there . . .) creates the right; this principle is justified – and hidden – based on a circumstantial interpretation of the law of nations. The law of nations contained a relationship between might and right, hidden in natural and Christian principles. Hans Morgenthau, whose works belong to the tradition of realism in international relations theory, suggests in the phrase in the epigraph to this text that such uses of natural law – a "dynamic ideology,"[151] as he puts it, precisely because its "ideological" use is always circumstantial – lasted until the great imperial wars of the mid-twentieth century, but certainly still later (and even more recently, when it occasionally became associated with theology again). Correspondingly, the distinctiveness of the situation of the Tapuias of Ibiapaba shows that natural law and the values underlying it have rarely served the "bottom" of colonial society, except when they had the power to shape law according to their needs and interests.

Bibliography

Primary Sources

de Acosta, José. *De procuranda indorum salute* (Madrid: Consejo Superior de Investigaciones Científicas, 1984–1987).

Agostinho. *De Trinitate. Livros IX–XIII*, trans. Arnaldo do Espírito Santo, Domingos Lucas Dias, João Beato and Maria Cristina Castro-Maia de Sousa Pimentel (Covilhã: Universidade da Beira Interior, 2008).

de Anchieta, José. *Arte de Grammatica da lingoa mais usada na costa do Brasil* (Coimbra: por Antonio de Mariz, 1595).

de Anchieta, José. *Obras Completas*, 13 vols. (São Paulo: Loyola, 1970–1989).

149 Vieira, "Voto sobre as dúvidas": 355. See the passage corresponding to note 110, above.

150 I have analyzed these changes in Vieira's position in Zeron, "Antônio Vieira e os 'escravos de condição'."

151 Hans J. Morgenthau, *Politics among Nations: The Struggle for Power and Peace* (New York: Alfred A. Knopf, 1946): 65.

de Anchieta, José. *Cartas, Informações, Fragmentos Históricos e Sermões* (Belo Horizonte: Itatiaia, 1988).
Aristóteles. *Política*, trans. Mário da Gama Kury (Brasília: Editora Universidade de Brasília, 1997).
Aristóteles. "Ética a Nicômaco," trans. Leonel Vallandro and Gerd Bornheim, in *Os pensadores* (São Paulo: Abril Cultural, 1973): 245–436.
Aristotle. *Politics*, trans. Harris Rackham (London: William Heineman; Cambridge: Harvard University Press, 1959).
Aristotle. *Nicomachean Ethics*, trans. Harris Rackham (Cambridge, MA: Harvard University Press; London: William Heinemann Ltd., 1934).
de Azevedo, João Lúcio. *História de António Vieira* (Lisbon: Clássica editora, 1992).
de Berredo, Bernardo Pereira. *Anais históricos do Estado do Maranhão, em que se dá notícia do seu descobrimento, e tudo o mais que nele tem sucedido desde o ano em que foi descoberto até o de 1718* (Lisbon: na Officina de Francisco Luiz Ameno, 1749).
de Berredo, Bernardo Pereira. *Anais históricos do Estado do Maranhão, em que se dá notícia do seu descobrimento, e tudo o mais que nele tem sucedido desde o ano em que foi descoberto até o de 1718*, 4th ed. (Rio de Janeiro: Tipo editor Ltda., 1988).
Bíblia de Jerusalém (São Paulo: Paulus, 2017).
Bluteau, Raphael. *Vocabulário portuguez e latino* (Coimbra: no Colégio da Companhia de Jesus, 1712–1728).
Herbermann, Charles G., Edward A. Pace, Condé Bénoist Pallen, Thomas J. Shahan, John J. Wynne and Andrew Alphonsus MacErlean, eds. *The Catholic Encyclopedia: An International Work of Reference on the Constitution, Doctrine, Discipline, and History of the Catholic Church* (New York: Robert Appleton Co., 1912).
Las Casas, Bartolomé de. *La controverse entre Las Casas et Sepúlveda*, trans. Nestor Capdevilla (Paris: Vrin, 2007).
de Loyola, Ignace. *Écrits*, trans. Maurice Giuliani (Paris: Desclée de Brouwer, 1991).
de Molina, Luis. *De Justitia et Jure*, 3rd ed. (Cologne: n.p., 1613–1614).
Monumenta Brasiliae, ed. António Serafim Leite, 5 vols. (Rome: Monumenta Historica Societatis Iesu, 1957–1968).
Quintiliano, Marcos Fábio. *Instituição oratória*, trans. Bruno Fregni Bassetto (Campinas: Editora da Unicamp, 2015).
de Sepúlveda, Juan Ginés. *Democrates segundo, o de las justas causas de la guerra contra los indios*, trans. Angel Losada (Madrid: Consejo Superior de Investigaciones Científicas; Instituto Francisco de Vitoria, 1984).
Serafim Leite, António, ed. *História da Companhia de Jesus no Brasil*, 10 vols. (Lisbon: Portugália, 1938–1945).
de Solórzano Pereira, Juan. *De indiarum iure (liber III: De retentione indiarum)* (Madrid: Consejo Superior de Investigaciones Científicas, 1994).
Sommervogel, Carlos. *Bibliothèque de la Compagnie de Jésus*, 12 vols. (Paris: A. Picard, 1932).
de Soto, Domingo. *Relecciones y opusculos*, vol. 1, *Introducción general, De dominio, Sumario, Fragmento: An liceat civitates infidelium seu gentilium expugnare ob idololatriam*, trans. Jaime Brufau Prats (Salamanca: Editorial San Esteban, 1995).
Suárez, Francisco. "De mediis quibus infideles possint licite ab hominbus ad fidem adduci," in *De bello contra insulanos. Intervención de España en America*, vol. 2, ed. Juan de la Peña (Madrid: Consejo Superior de Investigaciones Científicas, 1982): 384–407.
Suárez, Francisco. *Defensa de la Fe Católica y Apostólica contra los errores del Anglicanismo. Reproducción anastática de la edición príncipe de Coimbra 1613*, 4 vols., trans. José Ramón Eguillor Muniozguren (Madrid, Instituto de Estudios Políticos, 1970–1971).
Suárez, Francisco. *De Legibus* (Madrid: Consejo Superior de Investigaciones Científicas, 1971–1981).
Suárez, Francisco. *Disputazioni metafisiche I–III*, ed. Costantino Esposito (Milano: Bompiani, 2007).
Tomás de Aquino. *Suma teológica*, 4rd ed. (São Paulo: Loyola, 2014).

de Vasconcelos, Simão. *Crônica da Companhia de Jesus do Estado do Brasil (com as Notícias Curiosas e Necessárias das Cousas do Brasil)*, 3rd ed. (Petrópolis: Vozes, 1977).
Vieira, António. *Obras várias do Padre António Vieira* (Lisbon: J.M.C. Seabra & T.Q. Antunes, 1856).
Vieira, António. "Sermão da Sexagésima," in *Sermões*, vol. 1 (Lisbon: Lello e Irmão, 1945): 1–36.
Vieira, António. *Obras escolhidas: obras várias (III) em defeza dos índios*, vol. 5. (Lisbon: Livraria Sá da Costa, 1951).
Vieira, António. *Obras escolhidas: História do future*, vol. 8–9 (Lisbon: Livraria Sá da Costa, 1953).
Vieira, António. *Clavis prohetarum. Chave dos profetas. Livro III*, ed. Arnaldo do Espírito Santo (Lisbon: Biblioteca Nacional, 2000).
Vieira, António. *Obra completa do Padre António Vieira*, ed. Pedro Calafate and José Eduardo Franco (São Paulo: Loyola, 2014).
de Vitoria, Francisco. *Leçons sur les Indiens et sur le droit de guerre*, trans. Maurice Barbier (Genève: Droz, 1966).
de Vitoria, Francisco. *Political Writings* (Cambridge: Cambridge University Press, 2010).
de Vitoria, Francisco. *Relectiones: sobre os índios e sobre o poder civil*, trans. Paulo Sérgio de Vasconcellos (Brasília: Editora Universidade de Brasília, 2016).
Vocabulário na língua brasílica (São Paulo: Coleção do Depto. de Cultura, 1938).

Secondary Literature

Adler, Mortimer J., and William Gorman, eds., *The Great Ideas. A Syntopicon of Great Books of the Western World*, vol. 2 (Chicago: Encyclopaedia Britannica, 1952).
Barcia Trelles, Camilo. "Francisco de Vitoria et l'école moderne du droit international," in *Recueil des cours*, vol. 17, ed. Académie de Droit international (Paris, n.p., 1928): 136–48.
D'Oca, Fernando Rodrigues Montes. "Francisco de Vitoria e a teoria aristotélica da escravidão natural," *Thaumazein* 7, no. 14 (2014): 3–31.
Eisenberg, José. *As missões jesuíticas e o pensamento político moderno: encontros culturais, aventuras teóricas* (Belo Horizonte: Universidade Federal de Minas Gerais, 2000).
Esposito, Costantino. "Suárez and the Baroque Matrix of Modern Thought," in *A Companion to Francisco Suárez*, ed. Victor M. Salas and Robert Fastiggi (Leiden: Brill, 2015): 124–47.
Fastiggi, Robert. "Francisco Suárez and the non-believers," *Pensamiento* 74, no. 279 (2018): 263–70.
Fernandes, Florestan. "Formação e desenvolvimento da sociedade brasileira," in *O Brasil de Florestan*, ed. Florestan Fernandes and Antônio David (Belo Horizonte: Autêntica, 2018): 99–115.
Gama, José Gonçalves. "Vieira e a vaidade: da tentação fazer remédio," in *Padre António Vieira. Colóquio*, ed. José Cândido de Oliveira Martins (Braga: Universidade Católica Portuguesa, 2009): 209–15.
Godelier, Maurice. *L'idéel et le materiel: Pensée, économies, sociétés* (Paris: Fayard, 1984).
Godelier, Maurice. *The Mental and the Material: Thought, Economy and Society*, trans. Martin Thom (Thetford: Verso, 1986).
Hansen, João Adolfo. "Ler & ver: pressupostos da representação colonial," *Veredas. Revista da Associação Internacional de Lusitanistas* 3, no. 1 (2000): 75–90.
Hansen, João Adolfo. *Manuel da Nóbrega* (Recife: Fundação Joaquim Nabuco; Editora Massangana, 2010).
Hansen, João Adolfo. "Vieira e os estilos cultos: *ut theologia rhetorica*," *Letras* 21 (2011): 25–62.
Hansen, João Adolfo e Moreira, Marcello. *Para que todos entendais: poesia atribuída a Gregório de Matos e Guerra: letrados, manuscritura, retórica, autoria, obra e público na Bahia dos séculos XVII e XVIII* (Belo Horizonte: Autêntica, 2013).
Lukács, György. *Prolegômenos para uma ontologia do ser social* (São Paulo: Boitempo Editorial, 2010).

Marcocci, Giuseppe. "Machiavelli, la religione dei romani e l'impero portoghese," *Storica*, 41–42 (2008): 35–68.

Marcocci, Giuseppe. "Construindo um império à sombra de Maquiavel," in *Maquiavel no Brasil: Dos Descobrimentos ao século XXI*, ed. Rodrigo Bentes Monteiro and Sandra Bagno (Rio de Janeiro: Editora Fundação Getúlio Vargas, 2015): 57–80.

de Matos, Antônio. "Informação do Colégio do Rio de Janeiro pelo Padre António de Matos," in *História da Companhia de Jesus no Brasil*, vol. 6, ed. António Serafim Leite (Lisbon: Portugália, 1938–1945): 563–68.

Meihy, José Carlos Sebe. *Escritos instrumentais sobre os índios do padre Antônio Vieira* (São Paulo: EDUC/Loyola/Giordano, 1992).

Morgenthau, Hans J. *Politics Among Nations: The Struggle for Power and Peace* (New York: Alfred A. Knopf, 1946).

Pagden Anthony R. *The Fall of Natural Man: The American Indian and the Origins of Comparative Ethnology* (New York: Cambridge University Press, 1986).

Pich, Roberto Hofmeister. "*Dominium* e *ius*: sobre a fundamentação dos direitos humanos segundo Francisco de Vitoria (1483–1546)," *Teocomunicação* 42, no. 2 (2012): 376–401.

Ribeiro, Darcy. *Estudos de antropologia da civilização: as Américas e a civilização, processo de formação e causas do desenvolvimento desigual dos povos americanos* (Petrópolis: Vozes, 1983).

Ribeiro, Darcy. *O povo brasileiro* (São Paulo: Companhia das Letras, 1995).

Sande, Antonio Paes. "Relatório do Governador Antonio Paes de Sande, em que indica as causas do malogro das pesquizas das minas do Sul e propõe o alvitre para se obter de uma maneira segura o seu descobrimento," *Anais da Biblioteca Nacional do Rio de Janeiro* 39 (1917): 197–200.

Sartre, Jean-Paul. *Critique de la raison dialectique (précédé de Question de méthode)*, 2 vols. (Paris: Gallimard, 1960–1985).

Valdez, Ana T. "Tracking António Vieira's *Clavis Prophetarum*: The St. Bonaventure, Franciscan Institute, Manuscript 28," *The Catholic Historical Review* 103, n. 4 (2017): 663–97.

Villey, Michel. *Questions de Saint Thomas sur le droit et la politique* (Paris: Presses Universitaires de France, 1987).

Wilde, Guillermo. *Religión y poder en las misiones de guaraníes* (Buenos Aires: SB, 2009).

Zeron, Carlos A. de M. R. "Les *aldeamentos* jésuites au Brésil et l'idée moderne d'institution de la société civile," *Archivum Historicum Societatis Iesu* 76, no. 151 (2007): 38–74.

Zeron, Carlos A. de M. R. *Ligne de foi. La Compagnie de Jésus et l'esclavage dans le processus de formation de la société coloniale en Amérique portugaise (XVIe–XVIIe siècles)* (Paris: Honoré Champion, 2009).

Zeron, Carlos A. de M. R. "A construção de uma ordem colonial nas margens americanas do império português: discussões sobre o 'bem comum' na disputa de moradores e jesuítas pela administração dos índios (séculos XVI–XVIII)" (habilitation thesis, Universidade de São Paulo, 2010).

Zeron, Carlos A. de M. R. *Linha de fé: a Companhia de Jesus e a escravidão no processo de formação da sociedade colonial (Brasil, séculos XVI e XVII)*, trans. Antonio de Padua Danesi (São Paulo: Edusp, 2011).

Zeron, Carlos A. de M. R. "From Farce to Tragedy: António Vieira's Hubris in a War of Factions," *Journal of Jesuit Studies* 2, no.3 (2015): 387–420.

Zeron, Carlos A. de M. R. "Mission et espace missionnaire: les bases matérielles de la conversion," *Archives des Sciences Sociales des Religions* 169 (2015): 307–34.

Zeron, Carlos A. de M. R. "Antônio Vieira e os 'escravos de condição': os aldeamentos jesuíticos no contexto das sociedades coloniais," in *A Companhia de Jesus e os índios*, ed. Eunícia Barros Barcelos Fernandes (Curitiba: Prismas, 2016): 235–62.

Zeron, Carlos A. de M. R. "Different Perceptions on the Topic of Forced Conversion, after the South Atlantic Experience," in *Compel People to Come In: Violence and Catholic Conversions in the Non-European World*, ed. Vincenzo Lavenia, Stefania Pastore, Sabina Pavone and Chiara Petrolini (Rome: Viella, 2018): 49–68.

Zeron, Carlos A. de M. R. "Vieira in movimento: Dalla distinzione tra Tapuias, Tupis e negri alla rottura nella dottrina cristiana sulla schiavitù e sulla legge naturale," in *Schavitù del corpo e schiavitù dell'anima*, ed. Carlos A. de M. R Zeron, Emmanuele Colombo, Marina Massimi and Alberto Rocca (Rome: Bulzoni; Milano: ITL-Biblioteca Ambrosiana, 2018): 139–65.
Zeron, Carlos A. de M. R. "Political Theories and Jesuit Politics," in *The Oxford Handbook of the Jesuits*, ed. Ines G. Zupanov (New York: Oxford University Press, 2019): 193–215.
Zeron, Carlos A. de M. R. "Salamanca em contexto colonial: a teologia política de Manuel da Nóbrega (1517–1570)", in *La Escuela de Salamanca: la primera versión de la modernidad*, ed. David Torrijos-Castrillejo and Jorge Luis Gutiérrez (Madrid: Ediciones San Dámaso e Editorial Sindéresis, 2022): 285–300.

Contributors and Editors

Martha Abreu (PhD, University Estadual de Campinas, 1996) is a professor of history at the Universidade Federal Fluminense (Rio de Janeiro, Brazil), a researcher at Universidade Estadual do Rio de Janeiro (UERJ/FFP) and at Conselho Nacional de Pesquisa (CNPq). She has experience in the history of Brazil and the African diaspora in the Americas, focusing on popular culture, black music, cultural heritage, post-abolition, the memory of slavery, and race relations. She was one of the curators of the Museum of Afro-Brazilian History and Culture (MUHCAB). She is the co-director of the public digital project *Past Presents. Memories of Slavery in Brazil* (http://passadospresentes.com). Her latest publications include *Da Senzala Ao Palco: Canções Escravas e Racismo Nas Américas, 1870–1930* (Campinas: Universidade Estadual de Campinas. Editora, 2017); Cultura negra: novos desafios para os historiadores, 2 vols (ed., with Giovana Xavier, Lívia Monteiro and Eric Brasil, (Niterói: Eduff, 2018); and Monteiro Lopes e Eduardo das Neves: histórias não contadas da primeira república (with Carolina Dantas, Niterái: Eduff, 2020).

Crislayne Alfagali has a bachelor's degree in history (2009, Universidade Federal de Ouro Preto), a master's degree in the social history of culture (2012), and a PhD in the social history of Africa (2017, both from the Universidade Estadual de Campinas). She teaches at the history department of the Pontifícia Universidade Católica do Rio de Janeiro (PUC-Rio). Her main areas of interest are the colonial history of Brazil and the history of Africa, concentrating on themes such as the historical and cultural connections between Africa and Brazil, the material elements of culture, the history of labor, and the history of Angola. In 2018, she published the book *Ferreiros e Fundidores da Ilamba. Uma História Social da fabricação de ferro e da Real Fábrica de Nova Oeiras (Angola, segunda metade do século XVIII)* (Luanda: Fundação Dr. Antón).

Stephan Conermann (PhD University of Kiel, 1996) is spokesperson of the Bonn Center of Dependency and Slavery Studies and director of the department of near eastern history and languages at Bonn University. His research interests include slaveries, narrative strategies in historiographic texts, transition periods, mobility and immobility, global history, and rule and power. He focuses on the Mamluk and Delhi sultanates, the Mughal and Ottoman empires, and the crossroads area "Transottomanica." His latest publications include (ed., with Michael Zeuske), *The Slavery/Capitalism Debate Global. From 'Capitalism and Slavery' to 'Slavery as Capitalism'* = Comparativ – Zeitschrift für Globalgeschichte und vergleichende Gesellschaftsforschung (Special Issue) 30, no. 5–6 (2020): 447–636; (ed., with Gül Şen): *Slaves and Slave Agency in the Ottoman Empire* (Göttingen: V&R unipress, 2020); (ed., with Toru Miura): *Studies on the History and Culture of the Mamluk Sultanate (1250–1517). Proceedings of the First German-Japanese Workshop Held at Tokyo, November 5–6, 2016* (Göttingen: V&R unipress, 2021); and (ed., with Gül Şen): *The Mamluk-Ottoman Transition II. Continuity and Change in Egypt and Bilād al-Shām in the Sixteenth Century* (Göttingen: V&R unipress 2022).

Roberto Hofmeister Pich (PhD, University of Bonn, 2001) is professor of the graduate programs in philosophy and in theology of the Pontifical Catholic University of Rio Grande do Sul (Porto Alegre, Brazil). He is a researcher of the Brazilian National Council for Scientific and Technological Development (CNPq), Level 1B, and of the Bonn Center for Dependency and Slavery Studies. He is also a fellow of the Alexander von Humboldt-Foundation and of the Fulbright Commission. In 2018, he holds the chair CAPES/University of Bonn, and since 2019 he has been distinguished as ambassador of that university. He has written and edited books about the philosophy of religion, medieval philosophy, and the reception of medieval "schools" in Latin American scholasticism. He is one of the leaders of the project "*Scholastica colonialis*: Reception and Development of Baroque Scholasticism in Latin America, 16th to 18th Centuries" and since 2018 has focused his research on the philosophical and theological background of the ideology of black slavery in Latin American history. Among his latest publications are: "Race, Religion, and Slavery in Alonso de Sandoval's S. J. *De instauranda Aethiopum salute*," *Entangled Religions – Exploring Words: The Impact of the*

https://doi.org/10.1515/9783111026527-014

Colonization Period on the Development of a Religious Language 13, no. 4 (2022): 1–36; "Francisco José de Jaca's (*c.* 1645–1689) and Epifanio de Moirans's (1644–1689) Plea for the Liberation of Enslaved Black People in Latin America," in *Civilization – Nature – Subjugation. Variations of (De-)Colonization*, ed. Christoph Haar, Matthias Kaufmann and Christian Müller (Berlin: Peter Lang, 2021): 69–110; "Probabilismo e escravidão Negra," in *Humanidades: Revista de la Universidad de Montevideo* 8 (2020): 17–67; (ed., with Alfredo Storck and Alfredo Culleton), *Homo – Natura – Mundus: Human Beings and Their Relationships* (Turnhout: Brepols, 2020); and (ed., with Michael Schulz), *Philosophy of Religion in Latin America and Europe* (Göttingen: V&R unipress, 2020).

Maria Helena P.T. Machado is full professor in the history department of the University of São Paulo, researcher at the Brazilian National Research Council, and Leverhulme Trust Visiting Professor at Reading University (UK) in 2022. She is the author of several books and articles on slavery, abolition, and post-emancipation in Brazil. She has published catalogs and curated various exhibitions, individually and in partnership, for the Louis Agassiz Brazilian Photographic Collection and other Brazilian slavery photograph collections. She currently carries out research on the interrelations between slavery, abolition, and gender. Her publications in the last two years include: (ed., with Antonio Alexandre Cardoso), *Geminiana e seus filhos. Escravidão e morte; infância e maternidade* (Rio de Janeiro: Bazar do Tempo, in press); (with Iamara Viana), "Dos corpos negros: escravidão, raça e pós-abolição em perspectiva comparada," in *Revista de História Comparada da Universidade Federal do Rio de Janeiro* (2022); "Maria Firmina dos Reis, Século XIX, Maranhão Brasil," in *Revista de História Comparada da Universidade Federal do Rio de Janeiro* (2022); "Body, Gender, and Identity on the Threshold of Abolition. A Tale Doubly Told by Benedicta Maria da Ilha, a Free Woman, and Ovídia, a Slave," in *The Boundaries of Freedom. Slavery, Abolition, and the Making of Modern Brazil*, ed. Brodwin Fisher and Keila Grinberg (Cambridge: Cambridge University Press, 2022): 163–82; and (ed., with Flavio Gomes, Iamara Viana, and Luciana Brito), *Ventres Livres? Gênero, Maternidade e Legislação* (São Paulo: Ed. da Unesp, 2021).

Beatriz Mamigonian (PhD, University of Waterloo, 2002) is professor of history at the Federal University of Santa Catarina in Brazil. She has been a fellow of the Gilder Lehman Center for the Study of Slavery, Resistance and Abolition (Yale) and visiting scholar at the Ecole des Hautes Études en Sciences Sociales (EHESS-Paris). Her research interests include slavery, the slave trade, abolition, illegal enslavement, coercive labor, and individual trajectories. She is the author of *Africanos livres: a abolição do tráfico de escravos no Brasil* (São Paulo: Companhia das Letras Companhia das Letras, 2017) and the co-editor of *The Human Tradition in the Black Atlantic and The Human Tradition in the Atlantic World* (Lanham, MD: Rowman and Littlefield, 2009 and 2010), as well as *História Diversa: africanos e afrodescendentes na Ilha de Santa Catarina and Revisitar Laguna: Histórias de conexões atlânticas* (Florianopolis: Editora da UFSC, 2013 and 2021). She coordinates the Santa Afro Catarina public history project on the African presence in Santa Catarina.

Mariana Dias Paes is research group leader at the Max Planck Institute for Legal History and Legal Theory. Her research interests include slavery, ownership, land, court cases, global history, and legal history. She focuses on Brazil, Angola, and Portugal. Her latest publications include *Esclavos y tierras entre posesión y títulos: la construcción social del derecho de propiedad en Brasil, siglo XIX* (Frankfurt am Main: Max-Planck-Institut für Rechtsgeschichte und Rechtstheorie, 2021); "Shared Atlantic Legal Culture: The Case of a Freedom Suit in Benguela," in *Atlantic Studies, Global Currents* 17:3 (2020): 419–40; "Legal Files and Empires: Forms and Materiality of the Benguela District Court Documents," in *Administory. Zeitschrift für Verwaltungsgeschichte* 4 (2019): 53–70; and *Escravidão e direito: o estatuto jurídico dos escravos no Brasil oitocentista, 1860–1888* (São Paulo: Alameda, 2019).

Tâmis Parron is assistant professor of the History Institute at the Universidade Federal Fluminense (Rio de Janeiro, Brazil). He is member of the UFF Center on Global Inequalities and coordinates the research group COMMUN on World Comparative History at the same university. Parron's research focuses on the history of slavery, state building, and capitalism in the nineteenth century from the perspective of world system, conceptual history, and critical theory. He wrote *A política da escravidão no Império do Brasil, 1826–1865* (Rio de Janeiro: Civilização Brasileira, 2011), co-authored (with Rafael Marquese and Márcia Berbel) *Slavery and Politics: Brazil and Cuba* (Albuquerque: University of New Mexico Press, 2016), and is the editor of the book series *Narratives from Slavery* (2020). His latest publications in English include "Transcending the Capitalism and Slavery Debate: Slavery and World Geographies of Accumulation," in *Theory and Society*, 2022 (online), 2023 (v. 22); "The Great Transformation: World Capitalism and the Crisis of Slavery," in *The Atlantic and Africa: The Second Slavery and Beyond*, ed. Dale Tomich and Paul Lovejoy (New York: State University of New York Press, 2021): 19–47; and "The British Empire and the Suppression of the Slave Trade to Brazil: A Global History Analysis," in *The Journal of World History* 29 (2018): 1–36.

Ricardo Pirola is professor of Brazilian history at UNICAMP University (Brazil). He has published two books on social history of slavery in nineteenth-century Brazil: *Senzala insurgente: malungos, parentes e rebeldes nas fazendas de Campinas (1832)* (Campinas, SP: Editora UNICAMP, 2011) and *Escravos e rebeldes nos tribunais do império: uma história social da lei de 10 de junho de 1835* (Rio de Janeiro, RJ: Ministério da Justiça, Arquivo Nacional, 2015). His book *Escravos e rebeldes nos tribunais do Império* won the Brazilian National Archives Prize for the originality of its historical research. Pirola is currently working on law and the phenomenon of lynching in comparative perspective between Brazil and USA (nineteenth century).

Fabiane Popinigis (PhD, University of Campinas – UNICAMP, 2003) is associate professor of the history department at the Rural Federal University of Rio de Janeiro (UFRRJ) and coordinator of the graduate program in history at the same university. Her research interests include the history of slavery and freedom, labor history, and the relationship between race, gender, and class. Her latest publications include: (with Paulo Cruz Terra), "Classe, raça e a História social do trabalho no Brasil (2001–2016)," in *Estudos Históricos* 32, no. 66 (2019): 307–28; (with Henrique Espada Lima), "Maids, Clerks, and the Shifting Landscape of Labor Relations in Rio de Janeiro, 1830s-1880s," in *International Review of Social History* 1 (2018): 1–29; and "Trabajo, libertad y esclavitud: estrategias y negociaciones en el sur de Brasil, siglo XIX," in *Trashumante. Revista Americana de Historia Social* 6 (2015): 146–68.

Lilia Moritz Schwarcz is full professor in anthropology at the University of São Paulo and global scholar and visiting professor at Princeton. She published several books, such as (with Heloisa Murgel Starling) *Brasil: uma biografia* (São Paulo: Companhia das Letras, 2015) – Engl. trans. *Brazil: a Biography* (London: Allen Lane, 2018); (ed. with Flavio Gomez), *Dicionário da escravidão e liberdade: 50 textos críticos* (São Paulo: Companhia das Letras, 2018); *Sobre o autoritarismo brasileiro* (São Paulo: Companhia das Letras, 2019) – Engl. trans. *Brazilian Authoritarianism. Past and Present* (Princeton: Princeton University Press, 2022); and (with Heloisa Murgel Starling), *A bailarina da morte: a gripe espanhola no Brasil* (São Paulo: Companhia das Letras, 2020). She was a curator of exhibitions like *Sexuality Histories* (2017, São Paulo), *Afro-Atlantic Histories* (2018, São Paulo), *Women Histories* (2019, São Paulo), *Black Encyclopedia* (2021, Pinacoteca de São Paulo, 2022 Museu de Arte do Rio), *Contra memória* (2022, Theatro Municipal), *Retratos brasileiros: Dalton Paula* (2022, Masp), and *Histórias brasileiras* (2022, Masp). She was a fellow at the Guggenheim Foundation (2006/2007) and the John Carter Brown Library (2007), as well as visiting professor at Oxford, Leiden, Paris, Berlin, and Brown University. She holds the commendation of the Brazilian Order of Scientific Merit presented by the Presidency of the Republic (2010) and takes part in the American board of Human Rights Watch. She writes regularly for Brazilian newspapers such as: *Folha de S Paulo*, *Estado de S. Paulo*, and *Nexo*. Since 2015, she has been a co-curator (for history) at MASP (Museum of Modern Art of São Paulo)

Paulo Cruz Terra is a professor in the history department at Fluminense Federal University in Brazil. He is a scholar productivity researcher at CNPq (National Council for Scientific and Technological Development, Brazil) and a "Young Scientist of Our State" at FAPERJ (Carlos Chagas Filho Foundation for Supporting Research in the State of Rio de Janeiro). Between 2019 and 2022, he was a guest fellow at the Bonn Center for Dependency and Slavery Studies, as well as a fellow of Capes and the Alexander von Humboldt Foundation. Terra is the author of *Cidadania e trabalhadores: cocheiros e carroceiros no Rio de Janeiro (1870–1906)*, awarded by the General Archive of the City of Rio de Janeiro, and has several publications on labor history in Brazil. More recently, he has focused on the relationship between vagrancy, punishment, and laws in Brazil and Portuguese Africa and published the article "Anti-Vagrancy, Punishment and Labor Relations in the Context of the Abolition of Slavery in Brazil and the Portuguese Empire (1870 –1910)," in *Revista Brasileira de História* in 2021. He is currently one of the editors of the book series "Social History of Punishment and Labor Coercion" by Amsterdam University Press.

Carlos Zeron is full professor at the Universidade de São Paulo and a member of the Accademia Ambrosiana, Classe di Studi Borromaici (Milan, Italy). He was a visiting professor at the Ecole des Hautes Etudes en Sciences Sociales (1997, 2002, 2007, 2013, 2014, 2016), at the Universidad Internacional de Andalucía (2004), and the Pontificia Universidad Católica de Chile (2021); he was also a guest researcher at the Musée du Quai Branly (2009). He was the director of the Biblioteca Brasiliana Guita e José Mindlin (2016–2022) and has been a researcher of the Conselho Nacional de Pesquisa since 2003. Zeron conducts research on Amerindian and African slavery, colonial legislation, political theology, and modern juridical thought. He published *Ligne de foi. La Compagnie de Jésus et l'esclavage dans le processus de formation de la société coloniale en Amérique portugaise (XVIe-XVIIe siècles)* (Paris: Honoré Champion/Classiques Garnier Numérique, 2009; trad. port. São Paulo: Edusp, 2011). His latest publications include (ed., with Emmanuele Colombo, Marina Massimi and Alberto Rocca) *Schavitù del corpo e schiavitù dell'anima. Chiesa, potere politico e schiavitù tra Atlantico e Mediterraneo (sec. XVI-XVIII)* (Rome: Bulzoni; Milano: ITL Editore/Biblioteca Ambrosiana, 2018); "Usos contraditórios da autoridade de Juan de Solórzano Pereira por Antônio Vieira, Paulo da Silva Nunes e Francisco Xavier de Mendonça Furtado," in *Espaços coloniais: domínios, poderes, representações*, ed. Carmen Alveal and Thiago Dias (São Paulo: Alameda, 2019): 107–36; "Political Theories and Jesuit Politics," in *The Oxford Handbook of the Jesuits*, ed. Ines G. Zupanov (New York: Oxford University Press, 2019): 193–215; (with Antônio David) "Le jusnaturalisme en Europe et en outre-mer: Antonio Vieira face au droit naturel et à l'esclavage des Indiens de São Paulo (1694)," *in Clio@Themis* 22 (2022); and "Vieira em movimento: subjacências da distinção entre tapuias, tupis e negros," in *Estudos avançados*, vol. 33, no. 97 (2019).

Index

https://doi.org/10.1515/9783111026527-015

Printed and bound by CPI Group (UK) Ltd, Croydon, CR0 4YY
13/09/2026
14961095-0001